Introduction to Contemporary Special Education

New Horizons

Second Edition

Deborah Deutsch Smith
Claremont Graduate University

Naomi Chowdhuri Tyler
Peabody College, Vanderbilt University

Kimberly Garner Skow
Peabody College, Vanderbilt University

 Pearson

330 Hudson St, NY NY 10013

Director and Portfolio Manager: Kevin M. Davis
Content Producer: Janelle Rogers
Senior Development Editor: Jon Theiss
Media Project Manager: Daniel Dwyer
Portfolio Management Assistant: Anne McAlpine
Executive Field Marketing Manager: Krista Clark
Executive Product Marketing Manager: Christopher Barry
Procurement Specialist: Carol Melville
Full-Service Project Management and Composition: Cenveo® Publisher Services
Full-Service Project Manager: Kathy Smith
Cover Designer: Brenda Knight Trevethan
Cover Image: © Monkey Business Images/Shutterstock; Syda Productions/Shutterstock; Business stock/
Shutterstock; Yuriy Kulik/Shutterstock; Anton Petrus/Shutterstock; arka38/Shutterstock
Printer/Binder: LSC Communications
Cover Printer: Phoenix Color/Hagerstown
Text Font: Palatino LT Pro

Credits and acknowledgments for material borrowed from other sources and reproduced, with permission, in this textbook appear on the appropriate pages within the text.

Every effort has been made to provide accurate and current Internet information in this book. However, the Internet and information posted on it are constantly changing, so it is inevitable that some of the Internet addresses listed in this textbook will change.

Cataloging-in-Publication Data is available on file at the Library of Congress.

1   18

ISBN 10: 0-13-489508-8
ISBN 13: 978-0-13-489508-6

To our families:
Jim, Steve, Sarah, and the girls – Emma and Mary
Ken, Kyra, and Kailyn
Vaughn, Ashley, and Callie

And to students with exceptionalities, your families, friends, and the professionals in your lives:
This book has always been for you.

Brief Contents

1 Thinking About Exceptionalities   1

2 Supporting All Learners   26

3 Culturally and Linguistically Diverse Learners   47

4 Basic Guarantees, Individualized Programs, and Special Services   71

5 Speech and Language Impairments   101

6 Learning Disabilities   136

7 Attention Deficit Hyperactivity Disorder   167

8 Autism Spectrum Disorder   202

9 Intellectual Disability   241

10 Emotional and Behavioral Disorders   276

11 Physical and Health Disabilities   313

12 Deafness and Hard of Hearing   342

13 Visual Disabilities: Low Vision and Blindness   375

14 Other Low-Incidence Disabilities   410

15 Gifted and Talented   440

Appendix   481

Glossary   488

References   499

Index   537

Contents

1 Thinking About Exceptionalities   1

Putting Exceptionalities Into Perspective   2
- 1.1 All Students   3
- 1.2 Students With Disabilities   5
- 1.3 Students Who Are Gifted and Talented   8

Disabilities and Social Justice   9
- 1.4 Issues of Social Justice   10
- 1.5 Disability as a Minority Group   12
- 1.6 Participation in Education   14

Making a Difference   16
- 1.7 Perceptions Matter   16
- 1.8 Words Matter   18

The Changing Landscape   19
- 1.9 Academic Outcomes   20
- 1.10 Post-Secondary Accomplishments   21
- 1.11 Community Presence   23

Summary   **25**
- Addressing CEC Standards   25

2 Supporting All Learners   26

High-Quality Instruction   27
- 2.1 Introduction   28
- 2.2 Evidence-Based Practices   30
- 2.3 Universal Design for Learning (UDL)   32
- 2.4 Differentiated Instruction   35
- 2.5 Data-Based Decision Making   37

Multi-Tiered Systems of Support   40
- 2.6 Response to Intervention (RTI)   41
- 2.7 Positive Behavioral Interventions and Supports (PBIS)   43

Summary   **46**
- Addressing CEC Standards   46

3 Culturally and Linguistically Diverse Learners   47

Diverse Learners   48
- 3.1 The Diverse Landscape   49
- 3.2 Issues of Social Justice   52
- 3.3 Understanding Disproportionality   55

Cultural Diversity   57
- 3.4 Understanding Cross-Cultural Dissonance   58
- 3.5 Preventing Cross-Cultural Dissonance   60
- 3.6 Providing Culturally Responsive Instruction   62

Linguistic Diversity   64
- 3.7 Understanding Second-Language Acquisition   65
- 3.8 Effective Practices for ELs   67

Summary   **70**
- Addressing CEC Standards   70

4 Basic Guarantees, Individualized Programs, and Special Services   71

Educating Students With Disabilities   73
- 4.1 Federal Legislation   74
- 4.2 Basic Guarantees   77
- 4.3 Child Find and Initial Referrals   79
- 4.4 Steps in the IEP and Section 504 Processes   81

Individualized Education: Plans and Programs   83
- 4.5 IFSPs and IEPs   84
- 4.6 Basic Elements of IFSPs and IEPs   86
- 4.7 Additional IEP Components for Behavior and Secondary Transition   88
- 4.8 Accommodations vs. Modifications   89

Services, Personnel, and Settings   92
- 4.9 Individualized Services   92
- 4.10 Specialized Personnel   94
- 4.11 Continuum of Settings   97

Summary   **99**
- Addressing CEC Standards   100

5 Speech and Language Impairments   101

Speech and Language Impairments Described   102
- 5.1 Speech and Language Impairments Defined   103
- 5.2 Types of Speech and Language Impairments   106
- 5.3 Characteristics   109
- 5.4 Prevalence and Placement   111

Special Education   113
- 5.5 Challenges and Their Solutions   114
- 5.6 Accommodations   118
- 5.7 Early Intervention   119
- 5.8 School Years   123
- 5.9 Transition   125

People and Situations   127
- 5.10 Origins and History   127
- 5.11 Personal Stories   128

Future Perspectives   130
- 5.12 Prevention: Medical and Environmental Interventions   130
- 5.13 Technology: Improving Communication   132

Summary   **135**
- Addressing CEC Standards   135

6 Learning Disabilities   136

Learning Disabilities Described   137
- 6.1 Learning Disabilities Defined   138
- 6.2 Types of Learning Disabilities   140
- 6.3 Characteristics   143
- 6.4 Prevalence and Placement   144

Special Education   148

  6.5   Challenges and Their Solutions   149

  6.6   Accommodations   151

  6.7   Early Intervention   153

  6.8   School Years   154

  6.9   Transition   156

People and Situations   157

  6.10 Origins and History   158

  6.11 Personal Stories   160

Future Perspectives   161

  6.12 Prevention: Health Care and
     Technology Advances   162

  6.13 Technology: Selecting Appropriate
     Assistive Technology   164

Summary   **166**

  Addressing CEC Standards   166

7   Attention Deficit Hyperactivity Disorder   167

Attention Deficit Hyperactivity Disorder Described   168

  7.1   Attention Deficit Hyperactivity
     Disorder Defined   169

  7.2   Types of Attention Deficit
     Hyperactivity Disorders   171

  7.3   Characteristics   174

  7.4   Prevalence and Placement   175

Special Education   178

  7.5   Challenges and Their Solutions   180

  7.6   Accommodations   183

  7.7   Early Intervention   185

  7.8   School Years   187

  7.9   Transition   190

People and Situations   192

  7.10 Origins and History   193

  7.11 Personal Stories   194

Future Perspectives   196

  7.12 Prevention: Emerging Research   197

  7.13 Technology: Selecting Appropriate
     Assistive Technology   199

Summary   **201**

  Addressing CEC Standards   201

8   Autism Spectrum Disorder   202

Autism Spectrum Disorder Described   203

  8.1   Autism Spectrum Disorder Defined   204

  8.2   Types of Autism Spectrum Disorder   206

  8.3   Characteristics   207

  8.4   Prevalence and Placement   210

Special Education   213

  8.5   Challenges and Their Solutions   214

  8.6   Accommodations   217

  8.7   Early Intervention   219

  8.8   School Years   221

  8.9   Transition   225

People and Situations   228

  8.10 Origins and History   229

  8.11 Personal Stories   231

Future Perspectives   235

  8.12 Prevention: Emerging Research   235

  8.13 Technology: Selecting Appropriate
     Assistive Technology   237

Summary   **239**

  Addressing CEC Standards   240

9   Intellectual Disability   241

Intellectual Disability Described   242

  9.1   Intellectual Disability Defined   243

  9.2   Types of Intellectual Disability   246

  9.3   Characteristics   249

  9.4   Prevalence and Placement   250

Special Education   253

  9.5   Challenges and Their Solutions   254

  9.6   Accommodations   258

  9.7   Early Intervention   259

  9.8   School Years   261

  9.9   Transition   263

People and Situations   264

  9.10 Origins and History   265

  9.11 Personal Stories   267

Future Perspectives   269

  9.12 Prevention: Environmental Protections   270

  9.13 Technology: Connecting and Scheduling   272

Summary   **274**

  Addressing CEC Standards   275

10   Emotional and Behavioral Disorders   276

Emotional and Behavioral Disorders Described   277

  10.1 Emotional and Behavioral Disorders Defined 278

  10.2 Types of Emotional and Behavioral Disorders 280

  10.3 Characteristics   282

  10.4 Prevalence and Placement   283

Special Education   287

  10.5 Challenges and Their Solutions   288

  10.6 Accommodations   291

  10.7 Early Intervention   292

  10.8 School Years   295

  10.9 Transition   299

People and Situations   301

  10.10 Origins and History   302

  10.11 Personal Stories   305

Future Perspectives   307

  10.12 Prevention: Appropriate Access
     to Mental Health Services   308

  10.13 Technology: Current Considerations
     and Future Possibilities   310

Summary   **311**

  Addressing CEC Standards   312

11 Physical and Health Disabilities — 313

Physical and Health Disabilities Described — 314
11.1 Physical and Health Disabilities Defined — 315
11.2 Types of Physical and Health Disabilities — 317
11.3 Characteristics — 318
11.4 Prevalence and Placement — 319

Special Education — 321
11.5 Challenges and Their Solutions — 322
11.6 Accommodations — 325
11.7 Early Intervention — 327
11.8 School Years: Managing Health Emergencies, Including Seizures — 328
11.9 Related Services: Collaboration with School Nurses, Physical Therapists, and Occupational Therapists — 330

People and Situations — 332
11.10 Origins and History — 332
11.11 Personal Stories — 335

Future Perspectives — 337
11.12 Prevention: Accidents and Disease — 337
11.13 Technology: Prosthetics and Robotics — 339
Summary — **341**
Addressing CEC Standards — 341

12 Deafness and Hard of Hearing — 342

Deafness and Hard of Hearing Described — 343
12.1 Deafness and Hard of Hearing Defined — 344
12.2 Types of Hearing Loss — 346
12.3 Characteristics — 348
12.4 Prevalence and Placement — 351

Special Education — 353
12.5 Challenges and Their Solutions — 354
12.6 Accommodations — 357
12.7 Early Intervention — 359
12.8 School Years — 360
12.9 Transition — 362

People and Situations — 363
12.10 Origins and History — 364
12.11 Personal Stories — 366

Future Perspectives — 368
12.12 Prevention: Universal Screenings and Exposure to Environmental Noise — 369
12.13 Technology: Improved Devices and Medical Advances — 370
Summary — **373**
Addressing CEC Standards — 374

13 Visual Disabilities: Low Vision and Blindness — 375

Low Vision and Blindness Described — 376
13.1 Low Vision and Blindness Defined — 377
13.2 Types of Low Vision and Blindness — 379

13.3 Characteristics — 382
13.4 Prevalence and Placement — 385

Special Education — 386
13.5 Challenges and Their Solutions — 387
13.6 Accommodations — 389
13.7 Early Intervention: Motor and Concept Development — 392
13.8 School Years: The Expanded Core Curriculum — 394
13.9 Transition — 398

People and Situations — 402
13.10 Origins and History — 403
13.11 Personal Stories — 404

Future Perspectives — 406
13.12 Prevention: Medical Advances — 406
13.13 Technology: Assistive Technology, Apps, and Software — 408
Summary — **409**
Addressing CEC Standards — 409

14 Other Low-Incidence Disabilities — 410

Other Low-Incidence Disabilities Described — 412
14.1 Multiple Disabilities — 413
14.2 Traumatic Brain Injury (TBI) — 414
14.3 Deaf-Blindness — 416
14.4 Prevalence and Placement — 417

Special Education — 420
14.5 Accommodations — 421
14.6 Early Intervention — 423
14.7 School Years — 425
14.8 Transition — 427

People and Situations — 429
14.9 Origins and History — 430
14.10 Personal Stories — 431

Future Perspectives — 433
14.11 Prevention: TBI — 434
14.12 Technology: Improving Access — 436
Summary — **439**
Addressing CEC Standards — 439

15 Gifted and Talented — 440

Gifted and Talented Described — 441
15.1 Gifted and Talented Defined — 442
15.2 Types of Giftedness — 446
15.3 Characteristics — 449
15.4 Prevalence and Placement — 451

Special Education — 453
15.5 Challenges and Their Solutions — 454
15.6 Accommodations — 457
15.7 Early Intervention — 460
15.8 School Years — 462
15.9 Transition — 465

People and Situations   467
  15.10 Origins and History   468
  15.11 Personal Stories   470
Future Perspectives   472
  15.12 Issues to Resolve   473
  15.13 Technology: Expanding Options   477
Summary   **479**
  Addressing CEC Standards   480

Appendix

CEC Initial Level Special Educator
Preparation Standards   481

Glossary   488

References   499

Index   537

Preface

Vision of the Book

We are so excited about this second edition of *Introduction to Contemporary Special Education: New Horizons*!

If you are a college student, this introductory course is often the first step toward becoming a highly effective elementary, secondary, or special education teacher or other education professional (e.g., school principal, related service provider). For too many of you, this is the only exposure you will have to information about students with disabilities. Our aim is to set you on the best path possible. We want you to be engaged, independent, and critical learners who continue to seek better ways to improve results for all students throughout the span of your careers.

The content we included in this text reflects our shared vision: that we can provide a truly responsive and effective education to students with special needs. So many people are positively affected by such an education: the student, family members, friends, advocates, future co-workers, and neighbors. However, schooling and educational services can be truly special only when professionals value each child and utilize evidence-based practices with fidelity.

We are very excited about how the content is presented in this edition. Most students currently enrolled in teacher preparation courses are accustomed to learning in a very different way from their predecessors. While the expansion of technology into our daily lives impacts us all, it has particularly influenced those who have grown up during this period of vast technological innovation. Students expect learning to be engaging, interesting, and as interactive as possible. They want to *see* and *hear* the perspectives of individuals with exceptionalities, their family members, and their teachers. They want to see demonstrations of effective practices executed with fidelity. They want content presented in "nuggets" of information with guided opportunities to expand learning that capitalizes on *their* interests. They want text supported with strong visuals and key points highlighted through graphs, diagrams, tables, bullet points, and succinct summaries.

This text was created to meet these demands. It represents our beliefs about what today's "textbooks" should be. These beliefs stem from these experiences: (1) our own college course instruction, (2) our experience authoring seven editions of a traditional textbook, *Introduction to Special Education*, (3) our development of the first edition of *Introduction to Contemporary Special Education: New Horizons* and the unique, technological aspects of writing an e-text, (4) our history of developing interactive Web-based instructional Modules at the IRIS Center, and (5) our experience

in providing assistance to hundreds of professors as they design technology-enhanced coursework at IRIS workshops and seminars. These experiences have taught us many things about today's students and the application of technology in postsecondary instruction. This second edition of *Introduction to Contemporary Special Education: New Horizons* integrates these experiences, allowing us to develop an innovative alternative to conventional texts.

Organization of the Book

The book is composed of fifteen chapters. The first four chapters present foundational information about all students, and about those who struggle to reach their academic potential, even when provided with instruction designed for typical learners. In the first chapter, students learn about the progress individuals with disabilities have made, yet come to understand that their full attainment of social justice has yet to be achieved. In Chapters 2 and 3, readers learn key components of effective instruction for all students and how teachers can address the needs of struggling learners and those with other learning considerations (i.e., culturally and linguistically diverse learners). When consistently applied, procedures such as Universal Design for Learning, differentiated instruction, culturally responsive education, and multi-tiered systems of support will prevent many students from incorrectly receiving special education services. We then explain the requirements of legislation (e.g., the Individuals with Disabilities Education Act) and the need for an individualized education for students with disabilities (Chapter 4).

Each of the remaining eleven chapters presents basic information about a specific exceptionality, including giftedness. In these chapters, we describe each special education category, the educational challenges created by these exceptionalities, and evidence-based solutions to address these common challenges. Each chapter follows the same structure and is organized into four key issues that are further divided into two to five topics. References do not break up the reading. Instead, they are available at the end of the book (organized by chapter).

Now, here's the part that's important for course instructors to understand. These chapters were written sequentially, with scaffolded content that builds from chapter to chapter, particularly in the topics of early childhood, secondary transition, and assistive technology. For that reason, we highly recommend assigning these chapters *in chronological order*. We know that many instructors like to start the categorical portion of their courses with intellectual disability (Chapter 9) or autism spectrum disorder (Chapter 8) because so many students have prior knowledge of those two disabilities. Yet, it's exactly that prior knowledge that can serve as a foundation to better understand the characteristics of speech and language impairments (Chapter 5), which most individuals with intellectual disabilities or autism spectrum disorder also exhibit. And because so many students with other exceptionalities also have speech and language impairments, readers will have a consistent knowledge foundation for the remaining chapters. Trust us on this!

Special Features

Every chapter begins with a personal vignette. Some focus on an individual who has made a substantial contribution to advances in social justice or who provides an important message or example about individuals with special needs. Each chapter opener also includes an advance organizer that provides the learning outcomes for the chapter.

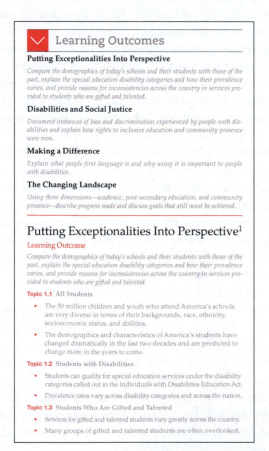

Learning Outcomes

Putting Exceptionalities Into Perspective

Compare the demographics of today's schools and their students with those of the past, explain the special education disability categories and how their prevalence varies, and provide reasons for inconsistencies across the country in services provided to students who are gifted and talented.

Disabilities and Social Justice

Document instances of bias and discrimination experienced by people with disabilities and explain how rights to inclusive education and community presence were won.

Making a Difference

Explain what people first language is and why using it is important to people with disabilities.

The Changing Landscape

Using three dimensions—academic, post-secondary education, and community presence—describe progress made and discuss goals that still must be achieved.

Putting Exceptionalities Into Perspective[1]

Learning Outcome

Compare the demographics of today's schools and their students with those of the past, explain the special education disability categories and how their prevalence varies, and provide reasons for inconsistencies across the country in services provided to students who are gifted and talented.

Topic 1.1 All Students

- The 50 million children and youth who attend America's schools are very diverse in terms of their backgrounds, race, ethnicity, socioeconomic status, and abilities.
- The demographics and characteristics of America's students have changed dramatically in the last two decades and are predicted to change more in the years to come.

Topic 1.2 Students with Disabilities

- Students can qualify for special education services under the disability categories called out in the Individuals with Disabilities Education Act.
- Prevalence rates vary across disability categories and across the nation.

Topic 1.3 Students Who Are Gifted and Talented

- Services for gifted and talented students vary greatly across the country.
- Many groups of gifted and talented students are often overlooked.

Several special features are included in most chapters. Charts, graphs, and diagrams illustrate important concepts and facts. *On the Screen* features allow students to assess the portrayals of exceptional individuals reflected in movies and television and to consider the subsequent impact on society's awareness and knowledge. *Tips for Teachers* supply key points that help create more effective learning environments and *A Closer Look at*

Research-Based Practices provide instructions on ways to implement evidence-based strategies and techniques. The *Characteristics-Challenges-Solutions* graphics, found in most chapters, identify many typical challenges a disability often presents and provide specific solutions that address those challenges.

> **On the Screen:** *A Brief History of Time*
>
> https://youtu.be/5_y13Pbo4qs
>
> This film depicts the life of the brilliant theorist Stephen Hawking (see chapter opener) who, despite his physical and health disabilities, contributes to human understanding of the origins of the universe. The film shows the overwhelming personal and professional challenges he faced and overcame. This very human story illustrates the joys and tragedies of his personal life, but it also centers on his great achievements and the respect he received from the public and the academic community.

New features take advantage of digital technology to enhance students' learning: embedded video clips demonstrate important methods or key points; interactive widgets provide extra practice with essential concepts (e.g., delineating between accommodations and modifications); *Check Your Understanding* quizzes assess student knowledge and provide further feedback on each chapter's content. Each chapter is peppered with links to additional resources for students or instructors who wish to delve deeper into the content: IRIS Center Modules; statistics from the IDEA Data Center; and relevant resources from reputable organizations. Each chapter concludes with a chapter summary and standards from the Council for Exceptional Children that connect to the content.

> **Check Your Understanding 13.3**
>
> Click here to gauge your understanding of the concepts in this section.

Additional Resources

Advanced Data and Performance Reporting Aligned to National Standards

Advanced data and performance reporting help instructors quickly identify gaps in student learning and gauge and address individual and classroom performance. Instructors easily see the connection between coursework, concept mastery, and national teaching standards with highly visual views of performance reports. Data and assessments align directly to CEC Standards and support reporting for state and accreditation requirements.

IRIS Center Resources

The IRIS Center at Vanderbilt University (https://iris.peabody.vanderbilt.edu), funded by the U.S. Department of Education's Office of Special Education Programs (OSEP), develops instructional resources for preservice and practicing teachers. The Center works with experts from across the country to create challenge-based interactive modules, case study units, and other resources that provide research-validated information about working with all students, struggling learners, and those with disabilities. Because we direct the IRIS Center, we are able to write chapter content that dovetails with the information in recommended IRIS Modules, thus enhancing the learning process for readers.

Supplementary Materials

The following resources are available for instructors to download on www.pearsonhighered.com/educators. Instructors search for the book by author or title, select the book, and then click on the "Resources" tab to log in and download textbook supplements.

Test Bank (0-13-451635-4)

The Test Bank includes a robust collection of test items. Some items (lower-level questions) simply ask students to identify or explain concepts and principles they have learned. But many others (higher-level questions) ask students to apply those same concepts and principles to specific classroom situations—that is, to actual student behaviors and teaching strategies.

TestGen® (0-13-451636-2)

TestGen® is a powerful test generator that instructors install on a computer and use in conjunction with the TestGen testbank file for the text. Assessments, including equations, graphs, and scientific notation, may be created for both print or testing online.

TestGen is available exclusively from Pearson Education publishers. Instructors install TestGen on a personal computer (Windows or Macintosh) and create tests for classroom testing and for other specialized delivery options, such as over a local area network or on the Web. A test bank, which is also called a Test Item File (TIF), typically contains a large set of test items, organized by chapter and ready for use in creating a test, based on the associated textbook material.

The tests can be downloaded in the following formats:

TestGen Testbank file - PC
TestGen Testbank file - MAC
TestGen Testbank - Blackboard 9 TIF
TestGen Testbank - Blackboard CE/Vista (WebCT) TIF
Angel Test Bank
D2L Test Bank
Moodle Test Bank
Sakai Test Bank

PowerPoint® Slides (0-13-451640-0)

The PowerPoint slides include key concept summarizations, diagrams, and other graphic aids to enhance learning. They are designed to help students understand, organize, and remember core concepts and theories.

Acknowledgments

We want to take this opportunity to thank some very important people who joined us on this long and challenging journey. First to our families, whose patience and support surpassed what anyone could ever expect. Thank you for your tolerance and for being so understanding of our collective crankiness. To our husbands, Jim, Ken, and Vaughn: We owe you many date nights. To our children, Steve, Kyra, Kailyn, Ashley, and Callie: This text is to honor the five of you. We are ever grateful for your involvement in the development of this text and its various elements. Steve, thank you for your continued involvement in the *On the Screen* features found in the text. Ashley, for your detail-oriented help all along the way, from assisting us with the initial document preparation to creating the PowerPoint supplement, thank you!

We want to express our gratitude to Brenda Knight Trevethan, whose keen eye and artistic talents have left an indelible mark on this edition. Brenda's talents are evident throughout this edition, from the cover to the wonderful *Characteristics-Challenges-Solutions* figures to graphics that support so many segments of text. We thank you for your creativity, problem solving, and willingness to always take on one more task. We also want to give a special thanks to those remarkable individuals who allowed us to share their stories: Sara Solomon, Belinda Butler, Helen Pandey, and Steph Zundel.

We also want to take this opportunity to acknowledge the members of the Pearson Team who contributed their time and expertise to the creation of the print and REVEL versions of this text. We would like to recognize Ann Davis, our long-time editor who worked with us over so many previous texts. Her vision and partnership during the first edition of *New Horizons* and during the initial phase of this edition shaped the end result. We want to thank Kevin Davis for taking the reins from Ann and believing in our ability to contribute to the development of an interactive, digital text that represents today's best publishing technology. We also want to acknowledge Jon Theiss (our Digital Dumbledore) who guided this REVEL product from the beginning. Even though the development "rules" seemed to be in constant flux, he retained a positive tone that kept us going. To Kathy Smith (our printed-page Yoda), we owe a special thank you for ensuring that the print version is appealing and as user-friendly as possible. Kathy's expertise in managing a complicated project with so many discrete elements is evident in the final product. Thanks to the entire Pearson team. Because of your contributions and confidence in this project, we are sure that the unique designs and features of this innovative, interactive text will help make the next generation of teachers and practicing educators more skilled and informed about students who face learning and behavior challenges.

Finally, we would like to thank the following reviewers for their insightful comments and suggestions: Jasmine Begeske, Purdue University; Bonnie Butcher, University of the Cumberlands; Rebecca Cohen, Pima Community College; Veda Jairrels, Clark Atlanta University; and Elizabeth A. Montanaro, Catholic University of America.

We conclude with one final explanation of our enthusiasm for this project. We were able to incorporate our beliefs about *what* is important for the next generation of education professionals to know, *why* they need to be continually curious about ways to improve their instruction and to become excellent consumers of research, and *how* this information

should be packaged. We believe that when these synergies are achieved, more students with disabilities will benefit, be college- or career-ready after high school, and achieve their dreams. To be honest, however, it may well be that our excitement lies in the fact that this project's long developmental journey is complete. It took over two years to complete this revision. The product has finally evolved from a set of ideas into being a reality. We hope you are as pleased with the outcome as we are.

DDS, NCT, & KGS

Chapter 1
Thinking About Exceptionalities

Jim Spellman/WireImage/Getty Images

LeDerick Horne is a poet, playwright, inspirational speaker, advocate, entrepreneur, and a person with a disability. In third grade he was identified as having a neurological impairment because he seemed unable to learn to read or spell. Though he struggled in school, he was determined to go to college, graduate, and become a successful writer. Today, not only is he a college graduate, a successful writer, a keynote speaker, a husband, and a father, but also he is a role model to all people with differences. His insights into disabilities, education, and his own life experiences make him a sought-after presenter on the college speaking circuit. He has presented at the White House, the United Nations, Harvard University, and many government meetings. Through his work, Mr. Horne helps us all develop a better perspective about people who learn differently. He teaches us how attitudes evolve and how they are reflected in culture, society, and language. He wisely counsels us that attitudes are changed by people's inspiration and will.

Mr. Horne speaks on behalf of many, and he challenges everyone to dare to dream, reach out, and grab opportunities. He also encourages all persons to insist on the best from themselves, from others, and from society. Such attitudes serve people with disabilities well.

To learn more about Mr. Horne, visit his Website: www.lederick.com

---

Watch LeDerick Horne as he shares his poem, "Dare to Dream," in this video:

▶ **"Dare to Dream"**

https://www.youtube.com/watch?v=HbOxNvuwabo

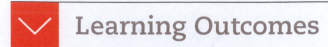

Learning Outcomes

Putting Exceptionalities Into Perspective

Compare the demographics of today's schools and their students with those of the past, explain the special education disability categories and how their prevalence varies, and provide reasons for inconsistencies across the country in services provided to students who are gifted and talented.

Disabilities and Social Justice

Document instances of bias and discrimination experienced by people with disabilities and explain how rights to inclusive education and community presence were won.

Making a Difference

Explain what people first language is and why using it is important to people with disabilities.

The Changing Landscape

Using three dimensions—academic, post-secondary education, and community presence—describe progress made and discuss goals that still must be achieved.

Putting Exceptionalities Into Perspective[1]

Learning Outcome

Compare the demographics of today's schools and their students with those of the past, explain the special education disability categories and how their prevalence varies, and provide reasons for inconsistencies across the country in services provided to students who are gifted and talented.

Topic 1.1 All Students

- The 50 million children and youth who attend America's schools are very diverse in terms of their backgrounds, race, ethnicity, socioeconomic status, and abilities.

- The demographics and characteristics of America's students have changed dramatically in the last two decades and are predicted to change more in the years to come.

Topic 1.2 Students with Disabilities

- Students can qualify for special education services under the disability categories called out in the Individuals with Disabilities Education Act.

- Prevalence rates vary across disability categories and across the nation.

Topic 1.3 Students Who Are Gifted and Talented

- Services for gifted and talented students vary greatly across the country.

- Many groups of gifted and talented students are often overlooked.

---

[1]References for Chapter 1 are found at the end of this text.

Roger Bacon/Reuters/Alamy Stock Photo

The Axis Dance Company performs worldwide with the purpose of changing the face of dance and disability. To learn more about this exciting group of performers, go to their Website: www.axisdance.org

Topic 1.1 All Students

- The 50 million children and youth who attend America's schools are very diverse in terms of their backgrounds, race, ethnicity, socioeconomic status, and abilities.

- The demographics and characteristics of America's students have changed dramatically in the last two decades and are predicted to change more in the years to come.

Who are America's children and where do they receive their education? The vast majority of America's schoolchildren do not have disabilities. Most of them thrive, achieve, and find their places in society as productive adults. Despite these positive outcomes for most, too many others struggle in school because of their life circumstances.

Although this text focuses on children and youth with disabilities, it is important to put them into proper perspective and understand the **demographics** of all of America's youth and their educational situations. Many of us have preconceived notions about America's schoolchildren, often obtained from media headlines, which may not always represent the full picture. It is vital to base educational knowledge and decisions about instructional practices or policies on real data from reliable resources. Sometimes, those data can be surprising, prompting us to reconsider what we thought was fact, to re-examine our own perceptions, and to question our information sources. Let's look at some data that present a picture of all of America's children and the education they receive. As you read along, ask yourself if the information presented aligns with your beliefs.

Approximately 50 million children and youth attend U.S. schools. They are diverse in respect to background, race and ethnicity, **socioeconomic status**, abilities to perform well, and type of education provided to them through the educational system. While White children accounted for 63% of the school population in 1997, they now

America's students come from different backgrounds, experiences, and abilities; but they share dreams of success at school and in life.

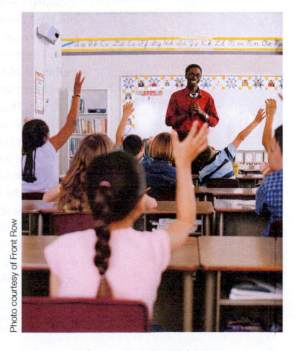

Photo courtesy of Front Row

make up less than 50% of the overall national school population. The figure illustrates the racial/ethnic composition of schools for the 2014–2015 school year. However, the U.S. Department of Education predicted that for the 2015–2016 school year, the nation's school population will change to a "minority–majority" status.

Demographics of U.S. Public School Students, 2013–2014 School Year

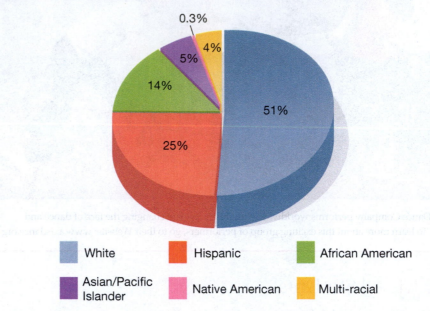

SOURCE: U.S. Department of Education, National Center for Education Statistics, *The Condition of Education*, 2015, 2016.

Most of America's children receive their education through the public school system. About 50 million schoolchildren attend public elementary or secondary schools; an additional 5 million students attend private schools. Because charter schools are considered public schools, their students are counted with all other public school students. Despite all the attention on charter schools, it may be surprising to learn that in 2014 less than 5% of public school students attend these alternate educational institutions.

The federal government predicts that the overall public school enrollment will increase 7% between 2012 and 2020, which is less than the overall trend seen over the past three decades. Elementary enrollment—pre-kindergarten through eighth grade—increased 30% between 1985 and 2012, while secondary enrollment increased 19%. The most dramatic enrollment increase, 745%, was noted for preschool, participation in which is optional. Two primary reasons for the large increases in preschool enrollment are (1) an overall population increase and (2) a greater preschool participation rate. The participation rate of three- to five-year-olds in preschool increased from 59% in 1990 to 65% in 2013. In what may be a hopeful sign of better school readiness (which leads to later school success), the percentage of children enrolled in full-day, rather than half-day, programs has increased from 39% to 60%.

What kinds of changes have occurred in the public school population? Across the past 40 years, the demographics and life conditions of America's children have changed greatly, mostly due to two groups of youngsters: Latinos/Hispanics[2] and Asians. Since 1997, the number of Hispanic students has doubled and the number of Asian students has increased some 46%. You might be surprised to learn that this growth is due to the number of students born to families in the United States, *not* due to immigration. While rates of immigration vary by state, with Texas, California, and Florida

---

[2]Across the United States many different terms are preferred when discussing race and ethnicity. In this text we attempt to reach a balance in the use of these terms.

having much higher percentages, almost all children from diverse backgrounds are born in the United States. Although their parents may be immigrants, less than 5% of America's children are themselves immigrants. This fact challenges many people's assumptions about Latino/Latinas in particular, in part because of continual media reports about immigration issues and undocumented workers. In fact, recent research findings challenge other commonly held misperceptions. The majority of U.S.-born Latinos come from English-speaking or bilingual (Spanish- and English-speaking) homes; English proficiency is at an all-time high. While first-generation immigrants do tend to struggle economically, second-generation Latino/Latinas fare much better than their parents did. Although not yet on par with their White peers, Latinos are completing high school, graduating from college, working in a wide range of jobs, and joining the middle class. Education is a priority for these students and their families, and their post-school successes indicate that this focus is paying off.

Why is this information important for you to know? Because it is human nature to make rash judgments about people, often based on stereotypes or on missing, inaccurate, or incomplete information. A teacher might assume that a Latino student in her class comes from a poor family, that he and his parents are immigrants, or that he does not speak English well. Instead, educators must guard against making stereotypical assumptions about any student, every one of whom deserves a high-quality education that challenges them and provides opportunities to excel.

Although the proportion of children born outside the United States is low, at around 5%, a slightly larger percentage (9%) of all students are English language learners (ELLs), also referred to as English learners (ELs)—they do not speak English at home. The percentage of ELLs includes students who speak languages other than Spanish (e.g., Chinese, Tagalog, Vietnamese, Korean, Arabic). As you will learn in Chapter 3, these students are not proficient in English and thus require language supports to benefit from classroom instruction.

Topic 1.2 Students With Disabilities

- Students can qualify for special education services under the disability categories called out in the Individuals with Disabilities Education Act.

- Prevalence rates vary across disability categories and across the nation.

Who are students with disabilities? Within the overall population of American schoolchildren, a subset of students have disabilities. Some 8% of all school-age children qualify for and receive special education services. In Chapter 4, you will learn about the national laws that guide states and school systems regarding the services these students are entitled to receive. For now, know that the federal government—through a national law called the Individuals with Disabilities Education Act of 2004 (IDEA '04, or simply IDEA)—guarantees students with disabilities a free public education that is appropriate to meet their educational needs, referred to as *special education* or *special education services*. In IDEA, the government outlines 13 specific disability categories under which students can qualify for special education services; however, the categories of deafness and hearing impairments are often combined. In addition, the category of developmental delay is a general category for young children (up to the age of nine) whose specific disability may not have yet been identified. The table provides a listing and brief explanation of the terms used to describe the disabilities included in IDEA. Be aware that sometimes the terms used by the federal government do not match those used by parent groups, professional organizations, states, or the public. For example, the federal government uses the term *emotional disturbance,* although most professional organizations and some states use the term *emotional and behavioral disorders.*

IDEA Disability Categories in Order of Prevalence

IDEA Term	Other Terms	Comments
Speech or language impairments	Speech disorders or language disorders; communication disorders	Divides speech impairments (articulation, fluency problems or stuttering, and voice problems) from language impairments
Specific learning disabilities	Learning disabilities (LD)	Includes reading/learning disabilities, mathematics/learning disabilities, unexpected underachievement
Other health impairments	Health impairments; special health care needs	IDEA includes attention deficit/hyperactivity disorder (ADHD) in this category, causing overall prevalence to reflect high incidence
Autism	Autism spectrum disorders (ASD)	Affects social interactions and communication with restricted, repetitive patterns of behavior
Intellectual disabilities	Intellectual and developmental disabilities; cognitive disabilities	Ranges from mild to severe, but often occurs with other disabilities
Emotional disturbance	Emotional and behavioral disorders (EBD)	Does not include conduct disorders as a reason for special education services
Orthopedic impairments	Physical impairments (PI); physical disabilities	Includes neuromotor impairments and muscular/skeletal conditions
Deafness; hearing impairments*	Hard of hearing and deaf	Deafness and hearing impairments are listed as separate categories in IDEA, but are often combined for reporting and data purposes
Visual impairments	Visual disabilities; low vision and blind	Includes full range of visual loss
Multiple disabilities	Multiple-severe disabilities; severe disabilities	Does not include all students with more than one disability; varies by state's criterion
Deaf-blindness	Deafblind	Criterion does not require both deafness and blindness
Traumatic brain injury (TBI)		Must be acquired after birth
Developmental delay		Allows for noncategorical or non-specific identification between the ages of 3 to 9

*Deafness and hearing impairments are called out in IDEA as two separate disabilities.

You will learn the definitions and eligibility criteria for special education services for each disability category in the disability-specific chapters later in this text. In general, it is important to know that simply having a disability does not automatically qualify a student for services. For example, a student who has a vision loss and uses glasses does not always require special services. However, if that student's educational performance is negatively affected in a substantial way by the vision loss, even when wearing glasses, then the student is probably eligible for special education services, most likely provided by a vision specialist (i.e., a teacher of students with visual impairments, or TVI).

How common are disabilities among public schoolchildren? Every year since IDEA was first passed in 1975, the federal government has collected data from each state about students who receive special education services. These data, summarized in the *Annual Reports to Congress*, capture all types of information, including age, disability category, and race/ethnicity. Having such national data collected from every state, every year, has several advantages.

First, the data help us to determine the number or **prevalence** of students who receive special services. The most recent data reported in the *Annual Report to Congress* indicate that roughly 8% of America's public schoolchildren between the ages of 6 and 21[3] receive special education services. This prevalence rate has decreased slightly across time—in 2004, 9% of all public school students ages 6 to 21 received special education services. In addition to identifying the overall prevalence rates of students who receive special services, these data reveal the national and state prevalence rates for each disability category. Overall trends for disabilities across time show interesting changes. Here are some specifics. For many years, learning disabilities represented over half of all school-age disabilities. Although the learning disabilities category has the highest rate, its prevalence has been declining over recent years, in part because of new early intervening techniques and the implementation of research-based practices (some of which you will learn about in Chapters 2 and 6). In contrast, the prevalence

---

[3]Students with disabilities are eligible for special education services through age 21, due to the extended length of time it may take them to prepare for post-school options.

of autism spectrum disorder (ASD) has been increasing dramatically, due to both the increasing occurrence and the application of a broader definition than was used historically, which allows more children to qualify. Some conditions like physical disabilities and traumatic brain injury (TBI) have increased incidence rates, but improved medical treatment procedures have kept the need for a special education response consistently low across time. The graph shows the proportion or percentage of students identified within each disability category who receive special education services, while the box titled *Prevalence Rate vs. Severity* introduces issues for consideration. For more about the prevalence of students with disabilities, visit http://nces.ed.gov/programs/coe/indicator_cgg.asp.

Order of Disabilities by Prevalence

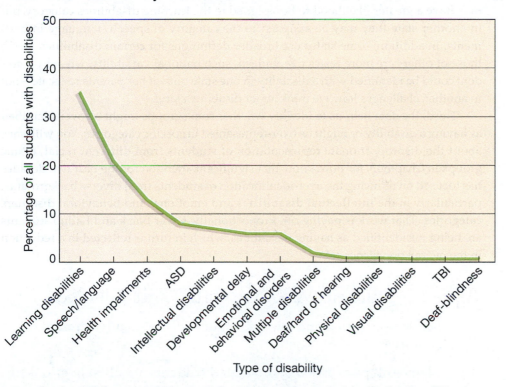

SOURCE: Data from U.S. Department of Education, National Center for Education Statistics, *The Condition of Education, Children and Youth with Disabilities, 2016,* http://nces.ed.gov/programs/coe/indicator_cgg.asp Data Analysis

Prevalence Rate vs. Severity

Many people incorrectly assume that a disability with a high prevalence rate, often referred to as a **high-incidence disability**, is milder, or less severe, than one that occurs less frequently (a **low-incidence disability**). This perception is not accurate. Every type of disability can manifest with a range of characteristics, from mild to severe. Also, considering prevalence data alone fails to take other key considerations into account. One consideration is that many students have co-existing disabilities; for example, it is possible for a student who is blind to also have a speech impairment. Yet, that student would be counted in only one disability category—the one viewed as his or her primary disability—which would not be reflected in state or national prevalence

data. Another point is that specific data within some disability categories are not immediately obvious. For example, most health impairments, such as sickle cell anemia, epilepsy, and cancer, are rare among children. More frequently occurring conditions like asthma, while responsible for a high rate of absenteeism, do not usually require special education services and are *not* part of the health impairments category. However, the health impairments disability category also includes students with attention deficit hyperactivity disorder, which is more common and makes the prevalence rate of this category exceptionally high and could give the initial impression that a larger proportion of U.S. schoolchildren are dealing with significant illnesses.

A second advantage to national data collection is that policy makers can detect state-by-state differences in prevalence. An analysis of the percentage of the school population between the ages of 6 and 21 who receive special education services shows some surprising variations. For example, roughly 6% of all schoolchildren receive special education services in Idaho and Hawaii. However, the rates in those states are much lower than in Massachusetts and New Jersey, where approximately 11% of all schoolchildren receive these services. It is unclear why these discrepancies exist. Also puzzling are the categorical differences between states. For example, Iowa reports that slightly more than 60% of its students who receive special education services have learning disabilities, while Kentucky's learning disability percentage, at 18%, is much lower. Comparable inconsistencies exist in almost every special education category. One potential reason for such variability in identification rates across states rests with procedural differences. For example, in one state, students with language disorders may have a greater likelihood to be assigned to the learning disabilities category, but in another state they may be assigned to the category of speech/language impairments. In addition, some states use broader definitions for certain disabilities, while those of others are more restrictive. Indeed, such national variability, whereby a student could be identified with a disability in one state but—if her parents re-locate—not in another, challenges how we think about disability status.

Third, the data help us to identify whether some groups might be over-identified as having a disability or might be over-represented in specific categories. You will learn about the disproportionate representation of students from different racial/ethnic groups in Chapter 3; for now, know that significant attention for the past two decades has focused on reducing the over-identification of students from diverse backgrounds, particularly in the **intellectual disabilities** and emotional and behavioral disorders categories. That work is paying off. Proportionally, fewer Black and Latino students are being misidentified as having disabilities, which in turn is reflected in a reduction in the overall prevalence rate.

Topic 1.3 Students Who Are Gifted and Talented

- Services for gifted and talented students vary greatly across the country.
- Many groups of gifted and talented students are often overlooked.

Who are children with academic gifts and exceptional creative talents? The federal government does not collect data on giftedness because these students, unlike those with disabilities, are not guaranteed special education services. There is no federal requirement for states to offer special services to these students; therefore, no reporting requirements are in place. That is why giftedness, creativity, and talents are not included in the figure in Topic 1.2. Experts estimate, however, that 3% to 5% of all students across the nation need some type of special educational programming because of their high levels of intelligence, creativity, or extraordinary talents.

Although students with special gifts and talents are often thought of as being exceptional and requiring unique services, decisions regarding the types of education programs available for them rest at the state, rather than the federal, level. In many states, students who qualify are provided with special education services similar to those for students with disabilities. However, these services are delivered without the federal legal requirements or the extra funding provisions guaranteed to states and school districts by the federal government. In other states and school districts, students with special gifts and talents do not receive any special accommodations, services, or supports.

Why do many students who are gifted and talented need special attention during their school years? While popular belief holds that students who are gifted and talented do not need special attention to achieve their potential, the facts tell a different story. Some experts hypothesize that half of all gifted students underperform in school, not living up to their talents or potential. And, those whose unique talents are evident early on often find themselves bored with the general education curriculum. Even though they are highly intelligent, scoring in the top 3% to 5% of all children, or show remarkable levels of other talents, they often flounder or don't achieve to the levels expected. They find themselves in what are now being called **excellence gaps**. Such gaps occur when schools focus on low-achieving students, trying to close the "**achievement gap**" or raise the academic performance of students who attend poor, underperforming schools. This approach can result in ignoring the needs of gifted students. Another group of gifted students who typically do not receive the attention they require comprises gifted students with disabilities. Without special differentiation, enrichment, or acceleration programs that challenge their unique abilities, they, too, often underachieve. More information about their special circumstances is found in the box *Something to Think About: Twice Exceptional*.

Sadly, gifted underachievers report that they find little value in their school experiences and many drop out. Some estimates indicate that up to one-fourth of all high school dropouts are gifted students. The results are tragic for the individuals involved and their families. The missed potential and societal contributions can only be imagined: the solution to climate change, a vaccine that prevents cancer, an exquisite song, a striking mural, innovative water management techniques for drought-stricken areas, or something so far beyond present understanding that we cannot even imagine it.

Something to Think About: Twice Exceptional

Many gifted and talented students fail to receive any specialized educational services because they are never identified as having special gifts or talents. Some individuals, like LeDerick Horne (from this chapter's opener), are **twice-exceptional**—they are gifted or have special talents and also have a disability. However, the disability often masks the giftedness, which causes them to be overlooked for gifted referrals, making twice-exceptional students an under-represented group in gifted education. Other under-represented gifted students are those from diverse ethnic and racial groups and those who attend poor schools where advanced opportunities are not readily available.

Check Your Understanding 1.1

Click here to gauge your understanding of the concepts in this section.

Disabilities and Social Justice

Learning Outcome

Document instances of bias and discrimination experienced by people with disabilities and explain how rights to inclusive education and community presence were won.

Topic 1.4 Issues of Social Justice

- Across time, and even today, there are many examples of how people with disabilities have been poorly treated and faced considerable bias and discrimination.

- Such biases and changing attitudes can be traced through film.

Topic 1.5 Disability as a Minority Group

- People with disabilities, like other historically under-represented groups, constitute a minority group.

- People with disabilities have become their own advocates to fight discrimination and unfair treatment.

Topic 1.6 Participation in Education

- Data from the 1960s and 1970s demonstrated to the public and to policy makers that children and youth with disabilities were routinely denied an education.

- Across the past 30 years students with disabilities have been increasingly included in general education.

Topic 1.4 Issues of Social Justice

Photo from the World Institute on Disability, www.wid.org

Ed Roberts, one of the founders of the disability rights movement, protesting for social justice for people with disabilities in the 1960s.

- Across time, and even today, there are many examples of how people with disabilities have been poorly treated and faced considerable bias and discrimination.

- Such biases and changing attitudes can be traced through film.

Have people with disabilities experienced unjust treatment across time? The answer is a sad, and often horrific, "yes." The history of disabilities documents the terrible treatment these individuals endured. A few examples follow. During the Middle Ages, some little people (formerly called midgets) were kept by the royal courts to serve and entertain as jesters; most, however, were shunned and abandoned. In the eighteenth century, people often left "defective" babies in the woods to die or placed them in bags and threw them over bridges into rushing rivers. At various points in history, many people held the misguided belief that society needed protection *from* those with intellectual disabilities. Subsequently, these individuals were locked away in institutions; sterilization was common practice to prevent them from having children of their own. During World War II, the Nazis sent people who were not deemed intellectually or physically perfect to concentration camps for extermination. Even people in positions of power, like President Franklin Delano Roosevelt (FDR), sought to hide their disabilities for fear they would be construed as signs of weakness. Films like *Warm Springs*, featured in this chapter's *On the Screen*, teach us important lessons from history, reminding us how people with disabilities had to hide their challenges from the public.

On the Screen: *Warm Springs*

The HBO Film *Warm Springs* tells the story of the personal life of Franklin Delano Roosevelt (FDR), the 32nd president of the United States (1933–1945) who brought America out of the Depression and World War II. This film also portrays the struggles that people with disabilities faced even as recently as the twentieth century. FDR had a physical disability, caused when he contracted polio at age 39, that substantially impaired his mobility. FDR hid his disability from the public throughout his presidency. Only two photos exist today that show FDR using a wheelchair. Even in 1997, when FDR's memorial was dedicated, a statue of him in a wheelchair was not included. The National Organization on Disability fought for such a statue, which was added in 2001. For a preview of this film, click here: **www.youtube.com/watch?v=sUQQqMr_big**

–Provided by Steven Smith

Such discrimination is not relegated to the distant past. For decades, when an infant with disabilities was born, parents were often told by their doctors to institutionalize their child; they nearly always complied. That practice began to diminish after 1967, when Burton Blatt published his famous book, *Christmas in Purgatory*, which brought to public attention the abhorrent conditions of institutionalization. This photographic essay chronicled the treatment of people with intellectual disabilities in state institutions. In such living centers, which were home to almost 200,000 persons with disabilities, these individuals were segregated and isolated, abandoned and forgotten. Typically, they received no education or rehabilitation services. Family members did not know that their relatives with disabilities all too often were provided only minimal food, shelter, and clothing.

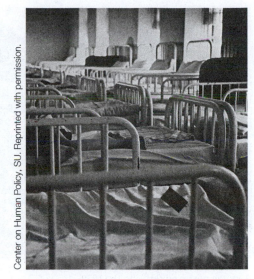

Center on Human Policy, SU. Reprinted with permission.

This photo of a dormitory at an institution for individuals with intellectual disabilities was part of Burton Blatt's photo essay that exposed the horrors of congregate living arrangements.

Abuse in these large, congregate settings was widespread because such residences and their occupants were out of the public's view. No wonder that when the institutions closed and the residents were released, they did not have the skills to live independently. Although institutions in the United States are not outlawed today, fewer of them exist, and calls for the closure of the few remaining institutions continue. Unfortunately, residential institutions are still prevalent in other countries, and abuses tend to persist. For example, in 2010 and 2011, atrocious and abusive conditions were reported in residential institutions and treatment centers for people with disabilities in Mexico, Romania, and many other countries. Watchdog groups like Disability Rights International and Human Rights Watch bring appalling and horrifying conditions to the public's attention, including people neglected in institutions, the homeless forced to fend for themselves on the streets, and those hidden from society. In 2015, Disability Rights International reported that 100% of the girls in at least one Mexican institution were sterilized. Although laws provide the foundation for society's right and wrong actions, it is everyone's job to ensure **social justice**, where equity and equality are part of the day-to-day rhythm of life. For more about worldwide advocacy, go to www.disabilityrightsintl.org and the Human Rights Watch at www.hrw.org.

How are society's perceptions of disability reflected in film? For many people, their only introduction to or knowledge of disability comes from what they see on TV or in the movies. Sometimes, these portrayals are negative or inaccurate. Films often mirror the beliefs and attitudes of society at the time they were made. A retrospective look at media portrayals of people with disabilities gives us a better understanding of how society's views have changed across time. As disability advocate and author Paul Longmore observed, films produced at the beginning of the twentieth century rarely depicted people with disabilities in a positive light. Most characters were villainous, evil, self-pitying, or bitter, and their disabilities often reflected a punishment from God for some sin, either their own or that of a family member.

Fortunately, films also have the ability to positively influence the way people think about and interact with others. Today, most characters with disabilities in cinema and TV are shown in a positive light. Many are part of an ensemble cast in which no special notice is paid to their disabilities at all. For some advocates, this is positive evidence that disabilities are more openly accepted, as much a part of the human condition as being short or tall, young or old.

The original and remakes of the movie *The Hunchback of Notre Dame* illustrate how perceptions have changed over time. In early versions of this movie, Quasimodo was a frightening and horrible creature, but across remakes, as in the most recent version created by Disney Films, he is more human and endearing, transcending his disabilities.

Although today's inclusion of characters with disabilities in TV and film reflect more positive and natural depictions, there still are not enough leading or supporting

A movie poster advertising the 1939 version of the movie, *The Hunchback of Notre Dame*, that depicted Quasimodo as a frightening, sad, and isolated character who was condemned to live in the church's bell tower.

roles to adequately portray the everyday lives of people with disabilities. According to the Screen Actors Guild, in 2011 less than 1% of all characters in TV shows had a disability; in the same year, only three prime time TV shows featured actors with Down syndrome. Too often, characters with disabilities are played by actors without disabilities. Movies like *One Flew Over the Cuckoo's Nest*, *The Miracle Worker*, and *Born on the Fourth of July* are just a few notable examples of movies in which the key actor did not have a disability but either was nominated for or won an Academy Award for the portrayal. Lawrence Carter-Long, an advocate with disabilities and an advisor to the Alliance for Inclusion in the Arts, leads the call for actors with disabilities to be cast in appropriate parts (similar to criticisms of the past regarding the casting of White actors to play American Indians). Results have been positive; the Screen Actors Guild and the American Federation of Television and Radio Artists, two of the entertainment industry's organizations for actors, have established a national committee that advocates for increased opportunities for auditions and casting of performers with disabilities.

Topic 1.5 Disability as a Minority Group

- People with disabilities, like other historically under-represented groups, constitute a minority group.
- People with disabilities have become their own advocates to fight discrimination and unfair treatment.

Do similarities exist among the experiences of people with disabilities and other minority groups in America? The civil rights movement of the 1950s and 1960s, which fought against the discrimination, bias, and segregation experienced by African Americans, set the stage for the inclusion and civil rights movement for people with disabilities. In the 1950s, the Supreme Court ruled in *Brown v. Board of Education* that schools separating children by race were not equal and subsequently mandated the integration of African American students to attend school side-by-side with their peers of different racial and ethnic backgrounds. The Civil Rights Act of 1964 opened the door to full participation in American society for all people of color. So both the courts and legislation affirmed that discrimination against people from minority groups was not only morally wrong but also illegal.

As with other minority groups, people with disabilities have faced, and continue to experience, bias. Like other historically under-represented groups in the United States, people with disabilities have been excluded from fair treatment, participation, and a full **community presence**. While acknowledging the existence of a *disability* (the literal lack of a specific ability), many individuals believe that society is what **handicaps** them because of their conditions and challenges. Society presents and creates barriers; society can remove them; and, therefore, society produces the events that handicap and restrict individuals with disabilities from achieving their potential.

How have individuals with disabilities increased public awareness of discrimination and bias? The lessons learned from the civil rights movement taught people with disabilities, their families, and their friends that they have to fight to get their voices heard and their opinions put forth. It often takes protests and public awareness efforts, such as through TV and social media, to expose abuses and to make positive and substantial changes.

In the video below, early disability advocates—including Ed Roberts and Justin Dart, initiators of the Disability Rights Movement—explain their struggles to achieve civil rights and social justice:

▶ **It's Our Story**

www.youtube.com/watch?v=fWDaRN490BI&feature=relmfu

John Duricka/AP Images

Ed Roberts and Judy Heumann, disability rights activists, at a landmark meeting where they advocated for the civil rights of people with disabilities. Both Roberts and Heumann, like many of the early advocates, contracted polio as children and had to fight to be included in the educational system. In 1983 they co-founded the World Institute on Disability, which is still doing important work to guarantee civil rights to people with disabilities. Although Ed Roberts died in 1995, Judy Heumann continues to work today to ensure such rights on an international level for all people with disabilities. To learn about the current activities of the World Institute on Disability, go to: http://wid.org/

An important shift in disability advocacy has developed in the past few decades. Originally, parents, brothers and sisters, other family members, and professionals were the advocates for individuals with disabilities. However, since the 1980s, individuals with disabilities themselves have become vocal, demanding social justice and civil rights. Here's a remarkable story about one of the first disability rights activists who demanded changes in access and equality in everyday life. At the age of 14, Ed Roberts almost died of polio. In the early 1960s, after considerable struggle and persistence, he was ready to attend college. However, the University of California (UC) at Berkeley declared that he was "too disabled" for the campus to accommodate. And, despite the fact that the California Department of Vocational Rehabilitation existed solely to provide support for adults with disabilities, that department would not pay for his education because Roberts, who had quadriplegia and used a wheelchair, was "too handicapped." Despite this rejection, Roberts paid for his own personal care attendants and became known on campus as one of the "Rolling Quads." After receiving his bachelor's and master's degrees, he eventually became director of the very agency that had refused to assist with his college education expenses. Much later, he co-founded the World Institute on Disability, an event that many mark as the formal beginning of the civil rights movement for people with disabilities. It was his advocacy and that of other individuals with disabilities that brought public attention to the systematic denial of access to society experienced by this group of people.

Deaf students of Gallaudet University took their complaints to the U.S. Congress in protest of the selection of a hearing president who did not know how to communicate using American Sign Language.

Courtesy of Gallaudet University Archives

Here is another groundbreaking example of disability advocacy. Gallaudet University, located in Washington, DC, is the nation's premier university dedicated to providing a liberal arts education and career development for Deaf students. In 1988, students protested because they disapproved of the newly appointed university president. She was a person without hearing loss, did not know or use American Sign Language, was not involved in Deaf culture, and was hired without their input. The students' weeklong protest and march from Gallaudet's campus to the U.S. Capitol brought their issues to the nation's attention. The result? The Board of Trustees reversed its position and immediately selected I. King Jordan as president. That event is referred to as Deaf President Now (DPN) and is still a rallying cry for people around the world. Jordan, who is a member of the Deaf community, has brought international attention to the importance of Gallaudet University. He challenges everyone to examine his or her attitudes toward people with disabilities.

Timeline for Disability Advocacy

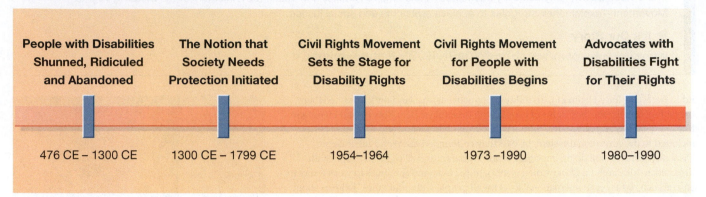

People with Disabilities Shunned, Ridiculed and Abandoned	The Notion that Society Needs Protection Initiated	Civil Rights Movement Sets the Stage for Disability Rights	Civil Rights Movement for People with Disabilities Begins	Advocates with Disabilities Fight for Their Rights
476 CE – 1300 CE	1300 CE – 1799 CE	1954–1964	1973 –1990	1980–1990

Topic 1.6 Participation in Education

- Data from the 1960s and 1970s demonstrated to the public and to policy makers that children and youth with disabilities were routinely denied an education.

- Across the past 30 years students with disabilities have been increasingly included in general education.

How were children with disabilities educated differently than their peers without disabilities? Positive attitudes about the benefits of educating students with disabilities began to develop centuries ago with Itard's famous work in France during the late 1770s with the "Wild Child," Victor. Information about this pioneering work is found in Topic 9.10. Despite these early efforts to educate students with disabilities, many U.S. students were denied access to a free appropriate public education until the mid-1970s. The following data were collected in the early 1970s, when Congress set out to investigate the situation. Its key finding was that although some students with disabilities received educational services, *most did not.* Here is some of the information collected.

Denial of educational opportunities was historic:

- In 1948, only 12% of all children with disabilities received special education services.
- As late as 1962, only 16 states had laws that included students with even mild cognitive problems under mandatory school attendance requirements.

Bias, discrimination, segregation, and exclusion were pervasive in the 1960s and 1970s at the time of the investigation:

- Many states had laws directing that some children be excluded from school, including those with profound hearing loss, intellectual disabilities, and emotional disturbance.
- In 1970, U.S. schools educated only one in five children with disabilities.
- One million children with disabilities in the United States were excluded entirely from the public school system.
- More than half of the eight million children with disabilities in the United States were not receiving appropriate educational services.
- The special educational needs of these children were not being fully met because they were not receiving necessary **related services** (e.g., speech therapy, physical therapy).
- Services within the public school system were inadequate and forced families to find services outside the system, often at great distance from their residence and at their own expense.

- If given appropriate funding, state and local educational agencies could provide effective special education and related services to meet the needs of children with disabilities.

Collectively, these findings caused Congress to take action. No longer could students with disabilities be excluded and denied their right to receive a free public education. In 1974, Congress put basic guarantees in place by passing a national law, the Individuals with Disabilities Education Act, which ensured all children with disabilities the right to a free public education that was appropriate to meet their educational needs. This law has been reauthorized multiple times, improving and expanding these fundamental rights to children and youth with disabilities, and is still in effect today.

Why is it important to consider where students with disabilities receive their education? In the 1970s and 1980s, great strides were made to ensure that *not a single* student with a disability was denied the right to attend public school. The focus was on providing an education deemed appropriate to meet the needs of each student. In many cases, the decision was made for the student to attend a separate, specialized school where his or her complex needs could be addressed. For example, these schools often had specially prepared teachers, physical therapists, speech and language pathologists, occupational therapists, and paraprofessionals who assisted teachers and related service providers. The schools were fully equipped with specialized equipment, often even with therapeutic swimming pools. Even though students attended separate schools, most professionals and parents felt that students received the best education possible. Their intentions were good, but the outcome was that children were segregated—separated from the community, typically developing peers, and from the general education curriculum.

These practices continued for years. Sometimes a school district or a group of them formed special schools for students with specific disabilities, such as those with physical disabilities, those with intellectual disabilities, or those who had difficulties with toileting or mobility. Other schools had special classes, sometimes located in remote areas of the school (e.g., in portable buildings at the far end of the school property) for students with learning disabilities, emotional or behavioral disorders, and other disabilities. As a result, public attention soon shifted to *where* students with disabilities received their education. In part because of the advocacy of adults with physical challenges—many of whom had cerebral palsy or had contracted polio as children—and parent organizations, the call for inclusive education soon emerged. The idea was, and is, that children should attend their neighborhood schools with their brothers, sisters, and neighborhood friends and, as much as possible, should access the general education curriculum in the general education classroom. Consequently, special education is now thought of as a service and *not* a place. The overarching goal for students with disabilities, like that for all schoolchildren, is to be college- or career-ready at the completion of their public school education.

National Archives and Records Administration

In the 1960s, students with disabilities who did receive a public education attended separate schools in segregated settings, often long distances from their homes and neighborhood schools.

Making a Difference

Learning Outcome

Explain what people first language is and why using it is important to people with disabilities.

Topic 1.7 Perceptions Matter

- Perceptions and attitudes influence how individuals and society respond to disabilities and abilities.

- Three perspectives—deficit, cultural, and sociological—can be used to think about disabilities.

Topic 1.8 Words Matter

- The words we use to communicate attitudes and perceptions are important.

- Most people with disabilities prefer that the words used to describe their disability express a condition or situation, like *using a wheelchair*, rather than define who they are.

The outcomes are amazing when everyone helps each other, respects each other, and works together!

Topic 1.7 Perceptions Matter

- Perceptions and attitudes influence how individuals and society respond to disabilities and abilities.

- Three perspectives—deficit, cultural, and sociological—can be used to think about disabilities.

How do perceptions and attitudes impact people with disabilities? Throughout history, many examples demonstrate repeatedly that perceptions and attitudes affect the way people are treated. Differences between groups can be celebrated or viewed as problems. Unfortunately, negative perceptions often turn into bias and discrimination, which too often lead to the awful treatment of others. Differences in religion, race, ethnicity, and (dis)abilities have all been the basis of such mistreatment. The Holocaust is an obvious example; intolerance of differences in religion, ethnicity, and disabilities resulted in the torture and death of an estimated 11 million people. Other examples may not be as well known, but they are just as horrific. The way people are treated can either create barriers that restrict their abilities to achieve or provide opportunities and supports that allow them to flourish. Throughout this text, we will continue to call attention to biases and discrimination that people with disabilities face, as well as to highlight successes that occur when people are treated with respect and allowed appropriate supports.

What are some of the differing perspectives on disability? One important fact is that disability is not a universally agreed-upon concept. How one thinks about disabilities sets the path for one's actions.

Work through the IRIS Module *What Do You See? Perceptions of Disability* and explore your own attitudes and beliefs about people with disabilities.

▶ IRIS Module: What Do You See? Perceptions of Disability
http://iris.peabody.vanderbilt.edu/module/da/

Three perspectives are used to explain society's reaction to the concept of difference due to disability. These perspectives or orientations provide frameworks to understand various actions and reactions relating to disabilities or special needs. Let's consider these three different orientations or perspectives.

The *deficit perspective* suggests that human behavior and characteristics are distributed along a continuum called the **normal curve**, or **bell-shaped curve**, as shown in the diagram. Scores or measurements across a large group of people tend to create a distribution in which the majority of people fall in the middle of the distribution; they are considered "average." For example, people are of different heights. Some people are extremely short, others exceptionally tall, but most heights fall somewhere in the middle; the average of everyone's height is at the center of the distribution. Such is the case with most characteristics, but the problem with this way of thinking is that—for any single characteristic—this orientation puts half of us below average, or not normal.

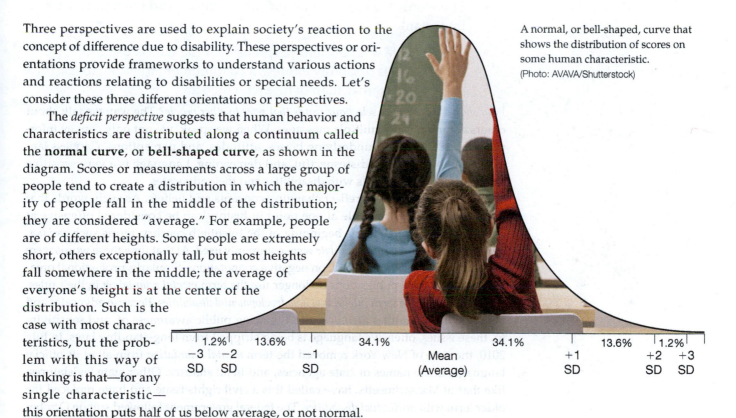

A normal, or bell-shaped, curve that shows the distribution of scores on some human characteristic.
(Photo: AVAVA/Shutterstock)

	1.2%	13.6%	34.1%	34.1%	13.6%	1.2%
	−3 SD	−2 SD	−1 SD	Mean (Average)	+1 SD	+2 SD +3 SD

Another way of conceptualizing disabilities reflects a *cultural perspective.* Often people from different cultures have a variety of views about difference and disability. This is a very important point for educators to recognize because students and their families come to school with different beliefs about what causes disabilities, and what the families' or schools' proper response should be. For example, many parents from Native and American Indian cultures believe that having a child with a disability is a blessing, while some from the Caribbean believe that such children are a curse from the devil. Knowing that not all cultures share the same concept of disability helps us understand why families, when informed that their child has a disability, respond to education professionals differently.

The third way to think about disability is socially constructed and is called the *sociological perspective.* Central to this view is the idea that disability results from society's need to stratify individuals, making many people subservient to a few. It is the way that society treats individuals, not a condition or set of traits or characteristics, that handicaps groups of people. In other words, according to this perspective, disability does not really exist; it results when individuals are treated differently. Taken to its extreme, this perspective implies that the application of special education services causes disabilities, as opposed to being a response to disabilities. While some believe that the sociological perspective explains disability, others feel that this is a dangerous position because the result could be that no special attention or services would be provided to students and adults with disabilities.

Reflect on the message of this French video about disabilities and how they are perceived in society:

▶ **Disability Awareness**
www.youtube.com/watch?v=wzRQOfVvVh4&feature=related

Topic 1.8 Words Matter

- The words we use to communicate attitudes and perceptions are important.

- Most people with disabilities prefer that the words used to describe their disability express a condition or situation, like *using a wheelchair*, rather than define who they are.

Why should we carefully select our words that refer to other people? The way we talk about others communicates multiple messages. When we speak, we not only convey information but also reveal underlying biases, attitudes, and perceptions. Careless language can be offensive, disrespectful, and demeaning. Language is a very sensitive issue for many individuals with disabilities and their advocates.

Language evolves to reflect changing concepts and beliefs. As such, words that might be socially acceptable at one point in history can be considered offensive at another. For example, at the beginning of the twentieth century, terms such as *idiot, imbecile, moron,* and *mental retardate* were commonly used. At that time these words were *not* offensive, but later they took on negative connotations. Similarly, professional organizations and their publications no longer use the term *mental retardation* in their titles, and instead use the term *intellectual and developmental disabilities*. Because advocates and people with disabilities are successfully raising public awareness of, and sensitivity to, these issues, offensive language is being stripped from long-standing laws. In July 2010, the state of New York removed the term *mental retardation* from all of its official language, in the names of state agencies, and in all statutes. Other state legislatures, like that of Massachusetts, have called this a civil rights issue and have replaced the older term with *intellectual disabilities*. The federal government followed suit on October 5, 2010, retroactively replacing the term *mental retardation* with *intellectual disabilities* in all federal statutes. That federal law is referred to as "Rosa's Law" and is considered by many in the disability community to be a major milestone in the ongoing battle for dignity and respect for people with intellectual disabilities. (We talk more about Rosa's Law and related issues for people with intellectual disabilities in Chapter 9.)

It is important to recognize that the term *intellectual disabilities*, while preferred today, will probably become offensive sometime in the future. In fact, advocates and scholars are confident that such will be the case and that everyone must be alert to words and phrases that become disrespectful or negatively classify people. Such discussions are currently being held about the word *disorder*, which is used in the World Health Organization's diagnostic tool used to identify disabilities.

Unfortunately, many terms and phrases considered insulting or derogatory are still used in the media. Now that your awareness has been raised, you will notice these terms in newspaper and magazine articles, online, and on social media. Think about the wording you see and hear in the press and decide how references to people should be improved. How can you promote the use of more positive language?

What language should we use when referring to people with disabilities? **People-first language** is a set of guidelines that helps us refer to people respectfully by considering the following: (1) *which words to use* and (2) *in what order those words are placed.* When using people-first language, mention the person first and the disability second, which builds on the idea that *disabilities do not define the individual.* The principles of people-first language place the primary focus on the person, rather than implying that the disability is primary and the individual is secondary. Just as someone can have brown hair or green eyes, a disability is something an individual has, not something the person is. If someone has a cold, we do not call him or her a "cold person"; we indicate that he or she has a cold.

People-First Language

Do Say	Don't Say
People with disabilities	The disabled
A student with a learning disability	A learning disabled student
A person who uses a wheelchair	A person confined to a wheelchair or someone who is wheelchair bound
A person who has cerebral palsy	A person who suffers from cerebral palsy
A child with intellectual disabilities	Retard

As with all guidelines, some exceptions apply. For example, Deaf Americans who use American Sign Language as their primary means of communicating prefer to capitalize the "d" in *deaf* and—as we used in the beginning of this sentence—to place *Deaf* first. To members of the Deaf community, their heritage and culture are the foremost priority (Deaf culture is discussed more in Chapter 11.) In another example, some people with autism spectrum disorder and their advocates, though not all, believe that autism does define them and that, in contrast to people-first language, the disability should come first. As such, the preferred terms should be an *autistic person* or an *ASD individual.* Others are more comfortable with phrases such as *a student with ASD.* Such disagreement also exists for people with visual disabilities. Some prefer to be called blind individuals, while others do not. As these examples illustrate, not everyone agrees about preferred language, even when from the same community.

Check Your Understanding 1.3

Click here to gauge your understanding of the concepts in this section.

The Changing Landscape

Learning Outcome

Using three dimensions – academic, post-secondary education, and community presence – describe progress made and discuss goals that still must be achieved.

Topic 1.9 Academic Outcomes

- More students with disabilities are benefiting from an inclusive education in elementary and secondary schools and becoming more college- and career ready for adult life.
- Challenges with academic achievement and access to post-secondary education still exist, however, and must be overcome.

Topic 1.10 Post-Secondary Accomplishments

- Trends are positive: more individuals with disabilities are attending post-secondary schools, including community colleges and four-year colleges and universities.

- Transition planning during high school and supports at post-secondary schools are helping individuals with disabilities achieve their dreams of a college education.

Topic 1.11 Community Presence

- Compared to the past, people with disabilities are assuming a community presence, living independently, and securing competitive employment.

- Welcoming attitudes, the ADA law, and removal of physical and social barriers have contributed to this progress.

Inclusive education—where students with disabilities participate in education with their peers and access the general education curriculum—contributes to improved academic accomplishments.

Topic 1.9 Academic Outcomes

- More students with disabilities are benefiting from an inclusive education in elementary and secondary schools and becoming more college- and career ready for adult life.

- Challenges with academic achievement and access to post-secondary education still exist, however, and must be overcome.

What does the education of students with disabilities look like today? Never before have so many individuals with disabilities found success in the elementary and secondary educational system. More of these students are college- or career-ready when they move on from high school. Many factors contribute to such improvements: (1) attitudes about what students with disabilities can achieve have become more positive; (2) a greater percentage of these students are accessing the general education curriculum; (3) inclusive educational settings are more responsive to individual needs; and (4) the implementation of proven instructional practices is helping to prevent school failure and avoid referrals to special education.

Improved educational outcomes are seen in many areas. Evidence shows that well-prepared and highly qualified teachers contribute to the improved outcomes of students with disabilities. New **evidence-based instructional practices** have been identified and are being implemented. Increased accountability and frequent measurement of students' progress ensure that time is not wasted on ineffective instructional methods. In addition, students with disabilities are allowed to use **accommodations** that help them compensate for challenges caused by their disabilities. As a result, 64% of those who do qualify for special education through the learning disabilities category are graduating from high school with a regular diploma (up from 52% a decade ago).

Some major accomplishments can be quickly summarized:

- First, 95% of all students with disabilities attend their neighborhood schools.
- Second, 60% access the general education curriculum and receive their education in the general education classroom at least 80% of the school day.
- Third, over the past 10 years, a 16% increase in rates of graduation with a standard high school diploma has occurred.
- Fourth, 21% fewer drop out of school.

Can we improve on these accomplishments? Yes, there is a lot of room for more students to make even greater gains. In fact, experts strongly believe that with appropriate accommodations and instruction, some 80% of students with disabilities are capable of attaining grade-level proficiency. However, such accomplishments will take considerable effort; the validation of more evidence-based practices; and possibly more intensive, individualized, and sustained services. For a number of reasons, we should *not* be satisfied with present levels of success:

- As a group, students without disabilities substantially outperform students with disabilities.
- While the achievement gaps between students with and without disabilities are narrowing at the elementary school level, the gaps are still unacceptable and averaging up to 41% during middle school and high school.
- Only 11% of students with disabilities scored "proficient" or above in fourth grade reading, and only 16% in fourth grade math.
- Although dropout rates among youth with disabilities have decreased, 23% of youth with disabilities still leave school before graduation, a rate twice that of their peers without disabilities.

One test of whether the normal rhythm of life has been achieved is when everyone has a chance to participate.

Topic 1.10 Post-Secondary Accomplishments

- Trends are positive: more individuals with disabilities are attending post-secondary schools, including community colleges and four-year colleges and universities.
- Transition planning during high school and supports at post-secondary schools are helping individuals with disabilities achieve their dreams of a college education.

Are more individuals with disabilities pursuing post-secondary education? More students in the United States are attending post-secondary schools (e.g., community college, university), particularly students from historically under-represented groups, including those with disabilities. Here are some data to support this claim:

- Almost 11% of all undergraduates have a disability.
- The percentage of students with disabilities attending college continues to increase over time.
  - In 2005, some 46% of students with disabilities attended a post-secondary college or university within four years after graduating from high school, up from 26% in 1990.
  - Over 50% of all 2009 ninth graders with disabilities were attending either a two-year or a four-year institution of higher learning four years later, in 2013.
- Of all students with disabilities, those with visual disabilities have the highest rate of attendance at two- and four-year colleges and universities (26% attend two-year colleges; 43% attend four-year colleges).
- In 2013, people with disabilities earned 5.8% of all doctoral degrees, up from 1.5% in 2008.
- In 2013, 10.5% of those earning a doctorate in special education are people who self-identified as having a disability, almost double the proportion they represent in other fields of study.

What are some of the supports that have made this success possible? More students with disabilities are succeeding in high school and continuing this success at the college and university level. They are benefiting from transition planning and services offered in high school, which prepare them to request and benefit from accommodations and supports now available in post-secondary settings. Even students with considerable cognitive struggles are finding their places on college campuses.

Although the legal requirements of IDEA '04 do not extend to post-secondary schools, more and more colleges and universities have special offices that provide supports to students with disabilities. Staff members from these offices help these students access important accommodations and supports, which are continually increasing in number and type: extended time for exams, note takers, lecture notes provided by faculty, help with study skills, alternate test forms, adaptive equipment, and assistive technology.

Some universities have designed unique programs for students with disabilities. For example, the University of Illinois at Urbana-Champaign has a first-of-its-kind, state-of-the-art dormitory that allows students with disabilities to live and study alongside their classmates without disabilities. Other colleges, like Iowa State University, have developed special programs in which students with intellectual disabilities live in dormitories on campus and attend classes that focus on independent living.

The important point is that greater percentages of individuals with disabilities are pursuing post-secondary education, particularly as colleges and universities are becoming more welcoming and are providing improved services. Yet, still more work is required to ensure access for all, and in more areas than just college or university attendance.

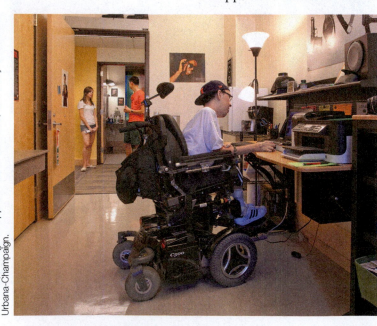

Photo courtesy of the Division of Disability Resources and Educational Services, College of Applied Health Sciences, University of Illinois at Urbana-Champaign.

Living in an accessible dorm room supports this young man's dreams of being a college student and, soon, a college graduate.

Topic 1.11 Community Presence

- Compared to times in the past, people with disabilities are assuming a community presence, living independently, and securing competitive employment.

- Welcoming attitudes, the ADA law, and removal of physical and social barriers have contributed to this progress.

What type of progress has been made to fully integrate people with disabilities into society and daily life? A lot of progress has occurred in this area, but challenges remain. Individuals with disabilities are finding their way in society and developing a community presence. More of these persons than ever before are securing competitive employment, living independently, and enjoying the benefits of community activities. These individuals include poets, writers, supervisors, inventors, entrepreneurs, teachers, and scientists. However, such achievements have not come easily. You may recall that the history of disabilities is fraught with discrimination, bias, and appalling treatment. Not that long ago, many Americans harbored negative, unfounded perceptions of individuals with disabilities (remember our earlier discussion regarding media portrayals). Such attitudes had terrible, probably unintended consequences. Individuals with disabilities were excluded from all aspects of society: schools, community living, recreation, and competitive employment. In Topic 1.5, you learned that individuals with disabilities have had to fight for attainment of civil rights. You learned in Topic 1.6 that most were excluded from education and, even after those rights were won, students were segregated in separate schools and separate classes.

The struggle for community presence continues today. While 61% of all individuals with disabilities are competitively employed at present, that percentage was almost 80% before the economic downturn. Surprisingly, up to eight years after high school graduation, only 36% are living independently, which includes living in a college dormitory. Despite what clearly seems like the "right thing to do," sometimes it takes federal action to ensure social justice for people with disabilities. One such example is the Americans with Disabilities Act (ADA), in part authored by Senator Tom Harkin, who is featured at the beginning of Chapter 4. The benefits of this law—meant to guarantee full access to American life—are still unfolding, but people with disabilities face less discrimination in employment, public accommodations, and telecommunications as a result. Because of the ADA, more restaurants, theaters, hotels, stores, banks, and college buildings are being remodeled or constructed to meet or exceed its accessibility requirements. These changes allow more people with disabilities to be included in all aspects of daily life. As a consequence, more people live with greater independence and have possibilities for full community participation. For example, they go to cafés with friends, enjoy drinks after work, see movies at their local theaters, and even travel the world. They live in houses and apartments in the community and commute to and from work. Merchants, the travel industry, and leisure-time businesses have become aware of this relatively new clientele and, in part due to the realization of the profit potential, are catering to them. For example, buses with accessibility features for wheelchairs have expanded ridership, parks with accessible trails and museums with tactile exhibits have increased patronage, and cruise lines and tour groups now design events in which people's special needs are met.

Even with such progress, negative attitudes remain and result in unwelcoming behavior. Consequently, more effort must be expended to achieve a real community presence for individuals with disabilities.

Society can handicap people and restrict their access more than disabilities do. Unfortunately, barriers like steps to access classrooms, advisors' offices, and public buildings still exist.

Monkey Business Images/Shutterstock

For instance, homeowners often fight changes in zoning ordinances that would allow building a **group home**, a community-based living center for a small group of individuals with disabilities, in their neighborhood. Shopping center developers put in the fewest elevators and ramps allowable, meeting the letter, but not the spirit, of the Americans with Disabilities Act. City and county government officials and college administrators delay the remodeling of public buildings so they do not have to spend the funds needed to make an entire building accessible. Can you identify such barriers on your college campus?

What are other examples of environmental alterations that have improved community access for people with disabilities? Collectively, many different adaptations, accommodations, and modifications to the environment contribute to a better life for individuals with disabilities. Even though some innovations target specific disabilities—like robotics that help amputees re-create their mobility—perhaps an important lesson is that many people benefit from these innovations, not just those with disabilities. For example, **open captioning,** which shows the words being spoken at the bottom of TV screens, allows people with hearing impairments to watch TV. However, it also helps people without hearing loss watch the news or a sporting event at a busy and noisy airport. As another example, **curb cuts** and ramps are designed to permit wheelchairs and their users to cross streets, enter buildings, and move more freely to access daily life. But they also make it easier for everyone to guide carts, roll luggage, push strollers, and even skateboard when crossing streets.

Although the above examples were specifically developed for people with disabilities, many products intended for mass markets also have great benefits to those with disabilities. Think about the technology you use on a daily basis. Cell phones, with us at all times, allow constant, immediate connection to family and friends. The Internet provides the convenience of online banking and personal shopping without having to leave home and lets us easily access information and communicate with others far and wide. Laptop computers and tablets like the iPad allow us to write without revealing poor handwriting; autocorrect features, though often annoying, prevent many misspellings. GPS devices permit travel without fear of getting lost. Applications of these technologies have even greater benefits for people with disabilities. A cell phone call, whether for help or for a pizza, is possible from virtually any location. Online banking eliminates the need to write checks or calculate financial balances. Laptop computers and personal readers have the capability to enlarge type size or provide auditory output. Computers also assist those with organizational difficulties when they need to format papers and assignments. Laser canes equipped with GPS systems and speech output enable easier orientation and mobility for people with visual disabilities.

When potential markets are large, businesses invest through research and development. Given that people with disabilities have considerable spending power, it is a good business strategy to develop products that are appealing and accessible to everyone. A growing number of technologies, both hardware and software, are being developed in multiple versions to better meet the needs of all individuals. For instance, one video game, *Perception,* is being developed by The Deep End Games company with two versions: one for people with visual disabilities and another for those without them. Both versions, however, have many people with and without disabilities represented in the game, providing equal treatment and equal exposure to integrated life.

In January of 2016, news outlets excitedly announced the addition of a Lego figure in a wheelchair, making the toys more reflective of the children who play with them. As you consider community access, think about it in terms of visibility. How often do you see individuals with disabilities in commercials or in Web, newspaper, or magazine ads? What other toy characters with disabilities have you seen? Just as importantly, did you notice that people with disabilities were missing from these depictions (until we mentioned it just now)?

Ekaterina Minaeva/Alamy Stock Photo

Given the historical treatment of individuals with disabilities and the momentous strides in attitudes, perceptions, educational services, and community presence, imagine the future possibilities and new horizons before us. Only our collective imaginations can envision how new technology and research will take us beyond what currently lies at our doorsteps with innovations that will enrich everyone's lives.

Check Your Understanding 1.4

Click here to gauge your understanding of the concepts in this section.

Summary

Putting Exceptionalities into Perspective

Although there is much room for improvement, most of America's 50 million students thrive, succeed, and find their places in society as adults.

- The nation's school population is becoming more diverse; students come from a variety of racial, ethnic, linguistic, and socioeconomic backgrounds, all of which have implications for school performance.

- Some 8% of America's children and youth receive special education services through one of the 14 eligible categories (13 disability categories and *developmental delay*) outlined in the national law, the Individuals with Disabilities Education Act of 2004 (IDEA '04).

- Between 3% and 5% of all schoolchildren have exceptional academic abilities or creative talents, but often their special needs are overlooked because of inconsistent availability of enrichment, acceleration, or special educational opportunities.

Disabilities and Social Justice

Although equity and equality are improving, social justice still is not automatically granted to people with disabilities.

- The history of disabilities, even in the recent past, is replete with examples of appalling treatment, bias, and discrimination, often reflected in films produced across time.

- Like other historically under-represented groups, people with disabilities have had to fight for basic civil rights.

- Before the 1970s, millions of children were denied a right to public education, which, when it was offered, was often provided in segregated settings and not appropriate for individual needs, thus restricting their chances to achieve their potential and take their places in American society.

Making a Difference

Working both collectively and as individuals, everyone can make a difference in the lives of people with disabilities.

- The way society perceives disabilities impacts the treatment of and opportunities afforded to people with disabilities.

- The language we use reflects our perceptions, including concepts of dignity and respect for people with disabilities.

The Changing Landscape

Although recent accomplishments of individuals with disabilities have been remarkable, they only hint at what will be possible when improved services are fully in place and actualized.

- Because of improved attitudes and increased access to the general education curriculum, inclusive education, and new evidence-based practices, more students with disabilities are college- and career-ready.

- More students with disabilities are attending colleges and universities and succeeding in post-secondary educational experiences.

- Individuals with disabilities are beginning to achieve a strong community presence, working and living among all of us.

Addressing CEC Standards

Council for Exceptional Children (CEC) knowledge standards addressed in this chapter: 6.2, 6.3, 5.5.

See the Appendix for the complete CEC Initial Level Special Educator Preparation Standards.

Chapter 2
Supporting All Learners

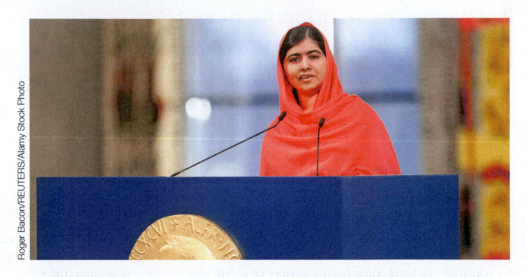

It is not time to tell the world leaders to realise [sic] how important education is—they already know it—their own children are in good schools... Leaders must seize this opportunity to guarantee a free, quality, primary and secondary education for every child. Some will say this is impractical, or too expensive, or too hard. Or maybe even impossible. But it is time the world thinks bigger.

—Malala Yousafzai, age 17, from her 2014 Nobel Peace Prize acceptance speech

From "Malala Yousafzai–Nobel Lecture." by Malala Yousafzai. Published by The Nobel Foundation © 2014.

Malala Yousafzai was 15 years old when a Taliban gunman shot her in retaliation for her educational activism. At that young age, she had already been speaking out in favor of Pakistani girls' rights to education for several years. In recognition of her continuing advocacy for education, Malala was the co-recipient of the 2014 Nobel Peace Prize. Access to a free public education is guaranteed in the United States; however, Malala's challenge to provide a *quality* education—at both the elementary and the secondary levels—for *every* child is an issue that we have not yet resolved.

 ## Learning Outcomes

High-Quality Instruction

Describe three areas of U.S. education in which there is room for improvement; define an evidence-based practice; and explain how the use of UDL, differentiated instruction, and data-based decision making can set a strong foundation of high-quality education for all students.

Multi-Tiered Systems of Support

Understand the conceptual framework of multi-tiered systems of support, and describe the specific processes involved in the RTI framework for academics and the PBIS framework for behavior.

High-Quality Instruction[1]

Learning Outcome

Describe three areas of U.S. education in which there is room for improvement; define an evidence-based practice; and explain how the use of UDL, differentiated instruction, and data-based decision making can set a strong foundation of high-quality education for all students.

Topic 2.1 Introduction

- Despite our knowledge about effective instructional and behavioral practices, too many students—particularly those with disabilities—fall behind academically, drop out, or face bullying at school.

- A solid educational foundation for students with disabilities depends on the provision of a high-quality education for all students: those with and without disabilities, those who struggle, and students who are gifted, talented, and creative.

Topic 2.2 Evidence-Based Practices

- Evidence-based practices have been proven effective by rigorous research.

- Evidence-based practices must be implemented with fidelity, using the same procedures that researchers used to develop them.

Topic 2.3 Universal Design for Learning (UDL)

- The implementation of evidence-based practices is only one component of high-quality instruction for a student population with a wide range of learning needs.

- Universal Design for Learning (UDL) can reduce or eliminate barriers to students' learning.

Topic 2.4 Differentiated Instruction

- Teachers who provide differentiated instruction (DI) adjust various aspects of the educational process to meet students' learning needs.

- Whereas UDL is a proactive measure implemented when designing the curriculum, differentiated instruction is a responsive measure that is incorporated when planning and implementing instruction.

Topic 2.5 Data-Based Decision Making

- Teachers should use data gathered from diagnostic, formative, and summative assessments to plan and modify instruction.

- Several types of formative assessments allow teachers to quickly gather information on students' progress.

---

[1]References for Chapter 2 are found at the end of this text.

Kindergarten students arrive at school excited and eager to learn. Unfortunately, too many students lose that enthusiasm early on. We need to work harder to ensure that all students remain engaged in their learning from their first day of school through graduation.

Topic 2.1 Introduction

- Despite our knowledge about effective instructional and behavioral practices, too many students—particularly those with disabilities—fall behind academically, drop out, or face bullying at school.

- A solid educational foundation for students with disabilities depends on the provision of a high-quality education for all students: those with and without disabilities, those who struggle, and students who are gifted, talented, and creative.

How well are we educating America's students? The future quality of life for today's students depends more than ever on how well their K–12 education has prepared them for **post-secondary education** options such as college or vocational training (also referred to as **college- and career-readiness**). Fortunately, the knowledge base regarding effective instructional and behavioral practices has grown substantially over the past few decades. Technological advances allow us to share that information quickly and easily. We are far better equipped than previous generations to provide a high-quality education for every single student in this country.

Yet all students are not achieving to their expected levels. The National Assessment of Educational Progress (NAEP) reports on the yearly performance levels of students in the United States. Ideally, students should score in the *Proficient* range, an indication of solid academic performance. In 2015, only 36% of fourth graders, 34% of eighth graders, and 37% of twelfth graders scored at the *Proficient* level or above in reading. The scores in mathematics were similarly disappointing, with only 40% of fourth graders, 33% of eight graders, and 25% of twelfth graders scoring at the *Proficient* level or above. The scores for the remaining students, who represent the majority of U.S. students, are troubling. In 2015,

- 64% of fourth graders and 66% of eighth graders scored at the *Basic* level—reflecting only partial mastery of the requisite knowledge or skills—or below in reading; and
- 60% of fourth graders and 67% of eighth graders performed at the *Basic* level or below in mathematics.

NAEP scores provide a snapshot of student performance at the elementary and middle school levels, with academic repercussions that continue through high school. Despite the fact that the high-school dropout rate is at an all-time low (6.5%), it still reflects nearly 2.5 million individuals between the ages of 16 to 24 who are not in school and have not earned a diploma or equivalency credential. Here are more troubling statistics:

- Roughly 56% of these dropouts are students of color (an issue discussed in more detail in Chapter 3).

- The dropout rate for students from low-income families is more than twice that of those from high-income families.

- Students who leave high school are more likely to be unemployed, live in poverty, receive public assistance, be incarcerated, experience poor health, and have lower life expectancies.

The actual departure from high school does not happen as a single, dramatic event; rather, dropping out is a process that transpires over time, sometimes starting as early as elementary school. Some factors (e.g., homelessness, parental incarceration) are generally outside most educators' influence. However, the educational environment—factors like academically challenging and engaging instruction and adults' expectations—and a student's school performance are also correlated with non-completion rates. The majority of dropouts report doing little homework and being bored, disengaged, and disconnected from a school environment where they felt educators did not care about them. Most skipped classes and had a history of truancy in the year prior to dropout. Sadly, dropouts also report that they would have worked harder if adults' expectations had been higher, and most believe they could have graduated if they had tried.

One final problematic issue must also be addressed: large numbers of students do not feel safe in school because of **bullying**—repeated, intentional, aggressive behavior, which usually involves an imbalance of power and is meant to physically or emotionally hurt someone who is unable to effectively defend himself or herself. Students perceived as being weak or "different" are more likely to be targeted due to characteristics such as disability, sexual orientation, obesity, physical frailty, or awkward social skills. The statistics are alarming:

- Approximately one out of every three students reports being the victim of bullying, most of which occurs at school (as opposed to bullying that occurs during leisure activities—in their neighborhoods, youth sports, or clubs).

- Because they are afraid, 160,000 students stay home from school each day.

- In their decision to leave school, 10% of high school dropouts report safety concerns as a key factor.

- Victims are two to nine times more likely to report suicidal thoughts.

- Victims often experience depression, low self-esteem, poor grades, and other stress-related health problems.

- Bystanders may also experience powerful negative feelings such as fearfulness, powerlessness, and guilt.

If this ninth grade classroom is representative of national norms, 19 of these 30 students are lacking basic proficiency in reading and math and 2 of them will drop out of school. Ten of these students are experiencing bullying. There is clearly room for improvement in our nation's schools.

The stopbullying.gov Website has a lot of helpful information for students, parents, and teachers that can increase awareness of the different types of bullying, risk factors, warning signs, and effective prevention programs.

What does all of this information have to do with the education of students with disabilities? As you learned in the previous chapter, students with disabilities are entitled to an individualized education. For the majority of these students, this involves receiving most of their instruction in the general education classroom, with additional, often more intensive, supports and accommodations. Yet if, as the NAEP scores indicate, a large proportion of students are not receiving high-quality instruction that results in

Hero Images/Getty Images

academic skill proficiency, then the general education foundation on which the more intensive special education services are built is inadequate. As such, students without disabilities may be misidentified as having disabilities because of their poor academic performance and may subsequently receive special education services despite policies and procedures aimed at preventing just such circumstances.

We currently have the knowledge and capability to provide students with a better education than at any previous time in history. Yet, too many teachers are unaware of effective practices they can use to improve learning outcomes for every student, starting with the initial planning stages of their instruction. They may not realize or be able to identify when students begin to struggle academically or fall behind, or they may not be knowledgeable about the responsive steps they can take to reverse that downward trend and bring students back on track. Issues of physical and emotional safety negatively affect school learning as well. Bullying creates a threatening school environment; students don't learn well when they don't feel safe, and students with disabilities are bullied at a higher rate than their typically developing peers. Other students struggle with emotional or behavioral issues that can be addressed within school-wide support systems, if teachers have the knowledge and skills to address them. Finally, students who struggle academically, including those with disabilities, or who feel disconnected from the school community are at greater risk of dropping out, which is obviously a negative factor in educational achievement.

The topics in this chapter address some of these issues with the intent that, when these foundational systems are in place

- the educational performance of all students will improve; and

- special education services can then be provided to those who truly need them—students with disabilities who require more than general education instruction to be successful.

We provide only an introduction to each topic in this chapter, as you will receive more in-depth coverage in other courses. But we feel they must be mentioned, for we truly believe that when all students receive a high-quality education—using responsive instructional techniques that address the needs of students who are struggling with academic and/or social-emotional challenges—they can reach their full potential. It is not our intent to come across as negative or critical of the U.S. educational system, particularly given how far we have come in educating all students, compared to many other countries. But you, as a future educator, cannot be expected to keep improving our educational system if you are unaware of the problems that currently exist. And we are confident that our next generation of educators will indeed remedy most, if not all, of these challenges.

Topic 2.2 Evidence-Based Practices

- Evidence-based practices have been proven effective by rigorous research.

- Evidence-based practices must be implemented with fidelity, using the same procedures that researchers used to develop them.

What should teachers consider when using instructional and behavioral practices? Probably thousands of instructional and behavioral techniques have been developed over time; however, not all of them are equally effective. In fact, some are quite ineffective. To ensure that students make the largest learning gains possible during each school year, teachers should use **evidence-based practices (EBPs)**. In education, an evidence-based practice (also referred to as research-validated or empirically validated) is one proven effective through rigorous research with data to verify its effectiveness.

The evidence-based practice movement originated in the field of medicine, so let's consider our issue from that perspective. Imagine that you have been diagnosed with cancer. Would you want your doctor to treat you using techniques that were popular

50 or even 100 years ago, or would you prefer a technique shown by current research to be effective in the majority of cases today? The same philosophy holds true in education. Unfortunately, too many teachers continue to use outdated instructional strategies that were popular decades ago but have not been proven effective through research.

The U.S. Department of Education considers the "gold standard" for rigorous research to be one that uses **randomized controlled trials**—studies in which students are randomly assigned to either an intervention (the practice being studied) or a control ("business as usual") group. In these studies, the gains for the two groups are compared to see if the intervention group does better than the control group. An evidence-based practice would consistently show better gains for the intervention group than for the control group.

In some cases, it is not possible to randomly assign large numbers of students with key characteristics—students with low-incidence disabilities, for example—to intervention and control groups. In these situations, **single-case design** studies can be used with small groups or with individual students. To be considered effective, the positive outcomes for the interventions researched in these studies must be replicated across different conditions.

If the teacher (right) does not follow the same procedures for the EBP that the researcher (left) used, her students will most likely not show the same positive gains as those in the research study. If this happens, she may incorrectly assume that the EBP was ineffective instead of realizing that her own implementation was at fault.

What other factors need to be considered when using evidence-based practices? Teachers must implement evidence-based practices with **fidelity** (also known as **fidelity of implementation**), which means they must accurately follow the same procedures used by the researchers when they validated the practice. This includes implementing all of the steps or components in order and adhering to the stipulated guidelines for length and frequency of instructional sessions and other important components. Think back to our earlier medical analogy. If the validated cancer protocol stipulated that patients receive two treatments per week for 24 weeks, how would you feel if your doctor prescribed treatment only once a week for 12 weeks? Do you think you would experience the same cancer-free results as the patients in the research studies? Similarly, if a teacher shortens an instructional period from 90 minutes to 60 minutes, or skips steps in an intervention, or reduces a four-session-per-week regimen to two sessions per week, her students are not likely to make the same positive educational gains as the students in the research studies that validated the intervention.

The information in the box below shows how teachers can determine whether an instructional technique or intervention has sufficient evidence to support its use. Teachers who use evidence-based practices and implement them with fidelity have set a strong foundation on which their students' education is built. If the foundation is not solid—that is, if a teacher is using a practice that has not been validated or is implementing an evidence-based practice without fidelity—then any subsequent student learning is compromised.

How to evaluate whether an educational intervention is supported by rigorous evidence: An overview

Step 1.	**Is the intervention backed by "strong" evidence of effectiveness?**

Quality of studies needed to establish "strong" evidence:

- Randomized controlled trials that are well-designed and implemented.

$+$

Quantity of evidence needed:

Trials showing effectiveness in
- Two or more typical school settings,
- Including a setting similar to that of your schools/classrooms.

$=$ "Strong" Evidence

Step 2.	**If the intervention is not backed by "strong" evidence, is it backed by "possible" evidence of effectiveness?**

Types of studies that can comprise "possible" evidence:

- Randomized controlled trials whose quality/quantity are good but fall short of "strong" evidence; and/or
- Comparison-group studies in which the intervention and comparison groups are *very closely matched* in academic achievement, demographics, and other characteristics.

Types of studies that do not comprise "possible" evidence:

- Pre-post studies.
- Comparison-group studies in which the intervention and comparison groups are not closely matched.
- "Meta-analyses" that include the results of such lower-quality studies.

Step 3.	**If the answers to both questions above are "no," one may conclude that the intervention is not supported by meaningful evidence.**

SOURCE: Coalition for Evidence-Based Policy. (2003, December). *Identifying and Implementing Education Practices Supported by Rigorous Evidence: A User Friendly Guide*, p. v. U.S. Department of Education. Retrieved from www.ed.gov/rschstat/research/pubs/rigorousevid/rigorousevid.pdf

Topic 2.3 Universal Design for Learning (UDL)

- The implementation of evidence-based practices is only one component of high-quality instruction for a student population with a wide range of learning needs.

- Universal Design for Learning (UDL) can reduce or eliminate barriers to students' learning.

Why is the use of evidence-based practices not enough? Although the use of evidence-based practices increases the likelihood of student academic success, it is only one component of high-quality instruction. Students in today's classrooms have a wide range of learning abilities and characteristics: those who are gifted, have disabilities, are learning English as their second language, or have cultural differences. Further, some are passive learners, while others are active learners; some are eager to learn, while others are completely disengaged. Even those who fall within the "typical" learner category display a wide range of learner characteristics: weak versus strong vocabularies, reading comprehension skills, note-taking abilities, and more. In acknowledgment of the need to address the learning requirements of a diverse student population, policy makers have endorsed **Universal Design for Learning** in key federal legislation:

- Individuals with Disabilities Education Act of 2004
- Higher Education Opportunity Act of 2008
- Every Student Succeeds Act of 2015

What is Universal Design for Learning? The school **curriculum** is composed of goals, methods, materials, and assessments, each of which can present barriers for some students. Universal Design for Learning, or UDL, refers to a framework through which teachers proactively reduce potential educational barriers and make the curriculum accessible to as many students as possible. Through the UDL framework, teachers intentionally provide flexible options within each of the curricular elements to address students' different learning needs. For example, text-based materials can create barriers for a number of students, such as those with visual disabilities, those who have difficulty decoding and comprehending text, and those who struggle with processing visual information. A UDL curriculum would provide options for accessing the content in these materials, such as videos or digital texts that allow users to listen to the text as it is read aloud.

UDL is based on three principles, derived primarily from research in cognitive science, cognitive neuroscience, neuropsychology, and neuroscience.

Principle 1: Provide multiple means of representation (the way that content is provided, the "what" of learning)

Principle 2: Provide multiple means of action and expression (the way that students demonstrate what they have learned, the "how" of learning)

Principle 3: Provide multiple means of engagement (the ways in which students are motivated by or interested in their own learning, the "why" of learning)

The following figure includes guidelines for each of the principles.

Universal Design for Learning Guidelines

I. Provide Multiple Means of **Representation**	II. Provide Multiple Means of **Action and Expression**	III. Provide Multiple Means of **Engagement**
1: Provide options for perception 1.1 Offer ways of customizing the display of information 1.2 Offer alternatives for auditory information 1.3 Offer alternatives for visual information	**4: Provide options for physical action** 4.1 Vary the methods for response and navigation 4.2 Optimize access to tools and assistive technologies	**7: Provide options for recruiting interest** 7.1 Optimize individual choice and autonomy 7.2 Optimize relevance, value, and authenticity 7.3 Minimize threats and distractions
2: Provide options for language, mathematical expressions, and symbols 2.1 Clarify vocabulary and symbols 2.2 Clarify syntax and structure 2.3 Support decoding of text, mathematical notation, and symbols 2.4 Promote understanding across languages 2.5 Illustrate through multiple media	**5: Provide options for expression and communication** 5.1 Use multiple media for communication 5.2 Use multiple tools for construction and composition 5.3 Build fluencies with graduated levels of support for practice and performance	**8: Provide options for sustaining effort and persistence** 8.1 Heighten salience of goals and objectives 8.2 Vary demands and resources to optimize challenge 8.3 Foster collaboration and community 8.4 Increase mastery-oriented feedback
3: Provide options for comprehension 3.1 Activate or supply background knowledge 3.2 Highlight patterns, critical features, big ideas, and relationships 3.3 Guide information processing, visualization, and manipulation 3.4 Maximize transfer and generalization	**6: Provide options for executive functions** 6.1 Guide appropriate goal-setting 6.2 Support planning and strategy development 6.3 Facilitate managing information and resources 6.4 Enhance capacity for monitoring progress	**9: Provide options for self-regulation** 9.1 Promote expectations and beliefs that optimize motivation 9.2 Facilitate personal coping skills and strategies 9.3 Develop self-assessment and reflection
Resourceful, knowledgeable learners	**Strategic, goal-directed learners**	**Purposeful, motivated learners**

SOURCE: From "Universal Design for Learning Guidelines version 2.0." Published by CAST © 2011.

Let's see what UDL looks like in a classroom. In this video, a fifth grade language arts teacher incorporates the principles and guidelines of UDL, while experts in UDL provide feedback.

▶ **UDL Guidelines in Practice: Grade 5 Language Arts**
https://www.youtube.com/watch?v=zE8N8bnIlgs&spfreload=10

Naomi Tyler

These fountains have several elements of universal design. The large buttons in front are easier to push than smaller buttons on top. Some fountains have sensors that turn on the water when the user is close, removing the need to push buttons at all. The varied heights are accessible to people of all sizes and to wheelchair users. The open space underneath the fountain provides easier access for a wheelchair user.

To understand UDL, it may be helpful to understand aspects of **universal design**, the architectural concept on which UDL is based. From the initial planning phase, universally designed structures are barrier-free and accessible to everyone, including people with physical disabilities. For example, ramps reduce barriers for people who use wheelchairs or walkers, but they are also beneficial for people pushing strollers or dollies. Similarly, UDL carries the concepts of universal design into the classroom by purposefully designing the curriculum to be barrier-free for all students.

Positive student academic outcomes appear to be more likely when the UDL principles are carefully constructed in concert with evidence-based practices and the options for accessing content or demonstrating knowledge are carefully implemented with a specific goal in mind. Technology, which is frequently used as a means to provide options within each principle, has been correlated with higher student engagement; however, its use—without careful planning and precise, goal-oriented implementation—does not necessarily lead to significantly stronger academic outcomes. On the other hand, research on UDL tends to show overall strong student engagement.

Research Feature: Universal Design for Learning

- Adolescents who struggle with reading, students who are deaf, students with cognitive disabilities, and English language learners benefit from digital reading environments designed according to UDL principles. Results show that these students outperformed their peers who received instruction using printed text on standardized tests of comprehension *(Rose & Gravel, 2010)*.

- High school students with and without learning disabilities showed significantly higher gains in social studies vocabulary and concepts when taught using a multimedia-based intervention that combined evidence-based practices and UDL principles. Further, the students with learning disabilities who were taught with this approach were able to reduce the educational performance gap between their group and the

students without disabilities who did not receive the UDL intervention *(Kennedy, Thomas, Meyer, Alves, & Lloyd, 2014)*.

- High school students with high-incidence disabilities in a UDL treatment condition performed better on chemistry post-tests than their counterparts in the typical instruction condition. However, their general education peers without disabilities showed no substantial differences between the UDL and typical instruction conditions *(King-Sears et al., 2014)*.

For more information on UDL, visit the National Center on Universal Design for Learning (udlcenter.org) and CAST (cast.org) Websites.
Source: From *Technology and learning: Meeting special students' needs,* 2010; From *Using evidence-based multimedia to improve vocabulary performance of adolescents with LD: A UDL approach,* 2014; From *Using evidence-based multimedia to improve vocabulary performance of adolescents with LD: A UDL approach,* 2014.

The following module examines the three principles of UDL and discusses how to apply these principles to curricular components (goals, instructional materials, instructional methods, and assessments).

▶ **IRIS Module: Universal Design for Learning: Creating a Learning Environment that Challenges and Engages All Students**
http://iris.peabody.vanderbilt.edu/module/udl/

Topic 2.4 Differentiated Instruction

- Teachers who provide differentiated instruction (DI) adjust various aspects of the educational process to meet students' learning needs.

- Whereas UDL is a proactive measure implemented when designing the curriculum, differentiated instruction is a responsive measure that is incorporated when planning and implementing instruction.

What is differentiated instruction? **Differentiated instruction,** or **DI**, is an educational approach in which teachers adjust the curriculum, instruction, and assessment to address the learning needs of all students. To align instruction with their students' learning needs, teachers must be knowledgeable about each student's *readiness*—academic skill levels (including special needs) and background knowledge about the topic; *interests*—topics of interest or motivation; and *learning profiles*—preferences for learning (e.g., visual, auditory, kinesthetic), grouping (e.g., independent, small or large group), and environment (e.g., quiet working space). Note that learning profiles are not synonymous with *learning styles*, an unvalidated theory which suggests that a student consistently and most effectively learns or processes information in a prescribed manner (e.g., visually, by touching). In fact, most students prefer different methods based on the content or concepts they are learning. Keep in mind that a student's preferences for learning do not necessarily translate into higher academic gains. Rather, teachers gather learning preferences information to make their instruction engaging and relevant for students.

When differentiating instruction, teachers adjust three instructional elements: **content**, **process**, and **product**.

CONTENT.   The *content* is the required knowledge or skills for a particular unit of study. When teachers differentiate content, students learn the same concepts or skills but the difficulty level or depth of coverage might vary for different students. To differentiate content, teachers might incorporate:

- A variety of materials—using texts with different reading levels or varying depths of coverage, as well as supplemental materials (e.g., videos, computer simulations).

- **Tiered content**—having all students complete the same instructional activity (worksheet, learning center), but varying the difficulty level of the content, based on student readiness levels. For example, when calculating multiplication problems that contain decimals, one group of students works problems like 24×1.4. Another group, who picked up the first skill easily, calculates problems with more digits (137×2.35) and uses those calculations to solve advanced word problems (e.g., finding the cost of various lengths of cloth at \$5.95 per yard). A third group needs extra practice, which is obtained using an engaging computer activity.

H. Mark Weidman Photography/Alamy Stock Photo

While the teacher works with a group of their classmates, these students work through learning center activities to help them apply advanced concepts.

PROCESS.   The *process* is the way a student accesses academic content or material. A teacher who differentiates the process expects all students to learn the same content, but the methods through which students access or learn that content can vary. To differentiate process, teachers might incorporate:

- **Learning centers**—a variety of activities, located in a specific area of the classroom, that are focused on a particular topic. Students can work independently, in pairs, or even in small groups to deepen their knowledge or build on or reinforce newly learned skills.

- **Tiered activities**—instructional tasks that are designed to teach and challenge students at different levels of readiness (low, middle, and high levels) for the same content or skills. These tasks can differ in level of complexity, depth of information conveyed, or level of abstraction.

PRODUCT. The *product* is the end result of the learning process that shows what a student understands. When teachers differentiate the product, they evaluate student comprehension of the same concept or skill, allowing students to demonstrate what they have learned in a variety of ways. To differentiate process, teachers might incorporate:

- **Tiered products**—assessments that are designed to challenge students at different levels of readiness (low, middle, and high levels) as they demonstrate their knowledge of the same content or skills.
- **Learning menus**—a list of choices related to learning objectives from which students can select the option that they would like. At the end of a unit, for example, students might be able to select the way in which they demonstrate what they have learned by taking a traditional test, writing a paper, making a presentation, making a short video, or putting on a short skit.

Differentiated classrooms are quite different from traditional classrooms, so teachers may be hesitant to change. However, they can start with one element (e.g., content, process, product), one subject area, or even one activity, and then gradually increase the amount of differentiation they incorporate into their instructional practices. Given the positive learning outcomes associated with differentiated instruction, it is a logical method to support all learners.

Research Feature: Differentiated Instruction

- Strategies used to differentiate instructional and assessment tasks were effective for all students in the classroom, including English language learners, gifted students, and struggling students (*McQuarrie, McRae, & Stack-Cutler, 2008*).
- Students with learning disabilities received more benefits from differentiated instruction than did their grade-level peers (*McQuarrie, McRae, & Stack-Cutler, 2008*).
- In a study conducted with 24 elementary classrooms, the students in the mixed ability classrooms who received differentiated instruction had higher levels of achievement than students in classrooms that did not receive this type of instruction (*Stavroula, Leonidas, & Koutselini, 2011*).
- In a study with approximately 1200 second- through fifth-grade students in five elementary schools, teachers replaced whole-group reading instruction with differentiated instruction. In two schools, the students' reading fluency increased significantly, and in one school the students' reading comprehension improved (*Reis, McCoach, Little, Muller, & Burcu, 2011*).

How does differentiated instruction differ from UDL? There are some definite similarities between UDL and DI: both are educational frameworks in which teachers implement a variety of strategies and evidence-based practices to increase student engagement and to maximize students' outcomes. Like UDL, differentiated instruction enhances learning not only for typical students but also for those with special learning needs, such as those who are gifted, have disabilities, or are English language learners.

Key differences between UDL and differentiated instruction involve when and how changes are made to address students' needs. UDL is a proactive measure that is implemented when designing the curriculum. With the aim of preventing barriers to learning and assessment, UDL builds resources and options into the curriculum *in anticipation of* a variety of student needs. In contrast, differentiated instruction is a responsive measure that is incorporated when planning and implementing instruction. Differentiated instruction involves adjustments or adaptations made by a teacher *in response to* students' academic abilities, learning profiles, and interests.

In the following video, teachers use quick checks at the end of class to determine how well students understand key concepts. They then use this information to differentiate instruction for their students, allowing some to delve into topics more deeply while others receive additional supports.

▶ **Exit Tickets: Checking for Understanding**

https://www.youtube.com/watch?v=Hp4quoyU7JI&list=PLnEDDaGQyuyHJOciV6WdkpzTIG4bPTI_X

Topic 2.5 Data-Based Decision Making

- Teachers should use data gathered from diagnostic, formative, and summative assessments to plan and modify instruction.
- Several types of formative assessments allow teachers to quickly gather information on students' progress.

How can teachers use data to make informed instructional decisions? Often teachers assess their students at the beginning of the year to determine the skills the students have mastered and those that need to be taught. Although this is a strategic way to plan for instruction, it does not provide insight into how to teach or adapt instruction throughout the year. Instead of teaching content and skills in the hope that most students will acquire them, teachers should be collecting data on students' progress and using those results to help guide their instruction and thereby ultimately improve students' skills and learning outcomes. This is referred to as **data-based decision making**. The teachers at Hampton High School (featured in the video in the previous topic) did this when they used information from students' exit tickets on one day to differentiate their instruction the next day. Three common types of assessments yield helpful data for teachers, each with different benefits.

- **Diagnostic assessments**—Conducted before an instructional period begins, these assessments (e.g., reading inventory) identify a student's areas of strength and the skills that are presenting difficulty. The teacher can use this information to plan instruction.

- **Formative assessments**—Conducted as instruction progresses, these assessments (e.g., teacher-made tests, progress monitoring) indicate how students are responding to instruction. Using these results, the teacher can measure students' progress on the skill or content being taught and can identify those who need additional instruction. Additionally, the teacher can evaluate her own instruction: if all students are struggling with the same concept, then the instruction was not clear and the concept needs to be retaught.

- **Summative assessments**—Conducted at the end of an instructional period, these assessments evaluate how well students learned the content. These assessments include chapter and unit tests as well as end-of-year state assessments (high-stakes tests). Because these tests are administered at the end of an instructional period, it is usually too late to remediate skills for students who perform poorly.

Types of Assessments

Type of Assessment	When Collected?	What Is Assessed?
Diagnostic	Before instruction	Needs of individual students
Formative	During instruction	Whether students are responding to instruction
Summative	After instruction	Students' mastery of skills and content

SOURCE: Adapted from R. Zumeta. (n.d). Understanding types of assessment within an RTI framework. In *RTI Implementer Webinar Series*. National Center on Response to Intervention. Retrieved from http://www.rti4success.org/video/implementer-series-understanding-types-assessment-within-rti-framework

How can teachers determine if students are responding to instruction? Teachers can use a type of formative assessment referred to as **progress monitoring** to assess student performance. By administering short tests (often referred to as progress monitoring measures or **probes)** frequently—monthly, weekly, or even daily— teachers can ascertain whether students are learning the skills or content being taught. Using the results of the assessment, teachers can determine if they need to make adjustments to their instruction or to add extra supports for **struggling learners**. There are two types of progress monitoring:

- **Mastery measurement (MM)**—This type of progress monitoring evaluates student achievement on a specific skill set (e.g., adding fractions) or the current instructional content. The content or skill sets being assessed change constantly as teachers move through each unit in the curriculum.

- **General outcome measures (GOM)**—This type of progress monitoring, often referred to as **curriculum-based measurement (CBM)**, covers a sampling of skills in one academic domain (e.g., mathematics, reading, writing) across the entire year's curriculum. A teacher uses a different version of the CBM measure containing problems or questions of equal difficulty each time the students are assessed. At the beginning of the year, students' scores will be relatively low, as they have had little exposure to the content. But week after week, those scores should steadily increase as students become more proficient. Because they contain content from across the entire year, GOMs evaluate retention of previously taught skills or content. Additionally, they gauge whether students can generalize what they have learned to skills or content that will be introduced later in the instructional sequence.

Two sample mathematics probes are shown below. Notice that the mastery measurement probe covers one skill (adding fractions), while the CBM probe covers a range of skills (adding and subtracting whole numbers and fractions, multiplication, and division).

Sample Probes

Sample Mastery Measurement Probe
Name_____ Date_____

a. $\dfrac{3}{5}+\dfrac{1}{5}=$ b. $\dfrac{2}{8}+\dfrac{5}{8}=$ c. $\dfrac{1}{3}+\dfrac{1}{3}=$

d. $\dfrac{2}{6}+\dfrac{2}{6}=$ e. $\dfrac{7}{15}+\dfrac{6}{15}=$ f. $\dfrac{1}{2}+\dfrac{1}{2}=$

g. $\dfrac{9}{16}+\dfrac{3}{16}=$ h. $\dfrac{1}{4}+\dfrac{1}{4}=$ i. $\dfrac{17}{32}+\dfrac{13}{32}=$

j. $\dfrac{18}{23}+\dfrac{4}{23}=$ k. $\dfrac{9}{18}+\dfrac{3}{18}=$ l. $\dfrac{2}{7}+\dfrac{4}{7}=$

m. $\dfrac{3}{9}+\dfrac{4}{9}=$ n. $\dfrac{5}{12}+\dfrac{4}{12}=$ o. $\dfrac{13}{17}+\dfrac{3}{17}=$

p. $\dfrac{2}{6}+\dfrac{1}{6}=$ q. $\dfrac{14}{20}+\dfrac{4}{20}=$ r. $\dfrac{1}{10}+\dfrac{7}{10}=$

s. $\dfrac{7}{13}+\dfrac{4}{13}=$ t. $\dfrac{3}{30}+\dfrac{22}{30}=$ u. $\dfrac{9}{15}+\dfrac{5}{15}=$

Sample CBM Probe
Name_____ Date_____

a. $8\overline{)23}$ b. $\begin{array}{r}41741\\+53697\end{array}$ c. $\begin{array}{r}8\\\times9\end{array}$

d. $3\overline{)61}$ e. $\begin{array}{r}7174\\3293\\+89\end{array}$ f. $5\overline{)25}$

g. $\begin{array}{r}24\\\times63\end{array}$ h. $\begin{array}{r}3\\\times4\end{array}$ i. $\begin{array}{r}6\\\times8\end{array}$

j. $\begin{array}{r}487\\\times32\end{array}$ k. $\begin{array}{r}21\\\times12\end{array}$ l. $\begin{array}{r}7\\\times5\end{array}$

m. $4\overline{)64}$ n. $5\overline{)40}$ o. $\begin{array}{r}24\\\times46\end{array}$

p. $\begin{array}{r}916\\\times2\end{array}$ q. $\dfrac{23}{30}-\dfrac{17}{30}=$ r. $\begin{array}{r}305\\-33\end{array}$

s. $\begin{array}{r}345\\-38\end{array}$ t. $\begin{array}{r}7\\-3\end{array}$ u. $\dfrac{3}{4}-\dfrac{2}{4}=$

The box below outlines the steps for using CBM to evaluate student progress.

CBM Steps

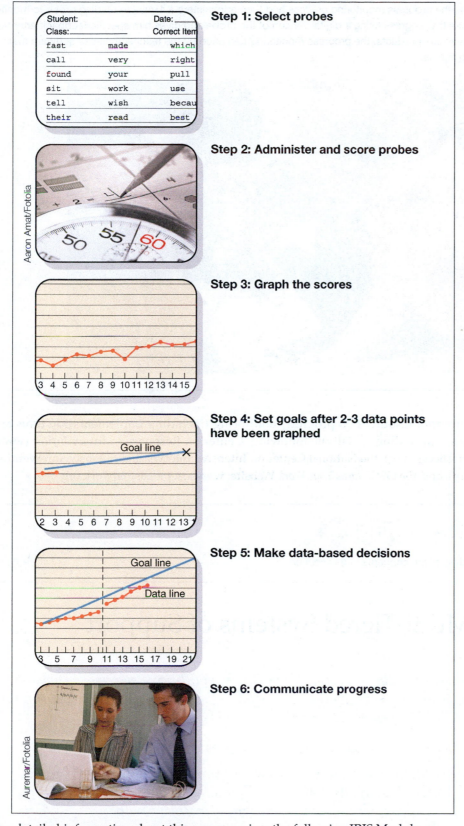

Step 1: Select probes

Step 2: Administer and score probes

Step 3: Graph the scores

Step 4: Set goals after 2-3 data points have been graphed

Step 5: Make data-based decisions

Step 6: Communicate progress

For detailed information about this process, view the following IRIS Module.

▶ **IRIS Module: Classroom Assessment (Part 1): An Introduction to Monitoring Academic Achievement in the Classroom**
http://iris.peabody.vanderbilt.edu/module/gpm/

DIBELS: Program Monitoring

In the video below, a teacher explains the progress monitoring process and then administers a 1-minute reading probe to monitor a student's reading fluency. She tracks his progress using a digital version of the probe and gives him specific feedback after he reads. As with many commercially available products, the progress monitoring tool used by the teacher includes software that automatically graphs the student's progress.

For more resources on progress monitoring (including implementation tools and research findings), visit the following: Center on Response to Intervention (www. rti4success.org), the National Center on Intensive Intervention (intensiveintervention. org), and the OSEP *Ideas That Work* Website: www.osepideasthatwork.org

Check Your Understanding 2.1

Click here to gauge your understanding of the concepts in this section.

Multi-Tiered Systems of Support

Learning Outcome

Understand the conceptual framework of multi-tiered systems of support, and describe the specific processes involved in the RTI framework for academics and the PBIS framework for behavior.

Topic 2.6 Response to Intervention (RTI)

- Multi-tiered systems of support provide high-quality instruction for all students, followed by increasingly intensive levels of support for those who need more intensive help.

- RTI is one type of MTSS that can be used to identify struggling learners and provide them with academic supports, as well as identify students with learning disabilities.

Topic 2.7 Positive Behavioral Interventions and Supports (PBIS)

- PBIS is a multi-tiered system of supports for behavior management.

- In a PBIS framework, all students receive specific instruction on behavioral expectations in order to prevent problems from arising; more intensive, evidence-based interventions are provided to students who require them.

Even when teachers use evidence-based practices in conjunction with UDL, differentiated instruction, and progress monitoring, some students will need additional supports. We will explore some of these within a framework of multi-tiered systems of support.

Topic 2.6 Response to Intervention (RTI)

- Multi-tiered systems of support provide high-quality instruction for all students, followed by increasingly intensive levels of support for those who need more intensive help.

- RTI is one type of MTSS that can be used to identify struggling learners and provide them with academic supports, as well as identify students with learning disabilities.

What are multi-tiered systems of support? **Multi-tiered systems of support (MTSS)** incorporate multiple levels of support for students; the most common framework has three levels, or tiers. Each level provides increasingly intensive supports for students who struggle with academic or behavioral issues. **Response to intervention (RTI)** is the multi-tiered framework for addressing academic skills. The first tier, referred to as **primary instruction** or **primary prevention**, is the high-quality instruction that all students receive in the general education classroom. The second level, **secondary intervention** or **secondary prevention**, provides additional supports of moderate intensity to students who are not making adequate progress with primary instruction alone. The third tier, **tertiary intervention** or **tertiary prevention**, provides intensive, individualized interventions to students for whom secondary supports are still

In addition to primary instruction, these students receive secondary intervention in a small group setting to help improve their academic performance.

insufficient. Students receive more or less intensive interventions based on whether they show adequate growth—or *responsiveness*—to the instruction or intervention provided. Teachers must implement evidence-based practices at each level and collect progress monitoring data, which you learned about in Topic 2.5, to determine whether or not a student's growth is adequate.

How does the RTI process work? RTI follows a systematic process for identifying struggling learners, providing increasingly intensive supports, and monitoring student progress.

1. *Universal screening.* All students are given a **universal screening** at the beginning of the school year to identify those whose skills are not at required or expected levels, and thus are at risk for academic failure. Screenings may be given again later in the year (e.g., second, third, or fourth quarter) to identify students who started out with adequate skills but later fell behind.

2. *Primary instruction.* All students receive high-quality instruction—using evidence-based practices—in the general education classroom. Ideally, the curriculum has been planned according to UDL principles and differentiated instruction is in place to make adjustments based on students' needs. Teachers use weekly progress monitoring to track the improvement of at-risk students (i.e., those identified through universal screenings). With good instruction, many of these students will show improvement or recover skills lost over the summer. However, a small number will not demonstrate adequate gains.

3. *Secondary intervention.* An estimated 10% to 15% of students will not make adequate progress at the primary instruction level and will require additional support, with continuous progress monitoring. This support consists of small-group instruction with validated interventions that target weak skill areas; secondary intervention sessions can range from 20 to 40 minutes of extra instruction per day, three or four times per week, for between 10 and 15 weeks. When progress-monitoring data show that a student's skills have sufficiently improved, secondary intervention can be reduced or eliminated. However, a few students will still make inadequate progress.

4. *Tertiary intervention.* After receiving secondary intervention, approximately 5% of students will continue to make inadequate progress and will subsequently receive intense, individualized intervention, with continuous progress monitoring. School professionals may use the progress monitoring data to show inadequate response to instruction or intervention, or they may conduct a formal evaluation to determine eligibility for special education services. Consequently, tertiary interventions may fall under general education or special education services, depending on a school's or district's policies.

The RTI framework serves two purposes. First, it allows educators to provide **early intervening** services to struggling learners. By providing these services at the first sign of academic difficulties, teachers can decrease the likelihood that the problems will worsen. Second, RTI can be used to identify students who have learning disabilities, something you'll learn more about in Chapter 6. In either case, RTI combines many of the educational practices you've learned about in this chapter—high-quality instruction that uses evidence-based practices, implementation fidelity, and progress monitoring—into a framework that is responsive to students' needs, works to prevent academic problems, and provides better learning opportunities for all students. Keep in mind, however, that the entire RTI framework depends on the premise that high-quality instruction using evidence-based practices has occurred at the primary instruction level (Tier 1). When primary instruction has been poor, students may be inappropriately identified as at-risk. If large numbers of students are identified as needing secondary interventions, then it is likely that they are receiving poor primary instruction.

RTI Tiers

In this diagram, progress-monitoring data have identified five students who are in need of additional Tier 2 supports. After receiving Tier 2 interventions, two of those students still require more intensive supports. Consequently, those two students receive Tier 3 services.

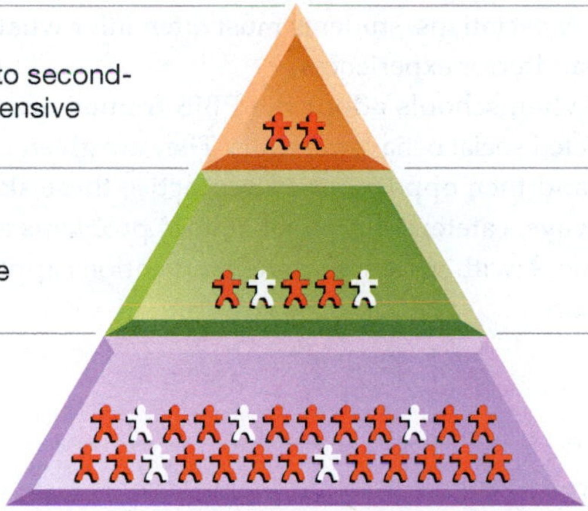

Tertiary Intervention:
Students not adequately responding to secondary intervention receive even more intensive individualized instruction.

- Intensive, individualized Intervention
- Progress monitoring
- Data-based decision making
- Fidelity

Secondary Intervention:
Students not making adequate progress in primary prevention receive additional support.

- Small-group targeted instruction
- Progress monitoring
- Data-based decision making
- Fidelity

Primary Instruction:
Students receive high-quality instruction in the general education setting, via validated practices.

- High-quality instruction
- Universal screening
- Progress monitoring
- Data-based decision making
- Fidelity

SOURCE: Adapted with permission from the IRIS Center, http://iris.peabody.vanderbilt.edu/module/rti-math/

In the following video, teachers, students, and parents discuss how implementation of RTI has helped address the needs of struggling learners, improved their school's ranking, and reduced the number of students who need special education services.

▶ **Response to Intervention: Collaborating to Target Instruction**

https://www.youtube.com/watch?v=cpPZjcFw7xc

The IRIS Center has a seven-Module in-depth series on RTI in regard to assessment, reading instruction, Tier 3, mathematics instruction, and considerations for school leaders. The first in the series contains information about the advantages of the RTI framework, its different uses, and a synopsis of each tier.

▶ **IRIS Module: RTI (Part 1): An Overview**

http://iris.peabody.vanderbilt.edu/module/rti01-overview/

Topic 2.7 Positive Behavioral Interventions and Supports (PBIS)

- PBIS is a multi-tiered system of supports for behavior management.

- In a PBIS framework, all students receive specific instruction on behavioral expectations in order to prevent problems from arising; more intensive, evidence-based interventions are provided to students who require them.

What is PBIS and how does it fit within a multi-tiered framework? PBIS stands for **Positive Behavioral Interventions and Supports** (also referred to as school-wide PBIS, or SWPBIS), a multi-tiered framework aimed at preventing problem behaviors and providing evidence-based interventions when problems do occur. Its overarching goal is to improve social behavioral outcomes for all students.

When students start school, we do not expect them to have already mastered all the academic content they need to know. Instead, teachers provide carefully planned, systematic, **scaffolded instruction** to teach students the necessary content. In contrast, we all too often assume that students start school with an understanding of expected school behavior and the necessary social skills to get along with peers. We also expect them to interact appropriately with teachers. Unfortunately, because we do not provide carefully planned, systematic, scaffolded instruction with regard to our behavioral expectations, students must often infer what they are or figure them out through trial-and-error experiences.

When schools adopt the PBIS framework, students are explicitly taught the expected social behavioral skills. They are given concrete examples of expected behaviors and then opportunities to practice these skills in various settings (classrooms, hallways, cafeteria). Any behavioral problems are addressed using evidence-based practices, with more intensive interventions applied to students who need additional support.

Core Principles of PBIS

The PBIS framework is built on seven guiding principles:

1. *All* children can be taught to engage in appropriate behavior.
2. Intervene early, before or as soon as problem behaviors arise.
3. Use a multi-tiered model to deliver services.
4. Use evidence-based interventions.
5. Monitor student progress frequently.
6. Make data-based decisions about the effectiveness of the interventions.
7. Use assessments for:
   a. Screening of daily and monthly office referrals.
   b. Analysis of data by time of day, behavior, and location (e.g., during lunch, fighting, in the cafeteria).
   c. Progress monitoring to determine if interventions are creating the desired behavioral outcomes.

What are the components of the PBIS framework? Like RTI, PBIS has three tiers: primary (also referred to as universal), secondary, and tertiary. Primary prevention, designed to prevent problem behaviors by teaching students the behavioral expectations for the school setting, is effective for roughly 80% of students. The main components of primary prevention are:

- A schoolwide approach to discipline that everyone (school personnel, students, parents) agrees to
- A positive statement of purpose
- Positively stated expectations for students and staff
- Specific procedures for teaching expectations to students
- A variety of measures for encouraging rule-abiding behaviors
- A variety of measures for discouraging rule-breaking behaviors
- Procedures for monitoring, evaluating, and modifying the PBIS system

About 15% of all schoolchildren require secondary prevention services because they do not respond adequately to primary prevention. These are students who may receive two to five office referrals per year and are at risk for engaging in more serious problem behavior. Secondary supports may include targeted interventions for small groups of students (e.g., social skills training) or individual supports (e.g., **Check In/ Check Out [CICO]**, individual PBIS plans that include **functional behavioral assessments [FBA]**).

Tertiary prevention is intended for students who show repeated patterns of problem behaviors—the roughly 5% of students who need more than secondary prevention support. These students may exhibit behaviors that are dangerous, that disrupt the learning process, or that cause them to be excluded from peer or social groups. At the tertiary level, a team of professionals works together to conduct a functional behavioral assessment to determine the reasons why the student engages in inappropriate behaviors. Using the results of the FBA, the team develops and implements a behavior plan that:

- Helps the student replace unwanted behaviors with appropriate behaviors.

- Adjusts the instructional, physical, or social environments to eliminate triggers for the unwanted behaviors while promoting and encouraging replacement behaviors.

- Allows for the monitoring, evaluation, and revision of the behavior plan as needed.

As the diagram below illustrates, similarities exist between the RTI and PBIS frameworks. Like RTI, PBIS combines many of the educational practices you've learned about in this chapter—evidence-based practices, implementation fidelity, and progress monitoring—into a system that is responsive to students' needs and that works to prevent behavioral problems so all students can be more engaged in the learning process and benefit from high-quality instruction.

RTI/PBIS Tiers

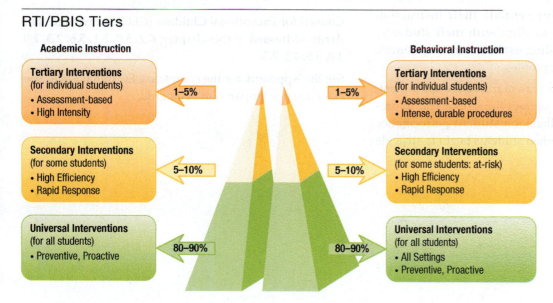

SOURCE: OSEP Technical Assistance Center for Positive Behavioral Interventions and Support. Retrieved from http://www.pbis.org/school/rti.aspx

The Technical Assistance Center on Positive Behavioral Interventions and Supports has helpful information on PBIS, including research findings and training information. For more information, go to: pbis.org

Check Your Understanding 2.2

Click here to gauge your understanding of the concepts in this section.

Summary

High-Quality Instruction

High-quality instruction must first be provided to all students, before an individualized education can be provided to students with disabilities.

- Although the knowledge base regarding effective instructional and behavioral practices has grown substantially, the U.S. educational system still needs improvement in guaranteeing that all students have the requisite academic skills, feel safe at school, and remain in school until they graduate.

- Teachers should use evidence-based practices that they implement with fidelity to increase their students' likelihood of academic success.

- In addition to the use of EBPs, teachers can proactively reduce potential educational barriers and make the **curriculum** accessible to as many students as possible by incorporating the Universal Design for Learning (UDL) principles.

- Teachers can then differentiate their instruction throughout the year to align with their students' learning needs, including each student's readiness, interests, and learning profiles.

- Progress monitoring, a type of formative assessment, occurs frequently throughout the school year to provide continuous feedback on student performance and to alert teachers when students begin to struggle with the content.

Multi-Tiered Systems of Support

Multi-tiered frameworks incorporate multiple levels of support for students; the most common framework has three levels, or tiers. Each level provides increasingly intensive supports for students who struggle with academic or behavioral issues.

- Response to intervention (RTI) is the multi-tiered framework that addresses academic skills. It serves to identify struggling learners and provide early intervening services immediately to prevent school failure, as well as to identify students who have learning disabilities.

- Positive Behavioral Supports and Interventions (PBIS) is the multi-tiered framework that addresses behavioral skills through three levels of increasingly intensive interventions.

Addressing CEC Standards

Council for Exceptional Children (CEC) knowledge standards addressed in this chapter: 6.2, 5.0, 5.1, 5.6, 2.3, 2.0, 3.0, 5.5, 4.2, 7.3.

See the Appendix for the complete CEC Initial Level Special Educator Preparation Standards.

Chapter 3
Culturally and Linguistically Diverse Learners

Sonia Nieto

"Many teachers and schools, in an attempt to be color-blind, do not want to acknowledge cultural or racial differences. 'I don't see Black or White,' a teacher will say, 'I see only students.' This statement assumes that to be color-blind is to be fair, impartial, and objective because to see differences, in this line of reasoning, is to see defects and inferiority. Although it sounds fair and honest and ethical, the opposite may actually be true. If used to mean nondiscriminatory in attitude and behavior, color-blindness is not a bad thing. On the other hand, color-blindness may result in *refusing to accept differences* and therefore accepting the dominant culture as the norm.... [T]hese attitudes result in denying the identities of particular students, thereby making them invisible."

—Sonia Nieto and Patty Bode

Affirming Diversity: The Sociopolitical Context of Multicultural Education, 6th ed., copyright 2012. Reprinted and electronically reproduced by permission of Pearson Education, Inc., New York, NY.

Differences can make us uncomfortable. When we see people whose features are different from ours or who behave differently from what we are accustomed to, we may feel uneasy. Yet, the reason for our discomfort is often a lack of knowledge. The more we know and recognize about each other—including our differences—the less discomfort we experience. Instead, we can celebrate the uniqueness in each person and take advantage of opportunities to learn from others' knowledge, and gain from their experiences.

Learning Outcomes

Diverse Learners

Describe the ways in which U.S. students are diverse, explain factors that contribute to an inequitable education for these students, and explain concerns regarding their disproportionate representation in special education.

Cultural Diversity

Explain how cultural differences can create conflicts in school, list at least two steps that teachers can take to prevent cross-cultural dissonance, and describe culturally responsive instruction.

Linguistic Diversity

Understand the process of second-language acquisition and describe effective programs and strategies for teaching English learners.

Diverse Learners[1]

Learning Outcome

Describe the ways in which U.S. students are diverse, explain factors that contribute to an inequitable education for these students, and explain concerns regarding their disproportionate representation in special education.

Topic 3.1 The Diverse Landscape

- U.S. schools have a long history of educating students from diverse cultural and linguistic backgrounds.

- America's schoolchildren are becoming increasingly diverse.

Topic 3.2 Issues of Social Justice

- Sociocultural disparities in key areas like parental education and income levels put students at risk for school failure.

- Schools in low-income areas often provide an inequitable education for those students.

---

[1]References for Chapter 3 are found at the end of this text.

Topic 3.3 Understanding Disproportionality

- One concern about equitable education for students from diverse backgrounds relates to their disproportionate representation in special education.

- Investigations of disproportionate representation in special education analyze identification and placement rates, as well as disciplinary actions.

The increasing racial, cultural, ethnic, and linguistic diversity that U.S. students bring to school provides exciting opportunities to expand all students' knowledge and experiences.

Topic 3.1 The Diverse Landscape

- U.S. schools have a long history of educating students from diverse cultural and linguistic backgrounds.

- America's schoolchildren are becoming increasingly diverse.

Who are diverse students, and how long have they been part of U.S. classrooms? In this chapter we continue the conversation about supporting all learners, specifically those from racially, ethnically, culturally, or linguistically diverse backgrounds. Because many such students have backgrounds and cultures that do not represent the dominant or mainstream American culture, or speak languages other than English, they may require additional educational considerations beyond those addressed in the previous chapter. Some of these students and their families are recent immigrants to the United States; others have been here for generations.

Students from other cultures and those who speak multiple languages have been part of U.S. classrooms throughout the country's history. In the 1800s, the nation was already composed of people from many countries, so non-English or dual language instruction was common, offered in over a dozen states and in more than 10 different languages. Toward the end of the nineteenth century, immigrants—who were mainly Catholic—began arriving from southern, central, and eastern Europe.

Immigrants from diverse backgrounds have been part of U.S. classrooms since the founding of this country.

Prior immigrants from northern and western Europe—who were predominantly Protestant—felt threatened by the newcomers. As a result, the newer immigrants became victims of **nativism**, a movement to further the interests of those who considered themselves native inhabitants (even though many were immigrants themselves!) and to "protect" American culture. Newer immigrants were treated with great suspicion; instruction in languages other than English was prohibited in many schools, and children speaking these languages did not fare well academically.

During World War I, "Americanization" led to the idea of a **melting pot**: a country where individuals abandoned their home languages and cultures to become part of a new, homogenized nation. But instead of creating a harmonious culture, each new immigrant group experienced racism, segregation, and aggression. These negative sentiments were also expressed toward American Indians and African Americans who had lived in this country for centuries under domination of the mainstream group. In the 1950s and 1960s, the civil rights movement brought national awareness to the inequities suffered by these dominated groups. **Cultural pluralism**—the idea that people should maintain their ethnic languages, cultures, and customs while still participating in and being accepted by society as a whole—emerged in the 1960s. During

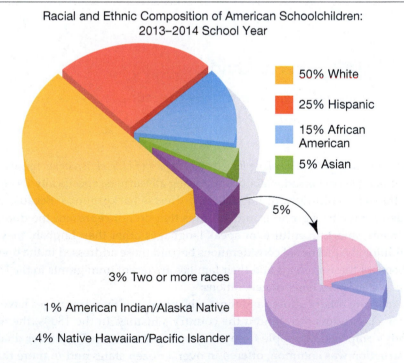

Racial and Ethnic Composition of American Schoolchildren: 2013–2014 School Year

- 50% White
- 25% Hispanic
- 15% African American
- 5% Asian

5%

3% Two or more races

1% American Indian/Alaska Native

.4% Native Hawaiian/Pacific Islander

SOURCE: Data from U.S. Department of Education, National Center for Education Statistics, Common Core of Data (CCD), "State Nonfiscal Public Elementary/Secondary Education Survey," 2013–14 v.1a.

the 1980s, **multicultural education** emerged as a way to help *all* students learn to appreciate and respect others' cultures and to produce citizens who can communicate and work within a global economy. In turn, economic globalization allows U.S. companies to recruit workers with high-demand skills from other countries who relocate with their families, adding to student diversity in U.S. schools. Additionally, over the past 25 years natural disasters, worsening economic conditions, genocide, and civil wars have resulted in the largest global human displacement in history. Migrants, refugees, and those seeking better lives for their families come to the United States. Students from these groups, and their families, make up the rich fabric of America, offering vibrant contributions to classroom and school experiences.

How diverse are students in U.S. schools? U.S. students are very diverse, racially, ethnically, culturally, and linguistically. Let's look at some statistics:

- The public schools enroll roughly 50 million students: 25 million (50%) are White, and the other half are students of color.

- In 16 "minority-majority" states and the District of Columbia, White students are the minority, making up less than half of the student population (see purple and red states in the map below).

- About 9% (4.4 million) of U.S. students participate in programs for **English language learners (ELLs)**, also referred to as **English learners (ELs)**.

- In many school districts, students and their families speak over 100 different languages; nearly 170 different languages are spoken in New York City schools.

- The majority of ELLs speak Spanish.

Diverse Student Enrollment

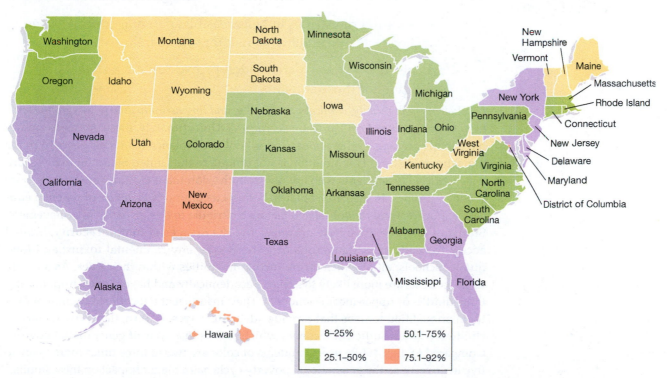

Legend:
- 8–25%
- 25.1–50%
- 50.1–75%
- 75.1–92%

SOURCE: Data from U.S. Department of Education, National Center for Education Statistics, Common Core of Data (CCD), "State Nonfiscal Public Elementary/Secondary Education Survey," 2013–14 v.1a.

Words Matter: Politically Correct, Geographically Correct, and Other Terminology Considerations

Similar to the issues of terminology for people with disabilities (see Chapter 1), terms used in reference to racial, ethnic, or cultural groups of people may be appropriate or inappropriate.[2] And, as with disability-related terminology, the preferred words change over time. In the United States, the federal government classifies individuals into one of the following racial categories:

- White: origins in Europe, the Middle East, or North Africa
- Black or African American: origins in any of the Black racial groups of Africa
- American Indian or Alaska Native: origins in North and South America (including Central America) and maintaining an affiliation with a tribe or community
- Asian: origins in the Far East, Southeast Asia, or the Indian subcontinent
- Native Hawaiian or Other Pacific Islander: origins in Hawaii, Guam, Samoa, or other Pacific Islands

Different terms that reflect broad membership in an ethnic group are often used in various geographic regions (e.g., Anglo, Latino/Latina, Chicano/Chicana). Further, many people prefer more specific terms that relate directly to their tribe (e.g.,

Navajo, Apache) or country of origin (e.g., Mexican, Guatemalan). Yet even this level of specificity can be problematic when political changes result in a name change for a country, such as the change from Burma to Myanmar, which is still being debated years later. Those who have lived in the United States for longer periods will often use terminology reflective of both countries or cultures (e.g., Mexican American). The term *historically underrepresented* has replaced *minority*, a term that carries a negative connotation associated with historically dominated groups. *Minority* is also mathematically incorrect in many communities and school districts where these individuals make up more than 50% of the population. The term **students of color** refers to those from non-White backgrounds. Note, however, that the federal government's definition of *White* includes those with origins in the Middle East; as such, the term *students of color* would exclude students from Iran, Iraq, Afghanistan, and their neighboring countries, which runs contrary to many people's perceptions. In the end, regional, group, and individual preferences all play a role in preferred terminology, which changes over time. So, how does one best determine which terms to use? Ask the person or group of people to whom you are referring which terms they prefer.

Topic 3.2 Issues of Social Justice

- Sociocultural disparities in key areas like parental education and income levels put students at risk for school failure.

- Schools in low-income areas often provide an inequitable education for those students.

Do students from racially, ethnically, culturally, and linguistically diverse backgrounds perform as well as those from the dominant culture? Unfortunately, these students tend to have lower academic achievement and school performance than their peers from the mainstream culture. This situation is not unique to the United States; in many countries worldwide, students who are not from the dominant culture demonstrate poor school outcomes. In the United States, both sociocultural (e.g., levels of parental education, poverty) and school-related factors contribute to this disparity in achievement. Students who live in poverty are subject to the ravages of **food insecurity**, limited access to health care, dangerous neighborhoods, environmental toxins, and low-quality schools, all of which create further inequities within their lives. As a result, these students are more likely to struggle academically and have higher dropout rates than middle- or upper-income students. Their insufficient educational training makes them unqualified for jobs that provide adequate wages. In turn, they raise their own children without sufficient incomes, which results in a cycle of generational poverty. Compared to their White peers, students of color are two to three times more likely to live in poverty, so the generational poverty cycle has a bigger impact on these families and their communities.

---

[2] The terminology used in this text reflects both national and regional preferences.

Lead Poisoning in Flint, Michigan

In 2015, a news story about toxic water in Flint, Michigan, illustrated the unjust circumstances of families living in poverty. Flint has a population of roughly 100,000 people, 56% of whom are African American and 40% of whom live below the poverty line. To save the state money, Flint's water supply was switched from Lake Huron to the infamously polluted Flint River. Worse, the water was not treated with a required anti-corrosive agent, so lead seeped from corroded pipes into the water supply. Lead poisoning is irreversible; it can cause intellectual disabilities and serious medical conditions. Although residents exhibited symptoms like hair loss, rashes, and other health concerns, public officials did not acknowledge the problem for 18 months, and then only after external researchers independently tested the water and released their findings. A class-action lawsuit was filed on behalf of the citizens of Flint, many of whom questioned whether the state would have made the same changes to the water supply if Flint were a higher-income, predominantly White community. Regardless of the outcome of the lawsuit, the long-term effects of lead poisoning on the residents and their children will be profound.

Rebecca Cook/Reuters

How do schools in low-income neighborhoods differ from those in middle- and upper-income neighborhoods? School-related disadvantages are a result of inadequate public education. Over 50 years ago, the Supreme Court ruled that separate schools for White and African American students were not equal (*Brown v. Board of Education*). Yet, White students and students of color are often still educated separately. Students of color frequently attend low-income schools. Poor schools tend to be larger, have higher student-teacher ratios, and have fewer human and financial resources (e.g., limited materials, few or no **advanced placement (AP) courses** or college-prep classes, limited after-school activities). In fact, annual differences in spending between a state's wealthiest and poorest school districts can reach a scandalous $40,000 *per student*.

Low-income schools have great difficulty attracting and retaining highly qualified teachers. As a result, these schools have more than their fair share of the least-prepared, inexperienced, and uncertified teachers. Because they lack preparation, these teachers have great difficulty providing motivating, culturally responsive, high-quality instruction in well-managed classroom environments. These schools have high rates of both teacher turnover and student dropout. The cumulative effects of these disparities—low-income, inferior schools and teachers with inadequate preparation—create huge challenges for students, referred to by social scientists as the **opportunity gap**. The result is unconscionable. Consider this: one research study found that weak instruction in poor schools resulted in students receiving the equivalent of 57 weeks less instruction by sixth grade than their higher socioeconomic status (SES) counterparts, resulting in an achievement gap of 3.5 grade levels by sixth grade!

Finally, bias and discrimination contribute to poor student outcomes. Some educators have low expectations for racially, ethnically, or culturally diverse students, compounding the effects of challenging life circumstances, poor schools, and inexperienced teachers. These perceptions influence teaching behaviors. Consider the differences in the teaching behaviors outlined in the table below. How would you feel if you were the student of a teacher who displayed the behaviors in the left column rather than the right column? In whose class do you think you would perform better?

Teacher Expectations and Instructional Behaviors

Teachers with High Expectations	Teachers with Low Expectations
Provide many opportunities to respond in class	Ask fewer questions
Give sufficient time to think through and respond to questions (i.e., **wait time**)	Give less wait time
Deliver positive feedback on correct responses	Provide little feedback on student responses
Guide students who give incorrect answers and help them reason through to obtain a correct answer	Simply call on someone else when a student gives an incorrect answer

The Achievement Gap

As shown in the accompanying graphs, the **achievement gap** between students of color and their White counterparts is apparent. The graphs show data from the 2013 National Assessment of Educational Progress (NAEP) in reading, using three key indicators: race, parental income, and eligibility for free or reduced-price lunch (an indicator for low-income households). Note the differences, or gaps, between the different groups.

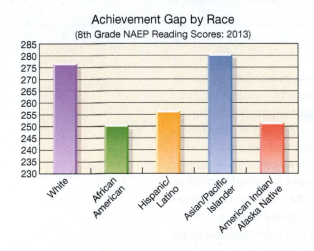

Achievement Gap by Race
(8th Grade NAEP Reading Scores: 2013)

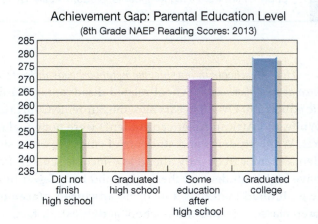

Achievement Gap: Parental Education Level
(8th Grade NAEP Reading Scores: 2013)

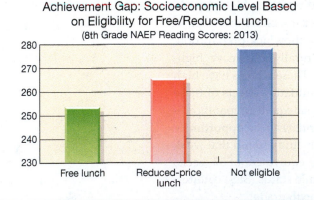

Achievement Gap: Socioeconomic Level Based on Eligibility for Free/Reduced Lunch
(8th Grade NAEP Reading Scores: 2013)

SOURCE: U.S. Department of Education, National Center for Education Statistics, *The Condition of Education 2015* (NCES 2015-144). Retrieved from http://nces.ed.gov/pubs2015/2015144.pdf

Research shows that low expectations or negative attitudes are often based on non-relevant information (e.g., dialect, movement styles) or stereotypical perceptions of their families based on a single piece of unverified information (e.g., mother uses illegal drugs). Students often internalize these negative perceptions and become disengaged, perform poorly, or engage in defiant behavior, which in turn reinforces the teachers' low expectations.

Equal vs. Equitable Education

An **equal education** is one in which all students receive the same education. But in order to reduce the achievement and opportunity gaps, educators must strive to give students an **equitable education**, one in which those from different backgrounds receive the education and supports necessary to achieve equal outcomes. In recognition of the need for equitable education, the U.S. Department of Education has implemented the Excellent Educators for All Initiative, not only to provide all students with a high-quality education but also to provide "great educators for the students who need them most." You can read more about this initiative through this link, http://www.ed.gov/news/press-releases/us-education-secretary-announces-guidance-ensure-all-students-have-equal-access-educational-resources, or through the Office of Civil Rights' Fact Sheet on Education Equity: http://www2.ed.gov/about/offices/list/ocr/docs/dcl-factsheet-resourcecomp-201410.pdf.

Topic 3.3 Understanding Disproportionality

- One concern about equitable education for students from diverse backgrounds relates to their disproportionate representation in special education.

- Investigations of disproportionate representation in special education analyze identification and placement rates, as well as disciplinary actions.

Why is placement in special education of particular concern for students from diverse backgrounds? As you learned in the previous topic, too many children from diverse backgrounds are receiving an inequitable education. In some cases, this can result in the inappropriate placement of students into special education programs, even though they do not have disabilities. In the 1970s, despite what was thought to be an improving climate for diversity, the harsh reality was that racial, cultural, and language differences resulted in too many students being inappropriately labeled as having intellectual disabilities. Important court cases involving diverse students and education centered on examples of discrimination in which these students inappropriately received special education services.

Landmark Court Cases

Year	Case	Findings
1970	*Diana v. State Board of Education*	Using IQ tests to identify Hispanic students as having intellectual disabilities was discriminatory.
1971	*Larry P. v. Riles*	Culturally biased testing resulted in overrepresentation of African American children in classes for students with intellectual disabilities.
1974	*Lau v. Nichols*	Schools must offer services to help ELL students overcome language barriers.

Given that special education services provide individualized instruction, why was it problematic that the students represented in these court cases received special education services? The answer is simple: it is wrong to place students who have no disabilities in special education. Unnecessary placement in special education

- often means removal from the general education setting and, in the case of students from diverse backgrounds, placement in a more restrictive setting with lowered expectations for achievement;

- burdens the special education system, when the students' educational needs can and should be met through other means; and

- needlessly exposes students to the societal stigmas, negative perceptions, actions, and comments of those who do not fully understand disabilities.

Would you be concerned to find out that this is a segregated special education classroom in a school whose student population is mostly White? Why or why not?

What is disproportionality, and how is it determined? Because of concerns tied to racial and ethnic discrimination in special education, educators and policy makers began investigating the incidence of **disproportionate representation**, or the variance between a group's presence in the general population and its presence in special education. IDEA requires school districts and states to gather data using students' racial and ethnic categories, adding the categories of *Hispanic/Latino* and *two or more races* to the five categories you learned about earlier (White, Black/African American, American Indian/Alaska Native, Asian, and Native Hawaiian/Other Pacific Islander). There are many ways to calculate disproportionality, some more complex than others, and beyond the scope of this chapter. However, at the most basic level, the data are analyzed to determine whether certain groups of students receive special education services at a higher rate than expected (**overrepresentation**) or at a lower rate (**underrepresentation**).

Let's use the enrollment data for Central School District to consider disproportionality (see the table below). If African American students make up 15.6% of the total school population, we would expect to see that 15.6% of the special education student population is African American. Given that they represent 16.6% of the special education population, it would appear the proportion of African American students in special education is slightly higher. However, if we examine the data more closely, African American students represent 25% of students in the emotional disturbance category and 30% of students in the intellectual disabilities category, which would indicate overrepresentation. Conversely, students with Asian backgrounds constitute 4.6% of the school population but only 2.2% of the special education population and only 1.1% of students with intellectual disabilities—a case of underrepresentation. Using the data for Central School District, do you notice any other areas of concern?

Enrollment data for Central School District (selected disabilities)

	Identification Data						
	American Indian/Alaska Native	Asian	Black (non-Hispanic)	Hispanic	Native Hawaiian/ Other Pacific Islander	White (non-Hispanic)	Two or More Races
Total public school enrollment	1.2%	4.6%	15.6%	15.7%	0.9%	60.5%	1.5%
All disabilities	1.5%	2.2%	16.6%	16.7%	2.1%	60.3%	0.6%
Specific learning disabilities	2.8%	1.7%	18.5%	20.1%	1.8%	54.8%	0.3%
Speech or language impairments	2.4%	3.7%	12.5%	17.0%	2.0%	61.5%	0.9%
Intellectual disability	1.3%	1.1%	30.0%	14.1%	1.9%	50.9%	0.7%
Emotional disturbance	1.6%	0.9%	25.0%	11.7%	1.6%	58.7%	0.5%
Autism spectrum disorder	0.7%	4.4%	13.4%	11.5%	1.0%	67.9%	1.1%

As we learned from Central School District's data, the enrollment percentages vary considerably when we compare overall special education enrollment to those in specific disability categories. Because of this, IDEA requires states to examine their enrollment data for each district and identify those with disproportionate representation in special education and within specific disability categories. Further, states must examine disproportionality with regard to placement (i.e., educational settings and the amount of time spent with typically developing peers) and disciplinary actions. For example (using the data from Central School District above), American Indian/Alaska Native and Native Hawaiian/Other Pacific Islander students each make up 1.6% of the students in the emotional disturbance category. However, if the majority of the American Indian/Alaska Native students are placed in segregated classrooms with little interaction with their peers, yet most of the Native Hawaiian/Other Pacific Islander students are educated in general education classrooms for the majority of the school day, then the district has cause for concern regarding its placement decisions. With regard to disciplinary actions, disproportionality would occur if Hispanic students make up only 15.7% of the total school population and 16.7% of the students with disabilities but account for nearly 44% of all suspensions and expulsions.

Recent research studies have found conflicting results regarding disproportionate representation of racially, culturally, or linguistically diverse students in special education. The studies vary by sample size (district, state, or national student data sets), type of disability, racial or ethnic group, and consideration of relevant family factors (poverty, education levels). Some studies have found clear patterns of overrepresentation, whereas others—when compared to White students with matching background characteristics such as poverty and parental education and income levels—have found that students from diverse backgrounds are underrepresented in special education. To address these issues, the federal government has multiple initiatives and investments in place that provide training for districts and require them to examine their enrollment data and look for disproportionality. For those interested in learning more, the Civil Rights Data Collection Website provides data on the enrollment patterns for individual schools and districts: http://ocrdata.ed.gov. The data are disaggregated by race/ethnicity, gender, level of English proficiency, and disability.

Check Your Understanding 3.1

Click here to gauge your understanding of the concepts in this section.

Cultural Diversity

Learning Outcome

Explain how cultural differences can create conflicts in school, list at least two steps that teachers can take to prevent cross-cultural dissonance, and describe culturally responsive instruction.

Topic 3.4 Understanding Cross-Cultural Dissonance

- Many of the behaviors we expect of children at school are based on cultural norms that students from other cultures or countries may not know.

- As a result of these cultural differences, students may experience difficulties in school.

Topic 3.5 Preventing Cross-Cultural Dissonance

- Teachers who engage in critical self-reflection can anticipate where cross-cultural dissonance may occur.

- Teachers who understand their students' cultures may prevent culturally based problems from arising.

Topic 3.6 Providing Culturally Responsive Instruction

- Teachers must be culturally competent, which includes being knowledgeable about students and their home cultures.

- Culturally responsive instruction teaches to the strengths of each student while validating and affirming his or her culture.

When students learn about and appreciate the cultures of other students, they are better prepared to work in a multicultural society.

Topic 3.4 Understanding Cross-Cultural Dissonance

- Many of the behaviors we expect of children at school are based on cultural norms that students from other cultures or countries may not know.

- As a result of these cultural differences, students may experience difficulties in school.

What is cultural diversity, and how can it influence the classroom learning environment? Students whose backgrounds differ from American mainstream society (i.e., White, middle-income) are thought of as **culturally diverse**. It is estimated that America's students come from over a thousand different cultures. Culture influences everything we do. Yet, for many of us, our culture is something we take for granted and thus don't think about. Consider one of our most basic interactions: meeting a new person. In the dominant American culture, we may shake the person's hand, look him or her in the eye, and exchange expected pleasantries (e.g., "Hi, it's nice to meet you."). Our culture dictates how close we stand to the person, how firmly and how long we hold his or her hand during the handshake, the length of time and the intensity of eye contact, the tone and volume of our voice, and the questions we ask. Now, think about how many ways this simple interaction could be misinterpreted when meeting someone from a different culture. If he stands too close (for our culture but not for his), we interpret it as aggression or inappropriate intimacy; if he stands too far away, he is aloof. If he holds our hand too long during the handshake, we tend to feel uncomfortable. If he lets go too soon, we assume he is uninterested. Lack of eye contact can be considered rude, but so can holding the gaze too long. Play this scenario all the way through, considering all aspects, and you realize how cultural differences can hinder a small, seemingly inconsequential interaction and leave the participants with negative first impressions of each other. Now, consider all of the interactions that students and teachers have throughout a typical school day and you realize how even minor, culturally based misperceptions can leave students feeling as though they are learning in an unwelcoming or even hostile environment (see the table).

Examples of Culturally Based Misinterpretations in the Classroom

Action	Possible Misinterpretation
A teacher gives a thumbs-up sign to indicate that a student answered a question correctly.	Students from some Middle Eastern countries, Nigeria, and Australia believe this is an obscene gesture, equivalent to the American middle-finger sign.
A teacher uses a passive communication style with her students, with phrases such as "Let's all think quietly" or "Jada, would you like to sit down?"	Many African American students are used to a straightforward communication style. Without a clear directive ("Jada, sit down"), they may not understand that the teacher is actually giving them a command. The teacher misinterprets this as defiance.
A student looks at the floor while a teacher is speaking to him, a sign of respect in many cultures.	The teacher believes the child is not listening to her or is uninterested in the conversation.
A student from Southeast Asia smiles when being scolded by a teacher as a sign that she admits her misbehavior and holds no hard feelings.	The teacher interprets the smile as a smirk and a sign that the child thinks the situation is funny or is not taking her seriously.

SOURCES: *Multicultural Manners: Essential Rules of Etiquette for the 21st Century,* by N. Dresser, 2005, Hoboken, NJ: John Wiley & Sons, Inc.; and "Toward a Conception of Culturally Responsive Classroom Management," by C. S. Weinstein, S. Tomlinson-Clarke, and M. Curran, 2004, *Journal of Teacher Education, 55*(1), pp. 25–38.

Dimensions of Cross-Cultural Communication

The video below details areas in which potential miscommunication might occur in the classroom, whether through cultural communicative differences or through literal translations of teacher language.

In what educational areas can cross-cultural conflicts occur? For some students, their cultural characteristics, behaviors, and actions are often at odds with the classroom culture or with teachers' expectations (referred to as **cross-cultural dissonance** or **cultural discontinuity**), creating situations and environments in which students perform poorly. The box summarizes four areas in which cross-cultural dissonance can occur.

Four Potential Areas for Cross-Cultural Dissonance

Learning Experiences and Preferences

Cultural differences exist in the ways students are traditionally taught (e.g., memorization vs. problem solving).

Behavioral Expectations

Different cultures have different behavioral norms.

Communication Styles

Differences in communication styles can include non-verbal norms, questioning techniques, nuances, and appropriate vs. inappropriate topics.

Curricular Representation

Curricula, lessons, and materials should reflect the diversity of the classroom.

Topic 3.5 Preventing Cross-Cultural Dissonance

- Teachers who engage in critical self-reflection can anticipate where cross-cultural dissonance may occur.

- Teachers who understand their students' cultures may prevent culturally based problems from arising.

How can teachers anticipate where cross-cultural dissonance might occur? As discussed in the previous topic, culture affects the way we communicate, process information, and learn, which describes nearly every activity during a school day! Teachers must first recognize that differences can make us uncomfortable. Yet, as the previous examples in the box indicated, the reason for our discomfort is often a lack of knowledge that can cause misunderstandings.

To prevent these negative responses, teachers must understand the roles that race, ethnicity, culture, and language can play in the learning process. Good teachers engage in reflective self-examination of their attitudes and assumptions. They also consider the subsequent impact of those beliefs on classroom instruction and activities, as well as on personal interactions, behaviors, or communication styles. The table below provides examples of self-reflection starting points regarding race. These questions can easily be adapted for self-reflecting on attitudes and assumptions about individuals with cultural and linguistic differences.

Think back to the example of the many ways a simple introduction could be culturally misconstrued. To avoid similar miscommunications in other types of classroom interactions, teachers who engage in self-reflection ponder their own teaching practices ("What types of questions do I typically ask, and how do I expect students to respond? Do I expect students to sit quietly while they work, or do I allow them to ask each other for help?"). They also consider their assumptions regarding what students know about the school culture ("I tell my students to study, but do they really know what that means?"). Understanding how culture shapes their own attitudes, assumptions, and behaviors will allow teachers to provide more effective and responsive instruction.

Guiding Questions for Teacher Self-Reflection

Self-Reflection on Teaching and Race	Reflection on Students, Race, and Social Context
How does my race influence my work with students, especially those whose race is different from my own?	How will my students' race(s) influence their work with me as their teacher? What conflicts might emerge due to racial differences and disconnections?
What is the effect of my race on my thinking, beliefs, actions, and decision making?	What matters are most important to my students and to me? What is the relevance of race to these important issues?
How do I situate myself in the education of students? How do I negotiate the power structure in my class to allow students from all racial backgrounds to feel a sense of worth?	To what degree are my role as a teacher and my experiences superior to the experiences and expertise of students? What knowledge can be learned from my students? How might race shape these roles?
How do I situate and negotiate students' knowledge, experiences, and race with my own?	Am I willing to speak about race on behalf of those who might not be present in the conversation, both inside and outside school? Am I willing to express what I find to be unjust regarding race and racism in difficult spaces?

SOURCE: *Start Where You Are, but Don't Stay There*, by H. R. Milner, 2012, Cambridge, MA: Harvard University Press. Adapted with permission.

What should teachers do after they have identified areas in which cross-cultural dissonance might occur? An important first step is for teachers to know their students. Recognizing what mainstream cultural knowledge their students may be missing allows teachers to fill in those gaps. When teachers learn about and understand their students' families, backgrounds, and beliefs, the potential for conflict is reduced. Clearly, for teachers who have students from many different backgrounds and cultures, this will not happen immediately but instead will require gradual information gathering.

Teachers should also be aware of the tendency to stereotype certain groups. For example, a teacher may think, "Sergio's parents are from Mexico, so Sergio will exhibit particular learning and behavioral characteristics and communication styles." Yet, it is important *not* to stereotype groups of individuals or assume that all people from the same culture hold similar beliefs and traditions. These can be influenced not only by the cultural background of students but also by such factors as the length of time the family has been in America; the geographic region of the country in which they live; the age, gender, and birth order of the child; the language spoken at home; the religion practiced by the family; the proximity to other extended family members; and the **socioeconomic level** of the family. So Sergio, an American-born child of Mexican heritage, may maintain a different cultural belief system than if he were a recent Mexican immigrant.

Although these students may appear to share the same cultural background, they are quite different. Some are recent immigrants who are learning English, others come from families who have lived here for generations and speak only English.

On the Screen: *McFarland, USA*

The film *McFarland, USA* chronicles the true story of high school teacher and coach Jim White, who initially knows little about the home backgrounds and cultures of the Mexican American students in his classes. As a result, he makes many mistakes: he has low expectations; he commits social gaffes with the students and their families based on inaccurate stereotypes; he inadvertently insults them when he cannot pronounce their names correctly. Yet, as he gradually learns more about the students and their culture, he is able to use their strengths—which include strong family and community support—to build an award-winning cross-country team.

Although the film focuses on several siblings from the Diaz family, it only alludes to their parents' dedication to the children's education and the close-knit relationship between the Diaz and White families. In reality, that strong familial and educational support system enabled all seven Diaz children to attend college and then return to their hometown as adults; six of the siblings now work in education.

https://www.youtube.com/watch?v=j-VAOIHGE6Q

Topic 3.6 Providing Culturally Responsive Instruction

- Teachers must be culturally competent, which includes being knowledgeable about students and their home cultures.

- Culturally responsive instruction teaches to the strengths of each student while validating and affirming his or her culture.

What is a culturally competent teacher? Teachers who are **culturally competent** can provide effective instruction to students from other cultures. Culturally competent teachers acknowledge students' differences (e.g., race, ethnicity, language, socioeconomic level) and recognize that these differences may influence how students learn. These teachers become knowledgeable about the backgrounds, heritages, traditions, and cultural expectations of students and their families and adjust their teaching accordingly.

A culturally competent teacher:

- Understands culture and its role in education.
- Engages in self-reflective examination of his or her own cultural attitudes and assumptions and their subsequent impact on classroom instruction and activities.
- Takes responsibility for learning about students' culture and community.
- Uses student culture as a basis for learning.
- Enriches classroom instruction with examples of students' home culture and involves community and family members.
- Creates learning environments that are culturally responsive, where the curriculum includes multiple perspectives and examples from many cultures.

One of the first responsibilities of a culturally competent teacher is to understand a student's culture. This cultural understanding includes knowing the family's perceptions of the role of education as well as other forces in the community that could affect a student's ability to perform well in school.

How Does Culture Affect Students' Attitudes toward School?

The video below discusses cultural knowledge and school performance in more detail.

Video

How does culturally responsive instruction help students succeed in school? **Culturally responsive instruction** is the process through which teachers demonstrate their cultural competence in the classroom. Culturally responsive instruction acknowledges and legitimizes different cultural heritages, using students' strengths to enhance learning. Rather than seeing a lack of mainstream knowledge as a deficit, teachers engaging in culturally responsive instruction recognize the prior knowledge, skills, and experiences that students bring to the learning environment and use them to connect meaning to new classroom materials and activities. Further, these teachers incorporate a wide variety of instructional techniques that take into consideration varied learning needs, preferences, and communication styles (recall what you learned about UDL and differentiated instruction in Chapter 2).

Culturally responsive instruction incorporates multicultural knowledge, resources, and materials in all subjects, not just in social studies classes or when certain holidays occur (e.g., Cinco de Mayo). As a result, one benefit is that students learn to understand and appreciate the cultural heritages of others, in addition to their own. This increased understanding and appreciation can further reduce cross-cultural dissonance in the school environment by preventing culturally based misunderstandings resulting from communication or behavioral differences. Many students are unaware that the communication and behavioral expectations of school differ from those of their homes and communities. While cultural differences do not explain all behavioral infractions that teachers have to deal with,

Tips for Culturally Responsive Teaching

Teachers who engage in culturally responsive instruction:

1. Recognize their own cultural beliefs and assumptions.
   a. Acknowledge that their personal beliefs and assumptions are not universally accepted.
   b. Understand how their personal beliefs influence their behavior and expectations for students.
   c. Identify potential sources of cross-cultural conflict.
   d. Monitor their equitable treatment of students.
2. Develop genuinely respectful, caring relationships with their students.
   a. Share information about themselves.
   b. Show a sincere interest in their students' lives, in and out of the classroom.
3. Actively learn about students' cultural backgrounds and use that knowledge in the classroom.
   a. Understand the impact of factors like family background and structure, relationship styles, discipline, perceptions of time, and interpersonal space on student behavior.
   b. Use communication styles (verbal and nonverbal) that are familiar to students (e.g., common expressions, verbal **call-and-response** patterns, straightforward directives).

4. Use culturally appropriate classroom management strategies.
   a. Clearly define classroom expectations (e.g., rules, procedures, consequences), particularly if they differ from those to which students are accustomed.
   b. Hold students accountable to classroom expectations.
   c. Focus on positive behavior.
   d. Communicate in a calm and respectful manner.
   e. Deal with inappropriate behavior immediately, consistently, and fairly.
5. Build caring classroom communities.
   a. Set clear, high expectations for all students.
   b. Help students learn about each other.
   c. Demonstrate and reinforce expectations of respect and kindness.
   d. Nurture personal development.

Sources: Adapted from "Creating Environments of Success and Resilience: Culturally Responsive Classroom Management and More," by E. Bondy, D. D. Ross, C. Gallingane, and E. Hambacher, 2007, *Urban Education, 42*(4), 326–348; "Culturally responsive classrooms for culturally diverse students with and at risk for disabilities," by G. Cartledge and L. Kourea, 2008, *Exceptional Children, 74*(3), 351–371; and "Toward a Conception of Culturally Responsive Classroom Management," by C. S. Weinstein, S. Tomlinson-Clarke, and M. Curran, 2004, *Journal of Teacher Education, 55*(1), 25–38.

understanding the basis for some of the problems can lead to more effective solutions. When genuine misbehavior does occur, research shows that teachers who are "warm demanders"—dealing with students in a consistent, caring, yet firm manner while maintaining high student expectations—have better classroom control. Furthermore, a positive environment, coupled with explicitly expressed commitment to help all students achieve, can prevent the psychological disengagement that can occur when students sense lowered expectations or inequitable treatment. In classes taught by culturally competent teachers, racially and culturally diverse students become self-disciplined, rather than rebelling against perceived unfair discipline. When **mutual accommodation** occurs in a classroom, teachers engage students in a culturally responsive and respectful manner. They acknowledge the appropriateness of certain behaviors outside the school setting but also explicitly teach classroom expectations to avoid misunderstandings, which helps students learn to "walk in two worlds."

If you are interested in learning more about cultural diversity, this IRIS Module examines the ways in which culture influences the daily interactions that occur across all classrooms and provides practice for enhancing culturally responsive teaching.

▶ **IRIS Module: Cultural and Linguistic Differences: What Teachers Should Know.**
http://iris.peabody.vanderbilt.edu/module/clde/

Check Your Understanding 3.2

Click here to gauge your understanding of the concepts in this section.

Linguistic Diversity

Learning Outcome

Understand the process of second-language acquisition and describe effective programs and strategies for teaching English learners.

Topic 3.7 Understanding Second-Language Acquisition

- Many terms are used to refer to students who speak a language other than English as their first language.

- Proficiency in a second language develops in stages; academic language proficiency is complex and takes significantly longer to develop than social language.

Topic 3.8 Effective Practices for ELs

- Many program options exist to help ELs improve their English skills; the most effective are bilingual programs.

- General education teachers can use strategies to help linguistically diverse students learn academic content while developing their English skills.

Vlad/Fotolia

Imagine how hard it would be to learn and study in another language, especially one in which the alphabet, characters, or words are nothing like those of your home language!

Topic 3.7 Understanding Second-Language Acquisition

- Many terms are used to refer to students who speak a language other than English as their first language.
- Proficiency in a second language develops in stages; academic language proficiency is complex and takes significantly longer to develop than social language.

What is linguistic diversity? In the United States, individuals whose home language or native language is not English are referred to as **linguistically diverse**. Many culturally diverse students are also linguistically diverse. Other terms used to describe these students include English language learners (ELLs), English learners (ELs), or **language minority students**. In the early childhood field, **dual language learners** refers to children who are learning more than one language simultaneously. The following table provides specific definitions used by the federal government.

Definitions of Linguistically Diverse Learners

Term	Definition	Source
English learner	1. An individual, aged 3–21, enrolled or preparing to enroll in an elementary or secondary school, a. who wasn't born in the United States or whose native language isn't English; b. who is a Native American or Alaska Native, or native resident of the outlying areas and comes from an environment where a language other than English has significantly impacted level of English language proficiency; or c. who is migratory, with native language other than English, from an environment where a language other than English is dominant; and 2. whose difficulties in speaking, reading, writing, or understanding English may be sufficient to deny the child a. ability to meet proficient level of achievement on state assessments; b. ability to successfully achieve in class where instruction is in English; or the c. opportunity to participate fully in society.	Every Student Succeeds Act, U.S. Dept. of Education
Dual language learner	Children who…acquire two or more languages simultaneously, and learn a second language while continuing to develop their first language. The term "dual language learners" encompasses other terms frequently used, such as Limited English Proficient (LEP), bilingual, English language learners (ELL), English learners, and children who speak a Language Other Than English (LOTE).	Office of Head Start (OHS)

SOURCES: PUBLIC LAW 114–95–DEC. 10, 2015, Every Student Succeeds Act; and Office of Head Start Definition of Dual Language Learners, HHS/ACF/OHS, 2009.

How does second-language acquisition occur, and how long does it take? Learning to speak English (or any second language) is complex. Second-language acquisition goes through five distinct stages, outlined in the following table.

Stages of Second-Language Acquisition

Stage	Characteristics	Vocabulary
1. Silent/receptive or pre-productive	Students are often silent during this stage and learn by listening to others. They tend to communicate by pointing or gesturing, and can give simple yes/no responses.	Receptive vocabulary of 500 words
2. Early production	Students can express their thoughts using very short (e.g., two-word) phrases and can respond to simple questions.	Receptive and expressive vocabulary of 1,000 words
3. Speech emergence	Students can use longer phrases and simple sentences and can ask simple questions, but they still have difficulty communicating their thoughts adequately, making frequent grammatical errors.	Receptive and expressive vocabulary of 3,000 words
4. Intermediate language proficiency	Students can express themselves using longer, more complicated sentences, which allows them to communicate more effectively. They are able to ask for clarification if they do not understand something.	Receptive and expressive vocabulary of 6,000 words
5. Advanced language proficiency	Students are able to understand and express themselves as well as their English-speaking peers. They are able to fully and successfully participate in learning activities.	Acquisition of content-level vocabulary

As students progress through these stages, they first develop **basic interpersonal conversation skills (BICS)** or conversational English, which allows them to communicate well on the playground and to interact socially with friends and teachers. These social language skills can be acquired within 2 to 3 years. However, **cognitive academic language proficiency (CALP)** or classroom English requires much more advanced skills. To be proficient with academic language, students must be able to understand content-specific vocabulary (e.g., *consensus, diffusion*), comprehend more complex sentence structures, and engage in discussions using advanced figures of speech (e.g., metaphors) and higher-order thinking skills (e.g., deductions, inferences). Academic language skills develop simultaneously with social language skills, but it takes 5 to 7 years of meaningful exposure and practice before students are proficient. And the mere ability to translate one language into another is not sufficient. Mastery of a language also requires an understanding of idioms, nuances, and non-verbal messages. With both social and academic language, **receptive language** skills develop sooner than **expressive language** skills, so EL students may understand more than they are able to convey. This makes sense if you consider your own second-language experiences. If you studied a foreign language in school, you probably find it easier to understand words, phrases, or brief snippets of conversation if you hear or read them (receptive language) than if you try to recall and speak those same words or phrases yourself (expressive language).

Lack of knowledge about the inherent differences between social and academic language can cause teachers to overestimate the English language proficiency of their EL students. For example, a teacher might hear a student talking with her friends in the hall or on the playground and incorrectly assume that her English skills are fully developed. Then, when this same student struggles in class, the teacher may not realize that her academic language skills are still developing and may incorrectly assume that she isn't trying hard enough, isn't studying, or has special learning needs. Or, in a very different scenario, teachers may be reluctant to refer an EL student who really does have a disability for special education testing because they

Social vs. Academic Language

Read through the examples below. Using your own second-language experience (e.g., high school foreign language classes), translate the examples into that language. Is it easier for the social language than for the academic language? What makes the academic language so much harder?

Skill Level	Examples
Social or conversational English (BICS)	• Can you push me on the swing? • I got a new race car video game yesterday. Do you want to come over this afternoon and test it out?
Academic or classroom English (CALP)	• Plants generate their own food using sunlight, carbon dioxide, and water through a process called photosynthesis. • Write a fraction with a denominator of 10 that equals ½. Now write that fraction as a decimal. Finally, write the number as a percent.

Many people are surprised at how hard it is to translate the science and math examples above, which come from elementary level content. How much harder do you think it would be to understand or translate high school level content, such as for chemistry or mathematics (with terms like *oxidation* or *trigonometric ratios*)?

assume that his struggles are due to second-language acquisition issues. To avoid these types of mistakes, teachers should have some understanding of the distinctions between language differences (e.g., a native Spanish speaker who struggles academically because she has not yet learned English) and language disorders (e.g., a student who struggles to understand, express, or manipulate language, regardless of whether it is his first or second language). We will discuss these differences more in Chapter 5.

Topic 3.8 Effective Practices for ELs

- Many program options exist to help ELs improve their English skills; the most effective are bilingual programs.

- General education teachers can use strategies to help linguistically diverse students learn academic content while developing their English skills.

What types of services are available to support linguistically diverse students? Schools offer a variety of different programs, dependent on factors such as the number of ELs in the school or district, availability of qualified personnel, funding, and district and state policies. The table below summarizes the different options in order of program effectiveness.

A comprehensive study with data from over 42,000 EL students found that two-way bilingual programs are the most effective. Contrary to public misperception, research shows that when students develop content knowledge and academic skills in their first language, the newly acquired knowledge transfers to the development of content knowledge and academic skills in their second language. Key predictors of success included

- cognitively complex, grade-level content instruction in a student's native language, combined with similarly complex content instruction in English; and

- supportive sociocultural environments for learning that utilize **additive bilingualism**.

Common Programs for ELs

Program	Characteristics	General Comments
• Two-way immersion (also known as two-way bilingual, dual language immersion)	• ELs *and* native English speakers learn side-by-side, using both first (L1) and second (L2) languages to learn academic content and a second language. • Goal is bilingualism and academic proficiency for both groups of students.	• Most effective program option. • Some concerns with recruitment and retention of native English speakers and long-term support from their parents.
• Developmental bilingual education	• Uses both L1 and L2 for content instruction for ELs. • Most programs start in K. • Students participate for as many years/grades as the program is available. • Most students need 4–7 years to achieve academic proficiency in their L2.	• Extended length of program is aligned with principles of academic language development. • Concerns exist regarding programming for late starters, early exiters, or transient students.
• Transitional bilingual education	• Provides L1 content instruction *and* L2 instruction for ELs. • Most start in K or first grade, with the goal of transitioning to L2-only instruction within two years. • Students are generally pulled out of the general education classroom to receive services.	• Teachers must be bilingual and able to teach academic content and English. • Limited time for L2 development is of concern. • Often negatively perceived (segregated, stigmatizing for students).
• English as a second language (ESL) or English for Speakers of Other Languages	• Instruction in L2 only for ELs. • Priority is to transition students to general education classrooms. • Students are generally pulled out of the general education classroom to receive services. • Little or no focus on learning content.	• Most frequently implemented program. • Least effective program option. • Teachers do not need to speak languages other than English.

NOTE: L1 is the native language; L2 is the second language.

The benefits of bilingualism cover the lifespan. Bilingual babies show precocious decision-making skills and advanced cognitive control. Students who develop academic proficiency in two languages often outperform their monolingual peers, as bilingualism is associated with greater cognitive flexibility, attention, working memory, metalinguistic awareness, and abstract reasoning. Bilingual adults have a competitive advantage in the global workforce. And for seniors, being bilingual appears to delay the onset of dementia symptoms by an average of four years.

What can general education teachers do to support ELs' success in class? General education teachers cannot assume that a student's English skills must be sufficiently developed in order to learn academic content, nor can they wait for this to occur. If they did so, the student would miss out on years of information. Instead, teachers must find ways to help ELs learn academic content at the same time that bilingual or ESL teachers are providing specialized English instruction. Fortunately, general education teachers can use certain instructional techniques in their classes to enhance learning opportunities for EL students. **Sheltered instruction** builds on components of effective instruction and UDL-like hands-on activities and manipulatives, cooperative learning, careful use of language (e.g., speaking slowly and clearly, monitoring vocabulary use to explain unfamiliar words), demonstrations, and multimodal means of presenting information.

Sheltered Instruction Observation Protocol (SIOP) is a research-based framework through which teachers provide sheltered instruction in a systematic and consistent format. In addition to the structured format, teachers who use the SIOP framework develop language objectives to support their lesson's content objectives. Consider these two lesson objectives:

- Content objective—Students will be able to calculate the perimeter and area of squares, rectangles, and parallelograms.
- Language objective—Students will be able to define the following terms: quadrilateral, square, rectangle, and parallelogram.

Comprehensible Input

The video below demonstrates how teachers can use sheltered instruction techniques—such as **comprehensible input**—to help students understand content-area information.

Although mathematics has been referred to as a "universal language," you can see that learners must understand much more than simple numeracy skills. Imagine how difficult it would be for an EL student to complete the content objective if she didn't understand the basic terminology. Adding a language objective promotes the acquisition of content knowledge while students continue to improve their English language skills.

Many instructional techniques or accommodations that are helpful to English learners can be implemented easily by classroom teachers, as demonstrated in the following IRIS Module. Highlights of the Module include videos of teachers providing typical lesson instruction and then re-teaching the lesson using sheltered instruction principles.

▶ **IRIS Module: Teaching English Language Learners: Effective Instructional Practices.**
http://iris.peabody.vanderbilt.edu/module/ell/

Check Your Understanding 3.3

Click here to gauge your understanding of the concepts in this section.

Summary

Diverse Learners

U.S. schools have a long history of educating students from diverse cultural and linguistic backgrounds.

- America's schoolchildren are becoming increasingly diverse. They speak hundreds of languages and represent over a thousand cultures.
- Many students from diverse backgrounds face inequitable life circumstances that put them at risk for school failure.
- One concern about equitable education for students from diverse backgrounds relates to their disproportionate representation in special education.

Cultural Diversity

Students whose cultures differ from that of mainstream America or from the dominant school culture are considered culturally diverse.

- Many of the behaviors we expect of children at school are based on cultural norms that students from other cultures or countries may not know, causing cross-cultural dissonance.
- Teachers who engage in critical self-reflection can anticipate where cross-cultural dissonance may occur and prevent problems from arising.
- Culturally responsive instruction teaches to the strengths of each student while validating and affirming his or her culture.

Linguistic Diversity

Students whose home language is not English (ELs, ELLs, language minority students) must learn English as their second language while also learning grade-level academic content.

- Proficiency in a second language develops in stages; academic language proficiency is complex and takes significantly longer to develop than social language.
- Many program options exist to help ELs improve their English skills; the most effective are bilingual programs.
- General education teachers can use strategies like sheltered instruction to help linguistically diverse students learn academic content while developing their English skills.

Addressing CEC Standards

Council for Exceptional Children (CEC) knowledge standards addressed in this chapter: 6.2, 1.2, 2.0, 1.1, 4.1, 6.3, 7.0, 7.1.

See the Appendix for the complete CEC Initial Level Special Educator Preparation Standards.

Chapter 4

Basic Guarantees, Individualized Programs, and Special Services

James Berglie/ZUMAPRESS/Alamy Stock Photo

Now retired Senator Tom Harkin of Iowa is a long-time advocate for individuals with disabilities. He was instrumental in creating landmark legislation that has improved and continues to improve the quality of life for all people with disabilities. Harkin's brother, Frank, lost his ability to hear at a very young age. Throughout his life, Senator Harkin saw how low expectations, lack of accessibility, and discrimination restricted his brother's participation in activities that most Americans take for granted. More than 25 years ago, as a junior member of the U.S. Senate, Harkin took the opportunity to craft groundbreaking legislation, the Americans with Disabilities Act, which provides vital civil rights to all people with disabilities. In his November 2010 speech at the 35th Anniversary of the Individuals with Disabilities Education Act, he reminded us all of how much work still needs to be done.

"Today, we celebrate a tremendously important and successful law. But, more fundamentally, we are celebrating a simple but radical idea: the idea that every child can benefit from an education, and has a right to a free and appropriate public education that is guaranteed by our nation's Constitution.

"But our job is by no means complete. In the years ahead, we must redouble our focus on high expectations for students with disabilities. We must ensure that the post-high school reality for students with disabilities includes opportunities for higher education.

"Our focus on students with disabilities cannot end when they complete school. We must build pathways into the workforce—with real opportunities for competitive, integrated employment, with decent wages and benefits, for all young people with disabilities.

"It bears remembering that, prior to 1975, children in the United States with intellectual disabilities, physical disabilities, and even sensory disabilities were not guaranteed access to a public education. Today, in America, we recognize that people with disabilities—like all people—have unique abilities, talents, and aptitudes. And that America is better, fairer, and richer when we make full use of those gifts."

Source: Harkin Honors 35th Anniversary of the Individuals with Disabilities Education Act, November 18, 2010, Press Files, Thomas R. Harkin Collection, Drake University Archives and Special Collections, Des Moines, Iowa.

 Learning Outcomes

Educating Students With Disabilities

Recognize the federal laws that govern the education of children and youth with disabilities in the United States, understand the basic guarantees provided to students through these laws, describe the processes through which students with disabilities are identified and referred for evaluation, and understand the steps through which students become eligible and receive special services.

Individualized Education: Plans and Programs

Understand when and for whom IFSPs and IEPs are developed, know the basic components that each document should contain, explain the purposes of behavior intervention plans and individualized transition plans, and understand how accommodations and modifications support the education of students with disabilities.

Services, Personnel, and Settings

Explain the concept of individualized services and how related services support them, describe the different types of specialized personnel who work with students with disabilities, and explain the continuum of settings in which the individualized services are delivered.

Educating Students With Disabilities[1]

Learning Outcome

Recognize the federal laws that govern the education of children and youth with disabilities in the United States, understand the basic guarantees provided to students through these laws, describe the processes through which students with disabilities are identified and referred for evaluation, and understand the steps through which students become eligible and receive special services.

Topic 4.1 Federal Legislation

- Two federal laws, Section 504 of the Rehabilitation Act and the Individuals with Disabilities Education Act, and several others that have additional influence, govern the education of children and youth with disabilities in the United States.

- Reauthorization of the Individuals with Disabilities Education Act and other federal legislation continually improves services for students with disabilities.

Topic 4.2 Basic Guarantees

- Section 504 and IDEA address the education of students with disabilities in different ways.

- IDEA provides six basic educational guarantees.

Topic 4.3 Child Find and Initial Referrals

- Infants and toddlers with disabilities are identified through the Child Find process.

- School-age students with disabilities are usually referred by school personnel for evaluation, although the Child Find mandate applies to them as well.

Topic 4.4 Steps in the IEP and Section 504 Processes

- The IEP process consists of eight steps.

- Some students with disabilities who do *not* qualify for special education services through IDEA can still receive supports and accommodations through Section 504.

---

[1]References for Chapter 4 are found at the end of this text.

Children with disabilities, from birth through age 21, are entitled to a free appropriate public education.

Topic 4.1 Federal Legislation

- Two federal laws, Section 504 of the Rehabilitation Act and the Individuals with Disabilities Education Act, and several others that have additional influence, govern the education of children and youth with disabilities in the United States.

- Reauthorization of the Individuals with Disabilities Education Act and other federal legislation continually improves services for students with disabilities.

What laws cover the education of children and youth with disabilities in the United States? As you learned in Chapter 1, Congress passes national laws to provide protections and guarantees to U.S. citizens. **Section 504** of the Rehabilitation Act of 1973 protects the civil rights of individuals with disabilities of all ages and ensures that their needs are met. It prohibits discrimination against people with disabilities and applies to an entity (e.g., agencies, organizations) that receives any kind of federal funding. Because public schools receive federal funding, they must adhere to Section 504, and therefore provide accommodations to students whose disabilities or conditions require some level of support.

However, in the early 1970s, Congress studied issues related to the education of roughly eight million children with disabilities in the United States and found that Section 504 was insufficient to meet their needs. More specifically, they found that:

- One million children with disabilities were excluded entirely from the public education system.

- Nearly half of all children with disabilities were not receiving appropriate educational services.

- Public school services were inadequate, forcing families to seek out other services, often at great distances from home and at their own expense.

- With appropriate funding, state and local education agencies could provide effective special education services to meet the needs of these children.

In 1975, Congress passed Public Law (PL) 94-142[2], the **Education for All Handicapped Children Act (EAHCA,** or simply **EHA)**. The initial goal of EHA was to ensure that students with disabilities received an individualized education with the least possible amount of segregation or isolation from their peers without disabilities. Over the past four decades, the law has been reauthorized numerous times, which included a name change; it is now referred to as the **Individuals with Disabilities Education Act (IDEA).**

President Bill Clinton signs the 1997 reauthorization of the Individuals with Disabilities Education Act.

How has federal legislation changed the education of students with disabilities over time? With each reauthorization of IDEA, officials utilized the most current research available at that time to improve the law. For example, the 1986 reauthorization (PL 99-457) added **early intervention services** for infants and toddlers because research indicated that the earlier instruction and intervention begin, the stronger the academic and behavioral gains are for students as they get older. Additional disability categories were also recognized in subsequent reauthorizations. For example, the category of autism (now referred to as autism spectrum disorder, or ASD) was added to the 1990 reauthorization (PL 101-476) because researchers realized that children with autism displayed unique characteristics that were markedly different from those in the existing disability categories. The table on the next page lists key federal legislation affecting individuals with disabilities. As you look at the list, note the many changes to IDEA over time.

The following video provides an historical overview of educational changes for students with disabilities from 1975 to 2015. The video is narrated by LeDerick Horne, whom you may remember from the opening for Chapter 1.

▶ **Celebrating the 40th Anniversary of IDEA**

https://www.youtube.com/watch?v=Oj4b9d4XAdY

If you would like more information about special education law, go to www.wrightslaw.com.

---

[2]Each federal law is referred to by two numbers. The first set of numbers is the session of Congress during which the law was passed; the second set of numbers is the law that was passed during that session. Thus, the EHA was the 142nd law passed by the 94th session of Congress.

Key Federal Legislation (Laws) Affecting Children and Adults with Disabilities

Law	Date	Name	Key Provisions or Changes
Section 504	1973	Rehabilitation Act of 1973, Section 504	• Guaranteed basic civil rights to all people with disabilities • Required the provision of accommodations
PL 94-142	1975	Education for All Handicapped Children Act (EAHCA or EHA)	• Guaranteed a free appropriate public education (FAPE) in the least restrictive environment (LRE) • Required each student to have an individualized education program (IEP)
PL 99-457	1986	EHA (reauthorized)	• Added provision of services for infants and toddlers • Required individualized family service plans (IFSPs) for these very young children and their families
PL 101-476	1990	Individuals with Disabilities Education Act (IDEA)	• Changed name of EHA retroactively to IDEA • Added requirement for transition plans • Added autism and traumatic brain injury as new disability categories
PL 101-336	1990	Americans with Disabilities Act (ADA)	• Barred discrimination in employment, transportation, public accommodations, public services, and telecommunications • Implemented principles of **normalization** • Required phased-in accessibility of school buildings • Directed the removal of barriers that inhibit access to and participation in society
PL 105-17	1997	IDEA '97 (reauthorized)	• Added ADHD to the "other health impairments" category • Added requirements for functional behavioral assessments and behavior intervention plans • Required that transition plans, formerly separate documents, become part of IEPs
PL 107-110	2001	Elementary and Secondary Education Act (ESEA, reauthorized; also known as No Child Left Behind or NCLB)	• Implemented a high-stakes accountability system based on student achievement • Required use of data-based practices and instruction • Required highly qualified teachers
PL 108-364	2004	Assistive Technology Act of 2004 (ATA) (reauthorized)	• Supported school-to-work transition projects • Continued a national Website on assistive technology • Created and supported programs that loan AT devices on a short-term basis

PL 108-446	2004	Individuals with Disabilities Education Act of 2004 (IDEA '04, reauthorized)	• Aligned with NCLB by requiring:
			  o Special education teachers to be highly qualified
			  o Students with disabilities to participate in annual state or district testing (with accommodations) or in alternate assessments
			• Eliminated IEP short-term objectives and benchmarks, except for students who take alternate assessments
			• Changed identification procedures for learning disabilities
			• Allowed any student to be placed in an interim alternative educational setting for weapons, drugs, or violence

PL 110-235	2008	Americans with Disabilities Amendments Act of 2008	• Broadened the definition of disability in both the ADA and Section 504 • Allowed impairments or conditions in remission to still be considered disabilities
PL 110-315	2008	Higher Education Opportunity Act (reauthorized)	• Supported improvements to better prepare future educators to work with students with disabilities • Created programs to support transition to college and to increase retention and graduation rates for students with disabilities • Encouraged development of post-secondary programs for students with intellectual disabilities at colleges and universities
PL 111-256	2010	Rosa's Law	• Retroactively changed all federal laws, replacing the term *mental retardation* with *intellectual disabilities*
PL 114-95	2015	Every Student Succeeds Act (ESSA, reauthorization of ESEA)	• Eliminated the highly qualified teacher language and the federally mandated teacher evaluation system from NCLB • Included considerations for gifted students • Ensured access to the general education curriculum for students with disabilities through: accommodations on assessments; UDL; use of EBPs; and protection from bullying, harassment, and aversive behavioral practices and interventions • Addressed issues of alternate diplomas for students with the most significant cognitive disabilities • Included protections and supports for certain groups, including those with disabilities, English learners, students from low-income backgrounds, and those who are homeless

Topic 4.2 Basic Guarantees

- Section 504 and IDEA address the education of students with disabilities in different ways.
- IDEA provides six basic educational guarantees.

In what ways do Section 504 and IDEA differ in their approaches to educating students with disabilities? Although Section 504 and IDEA both address the education of students with disabilities, they do so in very different ways. One primary difference is that Section 504 is a civil rights law that prohibits discrimination. It does not provide funding to support the education of eligible students; rather, schools that do not comply can lose their federal funding. In contrast, IDEA is a law that guarantees an appropriate education for students with disabilities and provides funding to states and school districts to help cover the costs of special education services for eligible students. The table below summarizes some of the other key differences between the two laws.

Key Differences Between Section 504 and IDEA

	Section 504	IDEA
Definition of disability	A mental or physical condition that limits one or more major life activities (see below); have a record of such impairment; or be regarded as having an impairment	Each of 13 disability-specific categories (see below) has its own definition; a category of "developmental delay" can be used for children ages three to nine who demonstrate delays in physical, cognitive, communication, social/emotional, or adaptive development
Conditions for eligibility	Must limit one or more major life activities: caring for oneself, performing manual tasks, seeing, hearing, eating, sleeping, walking, standing, lifting, bending, speaking, breathing, learning, reading, concentrating, thinking, communicating, and working	Must be eligible under one of the following categories: autism, deafness, deaf-blindness, hearing impairments, intellectual disabilities, multiple disabilities, orthopedic impairments, other health impairments, serious emotional disturbance, specific learning disabilities, speech or language impairments, traumatic brain injury, visual impairments, or developmental delay
Age range	All individuals with disabilities	Children and youth from birth through age 21
Educational impact	Effect on education is not required	Must adversely affect educational performance
Provision of services	Development and implementation of a 504 plan for accommodations	Development and implementation of an individualized family service plan (IFSP) or an individualized education program (IEP)

What are the basic guarantees that IDEA provides for students with disabilities? IDEA's educational guarantees differ depending on the age of the child. Because family members are a child's primary caregivers and first teachers, the guarantees for infants and toddlers with disabilities (up to age three) are tied closely to family involvement. Families of very young children are entitled to:

- *Multidisciplinary evaluation, identification, and intervention services.* These services must be appropriate to the child's needs and delivered in a timely manner.

- *An **individualized family service plan (IFSP)**.* This document states the goals for the child, services to be provided, and plans for transition to preschool or other appropriate programs. The IFSP should include key family information (e.g., their concerns, priorities, available resources).

- *Participation in the IFSP development as a member of the multidisciplinary team.* Many of the services are delivered in the family's home and depend on the family's ability to incorporate them into daily routines. As such, parental participation is critical to the success of the IFSP. Further, parents must give informed, written consent before services can begin.

- *Conflict resolution.* Also referred to as **due process**, these are procedures used to settle differences regarding the child's evaluation or services.

Most children and youth[3] who receive special education services under IDEA fall within the school-eligible age range of 3 to 21 years. IDEA has six guiding principles that entitle these students to:

1. *A free appropriate public education (FAPE)*. Special education services are provided at no cost to parents.

2. *An unbiased evaluation*. This evaluation is conducted by a team of knowledgeable professionals and assesses all areas of a suspected disability. It should include multiple assessments and sources of information that do not discriminate based on factors like socioeconomic level or cultural or linguistic differences.

3. *An individualized education program (IEP)*. This document provides details on the student's present levels of educational performance (as determined by the evaluation). A multidisciplinary team uses the evaluation results to set annual goals and benchmarking objectives and to then determine the special education services that will enable the student to reach those goals.

4. *Education and instruction in the least restrictive environment (LRE)*. In general, though not always, this means being educated alongside peers without disabilities to the greatest extent possible. If a student is not being educated in the general education classroom, a justification must be included in the IEP.

5. *Parent participation*. School personnel must work with parents and, when appropriate, the student, to develop the IEP. The input of the student and parents, including preferences and concerns, must be considered when determining goals, services, and so on.

6. *Procedural safeguards*. Parents of each student with a disability are guaranteed certain rights. These include being invited to all meetings about their child's educational program; giving permission for their child to be evaluated and to obtain an independent evaluation if they deem it necessary; having access to their child's educational records; resolving complaints through **mediation** and due process procedures; and receiving a written explanation (in their native language when possible) of these safeguards.

IDEA guarantees students with disabilities the right to a free appropriate public education (FAPE) in the least restrictive environment (LRE). FAPE is individually determined because what is appropriate for one student with a disability might not be so for another. LRE guarantees access to the **general education curriculum** with the least amount of separation or segregation possible. FAPE and LRE are interpreted in many different ways, with considerable debate over how to clarify these terms and how they should be balanced. At one end of the argument, the concept of **inclusion** is interpreted as the delivery of all components of the student's individualized education in the general education classroom. This model, *full inclusion*, gained popularity toward the end of the twentieth century and has many advocates. Those on the other side of the debate believe that individualized services are more appropriately delivered outside the general education classroom for some part, or even all, of the school day.

The balance between an appropriate education and the least restrictive environment can become a dilemma for many educators and families. Why might this be so? Here are a few examples:

- Gareth is Deaf and uses American Sign Language (ASL) to communicate. None of the other students in his class use ASL, making him dependent on his educational interpreter for social interactions, which is restrictive. Julian attends a separate

---

[3]The terms *youth* and *adolescent* are often used to refer to students at the upper end of this age range who are too old for the term *children*.

school for Deaf students where everyone—teachers; students; and custodial, cafeteria, and office staff—uses ASL and all instruction and extracurricular activities are geared toward students with hearing loss, so Julian is completely included.

- Melody and Sura are high school students with moderate intellectual disabilities. Melody's parents want her to be included in the everyday social and extracurricular activities of the school, so she receives most of her education in general education classes, with significant modifications. Sura's parents want her to have explicit instruction on a variety of life-related skills—using public transportation, holding a job, shopping at a grocery store—in the community settings where they actually occur.

- Ayame has a learning disability and requires intensive instruction in reading. Although the special education teacher can provide this instruction in the general education classroom, Ayame finds it difficult to concentrate in a large-group setting; she is also self-conscious about this arrangement. Therefore, her parents request—and her IEP stipulates—that her individualized reading instruction will take place outside the general education classroom for an hour each day, where the special education teacher can work with her in a small-group or one-on-one capacity. Clearly, decisions regarding FAPE and LRE must be made by considering the individual needs of students and families.

Balancing LRE and FAPE

Achieving a balance between free appropriate public education and least restrictive environment can be challenging.

Topic 4.3 Child Find and Initial Referrals

- Infants and toddlers with disabilities are identified through the Child Find process.
- School-age students with disabilities are usually referred by school personnel for evaluation, although the Child Find mandate applies to them as well.

How are infants and toddlers with disabilities initially identified? Some children with disabilities are identified at birth or at a very young age. In some cases, prenatal testing may have identified a chromosomal disorder (e.g., trisomy 21, which causes **Down syndrome**) before the baby is even born. Other cases are recognized immediately at birth because the disability is physically apparent: the infant may have clear facial differences caused by a specific condition or syndrome or may have misshapen or missing limbs. Some health conditions can be determined through **newborn screenings**, many of which are universally required and conducted before the newborn leaves the hospital. For example, **sickle cell disease** and **phenylketonuria (PKU)** can be identified by analyzing a few drops of blood taken from the baby's heel; early diagnosis and medical intervention can protect the infant from the life-threatening effects or resulting disabilities caused by these conditions (which you'll learn more about in Chapters 9 and 11). Other quick and simple screening procedures can identify conditions like congenital heart disease or hearing loss.

Some children have disabilities that are not identified at birth but instead become apparent during infancy or the toddler years. As they grow, most children progress through key developmental milestones (see the table on the next page). An infant or a toddler who has not achieved a milestone but is older than the age at which the skill is typically mastered shows signs of a developmental delay and might have a disability.

Sample Developmental Milestones

Age	Social/Emotional	Language/Communication	Cognitive	Physical
2 months	Smiles at people	Coos; turns head toward sounds or people speaking	Shows signs of boredom (crying, fussing)	When placed on tummy, can lift head and begin to push up with arms
4 months	Enjoys playing with people; may cry when playing stops	Begins babbling, imitating sounds and expressions of adults	Studies faces; can recognize familiar people	When placed on tummy, can push up onto elbows; initial eye-hand coordination develops (sees a toy and reaches for it with one hand)
6 months	Responds to others' emotions; enjoys looking in mirror	Responds when hears name; makes different sounds to show emotion; makes more sounds when babbling; engages in verbal turn taking ("conversation") with others	Is curious about objects; attempts to reach objects of interest that are beyond grasp	Can roll over in both directions (tummy to back, back to tummy); if placed in a standing position, can support weight on legs and bounce; may sit without support
9 months	Differentiates between familiar adults (may be clingy with) and strangers (may be afraid of)	Points at things; understands the word "no"; combines sounds ("dadada")	Looks for items that an adult "hides"; plays peek-a-boo; can pick up small items (e.g., cereal) using thumb and index finger	Crawls; sits without support; can maneuver into sitting position; stands while holding on to something for support
12 months	Has favorite people and items; shows fear, shyness, and nervousness	Responds to simple directions ("Bring me your shoes"); uses simple gestures (waves goodbye); can say "mama" and "dada," and uses simple expressions ("up" to be picked up); attempts to repeat words	Uses items (cup, brush) correctly; experiments with objects by banging, shaking, or throwing them; hears a word and looks at a picture of the item	Walks holding on to furniture; may stand independently; may take a few steps without support

The Centers for Disease Control Website (cdc.gov) provides detailed information on developmental milestones, which can be found by entering the search term *developmental milestones*. In addition to checklists of milestones at key ages, the site contains videos of children demonstrating these milestones and information on characteristics of concern. The video below shows some key milestones for older toddlers.

▶ **Early Recognition of Child Development Problems/Educational Video**

https://www.youtube.com/watch?v=KrUNBfyjlBk

Not all parents recognize these developmental delays, particularly if the infant is their first child or they have little contact with other infants or toddlers the same age. Instead, these delays might be picked up by a pediatrician at a **well-baby visit**, an observant neighbor, a child care provider, or another family member. But what should these people do when they have concerns? In order to ensure that every child with a disability is identified and receives appropriate services, IDEA's **Child Find** mandate requires states to implement a comprehensive system to identify, locate, and evaluate children who may need special education services. Through the Child Find system, anyone who suspects that a child has a disability can contact a designated agency to refer the child for further evaluation. Once identified, infants and toddlers with disabilities, ages birth to three, can receive early intervention services.

All states have similar Child Find processes, such as those found on Connecticut's Child Find program Website. Visit http://www.birth23.org for more information.

How are school-age students with disabilities initially identified? Some students have disabilities that are not recognized until they are in school and struggling with the academic or behavioral aspects of learning. The identification process for these students begins in the general education classroom, usually when they are not making adequate academic progress, despite receiving high-quality instruction using evidence-based practices. In these cases, a general education teacher, school counselor, or other school professional can initiate the **IEP process**. This process consists of a series of steps designed to identify students who have disabilities; determine whether they need special education services; and then develop, implement, and evaluate those services.

However, before a student is referred for the formal IEP process, teachers should try some pre-referral interventions first, to see if the student's needs can be met by making a few simple adjustments in the general education classroom. Teachers can incorporate pre-referral interventions through one of the following:

- *A multi-tiered system of support (MTSS) or response to intervention (RTI) framework.* Struggling students receive increasingly intense levels of instructional support until their performance shows that they need the individualized education provided through special education services. This is an approach you learned about in Chapter 2. IDEA allows this as an option specifically for identifying students with learning disabilities.

- *The **pre-referral process**.* A school-based team of individuals (which can have a variety of names, such as the *child study team* or *student support team*) reviews information on the student to determine whether other factors could be causing the difficulties, such as cultural or linguistic differences, or issues related to poverty or family stressors. The team members also consider whether minimal classroom or instructional adjustments, differentiated instruction, or minor supports would improve the student's performance to expected levels. If improvement does not occur, students are referred for an evaluation.

Both of these options attempt to rule out non-disability factors (e.g., need for eyeglasses, cultural or linguistic differences, poor instruction) as the reason for the student not performing well. Although most referrals for school-age children come from education personnel, the Child Find mandate also applies to this age group. So, coaches, scout leaders, church youth group leaders, and other adults who work with students outside school and suspect the presence of a disability can initiate referrals.

This IRIS Module highlights the benefits of the pre-referral process and outlines the stages most commonly involved in its implementation.

▶ **IRIS Module: The Pre-Referral Process: Procedures for Supporting Students with Academic and Behavioral Concerns.**
http://iris.peabody.vanderbilt.edu/module/preref/

Topic 4.4 Steps in the IEP and Section 504 Processes

- The IEP process consists of eight steps.
- Some students with disabilities who do *not* qualify for special education services through IDEA can still receive supports and accommodations through Section 504.

How is a student's individualized education provided under IDEA? For infants and toddlers (up to age three) who are eligible for early intervention services, a team of professionals works with the family to develop an IFSP. For students ages 3 through 21 who are eligible for special education services, a multidisciplinary team works with the family to develop an IEP, which provides the details of their individualized education and the other guarantees of IDEA. The IEP process is outlined in the table that follows.

Eight Steps of the IEP Process

Step	Purpose	Important Points
Step 1 Pre-referral	To ensure that students without disabilities are not needlessly referred for special education when minor adjustments can correct the situation	The general education teacher and the school's support team ensure that the student has received high-quality instruction and additional assistance (if necessary), and that other factors (e.g., lack of English proficiency, the need for eyeglasses, hunger) are not causing the difficulties. The team members also document how and when the student struggles, describe how the student responds to additional assistance, and monitor the student's progress by collecting classroom data.
Step 2 Referral	To refer the student for formal testing	A student whose academic performance is significantly behind that of his or her classmates is a prime candidate for referral, as are those who continually misbehave or disrupt the class. Parents must give written, informed consent for their child to be evaluated.
Step 3 Evaluation	To determine whether the student has a disability	The student is given multiple tests that assess all areas of concern. To eliminate cultural and linguistic concerns, tests must be unbiased and given in the language most likely to yield accurate results. Background information is also gathered from parents, teachers, and school and medical records, and classroom observations of the student are conducted.
Step 4 Eligibility	To determine whether the student qualifies for special education services	The test results are analyzed. A multidisciplinary team (also called the IEP team, and usually not the same team as in Step 1) determines whether a student qualifies based on two criteria: (1) the student has a disability that falls under either the broad category of developmental delay (for children ages three to nine) or 1 of the 13 disability-specific categories, and (2) the student's educational performance is adversely affected as a result.
Step 5 IEP development	To specify, in writing, the details of the student's individualized education	The IEP team, which includes the parents, outlines the student's special education services in a written document (the IEP). The team must also consider LRE when determining where the services will be provided. When appropriate, older students should attend the IEP meetings to advocate for themselves. The parents must consent, in writing, to the IEP.
Step 6 IEP implementation	To deliver the special education services outlined in the IEP	The student's individualized education begins. Services outlined in the IEP are provided by an array of personnel, including general education and special education teachers, and related service providers.
Step 7 Annual reviews	To ensure that the student is making acceptable progress	In most states, a student's IEP is reviewed annually to ensure he or she is meeting the outlined goals. At this time, necessary changes are made (e.g., updated goals, change in amount of time in general education classrooms) based on the student's progress.
Step 8 Re-evaluation	To gather updated information on the student's educational needs	Most students are re-evaluated every three years. The re-evaluation process repeats Steps 3 and 4 to obtain updated information on current performance and progress, and to determine whether the student continues to qualify as a child with a disability under an IDEA category and whether special education services are still necessary. The re-evaluation can be waived if the parents and the school district agree that it is not necessary (usually for students with the most significant disabilities).

What role does Section 504 play in the provision of services to students with disabilities? Not every student who goes through the IEP process qualifies for special education services. Some students who struggle academically do not have a disability. Others have a disability but do not qualify for special services because their disability does not adversely affect their educational performance. However, some students who have disabilities but do not require special education services can still benefit from accommodations or from related services. For these students, a multidisciplinary team develops a **504 plan** that includes the provision of needed accommodations and services. Consider the case of a student who uses a wheelchair and attends school in a two-story building that does not have an elevator. A simple accommodation would be to ensure that all of her classes were located on the first floor. She might require school nursing as a related service because she uses a **catheter**. (And if you picked up on the fact that the lack of elevators makes the school building inaccessible, a consideration under the Americans with Disabilities Act—a separate but related issue—good for you!) Another student with ADHD is easily distracted and disorganized. His 504 plan includes two accommodations. The first breaks longer assignments into sections, which he finds easier to complete. The second accommodation requires him to use an assignment notebook, which he carries from class to class and then home after school and which serves as a home-school communication tool. His teachers make sure he records his assignments and lists any supplies (books, notebooks) necessary to complete them. His parents use the notebook to monitor his homework completion.

The flowchart below might be helpful in understanding when a student would receive a Section 504 plan with accommodations rather than special education services through IDEA.

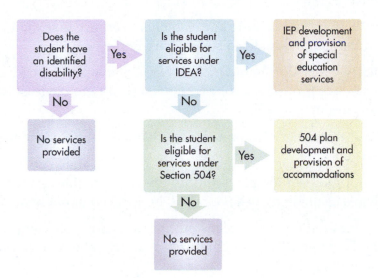

The American Diabetes Association has developed a sample 504 plan for students with diabetes, which can be downloaded and modified for other disabilities: http://www.diabetes.org/living-with-diabetes/parents-and-kids/diabetes-care-at-school/written-care-plans/section-504-plan.html

Check Your Understanding 4.1

Click here to gauge your understanding of the concepts in this section.

Individualized Education: Plans and Programs

Learning Outcome

Understand when and for whom IFSPs and IEPs are developed, know the basic components that each document should contain, explain the purposes of behavior intervention plans and individualized transition plans, and understand how accommodations and modifications support the education of students with disabilities.

Topic 4.5 IFSPs and IEPs

- Each child with a disability receives an individualized education, which is delineated in either an individualized family service plan

(IFSP) for infants and toddlers ages birth to 3 or an individualized education program (IEP) for students ages 3 to 21.

- All personnel responsible for the education of infants, toddlers, and students with disabilities should have access to these documents; however, confidentiality must be maintained.

Topic 4.6 Basic Elements of IFSPs and IEPs

- Every IFSP should include key elements to ensure that an infant's or toddler's individualized services are implemented.

- Similarly, every IEP should include key elements to ensure a student's free appropriate public education (FAPE) in the least restrictive environment (LRE).

Topic 4.7 Additional IEP Components for Behavior and Secondary Transition

- Behavior intervention plans specify the methods through which a student's challenging behaviors will be reduced or eliminated.

- Individualized transition plans outline transition goals and specify methods to transition a student from high school to work, college, and adult life.

Topic 4.8 Accommodations vs. Modifications

- Students with disabilities are entitled to a range of instructional and testing supports referred to as accommodations.

- When accommodations are not sufficient to help students achieve success, more support might be needed, such as that provided by modifications.

Topic 4.5 IFSPs and IEPs

- Each child with a disability receives an individualized education, which is delineated in either an individualized family service plan (IFSP) for infants and toddlers ages birth to 3 or an individualized education program (IEP) for students ages 3 to 21.

- All personnel responsible for the education of infants, toddlers, and students with disabilities should have access to these documents; however, confidentiality must be maintained.

What tools are used to ensure FAPE to children and students with disabilities? Mandated by IDEA, individualized family service plans (IFSPs) and individualized education programs (IEPs) are working documents that guide education professionals in the design and implementation of an individualized, free appropriate public education for infants, toddlers, and school-age students. These documents have many purposes, but their overarching goal is to provide the details of a student's individualized education, a sequence of successful early intervention and school experiences that will eventually prepare the student for a career or **post-secondary education**.

There are different documents for infants and toddlers than for school-aged students. As you learned earlier, the IFSP is a written document that guarantees FAPE to infants and toddlers (ages birth to three), often focusing on the entire family and providing guidance on how to deliver services in **natural environments** such as the home. Families with infants and toddlers who participate in early intervention programs often find these years to be intense; they encounter a steep learning curve about disabilities and services. Their lives are filled with many caring, concerned professionals who offer advice, training, guidance, and personalized services. The IFSP is helpful to families in keeping track of the services their child should receive. The IFSP is also used by the various service providers, who must coordinate services.

IDEA requires that toddlers with disabilities transition to preschool, or a similarly appropriate setting, at the age of three, which can be difficult and somewhat frightening for families. For many toddlers, services that were delivered primarily at the family's home will now be provided at a preschool, so parents may feel as though they have less control or involvement in their children's education or may worry about peer acceptance and interactions. To make this change go smoothly, IFSPs include specific plans to help the children and families transition from what they are used to and comfortable with—very intensive and individually delivered interventions in natural environments—to more traditional, less individualized preschool programs.

In the video below we meet Tamiya, a two-year-old with a disability, and her mother, who discusses her apprehensions about Tamiya's move from home-based services to a preschool setting.

▶ **CONNECT Video 2.2: The Family's Viewpoint**

https://www.youtube.com/watch?v=3kBKyA_TBbg

In contrast to an IFSP, an individualized education program (IEP) describes the special education and related services for a school-age student with a disability (from preschool—age 3—to age 21). This management tool is the cornerstone of every educational service planned for these students. The IEP reflects a unique array of special education services, accommodations, related services, and accountability measures.

Although IFSPs and IEPs ensure FAPE and the provision of special education and related services to children with disabilities, there are key differences between these two documents, as highlighted in the accompanying table.

Differences Between IFSPs and IEPs

Feature	IFSP	IEP
Population served	Infants and toddlers with disabilities (birth to 3 years) and their families	Preschoolers and students with disabilities (ages 3 to 21 years)
Settings	Natural environments (e.g., home, community settings), child care settings, clinics or service providers' offices, and hospitals	Schools, homes, and hospitals
Costs to families	Costs for some services may be charged to families (on a sliding scale according to income) or covered by their insurance	No cost to families, unless they elect other options (e.g., an independent evaluation)

Who should have access to IFSPs and IEPs? To begin with, parents should have a copy of their child's IFSP or IEP. Next, every school professional who works with the family or student must have access to these documents. Included are teachers, paraprofessionals, related service providers, and school administrators. These personnel need to know each student's goals, the accommodations and assistive technology used for instruction and for assessments, and details of the special education services to be delivered. They must also know the types of testing in which the student must participate.

IFSPs and IEPs are confidential, legal documents.

IFSPs and IEPs should not be located in a district office that is inconvenient for school personnel to access. Rather, they need to be readily available as a reference for the student's teachers and other relevant personnel throughout the year. However, access to IFSPs or IEPs must be balanced with the need for confidentiality. As with any document that contains personally identifiable information, IFSPs and IEPs should be kept in a locked file or drawer when they are not being used. Also, to maintain confidentiality, specific issues related to the student's education or IEP should not be discussed by adults in open areas (hallway, teachers' lounge) where others can overhear. (This is actually a good practice when discussing *any* student, not just those with disabilities.)

Topic 4.6   Basic Elements of IFSPs and IEPs

- Every IFSP should include key elements to ensure that an infant's or toddler's individualized services are implemented.

- Similarly, every IEP should include key elements to ensure a student's free appropriate public education (FAPE) in the least restrictive environment (LRE).

What basic elements should every IFSP contain? Every IFSP must include basic information that will guide the delivery of individualized services to the infant, toddler, and his or her family. The key components of IFSPs include:

- *Current functioning levels:* These levels describe the child's abilities in all relevant areas (physical development, cognitive development, speech and language development, psychosocial development, and self-help skills).

- *Family's strengths and needs:* These considerations outline how family members can support the development of the child as well as areas in which they might have difficulty or need assistance.

- *Expected outcomes:* This component specifies procedures, evaluation criteria, and a timeline for meeting goals.

- *Necessary services:* The necessary services category describes those services that the child and family will receive, as well as the location and schedule for their delivery.

- *Start date:* This specifies the date on which services will be initiated.

- *The name of the **service coordinator***: This person provides oversight and coordination of the services outlined in the IFSP.

- *A biannual review:* This review occurs every six months; the parents are updated on the child's progress, and changes to the IFSP are determined.

- *Transition plan:* This describes the well-planned methods for transitioning the child to preschool or other appropriate services at age three.

The Early Childhood Technical Assistance Center has samples of IFSP forms from many states, as well as numerous handbooks and instruction manuals on how to develop these documents: http://www.ectacenter.org

What basic elements should every IEP contain? Some elements of an IEP are similar to those of an IFSP. For example, the IEP must include a student's present levels of performance, similar to current functioning levels in an IFSP. However, most basic elements of the IEP are different from those in an IFSP, as would be expected given the different age span covered. At the very least, every student's IEP must describe:

- *Current performance:* This includes the student's present levels of academic achievement as well as information about how the student's disability influences participation and progress in the general education curriculum.

- *Goals:* Measurable goals—aligned with grade-level content standards—are related to participation in the general education curriculum or other educational needs resulting from the disability.

- *Special education and related services:* Specific educational services to be provided are outlined, including accommodations, program modifications, or supports that allow participation in the general education curriculum and extracurricular activities.

- *Participation alongside students without disabilities:* Explanation must be provided to justify situations where the student will not participate in general education classes and extracurricular activities alongside peers without disabilities.

- *Participation in state- and district-wide testing:* This component describes adaptations needed for these assessments, or, if the student will not be participating, lists reasons for non-participation and explains how the student will be alternately assessed.

- *Dates and places:* This information includes dates for initiation of services, where services will be delivered, and the expected duration of those services.

- *Transition service needs:* Beginning at age 16 (sooner if possible), a transition component is included in the IEP to identify post-school goals and to describe transitional assessments and service needs (further discussed in Topic 4.7).

- *Age of majority rights:* Beginning at least one year before the student reaches the age of majority (age 18 in most states), students must be informed of the rights that transfer to them.

- *Measuring progress:* This portion of the IEP states how the student's progress toward achieving IEP goals will be measured and how parents will be informed about this progress.

The following link takes you to a sample IEP for an eight-year-old student with a learning disability: http://www.education.com/reference/article/individualized-education-program-IEP/.

The next link takes you to a blank IEP form, provided by the U.S. Department of Education's Office of Special Education Programs (OSEP), available for anyone who would like practice in developing an IEP: http://idea.ed.gov/download/modelform1_IEP.pdf. The blank OSEP example contains the minimum federal requirements for IEPs; most states exceed these in their own requirements.

IFSPs and IEPs document the services that infants, toddlers, and students with disabilities receive.

Topic 4.7 Additional IEP Components for Behavior and Secondary Transition

- Behavior intervention plans specify the methods through which a student's challenging behaviors will be reduced or eliminated.
- Individualized transition plans outline transition goals and specify methods to transition a student from high school to work, college, and adult life.

Are there additional plans that support and complement IEPs? Two other plans are considered part of the IEP. The first is the **behavior intervention plan (BIP)**, which is developed for students with disabilities who have challenging behaviors or who have violated school conduct codes. In these cases, IDEA requires that the IEP team develop a BIP to reduce or eliminate the probability of future problem behavior. The BIP also includes techniques to help the student develop alternate, more appropriate ways of dealing with frustrating situations, negative or overwhelming feelings, or other triggers that lead to inappropriate behavior. To guide BIP development, a **functional behavioral assessment (FBA)** is conducted to help determine why a student behaves in a certain way (see the example in the box).

A Behavior Intervention Plan for Taz

Taz, a kindergarten student with social and language delays, screams and hits other students in his class. After gathering information (teacher interviews, classroom observations), the IEP team hypothesizes that these behaviors occur when other students try to play with Taz, uninvited. They further hypothesize that Taz lacks the language and social skills to vocalize his unhappiness, so he screams and hits. This behavior is reinforced when the other children run away, so Taz continues to behave this way. The IEP team develops a BIP that addresses this behavior by teaching Taz's peers to ask before joining him, and by teaching Taz specific phrases ("I don't want to play right now.") and alternate, appropriate behaviors (walking away) to use when his peers' behavior bothers him.

IDEA regulations include some guidelines regarding the use of BIPs:

- When a student's behavior interferes with learning, the IEP team should consider the use of positive behavioral interventions and supports (which you learned about in Topic 2.7), and other evidence-based strategies.
- When student behavior violates the conduct code, an FBA should be conducted and behavioral intervention services and modifications (which include a BIP) can be implemented, if appropriate.
- If the student's behavior is determined to be the result of the student's disability, then the IEP team must:
  o conduct an FBA and implement a BIP; or
  o review the previous FBA and modify the current BIP (for a student with an existing BIP), if necessary.

What type of plan addresses students' needs as they near the age of majority? Earlier we mentioned that each reauthorization of IDEA uses the most current research to improve individualized education for students with disabilities. Such was the case when policy makers required **individualized transition plans (ITPs)** in IEPs for older students during the 1997 reauthorization. Data at that time indicated poor post-school outcomes for students with disabilities: unacceptable high school dropout rates, low levels of employment, poor vocational training, and low enrollment in and graduation from college. The majority of young adults with disabilities lived at home with family members and engaged in leisure activities much less frequently than individuals without disabilities.

ITPs contain specific goals related to the next phase of adult life to prevent the dismal outcomes identified during the 1990s. Now, when a student turns 16, IDEA stipulates that the IEP in effect at that time must:

Without careful planning, many adolescents with disabilities do not attend college, find good jobs, or become engaged, productive members of their communities.

- Include appropriate, measurable, post-secondary goals based on age-appropriate transition assessments in the areas of training, education, employment, and, where appropriate, independent living skills.

- List transition services and coursework required to help the student meet those goals.

- Include a statement that the student has been informed about his or her rights as an adult (at least one year before the student reaches the age of majority).

- Include a summary of transition needs and accomplishments when the student exits high school.

There are outside agencies that provide supports for adults with disabilities; representatives from these agencies are part of the IEP team that develops the ITP. Such agencies and their representatives can support the transition to college, vocational training, the development of independent living skills, and more.

Once the ITP is developed, it is reviewed and updated annually. In addition to post-secondary options, the ITP should address social skills and participation in the community. Helping students advocate for themselves, gain work experience, and develop skills needed for independent living can be critical to post-high school success.

Some students with disabilities are not ready to leave high school at age 18. Some need extra time in school to acquire credits for graduation. Others require additional training to gain the vocational or independent living skills needed after high school. For these students, IDEA provides FAPE through the age of 21 (until their 22nd birthday). Even so, not all students with disabilities graduate with a regular high school diploma. Those with the most significant cognitive disabilities may instead receive an alternate diploma or a certificate of completion because their disabilities prevent them from mastering the high school content required for a regular diploma. All of this information—the length of time the student will remain in school, and whether the student will earn a regular diploma, an alternate diploma, or a certificate of completion—is included in the ITP.

Topic 4.8 Accommodations vs. Modifications

- Students with disabilities are entitled to a range of instructional and testing supports referred to as accommodations.

- When accommodations are not sufficient to help students achieve success, more support might be needed, such as that provided by modifications.

What are accommodations, and which students are entitled to such assistance? **Accommodations** are changes to *how* a student accesses instructional content and demonstrates learning. They do not change a student's learning expectations or the amount of work the student must complete. Accommodations simply assist in removing barriers presented by a student's disability to help the student access the general education curriculum and keep pace with peers without disabilities. For example, Brennan is a sixth grader who is blind. She is unable to complete the worksheets handed out in class. However, she can complete them if they are provided in braille or digitally and if she is allowed to use a braille typewriter (known as a brailler) or a computer to respond.

Although some people think that accommodations give students with disabilities an unfair advantage, this is not the case. Students who use approved accommodations do not always improve their test scores or get better grades in class. In other words, using accommodations does not guarantee better grades or create opportunities in which these students have an advantage over peers without disabilities.

Accommodations can be as simple as allowing a student with a vision problem to sit closer to the blackboard, but they can also be as complex as providing the student with additional time to complete assignments or allowing him or her to use a computer. Some accommodations, such as speech-to-text software, can be supported through assistive technology, which is also considered a related service. Accommodations, whether **instructional accommodations** or **testing accommodations**, are often categorized into four groups:

1. Presentation accommodations—changes to the way instruction is delivered or a test is presented
2. Setting accommodations—changes to the instructional or testing environment
3. Response accommodations—changes in the way students can respond to assignments or on tests
4. Scheduling or timing accommodations—changes to when a student completes an assignment or takes a test

The table below lists examples of frequently used instructional and testing accommodations for each of these four categories.

Examples of Frequently Used Accommodations

Presentation	Setting	Response	Scheduling or Timing
• Large print	• Small group	• Proctor/scribe	• Extended time
• Braille	• Separate room	• Computer or machine	• Breaks during testing
• Reading aloud (e.g., directions, passages)	• Seat location/proximity	• Write in test booklets	• Multiple sessions
• Signing	• Minimize distractions	• Tape recorder	• Testing at a time that is best for the student
• Highlighting	• Increase/decrease opportunity for movement	• Communication or speech device	• Testing over multiple days
• Re-reading or clarifying instructions	• Seat in carrel (to block out distractions)	• Spell checker	• Flexible scheduling
• Simplifying or paraphrasing		• Brailler	
• Prompting		• Sign responses	

SOURCE: Adapted from *2009 State Policies on Assessment Participation and Accommodations for Students with Disabilities* (Synthesis Report 83), by L. L. Christensen, M. Braam, S. Scullin, & M. L. Thurlow, 2011, Minneapolis, MN: University of Minnesota, National Center on Educational Outcomes.

Most students with disabilities require accommodations for success in the general education classroom. These accommodations must be specified in the student's IEP or 504 plan and must be used for both instruction and assessment. Note that accommodations are not specific to a given disability but should be determined based on a student's individual needs. Also, great variability exists across states and districts about what accommodations can be made available, particularly when used for state- and district-wide assessments.

What are modifications, and how do they differ from accommodations? For some students with disabilities, accommodations are not sufficient for success in the general education classroom. These students often require **modifications**. Like accommodations, modifications are changes to instruction, curriculum, or assessments. However, modifications differ in one major way: they alter *what* the student is expected to learn or demonstrate. It is important to understand that the student should still receive instruction on the same topic or subject as the other students in the class. For example, a sixth grade student with an intellectual disability might read at a first grade level. If the class is learning about the solar system, this student could read about the solar system in a text at a lower reading level, with simplified content. Some common modifications include:

- Reducing the level of difficulty (e.g., lower reading level material on the same topic, reduced number of answer choices on a multiple-choice test).

- Reducing the breadth and focus of an assignment (e.g., simplified vocabulary for a chapter, creating an outline instead of writing an essay).

- Reducing the amount of work the student completes (e.g., allowing the student to complete one assignment that can be turned in for two different classes).

Like accommodations, modifications must be specified in the student's IEP. They, too, are not specific to a given disability and should be determined based on a student's individual needs. Because accommodations and modifications are often confused and referred to interchangeably, it is important to understand the difference. Each scenario below contains a type of adaptation. See if you can correctly determine which are accommodations and which are modifications.

This student, who has a learning disability and ADHD, is receiving both timing and setting accommodations while she takes a test. She has extended time, because the learning disability affects her ability to read quickly, and she takes the test in a quiet location where she will not be distracted—or self-conscious—when the other students start turning their tests in.

Accommodation or Modification?

- The teacher reduces the number of division problems that Mia completes. She assigns only the odd problems so that Mia still encounters the more advanced problems.

- The teacher reduces the number of addition problems that Diego must complete, assigning the easiest problems.

- Garrett, who is blind, uses an audio version of the novel the class is reading.

- Lela, who has an intellectual disability, is using a science book from a lower grade level to learn about the same topic as her classmates.

- Caden, who has problems with fine motor skills, is allowed to type his responses instead of writing them by hand.

- Instead of completing a research paper for science class, Merrit's assignment is to write ten facts about his topic.

The following IRIS Module provides a more detailed overview of this topic; gives examples of presentation, response, setting, and timing and scheduling accommodations; and includes tips to help teachers determine and implement various accommodations.

▶ **IRIS Module: Accommodations: Instructional and Testing Supports for Students with Disabilities**
http://iris.peabody.vanderbilt.edu/module/acc/

Check Your Understanding 4.2

Click here to gauge your understanding of the concepts in this section.

Services, Personnel, and Settings

Learning Outcome

Explain the concept of individualized services and how related services support them, describe the different types of specialized personnel who work with students with disabilities, and explain the continuum of settings in which the individualized services are delivered.

Topic 4.9 Individualized Services

- Each student with a disability receives an intensive, individualized set of services.

- Related services provide additional, complementary supports that allow a student with a disability to benefit from an individualized education.

Topic 4.10 Specialized Personnel

- Special education services are provided by a multidisciplinary team consisting of professionals with different areas of expertise.

- Many types of related service providers are available to support the education of students with disabilities.

Topic 4.11 Continuum of Settings

- Special education services are delivered in a variety of settings, as required by IDEA, to provide a continuum from inclusive to more restrictive environments.

- The rates of participation in general education for students with disabilities have improved over time.

Topic 4.9 Individualized Services

- Each student with a disability receives an intensive, individualized set of services.

- Related services provide additional, complementary supports that allow a student with a disability to benefit from an individualized education.

What special education services are available to students with disabilities and their families? A wide array of special education services is available for students with disabilities, some of which were introduced in the prior section:

- *Early intervention services:* provided to infants and toddlers who have IFSPs to address developmental delays in physical development, cognitive development, speech and language development, psychosocial development, and self-help skills

- *Special education services:* provided to students with IEPs to address challenges in academic or behavioral areas

- *Transition services:* provided to adolescents whose IEPs have an ITP to support the transition from high school to post-secondary options such as vocational education, employment, and post-secondary education. Transition services also address functional skills needed to live independently and to engage in leisure activities and other aspects of community participation.

The special education services provided to students with disabilities are:

- *Intensive:* requiring more specialized instruction than that provided in the general education classroom (additional instructional time, smaller group size, or one-on-one instruction).

- *Individualized:* developed to meet the unique needs of the child or student.

A primary question that guides the delivery of these specialized services is this: what does the student need to achieve his or her IEP goals? The answers to this question determine what services will be provided. For example, if a student has an IEP goal related to improving reading skills, then intensive, individualized instruction in reading will be provided. A student who has an ITP goal related to riding the city bus independently to work each day will receive intensive, individualized instruction that will lead to his ability to do just that.

These intensive, individualized services can be combined in any number of ways to address the unique needs of each child or student with a disability. Some children require only a small amount of specialized instruction (e.g., an hour of daily instruction in mathematics). Others require more instruction and in several areas (e.g., daily instruction in reading, writing, and mathematics). Still others may spend most of their day receiving these specialized services.

What is the connection between related services, FAPE, and individualized education for students with disabilities? For many students with disabilities, general education and special education services are insufficient to meet their needs. Here is one example: Ciara, a student with cerebral palsy, does not have the arm strength to lift her books out of her backpack. She also does not have the finger dexterity necessary to turn the pages in her textbooks. Because her inability to do these things affects her education, she is eligible for **related services**. In this case, she might receive physical therapy (PT) and occupational therapy (OT) to improve her muscle strength and dexterity. Related services represent a wide range of disciplines that support and complement general and special education services, and they are tailored to the individual needs of each student. Some of the most common related services are speech-language therapy, PT, OT, social work services, and psychological services.

A few important points to know about related services are as follows:

- IDEA does not provide a precise list of related services because policy makers did not want to be too prescriptive; instead, these services are selected based on the specific needs of the individual.

- In many cases, students receive more than one related service, based on their needs.

- Usually, students do not receive related services every day. In many cases, the services are provided a few times per week.

- Related services **do** include medical services provided by school nurses but **do not** include those performed by physicians.

- In some cases, other professionals follow recommendations made by a related service provider (e.g., a physical education teacher reinforces physical therapy goals during physical education activities).

- With exceptions for very young children in some states, related services are provided at no cost to the student's family.

The figure below illustrates the differences between individualized services for infants and toddlers and those provided to school-age students.

If you are interested in learning more about related services, this IRIS Module offers descriptions of the five most commonly used related services, with an overview of the benefits they provide to students with disabilities. It also briefly highlights some of the other related services available.

▶ **IRIS Module: Related Services: Common Supports for Students with Disabilities.**
http://iris.peabody.vanderbilt.edu/module/rs/

Topic 4.10 Specialized Personnel

- Special education services are provided by a multidisciplinary team consisting of professionals with different areas of expertise.

- Many types of related service providers are available to support the education of students with disabilities.

Who is responsible for the education of students with disabilities? The education of students with disabilities is everyone's job. General educators, special education teachers, and related service providers work in partnership to ensure a high-quality education for students with disabilities.

- General education teachers provide the primary instruction for most of these students.
- Special education teachers support, reinforce, and supplement the instruction provided by general education teachers.
- Related service providers help students develop skills that are necessary to benefit from special education services.

In early childhood, a service coordinator—a special educator who specializes in early intervention—collaborates with child care teachers, related service providers (e.g., speech-language pathologist), and the parents to coordinate services that the child will receive. The service coordinator must be knowledgeable in the provisions of the state's early intervention system to ensure that all required services are provided to the infant or toddler.

For school-age students, special educators need to be knowledgeable about evidence-based instructional and behavioral practices, accommodations, and data-based decision making. They help design programs that improve the students' access to the general education curriculum and provide student supports through a variety of roles:

- Delivering individualized instruction directly to the student.

- Working as **consulting teachers** to general educators to ensure that students experience maximal integration and participation in school activities. For example, a consulting teacher might suggest instructional accommodations that the general education teacher can use for a blind student who cannot read notes off the board, or for a student with hearing loss who reads lips.

- Working primarily with one general education teacher through **co-teaching**, in which the two educators blend their expertise. The general education teacher has the content expertise (chemistry, literature, geometry), and the special education teacher has the expertise in intensive interventions. They work *together* to provide instruction, accommodations, modifications, and assessments. We highlight the term *together* because many co-teachers inadvertently fall into an ineffective classroom routine in which the special educator acts as an overqualified tutor for any struggling student in the classroom, rather than being a true partner in planning, implementing, and evaluating instruction.

- Supervising **paraprofessionals**, who provide instruction, guidance, monitoring, or support to a student under the special education teacher's supervision.

Special educators who work with students having ITPs are referred to as transition personnel. A **transition specialist** coordinates the transition services and acts as a liaison between various individuals and agencies. Some transition personnel (e.g., vocational rehabilitation specialists, job coaches) have expertise in teaching the vocational and life skills needed to live independently. Others support students in the college application and attendance process by overseeing high school course credit attainment, setting up visits to university campuses, and coordinating the transition process from the high school services provided in accordance with IDEA to the college supports offered through Section 504, the ADA, and the ESSA.

The animated video below was developed for high school students with disabilities to explain the vocational rehabilitation services that are available to them as part of their transition planning. Different vocational rehabilitation counselors are introduced in the video, with explanations of the many different roles they assume to help students succeed in their post-secondary endeavors.

▶ **Introducing Vocational Rehabilitation Services: Simply Said**

https://www.youtube.com/watch?v=vT9pKIcTQMg

What is the role of related service providers in the education of students with disabilities? Related service providers have specialized knowledge and skills in a given area (e.g., speech-language therapy, physical therapy). It is common for several related service providers to work with a student. Recall Ciara, the student with cerebral palsy discussed in Topic 4.9. We noted then that, due to her limited motor skills, which included strength and flexibility, she would work with an OT and a PT. In addition, her IEP team determines that she could benefit from other related services. Because her speech is difficult to understand, the team determines that a speech-language pathologist (SLP) will provide therapy to improve her speech and articulation, and an assistive technology specialist will help her master the use of a computerized speech synthesizer. The frequency, intensity, and duration of these services may vary across time as Ciara's skills improve. The following table lists some of the related services available and provides some information about each one.

Examples of Related Services and Providers

Related Service	Description	Provider	Percentage of All Related Service Providers
Psychological services (including diagnostic and evaluation services)	Administers psychological and educational tests (Steps 3 and 8 of the IEP process), participates in IEP meetings, consults with teachers regarding services and interventions	School psychologists	20%
Speech-language therapy	Provides services for the prevention and treatment of communicative disorders	Speech-language pathologist (SLP)	19%
Occupational therapy	Improves, develops, or restores the ability to perform tasks or function independently	Occupational therapist (OT)	12%
Social work	Mobilizes school and community resources and works in partnership with family members to resolve problems in a child's living situation that affect school adjustment	Social worker	10%
School health services	Provides health services designed to enable a student with a disability to participate in FAPE	Medical/nursing service staff	10%
Counseling services/ rehabilitation counseling	Provides psychological guidance services, including career development and parent counseling; develops positive behavior intervention strategies	Counselors, rehabilitation counselors	9%
Adaptive physical education (therapeutic recreation)	Assesses leisure function; provides therapeutic recreation and leisure education	Physical education teachers, recreation and therapeutic recreation specialists	8%
Physical therapy	Works to improve motor functioning, movement, and fitness	Physical therapist (PT)	5%
Educational interpreting	Translates oral language into some form of manual communication, such as finger spelling or American Sign Language for those who are deaf or hard of hearing	Interpreter	4%
Orientation and mobility training	Enables students with severe visual disabilities to move safely and independently at school and in the community	Orientation and mobility specialist	1%
Audiology services	Identifies and diagnoses hearing loss; determines proper amplification and fitting of hearing aids and other listening devices	Audiologist	<1%
Assistive technology	Assists with the selection, acquisition, or use of any item, piece of equipment, or product system used to enhance functional capabilities (assistive technology device)	Assistive technology specialist	No data available

The figure below illustrates how children and students with disabilities receive an array of services delivered by a wide range of personnel, including related service providers.

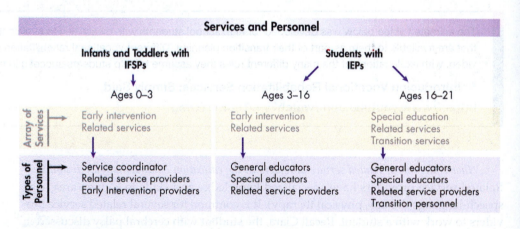

The video below shows a physical therapist working with a young child, Jake, to develop the strength and skills he needs to roll over. Notice how she encourages other children to join in, utilizing Jake's peers to model the skills he is working on, and to make the activity fun and reinforcing. Peer modeling and interaction are benefits of providing special education and related services in natural settings for infants and young children and in the general education classroom for school-age students.

▶ CONNECT Video 1.12: Routine in a Program—Rolling with Friends

https://www.youtube.com/watch?v=11StFJEzDf8

Topic 4.11 Continuum of Settings

- Special education services are delivered in a variety of settings, as required by IDEA, to provide a continuum from inclusive to more restrictive environments.

- The rates of participation in general education for students with disabilities have improved over time.

Where do students with disabilities receive their education? No single place is most appropriate for the education of students with disabilities. IDEA requires that infants and toddlers receive services in natural settings, whenever possible, which can include their homes, early childhood settings (e.g., child care, play groups), and more. Some related services might be provided in other locations, like a physical therapy clinic.

Unfortunately, many families of infants and toddlers experience difficulties when trying to find high-quality, inclusive early childhood programs, citing reasons such as:

- negative attitudes and false, stereotyped beliefs about children with disabilities;
- inadequate staffing, training, and expertise of early childhood personnel; and
- lack of comprehensive service provision in early childhood settings.

Recognizing these barriers to inclusion, the U.S. Department of Health and Human Services and the U.S. Department of Education released a joint policy statement that contains clear and specific expectations for states and local districts to increase the inclusion of infants, toddlers, and children with disabilities. The statement can be accessed at http://www2.ed.gov/policy/speced/guid/earlylearning/joint-statement-full-text.pdf.

IDEA requires that students with disabilities be educated with their peers and provided access to the general education curriculum to the greatest extent possible— referred to as the least restrictive environment, or LRE. Almost *all* students with disabilities attend general education classes for a significant part of their school day, but most receive at least some special education services outside the general education classroom. The federal government collects data on the various settings in which students with disabilities are educated. When analyzing the amount of time that students with disabilities spend in the general education setting, the data are divided into three categories:

- Inside the regular class 80% or more of the day
- Inside the regular class 40% through 79% of the day
- Inside the regular class less than 40% of the day

Throughout this text, we will provide data regarding the educational placements, or settings, of students with disabilities and will refer to these categories when we do so. For students whose education occurs in these settings, the remaining time spent outside the regular class involves individualized instruction with a special educator or related service provider. Depending on their educational, behavioral, or health needs, some students require instruction in more restrictive or segregated locations: separate special education school, residential setting, home, and hospital settings. Although some students with ITPs receive instruction on vocational and independent living in community settings (something we'll discuss in Chapters 9 and 14), these settings are counted within the separate special education classroom category. Finally, some students in the juvenile justice system receive their education in correctional facilities.

Continuum of Settings

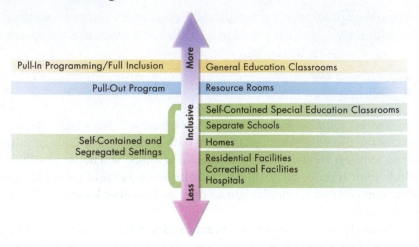

How have the educational placements for students with disabilities changed over time? Currently, over 60% of students with disabilities spend more than 80% of their school day learning in general education classrooms. And 96% do so at their neighborhood school, along with their siblings, neighbors, and friends. These rates of **inclusion** are very different from when IDEA was passed in 1975; at that time, over a million children were excluded from public schools. The next two figures illustrate the data in two very different ways. Compare these recent data with those of years past and think about the important inclusive trends they illustrate.

Educational Environments Across Time

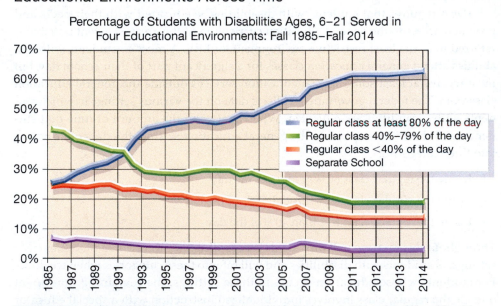

Percentage of Students with Disabilities Ages, 6–21 Served in Four Educational Environments: Fall 1985–Fall 2014

SOURCES: From the *21st* to *37th Annual Reports to Congress*, U.S. Department of Education, Office of Special Education Programs; and Accountability Data retrieved from www.ideadata.org

Finally, the figure on the next page illustrates the percentage of students who spend the majority of their days (80% or more) in the general education setting. Note the changes that have occurred over three decades.

Types of settings should not be associated with specific disabilities. For example, it should not be assumed that students with intellectual disabilities will be placed in separate special education classroom settings. Also, more restrictive settings like special schools should not necessarily be associated with more significant disabilities. The belief that a student with a significant disability should be educated in a separate special education classroom all day is just as inaccurate as the assumption that a student with a mild or moderate reading disability is best educated in the general education classroom for the entire school day. Instead, that student may need intensive and individualized reading instruction outside the general education setting for one hour, three days per week.

The figure below summarizes the ways in which infants, toddlers, and students with disabilities can receive an array of services, provided by personnel with expertise from many disciplines, and delivered in a continuum of settings. The many ways in which these options can be configured illustrates how truly individualized special education can be.

Changes in general education classroom participation: 1984 and 2014

1984 — 25%

2014 — 63%

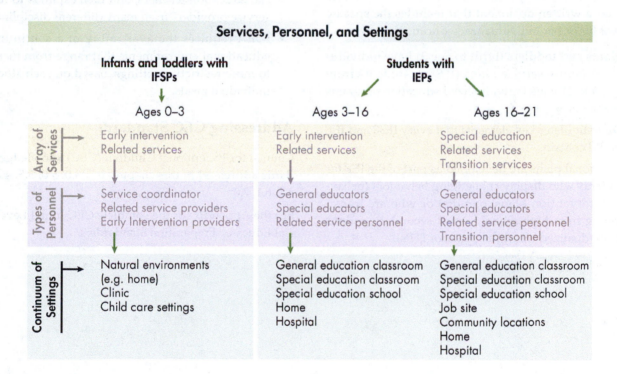

Services, Personnel, and Settings

	Infants and Toddlers with IFSPs	Students with IEPs	
	Ages 0–3	Ages 3–16	Ages 16–21
Array of Services	Early intervention Related services	Early intervention Related services	Special education Related services Transition services
Types of Personnel	Service coordinator Related service providers Early Intervention providers	General educators Special educators Related service personnel	General educators Special educators Related service personnel Transition personnel
Continuum of Settings	Natural environments (e.g. home) Clinic Child care settings	General education classroom Special education classroom Special education school Home Hospital	General education classroom Special education classroom Special education school Job site Community locations Home Hospital

Check Your Understanding 4.3

Click here to gauge your understanding of the concepts in this section.

Summary

Educating Students with Disabilities

Several federal laws guarantee a free appropriate public education (FAPE) for students with disabilities in the least restrictive environment (LRE).

- Section 504 of the Rehabilitation Act and the Individuals with Disabilities Education Act (IDEA) govern the education of children and youth with disabilities in the United States, and are reinforced by key components of the Americans with Disabilities Act (ADA) and the Every Student Succeeds Act (ESSA).

- IDEA provides six basic educational guarantees: FAPE, nondiscriminatory evaluation, an IEP, education in the least restrictive environment, parent participation, and procedural safeguards.

- Infants and toddlers with disabilities are identified through the Child Find process, while most school-age students are referred for evaluation by school personnel.

- The eight-step process through which school-age students receive services through IDEA includes: pre-referral, referral, evaluation, eligibility, IEP development, IEP implementation, annual review, and re-evaluation.

Individualized Education: Plans and Programs

Every infant, toddler, and student with a disability who is eligible to receive special education services through IDEA has a written document that includes the specific details of his or her individualized education.

- Infants and toddlers (birth to age 3) have individualized family service plans (IFSPs); students from ages 3 to 21 have individualized education programs (IEPs).

- IDEA stipulates key elements that every IFSP and IEP should contain.

- Additional plans are developed as part of the IEP for students who display challenging behaviors (behavior intervention plans, or BIPs) or who are transitioning from high school to post-secondary options (individualized transition plans, or ITPs).

- Students with disabilities are entitled to a range of instructional and testing supports (accommodations) or modifications when accommodations are insufficient.

Services, Personnel, and Settings

The services that students with disabilities receive, the personnel who provide those services, and the settings in which the services are delivered must all be determined based on each student's individual needs.

- Special education services are intensive, individualized, and include additional complementary supports called related services.

- A multidisciplinary team of professionals delivers special education services. This team starts with a collaboration between the general education and special education teachers, and then expands to related service providers from many different disciplines.

- IDEA requires the availability of a continuum of educational environments that range from inclusive to more restrictive settings, based on each student's individual needs.

Addressing CEC Standards

Council for Exceptional Children (CEC) knowledge standards addressed in this chapter: 6.2, 3.0, 5.0, 5.5, 4.4, 4.0, 4.2, 6.1, 7.0.

See the Appendix for the complete CEC Initial Level Special Educator Preparation Standards.

Chapter 5
Speech and Language Impairments

Mandoga Media/Alamy Stock Photo

Award-winning actor Samuel L. Jackson speaks openly about his stuttering. The following is an excerpt from his acceptance speech for the Freeing Voices, Changing Lives Award from the American Institute for Stuttering.

"Growing up a stuttering Black kid in segregated Chattanooga, TN, in the '50s didn't quite make me think I was going to end up in a place like this. I stuttered. My friends laughed. I beat them up. I got to school. People laughed, and I shut up. I shut up for about four years, from first grade through fourth grade. But I made better grades than all of them so they had to kind of catch up to that curve. So I found out the best revenge was not only beating them up, but being smarter. And that helped a lot.

"I'm not real sure when I made the decision to pretend to be other people who didn't stutter…I've done it so long that I'm not real sure that I am the person that I am standing before you because this person doesn't stutter. But, when I go back to being me, like I was the other day on the set of *Captain America* and they said, 'Action!' and I went 'g-g'. A 'g.' It was G day. So I have my days. I have G days, I have B days, I have T days, I have P days. I have S days and, I'm still a stutterer.

…It's OK to make people wait to hear what you have to say because what you have to say is important. Thank you all very much for making me understand that the things that I want to do were very much worth me going through those things so that I could be here. And that they will be worth that to a lot of you kids sitting here now. Everything you do makes you stronger. You're going to be stronger than those people out there who don't stutter, believe me."

—June 25, 2013

▶ **To view Samuel L. Jackson's entire acceptance speech, go to**
https://www.youtube.com/watch?v=YduYg4JleTQ

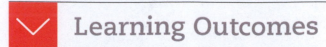

Learning Outcomes

Speech and Language Impairments Described

Explain the differences between speech and language impairments, know the different types of speech and language impairments, recognize the characteristics displayed by students with speech and language impairments, and understand the relationship between speech and language impairments and other disabilities.

Special Education

Explain the ways in which speech and language impairments can impact academic performance and interpersonal skills, describe the different accommodations that can lessen these challenges, understand methods that classroom teachers can use to reduce problems associated with speech and language disorders, and describe steps to take during the middle and high school years to promote a successful transition to college.

People and Situations

Explain how the education of students with speech and language impairments has changed over time, describe how people often have misconceptions about people with speech impairments, and describe how assistive technology can support communication in various settings.

Future Perspectives

Explain how the effects of speech and language impairments are being reduced or eliminated through parent training and medical and technological advances.

Speech and Language Impairments Described[1]

Learning Outcome

Explain the differences between speech and language impairments, know the different types of speech and language impairments, recognize the characteristics displayed by students with speech and language impairments, and understand the relationship between speech and language impairments and other disabilities.

Topic 5.1 Speech and Language Impairments Defined

- Speech and language impairments negatively influence an individual's ability to communicate effectively with others.

- Speech disorders affect an individual's ability to physically produce speech sounds; language disorders affect the ability to use or understand language.

---

[1]References for Chapter 5 are found at the end of this text.

Topic 5.2 Types of Speech and Language Impairments

- Speech impairments include problems with articulation, fluency, and voice.

- Language impairments affect communication in the areas of form, content, and use.

Topic 5.3 Characteristics

- Speech disorders do not cause academic difficulties, although social and self-esteem issues are common.

- Characteristics of language disorders include expressive and receptive language difficulties, as well as pragmatic skill deficits.

Topic 5.4 Prevalence and Placement

- More children have speech or language impairments than any other type of disability.

- As students get older and their language difficulties negatively affect school performance, many become eligible for special education services under the category of learning disabilities.

Sergey Furtaev/Fotolia

Many of us have fun playing the telephone game, laughing at the garbled message received at the end of the line. Unfortunately, for children with speech or language impairments, the difficulties in communicating clearly are no laughing matter.

Topic 5.1 Speech and Language Impairments Defined

- Speech and language impairments negatively influence an individual's ability to communicate effectively with others.

- Speech disorders affect an individual's ability to physically produce speech sounds; language disorders affect the ability to use or understand language.

How do speech and language impairments affect the communication process? Our society places a high value on verbal communication, which is a primary mode of interaction, a crucial part of life, and a fundamental aspect of the human condition. Note the emotions associated with conversations in college dining halls, in hallways at schools, and on cell phones. For most people, communicating effectively comes naturally. The communication process requires at least two people (a sender and a receiver), a shared desire to communicate, and a message. The sender translates his or her thoughts into a message and sends it to the receiver. Communication is successful only when the receiver understands the message just as the sender intended it.

Communication breakdowns occur when:

1. The sender incorrectly produces speech sounds and the receiver cannot understand the words.
2. The sender has difficulties using language correctly and the message is unclear to the receiver.
3. The receiver has difficulty interpreting or understanding the intent, even though the sender's message was clear.

Speech impairments are the root of the first communication breakdown, while **language impairments** cause the breakdowns in the two latter communications.

To understand how speech impairments are different from language impairments, you should first know the differences between speech and language. **Speech** is the physical act of producing verbal communication. A person with a speech impairment may have difficulty making speech sounds correctly or have voice or **fluency** problems that interfere with communication. The diagram below describes how several systems in the body work in concert to produce intelligible speech. Damage to any component can cause a speech impairment.

The Body's Systems for Generating Speech

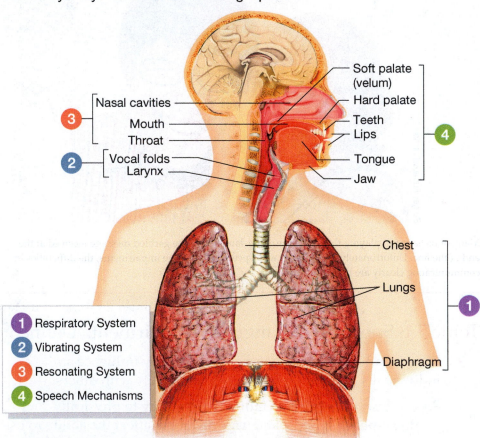

- ① Respiratory System
- ② Vibrating System
- ③ Resonating System
- ④ Speech Mechanisms

In contrast to speech, **language** is the complex, rule-based system of communication used to exchange thoughts and ideas with others. Language is the foundation for communication. We use it to express our thoughts and needs, describe our observations, and interact with others. Students with language impairments exhibit an impaired ability to express their thoughts, ideas, or needs so that others understand their intended message; they also have difficulty understanding the messages that others are trying to convey.

Speech and language problems are common for many students with disabilities. In fact, the majority of students with learning disabilities, intellectual disabilities, and autism spectrum disorders (ASD) also have co-occurring speech or language impairments.

How are speech and language impairments defined? These impairments can be referred to using numerous terms, each with its own definition. The table that follows compares IDEA's definition of speech or language impairment to several terms and definitions developed by the American Speech-Language-Hearing Association (ASHA), the leading organization for professionals in this field, and by the American Psychiatric Association.

Definitions of Speech and Language Impairments

Term	Definition	Source
Speech or language impairment	A communication disorder, such as stuttering, impaired articulation, a language impairment, or a voice impairment, that adversely affects a child's educational performance.	IDEA '04, U.S. Department of Education
Speech and language disorder	A speech and language disorder may be present when a person's speech or language is different from that of others of the same age, sex, or ethnic group; when a person's speech and/or language is hard to understand; when a person is overly concerned about his or her speech; or when a person often avoids communicating with others.	ASHA
Communication disorder[2]	A communication disorder is an impairment in the ability to receive, send, process, and comprehend concepts or verbal, nonverbal and graphic symbol systems. A communication disorder may be evident in the processes of hearing, language, and/or speech. A communication disorder may range in severity from mild to profound. It may be developmental or acquired. Individuals may demonstrate one or any combination of communication disorders. A communication disorder may result in a primary disability or it may be secondary to other disabilities.	ASHA
Speech disorder	A speech disorder is an impairment of the articulation of speech sounds, fluency and/or voice.	ASHA
Speech sound disorder	A. Persistent difficulty with speech sound production that interferes with speech intelligibility or prevents verbal communication of messages. B. The disturbance causes limitations in effective communication that interfere with social participation, academic achievement, or occupational performance individually or in any combination. C. Onset of symptoms is in the early developmental period. D. The difficulties are not attributable to congenital or acquired conditions, such as cerebral palsy, cleft palate, deafness or hearing loss, traumatic brain injury, or other medical or neurological conditions.	American Psychiatric Association
Language disorder	A language disorder is impaired comprehension and/or use of spoken, written and/or other symbol systems. The disorder may involve (1) the form of language (phonology, morphology, syntax), (2) the content of language (semantics), and/or (3) the function of language in communication (pragmatics) in any combination.	ASHA
Language disorder	A. Persistent difficulties in the acquisition and use of language across modalities (i.e., spoken, written, sign language, or other) due to deficits in comprehension or production that include the following: 1. Reduced vocabulary (word knowledge and use). 2. Limited sentence structure (ability to put words and word endings together to form sentences based on the rules of grammar and morphology). 3. Impairments in discourse (ability to use vocabulary and connect sentences to explain or describe a topic or series of events or have a conversation). B. Language abilities are substantially and quantifiably below those expected for age, resulting in functional limitations in effective communication, social participation, academic achievement, or occupational performance, individually or in any combination. C. Onset of symptoms is in the early developmental period. D. The difficulties are not attributable to hearing or other sensory impairment, motor dysfunction, or another medical or neurological condition and are not better explained by intellectual disability...or global developmental delay.	American Psychiatric Association

SOURCES: From 34 CFR Parts 300 and 303, *Assistance to States for the Education of Children with Disabilities and the Early Intervention Program for Infants and Toddlers with Disabilities*; Final Regulations, Section 300.8 (a)(11), U.S. Department of Education, 2006; "American Speech-Language-Hearing Association Definition of Speech or Language Impairments," in *Definitions of Communication Disorders and Variations*—10.1044/policy.RP1993-00208, © 1993, p. 1, www.asha.org/policy/RP1993-00208.htm; and American Psychiatric Association, *Diagnostic and Statistical Manual of Mental Disorders* (5th ed.) (DSM-5), 2013, pp. 42, 44.

---

[2]The term **communication disorder** is often used to refer to all disabilities that result in difficulties with speech, language, and hearing. IDEA, however, considers speech or language impairments as one disability category and hard of hearing and deafness as two additional, separate categories.

Types of Speech Impairments

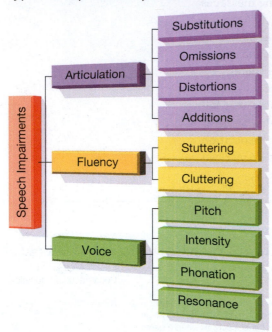

Note that IDEA uses the term *impairment*, while ASHA and the American Psychiatric Association use the term *disorder*. We use these two terms interchangeably in this text. Because speech impairments are very different from language impairments, we use the term *speech* **and** *language impairments* when referring to both disabilities at once, and *speech* **or** *language impairments* when differentiating between the two.

Topic 5.2: Types of Speech and Language Impairments

- Speech impairments include problems with articulation, fluency, and voice.

- Language impairments affect communication in the areas of form, content, and use.

What are the different types of speech impairments? The three types of speech impairments are articulation, fluency, and voice. Problems with any of these are distracting to listeners and can negatively affect the communication process.

Articulation problems (**misarticulations**), the most common type of speech impairment, are caused by the flawed production of speech sounds. There are four kinds of articulation errors—substitution, omission, distortion, and addition—which can be remembered using the acronym SODA. Because teachers are likely to encounter these errors, we have provided examples of each in the table below.

Four Types of Articulation Errors (Misarticulations)

Error Type	Definition	Example
Substitution	One sound or group of sounds is used instead of another.	Intended: *I see a rabbit.* Substitution: *I see a wabbit.*
Omission	A sound or group of sounds is left out of a word.	Intended: *I'm sleepy.* Omission: *I'm seepy.*
Distortion	A variation of the intended sound is produced in an unfamiliar manner.	Intended: *Can Susan come over on Friday?* Distortion: *The /z/ sound in Susan is pronounced /zh/ like in "measure".*
Addition	An extra sound is inserted.	Intended: *I miss her.* Addition: *I missa her.*

In some cases, students may correctly articulate a sound when it occurs in one position in words but not in others. For example, a young child might have difficulty pronouncing the /l/ sound at the beginning of a word ("*Y*et's go!" instead of "*L*et's go!"), but have no problem pronouncing it at the end of the word ("That's my ba*ll*.").

Fluency problems (**dysfluencies**) involve hesitations or repetitions of parts of words that interrupt the flow of speech. **Stuttering** is a type of dysfluency in which words or parts of words are repeated (e.g., "The b-b-boy w-w-went to the m-m-movies."). Another type of dysfluency is **cluttering,** which involves speech that is rapid; contains lots of pauses, starts, and stops; is disorganized; drops sounds or endings of words; and is often unintelligible.

Voice problems—uncommon in students—include **pitch** (high or low quality of voice), **intensity** (loudness or softness), **phonation** (the voice sounds too breathy, hoarse, husky, or strained), and **resonance** (too much or too little nasality).

Disfluency Example: Three-Year-Old Boy

In the video below, a three-year-old boy talks about going swimming and playing in the sprinklers. Although he demonstrates some dysfluencies at the beginning, notice how his fluency improves as he settles into the discussion. Young children often exhibit dysfluencies when they are excited, which should not be considered an indication of a speech impairment.

What are the different types of language impairments? For students with language impairments, communication is hindered by a breakdown in one of the three aspects of language—form, content, or use.

Form refers to the rule system used in all languages (oral, written, sign). In oral language, form has three components: **phonology**, **morphology**, and **syntax**. Students with language impairments may demonstrate problems with any or all of these elements. **Phonological awareness** skills develop during the preschool years and are a prerequisite for reading. These skills include being able to:

- Detect sound segments.
- Match beginning sounds to their respective words.
- Identify sound segments in words and phrases.
- Recognize and make rhymes.

Types of Language Impairments

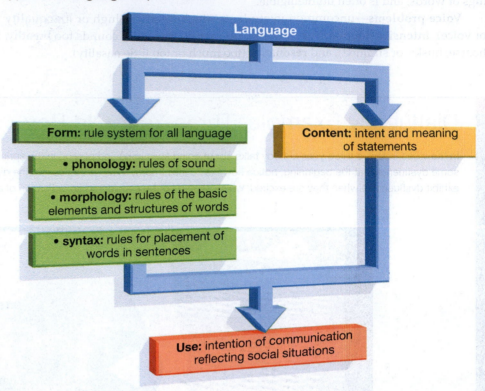

Morphology and syntax problems affect language skills in different ways. For example, a student with a language impairment:

- May misunderstand that a friend's story relates to something that happened in the past because he didn't pick up on the "-ed" suffixes on the verbs (morphology).
- Might communicate to listeners a very different message than intended because she used the wrong word order—"It is time to go" instead of "Is it time to go?" (syntax).

The second aspect of language, **content**, reflects the intent and meaning (i.e., **semantics**) of spoken or written statements. Communication can be direct ("That is a really ugly shirt.") or implied ("Are you sure you want to wear that shirt out in public?"). Students with language impairments have difficulty understanding or conveying the accurate intent or meaning of a communication, especially with indirect or implied statements. Further, these students often use vague referents without providing sufficient background information. For example, a child may only say, "I left it," when trying to explain that he forgot his jacket on the playground; without more detailed information, a teacher or parent may not understand what the child is trying to communicate. Children with language disorders will demonstrate these difficulties in both spoken and written language.

Form and content have a combined influence on **use**, the ability to apply language correctly in a variety of settings. The capacity to do this according to the social context of the situation is called **pragmatics**. Students with language disorders often display inappropriate social skills as a result of impaired pragmatic language. Pragmatics involves:

- Using language for different reasons (e.g., greeting someone, requesting something, explaining an answer).
- Modifying language or tone (e.g., speaking differently to an adult or person in authority than to a peer or a baby).
- Following socially accepted language rules (e.g., turn taking in conversations, staying on topic, recognizing and repairing communication breakdowns).

Topic 5.3: Characteristics

- Speech disorders do not cause academic difficulties, although social and self-esteem issues are common.

- Characteristics of language disorders include expressive and receptive language difficulties, as well as pragmatic skill deficits.

How do speech impairments affect students' school performance? Most students who have speech disorders (articulation, fluency, voice) attend general education classes and function well academically. Usually their disorder does not influence their academic learning. However, students with severe speech disorders, such as stuttering, may be reluctant to speak in class, which inhibits their ability to answer teachers' questions, work with partners or in small groups, or give presentations. Further, these students may experience feelings of inadequacy and low self-confidence, and therefore may feel uncomfortable or avoid interacting with peers in social situations that require talking (recall Samuel L. Jackson's comments in the chapter opener). Consequently, this can influence the friends they make, their relationships with others, the types of jobs they eventually seek, and their overall quality of life.

More information on speech impairments can be found at the following organizations' Websites: American Speech-Language-Hearing Association: www.asha.org and American Institute for Stuttering: http://www.stutteringtreatment.org.

How do language impairments affect communication? In contrast to speech disorders, children with language disorders may experience academic difficulties because of problems with **expressive language** (the ability to convey thoughts, feelings, or information), **receptive language** (the ability to understand information that is received), pragmatics (social language competence), or a combination of these. In the classroom, receptive language is important for gaining knowledge: comprehending lectures and written materials, understanding and following the teacher's instructions, and complying with classroom and school rules. A student with receptive language deficits might experience confusion when the teacher says, "Turn in your homework, gather your lab supplies from the list on page 147, and begin work on lab procedures 1 through 5." The three-step instructions may be confusing, especially with so many details. As a result, the student may complete only the first step or the last step—depending on whether she cognitively processes the first or last thing that she hears—which subsequently causes problems when she omits the other two steps.

Expressive language is necessary to demonstrate knowledge, such as answering the teacher's questions, taking tests, writing reports, and giving presentations. A student with an expressive language disorder may know the answer to a teacher's question but have difficulty formulating that knowledge into a spoken sentence. These students also have difficulty with word retrieval, similar to the experience of having something "on the tip of your tongue." For example, an 11-year-old may not be able to recall the word *rectangle* and works around her problem by describing it "like a square but with longer sides on the top and bottom." Students with expressive language problems may convey accurate information but not to the level of detail necessary for full understanding, as illustrated in the picture on the next page.

Pragmatics, necessary for social interactions, requires both linguistic and **communicative competence**. Effective social language is needed to engage in peer group activities, sustain appropriate interactions, negotiate and resolve conflicts, and develop friendships. Children who have problems with pragmatics may not ask to join a game at recess. Instead, they barge in, disrupt the game, and alienate their peers in the process. These students may also have difficulties understanding how to transition from one subject to another during a conversation, instead making what appear to be random comments that do not pertain to the topic at hand. Students with pragmatics difficulties may struggle with:

- Initiating and maintaining conversations.
- Interpreting body language and facial expressions.
- Recognizing the listener's need for more information or clarification.
- Engaging in common social customs (e.g., greetings, saying goodbye).
- Producing appropriate requests or responses.
- Developing positive peer relationships.

"Wow, big fish"

This boy's vague statement, indicative of an expressive language problem, does not convey the danger or urgency of their situation.

Cultural and Linguistic Considerations: Language Difference vs. Speech or Language Disorder?

Recall from Chapter 3 that students learning a second language go through the silent or pre-production stage in which they observe and listen to others. This is followed by the early production stage in which they express their thoughts using very short phrases. Students in the later stages—speech emergence and intermediate fluency—may continue to display grammatical errors in spoken and written communications. Teachers need to recognize these stages of English language development to avoid misinterpreting students' linguistic behaviors as characteristics of receptive or expressive language delays. Teachers must also consider that English has some sounds not found in other languages. For example, students whose first languages are Spanish, Chinese, Italian, or Japanese may struggle to say the *dg* sound (e.g., edge, dodge), but this would not indicate an articulation problem. Further, students from different regions of the country or from diverse cultures may speak with a dialect, which also should not be misinterpreted as a speech or language impairment.

The following questions can help guide teachers in assessing whether a student is exhibiting speech or language disorders or characteristics associated with cultural or linguistic differences:

- Does the student exhibit similar language delays in his or her home language?
- Does the student exhibit age-appropriate communication skills in his or her home language?
- Are language delays consistent with the stages of second-language acquisition?
- Are speech or language characteristics consistent with those of students from the same cultural or linguistic background?
- Does the student respond adequately to primary or Tier 1 high-quality instruction, as indicated by progress monitoring data?

If a student's characteristics are inconsistent with those of second-language development or cultural differences, then additional action by educators may be warranted (e.g., initiation of the pre-referral process, provision of Tier 2 or secondary intervention services).

Topic 5.4 Prevalence and Placement

- More children have speech or language impairments than any other type of disability.

- As students get older and their language difficulties negatively affect school performance, many become eligible for special education services under the category of learning disabilities.

How many students have speech or language impairments and where do they receive services? Speech and language impairment is a high-incidence disability category. These students make up the largest category of three- to five-year-olds with disabilities (44%) and the second-largest category (behind learning disabilities) for students between the ages of 6 and 21 (18%). Overall, however, more students have speech or language impairments than any other disability. How can this be? The federal government tallies students by their primary disability category only. Yet many students have more than one disability. In fact, students in nearly all disability categories exhibit communication difficulties. Although the majority can speak clearly enough to be understood (speech), many experience considerable difficulties expressing themselves, understanding others' communications, or interacting socially (language). When both primary and secondary disabilities are considered, students with speech or language impairments emerge as the largest group.

Students with speech or language impairments are typically educated in the general education classroom. In fact, the general education setting is where more than 85% of these students spend at least 80% or more of their school day. However, these percentages vary slightly for different age groups. As you learned in Chapter 4, more preschoolers receive services in their homes or at a service provider's location than in a classroom. Because these children are not yet in school, speech-language pathologists often work with them (and their families) in other settings. However, once these same children reach school age, most receive services at school and very few are given services in their homes or in clinical settings.

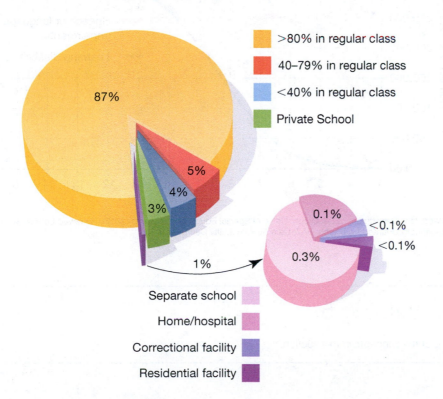

Separate school
Home/hospital
Correctional facility
Residential facility

Educational Placements for Students with Speech or Language Impairments, Ages 6–21 (2014 school year)

SOURCE: U.S. Department of Education. (2015). *Child Count and Educational Environments.* [IDEA Section 618 Data Products: State Level Data Files.] Retrieved from http://www2.ed.gov/programs/osepidea/618-data/state-level-data-files/index.html#bccee

If students with other disabilities also have speech or language impairments, how does that affect the prevalence of this disability over time? An interesting relationship exists between early identification of language impairments and later identification of learning disabilities. The figure shows the number of children who receive services under IDEA's speech or language impairments category compared to those identified with learning disabilities. Note that more young children have speech or language impairments, but as they get older, their diagnoses change to learning disabilities. This occurs for several reasons. As you'll learn in Chapter 6, many students' learning disabilities are identified when they start to struggle with reading. Very young children (toddlers and preschoolers) are too young to read, so these difficulties are not yet apparent. However, delayed language skills are evident, so these children are initially classified as having speech or language impairments. When they are older and in school, their language difficulties impact their ability to stay on par with their peers academically, particularly in subjects that require strong reading skills. As the figure below illustrates, at age three—when children with language delays are first identified—the speech or language impairments category is 50 times larger than the learning disabilities category. However, at fourth grade (age nine), when reading problems have become apparent, the learning disabilities category is almost the same size as the speech or language impairments category. From that point on, as reading becomes a more integral part of all schoolwork, the numbers in the learning disabilities category increase dramatically. And, as students with speech or language impairments go through the re-evaluation process (which occurs every three years), many are re-classified as having learning disabilities as their primary disability, causing the numbers in the speech or language impairments category to decrease.

From Speech and Language Impairments to Learning Disabilities

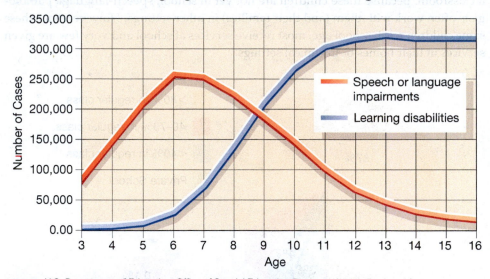

SOURCE: U.S. Department of Education, Office of Special Education Programs (2012). Retrieved from www .ideadata.org, adapted from Table BI-7; Data Accountability Center (2011).

Check Your Understanding 5.1

Click here to gauge your understanding of the concepts in this section.

Special Education

Learning Outcome

Explain the ways in which speech and language impairments can impact academic performance and interpersonal skills, describe the different accommodations that can lessen these challenges, understand methods that classroom teachers can use to reduce problems associated with speech and language disorders, and describe steps to take during the middle and high school years to promote a successful transition to college.

Topic 5.5 Challenges and Their Solutions

- Speech and language impairments create challenges in language-based academics as well as social and interpersonal areas.

- Speech-language pathologists provide explicit instruction in key areas, while classroom teachers can provide additional supports to reduce the impact of the disability.

Topic 5.6 Accommodations

- Students with speech impairments often require accommodations to help express themselves.

- Because language impairments negatively affect receptive and expressive language, students with language impairments typically require different accommodations than students with speech impairments.

Topic 5.7 Early Intervention

- The first signs of speech and language impairments appear when toddlers and preschoolers do not achieve typical developmental milestones.

- High-quality early intervention services that include collaboration with parents, language-rich environments, and early phonological awareness training can reduce the impact of language disorders.

Topic 5.8 School Years

- Learning strategies such as Collaborative Strategic Reading teach students how to be more effective learners.

- Teachers who recognize communication breakdowns and actively work to reduce language barriers in the classroom can prevent many language-related problems.

Topic 5.9 Transition

- Study skills instruction should occur in high school, or earlier, to prepare students for college.

- Self-advocacy skills are also important and should be included in students' individualized transition plans (ITPs).

Maskot/Getty Images

Difficulties caused by speech or language impairments can cause communication breakdowns and frustrations in social situations.

Topic 5.5 Challenges and Their Solutions

- Speech and language impairments create challenges in language-based academics as well as social and interpersonal areas.

- Speech-language pathologists provide explicit instruction in key areas, while classroom teachers can provide additional supports to reduce the impact of the disability.

What challenges do speech and language impairments create? Students with speech or language impairments show common developmental traits: As preschoolers, their language development is delayed or their speech may be difficult to understand. Students who are self-conscious about their speech disorders are often reluctant to talk or they avoid school and social situations that involve speaking. By third grade, those with language impairments often have difficulties learning to read, and throughout their schooling they continue to struggle with academic subjects that require language-related skills. As they become adults, problems with both speech and language can impede success in social and personal interactions.

Challenges: Speech Impairments

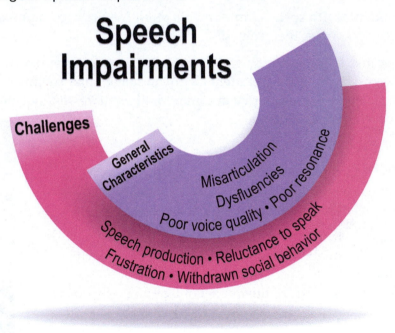

Although speech impairments do not affect the ability to learn academic material, language impairments can negatively affect learning when students have:

- Disorganized learning and study techniques.
- Problems with reading comprehension.
- Trouble communicating effectively.

Let's look at each of these in more detail.

Students with language impairments are often disorganized learners. More specifically, they are non-strategic learners. As an example, think about how you would go about memorizing the following list of words:

eggplant	*shark*	*tractor*	*penguin*
cheetah	*carrot*	*zucchini*	*gazelle*
motorcycle	*elephant*	*octopus*	*airplane*

Some people would group these words by categories: vegetables, animals, vehicles. They might even create animal subgroups (sea animals, land animals) to make memorization easier. Others might break the list into three- or four-word chunks. Still others might develop a **mnemonic** using the first letter or letters of each word (e.g., **e**at **chee**sy **m**eatballs to remember the words *eggplant, cheetah,* and *motorcycle*), or picture a cheetah riding a motorcycle while eating an eggplant. In contrast, a student with a language disorder might only read the words over and over, using no clear memorization strategy. Further, he might think he was studying hard and not even realize that he wasn't actually learning the words!

Another task that can be daunting for students with language impairments, many of whom have poor vocabularies, is reading textbooks. Texts are often written with complex sentence structures that can be hard to comprehend. Textbook passages contain content-specific vocabulary, and students with language impairments are less able to determine unknown word meanings using context cues. Keep these challenges in mind while you read the passage below about the Trail of Tears.

Trail of Tears Passage

Federal troops and state *militias* began to move the Cherokees into *stockades*. In spite of warnings to troops to treat them kindly, the roundup proved *harrowing*. A *missionary* described what he found at one of the collection camps in June:

The Cherokees are nearly all prisoners. They have been dragged from their houses, and *encamped* at the forts and military posts, all over the nation. In Georgia, especially, *multitudes* were allowed no time to take any thing with them except the clothes they had on. Well-furnished houses were left prey to *plunderers*, who, like hungry wolves, follow in the trail of the *captors*. These *wretches* rifle the houses and strip the helpless, *unoffending* owners of all they have on earth.

ORIGINAL SOURCE: *Baptist Missionary Magazine 18* (Sept. 1938); cited in Hoig, *The Cherokees and Their Chiefs, 167*. Retrieved from http://www.nps.gov/history/nr/twhp/wwwlps/lessons/118trail/118facts3.htm

This passage presents many problems for a student with a language impairment, who might:

- Have trouble decoding (reading) words like *militia* or *wretches*.
- Confuse synonyms (*pray* for *prey*).
- Not know the meanings of many of the italicized terms.
- Not be able to use context cues to figure out the meanings of unknown words.
- Not understand the comparison of plunderers to hungry wolves or the reference to "rifle the houses" and misinterpret these phrases (i.e., think that real wolves followed the captives, or that rifles were used to shoot at the houses).
- Think the last paragraph was part of the regular text rather than a quote from a missionary.

When you consider that this is only one small passage of a much larger assignment, you can understand how students might have problems understanding text assignments or become easily overwhelmed.

A third area affected by language disorders is effective communication. Language permeates everything that occurs in a classroom setting, so students with language impairments are at a distinct disadvantage. They are less likely to comprehend teachers' instructions, peers' social cues, or written directions. They are also less likely to accurately express their needs or feelings or to explain what they have learned from a lesson. The following table shows some examples in typical school situations of responses from a student with a language impairment. A teacher unfamiliar with the characteristics of language impairments might mistakenly believe that the student did not read the question carefully, was working carelessly, or was being rude or defiant.

Student Miscommunications

Test/Worksheet Question	Student Response	Additional Information
Using your periodic table, list the 7 noble gases.	Blue	The noble gases are all colored blue on the periodic table.
Look at the map below. How many cities have a population density of more than 100 people per square mile?	Atlanta	On the map, Atlanta is shown as having a population density >100 people per square mile.

Personal Interactions	Student Response	Additional Information
A teacher questions a student who is in the hallway during the lunch hour: "Where are you headed?"	"Duh, to the library."	The student has a hall pass to visit the library during lunch but doesn't realize the teacher lacks this background knowledge. Pragmatics issue: He is attempting to imitate other students' use of *duh*, not recognizing his inappropriate response to an authority figure.

Teachers and peers who do not recognize the signs of a language impairment may feel frustration due to these miscommunications, and students experience reduced academic outcomes or peer conflict and exclusion.

Challenges: Language Impairments

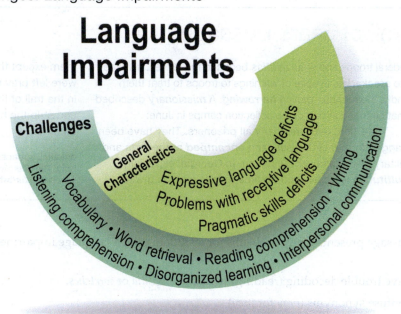

How can the challenges of speech and language impairments be lessened or overcome? Students with speech or language impairments will usually receive **speech-language therapy**. A **speech-language pathologist (SLP)**, a related service provider whom we introduced in Chapter 4, provides speech therapy to improve the articulation of students with speech impairments. The SLP will work with students to produce the sound correctly, providing lots of opportunities for practice. An SLP can help children reduce dysfluencies like stuttering by showing them how to control and monitor their rate of speech (e.g., slower, with less tension) and breathing.

When peers and teachers demonstrate understanding, sensitivity, and acceptance of a student's speech disorder, they help reduce much of the stress experienced by the child, which, especially in the case of dysfluencies, can reduce the occurrence of the problem. Peers and teachers can help by:

- Maintaining eye contact, rather than looking away, when a student is having difficulty communicating.
- Waiting for a student to finish her sentence or thought rather than interrupting or finishing a sentence for her.
- Providing a respectful, supportive environment where a student feels accepted.

Solutions: Speech Impairments

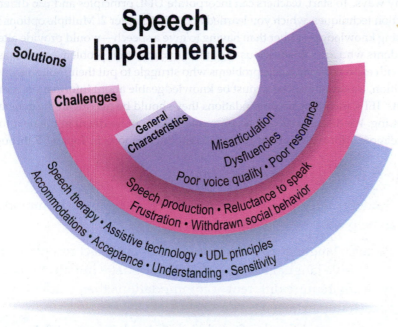

Students with language disorders can also benefit from working with an SLP, but they receive language therapy instead of speech therapy. An SLP can help the student with expressive, receptive, and pragmatic language issues and tie the therapy goals to common classroom situations such as answering questions, working with a partner or small group, or engaging in social activities. An SLP might also provide **explicit instruction** in areas where one might not think it necessary. For example, because students with language disorders often have difficulty interpreting body language or facial expressions, they need explicit instruction to correctly interpret these types of nonverbal communication. Further, using and understanding metaphors, analogies, and figures of speech (e.g., *speak your mind, time flies*) can be challenging, as students may interpret them literally. To reinforce the work of the SLP, teachers can integrate instruction about these conceptually difficult aspects of language into their classroom lessons.

Solutions: Language Impairments

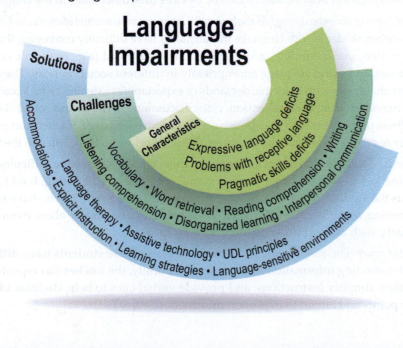

Classroom teachers can support students with speech and language impairments in many ways. To start, teachers can incorporate UDL principles and use differentiated instruction techniques, which you learned about in Chapter 2. Multiple options for demonstrating knowledge—rather than having to give a speech—would provide alternatives for students who are self-conscious about their articulation problems as well as for students with expressive language problems who struggle to put their thoughts into words. In addition, classroom teachers must be knowledgeable about information contained in students' IEPs, including accommodations they should be making in the general education setting. We discuss relevant accommodations in more detail in the next topic, and provide more information about general classroom supports in Topics 5.7 through 5.9.

Topic 5.6 Accommodations

- Students with speech impairments often require accommodations to help express themselves.

- Because language impairments negatively affect receptive and expressive language, students with language impairments typically require different accommodations than students with speech impairments.

What types of accommodations benefit students with speech impairments? As you learned earlier, students with speech impairments often experience difficulty with articulation, fluency, and voice. Because of the difficulty in expressing themselves, these students are often reluctant to participate or speak in class or to interact with peers inside and outside the classroom. To help them achieve more success in class, teachers can allow the use of response accommodations, such as those below, to complete an assignment or to communicate in class:

- *Alternate response to an assignment*—When a project is assigned that requires the student to present information orally, the teacher can allow the student to use an alternate method to present the information (e.g., PowerPoint presentation).

- ***Augmentative and alternative communication (AAC)***—Students with significant speech problems can use AAC, which is any method other than oral language used to communicate. Although AAC can include using gestures, writing, pictures, or symbols to communicate ideas, thoughts, and needs, these students often use augmentative devices such as **picture communication boards**, **symbol communication boards**, and electronic devices (discussed later in the chapter).

What types of accommodations do students with language impairments often receive? As you learned earlier, students with language impairments have difficulty conveying thoughts or information, understanding information that is presented (e.g., academic content, instructions), and using language appropriately in different social contexts. They often encounter challenges with academic demands or expectations: listening tasks, vocabulary, word retrieval, reading comprehension, class discussions, writing, and social skills. To help address problems related to expressive and receptive language, teachers can provide a number of accommodations, such as those described below and also listed in the table.

- *Visuals*—Because students with language impairments often have difficulty identifying key points, a teacher can use visual cues (e.g., highlighting, bold font) to focus the students' attention on what is important. For students who have trouble retrieving words or organizing their thoughts, teachers can also allow them to use visuals, such as illustrations, to express their ideas.

- *Verbal repetition, simplification, and cues*—Because these students have difficulty understanding information that is presented orally, the teacher can repeat information, simplify instructions, and provide verbal cues to help students identify key points and attend to important information.

Examples of Frequently Used Accommodations for Students with Language Impairments

Presentation	Setting	Response	Scheduling or Timing
• Previewing vocabulary • Advance organizers • Digital text • Verbal cues • Visual cues • Simplified directions • Repeating key information or directions	• Alternate setting • Preferential seating	• Alternate response options (includes AAC) • Graphic organizers • Increased wait time • Use of visuals	• Extended time • Visual schedule

Tips for Supporting Students with Speech and Language Impairments

Difficulty with Expressive Language
- Ask for clarification when a student uses non-specific vocabulary.
- Create opportunities for students to use new vocabulary and discuss concepts being learned.
- Encourage students to use new vocabulary words outside class.
- Model correct language when a student uses incorrect grammar or vocabulary.
- Provide extended wait time for students who experience word retrieval difficulties.

Difficulty with Receptive Language
- Rephrase directions (if student appears unresponsive) and instructions (if student appears confused).
- Repeat instructions, if necessary.
- Start with one-step instructions and gradually build to multi-step instructions.
- Provide physical cues when giving instructions (e.g., holding up the book they should be opening).
- Rather than ask students if they understand something (they will usually respond with "yes"), ask them to do one of the following:
  - Repeat the instructions back to you
  - Restate content in their own words
  - Show you what they are supposed to be doing
  - Work one or two problems and then check with you to be sure they are doing them correctly
- Have students partner during activities to provide support and enhance comprehension.
- Teach students to recognize when they do not understand something and how to verbalize that.

Difficulty with Pragmatics
- Teach and practice how to interpret facial expressions and body language.
- Teach scripted responses for certain social conventions.
- Teach the importance of different communication styles expected by different people (peers or siblings vs. adults in authority) and when and how to use them.
- Avoid using sarcasm, which can be interpreted literally.

Topic 5.7 Early Intervention

- The first signs of speech and language impairments appear when toddlers and preschoolers do not achieve typical developmental milestones.

- High-quality early intervention services that include collaboration with parents, language-rich environments, and early phonological awareness training can reduce the impact of language disorders.

Are there early indicators that a young child may have a speech or language impairment? Age is a critical factor when determining whether a child has a speech or language impairment. Let's consider each disorder separately.

As the figure below shows, correct production of speech sounds develops over time, so an articulation error that is developmentally normal at an early age may not be acceptable later. For example, the chart shows that most children start making the /k/ sound around age two and typically have mastered the sound by age four. So, although it would be normal for a three-year-old to have articulation difficulties with the /k/ sound, there would be cause for concern if that child were still not able to make the /k/ sound at age five. Similarly, it is normal for young children (below the age of six) to exhibit high rates of dysfluencies, particularly in exciting, stressful, or uncommon situations. However, 75% of preschoolers who stutter will eventually recover, so adults should consider a child's age when determining whether he or she might have a speech disorder. Concerns about speech disorders are warranted only when articulation or fluency errors are consistently age-inappropriate.

Sander's Chart, Indicating When 90% of All Children Typically Produce a Specific Sound Correctly

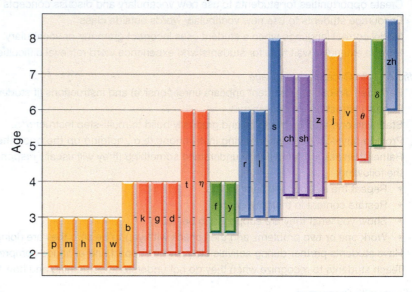

NOTES: Average-age estimates and upper-age limits of customary consonant production. The solid bar corresponding to each sound starts at the median age of customary articulation; it stops at the age level at which 90% of all children are customarily producing the sound.

The θ symbol stands for the breathed /th/ sound, as in the word *bathroom*. The δ symbol stands for the voiced /th/ sound, as in the word *feather*. The η symbol stands for the /ing/ sound, as in the word *singing*. The zh symbol indicates the sound of the medial consonant in *measure* or *vision*.

SOURCE: "When Are Speech Sounds Learned?" by E. K. Sander, 1972, *Journal of Speech and Hearing Disorders*, *37*, p. 62. © American Speech-Language-Hearing Association. Reprinted by permission.

Similar to speech sounds, language skills also develop in an orderly sequence across the first 18 months of life. **Language delays** during this time are a common indicator of disabilities. Late talkers (toddlers between 1½ and 2½ years of age) have language skills far below those of their same-age peers. These children:

- Are slow to acquire their first 50 words or to combine words into phrases.
- Understand fewer words than their peers.
- Have poor comprehension skills.
- Use few gestures when communicating.

Articulation Errors

In the video below, a young child, Callie, tells her mother how she would like to spend her day. As she speaks, she displays some consistent articulation errors. Can you identify them?

- What sounds is Callie mispronouncing?
- What types of articulation errors can you detect?
- Using Sander's chart (above), determine whether Callie's articulation errors are age appropriate if she is four years old. What if she is five years old? Justify your answer.

Compare the profiles and language milestones for children with typical and delayed language in the table below. Note that after age 3 (40 months), a typically developing child will use fairly sophisticated language, but a 40-month old with language problems is only beginning to use two-word combinations. The gaps between these two children widen quickly. In addition to delays, children with language disorders also display disjointed language skills (e.g., "The boy, and him, they go there," instead of "Matt and Spencer are playing on the slide.").

Comparison of Language Acquisition Skills

Age in Months		Skill	Example
Typical	Delayed		
8–12	17	First words	Mamma; Uh-oh; Doggie; Bye-bye; No!
18	38	50-word vocabulary	
18–26	40	First 2-word combinations	More juice; Here ball
22	48	Later 2-word combinations	Mommy purse; Cup floor
24	52	Mean sentence length of 2 words	Andy sleep.
24–30	55	First appearance of -ing	
30	63	Mean sentence length of 3.1 words	
30	66	First appearance of is	My car is gone!
37	73	Mean sentence length of 4.1 words	
38	76	Mean sentence length of 4.5 words	
40	79	First appearance of indirect requests	Can I get the ball?

Language Samples: Five-Year-Old Girls

In the video below, you will watch two five-year-old children talking. Callie, whom you met earlier, talks about her favorite scene from a movie. Then Diana, who has delayed language, plays with some toys so that an SLP can observe her language skills. Notice the differences between the length of the sentences and descriptions that Callie uses and the shorter phrases that Diana uses.

Recall from Chapter 4 that IDEA allows children younger than age nine to qualify for special education services under the category of developmental delay without being labeled—or mislabeled—with a specific disability. As a result, children who demonstrate language delays may not always be included in the speech or language impairments category.

How is high-quality early intervention provided? Early speech and language intervention is often provided in the child's home in collaboration with the parents. An SLP might work directly with the young child while also demonstrating techniques that the parents can implement during daily activities (playtime, meals, baths, bedtime). Parents can increase a child's vocabulary in many ways, such as teaching unknown words during play ("Look at this *zebra* [holding up a stuffed toy zebra]. It has *stripes*."). Parents can also foster children's expressive language development by asking questions, reinforcing responses, and encouraging them to expand their verbalizations:

Parent (holding up a stuffed toy zebra): Here's an animal friend! What kind of animal is this?

Child: D-

Parent: Yes, it's a zebra. Can you say "zebra?"

Child: Dee

Parent (tickling the child under the neck with the zebra): This zebra likes you! Can you say "ze-bra"?

Child (giggling): Dee-a.

Notice that the child's vocalization about the zebra increased from a single sound (*d-*) to a two-syllable utterance (*dee-a*) during this interaction. With repeated practice, the child's vocalizations will become closer to the actual word. And, if you check Sander's chart above, you'll see that the /z/ sound is one of the more difficult sounds that children master at an older age.

Effective early childhood teachers develop **language-rich environments** where young children have opportunities to explore, exchange ideas, and interact with both familiar and novel toys and objects. Good preschool teachers integrate language development into every lesson and engage students in interesting activities that motivate them to talk. These teachers also provide explicit instruction in pragmatics, which improves social skills and reduces subsequent negative peer interactions. Finally, they build early phonological awareness skills through everyday reading and language activities. Teachers can support children's language development by:

This SLP works with a toddler in his home, building speech and language instruction into everyday play activities by encouraging him to tell her what he is doing, to name the colors of his toys, and so on.

- Specifically teaching and modeling vocabulary that children will use in social interactions (e.g., *doctor*, *groceries*, *salon* and *firefighter* for dress-up or dramatic play, *slide* and *swing* for playground interactions).

- Placing some materials or toys out of reach so that children must ask for them.

- Setting up a silly situation (e.g., putting a coat on backwards) and having children explain how to fix it.

- Asking children questions and then expanding on their answers, modeling desired language (similar to the parent example above).

- Playing word games in which children clap for each "part" (syllable) of their names or practice rhyming words in songs.

Topic 5.8 School Years

- Learning strategies such as Collaborative Strategic Reading teach students how to be more effective learners.

- Teachers who recognize communication breakdowns and actively work to reduce language barriers in the classroom can prevent many language-related problems.

What strategies can teachers use to help students with language impairments who struggle with reading comprehension? As we mentioned earlier, students with language impairments can have problems with reading comprehension because of poor vocabulary skills or difficulty following long or complex sentences. Sometimes, these students do not even recognize that they don't understand what they've just read.

One effective intervention is to teach **learning strategies**. These strategies provide an explicit, specific process by which to learn information, replacing the disorganized or ineffective methods currently used by the students. A great benefit of learning strategies is that they can help *all* students, not just those with disabilities. Collaborative Strategic Reading (CSR) is one such learning strategy that improves students' reading comprehension skills.

Oksana Kuzmina/Shutterstock

A Closer Look at Research-Based Practices

Collaborative Strategic Reading (CSR)

CSR is a reading approach in which students use comprehension strategies in cooperative learning groups (small groups consisting of three to five students with mixed abilities). The goal is to improve students' reading comprehension skills, particularly for expository text such as that found in textbooks. CSR incorporates four strategies that students use before, during, and after reading a passage.

Preview: *Before reading a passage*, to activate prior knowledge, students write down everything they know about the topic and share their responses with the small group. They then skim the text, write down their predictions about what they think they will learn, and share these with their peers.

Click and clunk: *During passage reading,* students monitor their understanding of what they are reading. Students continue to read the assigned passage as long as they encounter text that is easily understood (i.e., clicks). However, as soon as they encounter difficult vocabulary (i.e., clunks) they should stop and use one or more of the following fix-up strategies to determine the meaning.

- Reread the sentence and try to find a synonym for the clunk.
- Reread the sentence and the preceding and following sentences to search for clues that help make sense of the clunk.
- Use prefixes or suffixes to help determine the clunk's meaning.
- Break the clunk into smaller words.

Get the gist: Also *during reading*, students identify the main idea of the passage and then restate it in 10 words or less.

Wrap up: *After reading the passage*, students generate and answer a list of questions. Next, they summarize what they have learned in writing and share their ideas with their peers. Worksheets such as the one below can guide students through the four strategies and provide a concrete record of what they learned.

CSR Learning Log

Topic: _Ecosystems_   Date: _03/10/XX_

BEFORE READING — Preview
1. What I already know about the topic: *An ecosystem is the environment.*   **2. What I think I will learn:**   *I will learn something about deserts and rain forests.*

DURING READING — Clunks and Gists

First Section	Second Section	Third Section
Clunks: _harmony_ – *in peace with each other*	Clunks: _interdependence_ – *relying on each other*	Clunks:
Gists: *The parts of an ecosystem rely on each other.*	Gists: *An ecosystem can be broken.*	Gists:

AFTER READING — Wrap Up
Questions about the important ideas in the passage: *What is an ecosystem?*   *What happens if a part of an ecosystem is damaged?*   **What I learned:**   *The ecosystems need to be taken care of.*

Worksheet courtesy of the IRIS Center. Retrieved from http://iris.peabody.vanderbilt.edu/module/csr/

This IRIS Module explores the components of CSR and provides details about classroom implementation.

▶ **IRIS Module: CSR: A Reading Comprehension Strategy.**
http://iris.peabody.vanderbilt.edu/module/csr/

How else can general education teachers support students with language impairments? Another way that teachers can address some of the challenges that students with language impairments face is to identify and prevent potential communication breakdowns. In the previous topic, you learned how to create language-rich preschool environments. Similarly, teachers who are aware of potential communication pitfalls can create **language-sensitive environments** that foster language development and support students' language needs.

When creating language-sensitive environments, effective teachers:

- Provide direct vocabulary instruction.
- Match their language to their students' comprehension abilities.
- Adjust, modify, and supplement instruction based on students' needs (e.g., break large amounts of information into smaller sections; add visual cues).
- Use relevant examples that are tied to students' experiences and cultures.
- Provide multiple examples to illustrate a point.
- Repeat or rephrase important concepts and instructions.
- Use specific referents ("Open your geography book to page 105." instead of just "Open your book to today's chapter.").
- Avoid indirect expressions (instead of "Do you get it?" say, "Do you understand how to complete your homework assignment?").

Let's revisit the student miscommunication examples from Topic 5.5. A teacher who is sensitive to a student's language impairment issues would recognize the potential for communication breakdown and respond accordingly, as illustrated in the table below.

Potential Teacher Responses to Student Miscommunications

Test/Worksheet Question	Student Response	Additional Information	Possible Teacher Response
Using your periodic table, list the 7 noble gases. Look at the map below. How many cities have a population density of more than 100 people per square mile?	Blue Atlanta	The noble gases are all colored blue on the periodic table. On the map, Atlanta is shown as having a population density >100 people per square mile.	Follow up with the student and ask, "How did you get this answer?" Then go over the wording in the question and explain how the student's response did not answer it.
Personal Interactions	**Student Response**	**Additional Information**	**Possible Teacher Response**
A teacher questions a student who is in the hallway during the lunch hour: "Where are you headed?"	"Duh, to the library."	The student has a hall pass to visit the library during lunch, but doesn't realize the teacher lacks this background knowledge. Pragmatics issue: He is attempting to imitate other students' use of *duh*, not recognizing his inappropriate response to an authority figure.	Calmly lead him through the reasoning steps necessary to realize that the teacher wouldn't know that he had permission to go to the library. Explain why his response was inappropriate.

Topic 5.9 Transition

- Study skills instruction should occur in high school, or earlier, to prepare students for college.
- Self-advocacy skills are also important and should be included in students' individualized transition plans (ITPs).

What academic supports do students with language impairments need to enhance the transition process? Recall from the previous sections that students with language impairments are disorganized learners and have difficulty identifying key information or relevant points. Such characteristics can create even greater challenges to academic success in college. These students can benefit from study skills instruction. Just as students may have difficulty in multiple areas, a variety of strategies can be used to address problems in those areas.

Students Who Have Difficulty With...	...May Benefit From Using
Receptive language (processing information that is heard or read and delineating between important information and supporting details)	Graphic organizers Comprehension strategies (like CSR) Note-taking strategies
Expressive language (explaining information)	Writing strategies
Remembering or recalling information	Mnemonics
Organization and time management	Organizational techniques
	Time management strategies

However, students with language impairments do not implicitly develop these strategies; in fact, most students don't. Teachers need to explicitly teach study skills strategies, monitor students' use, and give corrective feedback to ensure long-term retention and use.

The following IRIS Module examines the importance of effective study skills strategies, includes information on why some students struggle with those skills, and highlights why it's critical for teachers to explicitly teach such strategies.

▶ **Iris Module: Study Skills Strategies (Part 1): Foundations for Effectively Teaching Study Skills.**
http://iris.peabody.vanderbilt.edu/module/ss1/

Study skills instruction is essential and is best initiated early enough to improve middle school and high school academic outcomes, in preparation for future college attendance. Although learning academic content is the ultimate goal of improving study skills, students must also understand the importance of keeping an adequate grade point average (GPA) for college entrance requirements and scholarship eligibility.

Robin Nelson/PhotoEdit

As students get older, they should attend their IEP meetings, when appropriate. By taking part in her IEP meeting and making decisions about goals, classes, and accommodations, this student (in the orange shirt) is developing self-advocacy skills that will benefit her as an adult.

What other skills should be included in students' individualized transition plans? Because students with disabilities do not have the same guarantees and protections provided by IDEA when they attend college, they must learn to speak up for themselves, a skill referred to as **self-advocacy**. To do this effectively, they must understand their disability and their own strengths and areas of needed support. At the most basic level, this means that students must "own" their disability, which can be hard for those who have spent years trying to hide it from their peers. Students must comprehend how the disability affects them and be familiar with the accommodations they will need in college. Although most colleges have a disability services office, data indicate that many students fail to take full advantage of such services: they neglect check-ins with their counselors, do not request accommodations or choose not to use them even when they are available, and fail to inform professors of their disabilities. Fortunately, students who are taught self-advocacy during high school and who are actively involved in the planning and decision making that relate to their courses and future plans are more successful in college. The development of these skills should be included in their individualized transition plans.

Check Your Understanding 5.2

Click here to gauge your understanding of the concepts in this section.

People and Situations

Learning Outcome

Explain how the education of students with speech and language impairments has changed over time, describe how people often have misconceptions about people with speech impairments, and describe how assistive technology can support communication in various settings.

Topic 5.10 Origins and History

- Services for students with speech and language impairments started about 100 years ago but focused primarily on articulation disorders.

- Today, most students with speech or language impairments receive speech-language therapy as a related service to support their success in the general education classroom.

Topic 5.11 Personal Stories

- A person's speech impairment should not be considered an indication of his or her intellectual abilities.

- Teachers can support students with speech and language impairments in simple, respectful ways.

Topic 5.10 Origins and History

- Services for students with speech and language impairments started about 100 years ago but focused primarily on articulation disorders.

- Today, most students with speech or language impairments receive speech-language therapy as a related service to support their success in the general education classroom.

How long have speech and language disorders been recognized? Records dating before 1,000 BC reveal that individuals with disabilities were historically considered fools, buffoons, and sources of entertainment, often because of their speech or language problems. For example, during the Roman Empire, people with disabilities were exhibited in cages along the Appian Way—the main road into and out of Rome—for the amusement of those passing by. Families even planned special outings to see Balbus Balaesus the Stutterer, who would attempt to talk whenever a coin was thrown into his cage.

In the mid-1800s, Claudius Chervin, a French educator, engaged in some of the earliest speech intervention efforts. He successfully worked with a student to remediate stuttering. Buoyed by this success, he continued to study stuttering treatments and eventually founded the Institute of Stammering in Paris in 1867. In the United States, the foundation for specialized services for students with speech and language disabilities was laid at the beginning of the twentieth century. At that time, "speech correction" was offered in clinics, not at schools. The first school-based programs became available in 1910, when the Chicago public schools hired an itinerant teacher to help children who stuttered. In 1913, the superintendent of the New York City schools began a program of speech training for children with speech impairments. A year later, Smiley Blanton opened the first university speech clinic at the University of Wisconsin. Then, in 1925, a small group of professionals created the American Academy for Speech Correction (now called the American Speech-Language-Hearing Association, or ASHA) to share their ideas and research.

During the late 1950s and 1960s, speech-language pathologists (SLPs)—then called *speech therapists* or *speech clinicians* (notice the emphasis on the word *speech*)—worked in

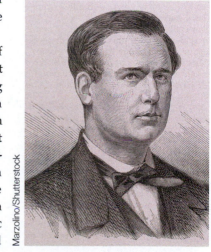

Claudius Chervin was one of the first educators to work with students with speech disorders.

Marzolino/Shutterstock

schools providing support services to teachers and direct services to students and their families. The majority of their time was spent with students who had articulation problems. Each SLP worked with more than 200 children per week, primarily in small groups and for as little as 30 minutes a day. Students with significant language and cognitive problems typically did not receive services from SLPs because, according to the general belief of that time, they were not considered developmentally able to profit from therapy.

How did services for students with speech or language impairments change after the passage of IDEA? After 1975, the roles of SLPs changed as more students with complex speech and language problems attended public schools. SLPs, whom IDEA identified as related service providers, began working with students who had a broader range of disabilities (e.g., learning disabilities, intellectual disabilities, autism spectrum disorders). Accordingly, ASHA coined the term *speech-language pathologist* to reflect the wider range of services these specialists now provided to students with many more types of conditions and disabilities. Because most teachers had little preparation in the area of language development, SLPs assumed a greater role in providing an appropriate education to students with significant language problems.

An SLP works with a student to improve his articulation. By looking in the mirror, the student can see how his mouth, lips, and tongue form sounds.

As service delivery models have evolved over time, SLPs now provide an array of services across a continuum of settings (something you learned about in Chapter 4). SLPs usually provide direct services to infants and toddlers in their homes or in clinic settings. They also work with parents, offering information on methods parents can use to support speech and language development at home. For school-age students, SLPs provide a continuum of services to improve communication skills in academic and school-related tasks. The IEP team for each student considers the intensity of the services needed, the goal of speech-language therapy, and the least restrictive environment (LRE, see Chapter 4). SLP service delivery can be:

- *Consultative/collaborative*—The teacher and SLP work together to meet an individual student's needs in the general education setting.
- *Classroom-based*—The SLP works in the general education setting with individual students or in small groups with other students who may or may not also have speech or language disorders.
- *Pull-out*—The SLP works with the student in a location away from the general education classroom (e.g., SLP office, library).

Topic 5.11 Personal Stories

- A person's speech impairment should not be considered an indication of his or her intellectual abilities.
- Teachers can support students with speech and language impairments in simple, respectful ways.

How are people with speech or language impairments treated in society? The answer to this question varies greatly. For example, many people mistakenly interpret a speech disorder, particularly slow, labored speech or misarticulation, as an indication of intellectual impairment, and they treat these individuals as though they have diminished cognitive capabilities. Stutterers are often regarded with compassion; yet they can also be treated with pity or ridicule. Students who stutter or have pragmatic or other communication difficulties are at risk for bullying. Because most people are unaware of the term *language impairment*, or of the characteristics of this disorder, they recognize that an individual has poor communication or social skills but do not understand why. As a result, they become frustrated and, in the case of children, select not to play or socialize with the child who has a language impairment.

Public perceptions of many disabilities are also based on what individuals read or see in the media. In that regard, good media portrayals can increase public awareness,

On the Screen: *The King's Speech*

https://www.youtube.com/watch?v=kYoSQkfrjfA

This film covers a period in the life of Great Britain's King George VI during which he worked with speech therapist Lionel Logue to overcome his stuttering. In addition to shedding light on the physical and psychological effects of stuttering, the film depicts the speech therapy techniques used by Logue, considered at the time to be unorthodox. In Chapter 1, we noted that many Academy Award–winning films have featured actors without disabilities portraying individuals with

disabilities. **The King's Speech** is one such film. It won four Academy Awards, including Best Performance by an Actor in a Leading Role for Colin Firth. Ironically, Colin Firth developed a stutter during his work on the film.

In the film, King George's crowning achievement was the delivery of a live radio broadcast speech as Great Britain entered World War II. You can listen to the original speech delivered by King George VI at www.youtube.com/watch?v=DAhFW_auT20

while poor portrayals can create misconceptions. Fortunately, the film *The King's Speech* made positive strides in increasing public understanding of stuttering.

What recommendations do individuals with speech or language impairments have for teachers? Sara Solomon is a gifted young woman with a long list of impressive accomplishments, including recognitions from President George W. Bush, the Tennessee State House of Representatives, the Council for Exceptional Children, *Black Enterprise Magazine*, and the Institute of Entrepreneurship. Sara also has cerebral palsy (CP), a condition you will learn more about in Chapter 11. CP, which usually results from damage to the brain that occurred at or before birth, can hinder one's abilities to control muscles for walking, writing, or forming speech sounds. Sara is a frequent guest speaker in university and medical school courses, sharing her experiences to help future teachers and medical personnel improve their instruction and care of people with disabilities. Many of her suggestions apply not only to students with speech and language disorders but also to those with other types of disabilities.

Sara's Suggestions

Sara Solomon

10. Be flexible! Everything doesn't always go according to plan. Adjust, accommodate, and try other ways of doing things.

9. Be helpful! Always ask me what would be most helpful when you are trying to help me…and then *do* help me!

8. Be responsible! If I have an educational assistant, don't depend on him or her to do your job. YOU are the teacher!

7. Be thoughtful! Just because I have an assistant doesn't mean they can read my mind. Please ask me!

6. Be patient! I might sound like I speak a foreign language, but that doesn't mean I don't understand everything

you say. If you don't understand me, please ask again (and maybe again).

5. Be mindful! All that equipment I have, I actually need it. Please keep it accessible for me when needed.

4. Be inclusive! Make sure you include me in everything.

3. Be there! When you go to an IEP meeting, stay long enough to actually learn my strengths as well as my needs. It isn't just about deficit areas.

2. Be communicative! Communicate and get to know me! I am more than just a student with a disability in your class!

1. Be confident! Have high expectations for me and I will live up to them.

Courtesy of Sara Solomon

Check Your Understanding 5.3

Click here to gauge your understanding of the concepts in this section.

Future Perspectives

Learning Outcome

Explain how the effects of speech and language impairments are being reduced or eliminated through parent training and medical and technological advances.

Topic 5.12 Prevention: Medical and Environmental Interventions

- Many conditions that cause speech impairments can be prevented or repaired through medical interventions.

- Preventive actions, such as prenatal folic acid supplements, prompt treatment of otitis media, and increased language stimulation in early childhood can reduce or eliminate the impact of language impairments.

Topic 5.13 Technology: Improving Communication

- For many students, assistive technology can be used to enhance expressive language.

- New technology apps can help with articulation, organization, writing, and other relevant skills.

ZUMA Press, Inc./Alamy Stock Photo

This young boy touches pictures and symbols on his communication device to express his thoughts. Using a synthesized voice, the device then "speaks" his thoughts aloud.

Topic 5.12 Prevention: Medical and Environmental Interventions

- Many conditions that cause speech impairments can be prevented or repaired through medical interventions.

- Preventive actions, such as prenatal folic acid supplements, prompt treatment of otitis media, and increased language stimulation in early childhood can reduce or eliminate the impact of language impairments.

What causes speech impairments, and can some of them be prevented? Speech impairments can result from many conditions, including damage to the respiratory or speech mechanisms or to the articulators (refer to the diagram in Topic 5.1). For example, a **cleft palate**—an opening in the roof of the mouth—allows excessive air and sound waves to flow through the nasal cavities, resulting in a nasal-sounding voice and difficulty producing speech sounds such as *s* and *z*. A **cleft lip**, in which the two sides of the upper lip do not connect, also results in an inability to form some speech sounds. A prenatal folic acid supplement, typically taken to reduce the risk of spina bifida and other neural tube defects, can reduce the incidence of cleft palates and cleft lips by 25% to 50%. When these conditions do occur, plastic surgeons, dentists, SLPs, and other professionals work together to help students overcome the resulting articulation problems and cosmetic issues. Surgery for cleft lips can be performed on children as young as 8 to 12 weeks of age. Surgeons can repair cleft palates by closing the gap between the oral and nasal cavities. This surgery is often performed on children between 9 and 12 months old, before they start forming words. However, some researchers advocate for surgery at even younger ages, as the cleft palate interferes with early babbling, the precursor to word development.

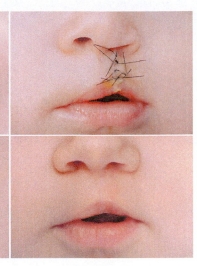

Malgorzata Ostrowska/Alamy Stock Photo

Surgery to repair a cleft palate helps improve a child's ability to eat and speak, and eliminates negative social stigmas tied to the physical appearance of the condition.

Making a Difference: Operation Smile

Children with cleft lips and cleft palates often experience rejection and ridicule. Unfortunately, the costs of reconstructive surgery are prohibitive for many children around the world.

Operation Smile, headquartered in Norfolk, Virginia, is an international children's medical charity that works in more than 60 countries, whose network of more than 5,000 medical volunteers from over 80 countries is dedicated to helping improve the health and lives of children. Since its founding in 1982, Operation Smile has provided more than 3.5 million health care evaluations and conducted over 220,000 free surgeries for children and young adults born with cleft lips, cleft palates, and other facial deformities. Operation Smile trains doctors and local medical professionals in its partner countries so they are empowered to treat their own local communities, donates medical equipment and supplies, and provides year-round medical treatment through Comprehensive Care Centers. Operation Smile has received many accolades, including the President's Call to Service Award (President George W. Bush), the President's Volunteer Action Award (President George H. W. Bush), and the Conrad N. Hilton Humanitarian Prize.

Learn more at Operation Smile's Website: www .operationsmile.org.

How can language impairments be prevented? Language impairments have many causes, including injury, genetic conditions, hearing impairments, illness, and lack of early language stimulation. Some cases can be prevented. For example, some instances of brain injury, which can produce conditions such as **aphasia**, can be prevented by wearing proper headgear during activities like biking or skating. In other cases, genetically based language disorders can impact brain development and the subsequent capacity for language development. Interestingly, the same prenatal folic acid supplements mentioned above that reduce the incidence of cleft lips and cleft palates may have neurological benefits. In a recent study, children whose mothers took folic acid supplements during pregnancy had half the incidence of severe language delays at age three than children whose mothers took no supplements or supplements without folic acid.

Impaired hearing, and the subsequent inability to listen to, imitate, and replicate language, can also negatively affect normal language development. For example, chronic **otitis media**, or middle ear infection, reduces opportunities for toddlers to hear and imitate others' language during key developmental periods and may result in difficulties with language development. Yet careful monitoring of children who display symptoms, and immediate medical attention when an ear infection does occur, can prevent related language delays.

The quality and quantity of early language exposure in the home environment can greatly affect a child's language development. Insufficient language exposure and stimulation can result in language delays. For example, some children are left alone often, are not spoken to regularly, or are not read to frequently. Some are ignored when they try to communicate or even punished for speaking because their parents view their talking as an annoyance. Many of these children have no reason to speak, nothing to talk about, and few experiences to share. Children raised in such language-deficient environments exhibit speech and language delays. Yet, because parents provide a child's earliest and most important language models, parental training on the importance and implementation of language-rich environments and other positive parenting behaviors is an effective measure that can prevent such unfortunate outcomes.

Topic 5.13 Technology: Improving Communication

- For many students, assistive technology can be used to enhance expressive language.

- New technology apps can help with articulation, organization, writing, and other relevant skills.

What types of assistive technology can provide supports for students with speech or language impairments? Typically, individuals with speech impairments require different technological supports than do those with language impairments. **Augmentative and alternative communication (AAC) devices** provide alternatives for individuals who cannot communicate through speech. AAC includes both **low-tech** and **high-tech** devices. A **communication board** is an example of a low-tech device; it contains pictures that represent often-used items (e.g., toys, books), phrases (e.g., "please" or "thank you"), or needs (e.g., hungry, bathroom). A child can point to the picture to communicate needs or desires. In contrast, a **speech synthesizer**—a high-tech device—can actually produce the speech sounds and words for students who cannot speak for themselves. Speech synthesizers can be used for anything from an immediate response to a teacher's question to programming an entire speech or presentation. Sara Solomon, whom you met earlier, has used both low- and high-tech devices throughout her life. On the next page, she discusses how her evolving communication skills influenced her choice of AAC devices over the years.

In addition to the considerations that Sara lists, parents and teachers must also account for a child's physical skills and age when selecting assistive technology devices. Some devices have buttons that need a certain amount of finger strength to push; others use a touch screen that requires little or no strength but greater finger dexterity. Younger children need sturdy technology that can withstand scrapes, drops, and spills, not to mention spaghetti-covered fingers, as seen in Luke's video on the next page!

Sara's Technology Supports

I have spastic quadriplegic cerebral palsy. Cerebral palsy affects motor skills and for me this included not only the fine and gross motor skills but also the oral motor skills associated with feeding, swallowing, and talking. This was a real problem for me as I liked to eat and I had a lot to say! When I was very young and began to develop words and sounds, it became clear that my receptive language far exceeded my expressive language. That is when my mom and my therapists really began to focus on my communication skills. They did everything, starting with [pointing to] very simple objects to make choices, to using simple photos to identify picture choices or preferences, to BIG books filled with picture cards. We had cards and photos for everything. But these books started to get hard to carry around.

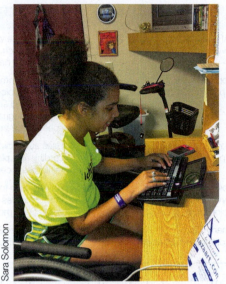

Sara Solomon

Sign language was a great option for communication. My non-verbal signing vocabulary grew rapidly to hundreds of words and it was great to get my wants and needs met this way. That's a powerful thing when you recognize that you are communicating! But my fine motor skills did not keep pace, so my signs were somewhat unique to me. I really wanted people to understand what I was saying verbally, too. My oral motor impairment really affected my articulation. It is hard to speak clearly when you can't get your lips together to form sounds.

So in preschool I got my first of many augmentative devices, an Alpha-Smart.

From pre-K through college I have had a number of augmentative devices (e.g., Delta Talker, Liberator™) that have helped supplement my spoken language. These devices have become more sophisticated over the years. As technology changes, so do my devices. These devices have allowed me to communicate freely with classmates, friends, family, and in the community. While I still prefer spoken language to express myself, it is great to have tools to help people like me communicate, regardless of whether the tool is a simple photo or object or a complicated piece of equipment.

(**SOURCE:** Courtesy of Sara Solomon)

As you view this video, recall the factors that must be considered in choosing assistive technology. Also, note the teacher's interactions with Luke and what she expects from him. When Luke used his device to ask for "more," his teacher probably realized that he wanted more spaghetti because his plate was empty. Yet, by asking "More what?" she encouraged him to provide more details ("More spaghetti.") and enhanced his communication. Also, did you notice that she required him to say "please"? She held Luke to the same standards for polite and respectful manners that she required from his classmates. This is not a small thing to overlook. Having high expectations for students with disabilities starts at the youngest of ages.

▶ **Luke's Assistive Technology**

https://www.youtube.com/watch?v=STjeXeDomsw

What types of apps are available to support students with speech and language impairments? The advent of smartphones and tablets has produced a host of apps for students with speech disorders. These apps serve many functions, ranging from articulation improvement to text-to-speech applications. Until recently, most synthesized voices were those of adults. Although many programs offered "children's voices," these were, in fact, digitally manipulated adult voices, so they never sounded natural.

In an exciting breakthrough, Proloquo2Go released a version with actual children's voices, which is demonstrated in the video below.

▶ **AssistiveWare—Giving Children a Voice of Their Own**

https://www.youtube.com/watch?v=qxMofds00Fg

A few apps that support speech and language are described in the table below.

Speech and Language Apps

Sample Apps	Description
DAF Assistant www.artefactsoft.com/iphonedaf.htm	Helps people who stutter to control their speech fluency, slow their rate of speech, and develop good speech habits; provides auditory feedback to help students' stuttering
iCommunicate http://a4cwsn.com/grembe-inc/	Creates communication boards, visual schedules, storyboards, routines, choice boards, and flashcards; comes pre-loaded with pictures and storyboards, routines, and daily schedules to help facilitate language comprehension; can record audio, use text-to-speech, use personal photos, and more
Language Builder http://a4cwsn.com/?p=2115	Uses audio clips to improve auditory processing; allows audio recording and playback to improve sentence structure and formation; reinforces receptive and expressive language skills
Proloquo2Go www.assistiveware.com/product/proloquo2go	An AAC app for people who have trouble speaking or cannot speak at all; provides over 7,000 symbols, natural-sounding text-to-speech voices, and more
Smarty Ears http://smartyearsapps.com/	Includes over 27 apps for special education and speech therapy, ranging in difficulty levels; addresses articulation and communication problems

Because students with language disorders typically have difficulties with expressive language, vocabulary, and organizing their thoughts, writing assignments can be a challenge. Apps like *Kidspiration*® (for young children in kindergarten through fifth grade) and *Inspiration*® (for students in grades 6 through 12) can be helpful. These programs can assist with creating graphic organizers, such as attribute webs (see the example below, which was developed by a high school freshman to study for a biology test). The software can also transform the web content into an outline to help students study for tests or write reports. A student using such programs can better organize writing assignments, and the end product enhances their ability to remember information.

Inspiration® Example

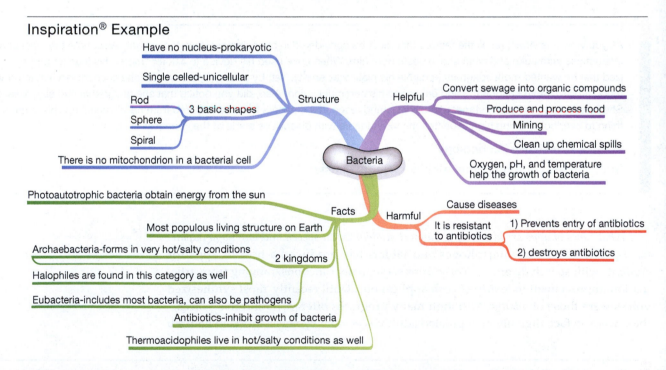

Check Your Understanding 5.4

Click here to gauge your understanding of the concepts in this section.

Summary

Speech and Language Impairments Described

Speech and language impairments are two types of disorders that negatively influence an individual's ability to communicate effectively with others.

- Speech disorders affect one's ability to physically produce speech sounds; language disorders affect one's ability to use or understand language.

- Speech impairments include problems with articulation, fluency, and voice; language impairments affect communication in the areas of form, content, and use.

- Speech disorders do not cause academic difficulties but may cause social and self-esteem issues; students with language disorders experience academic and social difficulties due to problems with expressive, receptive, and pragmatic language use.

- When both primary and secondary disabilities are considered, students with speech and language impairments make up the largest group of students with disabilities. Many students who are initially identified as having language disorders eventually become eligible for special education services under the category of learning disabilities when they are older and their language difficulties negatively affect school performance.

Special Education

The majority of students with speech and language impairments receive instruction in the general education classroom and are provided speech-language therapy as a related service.

- Speech-language pathologists provide explicit instruction in key areas, while classroom teachers can provide additional supports to reduce the impact of the disability.

- Students with speech impairments often require different accommodations than those with language impairments.

- The first signs of speech and language impairments appear when toddlers and preschoolers do not achieve typical developmental milestones; fortunately, high-quality early intervention services can reduce the impact of these disorders.

- Teachers who use learning strategies to teach language-based skills, recognize communication breakdowns, and actively work to reduce language barriers in the classroom can prevent many language-related problems.

- Instruction in study skills strategies and self-advocacy should occur in high school, or earlier, to prepare students for college.

People and Situations

Speech therapy services started about 100 years ago but focused primarily on articulation disorders, whereas services today address all speech and language disorders.

- Today, most students with speech and language impairments receive speech-language therapy as a related service that supports their success in the general education classroom.

- People with speech impairments are sometimes misjudged because of their poor articulation.

Future Perspectives

Medical advances can repair physical problems that interfere with communication and also can prevent some types of conditions. Technological advances can enhance communication for students with speech and language disorders.

- Parental awareness and training can reduce the incidence of language impairments caused by lack of language stimulation.

- AAC devices and smartphone and tablet applications offer alternatives for students who cannot speak clearly to express themselves and can improve their ability to understand information.

Addressing CEC Standards

Council for Exceptional Children (CEC) knowledge standards addressed in this chapter: 6.2, 1.0, 5.4, 5.3, 5.0, 4.0, 7.0.

See the Appendix for the complete CEC Initial Level Special Educator Preparation Standards.

Chapter 6
Learning Disabilities

INTERFOTO/Personalities/Alamy Photo Stock

"This idea of learning differently has always sort of been part of my life. And, for many years, teachers and educators and folks that I thought really had more information than they actually did, thought I was lazy. And put me in a slow class. Which gave other kids the idea that it was OK to call me stupid. And so for years, that was kind of my middle name. Stupid. And I couldn't quite figure out why they didn't get it because if you told me something I'd retain it. [But] if you wanted me to memorize a number, I couldn't do it. I still can't tell you what my phone number is, even with the smartphone.

. . . School was not my thing. And you kinda get tired of teachers just calling you names. And I get that they didn't know, but still…That's the other thing, people don't believe young people or kids when they say, 'It [writing] looks odd to me. This is how it looks.' And people go, 'No, you can't possibly be seeing [that].' 'But I am! I am! This is what it is!' And you spend so much time trying to convince people that you just give up.

. . . Slowly, people are starting to understand that this is real. That it's not kids being slow because they feel like being slow. No kid wants to not keep up . . . All kids want to be on par with other kids. So we just have to give them all the information and the utilities to do this."

—Whoopi Goldberg, May 16, 2014

Whoopi Goldberg, who has dyslexia, received Landmark College's inaugural LD Luminary Award, which recognizes those who work to educate the general public about learning disabilities. The excerpts above, from her acceptance speech, express common themes expressed by students with learning disabilities: the misperceptions of adults, the frustrations of students and sadly, the disconnection that causes too many to leave school. You can view her entire speech at https://www.youtube.com/watch?v=2aEKru4Uufw

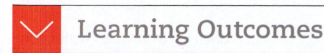

Learning Outcomes

Learning Disabilities Described

Define learning disabilities, describe the different types of learning disabilities, recognize the characteristics displayed by students with learning disabilities, and understand prevalence and placement data for students with learning disabilities.

Special Education

Explain the ways in which learning disabilities can impact academic performance and interpersonal skills, describe the different accommodations that can lessen these challenges, understand methods that early childhood and classroom teachers can use to reduce the problems associated with learning disabilities, and describe factors to consider during the high school years to promote a successful transition to college.

People and Situations

Describe the history of instruction for students with learning disabilities and identify resources for students with disabilities and their parents.

Future Perspectives

Explain how preventive measures can reduce the incidence of learning disabilities, describe how new technologies are identifying brain functions associated with learning disabilities, list some considerations when selecting assistive technology, and identify different types of AT that can be used as accommodations.

Learning Disabilities Described[1]

Learning Outcome

Define learning disabilities, describe the different types of learning disabilities, recognize the characteristics displayed by students with learning disabilities, and understand prevalence and placement data for students with learning disabilities.

Topic 6.1 Learning Disabilities Defined

- Individuals with learning disabilities have unexpected underachievement.

- Two methods for identifying learning disabilities are the IQ-achievement discrepancy model and response to intervention (RTI).

Topic 6.2 Types of Learning Disabilities

- Learning disabilities are often evident in three areas: reading, writing, and mathematics.

- Students with learning disabilities can struggle in more than one area.

---

[1]References for Chapter 6 are found at the end of this text.

Topic 6.3 Characteristics

- Students with learning disabilities often have problems with visual and auditory processing.

- Deficits in working memory are another characteristic of learning disabilities.

Topic 6.4 Prevalence and Placement

- Although learning disabilities constitute the largest special education category, the prevalence has declined over the past 15 years.

- Students with learning disabilities are typically educated in the general education classroom.

Monkey Business/Fotolia

Because students with learning disabilities have average or above average potential, teachers are often surprised to discover that they struggle with basic reading, writing, and mathematics skills.

Topic 6.1 Learning Disabilities Defined

- Individuals with learning disabilities have unexpected underachievement.

- Two methods for identifying learning disabilities are the IQ-achievement discrepancy model and response to intervention (RTI).

What are learning disabilities and how are they defined? In the broadest sense, students with **learning disabilities (LD)** have average or above average intelligence but have **unexpected underachievement**—academic performance significantly below what would be predicted from their talents and potential. This underachievement cannot be attributed to lack of effort, poor instruction, cultural or linguistic differences, or other extrinsic influences. Let's look at a few definitions to get a better sense of how this disability affects a student's educational performance.

Definitions of Learning Disabilities

Term	Definition	Source
Specific learning disability	Specific learning disability means a disorder in one or more of the basic psychological processes involved in understanding or in using language, spoken or written, that may manifest itself in an imperfect ability to listen, think, speak, read, write, spell, or to do mathematical calculations, including such conditions as perceptual disabilities, brain injury, minimal brain dysfunction, dyslexia, and developmental aphasia. The term does not include learning problems that are primarily the result of visual, hearing, or motor disabilities, intellectual disabilities, emotional disturbance, or environmental, cultural, or economic disadvantages.	IDEA '04, U.S. Department of Education
Learning disabilities	Learning disabilities are disorders that affect the ability to understand or use spoken or written language, do mathematical calculations, coordinate movements, or direct attention. Although learning disabilities occur in very young children, the disorders are usually not recognized until the child reaches school age.	National Institutes of Health
Specific learning disorder	A. Difficulties learning and using academic skills, as indicated by the presence of at least one of the following symptoms that have persisted for at least 6 months, despite the provision of interventions that target those difficulties: 1. Inaccurate or slow and effortful word reading 2. Difficulty understanding the meaning of what is read 3. Difficulties with spelling 4. Difficulties with written expression 5. Difficulties mastering number sense, number facts, or calculation 6. Difficulties with mathematical reasoning B. The affected academic skills are substantially and quantifiably below those expected for the individual's chronological age, and cause significant interference with academic or occupational performance, or with activities of daily living, as confirmed by individually administered standardized achievement measures and comprehensive clinical assessment.	American Psychiatric Association

Selected Types of Learning Disabilities

Term	Definition	Source
Dyslexia	Dyslexia is a brain-based type of learning disability that specifically impairs a person's ability to read. These individuals typically read at levels significantly lower than expected despite having normal intelligence. Although the disorder varies from person to person, common characteristics among people with dyslexia are difficulty with phonological processing (the manipulation of sounds), spelling, and/or rapid visual-verbal responding.	National Institutes of Health
Dysgraphia	Dysgraphia is a neurological disorder characterized by writing disabilities. Specifically, the disorder causes a person's writing to be distorted or incorrect. In children, the disorder generally emerges when they are first introduced to writing. They make inappropriately sized and spaced letters, or write wrong or misspelled words, despite thorough instruction. Children with the disorder may have other learning disabilities; however, they usually have no social or other academic problems.	National Institutes of Health
Dyscalculia	Dyscalculia affects a person's ability to understand numbers and learn math facts. Individuals with this type of learning disability may also have poor comprehension of math symbols, may struggle with memorizing and organizing numbers, have difficulty telling time, or have trouble with counting.	Learning Disabilities Association of America

SOURCES: 34 CFR Parts 300 and 303, Assistance to States for the Education of Children with Disabilities and the Early Intervention Program for Infants and Toddlers with Disabilities; Final Regulations on the Implementation of the Individuals with Disabilities Education Act (IDEA) (p. 1264), U.S. Department of Education, 2006, Federal Register, Washington, DC.

"What are learning disabilities?" NINDS Learning Disabilities Information Page by National Institutes of Health, National Institute of Neurological Disorders and Stroke, 2010, retrieved from www.ninds.nih.gov

"Specific learning disorder definition." American Psychiatric Association, *Diagnostic and Statistical Manual of Mental Disorders*, 5th ed., 2013, pp. 66–67.

"What is dyslexia?" NINDS Learning Disabilities Information Page by National Institutes of Health, National Institute of Neurological Disorders and Stroke, 2015, retrieved from www.ninds.nih.gov

"What is dysgraphia?" NINDS Dysgraphia Information Page by National Institutes of Health, National Institute of Neurological Disorders and Stroke, 2011, retrieved from www.ninds.nih.gov

"Dyscalculia." Learning Disabilities of America, 2016, retrieved from http://ldaamerica.org/types-of-learning-disabilities/dyscalculia/

How are learning disabilities identified? A student can qualify for services under the Individuals with Disabilities Education Act's (IDEA) category of *specific learning disability* in two ways. We have already alluded to the first: the **IQ-achievement discrepancy** approach. In this traditional method, a student must demonstrate a significant gap between his or her potential or ability (as determined by the score on an IQ test) and academic achievement. The theory behind this method is that a student with high potential but low achievement—a discrepancy that cannot be accounted for by other factors—has, by process of elimination, a learning disability. One problem with this approach is that it often takes years for the discrepancy to become large enough for students to qualify for special education services—often in third or fourth grade—causing them to struggle for years before they receive help.

Students with learning disabilities are often considered **resistant to treatment** or **resistant to instruction**. This does not mean that they are reluctant or unwilling learners, but rather that the instruction typically provided by their general

The Widening Performance Gap

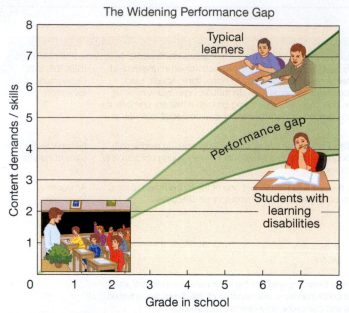

For students with learning disabilities, the gap between their actual performance and their expected performance grows larger over time. Unfortunately, it often takes many years of failure before the gap is large enough to qualify for services with the IQ-achievement discrepancy model, which can cause additional self-esteem and social-emotional issues.

education teachers is not effective for them. In consideration of those characteristics, IDEA also allows the use of the **response to intervention (RTI)** process, which you learned about in Chapter 2, to identify students with learning disabilities. You may recall that the RTI process is a multi-tiered system of supports. Students first receive high-quality instruction with progress monitoring in the general education classroom (primary instruction, or Tier 1). Because students with learning disabilities are resistant to treatment, they need more intensive services and interventions—at a minimum, the targeted supports at the secondary tier (Tier 2), and usually the intensive, individualized supports provided in the tertiary tier (Tier 3)—to make academic gains. Progress monitoring data are collected throughout the process, at each tier, and used to make data-based instructional decisions. Within the RTI process, students who consistently fail to respond to these interventions are referred for special education services. The RTI process can prevent years of school failure if students begin receiving more intensive interventions and special education services sooner. The quality of the first tier of instruction is critical. If the general education teacher is not providing evidence-based, high-quality instruction, then **false positives** occur: that is, students are incorrectly identified as having learning disabilities because they demonstrate poor academic performance.

You can find more information about RTI at www.rti4success.org.

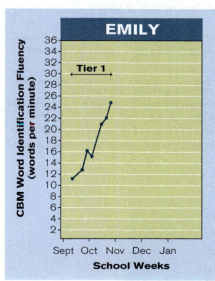

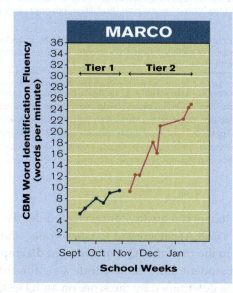

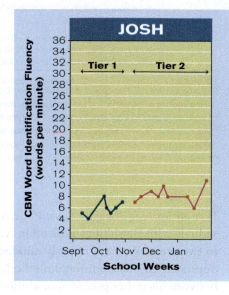

These progress monitoring data indicate that Emily made adequate progress with Tier 1 instruction; Marco was not making adequate progress in Tier 1 but did when Tier 2 interventions were implemented; Josh did not make adequate progress with Tier 1 or Tier 2 instruction or interventions. Josh requires Tier 3 services and might have a learning disability, so further testing is warranted.

Topic 6.2 Types of Learning Disabilities

- Learning disabilities are often evident in three areas: reading, writing, and mathematics.

- Students with learning disabilities can struggle in more than one area.

What are the different types of learning disabilities? New conceptualizations of learning disabilities focus on academic manifestations in the areas of reading, writing, and mathematics. Let's look at each of these more closely.

Students with **reading disabilities** have problems processing written language. More specifically, they have trouble recognizing combinations of print symbols (letters) and translating them into the sounds and words that the symbols represent. For many of these students, the struggle to decode words is a slow and laborious process, so their ability to comprehend what they read is also subsequently reduced. As a result, their reading abilities are significantly below those of their classmates without disabilities. Reading difficulty is the most common reason for referral to special education. Dyslexia is one type of reading disability; however, not all students with reading disabilities have dyslexia.

Students with **writing disabilities** have problems producing written language. In some cases, students with writing disabilities struggle with the physical act of holding a pen or pencil and forming letters on paper. In other cases, they are unable to translate the thoughts in their heads into words on paper. They often have poor spelling, so they may write words out phonetically, or choose to use simple words to avoid writing long words or making spelling errors. Here is an example. A student is writing a story and wants to write *The evil scientist laughed maniacally as his nefarious plan began to unfold.* Although she is creative and has strong vocabulary skills, she has difficulty getting the words down on paper. She struggles with spelling many of the words, erasing, rewriting, and substituting words until her paper is full of erasure marks and looks like this:

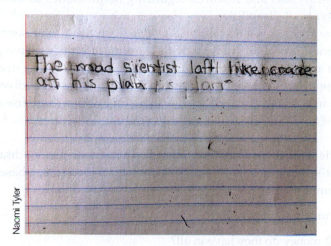

Not only is this far less descriptive than the sentence she intended, but this short sentence is all she has accomplished after 5 minutes of writing. At the end of the allotted time, her story is incomplete and far less detailed than those of her classmates. Dysgraphia is one type of writing disability; as with dyslexia, not all students with writing disabilities have dysgraphia.

Students with **mathematics disabilities** have problems understanding mathematics concepts (basic number sense, one-to-one correspondence), memorizing number facts, and performing calculations. These students often have difficulty understanding concepts of *greater than* and *less than,* count on their fingers for years after their peers have memorized number fact families, and inconsistently apply regrouping (borrowing and carrying) rules. Further, these students often have difficulty recognizing unreasonable or unrealistic answers. For example, when adding $5.50 and $15, a student with a mathematics disability might fail to add a decimal to the $15 (to make it $15.00), and instead calculate the answer like this:

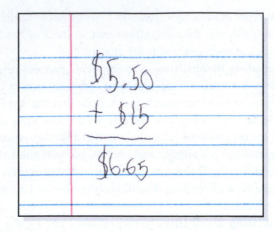

Although the failure to add and align the decimal for the $15.00 is a rather common mistake for many students, a student with a mathematics disability might not recognize that the answer is improbable and therefore might not backtrack to find the mistake. Dyscalculia is one type of mathematics disability. You might have been exceptionally observant and noticed that—in our table of definitions in Topic 6.1—the definitions for *dyslexia* and *dysgraphia* came from the National Institutes of Health (NIH), while the definition for *dyscalculia* came from the Learning Disabilities Association of America. This is because NIH has no definition for dyscalculia (as of this text's print/post date), one indication that the awareness and research regarding mathematics disabilities are far behind other types of disabilities.

Does overlap exist between the types of disabilities? Yes, and some sources estimate that roughly one-third of all students with learning disabilities have problems in more than one area. Remember that IDEA defines specific learning disability as "a disorder in one or more of the basic psychological processes involved in understanding or in using language." Because reading and writing both use overlapping language-related skills, many students with reading disabilities also have writing disabilities.

Many students with reading disabilities also have mathematics disabilities. You might be surprised to learn that much of mathematics is language-based. Consider this simple example:

Aretha has $6 and Franklin has $3.

> How much money do they have in all?
>
> What is the sum of their money?
>
> How much more money does Aretha have than Franklin?
>
> What is the difference in the amount of money they have?
>
> What fraction of Aretha's money does Franklin have?
>
> What percentage of Aretha's money does Franklin have?

Even these simple mathematics problems require a lot of language processing as well as a fair amount of reading. Notice that questions can be phrased in different ways but still have the same answer. Students must understand certain word cues (*in all*, *sum*, *difference*) in order to solve the problems. Do you remember the characteristics of language disorders that we discussed in the previous chapter? The example above shows why many students with language disorders are often classified as having learning disabilities as they get older—their language difficulties affect their ability to process and learn information.

Topic 6.3 Characteristics

- Students with learning disabilities often have problems with visual and auditory processing.

- Deficits in working memory are another characteristic of learning disabilities.

Do students with learning disabilities display common characteristics? Yes, regardless of which type, or combination of types, of learning disability (reading, writing, mathematics) they have, these students exhibit some commonalities. In addition to unexpected underachievement and specific academic deficits, students with learning disabilities often display problems with visual and auditory processing. This does *not* mean that these students have difficulties with their eyesight or their hearing, but rather the way in which their brains interpret the information they see or hear is impaired.

Visual processing refers to the way the brain interprets, understands, or processes visual information—that which is obtained through sight. Many students with learning disabilities have trouble with visual discrimination: they have trouble distinguishing between the letters *b, d, p,* and *q;* between *m* and *n;* or between similar numbers like *104, 140, 401,* and *410.* For some students, letters, words, and numbers seem to slide around on a page, making it difficult to sound words out or to perform calculations. Students with visual processing problems might also find it challenging to distinguish an object from its background: letters on the board, numbers on a page, or an object in a picture.

Auditory processing refers to the way the brain interprets, understands, or processes auditory information—that which is obtained through hearing. Many students with auditory processing problems have difficulty recognizing that words are made up of individual sounds (phonemes) and syllables; for example, they would have trouble identifying the individual phonemes in the word *cup* (/c/ /u/ /p/) or the syllables in the word *cupcake* (*cup-cake*). Conversely, if given the sounds /c/ /u/ /p/, they may not realize that, when put together, the sounds make the word *cup.* Recognizing that the words *cup, can,* and *cake* all start with the same sound, or that the words *cake, bake,* and *take* rhyme, also may present challenges. Finally, these students often struggle with tasks involving auditory memory, such as verbal instructions, remembering parts of a story, or repeating a series or sequence of items (like a phone number).

In addition to the type of processing (visual versus auditory), students with learning disabilities may display differences in processing speed. More specifically, these students often process information at a slower rate than their peers. For example, when shown a list of letters and asked to read them as quickly as possible (referred to as **rapid letter naming** or *rapid automatized naming*), students with learning disabilities show more pauses and delays, which result in fewer letters named during a specified time. These same types of pauses and delays cause students to take longer to complete academic tasks that require information processing.

What other types of characteristics do students with learning disabilities display? Students with learning disabilities often show deficits in **working memory**. Here are a few ways in which working memory affects academics:

- *Decoding skills (reading)*—Think back to the example above, in which the sounds /c/ /u/ /p/ combine to form the word *cup.* Although this was an auditory processing

Letter Name Fluency

P	t	s	z	c	r	H	y	e	f
j	a	D	u	V	F	M	J	X	g
x	F	v	J	c	q	u	T	e	v
g	o	B	K	l	W	n	k	R	p
L	b	U	w	V	n	e	j	q	S
f	T	Y	r	H	C	l	m	A	i
M	z	r	u	z	k	G	f	C	t
i	x	l	g	E	O	Z	h	d	l
d	h	A	W	o	P	N	s	y	p
D	s	K	x	a	Q	j	D	b	R

Mon. ☐ Tues. ☐ Wed. ☐ Thur. ☐ Fri. ☐

My goal: ☐

Rapid letter naming tests like this are used as progress monitoring probes for early readers. Students read as many letters as they can in 1 minute, and their scores are graphed to chart progress over time. Students with learning disabilities often show processing speed deficits when engaged in such tasks.

example, it also relates to working memory. A student who is sounding out a word puts each of those sounds in working memory. However, if he has working memory deficits and cannot remember the first sound, then he cannot blend it with the second and third sounds to make a word.

- *Note taking*—A science teacher says, "Today we are going to learn about three cell parts: the cell wall, cytoplasm, and the nucleus." A student with working memory problems would probably have difficulty remembering all three cell parts long enough to write them down on paper. Combine the working memory deficits with auditory processing problems and you can see why many students with learning disabilities have sparse, incomplete notes. Without detailed notes, the amount of information studied is compromised and they perform poorly on exams.

- *Mathematics calculations*—Here is a word problem from a math textbook: *Calculate the sale price of a $79.98 jacket that is 30% off.* Difficulties with working memory in mathematics can cause a student to incorrectly remember the numbers when she copies them onto a piece of paper. (Of course, her learning disability can also cause her to mix up the numbers or reverse their order. Are you beginning to see how many of these traits overlap?) If she does write the problem correctly, working memory problems might cause her to forget some of the steps involved in this multi-step problem. She might have trouble remembering the order of the steps in the multiplication problem, or she might calculate 30% of $79.98 correctly but then forget to subtract that answer from the original price to find the sale price of the jacket.

Working memory is associated with attention, so—not surprisingly—many students with learning disabilities who have working memory deficits also have problems focusing and maintaining attention. In some cases, these attention problems are minor and merely affect the amount of time it takes to complete tasks and assignments. In other cases, they are severe enough to result in a co-existing classification of attention deficit hyperactivity disorder (ADHD).

It is important to understand that this disability's neurological base can result in inconsistent student performance from day to day. For example, a student might appear to learn a skill or new information fairly well on one day, and then the next day have little recollection of what was learned, or struggle to perform the skill. Imagine how frustrating this would be for the student, particularly because he knows that he learned the information previously. These students might earn a high test grade for one unit—on a day when neurological processing is working well—and then fail a test on the next unit, when neurological blocks are occurring.

One last thing to be aware of is that the level of severity, or impairment, differs with each student. These students show inconsistent patterns of strengths and weaknesses and not every student with a learning disability will display all of the characteristics discussed above. One student may exhibit extreme difficulties in some areas, while a different one demonstrates very minor difficulties in the same areas, but severe impairments in others. Because these students exhibit a wide range of strengths, abilities, and weaknesses, they learn and respond to instruction in different ways. For professionals, this **heterogeneity** complicates teaching because no single type of differentiation, accommodation, or instruction is uniformly effective. Successful intervention requires an individualized approach, which is why special education services are needed.

Topic 6.4 Prevalence and Placement

- Although learning disabilities constitute the largest special education category, the prevalence has declined over the past 15 years.

- Students with learning disabilities are typically educated in the general education classroom.

How prevalent are learning disabilities? When we consider primary disability only, it is by far the largest category. The pie chart compares the two disabilities we have learned about so far—speech and language impairments and learning disabilities—to all of the remaining disabilities combined. Clearly, learning disabilities are a high-incidence disability.

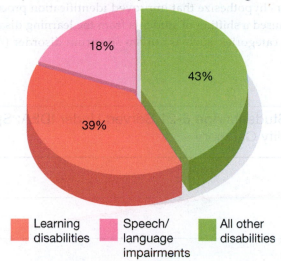

Percentage Comparison: Disability Prevalence, Ages 6–21

- 43% All other disabilities
- 39% Learning disabilities
- 18% Speech/language impairments

SOURCE: U.S. Department of Education, EDFacts Data Warehouse (EDW): "IDEA Part B Child Count and Educational Environments Collection," 2014–15. Data extracted as of July 2, 2015, from file specifications 002 and 089.

Here is another way of looking at the prevalence data. The graph below shows that the prevalence of learning disabilities among school-age students is double the size of the next largest disability category (speech and language impairments) and many times the size of other high-incidence disabilities. Note also that the prevalence of learning disabilities has declined in recent years.

Prevalence Comparison: High-Incidence Disabilities

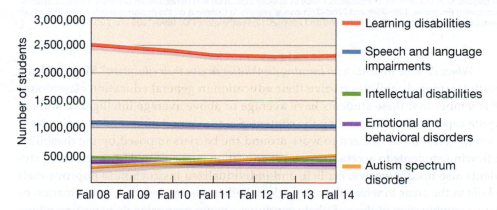

- Learning disabilities
- Speech and language impairments
- Intellectual disabilities
- Emotional and behavioral disorders
- Autism spectrum disorder

SOURCES: From the *22nd* and *23rd* Annual Reports to Congress, U.S. Department of Education Number of Students Served by Disability 1994 Through 2003; U.S. Department of Education, Office of Special Education Programs, Data Analysis System (DANS), OMB #1820-0043: "Children with Disabilities Receiving Special Education Under Part B of the Individuals with Disabilities Education Act" 2011; U.S. Department of Education, EDFacts Data Warehouse (EDW): "IDEA Part B Child Count and Educational Environments Collection," 2014–15. Data extracted as of July 2, 2015, from file specifications 002 and 089. U.S. Department of Education (2013–2015). Child Count and Educational Environments. IDEA Section 618 Data Products: State Level Data Files. Retrieved from http://www2.ed.gov/programs/osepidea/618-data/state-level-data-files/index.html#bccee

During the twentieth century, the numbers of students with learning disabilities steadily increased for decades. When IDEA was first passed, only about one-quarter of all students with disabilities were served in the learning disabilities category. Later, during the 1990s, students with learning disabilities represented half of all students with disabilities who received services under IDEA. However, during this century, the overall percentage of students with learning disabilities has steadily decreased, even though the total percentage of students with disabilities has remained fairly constant. Some experts theorize that the reduction in the prevalence of learning disabilities could reflect the effectiveness of the prevention and early intervention strategies of multi-tiered systems of support like response to intervention. Others hypothesize that improved identification procedures for other disabilities have caused a shifting of students from the learning disabilities category to other disability categories, such as autism spectrum disorder (ASD), which are showing increases.

Percentage of Students Age 6-21 Served Under IDEA: Specific Learning Disability Category

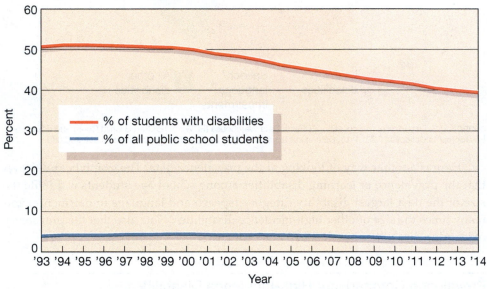

SOURCES: U.S. Department of Education, Office of Special Education and Rehabilitative Services, Office of Special Education Programs, *19th–20th* and *22nd–37th annual reports to Congress on the implementation of the Individuals with Disabilities Education Act, 1995–1998* and *2000–2015,* Washington, DC, 1996–1999 and 2001–2016.

Where do most students with learning disabilities receive their education? Most students with learning disabilities receive their education in general education classrooms. Remember that these students have average or above average intelligence and are quite capable of understanding the content. So, accommodations and assistive technology (AT) can be utilized to work around the barriers imposed by the disability, allowing students to access the general education curriculum. However, these students also need intensive, explicit, and individualized instruction to improve their skills in the areas in which they struggle, whether reading, writing, mathematics, or some combination of those. Debate continues among professionals regarding where these intensive, individualized services should be provided. Some argue that the general education setting is the optimal choice; others maintain that such specialized instruction is more effective in a resource room setting, where the student is pulled from the general education classroom for that portion of the school day. Students with learning disabilities also have mixed preferences in this regard. Some prefer to stay in the general education setting because they don't want to appear different from their peers. Others believe that they can learn better in a small group setting and feel less self-conscious when their peers have similar levels of skill. As with all students with disabilities, placement decisions and service provision must be individualized, based on what is best for each student.

Educational Placements of Students with Learning Disabilities

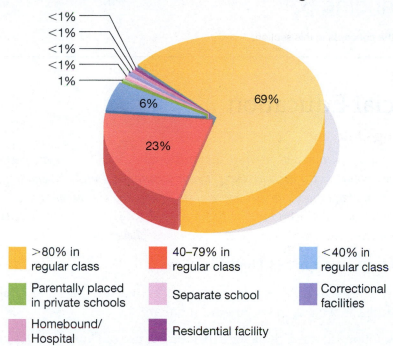

<1%
<1%
<1%
<1%
1%
6%
23%
69%

- >80% in regular class
- 40–79% in regular class
- <40% in regular class
- Parentally placed in private schools
- Separate school
- Correctional facilities
- Homebound/Hospital
- Residential facility

SOURCE: U.S. Department of Education. (2015). *2014 Child Count and Educational Environments, Part B* [IDEA Section 618 Data Products: State Level Data Files]. Retrieved from http://www2.ed.gov/programs/osepidea/618-data/state-level-data-files/index.html

Cultural and Linguistic Considerations: Identification of Students with Learning Disabilities

As we consider the prevalence data for students with learning disabilities, recall some of the concepts discussed in Chapter 3, *Understanding Disproportionality*. At present, there is no reliable method to distinguish between English learners who are struggling in school because of second-language issues and those who are struggling because of learning disabilities. As a result, the U.S. Department of Education reports instances of both over-representation and under-representation across various districts and states. Over-representation occurs when English learners are misidentified as having learning disabilities (false positives) because their poor academic achievement is actually caused by a lack of English proficiency. The opposite situation causes under-representation: educators mistakenly believe that students' poor academic achievement is due to lack of English proficiency when learning disabilities are actually the cause. In either case, students do not receive the appropriate services.

Use of the IQ-achievement discrepancy method can misidentify English learners when a lack of second-language proficiency causes their achievement to fall significantly below their potential. However, use of the RTI model can also misidentify these same students if the instruction in Tier 1 does not meet their second-language acquisition needs. These issues can be addressed by providing professional development for teachers regarding the characteristics and instruction of English learners and by improving referral and identification processes used by schools and districts to identify students with learning disabilities.

The following questions can guide teachers in considering whether a student's poor performance is caused by a learning disability or by characteristics associated with second-language acquisition:

- Is the instruction sufficient to support adequate progress while also addressing linguistic differences?

- How does the student's progress in skill areas (reading, writing, speaking, listening) compare to what would be expected for a student of that age, cultural acclimation, and English proficiency level?

- What other factors could be affecting the student's school performance (e.g., lack of sleep, need for eyeglasses, inconsistent educational opportunities)?

If a student's characteristics are inconsistent with those of second-language development or cultural differences, then additional action by educators may be warranted (e.g., initiation of the pre-referral process for the IQ-achievement discrepancy approach, provision of Tier 2 or secondary intervention services in the RTI process).

Check Your Understanding 6.1

Click here to gauge your understanding of the concepts in this section.

Special Education

Learning Outcome

Explain the ways in which learning disabilities can impact academic performance and interpersonal skills, describe the different accommodations that can lessen these challenges, understand methods that early childhood and classroom teachers can use to reduce the problems associated with learning disabilities, and describe factors to consider during the high school years to promote a successful transition to college.

Topic 6.5 Challenges and Their Solutions

- Learning disabilities create challenges in academics and related skills, as well as in social-emotional areas.

- Solutions to these challenges include the use of Universal Design for Learning (UDL), accommodations, explicit instruction, learning strategies, and other evidence-based practices.

Topic 6.6 Accommodations

- By implementing UDL, teachers can reduce many barriers that students with learning disabilities encounter when trying to learn new content or demonstrate their knowledge.

- Students with learning disabilities often require individualized accommodations to be successful in the classroom.

Topic 6.7 Early Intervention

- The early signs of learning disabilities are often apparent by age three.

- Early intervention during the preschool years can lessen the impact of a learning disability for many children.

Topic 6.8 School Years

- Explicit instruction and learning strategies can improve school performance for students with learning disabilities.

- The process of *how* to use a learning strategy must be explicitly taught for a student to use it effectively.

Topic 6.9 Transition

- In addition to focusing on study skills instruction and self-advocacy during high school, students with learning disabilities should make informed choices when selecting a college.

- Although IDEA does not apply to students in college, many universities offer supports through their offices of disability services.

Although learning disabilities present a number of challenges, many evidence-based practices, supports, and accommodations can reduce the impact of those challenges.

Topic 6.5 Challenges and Their Solutions

- Learning disabilities create challenges in academics and related skills, as well as in social-emotional areas.

- Solutions to these challenges include the use of Universal Design for Learning (UDL), accommodations, explicit instruction, learning strategies, and other evidence-based practices.

What challenges do learning disabilities create? By now, you should have a fairly good idea of the academic challenges faced by these students, particularly in the areas of reading, writing (which includes spelling), and mathematics. Deficits in visual and auditory processing and working memory also affect areas that support academics, like note taking, study skills, and memorization. Tied to these characteristics is difficulty with **generalization**—transferring or applying information or strategies from one situation to another. For example, a student may learn a reading comprehension strategy in social studies but fail to realize that the same strategy can be used in other classes like science or English literature.

Earlier in the chapter we mentioned that students with learning disabilities are resistant to instruction, do not make the same level of academic progress as their peers, and exhibit inconsistent performance—learning or testing well on one day but struggling on another, unable to remember what they have previously learned. Along with the frustration that accompanies such situations, these students often develop **learned helplessness**. Because of their inconsistent performance, they believe their efforts have no bearing on their learning outcomes. Instead, they attribute success or failure to external factors: luck, an easy test, or a teacher who doesn't like them. These attributions lead to passive learning and a lack of motivation; they believe that nothing they can do can make them successful. Often, these students do not ask questions or seek help, either because they do not want to call attention to their struggles or because they feel they have no control over their own learning. When students perform inconsistently, teachers and parents may incorrectly assume that they are "messing around," not trying, or even lying when they say they can't remember how to do something. Many students with learning disabilities complain that adults don't believe them in these situations and that they tire of hearing admonitions like, "You just need to try harder."

Finally, students with learning disabilities often have co-existing language or attention problems, which can cause many of the same social challenges as those for students with language impairments and ADHD (see the *Characteristics* sections for those disabilities in Topic 5.5 and Topic 7.5, respectively). As a result, students with co-existing language impairments may struggle with pragmatics: initiating interactions, engaging appropriately in conversations, or recognizing and repairing communication breakdowns. Students with co-existing attention problems may struggle with social situations in which they fail to process all of the information (conversations, playing games with rules, agreeing to meet friends at a specified time or location).

Challenges: Learning Disabilities

How can the challenges of learning disabilities be lessened or overcome? Approaches to working with these students are multi-faceted. Because these students are resistant to typical instruction, they require intensive, individualized, **explicit instruction** in their deficit areas. Specialists with extensive knowledge in evidence-based interventions for this population of students (i.e., special education teachers) must provide this instruction. However, instruction and learning in all other academic areas cannot be suspended while this remediation takes place. At the same time that special education teachers are working to remediate specific academic areas, these students must continue to receive instruction in the content areas—science, social studies, and so on—*without* letting the effects of the learning disability interfere with their academic progress. General education teachers can incorporate UDL and differentiated instruction to address some of their needs, while also implementing accommodations and using assistive technology to work around the barriers imposed by the disability.

General education and special education teachers can also teach these students **learning strategies**, which are helpful for all students, but particularly for those with learning disabilities. These **metacognitive** strategies teach them *how* to learn and make them more aware of their own learning processes, including their deficit areas and how to work around them. As students become more efficient learners, their negative attributions and feelings of learned helplessness decrease. We will discuss learning strategies in more detail in Topic 6.8, *School Years*. Additionally, because a number of these students have co-existing language disorders, many of the solutions for students with language impairments (discussed in Chapter 5) are also helpful.

Solutions: Learning Disabilities

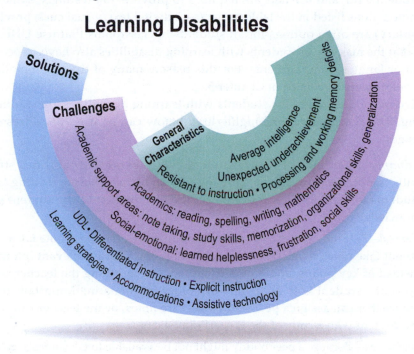

Topic 6.6 Accommodations

- By implementing UDL, teachers can reduce many barriers that students with learning disabilities encounter when trying to learn new content or demonstrate their knowledge.

- Students with learning disabilities often require individualized accommodations to be successful in the classroom.

How can UDL benefit students with learning disabilities? Recall that students with learning disabilities have difficulty processing and understanding visual or auditory information as well as organizing and writing ideas. In addition, due to years of academic failure, they become disengaged and unmotivated to learn. UDL offers flexible options that help reduce these challenges. As you learned in Chapter 2, when implementing UDL, teachers present the content in a variety of ways, allow different options for students to demonstrate their knowledge, and incorporate activities to engage and motivate students. For example, a student who has difficulty comprehending text, perhaps because of poor decoding skills, can access a digital version of the content that can be read aloud. Likewise, a student who struggles with putting his or her thoughts into cohesive and organized ideas in writing can demonstrate knowledge through another means, such as an oral report or a hands-on project. Simply presenting information in multiple ways, using a variety of instructional materials, and offering options to demonstrate learning often lead to increased engagement and greater in-depth learning.

If a teacher is implementing UDL, why would students need individualized accommodations? First, not all teachers implement UDL, and those who do typically start with a few lessons or classes and then gradually expand to other lessons and classes over a number of years. So, not all class sessions will have UDL options for every student. Second, teachers may not provide options that address the individual needs of students with learning disabilities. Although UDL reduces many barriers, these students might also benefit from accommodations, which are stipulated in a student's IEP and teachers are required to provide. Interestingly, some of the accommodations listed in the table below (e.g., digital text, visual cues, previewing vocabulary) are often options for all students in classrooms that use UDL. Also, recall that the majority of students with learning disabilities also have co-occurring speech or language impairments. For this reason, many of the accommodations listed below were also listed in Chapter 5.

Two major challenges for students with learning disabilities are reading and writing. The accommodations highlighted below can be used to address these challenges.

- *Advance organizers*—Because students with learning disabilities struggle with comprehension, advance organizers can be used before reading to alert students to main ideas and to connect the information to the student's prior knowledge.

- *Note takers*—Students with learning disabilities are often poor note takers; some do not take notes, some take incomplete notes or record irrelevant information instead of key points, and others try to record everything the teacher says. To prevent a student with a learning disability from missing important content, the teacher can assign a peer buddy to share notes, or the teacher can provide the student with a copy of the PowerPoint slides.

- *Digital pen*—Because a peer buddy might not be available to take notes (e.g., absent from school) or the teacher may forget to provide copies of slides or other information, a digital pen (also known as a smart pen) can be a great option. While the student is taking notes, this device collects digital data on the student's pen strokes and records the lecture. Later, the student can touch a pen stroke on the paper and listen to what the teacher was saying at the time that particular note was written. Alternatively, the student can upload the digitized notes to a computer and revisit and revise the notes as often as desired. See Topic 6.13, *Technology*, to learn more about this device.

- *Oral response*—Many students with learning disabilities have difficulty expressing their ideas in writing: they record few ideas with little elaboration; do not organize thoughts; have poor handwriting; and/or make spelling, punctuation, and capitalization errors. As an alternate means of demonstrating their knowledge, teachers can allow these students to respond verbally, dictate answers to a scribe, record their answers on a recording device, or use a computer (which is especially useful for students with poor handwriting, spelling, or grammar skills). Recall the student we mentioned earlier who wanted to write *The evil scientist laughed maniacally as his nefarious plan began to unfold.* She knew what she wanted to write, but her learning disability inhibited her capability to get those thoughts down on paper. Imagine how much more detailed and engaging her story would have been if she had been provided with an oral response accommodation!

The following table lists other accommodations that are commonly used for students with learning disabilities.

Examples of Frequently Used Accommodations for Students with Learning Disabilities

Presentation	Setting	Response	Scheduling or Timing
• Previewing vocabulary • Advance organizers • Digital text • Verbal cues • Visual cues (e.g., highlighting, color coding) • Study guides • Pre-teaching key information • Repeating key information or directions • Reader (text, test items)	• Noise-reducing headphones • Checklist of needed items • Quiet area in room or separate room • Testing in a small group	• Word processor • Graphic organizers • Increased wait time • Calculators • Concrete objects and manipulatives • Oral response • Note takers • Spelling and grammar tools • Respond in test booklet rather than on separate answer key • Digital pen	• Extended time for completing assignments and taking tests • Testing breaks • Multiple testing sessions

Topic 6.7 Early Intervention

- The early signs of learning disabilities are often apparent by age three.

- Early intervention during the preschool years can lessen the impact of a learning disability for many children.

What are some of the early warning signs of learning disabilities? Learning disabilities are usually not identified until children start school and are struggling with reading, writing, or mathematics. Although very few preschoolers are identified as having learning disabilities, parents and preschool teachers should be aware of some common early indicators. Because many of these children have language impairments, they exhibit the characteristics discussed in Chapter 5: they do not meet the normal developmental milestones for language acquisition, and they have speech delays and begin talking later than their peers without disabilities. The link between language development and reading is clear. Poor language development explains why so many children identified with language impairments during their preschool years are identified with learning disabilities during their school years.

Many other traits of a learning disability are evident at an early age. The table below summarizes areas in which young children with learning disabilities often demonstrate problems.

Early Warning Signs of Learning Disabilities

Young children with learning disabilities often have difficulty with:

Reading	Writing	Mathematics
• **Phonemic awareness** • **Phonological awareness** • Rapid letter naming	• Holding a pencil or crayon (pencil grip) • Forming letters • Leaving spaces between letters and words	• Counting objects (one-to-one correspondence) • Reading one-digit numerals • Recognizing that objects can be counted in any order and still equal the same number

How can early intervention reduce the impact of learning disabilities? Although the early warning signs listed above are indicative of learning disabilities, those skills are also the foundations for reading, writing, and mathematics. Explicit instruction in these areas during the preschool years has been shown to improve students' skills in these same areas later on. As with any of the disabilities we discuss in this text, the sooner early intervention can begin, the stronger the long-term outcomes will be for the child.

The video below shows early childhood teachers engaging in a range of phonological awareness activities with young students. This early instruction will help build the skills that are essential for the later development of reading.

▶ **REACH Workshop Series: Phonological Awareness**

https://www.youtube.com/watch?v=LucNw_2G_FU

Key Reasons to Intervene Early

- Students who fail to acquire the core skills of early reading during the preschool years often become poor readers for life.

- Students who fail to acquire foundational mathematics skills during the preschool years often find learning mathematics concepts across the school years difficult.

- Students who complete first grade without having mastered phonological awareness tend to be poor readers in fourth grade.

- Approximately 75% of readers who struggle in third grade will continue to struggle with reading in high school.

- Struggling readers do not catch up without intensive, individualized instruction.

- Intensive and explicit instruction on the core skills of reading (such as sound–symbol relationships), delivered early, often helps such students become better readers.

- High-quality instruction, frequent progress monitoring, and additional explicit instruction when the student signals problems learning mathematics skills and concepts can prevent years of school failure.

Topic 6.8 School Years

- Explicit instruction and learning strategies can improve school performance for students with learning disabilities.

- The process of *how* to use a learning strategy must be explicitly taught for a student to use it effectively.

What types of instruction are effective for students with learning disabilities? At the core of a successful education for students with learning disabilities is high-quality general education. The principles of UDL should be in place. Accommodations such as extended time for completing assignments and taking tests or being able to use word processing for written assignments can allow these students to demonstrate their learning. Additionally, students with learning disabilities require explicit instruction in the specific areas of weakness. As you learned in Topic 6.7, because young children with learning disabilities don't automatically "pick up" skills in phonemic or phonological awareness, teachers must provide explicit instruction in those skills. Similarly, school-age students require explicit instruction in reading (decoding, fluency, and comprehension), writing (spelling and composition), and mathematics (computation and problem solving). Further, because these students are resistant to instruction, they require more intensive interventions than those provided during typical instruction. This intensity can be accomplished through various means: giving extra instruction beyond that provided in general education, delivering interventions in a small group or one-on-one format, and increasing the amount of time that the student receives the additional interventions. Ongoing data collection (progress monitoring) must continue, with any instructional decisions being informed by the data.

As students enter the upper grades, the academic demands increase (e.g., reading for information, taking notes, expressing organized thoughts in writing). Students with learning disabilities often struggle and get further behind because they lack the strategies necessary to meet these demands. In Chapter 5, we introduced you to Collaborative Strategic Reading, or CSR, a learning strategy to improve students' reading comprehension skills. Recall that metacognitive strategies—many of which use **mnemonics**—are steps, rules, or methods that can be used for skills like learning information or completing a problem or task independently. They help students, including those without disabilities, learn *how* to learn as opposed to learning specific content. They are not tied to specific subjects, so students can use one strategy across multiple content areas. Because learning strategies are typically used with upper elementary and secondary students, they target the academic demands of those grades: comprehending written text, identifying main ideas and important information, and demonstrating knowledge through writing.

Examples of Learning Strategies

Academic Demand	Learning Strategy
Comprehend written text	RAP—**R**ead **a** paragraph. **A**sk yourself, "What was the main idea? What were two key supporting details?" **P**ut the main idea and details into your own words.
Remember main ideas and important information	First-letter mnemonic strategy—Using the first letter of words in a list or steps, students create another word (acronym) or sentence (acrostic). For example, HOMES is a mnemonic for the five Great Lakes: **H**uron, **O**ntario, **M**ichigan, **E**rie, and **S**uperior.

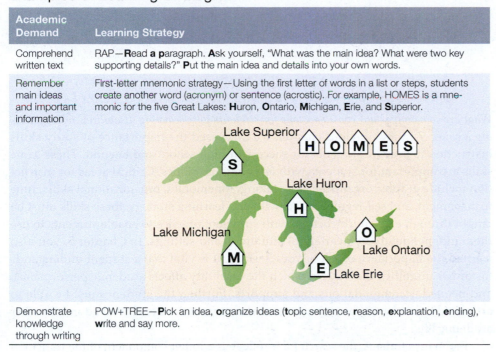

Demonstrate knowledge through writing	POW+TREE—**P**ick an idea, **o**rganize ideas (**t**opic sentence, **r**eason, **e**xplanation, **e**nding), **w**rite and say more.

How do students learn how to use learning strategies? Just as students with learning disabilities need explicit instruction to master skills in key areas, teachers must also explicitly teach learning strategies to students. In fact, teachers can use a strategic and sequential approach to teach their students how to use learning strategies. Learn more about it in the box below.

A Closer Look at Research-Based Practices

Self-Regulated Strategy Development

One approach that has proven effective for teaching learning strategies is Self-Regulated Strategy Development (SRSD). This approach combines teaching students how to use **self-regulation strategies** along with the following six steps for effectively teaching students a learning strategy:

- *Develop background knowledge*—help the student develop the skills needed to use the strategy
- *Discuss it*—discuss how the strategy will help the student and explain the strategy and when to use it
- *Model it*—demonstrate the steps of the strategy while verbalizing the thought processes that occur with each step
- *Memorize it*—require the student to learn the steps and what to do for each step
- *Support it*—provide support and specific feedback as the student is mastering the strategy and gradually fade (or withdraw) support
- *Establish independent practice*—monitor the student as he or she uses the strategy independently and provide opportunities to use the strategy in novel situations

SRSD can be used to teach any learning strategy. You can get more detailed information in the IRIS Module SRSD: Using Learning Strategies to Enhance Student Learning. This Module provides guidance on implementing each of the six steps of the Self-Regulated Strategy Development model to help students learn strategies and improve their academic performance.

▶ **IRIS Module: SRSD: Using Learning Strategies to Enhance Student Learning**

http://iris.peabody.vanderbilt.edu/module/srs/

Topic 6.9　Transition

- In addition to focusing on study skills instruction and self-advocacy during high school, students with learning disabilities should make informed choices when selecting a college.

- Although IDEA does not apply to students in college, many universities offer supports through their offices of disability services.

What are some important considerations for students with learning disabilities when selecting a college? In the previous chapter, we discussed the importance of study skills instruction to prepare students for success in high school and beyond. These same skills are important for students with learning disabilities. Critical areas for instruction include graphic organizers, note taking, mnemonics, organizational skills, time management, and self-regulation. As with any learning strategy, these skills must be taught through explicit instruction, with sufficient practice to enable students to use them independently in a variety of situations and settings. In Chapter 5, you also learned the importance of self-advocacy skills. It is vital that a student understands his or her disability, the ways in which the disability affects academic performance, and needed accommodations and supports. Further, the student must be able to articulate this information to teachers, counselors, and others involved in his or her academic life.

For many students, the search for a college is another component of the transition process. Finding the *right* college is critical to a successful experience. Like all students thinking about attending college, a student with a learning disability should consider these questions:

- Does a school have the academic programs and majors in which I'm interested?
- Where is the school located?
- What are the admissions standards?
- How big is the overall student body, and how many students are in the typical introductory courses?
- Does the school have extracurricular programs of interest to me?
- How much are tuition and fees, and what other expenses will be incurred?

For students with learning disabilities, these additional questions should be considered:

- How comprehensive is the university's office of disability services?
- What supports and services do I need for success?
- Are these types of supports and services offered at this school?

High school students with learning disabilities and their parents should start this process early and carefully research their options. In addition, there are a small but growing number of colleges that have specific programs for students with learning disabilities or that were designed for these students. One of these colleges is highlighted in the box below.

Higher Education for Students Who Learn Differently

Landmark College in Vermont was the first college founded specifically to serve students with dyslexia, expanding over the years to include students with ADHD and autism spectrum disorder. The faculty at Landmark incorporate many of the techniques you have learned about in this text—UDL, learning strategies, specific skill building, and assistive technology—to meet the diverse learning needs of their students. To learn more about Landmark, visit http://www.landmark.edu

What are the differences between services that students with learning disabilities are entitled to in high school and in college? In high school, students have IEPs to guide the delivery of their educational programs and supportive services. Because IDEA covers educational services only through high school, there are no IEPs for college. Section 504 of the Rehabilitation Act of 1973 does apply to students in college, prohibiting discrimination and guaranteeing accommodations, but it is not as comprehensive as IDEA. Nevertheless, more colleges and universities provide responsive and organized support services than in the past. These colleges and universities usually have an office of disability services and well-prepared staff that offer a range of assistance. Services include extended time for test taking, note takers, alternative places to take exams, and provision of some types of assistive technology. Many colleges and universities offer workshops that focus on time management and study skills for all students in order to improve their retention and graduation rates. In other cases, these workshops are provided by the offices of disability services and are designed specifically for students with disabilities, tailored to meet their disability-related needs.

To receive disability services in college, students must show proof of an identified disability. In many colleges, this proof must include an evaluation conducted within a specific, recent period (e.g., within the past two years). Students and their parents should investigate these requirements early in the college selection process to ensure that their evaluations fall within the requisite timeframe. If this is overlooked, students and their families may have to pay for an independent evaluation, which can be costly.

Tips for Transition to College

1. Learn and understand the differences between supports and services guaranteed through IDEA and those that can be obtained in college.

2. Clearly understand and be able to articulate one's disability and how it affects learning needs.

3. Know the accommodations and assistance needed for successful academic achievement.

4. Carefully analyze services available at colleges of interest and match those with individual needs.

5. Create a dossier of high school records, documentation of disabilities and IDEA or 504 eligibility, services and accommodations received, and success with those services.

6. Develop and practice self-regulation strategies, study skills, and organizational and time management practices.

7. Practice self-advocacy techniques.

Check Your Understanding 6.2

Click here to gauge your understanding of the concepts in this section.

People and Situations

Learning Outcome

Describe the history of instruction for students with learning disabilities and identify resources for students with disabilities and their parents.

Topic 6.10 Origins and History

- Early professionals pioneered techniques in explicit instruction, progress monitoring, and learning strategies.

- More recent work in the field has built on and refined evidence-based techniques within the RTI framework while improving transition services and those for English learners.

Topic 6.11 **Personal Stories**

- Many successful individuals with learning disabilities serve as role models for students.

- Eye to Eye and Understood are two organizations that provide support to students with learning disabilities and their families.

Weekend Images Inc./E+/Getty Images

Older students with learning disabilities can be positive role models and mentors for younger students.

Topic 6.10 Origins and History

- Early professionals pioneered techniques in explicit instruction, progress monitoring, and learning strategies.

- More recent work in the field has built on and refined evidence-based techniques within the RTI framework while improving transition services and those for English learners.

How long have learning disabilities been recognized? In the 1920s and 1930s, Samuel Orton, a specialist in neurology, developed theories and remedial reading techniques for children with severe reading problems. He attributed these reading difficulties to some sort of brain injury or central nervous system dysfunction. In the 1930s, Helen Davidson studied letter reversals—writing some letters (such as *b, d, q,* and *g*) backwards—a problem consistently observed in many students with learning disabilities. Before and after World War II, during the 1930s and 1940s, Wayne County Training School in Michigan became a major center of studies regarding the characteristics of students with learning disabilities, intellectual disabilities, and ADHD. There, psychologists like Sam Kirk, Alfred Strauss, and Laura Lehtinen developed specific instructional strategies in response to these students' learning problems. In 1961, the *Illinois Test of Psycholinguistic Abilities* (ITPA) was published. Sam Kirk, the ITPA's primary developer, sought to use it to identify students with learning disabilities and help prescribe instructional approaches based on the test's results regarding student strengths, weaknesses, and learning styles (i.e., whether they learned better by seeing or hearing information). Although the test was used for many years to identify students with learning disabilities, using the test results to guide learning-style–based instruction and remediation was unsuccessful and that theory was debunked. At a landmark meeting of parents and professionals in Chicago on April 6, 1963, Sam Kirk and others coined the term *learning disabilities*. As a result, some school services were then offered to these students. During the 1960s and early 1970s, professionals believed that learning disabilities could be resolved during the elementary school years if the condition were treated early. Therefore, when services for students with learning disabilities began, they were not available for middle and high school students.

During the 1970s, the field of learning disabilities was embroiled in heated debate about effective approaches for students. Referred to as the **process/product debate**, one group promoted instruction directed at improving students' perceptual abilities to remediate reading and other academic skills. The other group argued that explicit instruction would improve students' academic skills. Given the information you've read previously in this chapter, you know which side was correct! The dispute was resolved when research by Don Hammill and Steve Larsen showed that perceptual approaches were seldom effective but that explicit instruction of academic skills improved learning outcomes.

After the debate was put to rest, Tom Lovitt (University of Washington) and Stan Deno (University of Minnesota) conducted research that is the foundation for much of today's work: using explicit instruction to teach academic skills while monitoring students' progress through frequent and direct assessments of their academic work. This was the beginning of the work in **curriculum-based measurement (CBM)** and progress monitoring. Dan Hallahan (University of Virginia) and colleagues recognized the unfocused learning approaches utilized by many students with learning disabilities and developed methods to teach selective attention skills, which improved learning and comprehension.

In the 1980s, researchers found that many students with learning disabilities were not strategic in their approach to academic tasks. Don Deshler and his colleagues (University of Kansas) developed the first learning strategies. They continued to expand and refine this work for decades, with a particular focus on adolescents. The result was the Strategic Instruction Model™, or SIM. SIM addresses the needs of these students as they tackle literacy-related skills of content textbook reading comprehension and secondary writing.

What are some of the more recent advances in the field of learning disabilities? After the turn of this century, Lynn and Doug Fuchs (Vanderbilt University), Don Compton (formerly at Vanderbilt University and now at Florida State University), and Sharon Vaughn (University of Texas) and their colleagues expanded on the foundational work of Tom Lovitt and Stan Deno. They incorporated principles of curriculum-based measurement and progress monitoring in the development of the RTI approaches used in many classrooms today. They continue to refine these processes to help teachers identify struggling learners in Tier 1 more quickly and to make data-based instructional decisions across all tiers.

Research today continues to refine intensive intervention techniques in reading, writing, and mathematics as well as improve the use of accommodations in both instructional and testing settings. As the knowledge base in second-language acquisition grows, researchers now explore the intersection of language and disability and hone techniques accordingly. Other researchers focus on successful secondary transition processes to support the large numbers of students with learning disabilities who now enter post-secondary education settings. Finally, some researchers continue to delve into the neurological processes at the core of learning disabilities, investigating cognitive profiles associated with processing speed and working memory and searching for methods that can differentiate low-achieving students from those with learning disabilities in order to provide more individualized interventions.

Fads and Unproven Practices

Fads and invalidated practices were often promoted during the previous century, frequently with the promise of "curing" learning disabilities. Marianne Frostig developed materials to improve visual perception. She believed that reading abilities would improve if visual perception skills were enhanced—a theory that research did not validate. She was not alone in her inaccurate belief that indirect interventions using perceptual-motor approaches could improve reading skills. Another fad, promoted as a cure, was to have students, regardless of how old they were, use crawling exercises to "repattern" or retrain their brains. Other fads claimed that special diets or plants on students' desks improved academic and behavioral performance. These claims were not backed by scientific evidence.

Unfortunately, traces of these fads still exist today. Despite the lack of evidence that tying instruction to a student's learning style—visual, auditory, kinesthetic—will improve learning outcomes, many educators still believe in its effectiveness. High-tech versions of processing interventions, remnants from the process/product debate, are now available. New apps and computer games claim to increase working memory and improve processing speed (and even delay the onset of Alzheimer's disease). This promotion of invalidated procedures is one reason why current legislation like IDEA and ESSA insists that teachers use evidence-based practices.

Topic 6.11 Personal Stories

- Many successful individuals with learning disabilities serve as role models for students.

- Eye to Eye and Understood are two organizations that provide support to students with learning disabilities and their families.

Courtesy of Paul Orfalea

Paul Orfalea is the founder of Kinkos, and author of the popular book *Copy This!*

Are there positive role models for students with learning disabilities? Absolutely! Many successful individuals with learning disabilities talk openly about their lives—the struggles and the successes—and promote opportunities for others. Business entrepreneurs like Paul Orfalea, the creator of Kinkos, and Charles Schwab, the founder of the discount stock brokerage house, share the challenges they have overcome. In his book, *Copy This!*, Orfalea talks about how he flunked second grade, couldn't learn the alphabet, and attended a separate school for students with intellectual disabilities until he scored 130 on an IQ test. Nevertheless, he graduated at the bottom of his high school class of 1200 students. Possibly because he truly understands individual differences, he went on to develop a business that *Forbes Magazine* ranked for three years in a row as one of the best places to work.

Schwab, an icon in the financial world, admits that he made it through college by compensating for his weaknesses in reading with his strengths in mathematics and economics, and with the support of friends who took notes for him in class. Although he struggled in school, he didn't learn that he had dyslexia until his son was diagnosed with a learning disability.

The Website for the Yale Center for Dyslexia and Creativity (http://dyslexia.yale.edu/index.html) includes brief biographies of more than 60 successful individuals with learning disabilities. The list contains professionals from many fields: business, science, architecture, politics, entertainment, sports, and more. This impressive list is proof of what individuals with learning disabilities can accomplish when provided with the right supports.

What organizations provide support for students with learning disabilities and their families? Eye to Eye (http://www.eyetoeyenational.org) was founded by David Flink, who has a learning disability, and Jonathan Mooney, who has a learning disability and

ADHD. Eye to Eye pairs students with learning disabilities and/or ADHD with mentors who have the same disabilities. Their mission is to improve the life of every person with a learning disability through mentoring and advocacy, supporting his or her full inclusion in every aspect of society. Their overriding principle is that of empowerment through building self-esteem. The program seeks to facilitate academic achievement through self-advocacy, the development of metacognitive skills, and the use of learning strategies and academic accommodations. Through 57 chapters in 22 states, high school and college students mentor younger students through an arts-based program, helping them to learn about themselves, develop self-esteem, and acquire important self-advocacy skills.

Charles Schwab is the founder of Charles Schwab & Co., Inc., one of the nation's largest investment firms.

Understood (https://www.understood.org/) is a coalition of 15 organizations, including several that have already been referenced in this text (or will be in later chapters): National Center for Learning Disabilities (http://www.ncld.org); Learning Disabilities Association of America (http://ldaamerica.org/); CAST (http://www.cast.org/); and Benetech (http://benetech.org/), the host of Bookshare (https://www.bookshare.org/). This coalition, whose mission is to help the millions of parents whose children have learning and attention differences, is also guided by some of the top experts in the field, including Don Deshler, whom you read about in the previous topic. These groups work together to provide research-based, practical information for parents in an easy-to-understand format. In addition to information on characteristics, assessment, instruction, and parenting, the organization's Website has several interactive simulations that help parents (as well as teachers and other interested individuals) to experience first-hand the frustrations of having a learning disability or ADHD.

The Understood coalition's site also has some powerful videos of individuals sharing their personal stories. One of these is included below.

▶ **9-Year-Old Jade Shares Her Dyslexia Story**

https://www.youtube.com/watch?v=Q27DkM4V9rA

Check Your Understanding 6.3

Click here to gauge your understanding of the concepts in this section.

Future Perspectives

Learning Outcome

Explain how preventive measures can reduce the incidence of learning disabilities, describe how new technologies are identifying brain functions associated with learning disabilities, list some considerations when selecting assistive technology, and identify different types of AT that can be used as accommodations.

Topic 6.12 Prevention: Health Care and Technology Advances

- Although little is known about specific causes of learning disabilities, there are some preventive steps that can be universally beneficial to all children.

- New brain mapping technologies are identifying differences in brain functions of individuals with and without learning disabilities.

Topic 6.13 Technology: Selecting Appropriate Assistive Technology

- IEP team members should consider a few key factors when selecting appropriate AT for students with learning disabilities, to ensure maximum use.

- Other features should be considered when selecting apps, including whether they teach or reinforce skills or provide accommodations.

Andrey Popov/Fotolia

Advances in technology give students ways to work around the challenges of their disabilities.

Topic 6.12 Prevention: Health Care and Technology Advances

- Although little is known about specific causes of learning disabilities, there are some preventive steps that can be universally beneficial to all children.

- New brain mapping technologies are identifying differences in brain functions of individuals with and without learning disabilities.

Can learning disabilities be prevented? To prevent a disability, we must first determine what causes it. Unfortunately, specific causes for the neurological dysfunction of learning disabilities have not been clearly identified. What we do know is that multiple factors are *associated with* the presence of learning disabilities. This means that, when these factors are present, more children experience learning disabilities than would be expected. For example, an association appears to exist between genetics and learning disabilities because family members of students with learning disabilities often experience similar characteristics. We gave an example of this earlier: both Charles Schwab and his son have learning disabilities.

Similar to many of the disabilities that you will learn about in this text, there are some prenatal factors associated with learning disabilities, such as maternal

- illness
- drug or alcohol use
- malnutrition

When the supply of oxygen or nutrients is diminished, the growth and development of an unborn child (including his or her brain) is affected. For this reason, low birth weight is associated with many types of learning and developmental delays. Premature infants often have developmental delays; the earlier in the pregnancy the infant is born, the more severe the delays are. Complications during birth—prolonged labor, oxygen deprivation—can also damage a newborn's brain. For older children, exposure to toxins (lead poisoning) or malnutrition can result in brain damage as well. Finally, some learning disabilities have no discernible cause.

So, although definitive causes of learning disabilities are not known, preventive steps can be taken to improve the overall health and development of all children:

- *Reduce high-risk behaviors during pregnancy*—Despite public awareness campaigns about prenatal risks, too many pregnant women have unhealthy lifestyles (smoking, drinking, drugs), resulting in premature births and newborns with low birth weights.

- *Improve maternal prenatal health*—Simple preventive acts like washing hands after using the restroom (yes, we know, but this happens less often than it should), before meals, and after contact with others who are sick, and getting a flu shot can prevent many types of illnesses. Ensuring good prenatal nutrition and receiving prenatal checkups are other positive steps.

- *Address poverty-related challenges*—Children who live in poverty have higher rates of many types of disabilities, including learning disabilities. They are exposed to many of the risk factors listed above, as well as additional environmental factors such as lead-based paint and contaminated water.

Are there medical advances that can help prevent, or reduce the impact of, learning disabilities? Not yet. However, we are making headway with brain mapping technologies that help us understand brain characteristics and functions. A magnetic resonance image (MRI) provides a clear image of any body part that is scanned. Doctors and researchers use MRIs to learn how the brains of individuals with certain disorders, like learning disabilities, differ from the brains of those without the disorders. A functional magnetic resonance image (fMRI) can identify which portions of the brain are active by the amount of blood flow in those regions. Active regions have more blood flow than passive regions. By tracking blood flow while a person is engaging in certain tasks, researchers can identify the regions of the brain associated with those tasks (reading, computation), as well as distinguish differences in the brain functions of individuals with and without learning disabilities. In the future, these brain mapping technologies could help identify causes of neurological dysfunctions, which would then lead to the discovery of potential prevention and treatment methods.

Diffusion magnetic resonance imaging (dMRI) is one of the newest types of brain mapping. Researchers with the Human Connectome Project are using this technology to map the nerve fibers of the brain to track how information flows from one part of the brain to another. They also hope this technology will help them determine causes of breakdowns in these neural pathways and possibilities for repairing them.

This dMRI image, from the Human Connectome Project, shows the nerve fiber connections throughout the brain.

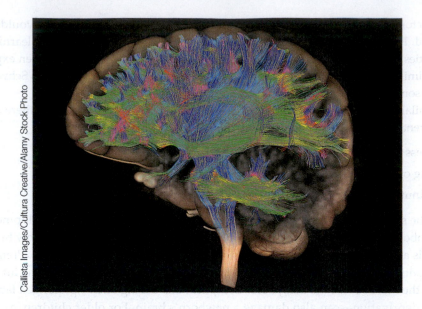

Callista Images/Cultura Creative/Alamy Stock Photo

Although brain mapping holds promise for the future, at present it does not lead to or connect with evidence-based instructional practices. We note this because, as with some of the fads and invalidated practices mentioned earlier in this chapter, there are companies that have begun advertising brain mapping technologies to parents, implying "cures" for their children's disabilities. Educators and parents must be vigilant and analyze claims against the evidence base for any intervention, product, or technology.

Topic 6.13 Technology: Selecting Appropriate Assistive Technology

- IEP team members should consider a few key factors when selecting appropriate AT for students with learning disabilities, to ensure maximum use.

- Other features should be considered when selecting apps, including whether they teach or reinforce skills or provide accommodations.

How can IEP teams select appropriate assistive technology for students with learning disabilities? One responsibility of an IEP team is to determine what types of assistive technology (AT) a student needs to be successful in school. This often involves selecting technology that can help compensate for, or work around, the effects of a student's disability. Unfortunately, many devices are used infrequently, or even abandoned, because IEP teams, parents, and students did not carefully determine whether these tools met key criteria. In other cases, devices are unused because teachers do not understand how or when to use them. The checklist below offers some questions to guide the selection of AT that will be used consistently and effectively and help produce desired outcomes.

Assistive Technology Checklist

- ❏ Does the device support an area of need for the student?
- ❏ Does the device have flexibility to meet a student's changing needs as he or she gets older?
- ❏ Is the device compatible with other AT that the student is using?
- ❏ Is the student willing to use it?
- ❏ Does the student have the necessary skills to use it?

- ❏ Can the student easily learn how to use the device?
- ❏ Are teachers willing to learn how to use the device?
- ❏ Are teachers willing to support its use in the classroom?
- ❏ Can teachers easily learn to use the device?
- ❏ Does the manufacturer (or other agency) provide training, technical support, and repair service for the device?

The IRIS Module below provides information on the various types of assistive technology available, explains how educators can determine appropriate AT devices and services, and shares ways that students' access to AT in the classroom can be expanded.

▶ **IRIS Module: Assistive Technology—An Overview**
(http://iris.peabody.vanderbilt.edu/module/at/)

What types of AT are available to support students with learning disabilities? As you learned in Chapter 5, AT devices come in both low-tech and high-tech options. A low-tech device can be as simple as a pencil grip to help a student with writing, while a high-tech device can be the digital pen that you learned about in Topic 6.6, *Accommodations.*

The video below highlights some of the key features of these digital pens, also known as smart pens.

▶ **Livescribe Echo ® Smartpen Introduction Video**
https://www.youtube.com/watch?v=Lg5QQHIepF0

In addition to AT devices, many other apps are available to help students with learning disabilities. Some of these apps can be used to teach or reinforce certain academic skills (e.g., math facts), while others can be used as accommodations (e.g., text-to-speech). When selecting apps, teachers and parents must consider several factors:

- purpose of the app (teach, reinforce, accommodate)
- age range or age group for which it was developed
- skill that the app addresses
- ease of use
- app's rating

Many organizations provide ratings for apps. Understood, the organization you read about in Topic 6.11, *Personal Stories,* provides ratings on its Website (understood.org). In addition to listing the grade level for which the app is appropriate and ratings on quality and learning, the site provides more in-depth information according to these categories:

- *What parents need to know*—provides a summary of the app and how it works, screenshots, price, compatible devices, and links for downloading
- *What kids can learn*—includes subjects, skills to be learned or reinforced, and physical requirements (tilting, swiping)
- *What's it about?*—an explanation of how the app works
- *Is it any good?*—a summary of helpful or not helpful features, and whether the app addresses the identified skills
- *How parents can help*—suggestions for ways in which parents can support or reinforce the skills that students learn with the app

Bookshare (www.bookshare.org) is another source of AT support for students with disabilities. Specifically, Bookshare supports individuals with print disabilities (those who have difficulty reading print due to learning disabilities, visual impairment, or physical disability) by providing over 488,000 textbooks, novels, magazines, and newspapers in a variety of accessible formats. Students with IEPs can receive these supports for free.

Check Your Understanding 6.4

Click here to gauge your understanding of the concepts in this section.

Summary

Learning Disabilities Described

A learning disability is a neurologically based disorder that results in unexpected underachievement, with uneven patterns of academic strengths and weaknesses, for students who have average or above average intelligence.

- Two methods for identifying learning disabilities are the IQ-achievement discrepancy model and response to intervention (RTI).

- Learning disabilities are often evident in three areas—reading, writing, and mathematics—and students can have disabilities in more than one area.

- Students with learning disabilities often have problems with visual and auditory processing and working memory deficits.

- Students with learning disabilities constitute the largest special education category, with most receiving their education in the general education setting.

Special Education

Students with learning disabilities require explicit instruction and individualized interventions in areas of academic weaknesses while simultaneously maintaining progress in other subjects with supports provided through UDL, differentiated instruction, learning strategies, and accommodations.

- Learning disabilities create challenges in academics and related areas such as note taking, study skills, and organizational skills.

- Because teachers cannot implement UDL methods in every lesson and for all subjects, students with learning disabilities also require individualized accommodations to be successful in the classroom.

- The early signs of learning disabilities are often apparent by age three, but early intervention during the preschool years can reduce their impact.

- Learning strategies can improve school performance for students with learning disabilities, but the process of *how* to use them must be explicitly taught for students to use them effectively.

- In addition to focusing on study skills instruction and self-advocacy during high school, students with learning disabilities should make informed choices when selecting a college, which includes finding out what supports are offered through each institution's office of disability services.

People and Situations

Much of the early work in the learning disabilities field laid the foundation for current evidence-based practices; however, unproven fads were also popular.

- Early professionals pioneered techniques in explicit instruction, progress monitoring, and learning strategies, while recent work has refined evidence-based techniques within the RTI framework, as well as improved services for secondary transition and those for English learners.

- Many successful individuals with learning disabilities serve as role models, and organizations exist that provide support to students with learning disabilities and their families.

Future Perspectives

Although little is known about specific causes of learning disabilities, some preventive steps can be universally beneficial to all children. Technological advances are helping researchers gain important knowledge as well as develop high-tech accommodations.

- New brain mapping technologies are identifying differences in brain functions of individuals with and without learning disabilities.

- IEP team members should consider certain key factors when selecting appropriate AT and apps for students with learning disabilities, to ensure maximum use and benefit.

Addressing CEC Standards

Council for Exceptional Children (CEC) knowledge standards addressed in this chapter: 6.2, 1.0, LD1K1, LD1K2, LD1K5, LD2K1, LD2K3, LD4S9, LD5S1, LD8S1, LD10K1, LD10K2.

See the Appendix for the complete CEC Initial Level Special Educator Preparation Standards.

Chapter 7
Attention Deficit Hyperactivity Disorder

Dee Cercone/Everett Collection/Newscom

"Throughout my life, I struggled with ADHD. It was hard for me at times to sit down, focus and get school work done. As a young adult and adult, I continued having difficulty in the studio as I was trying to write new songs and focus to complete my work. On the first album I remember very distinctly being stuck and not being able to focus. And I had 30 ideas floating through my mind and just couldn't document them . . . So many amazing thoughts, so many amazing ideas, just fall by the wayside."*

—Adam Levine

Nine Grammy nominations and three Grammy awards; platinum and gold album releases; multiple Billboard Music, American Music, and People's Choice awards; coach for the TV show *The Voice*—this list of accolades highlights the creativity and talent of Adam Levine, the lead songwriter and singer for Maroon Five. As you'll learn in this chapter, creativity is an often-recognized strength of individuals with ADHD. Yet even as successful adults, individuals with ADHD can struggle with an inability to focus or to complete an important task.

---

*Source of quotation: Low (2011), Adam Levine Talks About ADHD. Retrieved from https://www.verywell .com/adam-levine-talks-about-adhd-20602

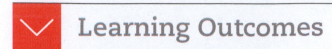

Learning Outcomes

Attention Deficit Hyperactivity Disorder Described

Define ADHD, describe the different types of ADHD, recognize the characteristics of students with ADHD, and understand prevalence and placement data for students with ADHD.

Special Education

Explain the ways in which ADHD can impact academic performance and interpersonal skills, describe the accommodations that can lessen these challenges, understand methods that parents and classroom teachers can use to reduce the problems associated with ADHD, and describe supports to help college students with ADHD stay in school.

People and Situations

Describe the history of instruction for students with ADHD and identify successful individuals with this disability.

Future Perspectives

Describe emerging research into causes of ADHD; identify some of the popular non-validated treatment fads for ADHD; and list some hardware, apps, and software options to help students with ADHD compensate for the effects of this condition.

Attention Deficit Hyperactivity Disorder Described[1]

Learning Outcome

Define ADHD, describe the different types of ADHD, recognize the characteristics of students with ADHD, and understand prevalence and placement data for students with ADHD.

Topic 7.1 Attention Deficit Hyperactivity Disorder Defined

- Students with ADHD demonstrate inattention, hyperactivity, and/or impulsivity to such an extent that their schoolwork is affected.

- The most commonly used definition, from the *DSM-5*, requires that the child demonstrate the behavior across multiple settings and for a prolonged period of time.

Topic 7.2 Types of Attention Deficit Hyperactivity Disorders

- Students with ADHD may demonstrate inattentiveness, or hyperactivity and impulsivity.

- Students can demonstrate attributes of more than one type of ADHD.

[1]References for Chapter 7 are found at the end of this text.

Topic 7.3 Characteristics

- Problems with executive functions are typical for students with ADHD and can negatively affect academics, behavior, and social skills.

- Students with ADHD also exhibit many strengths.

Topic 7.4 Prevalence and Placement

- Although prevalence data on children with ADHD is not collected under IDEA, experts estimate that 11% of U.S. children have ADHD.

- Not all students with ADHD receive special education services; many of those who do are classified under the other health impairments category.

Most people associate hyperactivity and impulsivity with ADHD. However, many do not realize that inattention is another key characteristic.

Topic 7.1 Attention Deficit Hyperactivity Disorder Defined

- Students with ADHD demonstrate inattention, hyperactivity, and/or impulsivity to such an extent that their schoolwork is affected.

- The most commonly used definition, from the *DSM-5*, requires that the child demonstrate the behavior across multiple settings and for a prolonged period of time.

What is ADHD and how is it defined? **Attention deficit hyperactivity disorder (ADHD)**[2] is a condition characterized by excessive inattentiveness, hyperactivity, or impulsivity. Many students, not just those diagnosed with ADHD, exhibit these characteristics. However, students diagnosed with ADHD exhibit them to such a marked degree that they interfere with many daily activities. These students often earn poor or failing grades because they are unable to maintain their attention long enough to read a text-book passage, turn in a worksheet or project, or finish a test. They may get in trouble

---

[2] Although many people refer to this condition as attention deficit disorder (ADD), the current term is attention deficit hyperactivity disorder (ADHD).

with their teachers because they are constantly out of their seats during class, interrupt or talk incessantly, or get distracted by seemingly inconsequential things.

There is no separate ADHD disability category in IDEA; instead, students with ADHD must qualify for special education services under the other health impairment (OHI) category[3]. Possibly because of this, the federal government provides little guidance to states and school districts about the definition to use when identifying students. In the United States, the most widely accepted and used definition of ADHD is the one developed by the American Psychiatric Association (APA) in its *Diagnostic and Statistical Manual of Mental Disorders,* fifth edition (*DSM-5*), which is much more detailed than the federal criteria. Let's look at a few definitions to get a better sense of how this condition can affect a student.

Definitions of ADHD

Term	Definition	Source
Other health impairment	Having limited strength, vitality or alertness, including heightened alertness to environmental stimuli, that results in limited alertness with respect to the educational environment that (i) Is due to chronic or acute health problems such as . . . attention deficit disorder or attention deficit hyperactivity disorder . . . and (ii) Adversely affects a child's educational performance.	IDEA '04, U.S. Department of Education
Attention deficit-hyperactivity disorder	A neurobehavioral disorder that affects 3–5 percent of all American children. It interferes with a person's ability to stay on a task and to exercise age-appropriate inhibition (cognitive alone or both cognitive and behavioral). Some of the warning signs of ADHD include failure to listen to instructions, inability to organize oneself and school work, fidgeting with hands and feet, talking too much, leaving projects, chores and homework unfinished, and having trouble paying attention to and responding to details. There are several types of ADHD: a predominantly inattentive subtype, a predominantly hyperactive-impulsive subtype, and a combined subtype. ADHD is usually diagnosed in childhood, although the condition can continue into the adult years.	National Institutes of Health
Attention-deficit/ hyperactivity disorder	A persistent pattern of inattention and/or hyperactivity-impulsivity that interferes with functioning or development, as characterized by (1) and/or (2) (1) **Inattention:** Six (or more) of the following symptoms have persisted for at least 6 months to a degree that is inconsistent with developmental level and that negatively impacts directly on social and academic/occupational activities [Note: The specific symptoms are listed in Topic 7.2]. (2) **Hyperactivity and impulsivity:** Six (or more) of the following symptoms have persisted for at least 6 months to a degree that is inconsistent with developmental level and that negatively impacts directly on social and academic/occupational activities [Note: The specific symptoms are listed in Topic 7.2].	American Psychiatric Association, *DSM-5* (partial definition)

SOURCES: From 34 CFR Parts 300 and 303, *Assistance to States for the Education of Children with Disabilities and the Early Intervention Program for Infants and Toddlers with Disabilities; Final Regulations* (p. 46757), U.S. Department of Education, 2006, *Federal Register,* Washington, DC; *"What Is Attention Deficit-Hyperactivity Disorder?"* NINDS Attention Deficit-Hyperactivity Disorder Information Page by National Institutes of Health, National Institute of Neurological Disorders and Stroke, 2015, retrieved from www.ninds.nih.gov; *"Attention-Deficit/Hyperactivity Disorder Definition."* American Psychiatric Association, *Diagnostic and Statistical Manual of Mental Disorders,* 5th ed., 2013, pp. 59–65.

The symptoms can be classified along a range from mild to severe. For U.S. children, the average age of diagnosis is seven years; however, for children who display severe symptoms, the average age is five. When ADHD characteristics are not cause for concern at a young age (mild symptoms), they often become noticeable when a child starts school and is unable to sit quietly or pay attention.

What other aspects are considered in an ADHD diagnosis? In addition to specific characteristics of inattention or hyperactivity/impulsivity, the *DSM-5* also lists the following requirements:

- Several inattentive or hyperactive-impulsive symptoms were present prior to age 12.

- Several inattentive or hyperactive-impulsive symptoms are present in two or more settings (e.g., at home, school, or work; with friends or relatives; in other activities).

- There is clear evidence that the symptoms interfere with, or reduce the quality of, social, academic, or occupational functioning.

- The symptoms do not occur exclusively during the course of schizophrenia or another psychotic disorder and are not better explained by another mental

---

[3] Although ADHD is not a distinct IDEA disability category, we include it as a separate chapter in this book because teachers are likely to encounter many students who exhibit the characteristics of this disorder.

disorder. (Source: *"Attention-deficit/hyperactivity disorder definition."* From "Diagnostic and Statistical Manual of Mental Disorders." Published by American Psychiatric Association © 2013, pp. 59–65.)

Let's take a closer look at how key components of the *DSM-5* definition can be applied to a fictional student named Jai. According to the *DSM-5*, ADHD is present only when characteristics are not developmentally appropriate and when they interfere with an individual's social, academic, or occupational performance. Symptoms of the condition must have been present before age 12, have endured for at least six months, and occur in two or more settings. So, if Jai is 13 years old and started exhibiting inattention and distractibility last month during reading class, ADHD would not be a consideration because (1) the characteristics were not present before age 12; (2) they have not endured for at least six months; and (3) they do not occur in more than one setting. However, if Jai's parents and teachers noted these symptoms from age eight, they have been ongoing ever since, and he displays these behaviors at home and in school (which cause significant academic and social difficulties), then ADHD could be a possibility. The following table provides more specificity regarding Jai's symptoms and the ADHD diagnostic criteria.

Application of Diagnostic Criteria

Diagnostic Criteria	Jai's Symptoms
Student displays: • ≥ Six symptoms of inattention.	Jai (13 years old): • Is easily distracted. • Makes careless errors. • Has trouble concentrating. • Is very disorganized. • Usually has incomplete homework. • Avoids activities requiring prolonged effort.
Behaviors must: • Have persisted six or more months. • Have been present before age 12. • Be present in two or more settings. • Be severe enough to affect social, academic, or occupational performance. • Not be caused by other disorders.	**Jai's behaviors:** • Have persisted for five years. • Have been documented by parents and teachers since age eight. • Are observed in most of his school classes, at home, and during baseball practices and games. • Are causing him to fail two subjects. • Are not caused by emotional or behavioral disorders, traumatic brain injury, or any other condition or disorder.

Topic 7.2 Types of Attention Deficit Hyperactivity Disorders

• Students with ADHD may demonstrate inattentiveness, or hyperactivity and impulsivity.

• Students can demonstrate attributes of more than one type of ADHD.

What are the different types of ADHD? Many people think that students with ADHD are basically hyperactive, which is a common misperception. There are actually three types of ADHD. Individuals with ADHD can display symptoms of extreme inattention (referred to in the *DSM-5* as *predominantly inattentive presentation*), hyperactivity and impulsivity (*predominantly hyperactive-impulsive presentation*), or a combination of traits (*combined presentation*).

Some students with ADHD demonstrate predominantly inattentive symptoms. While **inattention** is a characteristic commonly observed by parents and teachers, particularly when sustained effort is required, it is sometimes overlooked. Yet, carelessness, distractibility, and forgetfulness are all associated with this type of ADHD. An inattentive student may be unable to focus for the seemingly short time span required to complete a single math problem. As a result, she may miss many problems on a worksheet, even when it is clear that she has the skills needed to work them accurately. Inattentive students often cannot focus on smaller details, or they pay attention to the wrong features of the task. Problems with attention make it challenging to approach learning in an organized or efficient fashion or to shift from one task to another. The *DSM-5* lists symptoms of inattentive behavior, at least six of which must be present for an ADHD diagnosis (at least five for adolescents and adults over the age of 17):

- Often fails to pay close attention to details; makes careless mistakes in schoolwork, at work, or during other activities
- Often has difficulty sustaining attention in tasks or play activities
- Often does not seem to listen when spoken to directly
- Often does not follow through on instructions; fails to finish schoolwork, chores, or duties in the workplace
- Often has difficulty organizing tasks and activities
- Often avoids, dislikes, or is reluctant to engage in tasks that require sustained mental effort
- Often loses things necessary for tasks or activities
- Is often easily distracted by extraneous stimuli
- Is often forgetful in daily activities (Source: *"Attention-deficit/hyperactivity disorder definition."* From "Diagnostic and Statistical Manual of Mental Disorders." Published by American Psychiatric Association © 2013, pp. 59–65.)

To assist with diagnosis, the *DSM-5* also provides specific examples for each of these symptoms. Note that each symptom contains the word *often*. These symptoms do not occur occasionally; they are evident consistently in a student's daily life.

Some students with ADHD demonstrate symptoms of hyperactivity. **Hyperactivity** is the characteristic most commonly associated with ADHD. However, while this implies an excessive level of activity, teachers' and parents' judgments are often subjective about the concept of "too much." If the activity is admired, then the child might be viewed as energetic or enthusiastic. If the activity is annoying, teachers might describe the individual as fidgety, squirmy, or continually off task.

Some research indicates that hyperactivity diminishes with age as students learn to better control their behavior. However, when compared to their same-age peers, adolescents with ADHD still show significantly greater levels of restlessness and activity. Furthermore, adolescents and adults with ADHD may have ongoing challenges with distractions due to daydreaming, or an ongoing stream of thoughts and ideas flowing through their minds at times when concentration is important (e.g., during a college course or a meeting at work). Some individuals report that although excessive activity is reduced, it is replaced with feelings of internal restlessness.

Impulsivity can be described as an inability to control one's actions or reactions. Students with impulsivity tend to blurt out a quick response before thinking through a question. They may interrupt conversations, make random comments on whatever stray thought occurs to them, or jump into a new activity without finishing a previous one. These behaviors create frustration for their teachers and result in decreased social acceptance from their peers. And because they often act without thinking, these students are at greater risk for engaging in harmful or dangerous behaviors, such as running into the street without looking, jumping off playground equipment from a dangerous height, or trying cigarettes or drugs without considering the consequences.

To avoid some of the problems associated with subjective ratings of hyperactivity and impulsivity, the *DSM-5* provides symptoms, at least six of which must be present for an ADHD diagnosis (at least five for adolescents and adults over the age of 17):

- Often fidgets with or taps hands or feet or squirms in seat
- Often leaves seat in situations when remaining seated is expected
- Often runs about or climbs in situations in which it is inappropriate
- Often is unable to play or engage in leisure activities quietly
- Often is "on the go," acting as if "driven by a motor"
- Often talks excessively
- Often blurts out an answer before a question has been completed
- Often has difficulty waiting his or her turn
- Often interrupts or intrudes on others (Source: *"Attention-deficit/hyperactivity disorder definition."* From "Diagnostic and Statistical Manual of Mental Disorders." Published by American Psychiatric Association © 2013, pp. 59–65.)

Does overlap exist between the types of ADHD? Some students with ADHD will demonstrate a combined presentation of symptoms. Students diagnosed with *combined presentation* exhibit a combination of inattention and hyperactivity-impulsivity. For this diagnosis, students must display the required characteristics for predominantly *inattentive presentation* as well as the required features for predominantly *hyperactive-impulsive presentation*. The following figure illustrates the three types of ADHD and summarizes some of the defining features.

Three Types of ADHD

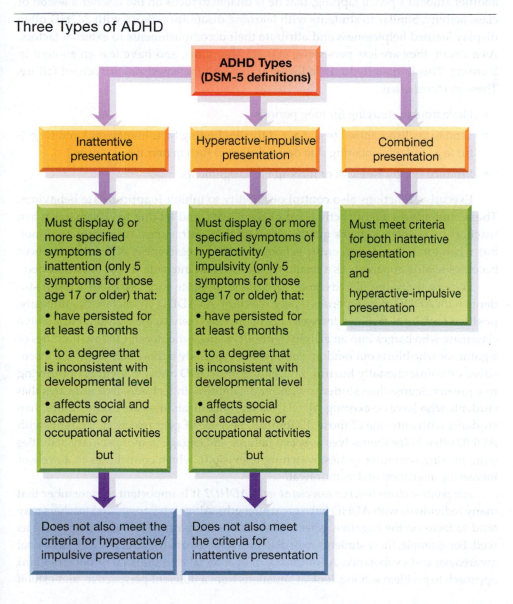

Topic 7.3 Characteristics

- Problems with executive functions are typical for students with ADHD and can negatively affect academics, behavior, and social skills.

- Students with ADHD also exhibit many strengths.

What do inattention, hyperactivity, and impulsivity have in common? The three defining traits of ADHD—inattention, hyperactivity, and impulsivity—are all related to **executive functions**, which are the cognitive abilities that enable us to plan, to self-regulate, and to engage in goal-directed activities. A student with ADHD has impaired planning or organization, which affects the ability to complete tasks or engage in systematic procedures. A child with ADHD may start many projects or chores (like cleaning her room, doing homework, or even drawing a picture) but never finish them. As a result, parents are often frustrated because they need to follow after the child to make sure things get completed. These same characteristics are evident at school, where executive dysfunction often causes problems in academic performance and with behavioral and social skills.

Many students with ADHD experience considerable difficulty with academic performance. Because of their distractibility and inability to focus, they spend less time engaged in academic tasks than their classmates without ADHD. For example, a student with ADHD may be so distracted by extraneous classroom events, such as another student's pencil tapping, that he is unable to focus on the teacher's lesson or class activity. Similar to students with learning disabilities, those with ADHD often display learned helplessness and attribute their accomplishments to external factors. As a result, they are less persistent, expend less effort, and have less enjoyment in learning. This frequently leads to lower grades and increased risk for school failure. These students often:

- Have trouble studying for long periods.
- Tend to be disorganized (e.g., have difficulty finding their homework) and forgetful (e.g., not remembering due dates, failing to turn in permission forms).
- Produce sloppy, careless, or incomplete assignments.

Executive functions also control our ability to inhibit inappropriate behaviors. These students are highly active, out of their seats, and talking to classmates when teachers want them to work quietly. Most of their infractions are relatively minor, but when totaled up for an entire school day, the excessiveness of the disturbances becomes readily apparent. As a result, teacher-student interactions are often strained.

Hyperactivity, impulsivity, and inattention influence social skills; as a result students with ADHD may experience peer rejection. As ADHD characteristics intensify, positive social interactions decrease. Peers are less likely to play with an impulsive classmate who barges into an activity without asking, who doesn't follow the rules of a game, or who blurts out random comments—especially if those comments are insensitive or unintentionally hurtful. Students with ADHD are also victims of bullying to a greater degree than students without disabilities. In fact, research indicates that students who have co-existing ADHD *and* learning disabilities are bullied more than students with only one of those disabilities. Because of peer rejection, students with ADHD often judge themselves as social failures and engage in more solitary activities (e.g., playing computer games, watching television), which contributes to a cycle of increasing alienation and withdrawal.

Are positive characteristics associated with ADHD? It is important to remember that many individuals with ADHD have great strengths. Although parents and teachers may tend to focus on the negative aspects of this disorder, positive features are present as well. For example, these students may display intense creativity, intuitiveness, emotional awareness, and exuberance. Additionally, they may take an unusual or non-standard approach to problem solving, look at situations from a different perspective, and exhibit an ability to "think outside the box." As a result, people with ADHD are highly represented among entrepreneurs, inventors, and artists (see Topic 7.11, *Personal Stories*).

You can learn more about these strengths in the video below and then, in the box that follows, see how they apply to David Neeleman's success.

▶ **Dr. Edward (Ned) Hallowell on ADHD: A Ferrari in Your Brain**

https://www.youtube.com/watch?v=i5D56Cg7y4I

David Neeleman

"If I could take a magic pill to get rid of it [ADHD], I wouldn't."
—DAVID NEELEMAN

Bloomberg/Getty Images

JetBlue CEO and airline entrepreneur David Neeleman exhibits the classic inattentive and impulsive characteristics of ADHD. He readily admits to being "out in space," and those who work with him confess it can be difficult to keep up with his constantly changing train of thought. Yet, Neeleman, who discovered that he had ADHD during his late thirties, considers his ADHD to be an asset. He regards his creativity (which helped him invent the e-ticket, a convenience that airline travelers now take for granted), energy, and ability to multi-task as positive reflections of his ADHD. However, he also uses specific strategies to counter the more frustrating aspects of the disorder. To keep himself organized, he develops routines, always puts important things such as his wallet and watch in the same place, and surrounds himself with highly organized people.

Topic 7.4 Prevalence and Placement

- Although prevalence data on children with ADHD is not collected under IDEA, experts estimate that 11% of U.S. children have ADHD.

- Not all students with ADHD receive special education services; many of those who do are classified under the other health impairments category.

How many students have ADHD? No national registry or required reporting system exists for ADHD, so exact numbers of children with this disorder are unavailable. Current estimates come from various sources, including national parent surveys conducted on behalf of the U.S. Centers for Disease Control and Prevention (CDC). Estimates of ADHD prevalence have been roughly 5% of children. However, the CDC recently released new figures, estimating that approximately 11% of children between the ages of 4 and 17 (6.4 million) have ADHD. Although these percentages indicate that the prevalence rates of ADHD may be higher than those of learning disabilities, not all students with ADHD require special education services. Boys are generally identified at nearly twice the rate of girls; however, some studies have shown that girls are under-identified, possibly due to a lack of awareness of how their behavioral characteristics differ from those of boys. For example, girls identified with ADHD are more likely to have the predominantly inattentive type. Because an inattentive child is less disruptive than a hyperactive or impulsive child, parents and teachers are less likely to notice the symptoms and seek additional supports.

► **ADHD in Girls and Boys: Is It Different?**
https://www.youtube.com/watch?v=TKwvcuRbkU8

According to the CDC, the number of students identified with ADHD has increased 5% annually during the period from 2003 to 2011. Because a historical record of the prevalence of ADHD does not exist, it is impossible to know with any confidence whether the number of students with ADHD is increasing more rapidly than the student population in general. While some speculate that we are over-identifying students with ADHD, others counter that less than half of all children with ADHD receive proper diagnosis and treatment.

Worldwide prevalence rates are approximately 5% but vary greatly. This variability is not associated with geographic location or cultural practices and perceptions, but rather is caused by differences in the definitions used and in the data collection methodology. The prevalence rates in Japan (up to 7%), China (6% to 8%), and New Zealand (up to 7%) are quite similar to previous U.S. estimates, while countries such as Germany (18%) and Ukraine (20%) have much higher rates. Here is an interesting prevalence study from Australia. Parent ratings alone identified 10% of all school-children as having ADHD, while teacher ratings alone identified 9%. At first glance, it would appear that the parent and teacher ratings corroborated each other, right? Wrong! In fact, only 2% of students met the criteria for ADHD when researchers required that both parent and teacher ratings had to agree. This example illustrates how decisions regarding eligibility requirements can cause significant differences in prevalence numbers. Even switching from one edition of the American Psychiatric Association's diagnostic manual to the next (e.g., the *DSM-III* to the *DSM-IV* or to the *DSM-5*) can change prevalence data. Such factors might explain the state-by-state variation in ADHD prevalence shown in the following map.

Percentage of Youth Aged 4–17 with Attention-Deficit/Hyperactivity Disorder by State: National Survey of Children's Health

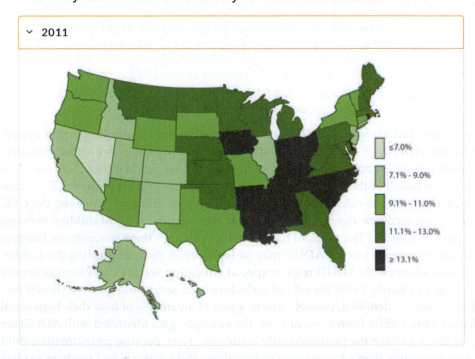

ˇ 2011

≤7.0%

7.1% - 9.0%

9.1% - 11.0%

11.1% - 13.0%

≥ 13.1%

SOURCE: The CDC, part of the U.S. Department of Health and Human Services, provides a wealth of information about ADHD: http://www.cdc.gov

How many students with ADHD receive special education services? The number of students with ADHD who receive special education services is—as you have probably guessed—also unknown. While many students with ADHD are included in the OHI category, it is only one of many conditions within that category (Chapter 11 discusses many of the others), and sub-categorical data are not collected. Because ADHD co-exists with many other disabilities, the problem is further complicated. As you learned in previous chapters, IDEA requires states to report annually on the number of students with disabilities that are served in each category (e.g., speech or language impairments, learning disabilities). However, states report only the number of students served by their *primary* disability. Thus, some students with ADHD are counted in the learning disabilities category, others in the emotional or behavioral disorders category, and so on.

The following graph shows the substantial growth of the OHI category over time. Although multiple health conditions are included in this category, many professionals believe that the dramatic increase in prevalence is tied to ADHD. Recall from Chapter 4 that ADHD was added to this category in the 1997 reauthorization of IDEA. Although the number of students in the OHI category markedly increased after that reauthorization, the increase actually started earlier. What happened at that time to influence this growth? After the 1990 reauthorization of IDEA, the U.S. Department of Education released a joint policy memorandum clarifying that students with ADHD (then referred to as ADD) could receive services under the OHI category if their ADHD resulted in limited alertness that adversely affected educational performance. The timing of the memorandum, coupled with the subsequent rise in the number of students in this category, leads many professionals to believe that the increases are due to the inclusion of students with ADHD.

Increase in Children Ages 6–21 Served Under IDEA: Other Health Impairments Category

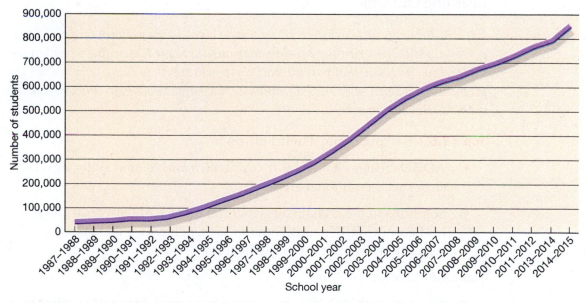

SOURCE: U.S. Department of Education. (2013–2015). *2012–2014 Child Count and Educational Environments*, Part B [IDEA Section 618 Data Products: State Level Data Files]. Retrieved from http://www2.ed.gov/programs/osepidea/618-data/state-level-data-files/index.html

The other health impairments category was a low-incidence category before students with ADHD were included. It is now a high-incidence category. As can be seen in the following chart, it is currently IDEA's third largest disability category, behind learning disabilities and speech and language impairments.

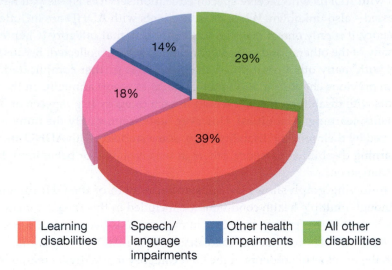

Disability Prevalence: 2014–2015 School Year

- Learning disabilities
- Speech/language impairments
- Other health impairments
- All other disabilities

Check Your Understanding 7.1

Click here to gauge your understanding of the concepts in this section.

Special Education

Learning Outcome

Explain the ways in which ADHD can impact academic performance and inter-personal skills, describe the accommodations that can lessen these challenges, understand methods that parents and classroom teachers can use to reduce the problems associated with ADHD, and describe supports to help college students with ADHD stay in school.

Topic 7.5 Challenges and Their Solutions

- ADHD creates challenges in academics and related skills, as well as in social-emotional areas.

- Solutions to these challenges include the use of Universal Design for Learning (UDL), accommodations, behavior therapy, self-regulation strategies, and medication.

Topic 7.6 Accommodations

- Students with ADHD who demonstrate predominantly inattentive symptoms often benefit from accommodations that address their inability to focus and their lack of organization.

- Students with ADHD who demonstrate hyperactivity and impulsivity may benefit more from accommodations that target their excessive activity and impulsivity.

Topic 7.7 Early Intervention

- Young children with ADHD display inattention, hyperactivity, and impulsivity at a more intense level than typical preschoolers and are usually diagnosed by a pediatrician or other health care provider.

- Behavior therapy is a validated practice in which both children and their parents learn more effective ways of dealing with ADHD-related behaviors.

Topic 7.8 School Years

- Not all students with ADHD receive services under IDEA; some have 504 plans, while others require no additional accommodations or interventions.

- Self-regulation strategies can help students learn to monitor and manage their own behavior.

Topic 7.9 Transition

- College students with ADHD must continue to use strategies and skills they learned in high school while taking advantage of disability services for which they are eligible.

- Several reputable organizations provide sound recommendations and resources for students as they move through the secondary transition process.

Success for adults with ADHD starts with strong supports in the early years that continue throughout their lives.

Topic 7.5 Challenges and Their Solutions

- ADHD creates challenges in academics and related skills, as well as in social-emotional areas.

- Solutions to these challenges include the use of Universal Design for Learning (UDL), accommodations, behavior therapy, self-regulation strategies, and medication.

What challenges are associated with ADHD? As we discussed earlier in the chapter, students with ADHD have impaired executive functioning, which makes sustaining attention difficult. So, these students often appear to be unfocused or daydreaming. Executive functions are also responsible for inhibiting inappropriate behaviors; the impulsivity that accompanies ADHD is directly tied to the lack of these skills. Without the self-control needed to inhibit problematic behaviors, these children often engage in risky and dangerous activities. And, these children sometimes display hyperactivity, which keeps them going long after they should have tired out. An introspective 12-year-old once explained her hyperactivity in this way: "It's like my brain is telling me that I should be tired, but my body wants to keep going!"

The combination of the three ADHD characteristics leads to additional problems besides the academic and social issues already mentioned. Imagine a common childhood situation in which a ball rolls into the street. A child with ADHD is much more likely to run into the street without looking because he (1) doesn't notice the oncoming cars (inattention), (2) does not think to stop and look both ways (impulsivity), and/or (3) simply needs to keep moving and running and doesn't want to stop (hyperactivity). As you might surmise, children with ADHD have more injuries, accidents, and visits to the hospital than those without ADHD. Further, their injuries are more serious; they also have a significantly greater likelihood of being hospitalized for accidental poisoning, of being admitted to intensive care units, and of having a resulting injury-induced disability (e.g., traumatic brain injury).

These children can create frustrating situations for family members: birthday parties are ruined when cakes, furniture, or even other children are knocked over during rough-housing; siblings and other relatives are unwilling to play with a child who won't stop moving and can't follow the rules; and parents may have difficulty hiring babysitters. Parents are often exhausted and feel they are somehow to blame for their child's uncontrollable behavior. Many of these same behaviors transfer to the school setting, where these students have difficulty making friends and cause frustration for their teachers.

For most students, ADHD co-exists with another disability, a situation commonly referred to as **comorbidity**. Researchers estimate that one-third to one-half of all students with ADHD also have learning disabilities, which cause the academic challenges you learned about in Chapter 6. Approximately one-fourth of students with ADHD also have emotional or behavioral disorders, including anxiety, depression, **oppositional defiant disorder (ODD)**, and **conduct disorder (CD)**. Boys exhibit more aggressive and antisocial behaviors, resulting in higher referral rates for this category. Although girls may show equal levels of impulsiveness, they are less likely to be referred to special education for emotional or behavioral problems because they often have lower levels of hyperactivity, aggression, defiance, and conduct problems. Additionally, as you'll learn when we discuss emotional and behavioral disorders in Chapter 10, their symptoms of anxiety and depression are often overlooked.

Challenges: ADHD

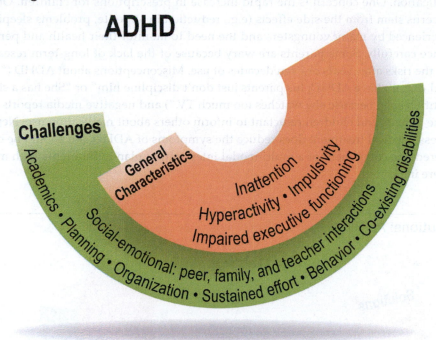

How can the challenges of ADHD be lessened or overcome? As with most students with disabilities, successful approaches are multi-faceted. General education teachers can incorporate UDL and differentiated instruction techniques to create a strong educational base for all of their students. Highly motivating instructional materials can help students stay focused and engaged (again, not just for those with ADHD), and accommodations and assistive technology can provide additional supports in problem areas. **Behavior therapy**, which includes a parent training component, is an effective intervention that will be discussed in Topic 7.7, *Early Intervention,* as the recommended first step for young children. Also, **self-regulation strategies**, a set of effective strategies that help students to monitor and manage their own behavior, will be described in Topic 7.8, *School Years.*

However, before students even begin to engage in learning activities, many need additional help through medication. Think of it this way: just as some students need glasses to see better, some students need medication to help them ignore distractions and pay better attention in class or to control their behavior. Nearly two-thirds of school-age children with ADHD take medication; **stimulant medication** is the most commonly prescribed medical intervention for ADHD. You may be wondering: why give stimulants to a student who is already hyperactive? Actually, the term *stimulant* can be misleading; the medications do not stimulate the entire child, but rather just the brain. These medications are thought to increase the arousal level of the central nervous system, enhancing blood flow or increasing electrical activity in the frontal lobes of the brain. These areas are linked to executive function, so aspects such as working memory, attention, planning, and self-regulation are improved. These stimulants are also believed to increase the levels of certain neurotransmitters that enhance brain functioning. Stimulants, such as Ritalin (methylphenidate), Concerta (methylphenidate), Adderall (dextroamphetamine/amphetamine), or Dexadrine (dextroamphetamine sulfate), are effective for 80% to 90% of students who take medications to help them control behavior. Non-stimulant options are available for children who do not respond well to stimulant medications.

Some controversy surrounds the interplay between ADHD, children, and medication. One concern is the rapid increase in prescriptions for children. Other concerns stem from the side effects (e.g., reduction in appetite, problems sleeping) experienced by many youngsters and the need to monitor their health and performance carefully. Some parents are wary because of the lack of long-term research and the risks after years or even decades of use. Misconceptions about ADHD ("The child doesn't have ADHD; his parents just don't discipline him" or "She has a short attention span because she watches too much TV.") and negative media reports can make parents and children reluctant to inform others about medication use. Nevertheless, medical treatment does reduce the symptoms of ADHD and should be considered one component of a multi-modal intervention plan for students with more severe indicators.

Solutions: ADHD

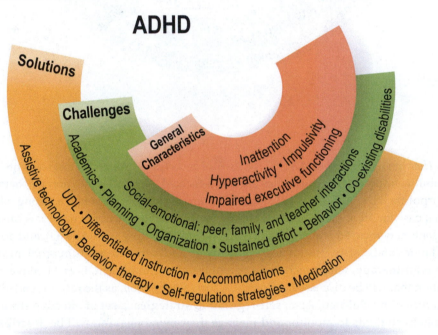

Medication: School-Home Communication

When students are taking medications, educators need to work closely with their families. Teachers spend up to seven hours per day with these students and are likely to notice changes in behavior. As families and medical providers work to select the right medication and adjust dosage levels for maximum benefit, teacher feedback is vital for several reasons.

- These medications are not uniformly effective. Some work better with particular individuals than with others. Families need feedback from teachers on whether the medication is having the desired effect.
- It may take several adjustments to achieve the appropriate dosage for optimum performance, and dosages change as

children grow. Teachers need to communicate their classroom observations to families after a dosage change.
- Parents depend on teachers to relate their observations on side effects because teachers are in contact with students for a large portion of the day.

Still, teachers and family members must keep in mind that, although medical treatment can alleviate the symptoms of ADHD, such treatment alone does not directly improve academic functioning. To make gains in both academics and behavior often requires a combination of behavioral and medical interventions.

Topic 7.6 Accommodations

- Students with ADHD who demonstrate predominantly inattentive symptoms often benefit from accommodations that address their inability to focus and their lack of organization.

- Students with ADHD who demonstrate hyperactivity and impulsivity may benefit more from accommodations that target their excessive activity and impulsivity.

Why do students with ADHD who display symptoms of extreme inattention often benefit from the same accommodations as students with learning disabilities? Recall that students with learning disabilities often share some of the same challenges as students with ADHD (inattentive symptoms). They are forgetful, have difficulty focusing on key features or pieces of information, and approach learning in an unorganized manner. For this reason, many accommodations that benefit students with learning disabilities (e.g., advance organizers, note takers, repeated instructions, visual and auditory cues) are effective for these students as well. In addition, students with ADHD who demonstrate inattentive behavior often make careless errors and have difficulty focusing long enough to complete a task. The accommodations listed below can help reduce barriers created by all of these challenges.

- *Reduced noise or distractions*—Because these students are easily distracted, simply reducing or eliminating distractions can allow them to focus on the task at hand. Two easily implemented accommodations are headphones to decrease noise and study carrels to reduce visual distractions.

- *Checklist of materials*—To address lack of organization (and forgetting important information or steps), teachers can provide a checklist of needed materials or of steps to complete a task.

- *Extra set of books for home*—Because students with ADHD are often forgetful with daily activities, it is not uncommon for them to leave school without needed textbooks and supplies. To help prevent students from getting behind in homework, teachers can provide an extra set of textbooks to be kept at home.

- *Brief assignments*—Because of their short attention span, these students may benefit from short assignments or may perform better if larger assignments are broken into smaller components. In either case, students should receive immediate feedback; this can alert them to careless errors, which they are prone to make.

Why might students with ADHD who demonstrate hyperactivity and impulsivity benefit from different accommodations? These students typically experience different challenges than students who present with inattentive symptoms. They have difficulty with restlessness, excessive activity, concentrating, and controlling their actions. This situation is a prime example of why all students in a given disability category should not be provided with the same accommodations. While all students with ADHD may benefit from some of the same accommodations, their needs vary greatly and their accommodations should be individualized. Following are a few accommodations worth considering for students who display hyperactive or impulsive symptoms.

- *Physical movement*—Often students with this type of ADHD have difficulty sitting still for extended periods and benefit from movement. Teachers can easily accommodate this in a number of ways: allowing the student to stand at his desk while working on classwork, sending him on a quick errand, or assigning a nonacademic task such as erasing the board or feeding the class pet. Certain sensory tools (e.g., hand-held stress ball, rubber band placed around the chair legs that a student can kick) offer students other opportunities for movement.

- *Frequent breaks*—Typically, these students also have difficulty concentrating for a long time. Allowing short breaks after activities, or during long activities or tests, can be beneficial.
- *Teacher proximity*—Students with ADHD are often off task and engage in inappropriate classroom behavior. When teachers are in close proximity to the student, she may be less likely to engage in these behaviors, and if she does, the teacher can more easily redirect her.

The following table highlights some commonly used accommodations for students with ADHD.

Examples of Frequently Used Accommodations for Students with ADHD

Presentation	Setting	Response	Scheduling or Timing
• Advance organizer • Verbal or visual cues • Prompts • Repeating instructions • Recorded instructions • Organized materials	• Quiet area or separate room • Reduced noise/distractions • Study carrels • Preferential seating • Checklist of needed materials • Small-group or one-on-one instruction • Extra set of books • Sensory tools	• Note-takers • Graphic organizers	• Extended time for tests • Frequent breaks • Multiple testing sessions • Shorter, more frequent study periods • Brief assignments (or broken into parts)

In addition to providing accommodations, teachers can make adjustments to classroom and instructional practices to help these students achieve greater success. The following table lists a few common situations that teachers may encounter and tips for dealing with them successfully.

Tips for Teachers

Common Problem Areas	Tips for Teachers
Academic	
Initiating work	• Gain student's attention. • Use clear, one-step instructions. • Provide directions orally and in writing.
Completing assignments	• Provide specific, positive reinforcement when each task is completed. • Set a standard for acceptable work. • Provide a rationale for completion. • Assign a peer assistant.
Behavioral	
Remaining on task	• Use hands-on activities. • Assign highly motivating activities. • Alternate instructional activities frequently.
Making transitions from one activity to another	• Give a 5-minute warning before changing from one activity to another. • Use a standard, predictable schedule. • Remind the student about requirements during transitions (e.g., clear items off desk, line up in small groups).

Topic 7.7 Early Intervention

- Young children with ADHD display inattention, hyperactivity, and impulsivity at a more intense level than typical preschoolers and are usually diagnosed by a pediatrician or other health care provider.

- Behavior therapy is a validated practice in which both children and their parents learn more effective ways of dealing with ADHD-related behaviors.

How are young children with ADHD identified? The defining characteristics of ADHD are inattention, hyperactivity, and impulsivity—common features of most preschoolers! For this reason, some parents might not recognize the early signs of ADHD, believing that the behaviors are typical for young children. Remember however that children diagnosed with ADHD exhibit these characteristics at a higher rate and with more intensity than typical children. Although the average age of identification for children with ADHD is seven years, the average age for children with severe symptoms is five, and toddlers are now being diagnosed as early as age two. For many of these children, parents and preschool teachers have been dealing with behaviors associated with ADHD for several years prior to an official diagnosis. In many cases, they feel frustrated with the child's behavior or with their own inability to manage or control it.

For concerns they have at home, parents often first seek help from their child's pediatrician or other health care professional. The pediatrician may handle the identification process or refer the family to a child psychologist or psychiatrist. These professionals use the *DSM-5* definition of ADHD, in conjunction with family and teacher interviews and behavioral checklists, to make a diagnosis. A child with a clinical diagnosis of ADHD does not automatically receive early intervention services or special education services when he or she starts school. To qualify for special education services, the student must have symptoms severe enough to adversely affect educational performance.

What are effective interventions for young children who have ADHD? The first recommended course of action is behavior therapy, also referred to as **behavior modification**, cognitive-behavioral intervention, or psychosocial treatment. Behavior therapy focuses on reducing or eliminating problem behaviors *and* on introducing and increasing positive behaviors. Consider this scenario: four-year-old Paolo likes to run in circles around the living room, jumping on the sofa and coffee table. His mother is frustrated and yells at him constantly, while his father implements various forms of punishment (time-out, sending him to his room, taking away toys). Both parents express heightened stress levels and end up arguing about how best to handle his behavior. In Paolo's case, the goals of behavior therapy would be to reduce his running and jumping behavior and increase more positive alternatives (e.g., walking and sitting; asking to go outside, where running and jumping are appropriate). Behavior therapists would also work with Paolo's parents, showing them effective, appropriate methods for intervening.

The parent training component of behavior therapy helps families:

- *Establish a structured home environment*—Students with ADHD require more structure than those without ADHD. By providing structure, parents help children understand expectations and consequences for when those expectations are not met.

- *Utilize positive reinforcement effectively*—Reinforcing positive behavior is important, and students with ADHD often have difficulty with delayed gratification. Therefore, providing specific, immediate feedback has shown greater effectiveness than giving feedback after a prolonged period.

- *Deliver consequences fairly and consistently*—Consequences must be laid out as part of a structured home environment. Any inconsistency in the delivery of consequences causes confusion for the child and inadvertently sabotages the process.

- *Intervene appropriately when a problem is present*—Without training, parents might resort to ineffective interventions (e.g., yelling, spanking) rather than those yielding a positive effect.

- *Communicate effectively with school and medical professionals*—Whenever possible, child care or preschool personnel should be working on the same behaviors that family members are targeting at home. Medical professionals can help monitor progress and recommend additional resources if necessary.

Behavior therapy is not a quick fix; it takes some time for behavioral changes to occur. The American Academy of Pediatrics and the CDC stress that behavior therapy should be the *first* intervention for young children and that medication should be added as a second treatment when behavior therapy alone is not enough. Here are some research findings that families should be aware of:

- For very young children, the effects of behavior therapy, when implemented consistently, are just as strong as medication.

- The positive effects of behavior therapy are still evident several years after treatment.

- Those who start behavior therapy first require lower doses if medication is eventually added.

- A multi-modal treatment approach that incorporates behavior therapy and medication has proved to be more effective than medication alone.

Unfortunately, as the following graph illustrates, current data indicate that far more young children are taking medication than are receiving behavior therapy. Because of this, the CDC has a public awareness campaign aimed at increasing the use of behavior therapy as the first course of action.

Treatment Types Among Young Children with Employer-Sponsored Insurance in Clinical Care for ADHD

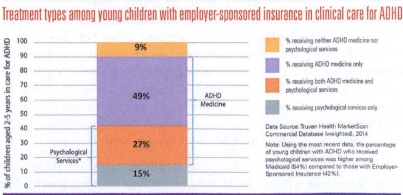

SOURCE: "ADHD in Young Children," Centers for Disease Control and Prevention, 2016, retrieved from http://www.cdc.gov/vitalsigns/adhd/

In the video below, Dr. Thomas E. Brown explains the advantages of behavior therapy and medical interventions for ADHD, as well as outcomes that stimulant medication *cannot* produce.

▶ **ADHD Treatment | ADHD Medication**

https://youtu.be/6dRjtOggw-c

Topic 7.8 School Years

- Not all students with ADHD receive services under IDEA; some have 504 plans, while others require no additional accommodations or interventions.

- Self-regulation strategies can help students learn to monitor and manage their own behavior.

What types of school services do students with ADHD receive? When it comes to school services, students with ADHD fall into three groups.

1. Some students perform adequately in the classroom and require no additional supports. These students may have received multi-modal interventions in which a combination of previous behavioral interventions and current medication dosages address their needs adequately. Another reason these students do not require additional supports is that they have been assigned a teacher who is highly structured and organized, follows predictable routines, and provides engaging and motivating instruction. In these cases, parents and teachers need only monitor progress to ensure that students continue to perform well.

2. Some students receive accommodations (e.g., extended time on tests or assignments) through Section 504 of the Rehabilitation Act but do not receive special education services. These students qualify for services through Section 504 if they have a "physical or mental impairment that substantially limits one or more major life activities." Learning is considered a major life activity. Rights guaranteed under Section 504 include assessment, an individualized education, due process, and some parental and due process proceedings. As you might remember from Chapter 4, Section 504 is a civil rights law, which guarantees individuals with disabilities access to society. Students with disabilities are denied access to an education when they encounter barriers to learning, which school personnel are subsequently required to remove. As such, school personnel must provide accommodations that reduce or eliminate the learning barriers called out in a student's **504 plan**. Typically, 504 plans are developed for students who do not qualify for special education services under IDEA.

3. Other students qualify for special education services under IDEA if it is determined that: (1) they have a disability, and (2) the disability negatively affects educational performance to the extent that they require specialized services. These students have an IEP that specifies the special services they receive, including accommodations to assignments or tests to compensate for the disability.

Service Options for Students with ADHD

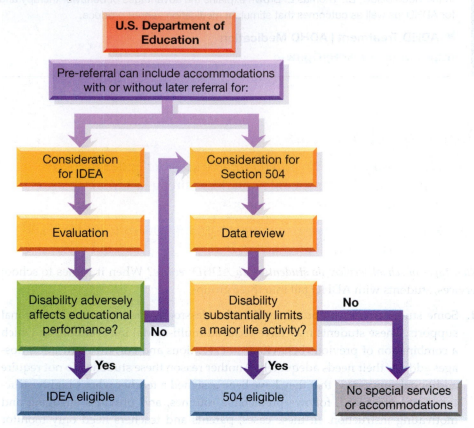

```
                    ┌──────────────────────┐
                    │  U.S. Department of  │
                    │      Education       │
                    └──────────────────────┘
                    ┌──────────────────────┐
                    │ Pre-referral can include accommodations │
                    │    with or without later referral for:  │
                    └──────────────────────┘
```

Consideration for IDEA	Consideration for Section 504
Evaluation	Data review
Disability adversely affects educational performance? → **No**	Disability substantially limits a major life activity? → **No**
↓ **Yes**	↓ **Yes**	→ No special services or accommodations
IDEA eligible	504 eligible	

SOURCE: Adapted from *ADHD and Education: Foundations, Characteristics, Methods, and Collaboration* (p. 16), by S. S. Zenthall. (2006). Upper Saddle River, NJ: Pearson Education, Inc.

Watches that have a silent vibrating alarm can be used in place of a pre-recorded audio beep (see the Self-Regulation box on the next page). When the watch vibrates, the student self-monitors and then checks the worksheet. Many of these watches contain multiple alarm settings that can be used as reminders for other tasks (leaving for school, taking medication [for older students and adults]).

How can teachers support students with ADHD in their classrooms? Students with ADHD, more than others, need structure to support learning and social performance. Teachers can help in many ways. First—and this benefits *all* students in class—they should have a comprehensive classroom behavior management plan that includes:

- Clear and concise rules.
- Descriptions of common classroom procedures.
- Consequences that are implemented consistently and fairly.

Students with ADHD perform better academically and behaviorally in highly structured classrooms with predictable routines. General behavioral supports can include clear directions, advance notice about upcoming changes in activities, and prompts for students who appear to be slipping off task.

Second, teachers can make assignments interesting and relevant to students' backgrounds and interests, as well as implement principles of UDL and differentiated instruction. Students with ADHD can maintain focus better when instruction and learning activities are varied. Because many students with ADHD also have language impairments or learning disabilities, their academic supports are similar to those you read about in Chapters 5 and 6. **Learning strategies** provide students with explicit and systematic methods for completing academic tasks, such as solving math problems, writing paragraphs or reports, or memorizing content area facts.

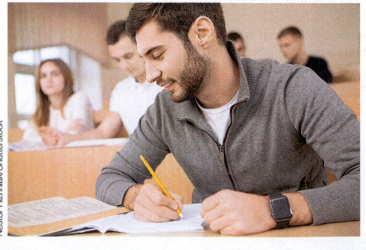

Graphic organizers can help students focus on and connect the important elements of the material. **Study skills** instruction is especially helpful for students who are passive learners, while instruction and coaching in organization and **time management** skills can reduce the clutter in students' desks and lockers, help them organize and use their time more effectively, and reduce the number of lost and incomplete assignments. Finally, and perhaps most importantly, training in self-regulation strategies can help students learn to monitor and regulate their own behavior. The box below describes this strategy in more detail.

A Closer Look at Evidence-Based Practices

Self-Regulation

Self-regulation strategies, sometimes referred to as **self-management strategies**, are procedures that a student can use to control his or her own behavior or improve academic performance. Typically, self-regulation strategies are grouped into four categories:

- **Self-monitoring**—A student assesses his own behavioral or academic progress and records the results, often using a checklist or a self-monitoring sheet (see example below).

- **Self-instruction** or **self-talk**—A student uses self-induced statements or words of encouragement to guide himself through a task or an activity (e.g., writing a paragraph, staying focused, coping with difficult situations, evaluating an answer, congratulating oneself on completing a task).

- **Goal setting**—A student, often with the help of a teacher, determines a goal, which can include a series of smaller sub-goals. This goal should be achievable (not too easy or too hard) and measurable.

- **Self-reinforcement**—A student selects a reinforcer and rewards himself once he has completed a task or achieved a pre-determined goal. Reinforcers can be tangible (e.g., pencil, pizza), social (e.g., working with a partner, a movie with friends), or activity-related (e.g., computer game).

  Although self-regulation strategies can be used independently, they also work in combination. Let's look at how these four strategies can be combined to help Hayden, who has difficulty staying focused during classroom instruction and frequently daydreams instead of completing independent work. To address these behaviors, the teacher meets

with her and explains that Hayden is now going to be responsible for self-regulating her own behavior. By using the self-monitoring sheet below, Hayden will keep track of her performance (being on task). Each time she hears a beep from pre-recorded audio, she asks herself, "Was I paying attention? Was I doing what I was supposed to be doing?" Hayden learns to evaluate her own behavior by determining whether it is appropriate (on task) or not (off task). She records this information by placing a check in the row designated ☺ (Yes) or ☹ (No). Collaboratively, Hayden and her teacher decide that Hayden's goal is to maintain on-task behavior for an entire class period. However, she will start with a smaller sub-goal of 7 minutes and gradually work up to the entire period. To keep herself on task during independent work, Hayden uses self-instruction statements such as, "Stay focused. Only five more questions to go." At the end of each class period, Hayden reviews her self-monitoring sheet. If she has at least seven checks indicating that she was on task, she then rewards herself (self-reinforcement) with a sticker.

Sample Self-Regulation Form for On-Task Behavior

Student's name: __*Hayden*__   Date: _11–6_

Ask yourself: **"Was I on task? Was I doing what I was supposed to be doing?"**

Check yes or no when you hear the beep.

	1	2	3	4	5	6	7	8	9	10
☺ YES	✔		✔	✔	✔		✔		✔	✔
☹ NO		✔				✔		✔		

You can learn more about self-regulation strategies in the following IRIS Module, which contains in-depth information and includes examples of self-monitoring, self-instruction, goal setting, and self-reinforcement.

▶ **IRIS Module: SOS: Helping Students Become Independent Learners**
http://iris.peabody.vanderbilt.edu/module/sr/

Topic 7.9 Transition

- College students with ADHD must continue to use strategies and skills they learned in high school while taking advantage of disability services for which they are eligible.

- Several reputable organizations provide sound recommendations and resources for students as they move through the secondary transition process.

What skills and supports benefit students with ADHD who transition from high school to college? Although professionals once believed that children and youth with ADHD would outgrow their problems, we now know that, for most individuals, the symptoms continue throughout their lives. The transition to college for students with ADHD begins with a strong foundation in high school. Yet, many of these students already show negative traits that sabotage their academic success. Recent research shows that, compared to their peers without disabilities, high school students with ADHD report significantly:

- More substance abuse.
- Lower academic engagement and less time studying.
- More emotional difficulties.
- More time partying, playing computer and video games, and engaging in online social activities.

When post-secondary goals and activities are considered, these students are:

- Less likely to apply for or enroll in post-secondary education.
- Less likely to attend a four-year college or university.
- More likely to receive failing grades.
- More likely to withdraw from classes.
- Less likely to earn a degree.

Given these statistics, it is clear that students with ADHD require a range of supports to become successful independent adults.

The transition planning process includes many of the same considerations mentioned in earlier chapters. In Chapter 5, we discussed the importance of preparing students for college: providing study skills instruction, helping them be aware of high school graduation requirements (e.g., minimum number of courses, GPA), and teaching them how to self-advocate. In Chapter 6, we discussed factors to consider when selecting a college: entrance requirements and eligibility for and provision of supports through a university's office of disability services. Once students are enrolled in college, the next step is to ensure that they are successful and earn their degrees.

Clearly, strong study skills are crucial for college success; yet those needed in college are different from those in high school. In college, students must study for courses that have only a few tests per semester, in contrast to the more frequent (e.g., monthly, unit) tests given in high school. College students have more independent reading than in high school and are expected to write more papers with greater page length requirements. The needed organization and time management skills also differ from those in high school. In college, the daily and weekly class rhythm is a change from the all-day schedule of high school. Students are also learning to manage evenings and weekends without curfews, to find time for independent living tasks (e.g., doing laundry), and more. This can be challenging for many students, even more so for those with ADHD.

Building on the information presented in the IRIS Module *Study Skills Strategies (Part 1)*, information on specific skills and strategies for students with ADHD and learning disabilities can be found in the second Module in the series. These strategies can be helpful for students in high school and in college.

▶ **IRIS Module: Study Skills Strategies (Part 2): Strategies that Improve Students' Academic Performance**
http://iris.peabody.vanderbilt.edu/module/ss2/

One of the most critical steps a student with ADHD can take to ensure college success is to utilize the offerings available through the college's office of disability services. However, too many students with disabilities do not take advantage of them. Further, they often do not use the accommodations to which they are entitled. In some cases, they merely want to see whether they can be successful without them or are reluctant to reveal their disability to professors and peers. In other cases, they do not understand the types of accommodations available or how to request them (which illustrates the need for strong self-advocacy skills). Sometimes, time management and organizational skills are required to access the accommodations, and lack of proficiency in these areas undermines success. For example, a student with ADHD has an accommodation to take her exams in the disability services office, where she can get extra time in a distraction-free environment. However, she must notify her professors several days in advance so that they can send a copy of the test to the disability service office counselors. Because her ADHD affects her advance planning skills, she forgets to notify her professors; takes the tests in the regular course classrooms, several of which are large auditoriums with many distractions; and fails them. Too often, students with disabilities request accommodations only after they are already failing, rather than from the beginning of the semester. If a student is failing, it can be difficult—or even impossible—to bring his or her grade up to a passing level, especially if the semester is nearly over.

Steps to Successful Post-Secondary Transition

What are the reputable resources and organizations available to help guide students with ADHD through the transition process? Many organizations and resources are available to students and their families. In addition to addressing concerns related to the transition to college, they also offer resources for adults with ADHD about transitioning to a job, supports in the workplace, and more. Here are a few:

- *Understood* (http://www.understood.org)—This organization (which you learned about in Chapter 6) devotes an entire portion of its Website to the transition process: Leaving High School. In addition to college considerations such as community college vs. four-year college and online vs. face-to-face, the site has good information on other post-secondary options: vocational programs, gap year, military, and entering the workforce immediately after high school. The site also describes programs at various universities that are specifically equipped to provide support services to students with ADHD.

- *Going to College* (http://www.going-to-college.org)—Adolescents can access a lot of information about the transition from high school to college through this Website, developed by Virginia Commonwealth University as a resource for teenagers with disabilities.

• *The National Resource Center on ADHD* (http://www.help4adhd.org)—This organization has an entire section of its Website devoted to adults with ADHD. The resources cover important topics like workplace issues, laws and legal protections, and living with ADHD across the lifespan.

Check Your Understanding 7.2

Click here to gauge your understanding of the concepts in this section.

People and Situations

Learning Outcome

Describe the history of instruction for students with ADHD and identify successful individuals with this disability.

Topic 7.10 Origins and History

• The first documented characteristics of ADHD occurred during the late 1700s.

• ADHD research is conducted by professionals from many different fields.

Topic 7.11 Personal Stories

• Many individuals with ADHD learn to channel their creativity and high energy into successful careers.

• Books about individuals with ADHD can educate and motivate young children.

Alexander Crichton and George Still were among the first physicians to document the symptoms of ADHD.

Topic 7.10 Origins and History

- The first documented characteristics of ADHD occurred during the late 1700s.

- ADHD research is conducted by professionals from many different fields.

Is ADHD a newly discovered disorder? No, characteristics of ADHD have been well documented for over 200 years. In 1798, Scottish physician Alexander Crichton published a description of attention disorders that included many aspects of the inattentive presentation recognized today. Crichton discussed an "inconstancy of attention," which referred to constant movement because of an inability to maintain attention. He even argued that some forms of inattention would decrease with age. In the 1840s, Dr. Heinrich Hoffmann of Germany published a children's book of playful poems and whimsical stories filled with characters such as Slovenly Peter and Idle Fritz, meant to teach young children about the pitfalls of improper behaviors. "The Story of Fidgety Philip," one of the more famous poems from the book, describes a child who clearly has many characteristics of ADHD. Nearly 60 years later, Dr. George Still, a British physician, described children who had problems with inattention and impulsivity, which he attributed to a "defect of moral control." In his classic 1902 article, Still noted that the prevalence was greater among boys than girls and that most cases were apparent in early childhood.

The Story of Fidgety Philip

The Story of Fidgety Philip
By Heinrich Hoffmann, 1845

"Let me see if Philip can
Be a little gentleman;
Let me see if he is able
To sit still for once at table."
Thus spoke, in earnest tone,
The father to his son;
And the mother looked very grave
To see Philip so misbehave.
But Philip he did not mind.
His father who was so kind.
He wriggled
And giggled,
And then, I declare,
Swung backward and forward
And tilted his chair,
Just like any rocking horse;-
"Philip! I am getting cross!"

See the naughty, restless child,
Growing still more rude and wild,
Till his chair falls over quite.
Philip screams with all his might,
Catches at the cloth, but then
That makes matters worse again.
Down upon the ground they fall,
Glasses, bread, knives forks and all.
How Mamma did fret and frown,
When she saw them tumbling down!
And Papa made such a face!
Philip is in sad disgrace.

SOURCE: Struwwelpeter Merry Tales and Funny Pictures, by Heinrich Hoffman, Project Gutenberg eBookRelease date April 23, 2004 [EBook #12116]

When did the focus change from physicians' anecdotes to research and education? Interest in ADHD heightened after a 1917–1918 encephalitis epidemic, when doctors noticed distinct behavioral and cognitive issues in children who had survived the brain infection, including problems with attention, activity regulation, and impulsivity. During the 1930s, Kurt Goldstein further documented learning and behavior issues associated with brain injury in his work with injured World War I German soldiers. American researchers Heinz Werner, Newell Kephart, Alfred Strauss, and Laura Lehtinen, influenced by Goldstein's work, posited a theory of brain injury in the late 1930s and 1940s, which was eventually modified to include milder terminology such as "minimal brain dysfunction" when no clear evidence of actual brain injury could be found. William Cruickshank built upon their work in his research with students with cerebral palsy, where brain injury could be positively established, and developed demonstration classrooms for students with average intelligence who exhibited characteristics such as hyperactivity and distractibility. Cruickshank's classroom environments were distraction-free: daily routines were strictly adhered to, students worked in cubicles, the walls had few decorations (if any), and even the wearing of jewelry by teachers was discouraged. While the results of his program were mixed—students showed gains in behavior but not academics—his classrooms were the forerunners for the highly structured learning environments recommended for students with ADHD today.

Research in the 1960s focused primarily on hyperactivity, while the 1970s saw increased awareness of the problems associated with poor attention span and impulse control. Although studies during this period became more rigorous, non-validated treatments that focused on the reduction of sugar and food additives in a child's diet became popular, as did the unfounded belief that hyperactivity could be attributed to poor childrearing practices. Luckily, studies in the 1980s confirmed the effectiveness of stimulant medication and also showed that the more negative and controlling parenting behaviors observed by researchers—and initially thought to have caused the child's behavior—were in fact developed in response to their children's inability to effectively control their own actions. Neuroimaging studies within the past 20 years have further verified a biological basis for this disorder, with clear indications of reduced activity in regions of the brain that control attention and inhibition.

ADHD continues to be the most researched childhood condition, with studies conducted by professionals in education, medicine, neuroscience, psychology, and more. Despite the abundance of research and worldwide prevalence, some people still continue to question its existence, blaming the impulsive and hyperactive behavior of children with ADHD on other factors (e.g., poor parenting, too much sugar, TV, video games).

Topic 7.11 Personal Stories

- Many individuals with ADHD learn to channel their creativity and high energy into successful careers.

- Books about individuals with ADHD can educate and motivate young children.

Who are some successful people with ADHD? Conduct an Internet search for "famous people and ADHD" and you'll probably be surprised at the names that appear. Many inventors and entrepreneurs are on this list, evidence of the creativity and ingenuity that we discussed earlier. A large number of entertainers and athletes also make the list, many of whom credit the arts and sports for helping them cope successfully with ADHD. As you read earlier, singer Adam Levine has ADHD. He is also the spokesperson for the "Own It" campaign, which seeks to increase awareness of adult ADHD. As you look at the chart below, you may recognize Paul Orfalea, the founder of Kinkos, whom you read about in Chapter 6. In fact, many of these individuals have co-existing learning disabilities, which is quite common.

Famous People with ADHD

Inventors	Entrepreneurs	Writers	Entertainers	Athletes
Thomas Edison	Henry Ford	Emily Bronte	Robin Williams	Terry Bradshaw
Benjamin Franklin	Bill Gates	Samuel Clemens (Mark Twain)	Will Smith	Cammi Granato-Ferraro
Alexander Graham Bell	Paul Orfalea	Leo Tolstoy	Justin Timberlake	Michael Jordan
Orville and Wilbur Wright	Richard Branson	Robert Frost	will.i.am	Jason Kidd

Debbie Phelps, a middle school principal and mother of Olympic swimmer Michael Phelps, is an advocate for parents and their children with ADHD. She speaks openly about her life parenting a distracted, energetic child who would often show up at the starting blocks without his goggles or swim cap! Like many parents, Debbie Phelps initially attributed Michael's high energy level to the stereotypical active behaviors of little boys. However, when teachers expressed their concerns year after year, she sought help. Michael was diagnosed with ADHD at age nine. Debbie attributes Michael's current success to a combination of factors that you have learned about in this chapter: medication, behavior therapy, constant praise and reinforcement, and swimming as an outlet for his energy. In an interview to promote her bestselling book, *A Mother for All Seasons*, she discussed the need for organization and structure in children's lives and stated, "whether they have ADHD or not they need boundaries, limitations, routine and consistency. That's what I tried to do with Michael. Every day after school, he would put his back pack in the same place in our house, maybe go shoot some hoops, come in for a nutritious snack, and then pack his bag for swim practice. He followed his daily schedule on a regular basis. He knew his stuff had to be done in order to go swimming."

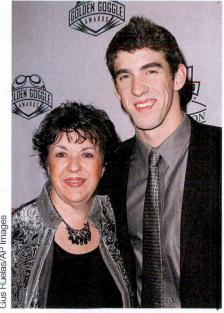

Gus Ruelas/AP Images

Olympic swimmer Michael Phelps, pictured with his mother, Debbie, has earned 28 Olympic medals (23 of which are gold), making him the most decorated Olympian of all time. He has brought attention to the strengths, as well as the pitfalls, of individuals with ADHD. Drug- and alcohol-related incidents have resulted in several suspensions from competitive swimming and a suspended jail sentence. The impulsivity and impaired ability to thoroughly think through the consequences of such actions are typical ADHD traits.

Where else can young people with ADHD turn for inspiration or information? Literature for children and adolescents can provide insight into ADHD. Through the title character's descriptive yet poignant storytelling, teachers and students who read *Joey Pigza Swallowed the Key* learn how much he wants to behave and cooperate and how desperately he craves the approval of the adults and peers in his life, despite his inability to sit still or remain quiet. Readers gain insight into the way his frenetic brain works as he moves from one uncompleted activity to the next, in part because his inability to focus is tied to his over-abundance of attention paid to everything else going on around him.

Percy Jackson, the teenage demigod hero of the *Percy Jackson and the Olympians* series, has ADHD and a learning disability. Throughout the series, Percy deals with the challenges of his disabilities with humor while appreciating the strengths that keep him and his friends alive as they move from one dangerous adventure to the next.

Inspirational Imperfect Heroes

> "Making Percy ADHD/dyslexic was my way of honoring the potential of all the kids I've known who have those conditions."
>
> —RICK RIORDAN

Bob Hallinen/Anchorage Daily News/MCT/Newscom

The best-selling novel series *Percy Jackson and the Olympians* began as a bedtime story for Rick Riordan's young son, Haley. Haley struggled in school and disliked reading. However, he loved Greek mythology, so his father, a middle school teacher and author, would recount the famous stories at bedtime. One night, when they had run out of new stories, Haley encouraged his father to make one up, and the premise for Percy Jackson was created. Later, when Haley was diagnosed with ADHD and dyslexia, Riordan decided to incorporate those characteristics into his demigod boy hero. In fact, all of the demigods in that series and its sequel series, *Heroes of Olympus*, have ADHD and dyslexia, indicators of their elite Olympian heritage. Scores of young readers with ADHD and dyslexia have written to Riordan, sharing how his books have changed their perceptions of themselves and of their abilities. Riordan hopes that his fictional heroes will motivate struggling students everywhere to define themselves by their strengths.

You can learn more about the characters in each of Rick Riordan's series at www.rickriordan.com

From "Rick Riordan on four ways to get kids with ADHD to read." by Rick Riordan. Published by Dow Jones © 2010.

Check Your Understanding 7.3

Click here to gauge your understanding of the concepts in this section.

Future Perspectives

Learning Outcome

Describe emerging research into causes of ADHD; identify some of the popular non-validated treatment fads for ADHD; and list some hardware, apps, and software options to help students with ADHD compensate for the effects of this condition.

Topic 7.12 Prevention: Emerging Research

- Researchers are currently investigating causes of ADHD, some of which appear to be interrelated.

- Some treatments are unproven through research, even though they are popular.

Topic 7.13 Technology: Selecting Appropriate Assistive Technology

- Smartphone and tablet apps can support time management and organization skills.

- Software applications that support study skills are helpful for students with ADHD.

Wavebreakmedia Micro/Fotolia

The growing number of tech devices and apps now provide many resources and supports for students with ADHD.

Topic 7.12 Prevention: Emerging Research

- Researchers are currently investigating causes of ADHD, some of which appear to be interrelated.

- Some treatments are unproven through research, even though they are popular.

Can ADHD be prevented? The exact causes of ADHD are unknown, so preventive efforts cannot yet be developed. Researchers believe the condition arises from multiple sources that could include some sort of brain injury (from trauma or infection), heredity (there appears to be a strong genetic component), and risk factors (e.g., prenatal exposure to alcohol or tobacco; childhood exposure to lead). Therefore, many of the universal recommendations for pregnant women listed in Chapter 6 are applicable: reducing high-risk behaviors such as smoking and drinking, improving prenatal health, and addressing poverty-related challenges. Greater efforts must also be undertaken to prevent childhood exposure to toxins. For example, medical professionals are well aware of the effects of lead ingestion on children. Yet, in the wake of the Flint, Michigan water crisis, dangerously high lead levels have been found in the water sources for homes, schools, and child care centers in other cities and states, causing renewed worry for parents.

Studies investigating precise neurological conditions related to ADHD have found that subjects with ADHD show:

- Decreased blood flow and electrical activity in the frontal lobes of the brain (areas responsible for executive functions).

- Anatomical differences in various regions of the brain.

- Differences in neurotransmitter levels (chemicals, such as dopamine, responsible for the transfer of messages from one part of the brain to another).

Emerging research has shown links between ADHD and exposure to pesticides. One study found that children with the highest levels of organophosphate pesticide residue (detected through urine samples) also had the highest rates of ADHD. Several concerns arose from the study:

- Organophosphates eliminate pests by affecting the nerve connections in their brains. Pesticide exposure in animal studies resulted in hyperactivity and cognitive impairments, so there are implications for similar effects on children.

- Because organophosphates are typically eliminated from the body within three to six days, the pesticide levels in this study indicate continuous exposure, most likely through commonly eaten fruits and vegetables.

- Children with marginally higher than acceptable levels of pesticide residue were twice as likely to exhibit ADHD traits, indicating that even low levels of the pesticide can cause adverse effects.

Although organophosphates are banned for residential use, they are still used commercially. However, residential pesticides that replaced organophosphates are also showing links to ADHD-like behaviors.

Are certain preventive and treatment measures invalid? As you learned earlier, despite the fact that ADHD is the most heavily researched childhood disorder, its history is replete with practices that were not research-validated but instead based on popular public opinion. Unfortunately, this trend still occurs today, especially with regard to special diets or supplements that are purported to alleviate the symptoms of ADHD. Here are a few research findings in this area:

- Despite subjective parental reports that additive- and preservative-free diets significantly reduced their children's symptoms, carefully controlled research studies have failed to confirm their effectiveness. These diets may be beneficial for a small sub-group of children who react adversely to additives and preservatives, but they are not a cure for ADHD.

- Hypoallergenic or elimination diets that remove possible sensitizing foods from children's diets have shown mixed results. The diets often restrict foods that include cow's milk, wheat cereals, eggs, chocolate, nuts, and citrus foods, so they are time-consuming and difficult for most families to implement. As with the diets above, these may be beneficial for a small subset of children with specific food allergies but cannot be generalized to the entire population of children with ADHD.

- A link exists between ADHD and low levels of polyunsaturated fatty acids. While omega-3 and omega-6 supplements have been researched as potential treatments, the results are not clearly demonstrated. Further research is warranted.

- Research has indicated that zinc supplements have potential for decreasing ADHD symptoms, but specifically for individuals in Middle Eastern countries with endemic zinc deficiencies. U.S. studies have shown that zinc supplements may enhance the effects of stimulant medications, but more research is needed.

- Studies investigating the correlation between low iron levels and ADHD have shown mixed results. Similar to zinc, iron supplements may enhance the effects of stimulants, but, again, more research must be conducted to increase knowledge in this area.

The takeaway from these research findings is that, although a healthy diet is beneficial for any child, restrictive diets or supplements have little effect on ADHD symptoms. Teachers and parents should use evidence-based practices—such as those discussed earlier in this chapter—to improve outcomes for children with ADHD.

Topic 7.13 Technology: Selecting Appropriate Assistive Technology

- Smartphone and tablet apps can support time management and organization skills.

- Software applications that support study skills are helpful for students with ADHD.

Can technology help students with ADHD work around some of their challenges? Absolutely! Advances in technology offer many possibilities for students with ADHD. Because many people with and without disabilities use devices such as tablets, smartphones, and even tech-saturated watches, these items do not call undue attention to an individual, which is a common concern for many students and adults with disabilities. Also, the proliferation of such devices has resulted in increasingly lower costs.

Many applications for smartphones and tablets are helpful for students with ADHD. A good number of these are standard on devices. For example, basic calendar apps allow a student to enter events such as upcoming project and assignment due dates, tests, appointments, and sports practices. These calendar apps come with options that allow users to color-code entries (e.g., chemistry/blue, algebra/green, sports/purple), set reminder alarms, and add notes (e.g., "Bring calculator for Algebra test"). Other apps allow students to write reminders, make checklists, and set time intervals within which to finish each item on the list. Workout apps with programmable interval timers can be used as self-regulation supports; the same beep designed to signal an athlete to change workout modes can signal a student to do a self-check of attention and to self-record progress.

Example of a Calendar App

Parents, teachers, and students can also find many apps that are designed and advertised for use by individuals with ADHD. As with any item, potential users should read the reviews and ratings before purchasing or downloading, as some do not live up to their advertising. As we mentioned in Chapter 6, www.understood.org provides ratings and other helpful information for many disability-specific apps. Here is a quick activity: Go to the app store and search "Pomodoro" (which means *tomato* in Italian, and is also a productivity technique in which tasks are broken down into 20- or

25-minute segments). Analyze the available apps, considering factors such as ratings, features, age range, price, and so on. Determine which one might be helpful for a student with ADHD, then compare to see how your ratings compare to those on www.understood.org. You might even find an app that can be helpful for you!

Are there other types of technology that can be helpful for students with ADHD? Software applications also benefit students with ADHD. Many students turn in work that has undecipherable handwriting or that contains disorganized or jumbled thoughts. In these cases, basic word processing software can help to eliminate sloppy handwriting and formatting, while also providing supports like spellcheckers. Software designed to help students write essays or reports can provide structure to organize scattered thoughts, place them in a logical sequence, and then produce a written document that is formatted and pleasing in appearance. As we noted in Chapter 5, programs such as *Kidspiration®* and *Inspiration®* assist students by facilitating their creation of graphic organizers for studying and writing reports.

Many school textbooks now have complementary Websites that offer interactive activities to supplement and enhance the text's content, such as these flashcards for beginning Spanish students. The combination of interactivity with audio and video links is appealing to students with ADHD who have shorter attention spans and may feel the need to switch activities more frequently.

Interactive Websites

Other technology supports are particularly suited to students with ADHD. Students can access information through Website pages that provide interesting text and stimulating pictures combined with video or audio clips. Being able to change activities frequently maintains their interest more than reading a book chapter or a handout packet for a prolonged period. Similarly, the ability to click on hyperlinks to access supplemental information or to engage in interactive learning activities provides further opportunities to shift attention frequently. As with any technology, teachers must make sure the software is easy to use. For example, some software programs are not intuitive to students; they may require training on how to input, access, or retrieve information. Similarly, not all online learning activities are equally accessible. The usefulness of all technology should be determined carefully, perhaps with help from a specialist in assistive technology.

Check Your Understanding 7.4

Click here to gauge your understanding of the concepts in this section.

Summary

Attention Deficit Hyperactivity Disorder Described

ADHD is a condition in which individuals demonstrate inattention, hyperactivity, and/or impulsivity to such an extent that their schoolwork, employment, or other areas of their lives are negatively affected.

- The most commonly used definition of ADHD, from the *DSM-5*, requires that a child demonstrate characteristics across multiple settings and for a prolonged period.
- Students with ADHD may demonstrate inattentiveness, hyperactivity and impulsivity, or a combination of characteristics.
- Although students with ADHD exhibit many strengths, problems with executive functions are typical and can negatively affect academics, behavior, and social skills.
- Not all students with ADHD receive special education services; many of those who do are classified under the other health impairments category.

Special Education

ADHD creates challenges in academics and related skills, as well as in social-emotional areas. Learning disabilities also create challenges in academics and related areas such as note taking, study skills, and organizational skills.

- Solutions to these challenges include the use of Universal Design for Learning (UDL), accommodations, behavior therapy, self-regulation strategies, and medication.
- Successful accommodations may vary, depending on whether the student is displaying predominantly inattentive symptoms or predominantly hyperactive and impulsive symptoms.
- Young children are usually diagnosed by a pediatrician or other health care provider.
- Not all students with ADHD receive services under IDEA; some have 504 plans, while others require no additional accommodations or interventions.

- Behavior therapy is a validated practice in which both children and their parents learn more effective ways of dealing with ADHD-related behaviors; self-regulation strategies can help students learn to monitor and manage their own behavior.
- College students with ADHD must continue to use strategies and skills they learned in high school while taking advantage of disability services for which they are eligible.

People and Situations

ADHD has been documented since the 1700s, with research conducted by professionals from many different fields.

- ADHD is the most researched childhood disorder.
- Many individuals with ADHD learn to channel their creativity and high energy into successful careers.

Future Perspectives

Researchers are currently investigating causes and treatments for ADHD.

- Universal prevention measures (e.g., good prenatal health and care) are helpful; however, some treatments are unproven through research, even though they are popular.
- Many smartphone and tablet apps can support time management and organization skills, while software applications can support study skills.

Addressing CEC Standards

Council for Exceptional Children (CEC) knowledge standards addressed in this chapter: 6.2, 1.0, 5.0, 5.5, 4.0, 7.0.

See the Appendix for the complete CEC Initial Level Special Educator Preparation Standards.

Chapter 8
Autism Spectrum Disorder

Belinda Butler

Belinda (left) and her daughter Helen (right) with Justin at his high school graduation.

Personal Perspective

Belinda Butler is the mother of three children, two of whom have autism spectrum disorder (ASD). Here, she shares her current thoughts about her older son, Justin.

"So what's he going to do now?" I am asked that question a lot now that Justin has graduated and received his special education diploma. The short answer is that Justin will continue to accompany his life skills classmates into the community to learn job skills at one of their work sites a couple of days per week. But I spend a lot of time thinking (and worrying) about what he will do after age twenty-one.

Everyone needs a "day program" to maintain his or her mental health. For some a day program is called a job; for some it's called parenting. For others it is volunteering or being a student. These endeavors provide a change of scenery, socialization with people outside the family, and a sense of purpose. These "day programs" give life texture and variation, providing a delineation between weekday and weekend, and between work and leisure.

I have toured local programs, and talked to countless parents in an effort to find a day program for Justin. The vast majority of options require a level of independence that Justin does not possess at this point in his life. Many options are prohibitively expensive. Many have waiting lists so long it feels futile to add his name at the bottom. And honestly, we haven't found a good fit.

So the long answer to the what's-he-going-to-do question is "I don't know, yet." Justin and I will continue to look, and hopefully we will find something that will allow new and purposeful experiences with friends and an appropriate level of support. Wouldn't it be great if we could all find that?

Over the years, Belinda has written personal perspectives for numerous editions of this book. We share several of them throughout this chapter, in the hope that her perspectives will help you understand the kinds of issues that families face at different times in their lives. In addition, Belinda's daughter, Helen, will share her personal perspective about growing up with two brothers who have ASD—Justin and her twin, Trevor.

Learning Outcomes

Autism Spectrum Disorder Described

Define autism spectrum disorder (ASD), describe the different types of ASD, recognize the characteristics of students with ASD, and understand prevalence and placement data for students with ASD.

Special Education

Explain the ways in which ASD can impact academic performance and interpersonal skills, describe accommodations that can lessen these challenges, understand methods that parents and classroom teachers can use to reduce challenges associated with ASD, and describe supports to help students with ASD transition to post-secondary options such as school, work, and independent living.

People and Situations

Describe the history of instruction for students with ASD and understand some of the fraudulent research claims that have plagued the field.

Future Perspectives

Describe emerging research into causes of ASD, identify some of the popular non-validated treatment fads for ASD, and understand how teachers and parents can select appropriate apps for students and themselves.

Autism Spectrum Disorder Described[1]

Learning Outcome

Define autism spectrum disorder (ASD), describe the different types of ASD, recognize the characteristics of students with ASD, and understand prevalence and placement data for students with ASD.

Topic 8.1 Autism Spectrum Disorder Defined

- Autism spectrum disorder is characterized by deficits in social interactions and communication skills and by fixated interests and repetitive behaviors; definitions differ based on the focus of the defining organization or agency.

- Several terms are used to refer to this condition, some of which purposely do not use people-first language.

Topic 8.2 Types of Autism Spectrum Disorder

- The levels of severity for ASD range from mild to severe.

- An individual may demonstrate a variety of severity levels across different skills and traits.

---

[1]References for Chapter 8 are found at the end of this text.

Topic 8.3 Characteristics

- Deficits in social communication and interaction create difficulties in interpersonal relationships for individuals with ASD.

- The need for sameness and restrictive, repetitive behaviors can cause problems in the execution of everyday activities.

Topic 8.4 Prevalence and Placement

- The prevalence of ASD is increasing at a dramatic rate.

- There are many hypotheses concerning the cause of the increase but no definitive answers.

Amelie-Benoist/BSIP/Alamy

A child who shows little or no interest in interacting or communicating with others might be exhibiting key characteristics of ASD.

Topic 8.1 Autism Spectrum Disorder Defined

- Autism spectrum disorder is characterized by deficits in social interactions and communication skills and by fixated interests and repetitive behaviors; definitions differ based on the focus of the defining organization or agency.

- Several terms are used to refer to this condition, some of which purposely do not use people-first language.

What is autism spectrum disorder, and how is it defined? **Autism spectrum disorder (ASD)** refers to a condition characterized by:

- Deficits in social interactions and communication skills.
- Fixated interests and repetitive behaviors.

ASD has many different definitions, each of which reflects the focus of the organization or agency for which it was developed. For example, the IDEA definition requires that the individual's educational performance be adversely affected in order to qualify for special education services (as you would expect based on what you have learned in previous chapters). The *DSM-5* definition reflects a more diagnostic focus—again, something you would expect based on what you learned in Chapter 7. In contrast, the definitions from the Office of Head Start and Autism Speaks are far less detailed. We include five definitions for comparison in the following table.

Definitions of ASD

Term	Definition	Source
Autism	*Autism* means a developmental disability significantly affecting verbal and nonverbal communication and social interaction, generally evident before age three, that adversely affects a child's educational performance. Other characteristics often associated with autism are engagement in repetitive activities and stereotyped movements, resistance to environmental change or change in daily routines, and unusual responses to sensory experiences. (i) Autism does not apply if a child's educational performance is adversely affected primarily because the child has an emotional disturbance [as defined by IDEA]. (ii) A child who manifests the characteristics of autism after age three could be identified as having autism if the criteria [above] are satisfied.	IDEA '04, U.S. Department of Education
Autism spectrum disorder	A. Persistent deficits in social communication and social interaction across multiple contexts, as manifested by the following, currently or by history. 1. Deficits in social-emotional reciprocity 2. Deficits in nonverbal communicative behaviors used for social interaction 3. Deficits in developing, maintaining, and understanding relationships B. Restricted, repetitive patterns of behavior, interests, or activities, as manifested by at least two of the following, currently or by history. 1. Stereotyped or repetitive motor movements, use of objects, or speech 2. Insistence on sameness, inflexible adherence to routines, or ritualized patterns of verbal or nonverbal behavior 3. Highly restricted, fixated interests that are abnormal in intensity or focus 4. Hyper- or hyporeactivity to sensory input or unusual interest in sensory aspects of the environment C. Symptoms must be present in the early developmental period (but may not become fully manifest until social demands exceed limited capacities, or may be masked by learned strategies in later life). D. Symptoms cause clinically significant impairment in social, occupational, or other important areas of current functioning. E. These disturbances are not better explained by intellectual disability (intellectual developmental disorder) or global developmental delay. Intellectual disability and autism spectrum disorder frequently co-occur; to make comorbid diagnoses of autism spectrum disorder and intellectual disability, social communication should be below that expected for general developmental level.	American Psychiatric Association, *DSM-5* (partial definition)
Autism	A child is classified as having autism when the child has a developmental disability that significantly affects verbal and non-verbal communication and social interaction, that is generally evident before age three and that adversely affects educational performance.	Office of Head Start
Autism spectrum disorder	Autism spectrum disorder (ASD) is a developmental disability that can cause significant social, communication and behavioral challenges. There is often nothing about how people with ASD look that sets them apart from other people, but people with ASD may communicate, interact, behave, and learn in ways that are different from most other people. The learning, thinking, and problem-solving abilities of people with ASD can range from gifted to severely challenged. Some people with ASD need a lot of help in their daily lives; others need less.	Centers for Disease Control and Prevention
Autism spectrum disorder Autism	Autism spectrum disorder (ASD) and autism are both general terms for a group of complex disorders of brain development. These disorders are characterized, in varying degrees, by difficulties in social interaction, verbal and nonverbal communication and repetitive behaviors.	Autism Speaks

SOURCE: From 34 CFR Parts 300 and 301, *Assistance to States for the Education of Children with Disabilities and Preschool Grants for Children with Disabilities*; Final Rule (pp. 1260–1261), U.S. Department of Education, August 14, 2006, *Federal Register*, Washington, DC; "*Autism Spectrum Disorder Definition.*" American Psychiatric Association, *Diagnostic and Statistical Manual of Mental Disorders*, 5th ed., 2013, pp. 50–59; "*Eligibility Criteria: Autism.*" 45 CFR Chapter XIII, Head Start Program Performance Standards; U.S. Department of Health and Human Services, Administration for Children and Families, Office of Head Start. p. 176; "*Facts About ASD.*" Centers for Disease Control, 2016, retrieved from http://www.cdc.gov/ncbddd/autism/facts.html; "*What Is Autism? What is Autism Spectrum Disorder?*" Autism Speaks, 2016, retrieved from https://www.autismspeaks.org/what-autism

What are some of the terms associated with ASD? You probably noticed that some definitions use the term *autism spectrum disorder*, while others use **autism**. There are two reasons for this. First, this represents another example of terminology that is constantly changing. In general, the term *autism* has been replaced with *autism spectrum disorder*; however, it takes time for changes to take hold. The second reason has to do with the source. Notice that both IDEA and the Office of Head Start—educational agencies—use the term *autism*. The Centers for Disease Control and Prevention (CDC) and the American Psychiatric Association—medical organizations—use the term *autism spectrum disorder*. It is possible that the educational term will change when IDEA is next reauthorized, but that is yet to be seen. Finally, Autism Speaks, an advocacy organization founded by the grandparents of a child with ASD, uses both terms in its definition, acknowledging both the educational and medical needs of individuals with ASD and the families that the organization serves.

There are also some people-first terminology considerations for individuals with ASD that are different from those discussed in Chapter 1. Although many prefer people-first language, quite a few in the ASD community feel defined by their condition and refer to themselves as an *autistic person* rather than *a person with ASD*. These individuals might also say, "I am autistic" rather than "I have autism." Further, you may have heard the terms *on the autism spectrum* or *on the spectrum*. The word *spectrum* in *autism spectrum disorder* refers to the variety of characteristics within ASD, each of which ranges in severity from mild to severe. As such, the phrases *a person on the autism spectrum* and *a person on the spectrum* also refer to an individual with ASD. Finally, variations of *neurodiversity* and *neurotypical* are emerging terms that refer to those with and without ASD, respectively.

Topic 8.2 Types of Autism Spectrum Disorder

- The levels of severity for ASD range from mild to severe.

- An individual may demonstrate a variety of severity levels across different skills and traits.

Are there different types of ASD? In 2000, the American Psychiatric Association (APA) included five disorders in what was often referred to as the ASD umbrella: autism, **Asperger's disorder** (also referred to as **Asperger's syndrome**), **pervasive developmental disorder–not otherwise specified (PDD-NOS)**, **childhood disintegrative disorder**, and **Rett's disorder** (also known as **Rett syndrome**). The current *DSM-5* definition of ASD no longer breaks this condition into different types; instead, it uses the over-arching definition presented in Topic 8.1, *Definitions of Autism Spectrum Disorder*. It does, however, identify three levels of severity for this disorder. Although the *DSM-5* refers to these as Level 1 (the least severe, requiring some supports), Level 2, and Level 3 (the most severe, requiring very substantial supports), severity is often discussed in non-clinical situations as ranging from mild to severe, or from high functioning to low functioning. Children at the ends of the spectrum are very different from one another. A child at the low functioning end of the spectrum may be completely nonverbal, while a child with high functioning ASD might have very strong verbal skills but use them inappropriately and be perceived as socially awkward. Roughly 30% to 60% of individuals with ASD have a co-existing intellectual disability (which you will learn about in the next chapter). Their social-communication, interaction, and behavioral symptoms are typically toward the severe, or low functioning, end of the spectrum.

A very small subgroup of individuals with ASD display unique behaviors known as **splinter skills**. These individuals are known as **autistic savants**. If you have seen the movie *Rain Man*, you might recall that Raymond, the main character, could instantly count the number of matches that had fallen on the floor, remember the dates of important events from previous decades, or recall the telephone numbers for all of the people in the phone book. Raymond's character was an autistic savant, and these are examples of splinter skills. In real life, these skills are exhibited in many intriguing ways: playing a complicated piece on the piano after hearing it only once, drawing an intricately detailed city scene from memory, instantly calculating the day of the week on which a future date will fall. While such splinter skills are fascinating to observers, they are rarely productive or functional for the individual.

Are the severity levels consistent across all of an individual's characteristics? Not always. An individual may display strengths in some areas but severe deficits in others, one example of why the term *spectrum* is included in *autism spectrum disorder*. The following figure provides an example of the ranges that various traits and abilities can fall within, and how they might present for one individual.

Example Range of Symptoms

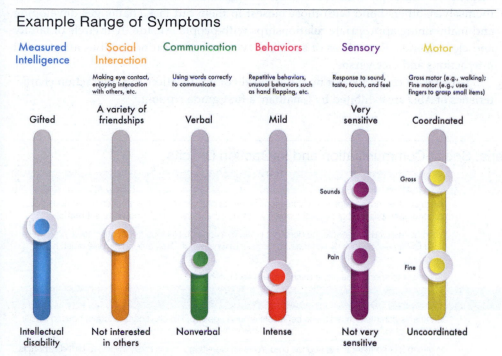

SOURCE: Adapted from *Example Range of Symptoms*, Centers for Disease Control and Prevention. http://www.cdc.gov/ncbddd/autism/signs.html

Because the characteristics displayed within each of the core areas are so widely disparate from one individual to the next, members of the ASD community often say, "If you've met one person with ASD, you've met one person with ASD." In other words, don't generalize what you think you know about ASD based on one person's characteristics because another person's traits will be much different.

Topic 8.3 Characteristics

- Deficits in social communication and interaction create difficulties in interpersonal relationships for individuals with ASD.

- The need for sameness and restrictive, repetitive behaviors can cause problems in the execution of everyday activities.

What are some characteristics of ASD related to social communication and interaction? IDEA refers to these characteristics as problems in "verbal and nonverbal communication and social interaction," while the *DSM-5* refers to them as deficits in "social communication and social interaction." The *DSM-5* includes three examples to help with diagnosis:

- *Social-emotional reciprocity*—These individuals may not initiate interactions, respond to greetings, or be able to engage in conversational turn taking (think back to what you learned about pragmatics in Chapter 5).

- *Nonverbal social communication*—Children with ASD might not maintain eye contact, might use atypical body language, or might have difficulty interpreting or displaying facial expressions.

- *Interpersonal relationships*—Children with ASD may not show interest in other children or in making friends, or may not engage in typical play (e.g., make believe).

In addition to communication issues, most individuals have difficulties interpreting social situations or understanding another person's perspective. As might be expected, those with ASD have fewer peer friendships than people without such disabilities. Although some individuals with ASD are totally withdrawn and isolate themselves, others bond with those closest to them but face challenges developing and maintaining appropriate relationships with people outside their circle of family and close friends. Regardless of severity level, communication abilities affect social interactions and vice versa.

Let's take a closer look at how the social-communication and interaction characteristics of ASD are exhibited by Jonathan, a first-grade student.

Application of Diagnostic Criteria: Social-Communication and Interaction Deficits

Examples	Jonathan's Symptoms
Social-emotional reciprocity	Jonathan does not engage in conversations unless spoken to first. When spoken to, he does not respond appropriately but instead repeats what the other person said (known as **echolalia**).
Nonverbal social communication	When he responds to people, he does not make eye contact. His face frequently shows no emotion. His demeanor does not change, regardless of whether children around him are quiet, happy, or sad.
Interpersonal relationships	He prefers to spend time alone during recess and lunch.
Other Diagnostic Criteria to Be Considered	
Evident at an early age	Jonathan's parents noticed these behaviors around age two. His child care teachers noticed similar behaviors at school.
Impairment in social, occupational, or educational areas	Jonathan has no friends. He spends time alone on weekends and is rarely invited to birthday parties or other social activities. Jonathan does not participate in large- or small-group activities in school. Instead, he sits by himself, rocking. Many of his classmates feel uncomfortable because he never initiates a conversation and exhibits unusual body language and few social behaviors. Often, he does not acknowledge when adults speak to him and inconsistently complies with the teacher's requests.
Not better explained by intellectual disability or global developmental delay	Jonathan does not have an intellectual disability or developmental delay.

What are some characteristics of ASD related to restrictive or repetitive behavior? IDEA refers to these characteristics as "repetitive activities and stereotyped movements." The *DSM-5* refers to them as "restricted, repetitive patterns of behavior, interests, or activities" and includes four examples to help with diagnosis:

- *Stereotyped or repetitive actions*—Hand flapping is a common stereotypical behavior for children with ASD, though the ways in which these children display stereotyped actions are as unique as each individual. For example, a child may repeat a movement, such as checking the straps on her backpack, over and over again. In other cases, children develop elaborate rituals that often start very simply: a child takes a bite of food and then puts his fork down; he takes a bite of food, puts his fork down, and makes a popping sound with his mouth; he takes a bit of food, puts his fork down, and makes two popping sounds. Before families or teachers realize it, the child has developed a 10- or 12-step ritual.

- *An insistence on sameness or an inflexible adherence to routines*—The need for sameness can cause children to want only certain foods at meals or wear only certain clothes (more on this issue momentarily). In some cases, the child may insist on others following a routine (e.g., the teacher must call students' names in the same order every day, a parent must always drive the same route to school or to the store). The child's reaction to any change, no matter how small, is often excessive.

- *Abnormally intense, restricted interests*—A child might focus on a certain interest (e.g., train engines) to the exclusion of all else. He might want to play only with train engines, not other railcars, cabooses, train sets, or toy train stations—only engines. Furthermore, his play may not be typical; he may line the engines up, take them apart, spin their wheels, but not run them on a track or have them pull other cars. He may draw engines and want to watch TV shows or movies about engines (or ignore or fast forward through all parts of a movie except scenes in which an engine appears). He may talk about engines, reciting trivia and minutiae that bore other people. Because he is unable to read facial expressions and body language, understand their perspective, or have compassion for their boredom (problems tied to social-communication and interaction deficits), he will return to the topic of train engines even when others change the topic.

- *Unusual reactions to sensory input*—These unusual reactions fall into three categories: **hyperresponsive** (overreaction), **hyporesponsive** (little or no reaction), and sensory seeking. In cases of hyperresponsiveness, children may show excessive reactions to what most people consider mild sensory stimuli, such as covering their ears or screaming at the sounds of small children's voices, a phone ringing, or someone playing the piano. For some children, excessive reactions are tied to their insistence on sameness for foods or clothing. When these children have highly averse reactions to the smells or textures of certain foods, they refuse to eat them, which in turn limits their diet. Similarly, certain clothing textures may feel too scratchy; tags in shirts or seams in socks seem unbearable. A child may refuse to wear the items, leading to lengthy and stressful morning routines for parents as they try to find acceptable clothes and still get to school and work on time. If they are unable to find clothing alternatives, the child may be cranky at school or have a meltdown because of the intolerable textures.

In cases of hyporesponsiveness, individuals with ASD may show little or no reaction to sensory stimuli. In some instances, this can cause injuries, as when a child does not instinctively pull his hand away from a hot stovetop burner. Sensory seeking behaviors, sometimes referred to as self-stimulatory behaviors, or **stims**, can include rocking, twirling, hand flapping, or even head banging that the child engages in to receive sensory input. Temple Grandin, a college professor and author with ASD whom you will learn about in Topic 8.11, explains that her stims, such as trickling sand through her fingers, helped her to calm down and drown out the noise, confusion, and stress of the world around her.

Let's revisit Jonathan, our first grader, to see how he exhibits characteristics of restricted or repetitive patterns of behavior.

Application of Diagnostic Criteria: Examples of Restrictive or Repetitive Behaviors

Examples	Jonathan's Symptoms
Insistence on sameness, inflexible adherence to routines	Jonathan's morning routine consists of getting dressed: socks first, then pants, then shirt, then shoes (which must be waiting at the foot of his bed); eating breakfast; brushing his teeth; and making his bed. He becomes upset if the routine is altered, as when his younger brother, who shares his room, has moved his shoes or when his mother asks him to make his bed before eating breakfast.
Unusual responses to sensory experiences	Jonathan refuses to eat foods with certain textures, which has resulted in a limited diet. He also complains about clothing that is stiff or that has zippers or buttons, preferring cotton t-shirts and sweatpants. Jonathan does not like walking barefoot on sand, which makes beach vacations difficult. He also does not like walking on grass, even with shoes on, so he often hovers on the blacktop basketball court or on the sidewalk that leads to the school playground during recess. Jonathan does not like high-pitched or loud sounds. When he was a toddler, he did not like to be around his infant brother. When the baby would cry, Jonathan would cover his ears, rock, and cry.

The following IRIS Module includes more information on the characteristics of ASD. It also provides information on the early signs of ASD, something you will learn more about in Topic 8.7, with comparison videos of young children with and without ASD, and an overview of the difference between a medical diagnosis and an educational determination.

▶ **IRIS Module: Autism Spectrum Disorder: An Overview for Educators**
http://iris.peabody.vanderbilt.edu/module/asd1/

Topic 8.4 Prevalence and Placement

- The prevalence of ASD is increasing at a dramatic rate.

- There are many hypotheses concerning the cause of the increase but no definitive answers.

How has the prevalence of ASD changed over time? As the accompanying graph indicates, the prevalence of ASD has shown a dramatic increase over the past 20 years. According to the CDC's Autism and Developmental Disabilities Monitoring (ADDM) Network, ASD increased 23% from 2006 to 2008 and 78% between 2002 and 2008. The CDC now reports that as many as 1 in 68 children in the United States has ASD. Although this is a significant increase from 1 in 150 only a few years ago, the numbers have held steady since 2010. The CDC also estimates that 1 in every 42 boys has now been diagnosed with ASD, which is 4.5 times higher than the prevalence for girls (1 in every 189). African American and Latino children tend to be identified at older ages, raising questions about early identification procedures in some communities.

ASD Prevalence on the Rise

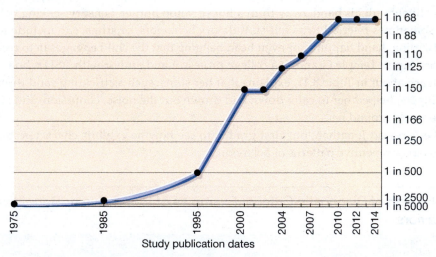

Study publication dates

SOURCE: Centers for Disease Control, March 31, 2016. Retrieved from http://www.cdc.gov/ncbddd/autism/data.html

Such soaring increases are being observed worldwide, though the rates vary substantially from country to country. Most countries in Asia, Europe, and North America have identified between 1% and 3% of their population as having ASD. The reason for some variance is thought to be due to differences in diagnostic methods and criteria used for identification. Other variance is due to cultural attitudes and perspectives on disability, which affect parents' inclination to seek help.

In the United States, prevalence rates vary greatly between those reported by the CDC and the U.S. Department of Education. According to IDEA data, 0.71% of all students, including those relatively few students between the ages of 18 and 21, have ASD and receive special education services. This prevalence rate is about half that reported by the CDC. Some differences could result from the more restrictive definition in IDEA, which includes the requirement that educational performance must be negatively affected.

As with the CDC data, IDEA data show great differences across states. Let's look at some of these differences on the map below. The state of Iowa reports the lowest rate of children with ASD. New Mexico reports a rate nearly 5 times higher than that in Iowa; Florida and Washington report rates 7.5 times higher. Although Massachusetts's prevalence rate is 10 times higher than Iowa's, any hypotheses that prevalence rates are affected by geographic location or region are disproved when one recognizes that Minnesota, Iowa's neighbor, also has a rate nearly 10.4 times higher.

Prevalence Rates: Selected States

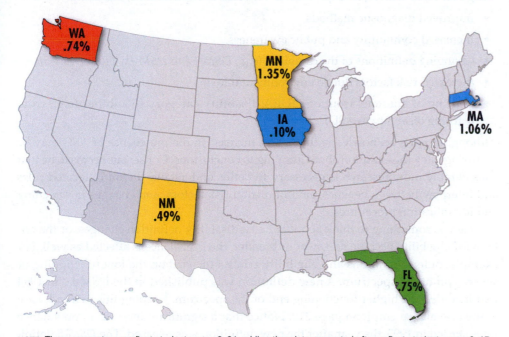

NOTE: These percentages reflect students ages 6–21, while other data presented often reflect students ages 6–17.

SOURCE: U.S. Department of Education. (2015). *Students Ages 6 through 21 Served under IDEA, Part B, as a Percentage of Population, by Disability Category and State* [IDEA Section 618 Data Products: Static Tables, 2014–2015 Part B *Child Count and Educational Environments*]. Retrieved from http://www2.ed.gov/programs/osepidea/618-data/static-tables/index.html#part-b

Regardless of the state-by-state discrepancies, students with ASD now make up the fourth largest disability category described in IDEA. The pie chart below shows the continued progression of eligibility categories you have learned about so far. Note that this chart shows the prevalence among children with disabilities, while the rates in the map above show the prevalence rates among all children.

Disability Prevalence: 2014–2015 School Year

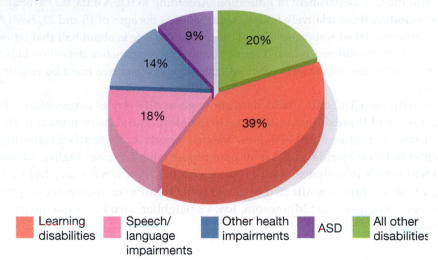

| Learning disabilities | Speech/ language impairments | Other health impairments | ASD | All other disabilities |

Why are prevalence rates increasing? No one really knows why more children are being identified with ASD. Experts offer a myriad of explanations, including:

- Improved diagnostic methods.
- Increased community and public awareness.
- Changing definitions of the disability (e.g., *DSM-IV* to *DSM-IV-TR* to *DSM-5*).
- Increased risk factors due to environmental toxins.
- Shifting of students from one IDEA disability category to another (e.g., from learning disability to ASD).

Although experts acknowledge that a true increase in the prevalence of ASD may be occurring, they raise caution about jumping to conclusions. Consensus seems to be that considerably more research is necessary to better understand the multi-faceted roles and interplay between genetics, environmental risk factors, and changes in screening and identification procedures.

Here is something to think about: when a disability definition changes, or the criteria for eligibility become narrower or broader, the prevalence is affected as well. For example, older definitions and eligibility criteria focused on the low functioning or severe end of the spectrum. A new definition was published in the *DSM-IV* in 1994 that included the higher functioning end of the spectrum. Keeping this in mind, look at the prevalence graph on page 210. Notice that a significant increase in prevalence rates started in 1995, the year after the new definition was released. The *DSM-5* definition of ASD was changed in 2013, so the prevalence data we have now are not exactly comparable to those for students whose ASD was diagnosed prior to 2013. Researchers will continue to monitor yearly prevalence rates; however, it may be difficult to determine whether changes are due to increases or decreases in the prevalence of ASD or to alterations to the definition and eligibility requirements.

The CDC's Autism and Developmental Disabilities Monitoring (ADDM) Network tracks prevalence rates of ASD across the United States. The network aims to:

- Describe the population of children with ASD.
- Compare prevalence rates in different parts of the United States.
- Identify changes in prevalence rates over time.
- Understand the impact of the condition in the communities.

You can obtain the most current prevalence rates from the ADDM at www.cdc.gov/ ncbddd/autism/addm.htm

Check Your Understanding 8.1

Click here to gauge your understanding of the concepts in this section.

Special Education

Learning Outcome

Explain the ways in which ASD can impact academic performance and interpersonal skills, describe accommodations that can lessen these challenges, understand methods that parents and classroom teachers can use to reduce challenges associated with ASD, and describe supports to help students with ASD transition to post-secondary options such as school, work, and independent living.

Topic 8.5 Challenges and Their Solutions

- In addition to social-communication and behavioral challenges, children with ASD often have physical and mental health concerns.

- Solutions to these challenges include applied behavior analysis (ABA) and the Picture Exchange Communication System (PECS), along with UDL, differentiated instruction, accommodations, assistive technology, and medical interventions.

Topic 8.6 Accommodations

- Teachers can provide accommodations for students with ASD to address barriers related to social communication and social interaction.

- Different accommodations may be required to address behavioral challenges.

Topic 8.7 Early Intervention

- ASD has clear early warning signs, many of which are evident by a child's first birthday.

- The Picture Exchange Communication System (PECS) is a validated practice used to improve expressive communication skills.

Topic 8.8 School Years

- Many of the strategies learned in earlier chapters can be used to address the communication, academic, and behavioral challenges of students with ASD.

- Evidence-based visual and auditory supports can address a student's need for order, sameness, and routine.

Topic 8.9 Transition

- Students with high functioning ASD should be exposed to a variety of post-secondary education options, career-awareness opportunities, and social skills training.

- Students with low functioning ASD will require transition plans that include different types of goals for employment and for independent living.

Belinda Butler

The noise-canceling headphones that Justin is wearing are a common accommodation for students with ASD who have extreme sensitivity to auditory stimuli. Recall that we also listed these head-phones as an accommodation for students with ADHD, to filter out distracting auditory stimuli. As you will learn in this section, many of the accommodations and interventions mentioned in previous chapters will also work for students with ASD.

Topic 8.5 Challenges and Their Solutions

- In addition to social-communication and behavioral challenges, children with ASD often have physical and mental health concerns.

- Solutions to these challenges include applied behavior analysis (ABA) and the Picture Exchange Communication System (PECS), along with UDL, differentiated instruction, accommodations, assistive technology, and medical interventions.

What challenges are associated with ASD? You have learned enough about ASD by now to recognize that the characteristics of ASD—social, communication, and behavioral deficits—create challenges within interpersonal and behavioral domains. Many of these characteristics interfere with learning and subsequent school academics. Additionally, some individuals with ASD have serious problems with their behavior. They might:

- *Inflict **self-injury**—*turn their behaviors inward and hurt themselves.

- *Demonstrate **aggression**—*turn their behavior outward and hurt others.

Sometimes, the behavior problems are tied to communication difficulties. Children, as well as adults, who have no way to explain that they feel frustrated, feel scared, or are in pain will act out in a variety of ways. Some are attempts to communicate; others are attempts to make the negative feelings go away.

One challenge we have not yet discussed is that of health-related concerns. We discuss two health-related challenges here: co-existing health conditions and access-ing health care. Individuals with ASD have a higher than normal rate of certain health conditions, such as seizure disorders. Many also have sleep disorders: they have dif-ficulty falling asleep or sleep much less than is typical. This can be physically draining for parents, particularly when they have children who require a lot of monitoring and supervision. Individuals with ASD also have a higher than normal rate of gastroin-testinal disorders, particularly severe constipation. And many have nutritional defi-cits, often tied to the food aversion issues discussed earlier. Even though many people with ASD have restricted diets because of food and texture aversions, they commonly exhibit **pica,** a condition in which individuals eat non-food items. So, a child with ASD and pica may eat only soft foods like mashed potatoes, pudding, and applesauce, yet also eat sticks, grass, and mulch when playing outside, or paperclips, crayons, and even bedsheets when inside. Pica is of particular concern when children ingest sharp, dangerous, or poisonous objects, requiring parents and teachers to be on constant alert.

In addition to physical health concerns, individuals with ASD also have higher rates of mental health issues, including anxiety, depression, and obsessive-compulsive disorder (OCD). One study found a significantly higher rate of suicide attempts among adults with ASD than among the comparison group of adults without ASD; yet, half of those who attempted suicide did not have depression diagnoses. These data led the researchers to hypothesize that rates of depression are under-diagnosed in this population.

Given the various health concerns associated with ASD, high-quality health care seems a necessity. However, many families find it difficult to provide these services for their children. Certain characteristics of ASD contribute to the difficulties. Think about your last trip to the dentist, and then imagine how hard it would be to get your teeth cleaned if you have sensory issues. Think about the bright lights above a reclining chair; the cloth around your neck; all the poking and prodding with sharp, shiny instruments; and the whirring of the machinery. A simple dental or well-child visit can cause a child with ASD to act out aggressively and result in stress for parents and health care professionals. In many cases, the child's communication deficits prevent him from being able to express why he is afraid or distressed. If the child is sick, he cannot communicate with the doctor to describe how he feels or which part of his body hurts. Conversely, if doctors and parents explain to a child why they are trying to clean his teeth or conduct a wellness checkup, he might not understand.

Providing mental health care to an individual with ASD is also challenging. Often, deficits in communication make it difficult for an individual to express how he or she is feeling—one contributing factor to the suspected under-diagnosis of depression discussed above. Psychiatrists who treat these disorders cannot depend on a patient's ability to communicate whether medication has had any effect on anxiety or depression levels, so they often rely on family members' perceptions, which may not be accurate.

ASD Challenges

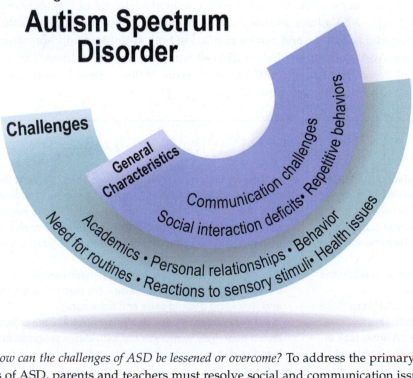

How can the challenges of ASD be lessened or overcome? To address the primary challenges of ASD, parents and teachers must resolve social and communication issues as well as behavioral ones. Each is equally important. Although we cannot discuss every solution in sufficient detail, throughout this chapter we will provide overviews of several that have proven effective: **applied behavior analysis (ABA)**, the **Picture Exchange Communication System (PECS)**, and **TEACCH (or structured TEACCHing)**. And, as you have learned in previous chapters, application of UDL principles, differentiated instruction, and accommodations are always helpful. We will provide an overview of ABA in this topic, and discuss PECS and TEACCH in Topics 8.7 and 8.8.

ASD Solutions

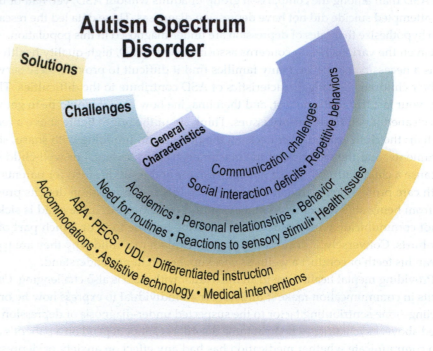

Applied behavior analysis (ABA) is a highly researched, validated method to increase desired behaviors and reduce or eliminate unwanted ones. It originates from B. F. Skinner's work and was further refined by teams of researchers across many decades. ABA addresses many skills—communication, social, play, motor, pre-academic, and self-care—and can be applied in both structured and non-structured situations. ABA is often provided for 25 to 40 hours per week and directed by a **Board Certified Behavior Analyst™ (BCBA)**. At the core of this approach are the key components described in the accompanying box.

Key Components of the Applied Behavior Analysis Approach

Functional Behavioral Assessment (FBA): Through an **ABC analysis**, a child's actions (i.e., behavior) are observed and recorded to identify the cause or purpose of the behavior, particularly unwanted ones. Specifically, the ABC analysis considers the:

- *Antecedent*—the events that precede the behavior.
- *Behavior*—the undesirable action(s).
- *Consequence*—the events that reinforce or maintain the behavior.

Task Analysis: A multi-step task or skill is broken into smaller steps that can be learned more easily.

Repeated Instruction (**discrete trials**): A small task or step that is part of the larger skill is presented and taught repeatedly until mastery is achieved. Then, the next task or step in the sequence is taught. The process continues until the entire skill is mastered. The steps in the sequence can be taught from beginning to end, referred to as forward chaining, or in reverse order from end to beginning, referred to as backward chaining.

Positive Reinforcement: Systematic rewards—including tokens, privileges, and praise—are earned for learning and executing desired skills and behaviors.

Direct Assessment or Measurement: Data are collected frequently to monitor the individual's progress in learning and mastering the skill or task.

Note that these are components; they are *not* steps. In other words, a teacher does not need to conduct an FBA first, then a task analysis next, followed by discrete trials, and so on. Rather, these key components can be used individually or in combination for desired results. The components are not unique to ABA; they are effective elements for teaching new skills or for differentiating skills for struggling learners and students with disabilities. For example, think back to when you learned to tie your shoes. You probably didn't learn how to do this as one complete process, but rather as a series of smaller steps (task analysis). You probably learned it through forward chaining, with crossing the laces as the first step and pulling the loops tight as the last step. Do you remember learning to use a zipper? You may have learned this skill through backward chaining; an adult started it for you by fitting the two pieces together and you completed the last step, which was to grasp the zipper and pull it up. Gradually, over time, you learned to fit the two pieces together until eventually you could perform the entire task independently. Ideally, someone even gave you positive reinforcement as you successfully completed each step!

ABA can be used to teach a wide variety of skills (see the following table). It is typically designed for preschoolers, although it has been used with older children. After two to three years of therapy, some children have gained the skills needed to succeed in inclusive education settings. Although ABA produces better results than other intervention approaches, it is not uniformly effective for all students with ASD. To date, no one understands why it is more powerful with some children than with others.

Applied Behavior Analysis

Uses	Examples
Teach new skills	Functional life skills (e.g., dressing, self-care, time management, making choices) Communication skills (e.g., increasing vocabulary) Social skills (e.g., sharing, playing)
Increase desired behaviors	Interact appropriately with peers Engage in cooperative play
Decrease undesired behaviors	Eliminate tantrums Stop fights
Generalize learning	Transfer learning to new settings Apply learning to new situations Use learned skills with new people

The video below demonstrates several components of ABA. It also includes examples of how technology can be used to support the instruction of students with ASD, something we will discuss further in Topic 8.13.

▶ **What Is ABA Therapy?**
https://www.youtube.com/watch?v=GC968hBJGz8

Topic 8.6 Accommodations

- Teachers can provide accommodations for students with ASD to address barriers related to social communication and social interaction.

- Different accommodations may be required to address behavioral challenges.

How do instructional accommodations for students with ASD compare to those used for students who have speech and language impairments or learning disabilities? Although individual needs vary, some of the same accommodations are often used for students in each of these disability categories. Two such supports are visual cues to support the presentation of information and allowing extra time for a student to respond (i.e., extended wait time). Because many students with ASD have difficulty with fine motor skills, they also benefit from the same accommodations often provided to students with learning disabilities to reduce barriers associated with handwriting (e.g., computers, alternate responses, note takers). In addition to these types of supports, which can help some students with ASD access the general education curriculum and succeed academically, all students with ASD can benefit from supports that can help reduce barriers related to communicating with others and engaging socially with peers. Depending on the student's level of functioning, one of the following accommodations can be used to address deficits in social communication and social interactions.

- *Augmentative and alternative communication (AAC) systems*—Students with little or no functional speech can be taught to use AAC systems to initiate conversations, exchange information, and express their wants and needs. One AAC system designed specifically for children with autism spectrum disorder is the Picture Exchange Communication System (PECS). With this system, a child exchanges a picture symbol or a sentence strip to request a desired item or activity, answer questions, and initiate conversations. PECS will be explored in more depth in Topic 8.7, *Early Intervention*.

- *Peer buddy*—Some students with ASD have a difficult time initiating interactions with peers, others prefer to play alone, and yet others display socially awkward or inappropriate behaviors. For this reason, it can be beneficial to pair the student with a peer who has strong social skills and can support the student during group work periods in class and during non-academic periods (e.g., lunch, recess). Once the student is comfortable initiating conversations with the peer buddy, the teacher can create structured activities involving a few more students, allowing the student to interact in a larger group, yet with the support of the peer buddy.

Because students with ADHD and ASD have behavioral challenges, can teachers use the same accommodations to address the needs of both groups? The answer is maybe, but it will depend on individual needs. Recall that challenges for students with ADHD are often associated with inattentive, hyperactive, or impulsive behavior. For students with ASD, behavioral challenges often result from the students' inability to handle changes in routine, interference with their repetitive actions, and hyperresponsiveness or hyporesponsiveness to sensory inputs. For both groups of students, noise and other distractions can interfere with learning new information and demonstrating that learning, so as a whole these students often benefit from accommodations such as separate rooms for testing or noise-reducing headphones. Because of their deficits in social communication and interaction, students with ASD often communicate through their behaviors, which can create additional difficulties. The two accommodations highlighted below can reduce behavioral challenges related to under-stimulation or over-stimulation and to the inability to handle changes in routines.

- *Decreased or increased stimulation*—As mentioned above, separate locations for testing and headphones can be effective means of reducing noise and auditory stimuli for students with autism spectrum disorder who are easily overstimulated. Interestingly, headphones can also be used to provide auditory stimuli, such as music, for students who are hyposensitive to sensory inputs and require extra stimulation.

- *Clearly established routines and schedules*—Typically, students with ASD like predictability. When activities follow a consistent pattern or occur at the same time each day, these students are less agitated and are more successful at school. To help students know what to expect throughout the day, the teacher can post a written schedule, or a visual schedule for those with limited language or reading skills, in the classroom.

The following table highlights commonly used accommodations for students with autism spectrum disorder.

Examples of Frequently Used Accommodations for Students with Autism Spectrum Disorder

Presentation	Setting	Response	Scheduling or Timing
• Advance organizers • Visual or written instructions • Visuals to accompany verbal information • Read-aloud instructions for tests	• Separate testing location • Reduced noise/distractions • Quiet area to take a time-out • Headphones	• Augmentative and alternative communication (AAC) systems • Adapted keyboards • Computer • Note taker • Alternative response methods • Increased wait time • Visual supports	• Extended time for tests or assignments • Brief assignments (or broken into parts) • Visual schedules • Syllabi • Clearly established routines/schedules

Topic 8.7 Early Intervention

- ASD has clear early warning signs, many of which are evident by a child's first birthday.

- The Picture Exchange Communication System (PECS) is a validated practice used to improve expressive communication skills.

What are the early indicators of ASD? IDEA's definition requires symptoms of ASD to be evident by age three, while the *DSM-5* requires them to be present during the early developmental period. Many early warning signs of ASD are evident as early as a child's first birthday. The CDC lists possible "red flags" that parents should watch for, summarized in the following table.

Early Warning Signs of ASD

In Many Cases, Young Children with ASD	
Will	**Will Not**
• Avoid eye contact or physical contact • Prefer to play alone • Become agitated with even minor changes in routine • Display **stereotypies** (repetitive behaviors such as hand flapping, spinning, or vocalizations)	• Respond to their names (by 12 months) • Point to objects of interest (by 14 months) • Respond or look when others point to objects of interest • Play pretend or imaginative games, like rocking a doll to sleep (by 18 months) • Engage in **joint attention**

The video below was developed to assist in the early identification of very young children with ASD. It contrasts the behaviors of one-year-olds with and without ASD. The differences—when you know what to look for—are clear.

▶ **Early Signs of Autism Video Tutorial—Kennedy Krieger Institute**

https://youtu.be/YtvP5A5OHpU

When a child is identified at a young age, early intervention services can include a range of supports and therapies, depending on the child's unique needs: speech-language therapy to improve communication, ABA to teach and reinforce skills, and occupational therapy to address sensory issues. As is typical for early intervention services, children who begin receiving these supports at a young age have better long-term outcomes—the earlier the better.

The ASD Toddler Initiative, a joint project between the Frank Porter Graham Child Development Institute at the University of North Carolina at Chapel Hill and Autism Speaks, has many useful resources to support early intervention. These include online modules about interventions such as prompting, functional behavior assessment, **video modeling** (which you'll learn more about later in this chapter), and more: http://asdtoddler.fpg.unc.edu/learning-modules

Is there a validated practice that can help students who have trouble developing functional communication skills? The Picture Exchange Communication System (PECS) was designed as an augmentative and alternative communication (AAC) system for students with ASD who have little or no functional speech. With years of research to support its efficacy, PECS relies heavily on applied behavior analysis to improve communication skills. Using this system, the child selects a picture that conveys the message. That picture is then handed to a person who can fulfill the request. So, if a child wants a cookie, he or she gives a picture of a cookie to the teacher, who in turn gives the child a cookie. PECS begins with one-word requests and eventually expands communications through sentence strips of pictures. The method not only fosters communication but also forces children to interact with other people if they want something. The six major steps or phases used in PECS are outlined in the box below.

A Closer Look at Evidence-Based Practices

Picture Exchange Communication System (PECS)

Prior to Implementation. Identify the individual's preferences and prepare picture cards that represent desired objects, actions, or needs.

Phase 1: Teach students *how to communicate*—Two trainers (a communication partner and a helper) assist the student in picking up a picture symbol and exchanging it for a desired item or activity. Initially, a desired item is placed out of reach of the student. When the student reaches for the item, the communication partner opens a hand to prompt the student to use the picture card and the helper physically helps the student perform the correct action. When the student is rewarded with the item, a trainer says its name. As the student learns the process, physical assistance and prompting are faded.

Phase 2: Promote *spontaneity* and *generalization*—The student is provided many opportunities to communicate with a single picture card in a variety of natural settings and with different communication partners (e.g., parents, siblings, teachers, peers). Additionally, a trainer uses two methods to encourage the student to travel greater distances to access the desired item. First, the trainer moves farther from the student, and then the picture cards are placed farther away. This phase is sometimes referred to as *distance and persistence*.

Phase 3: Teach students to *discriminate*—Pictures or symbols of two items, one preferred (e.g., book) and one

non-preferred (e.g., sock), are placed in a communication book. The communication partner interacts with both items. When the student selects the correct picture (i.e., the preferred item), the communication partner gives verbal praise, provides the item, and says the name of the item. The number of picture symbols in the student's communication book is gradually increased so that he or she has to discriminate among more pictures.

Phase 4: Introduce *sentence structure*—Once the student can use and discriminate among 12 and 20 pictures, he or she is taught how to use sentence strips (e.g., placing an "I want" symbol next to the desired item picture.) Again, physical assistance is provided and then faded, and the communication partner provides the item and reads aloud the sentence. Students are also taught how to expand their sentences, using adjectives, verbs, and prepositions.

Phase 5: Teach students to *answer questions*—The communication partner asks the student, "What do you want?" The student is taught to respond with a sentence strip, "I want" symbol and a picture of the desired item.

Phase 6: Teach students to *comment*—Communication partners begin by asking questions such as, "What do you see?" and the student is taught to respond by assembling sentences such as, "I see (item)." Once the student can answer questions without assistance, he or she is encouraged to initiate conversation by commenting on the environment.

SOURCE: "The Six Phases of PECS," retrieved from www.pecs.com. Adapted with permission from Pyramid Educational Consultants.

Example of a PECS Sentence Strip

SOURCE: Adapted from the *Picture Exchange Communication System* training manual by L. Frost and A. Bondy, 2002, Newark, DE: Pyramid Educational Products, Inc.

The official PECS Website (www.pecsusa.com) provides considerable information about the system and training, including many video examples. Click the following link and scroll down to **Part 3: Overview of the Phases of PECS®** to see how the six PECS phases are demonstrated with children of various ages. http://www.pecsusa.com/videos.php

Topic 8.8 School Years

- Many of the strategies learned in earlier chapters can be used to address the communication, academic, and behavioral challenges of students with ASD.

- Evidence-based visual and auditory supports can address a student's need for order, sameness, and routine.

What types of strategies and practices can teachers use to address the needs of students with ASD? Many of the interventions and services you have learned about in previous chapters are effective for students with ASD. Let's review how some of those interventions can address the characteristics associated with ASD.

- *Delayed language or communication difficulties*—Speech-language therapy is necessary to improve communication skills. In many cases, students start this therapy as young children and the services continue during the school years. PECS (which you learned about in this chapter) can be used in the classroom, as can various types of assistive technology, to help the child communicate.

- *Academic difficulties*—In addition to the types of accommodations you learned about earlier in this chapter, many of the same academic practices and strategies that are effective for students with learning disabilities will also work for students with ASD: UDL, differentiated instruction, explicit instruction, and learning strategies.

- *Behavior issues*—Behavior therapy and self-regulation strategies are both evidence-based practices that are effective for students with ASD. Earlier in this chapter you learned about ABA, which provides intensive supports to improve many skills, including behavior. In some cases, a functional behavioral assessment (FBA) may be necessary to determine why a child is behaving a certain way. If teachers can determine the function of the behavior (e.g., a child screams and hits other children when they make noises to which she is hypersensitive), then a **behavior intervention plan (BIP)** can be developed to replace the problem behavior with a more appropriate one.

In addition to providing the interventions and accommodations listed on a student's IEP or 504 plan, teachers can do a number of things to help students with ASD experience more success at school. A few practices that can be incorporated into the already established classroom routines are listed in the box below.

Tips for Teachers

- Incorporate the student's highly focused interests into class activities. Do you remember the student we discussed earlier who loves train engines? Information on their speed and acceleration can be incorporated into mathematics problems; he can meet a research paper requirement by writing about train engines; and so on.
- Do not require eye contact; over time eye contact may develop naturally or can be targeted as a skill to work on.
- Model acceptance of the student and immediately address teasing or bullying by other students.
- Offer choices, which allow the student to feel in control. For example, a student balks at eating lunch in a noisy cafeteria.

The teacher asks if he would rather start eating 5 minutes earlier than the rest of the class or go to lunch at the same time as the others. The student chooses the former, giving him a voice in the matter. This also addresses the problem in other ways. It allows him to eat half his lunch before other students arrive. The noise increases as the cafeteria fills up, and the student is able to adjust to the change gradually, rather than being hit with the noise as soon as he enters.
- Be aware of the student's sensory needs and alter the classroom if possible. For example, if a student is hypersensitive to visual stimuli, an overly decorated classroom can be over-stimulating.

What are some other evidence-based supports that can address characteristics more specific to ASD? A student's need for order, sameness, and routine can create challenges throughout the day, particularly during transitions when a student must stop what he or she is doing and move to a new activity. Fortunately, in such cases, teachers can turn to a variety of evidence-based practices, some of which were listed in Topic 8.6, and are summarized in the following table.

Types of Evidence-Based Supports

Type	Explanation	Example
		Visual Supports
Visual schedule	A summary of the schedule for a particular period of time (morning, afternoon, day), to help a student anticipate when changes will occur	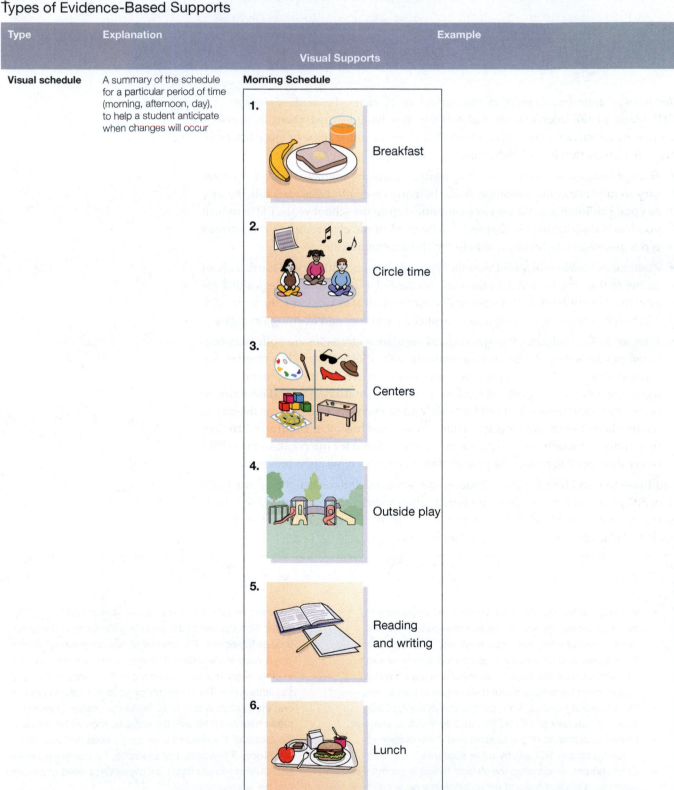

First/then board	Two pictures that depict a required behavior or action (often a non-preferred activity) that must be completed (first) to receive a preferred item or activity (then)	 First/Then board

Social story or social narrative	A story that is read with a student before an activity takes place; it presents an anticipated social situation, the social or behavioral cues that a student should notice, and the desired appropriate response or behavior

My name is Mack.

This is the playground at school.

When I am on the playground,
I stay inside the fence.

When I stay inside the fence,
I can play with my friends.

When I stay inside the fence,
I can see and hear my teacher.

When I stay inside the fence,
I am safe.

Video modeling or video priming	A video demonstration of desired skills or behavior, shown to the student immediately prior to a situation in which he or she will be expected to perform that skill	Peer interactions during small-group work make Neerav anxious. Right before small-group time, his teacher shows him a video of a student who says, "Excuse me for a minute. I need a break," and then walks around the room until he feels calm enough to return to the group.

(Continued)

Types of Evidence-Based Supports (*Continued*)

Type	Explanation	Example
		Visual Supports
Visual timer	Any type of time-keeping device that allows a student to see how much time has passed/is remaining before the start of a new activity	Saiko3p/Shutterstock

		Auditory Supports
Type	Explanation	Example
Verbal advance warning	A verbal statement that includes a time frame and the activity that will occur when the time frame has expired	"In 5 minutes, we will put our books and other things away and go to lunch."
Auditory cue	Any sound that signals the beginning or end of a specified time frame or activity	A timer beeps to indicate that it is time to put things away and go to lunch

The use of visual supports is a key component of the UNC TEACCH Autism Program, which involves providing structure to the environment to help individuals with ASD to make sense of the world. The aim is to organize the physical environment and provide visual cues that sequence activities to make them predictable and understandable. Once new skills are acquired, children are taught to perform them more and more independently as teacher prompts are faded. The structured TEACCH framework is based on four components:

1. Each individual has an individualized plan.
2. The physical structure and organization of the classroom or work area are arranged to meet the needs of the student while he or she is performing required tasks.
3. Visual schedules make daily schedules understandable and predictable.
4. Visual supports are used to explain individual tasks within the daily schedule.

You can learn more about TEACCH at http://teacch.com/

The following video shows how the TEACCH program works for a young girl named Alice.

▶ **The TEACCH Approach**

https://www.youtube.com/watch?v=vkymZzmg4jw

The National Professional Development Center on Autism Spectrum Disorder provides online summaries and interactive modules on evidence-based practices for children and youth with ASD, birth to age 22: http://autismpdc.fpg.unc.edu/evidence-based-practices.

Topic 8.9 Transition

- Students with high functioning ASD should be exposed to a variety of post-secondary education options, career-awareness opportunities, and social skills training.

- Students with low functioning ASD will require transition plans that include different types of goals for employment and for independent living.

What are post-secondary options for students with high functioning ASD? Students with high functioning ASD have the same post-secondary options as their peers without disabilities: college (two- or four-year options), vocational education, and employment. Transition assessments, which can help these students determine which path to take, should cover not only academic achievement but also vocational interests, as well as self-determination, adaptive behavior, and independent living skills. Some of these assessments are standard (you probably took a vocational interest inventory at some point during your high school career). Others are specialized, developed specifically for students with disabilities (e.g., adaptive behavior and independent living skills inventories). The results from these assessments can help students and their families determine career interests, whether post-secondary education or vocational training is needed, where the student will live, with whom he or she will live, skills to be developed, and the types and intensity of supports needed. Because most students will not have all the necessary skills they will need to be successful in post-secondary settings, the assessments also help guide instruction during the high school years to prepare students for life after graduation.

Transition plans for students will contain different goals, based on whether they are preparing for post-secondary education or for employment. For those looking toward college, transition planning includes many of the same components you have learned about in previous chapters: satisfying course requirements for high school graduation; learning and utilizing study skills to maintain required GPA eligibility requirements; careful college selection; and development of self-advocacy skills. Many colleges have developed programs to support students with ASD on campus. The LIFE Program at California State University at Long Beach (https://web.csulb.edu/divisions/students/dss/programs/autism_services/), the MoSAIC program at the University of Tennessee at Chattanooga (http://www.utc.edu/disability-resource-center/mosaic/aboutmosaic/index.php), and the Autism Support Program at the University of Arkansas (http://autism.uark.edu) are just a few of the many options that students with ASD and their families might consider.

In contrast, transition plans for students interested in post-secondary employment should include one or more of the following:

- *Career exploration*—This can include visits to local businesses and companies of interest to students, interviews with potential employers, and career fairs.

- *Job shadowing*—This provides opportunities to observe someone performing the job responsibilities of interest to the student, to learn about the workplace, and to observe the types of communication and interpersonal skills required for the job.

- *Work sampling*—This allows a student to spend meaningful time in the workplace engaged in job tasks that do not require specialized training or learning selected job tasks in an unpaid capacity.

- *Service learning*—A required expectation for many high school students and valuable for students with disabilities, volunteer service activities provide additional exposure to community and vocational opportunities.

- *Internships*—A more formal arrangement than the options above, students learn and perform specified jobs in the workplace during a given period. Internships can be paid or unpaid positions.

- *Apprenticeships*—Another type of formal arrangement in which a student learns trade-specific vocational skills, apprenticeships can be time-based (i.e., one year) or competency-based.

- *Paid employment*—Research indicates that holding a job during high school, including after-school and summer employment, is a consistent predictor of positive post-school employment outcomes for students with a range of disabilities, not just ASD.

Participation in many of these opportunities is maximized when IEP teams include members from places such as a **vocational rehabilitation agency**. Vocational rehabilitation counselors, who work with adults with disabilities to secure gainful employment, can help find job placements, provide job-related training, and more.

The U.S. Department of Labor's career exploration Website, http://www.careeronestop.org, provides information on hundreds of careers. The site has assessments for interests, skills, and work values; information on salaries; and career comparisons. The site has a video library, categorized by career clusters (e.g., Agriculture and Natural Resources), that allows students to virtually explore potential careers. Also included is information that helps students work through a step-by-step process to identify and pay for necessary training, apply for a job, prepare for an interview, and more.

In addition to technical or career-related skills, employers consistently rate social competencies (e.g., the ability to interact positively with others) as critical to job success. Yet students with ASD often have problems with social-communication skills such as engaging in conversations, behaving in a professional manner, or respecting personal space. These skill deficits can cause conflicts with co-workers and result in lack of promotion opportunities or even job termination. Therefore, explicit instruction in social-communication skills is necessary. Social narratives can be helpful, as can teaching scripted responses (e.g., teaching a student to shake hands and say, "It's nice to meet you," after being introduced to someone). Peers can also be taught to provide social cues, reinforcement, or even tutoring during social situations, a practice known as *peer-mediated instruction* and intervention.

The following IRIS Module focuses on the transition process from high school to post-secondary settings and includes information on IEP planning, helping students become their own advocates in the transition process, and collaboration with outside agencies such as vocational rehabilitation offices.

▶ **IRIS Module: Secondary Transition: Helping Students with Disabilities Plan for Post–High School Settings**
http://iris.peabody.vanderbilt.edu/module/tran/

Some of the behavioral characteristics of ASD can be vocational strengths. For example, strengths associated with a need for exact routines or repetition include a meticulous attention to detail and high levels of accuracy, persistence, and reliability. MindSpark Technologies is one of several tech companies to realize this potential. Originally founded to create "careers in high tech for people with specialized abilities," MindSpark provides outsourced IT services—specifically

software testing—via employees with ASD. The company provides vocational training through its MindSpark Training Academy. The MindSpark workplace environment is designed to accommodate sensory over-stimulation issues with headphones and quiet break rooms, includes flexible work hours, and addresses each employee's individual social-emotional needs.

In 2016, MindSpark partnered with AT&T and other global companies in *The 5000 Initiative: Autism in Tech Workforce,* whose goal was to train and employ more than 5,000 individuals with ASD in the tech field. Learn more about this innovative company at http://www.mindsparktech .com and about *The 5000 Initiative* at http://optimityadvisors .com/insights/news/initiative-plans-5000-technology-jobs-people-autism-2020

What are post-secondary options for students whose characteristics fall on the low function-ing end of the spectrum? For these students, most of whom have a co-existing intellectual disability, multiple options are possible. Students and their families can still plan for employment and independent living, each with a range of services based on the severity of the individual's characteristics. For example, students may plan for some type of full- or part-time paid employment (also referred to as competitive employment) or **supported employment**. Supported employment, as its name implies, provides individualized sup-ports (e.g., job training and coaching) for adults with significant disabilities. Individuals in *community-based supported employment* programs work alongside workers without dis-abilities and earn a competitive wage. Examples of community-based supported employ-ment include food service, supermarket stock clerk or bagger, and janitorial or custodial services. In contrast, *on-site supported employment* occurs in structured environments with other employees who have disabilities. Workers in on-site employment programs often earn lower salaries, and the jobs—contracted through local employers—require minimal skill sets (e.g., shredding documents, applying mailing labels). Employers receive federal tax credit benefits for participating in supported employment programs.

A continuum of living arrangements exists to serve individuals with severe ASD, including independent living, partially supported living, and fully supported living. Residential programs, whether providing partially or fully supported living arrange-ments, have been shown to increase community participation, independent functioning, and interpersonal behavior. However, the majority of individuals with severe ASD live at home with family members, usually their parents. As Belinda Butler indicated in the chap-ter opening vignette, finding an appropriate, long-term living option can be a challenge.

Cultural Considerations

As IEP teams work to develop individualized transition plans (ITPs), it is important to consider not only the needs of the student but also family beliefs, needs, and preferences within the context of their culture. For example, an IEP team may plan for Vanya, a student with ASD, to live in a supported living arrangement, yet her family intends for her to live with her parents, and then with siblings or other family members after her parents' deaths. In their Indian culture it is common for extended family members to live together, providing varying levels of support not just for the person with a disability but for

all family members. This practice runs counter to mainstream U.S. cultural norms, according to which adult children are expected to move out of the family home. In another case, a student, Tahir, is being trained to clean up in a local butcher shop. His parents object because he might have to handle pork products, which violates their religious beliefs. As both of these examples illustrate, IEP teams—of which the parents and students are members—must consider not only the student's academic, behavioral, and social-emotional factors when making decisions but those tied to culture as well.

Check Your Understanding 8.2

Click here to gauge your understanding of the concepts in this section.

People and Situations

Learning Outcome

Describe the history of instruction for students with ASD and understand some of the fraudulent research claims that have plagued the field.

Topic 8.10 Origins and History

- The history of ASD chronicles the evolution of research and perceptions of this disability.

- Misinformation about causes of ASD has had negative effects on children with ASD, their families, and—because of fraudulent research that falsely claimed a vaccine–autism link—even children without this condition.

Topic 8.11 Personal Stories

- Temple Grandin, a spokesperson for people with ASD, has provided a personal glimpse into this disorder by sharing her experiences.

- ASD can have a significant effect on the whole family: the child, parents, and other family members.

Anthony Devlin/PA Images/Alamy Stock Photo

Dr. Andrew Wakefield conducted a fraudulent study and made bogus research claims that he had discovered a link between vaccines and ASD. Sadly, this diverted attention and research funds from investigating real causes and effective treatments as researchers attempted unsuccessfully for years to replicate his findings.

Topic 8.10 Origins and History

- The history of ASD chronicles the evolution of research and perceptions of this disability.

- Misinformation about causes of ASD has had negative effects on children with ASD, their families, and—because of fraudulent research that falsely claimed a vaccine–autism link—even children without this condition.

Is ASD a new disability? Although ASD has always been part of the human condition, its actual identification is relatively recent. In 1911, Eugen Bleuler, a Swiss psychiatrist, coined the term *autism* to describe patients with schizophrenia who actively withdrew into their own worlds. A few decades later, in 1943, Leo Kanner, another psychiatrist, reported on 11 children who displayed "extreme autistic aloneness" and failed to communicate or to form normal social relationships with those around them. At that time, autism symptoms were not categorized as ranging from mild to severe, as they are now. Rather, the autism classification included only individuals with severe problems in language, cognition, and behavior.

At about the same time Kanner was characterizing autism, Hans Asperger, a psychiatrist working in Austria, described a related condition in which the individuals had autistic symptoms but were high functioning, often with special talents. Asperger referred to many of the children he studied as "little professors" because they were able to talk about their favorite subjects in great detail. Despite these splinter skills, they showed little empathy for others, were unable to make friends, and were often preoccupied with special interests. Many professionals considered this condition a mild form of autism and sometimes described it as "high functioning autism" because many of these individuals were able to hold jobs and live independent lives. The condition was eventually named after Hans Asperger, initially termed *Asperger's disorder* or *Asperger's syndrome*. It is currently referred to as Asperger syndrome. Throughout much of the twentieth century, psychiatry offered little hope for treating ASD.

In 1994, the APA added Asperger's disorder to its *DSM-IV* definitions. That version of the *DSM* used the term *pervasive developmental disorders* which included five separate disorders: Autistic disorder, Asperger's disorder, pervasive developmental disorder—not otherwise specified (PDD-NOS), Rett's disorder, and childhood disintegrative disorder (CDD). The 1994 edition of the *DSM* also broadened the definition to include high functioning autism, which, as mentioned earlier, contributed to a subsequent increase in prevalence rates. By 2005, the ideas about ASD changed again. Instead of five distinct disorders, typically only three were included as part of ASD: autism, Asperger's disorder, and PDD-NOS. New research findings, coupled with ongoing public and professional discussions and debate, led to the re-conceptualization of this disability in 2013, when the *DSM-5* was released and categorized ASD as one disability that ranges from mild to severe.

In the 1960s, researchers began to investigate the epidemiological basis for autism and its related disorders as well as to develop research-based practices to improve language, behavior, and social skills. No evidence was found to support the theory that autism was caused by bad parenting (discussed below). Instead, experts concluded that ASD resulted from neurobiological problems with a genetic basis. Research and development of behavioral teaching techniques during this time laid the foundation for many of the validated practices used with today's students who have ASD. Ivar Lovaas and other researchers began what has become over 40 years of research demonstrating the power of the applied behavior analysis approach for children with ASD. **The Young Autism Program (YAP)** grew out of this work. YAP is an intensive (up to 40 hours per week) program that relies on procedures discussed earlier, such as task analysis, discrete trials, positive reinforcement, and direct or explicit instruction. With YAP the child is taught one skill at a time until all the skills needed to participate independently in all facets of daily living are mastered. While considerable research supports YAP, it has been evaluated primarily in home-based rather than school-based settings.

Family members of those with ASD have also influenced the history of the field. Bernard Rimland was a psychologist who dedicated his career to studying ASD after his son was diagnosed with it. In 1965, Rimland formed a parent advocacy group called the National Society for Autistic Children, now called the Autism Society. Today, the organization's Website (http://www.autism-society.org) collects, organizes, and disseminates reliable information about the condition. Autism Speaks was founded by Bob and Suzanne Wright, grandparents of a child with ASD, in 2006. The Wrights' goal for their organization was to raise money for research to determine the causes, identify effective treatments, and find a cure for ASD. Their efforts have generated millions of dollars of private and federal funding for research, prevention, and treatment. The Autism Speaks Website (https://www.autismspeaks.org) is another reliable source of information about ASD.

Leo Kanner (left) brought autism to the attention of the scientific community with his study of 11 children, laying the foundation for the world's understanding of this condition. Ivar Lovaas (right), considered by many to be the father of applied behavior analysis, developed many of the validated, structured approaches used today.

How can misinformation affect the treatment of students with ASD and of children in general? Unfortunately, false claims regarding causes of ASD have done irreparable harm to children and their families. In 1967, a prominent psychologist, Bruno Bettelheim, proffered a theory that bad parenting caused infantile autism. In particular, he claimed that cold and distant "refrigerator mothers" produced the disorder because their emotional frigidity resulted in insufficient emotional bonding with their babies. He also placed the blame on those he considered absent or weak fathers. The promotion of Bettelheim's view of autism was devastating for families. Parents blamed themselves and one another for the disorder, and treatment efforts were focused on ineffective psychoanalysis methods and placements in institutions.

In a second case, medical fraud caused a multi-continent health crisis. In 1998, the respected medical journal *The Lancet* published an article by British researcher Andrew Wakefield, who claimed that the three-in-one measles, mumps, and rubella (MMR) vaccine caused gastrointestinal problems and autism. A media circus ensued and Wakefield traveled the world, presenting at conferences and giving interviews and urging a boycott of the MMR vaccine. As a result, thousands of British and American parents refused the vaccine, which put their children at great risk for those diseases and the disabilities they cause (e.g., intellectual disability, deafness, blindness) and even death.

While media coverage heated up and vaccination rates dropped, other medical researchers tried to replicate Wakefield's findings, without success. As study after study found no link between ASD and vaccines, British reporter Brian Deer began to investigate the circumstances around Wakefield's study and discovered unprofessional conduct and intentional fraud. For example:

- Wakefield's study had a weak methodological design, which reviewers and editors at *The Lancet* failed to catch, and included only 12 children.

- The study was funded by lawyers who intended to sue vaccine companies and Wakefield had a patent for a competing measles vaccine, two conflicts of interest that Wakefield did not disclose.

- The children were recruited for the study by anti–MMR vaccine activists. Parents of 11 of the 12 children already blamed the MMR vaccine for their children's conditions *before the study* and several were involved in the lawsuits.

- Wakefield falsified data, including symptoms, characteristics, and timelines reported in the study. For example, he reported that one child displayed autistic-like behavioral symptoms, when medical records indicated that the child actually had a chest infection.

The Lancet eventually retracted the paper, 12 years after it was published and in a small paragraph that received none of the media frenzy of the original article. Wakefield lost his medical license in 2011, but the damage had already been done. As parents refused to vaccinate their children, diseases that had been nearly eradicated resurfaced. Measles, mumps, and whooping cough outbreaks occurred in Europe and the United States. The numbers themselves attest to the effectiveness of vaccinations: in 2004, England experienced a mumps epidemic (56,000 cases) when vaccination rates sank to 85%. Ten years later, when vaccination rates had risen to 95%, England had only 137 cases of mumps.

Why do we dedicate so much space to this story? We do so because too many parents still withhold the vaccine from their children due to fabricated research findings that received heavier news coverage than the discovery that those findings were false. Today, most people have heard of the "vaccination–autism link," but very few have heard the follow-up story. Even now, when news agencies report that research has not found a link between vaccines and ASD, they fail to mention that the original study on which many of these beliefs were founded was falsified. We expect you, as future teachers, to seek out information from reputable sources, evaluate the information yourself when necessary (remember, *The Lancet* was a reputable source), and share research findings with your colleagues and the parents of your students. As you will learn in Topic 8.12, parents are confronted with many questionable treatments that are marketed to "cure" ASD or reduce the severity of symptoms. They may turn to you for advice, and you must have the knowledge to direct them to valid information.

merseysideskeptics.org.uk

Brian Deer receiving the British Press Award for his relentless investigative reporting that uncovered fraud by Andrew Wakefield and his colleagues and sloppy reviewing standards by the prestigious British medical journal, *Lancet*.

You can watch CNN's Anderson Cooper interview Brian Deer about his investigation into Wakefield's study, and some of Wakefield's response to the investigation, in the following video.

▶ **Brian Deer Talks to Anderson Cooper**
https://youtu.be/6dX4JTS4FoQ

Topic 8.11 Personal Stories

- Temple Grandin, a spokesperson for people with ASD, has provided a personal glimpse into this disorder by sharing her experiences.

- ASD can have a significant effect on the whole family: the child, parents, and other family members.

What is it like to have ASD? Because communication is one primary area affected by ASD, many individuals with this disorder are unable to adequately express how it affects them. Temple Grandin, a college professor and world-renowned animal husbandry expert, speaks openly about her experiences with ASD and provides a rare glimpse into this condition. In her book *Thinking in Pictures: My Life with Autism,* she explains how she thinks in pictures and how words are like a second language to her. In her mind, she translates spoken and written words into full-color videos and pictures, complete with sound. She stresses that she experiences emotions, but they are often childlike. She explains that when she was a child she had temper tantrums but they were not really expressions of anger or frustration but rather a result of "circuit overloads." She further describes her emotions: "When I get angry, it is like an afternoon thunderstorm; the anger is intense, but once I get over it, the emotion quickly dissipates. . . . I still have difficulty understanding and having a relationship with people whose primary motivation in life is governed by complex emotions, as my actions are guided by intellect" (p. 90).[2] Temple Grandin's story is the feature of an HBO film highlighted in this chapter's *On the Screen.*

On the Screen: Temple Grandin

https://www.youtube.com/watch?v=bnI_Y8PyTHM

Temple Grandin thinks in pictures, and this film helps viewers understand that, as many of the movie's scenes show the images she visualizes when she listens or looks at something. The film also depicts the struggles she faces when communicating with other people—reading facial expressions, understanding humor, dealing with physical contact—as well as some of the sensory overload she experiences. At the same time, we see how her unique vision and perseverance—two positive traits associated with her ASD—revolutionized livestock handling techniques in the United States.

Click here to listen to Temple Grandin speak about ASD.
https://www.youtube.com/watch?v=1qPFAT4p8Lc

How are family members affected by ASD? For many family members, including parents, siblings, and other relatives, the impact of ASD can be overwhelming and feel all-consuming. They spend inordinate amounts of time and money for supports like ABA and speech therapy beyond what is received at school, for setting the structure and routines needed, and for providing constant monitoring and supervision. Yet, the social and communication requirements of everyday interactions can cause problems in daily living activities: going to the store, walking in the neighborhood, watching a sibling's sporting event. Small changes in a child's routine can cause a tantrum and subsequent discomfort or embarrassment for family members. Some parents have expressed a desire to have their child wear a shirt that reads "I have autism" so that people will understand; others actually have small cards that explain their child's condition, which they pass out to bystanders during behavioral episodes. Sadly, some families restrict the amount of time they take their child out in public to avoid awkward or uncomfortable incidents.

Many families struggle with the costs associated with ASD—health care for the various medical and mental health conditions, as well as supplemental therapies (e.g., speech therapy, applied behavior analysis), creates an enormous financial strain. Recent data indicate that yearly costs to support a child with ASD can reach $60,000. The cost for a lifetime of support is $1.4 million, and rises to $2.4 million if the person also has an intellectual disability. When a child's disability falls on the severe end of the spectrum and he or she requires intensive supports, it is common for a parent to reduce work hours or even leave the workforce entirely, which places additional strain on the family's finances.

Remember Belinda Butler from the chapter opening vignette, who shared her personal perspective on concerns for Justin's future? We share two more personal perspectives below. The first is the chapter opener that Belinda wrote for this text six years ago. It captures how overwhelmed many parents feel, while also conveying empathy for Justin. The second perspective is from Belinda's 15-year-old daughter Helen, whose twin, Trevor, has ASD.

[2]Temple Grandin, *Thinking in Pictures: My Life with Autism.* Vintage Books, © 2010, p. 90

A Mother's Perspective

Today I was whining on the phone to Mom about how hard it is to parent a child with autism. I related Justin's total meltdown at the store today and how embarrassing and frustrating it was. I went on to complain about the stress and the expense of trying to get the services that Justin needs, the sleepless nights, being bitten and scratched, and the endless poop cleanup. I bemoaned the fact that he is just going to get bigger and stronger and less manageable. There were a few "why me's," and "I did not sign up for this" was said at least once.

Mom listened quietly until I was finished ranting. Then she said, "I know it's hard to be you. Think how hard it is to be him." I felt so ashamed. She's absolutely right. Since getting Justin's diagnosis I have been treating him like he is a problem to be solved. I have been focusing on how his autism is disrupting our lives and trying to "fix" him. I have been

Belinda Butler

dragging him from therapy to therapy, changing his food, and plying him with supplements. I have lost sight of the fact that he is a sweet little boy who is doing the best he can, given the circumstances.

I haven't tried to understand how he sees the world; it must be so terrifying and confusing for him. He has no way to know what is coming up next or how to prepare for it. He has no way to tell us that something is painful or scary. He has no way to ask for comfort or help. It's so easy to take it personally when he tantrums or lashes out; but, it's not personal—it's the only way he has to communicate. Instead of focusing on how "bad" he is being, I need to focus on what he is trying to say and help him learn a more appropriate way to say it.

Above all, I need to remember that he's just a little kid, and he's doing the best he can.

A Sister's Perspective

My relationship and involvement with my brothers has evolved over the years. When I was a toddler, my brothers and I were pretty much at the same level intellectually. We would chase one another around in our diapers and I would steal all of the pacifiers. As I began to talk, Trevor didn't. I took full advantage of this and would boss him around. I remember one time my mom told me, "Helen, I am the one in charge, stop bossing Trevor around." In response to that, I said to Trevor, "Did you hear that? Mom is in charge, you have to listen to her!" When kindergarten came along, we went to different schools. Everyone would always ask me why my brother didn't go to school with me. All throughout elementary school, I was proud of my brothers and I wanted everyone to know about them.

Fifth grade was a tough year for me, as a lot of changes were happening in my family. For the duration of middle school, I was embarrassed and burdened by my brothers. I was more hesitant in having people over and many people didn't even know that I had siblings. I would find refuge with my best friend, and she was supportive of not only me, but also my brothers. Once I started high school, my best friend moved across the country. Since I had no place to escape to or relieve my feelings, I became very rude and took a lot of things out on my mom. I became more hostile and wanted nothing to do with home. At school things were going okay. I had some good friends, but there was one girl who had it out for me. We were good friends and I made the mistake of letting her into my personal life and telling her about my brothers.

Belinda Butler

One morning after a sleepover she said to me, "Don't you think it's weird that your brothers have autism and you don't?" I was completely shocked by this statement, and I replied with something like, "I guess so, I don't know. I have never really thought about it that way."

She confidently asked me, "Are you sure you don't have autism too, because you are pretty awkward?" On the outside I stayed calm and collected, but strings of obscenities were running through my head. I actually responded with something along the lines of, "I don't think I am that awkward," and proceeded to text my mom to come and pick me up. I didn't curse my friend out or call out her ignorance, because I knew that my brothers would expect more from me. I have truly learned so much from them and they have made me a better person.

Oftentimes when people find out that I have a twin, they ask if we have twin telepathy or if we are best friends. Over the years I have gotten better at answering the constant stream of questions. Most people love to talk about their siblings, but for me it brings a rush of emotions. When I was younger, I was more public about my family situation and my brothers' conditions. I thought that my brothers were funny and I even told my whole class about how Trevor, my twin, stripped in front of a busy cafeteria. As I have gotten older I have become more private and only talk about my siblings when asked. However, I always feel as if I am lying when I tell people that I have brothers, but omit that which makes them the most unique, autism.

Although many stressors are associated with being the parent of a child with ASD, more supports for families are available now than ever before. This is due, in part, to the increased awareness of ASD.

A Mother's Perspective on Applied Behavior Analysis and Support from Her Daughter's School

In the video below, a mother explains how early intervention services, ABA, and other evidence-based supports have helped her family, and she describes the progress that her daughter has made over the years.

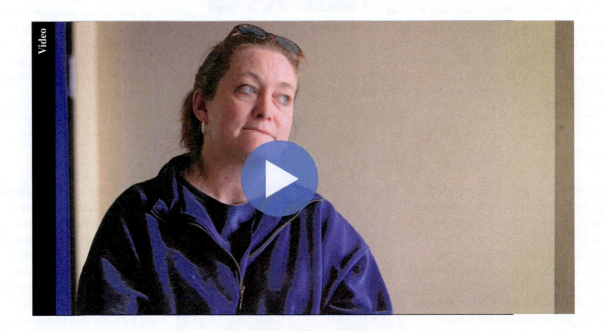

Check Your Understanding 8.3

Click here to gauge your understanding of the concepts in this section.

Future Perspectives

Learning Outcome

Describe emerging research into causes of ASD, identify some of the popular non-validated treatment fads for ASD, and understand how teachers and parents can select appropriate apps for students and themselves.

Topic 8.12 Prevention: Emerging Research

- Current research suggests that ASD is caused by a combination of multiple genetic factors and environmental associations.

- Parents should be wary of treatments that are not validated.

Topic 8.13 Technology: Selecting Appropriate Assistive Technology

- When selecting an app, consider its function over the disability for which it was developed.

- Apps and other technology resources are available to help teachers and parents with data collection and analysis.

Topic 8.12 Prevention: Emerging Research

- Current research suggests that ASD is caused by a combination of multiple genetic factors and environmental associations.

- Parents should be wary of treatments that are not validated.

Can ASD be prevented? Unfortunately, no single cause of ASD is known, so no preventive measures exist at this time. We do know that ASD clearly has a genetic component. Significantly higher rates of ASD occur among family members, and well over a hundred genes, genetic markers (gene or DNA sequences), and genetic mutations have been linked to the condition. Other factors are also associated with ASD, such as pre-term birth, low birth weight, delivery by cesarean section, and prenatal exposure to traffic-related air pollution (particularly during the third trimester). It is important to note that these factors are *associated* with ASD but are not causes. An association means that a higher number of cases of ASD occur when specific factors are present. However, they are not necessarily the cause. The ASD could have resulted from whatever condition or factor caused the pre-term birth or low birth weight. Current medical thinking is that ASD is first and foremost a genetic condition. In fact, researchers who studied thousands of twin pairs, with and without ASD, estimate that 56% to 95% of the effect is genetic. However, the researchers also noted environmental influences, lending support to the hypothesis that an individual can have a genetic predisposition to ASD that may be triggered by an environmental stimulus.

Given the above information, women who are planning to get pregnant can consider prenatal genetic counseling, particularly if they have a family history of ASD. One goal of prenatal genetic counseling is to help assess the risk for certain hereditary conditions. However, because the specific genetic contributions to ASD are still being investigated, the risk assessment is less precise than for other conditions. During pregnancy, the same health considerations listed in earlier chapters should be followed:

- Avoid tobacco, alcohol, and drugs.
- Maintain proper nutrition.
- Get proper prenatal medical care.

When a child is identified with ASD, early intervention services can significantly reduce the effects of the disorder. Therefore, universal screening for toddlers at 18 and 24 months is recommended to identify children with ASD as early as possible. These toddlers can then begin receiving services like speech-language therapy, ABA, and other supports that are individually tailored to their unique social-communication and behavioral needs.

What should parents know about new treatments that claim to cure ASD? First and foremost, any claim that a treatment can cure ASD is false. There is no known cure for ASD, only evidence-based interventions that can improve social-communication skills and reduce behavioral challenges. Unfortunately, parents are bombarded with misinformation through Website ads, testimonials, and blogs about treatments that have not been validated through rigorous research. Some of these treatments, such as dolphin-assisted therapy, are relatively safe and can be fun, though they produce no positive changes in ASD symptoms. Other treatments, such as bleach therapy (in which children are given oral doses or enemas containing diluted bleach) are extremely dangerous. One popular treatment that has not been validated is a gluten-free/casein-free (GFCF) diet. Gluten is a protein found in wheat, barley, and rye; casein is a protein found in dairy products. Despite consistent evidence that this diet has no effect on language, attention, activity and sleep levels, or bowel habits, it is estimated that anywhere from 50% to 75% of all families have put their children with ASD on this elimination diet.

Why, without hard evidence, would parents submit their children to ineffective treatments? Researchers hypothesize that the **placebo effect** plays a large role, particularly when parents have put significant effort into the diet. In other situations, the diet is implemented in conjunction with ABA and speech therapy, social skills training, and other validated interventions. Without a methodological process to determine what is causing behavioral changes (if any), parents often attribute the changes to the diet. In some cases, researchers have found that parents have such strong perceptions that they ignore evidence to the contrary. Another reason is that, without a vaccine or pill or other medical treatment for ASD, parents feel pressured to try alternative treatments out of fear that if they do nothing, they could miss an opportunity to help their child. Belinda Butler captures this pressure, and the sense of fleeting time constraints, in the box below—the first personal perspective she wrote for an earlier edition of this text. Notice the wide range of treatments she mentions, including ABA and speech therapy, which are validated interventions, and the many that are definitely not. You can learn the facts behind many of the unproven treatments she mentions (and more that were not on her list) on the Autism Science Foundation's Website: http://autismsciencefoundation.org/what-is-autism/beware-of-non-evidence-based-treatments/

The Maze

My husband and I have two boys with autism. Receiving a diagnosis of autism is difficult, in large part because there is no universally accepted treatment protocol at this time. The professional making the diagnosis does not say, "He has autism. This is what you should do…" Parents are left to research different interventions on their own, and most choose a course of treatment without much professional advice.

Imagine yourself in a maze—not the simple kind used with rats in the psychology lab, but something bigger and darker with dozens of choices at every turn. The well-being of your child—indeed his very future—rests upon your ability to navigate this maze successfully. You are being timed, and the penalties for standing still are stiff. At the entrance to each corridor is a gatekeeper who will charge you time and money to enter. Some of the most promising corridors are too expensive. Others have prohibitively long lines of people waiting to get in. Several corridors look inviting, but after investing your time and money, you find a dead end. Now here's the kicker: For most, the maze never ends. You can only hope to get as close to the jackpot as possible.

Since our first child was diagnosed two years ago, we have investigated applied behavioral analysis (ABA), speech therapy, occupational therapy, music therapy, auditory integration therapy (AIT), art therapy, and water therapy. We have looked into therapeutic riding, dolphin therapy, the Picture Exchange Communication System (PECS), megavitamin therapy, chelation, antifungal treatments, serotonin inhibitors, secretin, anti-yeast agents, and gluten-free/casein-free diets. We have had the boys tested for chromosomal abnormalities, allergies, lead poisoning, and mercury poisoning. Am I forgetting anything? Oh yes, we spoke with a doctor who prescribes blood thinners for children with autism despite the fact that he has no scientific data to back up his theories.

After two years of navigating the maze, my husband and I have decided that certain corridors are not worth investigating. We do not enter corridors that might be potentially harmful to our children. We steer clear of those choices that might benefit our sons at the expense of the family unit. Most important, we have learned to ignore the ticking of the ever-present clock. We have decided that success at any age is still success.

Trusted Resources

Throughout this chapter, we have provided multiple links to trusted organizations and their Websites as they pertain to or align with the content in that section. We thought it might prove helpful to provide them again, all together in one place, for ease of use.

- The ASD Toddler Initiative, http://asdtoddler.fpg.unc.edu

- The Autism Society, www.autism-society.org
- Autism Speaks, www.autismspeaks.org
- The Centers for Disease Control and Prevention, www.cdc.gov
- The National Professional Development Center on Autism Spectrum Disorder, http://autismpdc.fpg.unc.edu

Topic 8.13 Technology: Selecting Appropriate Assistive Technology

- When selecting an app, consider its function over the disability for which it was developed.

- Apps and other technology resources are available to help teachers and parents with data collection and analysis.

What should teachers and families consider when selecting apps for children with ASD? Developers have created dozens of apps for individuals with disabilities, some of which are advertised as particularly beneficial for, or developed exclusively for, students with ASD. Yet, a disability-specific app is not the key feature that consumers should consider. Rather, the focus on improvement of particular characteristics— social skills, self-regulation, use of speech—is more pertinent. When selecting apps to meet the unique needs of a student with ASD, remember to utilize information you learned in Topics 6.13 and 7.13: consider key factors of apps, such as purpose, age range, skill, ease of use, cost, and ratings or recommendations from reputable organizations (e.g., www.understood.org). The Autism Speaks Website contains a searchable app database that can sort by function (e.g., social skills, communication), age range, and device. Search results include supporting research (e.g., no data, anecdotal data, research with abstracts). The following table lists some common target areas for students with ASD and some current apps that address those needs. If Proloquo2Go sounds familiar, it is because we first introduced it in Chapter 5 for speech and language impairments. This particular app illustrates how the skill, not the disability, should be the primary selection consideration. Remember that technology changes quickly, so these apps are provided as illustrative examples; the list is by no means exhaustive.

Sample Apps for Children

Target Area	App	Description
Communication	Proloquo2Go www.assistiveware.com/product/proloquo2go	An AAC app for people who have trouble speaking or cannot speak at all, this app provides over 7,000 symbols, natural-sounding text-to-speech voices, and more.
	PECS III http://www.pecsusa.com/phase3.php PECS IV+App https://www.youtube.com/watch?v=9wRykZKrl7I	These apps are designed to resemble the PECS communication board and provide digital versions of this validated communication system.
Visual schedules, task management, organization	IMPACT Every Day https://impacteverydayapp.com	This app has an easy-to-use, visual platform through which students can schedule their entire day, add activities, set reminders, request help, and more. Activities can also be scheduled days, weeks, and months in advance.
Self-regulation	Calm Counter—Social Story and Anger Management Tool https://www.youtube.com/watch?v=NLVZmRkfeoE	This app uses a social story to teach children how to calm themselves down; it uses visual cues and strategies like counting backward and deep breathing. There is a free version for teachers.

Are there apps and other resources that parents and teachers can use? Absolutely! Again, the key is to select apps based on their function, ratings, ease of use, and cost, rather than simply choosing those that advertise themselves as autism-specific. For example, the Website www.wevideo.com is helpful for editing videos to use with video modeling. Teachers and parents can create a free account, upload their videos, and then use the site's tools to edit the videos, eliminating the need for specialized or expensive software. In other cases, parents and teachers may need resources that can help them develop visual schedules to provide support for ABA data collection and analyses. The following table provides a few examples.

Sample Apps for Parents and Teachers

Target Area	App	Description
Communication	iCommunicate http://a4cwsn.com/grembe-inc/	Creates communication boards, visual schedules, storyboards, routines, choice boards, and flashcards; comes pre-loaded with pictures and storyboards, routines, and daily schedules; can record audio, use text-to-speech, use personal photos, and more
Behavioral data collection	Behavior Tracker Pro www.behaviortrackerpro.com	Assists with data collection, including an option for functional behavioral assessments (FBAs); allows for selection of target behaviors; assists with data analysis and provides charts, graphs, and frequency tables of the data
	Skill Tracker Pro http://www.behaviortrackerpro.com/products/stp/STP-for-iPhone.aspx	Facilitates ABA implementation by tracking skill acquisition, scheduling retention checks, and exporting data to Excel worksheets; includes an option to video record intervention sessions that can be shared with teachers, IEP team members, and family members

Courtesy of Data Makes the Difference

Courtesy of Data Makes the Difference

The Behavior Tracker Pro app lets teachers and therapists collect data on precise behaviors of concern (left). It also puts the data into meaningful visual formats, such as frequency tables and graphs (right).

Check Your Understanding 8.4

Click here to gauge your understanding of the concepts in this section.

Summary

Autism Spectrum Disorder Described

Autism spectrum disorder (ASD) is a condition in which individuals demonstrate deficits in social interactions and communication skills as well as fixated interests and repetitive behaviors.

- An individual with ASD may demonstrate a variety of severity levels across different skills and traits.

- Deficits in social communication and social interaction create difficulties in interpersonal relationships for individuals with ASD, while the need for sameness and restrictive, repetitive behaviors can cause problems in the execution of everyday activities.

- Applied behavior analysis (ABA) is a highly researched, validated method to increase desired behaviors and reduce or eliminate unwanted ones.

- The prevalence of ASD is increasing at a dramatic rate, though there are no definitive answers to why this is occurring.

Special Education

ASD creates challenges in many areas: academics, behavior, physical and mental health, interpersonal relationships, and activities of daily or independent living.

- Solutions to these challenges include applied behavior analysis (ABA) and the Picture Exchange Communication System (PECS), along with UDL, differentiated

- instruction, accommodations, assistive technology, and medical interventions.

- Students with ASD will require different accommodations for symptoms related to social communication and social interaction than for those needed to address behavioral challenges.

- ASD has clear early warning signs, many of which are evident by a child's first birthday.

- The Picture Exchange Communication System (PECS) is a validated practice used to improve expressive communication skills.

- Many of the strategies learned in earlier chapters can be used to address the communication, academic, and behavioral challenges of students with ASD, while evidence-based visual and auditory supports can help with the need for order, sameness, and routine.

- Transition plans will be different for students with high functioning ASD (e.g., post-secondary education options, career-awareness opportunities, and social skills training) than for students on the low functioning end of the spectrum (e.g., employment and independent living).

People and Situations

ASD was first documented in 1911; much of the research comes from the field of psychiatry.

- Unfortunately, misinformation about causes of ASD has had negative effects on children with ASD, their families, and—because of fraudulent research that falsely claimed a vaccine–autism link—even children without this condition.

- ASD can have a significant effect on the whole family: the child, parents, and other family members.

Future Perspectives

At present, researchers are investigating causes and treatments for ASD. Current findings suggest that a combination of multiple genetic factors and environmental associations cause this condition, and there is currently no cure.

- Parents should be wary of treatments that are not validated.

- Whether selecting technology for students or for parents, the purpose or function should be the primary consideration.

Addressing CEC Standards

Council for Exceptional Children (CEC) knowledge standards addressed in this chapter: 6.2, 1.0, DDA1K1, DDA1K2, DDA1K3, DDA1K4, DDA1K5, DDA2K2, DDA4K2, DDA8K1, DDA10K1, DDA10S1.

See the Appendix for the complete CEC Initial Level Special Educator Preparation Standards.

Chapter 9
Intellectual Disability

Courtesy of Julie Petty

Julie Ann Petty, pictured here with her two sons, is a disability advocate who has a remarkable set of achievements. President Obama appointed Ms. Petty, along with actress Lauren Potter, one of the stars of the television show *Glee*, to the President's Committee on Intellectual Disabilities in 2012. They are the first people with intellectual disabilities[1] to be appointed to this important committee, which was established by President Lyndon Johnson in 1966 after the assassination of President John F. Kennedy. President Kennedy, whom you will learn more about in Topic 9.11, had been developing policies to better the life of each individual with an intellectual disability, but died before their implementation. The President's Committee on Intellectual Disabilities, which includes 21 citizens and 13 federal representatives, was put into place in part as a tribute to him. Ms. Petty advanced to chairperson of this important committee, which advises the president and the secretary of the U.S. Department of Health and Human Services, and completed her term at the end of 2016. She is a disability program specialist at the University of Arkansas Center on Disabilities. She received a bachelor of arts degree in journalism from the University of Arkansas. Accomplishments like hers and those of so many others clearly signal a brighter future. Ms. Petty is nationally recognized as an expert in self-advocacy.

---

[1] Many professional and advocacy organizations, as well as federal and state agencies, use the singular term *intellectual disability*, while others use the plural term, *intellectual disabilities*. In this chapter, we use the singular when referring to the condition and its definition and when we are talking about one person. We use the plural when referring to more than one person or a group of people.

Watch the following video to hear her important message.

▶ **Interview with Julie Petty**

https://youtu.be/bu8SM6wokAY

 Learning Outcomes

Intellectual Disability Described

Define intellectual disability, explain two ways to classify the types of intellectual disability, describe the relationship among the three characteristics of this disability, and discuss the prevalence and inclusion rates as compared to other disabilities.

Special Education

Explain the ways in which intellectual disability can impact learning and independent living, describe the different accommodations and modifications that can address these challenges, understand methods that early childhood and classroom teachers can use to reduce the problems associated with intellectual disability, and describe transition considerations for individuals with intellectual disabilities.

People and Situations

Describe the history of instruction for students with intellectual disabilities and discuss the effects of advocacy and changing attitudes

Future Perspectives

Explain how preventive measures can reduce the incidence of intellectual disability, discuss how inaccurate public information threatens the implementation of preventive measures, explain how technology can benefit individuals with intellectual disabilities, particularly in areas of independent living.

Intellectual Disability Described[2]

Learning Outcome

Define intellectual disability, explain two ways to classify the types of intellectual disability, describe the relationship among the three characteristics of this disability, and discuss the prevalence and inclusion rates as compared to other disabilities.

Topic 9.1 Intellectual Disability Defined

- Intellectual disability is a chronic, severe, and lifelong disability that emerges between birth and age 18.

- Three key areas of concern associated with intellectual disability are cognition, adaptive skills, and the need for supports.

---

[2] References for Chapter 9 are found at the end of this text.

Topic 9.2 Types of Intellectual Disability

- Intellectual disability ranges from mild to severe; however, over 95% of all cases are in the mild range.

- Two of the most common types, fragile X syndrome and Down syndrome, have a genetic cause; while the third most common type, fetal alcohol spectrum disorders (FASDs), is caused by alcohol consumption by pregnant women.

Topic 9.3 Characteristics

- Problems with cognition include difficulty with skills like remembering, reasoning, transferring learning from one task to another; problems with adaptive skills include areas such as social skills, living independently, and holding a job.

- A network of supports is needed to help individuals with intellectual disability address cognitive and adaptive skills.

Topic 9.4 Prevalence and Placement

- The size of the intellectual disability category is less than would be expected based on normal curve estimates.

- Students with intellectual disabilities experience less inclusion in general education than most other students with disabilities.

George Doyle/Exactostock-1491/Superstock

No one should limit his or her assumptions about the accomplishments individuals can achieve.

Topic 9.1 Intellectual Disability Defined

- Intellectual disability is a chronic, severe, and lifelong disability that emerges between birth and age 18.

- Three key areas of concern associated with intellectual disability are cognition, adaptive skills, and the need for supports.

What does it mean to have an intellectual disability? First, keep in mind that the terminology for this disability changed in recent years. Rosa's Law (discussed in Topics 1.8 and 9.11) requires all legislation using the outdated term *mental retardation* to retroactively change to the preferred term *intellectual disability*.

Two different definitions for **intellectual disability** are used in the United States today. Most states use the IDEA definition. However, many professionals prefer the definition adopted in 2010 by the American Association of Intellectual and Developmental Disabilities (AAIDD), the oldest professional organization in the United States working on behalf of these individuals. Notice that the second part of the name for the AAIDD refers to **developmental disability**. Developmental disability is an umbrella term that includes intellectual disability, but also other disabilities that appear in childhood and are chronic, severe, and lifelong. The individuals affected may have both a cognitive and physical disability. For example, a child with cerebral palsy who has both a physical and cognitive component would be considered to have a developmental disability. However, it is also important to remember that not all individuals with cerebral palsy have a cognitive or intellectual disability.

Both the federal and AAIDD definitions are provided in the following table. Look carefully at these two definitions. The AAIDD definition is more detailed and comprehensive than the federal government's definition. Further, the IDEA definition references the disability occurring during the developmental period, whereas the AAIDD definition specifies that the disability must occur *before* the individual's 18th birthday.

Definitions of Intellectual Disability

Term	Definition	Source
Intellectual disability	Intellectual disability means significant subaverage general intellectual functioning, existing concurrently with deficits in adaptive behavior and manifested during the developmental period that adversely affects a child's educational performance.	IDEA '04, U.S. Department of Education
Intellectual disability	Intellectual disability is characterized by significant limitations both in intellectual functioning and in adaptive behavior as expressed in conceptual, social, and practical adaptive skills. This disability originates before age 18. The following five assumptions are essential to the application of this definition: 1. Limitations in present functioning must be considered within the context of community environments typical of the individual's age peers and culture. 2. Valid assessment considers cultural and linguistic diversity as well as differences in communication, sensory, motor, and behavioral factors. 3. Within an individual, limitations often coexist with strengths. 4. An important purpose of describing limitations is to develop a profile of needed supports. 5. With appropriate personalized supports over a sustained period, the life functioning of the person with intellectual disability generally will improve.	American Association of Intellectual and Developmental Disabilities (AAIDD)

SOURCES: From *34 CFR Parts 300 and 303, Assistance to States for the Education of Children* with *Disabilities and the Early Intervention Program for Infants and Toddlers* with *Disabilities; Final Regulations* (p. 1263), U.S. Department of Education, 2006, *Federal Register,* Washington, DC; and *Intellectual Disability: Definition, Classification, and Systems of Supports* (p. 1), by R. L. Schalock, S. Borthwick-Duffy, V. J. Bradley, W. H. E. Buntinx, D. L. Coulter, E. M. Craig, S. C. Gomez, Y. Lachapelle, R. Luckasson, A. Reeve, K. A. Shogren, M. E. Snell, S. Spreat, M. J. Tassé, J. R. Thompson, M. A. Verdugo-Alonso, M. L. Wehmeyer, and M. H. Yeager, 2010, Washington, DC: American Association on Intellectual and Developmental Disabilities (AAIDD).

How do the three key areas of concern or limitations called out in the AAIDD definition help define intellectual disability? AAIDD refers to three areas of concern as the defining features or characteristics of this disability. The first area is **intellectual functioning**, the second is **adaptive behavior**, and the third is the **need for supports**.

Some think of intellectual or cognitive limitations as *the* defining feature of intellectual disability. In the past, only measures of intelligence or cognition were used to determine whether an individual had an intellectual disability. AAIDD broadened the definition to include not only limitations in intellectual functioning but also limitations in adaptive behavior and need for supports. To measure intellectual functioning, standardized tests of intellectual ability (IQ tests) are still often used today. Typically, individuals who score at least two standard deviations (at least 30 points) below the mean (a score of 100) on a test of intelligence meet one criterion of intellectual disability. However, parents and professionals have concerns about using these scores for identification purposes. First, although intelligence is complex and has many components (e.g., linguistic, logical-mathematical, spatial, musical, interpersonal), intelligence tests often address only a narrow aspect of cognition. Second, these tests contain inherent biases, particularly when the individual being tested is from a culturally or linguistically diverse background. That bias often results in a lower IQ score. Both of these issues can lead to the misidentification of intellectual disabilities in some students.

Adaptive behavior is the second defining feature of intellectual disability. The following figure illustrates components within the three adaptive behavior skill areas: conceptual, social, and practical. Note that these are all tied to skills needed to function independently. Difficulties in any of these areas can lead to significant issues across a lifetime. Problems with conceptual (basic thinking) skills result in challenges related to language, reading and writing, money, time, number concepts, and basic understanding. Problems with social skills interfere with interacting well with others, having positive self-esteem, and understanding concepts related to social responsibility. Problems with practical skills include difficulties with independent living, personal care, following schedules or routines, health care, holding a job, and transportation.

Examples of the Three Adaptive Skill Areas

The third defining feature of intellectual disability is the need for supports to achieve some level of independence. The response to this need is the creation of **systems or networks of supports**. These supports can take many forms, such as accommodations or direct assistance from a job coach, and are meant to unfetter the individual from challenges presented by this disability. The supports provided should not be controlling or restrictive. They must be individually determined and applied only to the level necessary for the individual to function as independently as possible. In addition, the individual should be involved in the selection of supports and should help to determine the activities in which supports are put into place. As discussed in Topic 9.8, it is important for individuals with intellectual disabilities to learn to make choices. For example, people with disabilities should be able to select what movies they want to see, what television shows they want to watch, and which leisure-time activities they want to pursue, rather than having decisions made for them by caregivers, teachers, family members, and others. These networks of supports, while important, should not impede an individual's ability to develop the skills necessary to live as independently as possible.

Topic 9.2 Types of Intellectual Disability

- Intellectual disability ranges from mild to severe; however, over 95% of all cases are in the mild range.

- Two of the most common types, fragile X syndrome and Down syndrome, have a genetic cause; while the third most common type, fetal alcohol spectrum disorders (FASDs), is caused by alcohol consumption by pregnant women.

What considerations are involved when determining the severity of intellectual disability? Remember, three areas of concern define intellectual disability: cognition, adaptive behavior, and need for supports. The severity of cognition and adaptive behavior limitations ranges from mild to profound; as severity increases, the need for more sustained and intensive supports becomes greater. Also, as cognition becomes more limited, typically so, too, does adaptive behavior. These characteristics are all interrelated. Although we all know very bright people with limitations in adaptive behavior, it is rare to find someone with considerable limitations in cognition who does not also have significant limitations in adaptive behavior.

When most people think about intellectual disability, they focus on cognitive limitations. For this reason, we'll consider this characteristic first. Historically, tests of intelligence (IQ tests) were exclusively used to determine intellectual disability. Despite criticism from the U.S. courts, parents, the federal government, and professional organizations, many school districts and countries around the world still rely on intelligence tests when identifying intellectual disability and its level of severity. IQ tests do provide quick answers to whether an intellectual disability exists and to its level of severity. Let's look at the foundation for these tests.

IQ tests are built on the idea that human characteristics, such as intelligence, height, and weight, are distributed in such a way that half of the population falls above and half falls below the average in ever decreasing segments in both directions. For example, a doctor might tell parents that their toddler is in the 50th percentile in weight and the 80th percentile in height. This means that their child's weight is more than or equal to that of 50% of the children her age and that she is taller than or equal in height to 80% of the children her age. A similar concept can be applied to scores from IQ tests.

A diagnosis of intellectual disability begins with scores more than two standard deviations (SDs) below the mean score of 100. A standard deviation is 15 points, so scores below 70 meet the IQ score criterion for intellectual disability. The further below the mean an IQ score falls, the more significant and complicated the disability. In theory, a "mild" classification of intellectual disability begins with scores less than

2 SDs below the mean (IQ score of 69), "moderate" begins at roughly 3 SDs below the mean, "severe" begins at approximately 4 SDs below the mean, and "profound" begins at around 5 SDs below the mean. The figure illustrates the normal curve and the distribution of IQ scores.

Normal Curve and Intellectual Disability

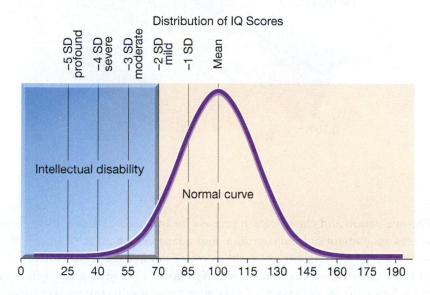

Although the theoretical classification of mild, moderate, severe, and profound intellectual disability is based on the number of standard deviations below the mean, in reality, the actual scores used are slightly different. The box shows the classification by severity level when using IQ scores.

Classifying Intellectual Disabilities by Severity

- *Mild intellectual disability:* IQ range of 50 to 69.

  Outcomes: Has learning difficulties, is able to work, can maintain good social relationships, contributes to society

- *Moderate intellectual disability:* IQ range of 35 to 49

  Outcomes: Exhibits marked developmental delays during childhood, has some degree of independence in self-care, possesses adequate communication and academic skills, requires varying degrees of support to live and work in the community

- *Severe intellectual disability:* IQ range of 20 to 34

  Outcomes: Has continuous need for supports

- *Profound intellectual disability:* IQ under 20

  Outcomes: Demonstrates severe limitations in self-care, continence, communication, and mobility; requires continuous and intensive supports

Study the figure showing the normal curve again. Most scores occur in the middle of the normal curve, and the largest group of scores falls between 1 SD above the mean and 1 SD below the mean. Notice that progressively fewer scores occur in each of the bands that fall further from the mean. As with almost all disabilities, most cases of intellectual disability are mild, and substantially fewer fall into the severe or profound range. The figure below compares the same data another way to reinforce the point that nearly all cases of intellectual disability (over 95%) fall into the mild range. This fact is important because many people incorrectly assume that all cases of intellectual disability are in the severe range, which is a mistake and can lead to lowered expectations for what these students are capable of achieving.

Prevalence of Intellectual Disability by Severity

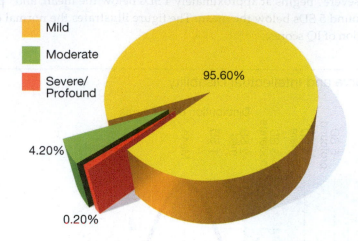

The evaluation and classification process for intellectual disability is complex. It involves assessment of both cognition and adaptive behavior. Although the two areas are often related, patterns of abilities vary from individual to individual. People with the same IQ score often show differences in the strengths of their adaptive behaviors. One person may have very strong social skills but weaker conceptual skills and will need supports in areas related to language; literacy; or money, time, and number concepts. Another person may have strong practical skills—the ability to use the transportation system and follow a schedule—but does not have equivalent strengths in skills that fall into the conceptual area. Professionals may find it difficult to conduct objective evaluations of adaptive behavior, so assessment tools can be helpful.

A careful analysis of information from the cognitive and adaptive behavior assessments leads to the selection and application of supports needed to enhance independence and community presence. The first assessment instrument developed in this area, the *Supports Intensity Scale,* was developed by AAIDD in 2002. It helps professionals think about the network of supports required by each individual. In Topic 9.5, we discuss how supports help solve many difficulties caused by intellectual disability.

What are the major known causes of intellectual disability? Another approach to classifying intellectual disability is by causation. Although the cause for about one-third of cases is unknown, several hundred causes for others have been discovered. Most can be grouped into five major categories:

1. Genetic or hereditary causes

2. Prematurity or low birth weight

3. Toxins

4. Diseases

5. Child abuse and neglect

Within the five causation categories, three major conditions are the most prevalent. First, **fragile X syndrome** (genetic or hereditary) is caused by a mutation on the X chromosome. This syndrome, first identified in 1991, is now recognized as the most common cause of intellectual disability (and some cases of autism). It affects about 1 in 4,000 males and 1 in 8,000 females. Individuals with this condition can have substantial cognitive problems and tend to have difficulty using complex sentences, reading, and speaking. Second, **Down syndrome** also has a genetic basis and is caused by a chromosomal abnormality in which the individual has too few or too many chromosomes. The condition is named after the English doctor, John Langdon Down, who first described an individual with the condition in 1866. In the most common type of Down syndrome, trisomy 21, the 21st set of chromosomes contains three chromosomes rather than the normal pair. The condition is more likely to occur when parents, particularly the mother, is older. Individuals with Down syndrome tend to have some distinct features (e.g., floppy muscle tone, similar flat facial features, small skin folds on the inner corner of the eyes, a single deep crease across the palm). They also are more likely to have a number of other issues, such as respiratory problems, cardiac issues, and hearing impairments. Third, **fetal alcohol spectrum disorders (FASDs)** is a group of conditions caused by mothers drinking alcohol during their pregnancies. **Fetal alcohol syndrome (FAS)** is the most severe disorder along this spectrum. Experts believe that FASDs are *the leading preventable cause* of cognitive problems. The severity of the effects on the child depends on when a woman drank alcohol during her pregnancy as well as how much was consumed. Typical problems of FASDs involve cognition, social skills, and understanding the consequences of one's behavior.

Topic 9.3 Characteristics

- Problems with cognition include difficulty with skills like remembering, reasoning, transferring learning from one task to another; problems with adaptive skills include areas such as social skills, living independently, and holding a job.

- A network of supports is needed to help individuals with intellectual disabilities address cognitive and adaptive skills.

Which two characteristics of intellectual disability set the stage for systems or networks of supports? You may recall from Topic 9.1, *Intellectual Disability Defined*, that AAIDD included three defining features or characteristics of intellectual disability in its definition:

1. Problems with cognition
2. Problems with adaptive behavior
3. Need for supports to sustain independence

As mentioned earlier, the most defining characteristic of intellectual disability is impaired **cognition**, defined as a score below 70 on a test of intelligence. Individuals with intellectual disabilities have cognitive abilities below those of 97% of their peers without disabilities. Impaired cognition makes simple tasks difficult to learn and can interfere with a person's ability to communicate well. Because cognition influences the ability to remember and the application of knowledge and skills already learned, students with intellectual disabilities need to be explicitly taught skills that others learn incidentally or almost naturally. Ultimately, the degree of cognitive impairment determines the type of educational curriculum content needed: academic, life skills, or both.

Problems with adaptive behavior constitute the second defining characteristic of intellectual disability. Adaptive behavior, which allows us to function independently in the community, is not just a problem area for people with intellectual disabilities. Think about people you know who are very smart, get great grades in school, but have awful social skills and cannot seem to manage daily life well. Friends and colleagues often consider these people disorganized, absent-minded, and sometimes even "too smart for their own good." Yet they are still able to get

Just like many adults without intellectual disability, these two friends enjoy the social aspects of getting together and having a drink, an aspect of normalization and community presence.

by, live independently, hold a job, and make friends. Such is not the case, however, for those with intellectual disabilities, which results in pervasive problems with adaptive behavior. Their lack of adaptive behavior skills impacts their ability to live independently, hold a good job, make friends, and participate in leisure-time activities in the community—all necessary to have a **community presence**.

How is the third defining feature or characteristic of intellectual disability related to the other two? The need for supports is the third feature or characteristic of intellectual disability identified by AAIDD. It is somewhat different from the other two defining characteristics. Remember that the first two defining characteristics, problems with cognition and adaptive behavior, result in the need for supports or assistance, the third defining characteristic. Often, individuals with intellectual disabilities use different types of supports that originate from various sources. For example, to have success on the job, some individuals might require help from a job coach, co-workers, and a transportation expert. All of their services come together to form a network of supports. You will learn in Topic 9.5 about the benefits of various types of supports and how they can help resolve or reduce the problems associated with the other two characteristics.

Do supports need to be individualized? Yes, it is important to remember that every person has distinctive strengths and abilities that must be addressed individually, so each person's network of supports will be unique.

It also must be recognized that specific syndromes or conditions often have additional features that the network of supports has to address. For example, most individuals with fragile X syndrome have difficulties with social communications, understanding non-verbal behaviors, using expressive language, and engaging in academic learning. Some may need assistive technology devices to help with communication challenges, as well as extra structure in their educational settings to address engagement issues. Individuals with Down syndrome usually face chronic health problems. Training on health care management, good nutrition, and appropriate exercise is an obvious support; however, you might not realize that they could also benefit from instruction on time management strategies and public transportation schedules to ensure timely arrival at doctors' offices. Students with FAS often have difficulty understanding the consequences of their actions. They might require specially designed behavior management programs in which functional behavioral assessments are integral components of their education plans.

Topic 9.4 Prevalence and Placement

- The size of the intellectual disability category is less than would be expected based on normal curve estimates.

- Students with intellectual disabilities experience less inclusion in general education than most other students with disabilities.

Are the prevalence rates for intellectual disability on par with other disabilities? The answer is a resounding "No." First, let's think again about what percentage of the school population would be expected to have intellectual disability. In Topic 9.2 you learned that when IQ is used to define intellectual disability, criterion for diagnosis begins with 2 standard deviations (SDs) below the mean IQ score of 100. Let's think about how this knowledge can be applied to the prevalence of disabilities as compared to all students' scores of intelligence or IQ scores. As the graph shows, 95.46% of all scores in a normal curve fall above the marker for 2 SDs below the mean score. Therefore, we would expect 4.54% of all students to meet the criterion for and be diagnosed with intellectual disability.

Distribution of IQ Scores along the Normal Curve

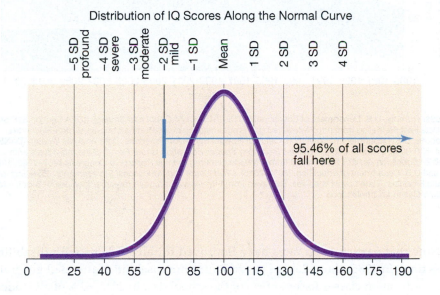

Distribution of IQ Scores Along the Normal Curve

95.46% of all scores fall here

Despite the statistical expectation of identifying more than 4% of all schoolchildren as having intellectual disabilities, substantially less than 1% (0.07%) receive special education services through the intellectual disability category. This is about half the number of students who received special education services through this category some 30 years ago.

Why would the expected percentage be so much greater than the actual percentage of students with identified intellectual disabilities? Here are two reasons. First, other disability categories like autism spectrum disorder and multiple disabilities also include students whose scores on tests of intelligence fall 2 SDs below the mean. Second, because of the stigma and segregation historically associated with intellectual disability, many educators are cautious about using this category to qualify students for special services, particularly those from diverse backgrounds.

Where do students with intellectual disabilities receive their education? Since the passage of IDEA in 1975, and particularly across the past three decades, more and more students with disabilities are included in general education classes at their neighborhood schools. However, as shown in the figure below, which compares placement or inclusion rates for all students who have disabilities (blue) with those who have intellectual disabilities (green), students without intellectual disabilities have greater rates of inclusive education. The data shown in the following graph compare the inclusion rates for all students with disabilities to those of students with intellectual disabilities since 1985.

Comparison of Inclusion Rates for All Students with Disabilities and Those with Intellectual Disabilities

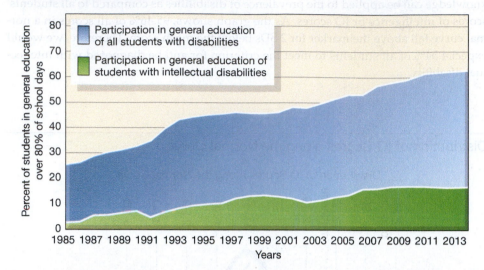

SOURCES: From the U.S. Department of Education. (2013-2015). *Child Count and Settings* [IDEA Section 618 State Level Data File]. Retrieved from http://www2.ed.gov/programs/osepidea/618-data/state-level-data-files/index. html#bccee; U.S. Department of Education, Office of Special Education Programs, Data Analysis System (DANS), OMB #1820-0043: *Children With Disabilities Receiving Special Education Under Part B of the Individuals With Disabilities Education Act-2011.* Retrieved from www.ideadata.org; *Annual Reports to Congress* 1987, 1992, 1997, 2007; and U.S. Department of Education. (2013-2015). *Child Count and Educational Environments.* IDEA Section 618 Data Products: State Level Data Files. Retrieved from http://www2.ed.gov/programs/osepidea/618-data/state-level-data-files/index.html#bccee

Note that participation rates have improved for all students with disabilities across time. In 1985, about 26% of all students with disabilities attended general or regular education classes for over 80% of the school day. In 2013, 62% of all students with disabilities attended general education classes in neighborhood schools for more than 80% of the school day. Across time, the inclusion rates for students with intellectual disabilities are consistently much lower than those for students with other disabilities. In 1985, their inclusion rates were dismal. Then, only 3% of students with intellectual disabilities attended general education classes for over 80% of the school day. In 2013, only 17% received services in the general education classroom for most of their school day.

Now let's take a closer look at where students with intellectual disabilities are educated. Study the following graph. Unlike most students with other disabilities, such as learning disabilities and others you have learned about already in this text, the majority of students with intellectual disabilities receive most of their education in non-inclusive settings. Today 49% attend separate special education classes and an additional 6% attend separate schools. Only 17% receive most of their education primarily in general education settings, with the remaining 26% receiving additional educational help through resource room services. Earlier you learned that over 95% of students have mild disabilities, so these data should be surprising to you. Some good reasons can explain these placement rates. For example, many students with intellectual disabilities participate in community-based instruction outside the typical school setting, particularly during high school years. Instruction is often delivered one-on-one in the natural or real-life setting (community). Through community-based experiences, students learn transportation, daily living, and work skills that are not part of the typical high school curriculum but are critical to independent living later in life.

Where Students with Intellectual Disabilities Are Educated

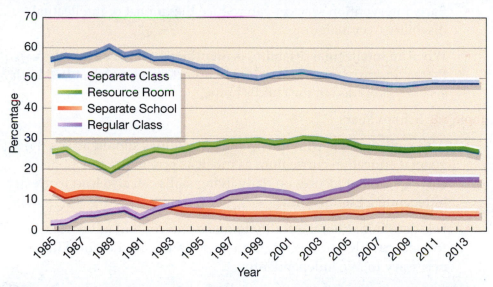

SOURCES: From U.S. Department of Education. (2013-2015). *Child Count and Settings* [IDEA Section 618 State Level Data File]. Retrieved from http://www2.ed.gov/programs/osepidea/618-data/state-level-data-files/index. html#bccee; U.S. Department of Education, Office of Special Education Programs, Data Analysis System (DANS), OMB #1820-0043: *Children with Disabilities Receiving Special Education under Part B of the Individuals with Disabilities Education Act-2011.* Retrieved from www.ideadata.org; *Annual Reports to Congress* 1987, 1992, 1997, 2007; and U.S. Department of Education. (2013-2015). *Child Count and Educational Environments.* IDEA Section 618 Data Products: State Level Data Files. Retrieved from http://www2.ed.gov/programs/osepidea/618-data/ state-level-data-files/index.html#bccee

Check Your Understanding 9.1

Click here to gauge your understanding of the concepts in this section.

Special Education

Learning Outcome

Explain the ways in which intellectual disability can impact learning and independent living, describe the different accommodations and modifications that can address these challenges, understand methods that early childhood and classroom teachers can use to reduce the problems associated with intellectual disability, and describe transition considerations for individuals with intellectual disabilities.

Topic 9.5 Challenges and Their Solutions

- Intellectual disability creates challenges in the areas of cognition and adaptive skills.

- In addition to being a characteristic of intellectual disability, systems or networks of supports are also partial solutions to these challenges.

Topic 9.6 Accommodations

- Students with mild intellectual disabilities might benefit from instructional and testing accommodations to overcome cognitive challenges.

- Students with the most severe cognitive impairments might also need adaptations such as alternative academic achievement standards along with alternative assessments.

Topic 9.7 Early Intervention

- Early intervention services can reduce the impact of intellectual disability over a lifetime.

- When an intellectual disability is identified at birth or shortly thereafter, early intervention services start immediately, often with services provided in the child's home.

Topic 9.8 School Years

- Although students with intellectual disabilities should access the general education curriculum as much as possible, a functional curriculum that focuses on daily living skills can also lead to greater independence as an adult.

- Self-determination, the ability to make choices and advocate for one's needs and desires, is an important collection of skills necessary to live independently.

Topic 9.9 Transition

- Being college- and career-ready are important transition goals to improve employment and independent living outcomes.

- Supported employment that often includes job coaches, help from co-workers, and concessions from employers not only provides opportunities for competitive employment but is also cost effective.

Students with intellectual disabilities can succeed when given the opportunities provided to everyone!

Topic 9.5 Challenges and Their Solutions

- Intellectual disability creates challenges in the areas of cognition and adaptive skills.

- In addition to being a characteristic of intellectual disability, systems or networks of supports are also partial solutions to these challenges.

What challenges often result from intellectual disability? First, remember that every person has unique abilities, strengths, limitations, and needs. Regardless, two of the defining characteristics of intellectual disability result in challenges that sometimes can seem overwhelming to individuals and their family members.

All those with intellectual disabilities, to a greater or lesser degree, have problems with cognition or intellectual functioning. One result can be difficulties with both comprehending and using language, which can affect communication, reading, and following instructions. Understanding the give and take of interpersonal relationships might also be affected. Another challenge is the inability to remember even simple routines, such as how to get ready for recess (e.g., putting away work, getting a jacket, and then lining up at the classroom door). Even though the vast majority of cases of intellectual disabilities fall within the mild range, the disability still affects thinking skills. Reasoning or thinking through complex tasks or situations (i.e., problem solving) is a challenge related to cognitive functioning, but it also impacts adaptive behavior, the second feature of intellectual disability.

Recall that the three adaptive skill domains are conceptual, social, and practical. Problems with adaptive skills affect an individual's ability to perform basic life skills. Many people without cognitive issues have difficulties with adaptive skills (e.g., arriving to work on time, spending within one's means) but—for most—these problems do not create major life problems. Further, they are often able to compensate for areas of weakness, or recognize the problems and correct them (getting up half an hour earlier or taking a different route to work, setting up a budget or getting a second job). In contrast, people with intellectual disabilities typically face challenges in at least one, if not all, of the adaptive skill domains to such a degree that their ability to function adequately or live independently is affected.

The third characteristic, need for supports or assistance, emanates from the two characteristics just reviewed. As you will learn next, supports can help resolve or lessen problems caused by limitations in cognition and adaptive behavior. The figure below highlights the challenges often presented by this disability.

Challenges of Intellectual Disability

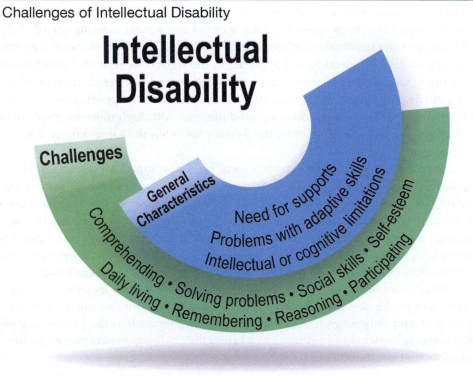

Can supports be both a component of the definition of intellectual disability and a main factor in its partial solution? Yes, when considering intellectual disability, the *need* for supports—resources and strategies that promote personal development and enhance functioning—is part of the disability's definition, while the *use* of supports can mitigate the effects of the disability. The idea to use networks of supports to resolve issues with thinking skills and adaptive behavior began in 2002, when AAIDD created a new definition of intellectual disability. For the first time, the concept of need for supports became part of the definition.

Receiving assistance can reduce or eliminate the differences between one's skills and ability levels and those required to meet the demands of life. For people with intellectual disabilities, systematic and sometimes intensive, individualized (personalized) supports allow them to live in the community, hold a job, participate in leisure-time activities, and enjoy life. In some cases, supports need to be intensive and sustained. In other words, some people may need continual, ongoing assistance throughout their lives. These supports may be needed in one area of their lives (e.g., transportation to get to and from work) or in multiple areas.

A network of supports, which puts multiple supports into place to address a variety of challenges, is one way to organize services. Professionals, and others like parents and friends, within the network have areas of expertise that can determine what types of help to offer so a person can accomplish what he or she wants or needs to do. This proactive approach is more positive and constructive than considering only the negative aspects of the disability. The system requires a balance between promoting dependency on others and simultaneously allowing the individual to participate in the planning process by encouraging and creating opportunities to make choices. For example, people who have problems with adaptive behaviors must learn to accept help from others, but they also need to be able to explain where they need help and where they do not.

We all use networks of supports in daily life. Where do these supports come from? Supportive relationships, many of which occur naturally, exist among people in almost every setting and in almost every aspect of life. People help each other in day-to-day tasks that range in complexity from simple to difficult. Assistance comes from family members, peers and professionals at school, co-workers, friends, neighbors, and, in some cases, a variety of social service agencies. For students and adults without disabilities, help comes in many areas of life: school crossing guards help students cross the street safely; school counselors help high school students navigate the complex task of selecting and applying to the right college; a co-worker offers guidance in using a new piece of equipment safely; a friend offers to drive to dinner and a movie. For people with intellectual disabilities, these supports must be carefully planned and sustained, often across a lifetime. Although more intensive than the supports used by most people, the sources are often the same: family, friends, peers at school, and co-workers.

In addition, some unique supports have been developed for adults who have intellectual disabilities. Many of these, like learning how to use a subway or bus system, are highly specialized and are often provided through city and local government programs. Social service agencies assist people in getting health care, housing, and job placements. Vocational rehabilitation agencies provide intensive supports in the workplace for training and for the creation of employment opportunities. Because the amount of necessary support varies for each individual and can change over time, it might be helpful to think of supports as a fluid concept, responsive to the needs of the individual by providing only as much assistance as needed, and only when necessary. The following figure lists the various people who make up networks of supports to address the challenges encountered by individuals with this disability.

Solutions to Characteristics Presented by Intellectual Disability

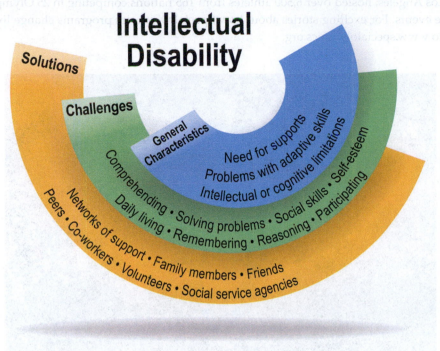

When considering networks of supports, we want to highlight a couple of service organizations that target supports in two important areas: inclusive education and leisure-time participation. **Best Buddies International** was founded by Anthony Shriver, a member of the Kennedy family you will learn more about in Topic 9.11. This organization is made up of middle school, high school, and college student-volunteers who help individuals with intellectual disabilities participate more fully at school and in the community. The organization encourages students without disabilities to form friendships with those who have intellectual disabilities. These volunteers might assist with schoolwork, attend a high school football game, or go to a movie. For more about Best Buddies International and how to get involved, go to www.bestbuddies.org.

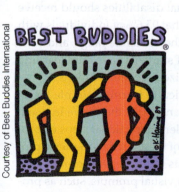

Volunteers who work with Best Buddies International help students with intellectual disabilities by building friendships that extend beyond school.

Special Olympics, another service organization started by the Kennedy family, provides networks of supports so that young people can develop athletic abilities, enjoy recreational activities, and engage in the same types of competitive events as other athletes. The Special Olympics organization hosts local, regional, national, and even international events that involve whole families and communities. The Special Olympics World Games are held every two years, with athletes who have intellectual disabilities participating from countries worldwide. The 2015 Summer Games, held in Los Angeles, hosted over 6,500 athletes from 165 nations competing in 25 Olympic-type events. For exciting stories about how Special Olympics programs change lives, go to www.specialolympics.org.

The excitement about competing in the Special Olympics Games is contagious, leaving everyone with great feelings of participation and achievement.

San Gabriel Valley Tribune/ZUMA Wire/Alamy Stock Photo

Topic 9.6 Accommodations

- Students with mild intellectual disabilities might benefit from instructional and testing accommodations to overcome cognitive challenges.

- Students with the most severe cognitive impairments might also need adaptations such as alternative academic achievement standards along with alternative assessments.

What types of accommodations are appropriate for students with mild intellectual disabilities? Because the severity of intellectual disability ranges from mild to profound, teachers might need to use a wide range of accommodations with this population of students. As is the case with any disability, students with intellectual disabilities should receive accommodations that meet their individual needs. Recall that 95.6% of individuals with intellectual disabilities fall within the mild range, 4.2% in the moderate range, and 0.2% in the severe/profound range. Clearly, the vast majority of students have mild learning challenges, many of which can be mitigated by individualized accommodations.

Students with mild intellectual disabilities have difficulty learning simple tasks, remembering information, and applying the knowledge and skills they have learned. Simple accommodations such as breaking tasks into smaller instructional steps or providing visual reminders can help students overcome some of these barriers. Because processing information can also be problematic, these students might benefit from having directions reread or simplified. Or they might benefit from visual prompts, such as providing pictures or outlining sequential steps for successful completion of a larger skill.

These students also might require accommodations to overcome reading difficulties. When the academic objective is to access the content, as opposed to decode words, it is often beneficial for another person to read text to the student or for the student to use a computer with text-to-speech software. For students struggling with spelling, constructing sentences, organizing information, or writing text by hand, accommodations such as graphic organizers, sentence frames with word options, or a word bank might prove beneficial. Allowing the student to use a computer to complete the task or a scribe to record responses can be a great support for students who have difficulty with handwriting. Finally, allowing more time to complete assignments or assessments can help these students achieve greater success.

Teachers should also be aware that many students with intellectual disabilities have difficulty focusing on and starting a new task, maintaining attention while working on a task, or identifying important information. Therefore, many of the accommodations you learned about in the ADHD chapter (Chapter 7) will also work for students with intellectual disabilities.

The accommodations mentioned above are only a few that can be used to support students with mild intellectual disabilities. The following table lists these accommodations, along with a few others, but is by no means exhaustive. You might notice that some of these have also been suggested for students with other disabilities. For example, the accommodations listed under the column "Setting Accommodations" can benefit students with ADHD. It is important to remember that one accommodation can work for many different disabilities, so any accommodation that supports an individual student's needs should be considered. It is also important to keep in mind that students should be provided the same accommodations during testing that they are provided during instruction.

Examples of Frequently Used Accommodations for Students with Mild Intellectual Disability

Presentation	Setting	Response	Scheduling or Timing
• Person or computer with text-to-speech software to read aloud text (directions, questions, passages) • Break tasks into pieces • Reread or clarify instructions • Simplify or paraphrase	• Headphones to reduce auditory distractions • Less distracting work area in the same room or in a separate room	• Proctor/scribe • Note taker • Computer • Write in test booklets • Tape recorder • Spell checker • Prompting • Cues or signals • Sentence frames with word options or a word bank	• Extended time • Breaks • Multiple sessions • Flexible scheduling

What types of supports might be appropriate for students with moderate and severe/profound cognitive impairments? Although students with moderate and severe/profound intellectual disabilities may benefit from many accommodations listed in the table above, they might require more substantial adaptations. For example, students with the most significant cognitive impairments (less than 1% of all students with disabilities) can receive instruction based on **alternate academic achievement standards**. These are achievement standards linked to the grade-level content; however, the content usually has been simplified or the amount or depth of the content has been reduced. This allows for slower-paced instruction and provides more time for students to grasp the targeted content and skills. Students whose instruction is based on alternate academic achievement standards will also be administered **alternate assessments**. Although these tests are related to grade-level content, they assess the student's knowledge of only a portion of the content or a more simplified version of the content.

Topic 9.7 Early Intervention

- Early intervention services can reduce the impact of intellectual disability over a lifetime.
- When an intellectual disability is identified at birth or shortly thereafter, early intervention services start immediately, often with services provided in the child's home.

Are early intervention services important to children with intellectual disabilities and their families? Early intervention services can reduce the severity and impact of cognitive disabilities. They occur at a time when the family is beginning its long involvement in the education of a child with a disability and when the student is developing important foundational skills. This is a time when language is beginning to develop, when social skills are forming, and when the understanding of causal relationships is taking shape. Many students who have cognitive challenges benefit from explicit instruction in these areas, when their friends without disabilities are learning them naturally. Preschool experiences provide the foundation for developing these important skills, which are useful later in school and in life.

The power of early intervention is remarkable, and early childhood education programs are essential not only for young children with disabilities, but also for young ones at risk for developmental delays or school failure. Attending preschool is associated with a 12% reduction in the rate of special education identification. In fact, adults with disabilities, including those with intellectual disabilities, who participated in preschool experiences outperform those who did not on all measures: IQ scores, high school graduation rates, income levels, home and car ownership, and citizenship (e.g., exercising their right to vote). Besides benefits to the individual, society benefits as well. Every tax dollar spent on the preschool experience provides an economic return of $17 from later educational savings, taxes on earnings, welfare savings, and reductions in some of the societal costs of crime. And, of course, these calculations do not fully reflect the human benefits. Additionally, findings from long-standing programs at the University of North Carolina–Chapel Hill clearly show that benefits of inclusive, high-quality preschools abound. In the following box, those quality indicators have been translated into tips for identifying high-quality preschool programs.

Tips: Selecting High-Quality Preschools for Young Children with Disabilities

- The atmosphere is welcoming to preschoolers with disabilities and their families.
- Children with and without disabilities learn together and are paired as buddies.
- People-first language is used.
- Parental involvement is at a high level.
- Classroom teachers plan and work together.
- Everyone collaborates and communicates well.
- Adults are involved in classroom activities.
- Individualized education programs drive instruction.
- Planning, space, materials, and instruction reflect and are adapted to individual children's needs and goals.
- Activities are balanced with structure, hands-on learning, outdoor time, opportunities for language development, and adult guidance.
- Transition from one activity to another is carefully planned.
- Ongoing program evaluation is in place.
- Focus is on everyone's success!

SOURCES: Adapted from *The Inclusive Classroom Profile*, by E. P. Soukakou, 2010, Chapel Hill, NC: Frank Porter Graham Institute. Retrieved from http://build.fpg.unc.edu/sites/build.fpg.unc.edu/files/resources/Soukakou-Inclusive-Classroom-Profile-sample-9-2010-1.pdf; "Measuring Quality in Inclusive Preschool Classrooms: Development and Validation of the Inclusive Classroom Profile (ICP)," by E. P. Soukakou, 2012, *Early Childhood Research Quarterly*, *27*(3), pp. 478–488; and *Selecting a Preschool: A Guide for Parents of Handicapped Children*, by P. Winton, A. Turnbull, and J. Blacher, 1984, Baltimore, MD: University Park Press, with permission by Pam Winton.

When and where should early intervention services be delivered? Many children with intellectual disabilities are identified at birth or soon thereafter. Some with certain genetic markers, like those of Down syndrome, are identified even before they are born. For these children and their families, early intervention services often begin during infancy with direct services from specialists in the development of language and motor skills (speech-language pathologists, physical therapists). Many babies and their families begin with services delivered in their homes and then transition to preschool programs upon their third birthday.

For students with intellectual disabilities, particularly those with more severe cases, inclusive education is more commonplace during the preschool and kindergarten years than during the elementary, middle, and high school years, when instruction in community settings, rather than at school, is more common. The preschool curriculum lends itself better to inclusive practices than does the curriculum in the higher grades, where achieving high scores on state and district achievement tests is a concern.

Topic 9.8 School Years

- Although students with intellectual disabilities should access the general education curriculum as much as possible, a functional curriculum that focuses on daily living skills can also lead to greater independence as an adult.

- Self-determination, the ability to make choices and advocate for one's needs and desires, is an important collection of skills necessary to live independently.

What should be included in educational programs for students with intellectual disabilities? As with all other students who have disabilities, there is no single answer. Each program must be designed to meet the needs of the individual. You have already learned in Topic 9.4 that these students do not participate in the general education curriculum at the same rates as other students with disabilities. Less inclusive education could be due to low expectations and assumptions about what these students can accomplish. It could, however, be the result of participation in a different curriculum to learn skills not typically taught in the general education classroom.

The general education curriculum provides many opportunities and sets the stage to learn the many complex skills needed to be successful adults. For example, basic reading skills set a path for literacy success, including basic survival skills needed to live and work independently in the community. In addition, the general education curriculum must address the academic abilities that are necessary for career and college readiness. However, most students with moderate to severe intellectual disabilities have learning needs not addressed through the general education curriculum. They must be explicitly taught daily living and job skills to be as independent as possible in adult life, which requires a different curriculum. In a **functional curriculum**, students' reading, writing, and mathematics instruction often focuses on practical skills. It addresses adaptive skills: those needed to hold a job; live in the community; have friends; and travel independently from home, to work, or to a recreational activity. Evidence shows that learning these important daily living and vocational skills in the natural setting (e.g., on the job, on the city bus) results in better mastery. So instruction is frequently individualized and conducted in the community, and is often referred to as **community-based instruction (CBI)**. A few examples of daily living skills are shown in the box.

Examples of Skills Learned in a Functional Curriculum

Reading Survival Words

- Street signs: walk, don't walk, stop
- Safety words: danger, poison, keep out

Writing

- Receiving information: taking phone messages, writing directions to get to a restaurant, taking notes on how to do a job
- Delivering information: leaving notes for someone else, providing instructions

Mathematics

- Time and money: telling time, counting money to pay for items
- Measurement: cooking measures, woodworking

What other skills do students with intellectual disabilities need to become successful adults? Unfortunately, many children with intellectual disabilities are denied opportunities to develop skills related to making good choices naturally. Instead of encouraging these children to pursue their interests and express their ideas and desires, teachers, parents, and family members too often make choices for them, even for the simplest decisions. As a result, they often do not develop an understanding of—or an ability to express—their own preferences, likes, and dislikes. Gaining these skills, referred to as **self-determination**, does not come naturally. Individuals with intellectual disabilities often require explicit instruction and practice in real-life settings to become independent adults. Fortunately, opportunities to teach these skills in conjunction with the general education curriculum abound. Such instruction does not have to take time from other content areas. Rather, what is really needed is a change in orientation about how instruction is delivered and what is integrated into the teaching routine. When given the chance, these students can learn how to make choices, explain their needs and desires, and participate in making decisions about their lives. Self-determination, an evidence-based practice that has been validated through considerable research, is described below.

A Closer Look at Evidenced-Based Practices

Self-Determination Instruction

An individual who is empowered is able to make informed choices and decisions about life—where and how to live, where to work, what to eat, and which leisure activities to pursue. Making such choices requires some complex abilities, such as knowing what activities and results are preferred, understanding the consequences of decisions, solving problems, advocating for oneself, and evaluating the results. To support self-determination in their students, education professionals can:

1. Help students understand themselves, their abilities, their needs, and their preferences.
2. Have students learn what supports and services should be available to them and participate in the decision-making process for the selection, implementation, and evaluation of services and supports.
3. Teach students how to make effective choices, including setting goals and self-monitoring their attainment.

Teachers can help students gain required skills by making and using a self-determination checklist to ensure that such activities are integrated into daily instructional opportunities.

Click the link below to see sample self-determination checklists that could be used in many different settings.

▶ **Sample Self-Determination Checklists for Students and Teachers**

Topic 9.9 Transition

- Being college- and career-ready are important transition goals to improve employment and independent living outcomes.

- Supported employment that often includes job coaches, help from co-workers, and concessions from employers not only provides opportunities for competitive employment but is also cost effective.

How do adults with intellectual disabilities fare in the workplace and in the community? Unfortunately, not as well as they should. Data reports on these individuals are typically not favorable. Adults with intellectual disabilities often do not hold good-paying jobs, nor do they live independently. For example, 83% of families state that their relative with intellectual disability is unemployed. Other reports indicate that only 52% of these adults work, are involved in job training programs, or go to school, which leads one to wonder how the other 48% are spending their days. Further, their lack of employment directly affects the ability to live independently. While 98% of all adults with intellectual disabilities live in the community, 78% live with a family member. Only 7% live independently. These poor adult outcomes signal a need for action.

One new approach provides college options for individuals with disabilities. This approach is making a difference, as individuals with intellectual disabilities who experience college life fare better than those who do not. A number of colleges and universities are offering innovative and uniquely designed programs where individuals with intellectual disabilities attend special programs housed on college campuses. One pioneering program, REACH, is based at the University of Iowa. Through this model program, individuals with intellectual disabilities can earn a two-year transition certificate. The program promotes self-determination and independent living. These students live in the dorm with typical college students. Classes are small, held on campus, and focus on life skills, technology, practical reading, and health and wellness. Because of the success of REACH and other such programs found on college campuses, a range of college options are now available, with more of these post-secondary education programs being developed across the nation.

The following link will help you learn more about college options for students with intellectual disabilities from Think College, a national center funded by the U.S. Office of Postsecondary Education: www.thinkcollege.net

Can special education services help improve the poor adult outcomes for those with intellectual disabilities? Yes, special education transition services and programs offer a more traditional approach to career-readiness. The outcomes of these programs are good: graduates of special education programs are more likely to be employed and to have higher earnings, particularly if they had vocational training, paid work experience, strong parental involvement, and inter-agency collaboration during their high school years. Job opportunities in the community are abundant, and many careers are begun through job training experiences during high school. People with intellectual disabilities who work in community businesses like grocery stores, veterinary clinics, or office supply companies express greater satisfaction than those who have jobs in settings where only people with disabilities work or than those who do not work at all. Developing the job skills necessary to succeed in competitive employment often requires a transition team during the school years and afterward. Because of these facts, transitional programming is an important part of older students' IEPs. (Review this information in Chapter 4.)

Here's how transition services operate for many of these students. During high school, they participate in a functional curriculum that includes learning how to get to and from work independently. They also work in a variety of jobs with assistance from a **job coach**, special education teachers, and networks of connections between schools and employers. One purpose of structured work experiences in high school is to learn important job-related skills. Another is to explore different career opportunities and develop preferences and interests regarding these options. As students gain greater experience, their preferences should be considered, and they should be allowed involvement in choosing types of employment and in placement decisions. Plentiful opportunities exist for developing self-determination and choice-making skills in applied community-based instructional situations.

The following IRIS Module includes more information about special education transition services and the importance of partnering with a variety of agencies.

▶ **IRIS Module Secondary Transition: Interagency Collaboration**
http://iris.peabody.vanderbilt.edu/module/tran-ic/

After high school or college, many individuals with intellectual disabilities require continuous assistance through systems or networks of supports to find and hold paid jobs in the community. In other words, transition services and training initiated during the high school years often need to continue into adulthood. This continuation of supports occurs in many different ways. Governmental agencies can assist individuals who could not otherwise hold a competitive job through **supported employment** programs. These programs help them locate a job, learn the skills required for that position, and understand how to keep the job. Job coaches might work alongside the individual, helping her or him to learn all parts of the job. Additionally, co-workers are trained to assist their associates with disabilities. To promote employment for these adults, employers can receive tax benefits for hiring individuals with disabilities. Supported employment programs began in the 1980s, have evolved over the years, and pay off with dividends far exceeding early predictions. The cost-benefit ratio of supported employment is 2:1. In other words, for every $500 spent, the benefits in workers' compensation are $1000. These employees work decent hours, pay taxes, and earn wages. The system not only is cost-effective but also contributes to better overall adult outcomes and satisfaction. Employers report that people with disabilities, who previously were considered unable to work in the community, are productive workers.

Check Your Understanding 9.2

Click here to gauge your understanding of the concepts in this section.

People and Situations

Learning Outcome

Describe the history of instruction for students with intellectual disabilities and discuss the effects of advocacy and changing attitudes.

Topic 9.10 Origins and History

- Special education began in France in 1798 when farmers found a wild boy in the woods in Avignon and brought him to Dr. Itard in Paris for care and treatment.

- The stigma historically associated with intellectual disabilities remains a major challenge and barrier to social justice for this group of individuals.

Topic 9.11 **Personal Stories**

- The changes in language over the years reflect changes in society's attitudes toward individuals with intellectual disabilities.

- Commitment and advocacy by the families of individuals with intellectual disabilities have had positive effects on the lives of many others.

Feeling isolated and without friends is a major issue for many people with intellectual disabilities. Welcoming environments and supports from peers can make a real difference in the lives of so many!

Topic 9.10 Origins and History

- Special education began in France in 1798 when farmers found a wild boy in the woods in Avignon and brought him to Dr. Itard in Paris for care and treatment.
- The stigma historically associated with intellectual disabilities remains a major challenge and barrier to social justice for this group of individuals.

Is intellectual disability new to modern society? Intellectual disability has always been a part of human history. However, systematic efforts in education and treatment did not begin until the 1700s, when Jean-Marc-Gaspard Itard, a French physician, observed the basic characteristics of this disability in his pupil, Victor. Considered by many as the first special education student, Victor had challenges with cognition, adaptive skills, and language development, and needed continued supports. His story is portrayed in *The Wild Child,* or *L' Enfant Sauvage,* described in *On the Screen.* Local farmers found Victor in the woods of rural France when he was about age 12. He was living much like an animal, fending for himself, walking on four limbs, and unable to speak. The film shows how Itard and his housekeeper worked with the boy, pioneering many of the instructional interventions used today. While Victor made remarkable progress, Itard ultimately considered his efforts a failure because he was unsuccessful in making Victor a truly independent gentleman of the times. Regardless, his work marks the beginning of the education and humane treatment of individuals with intellectual disabilities.

On the Screen: *In the Beginning*

The film *L' Enfant Sauvage* (*The Wild Child*) tells the true story of the beginning of special education. The discovery in rural France of the "Wild Child," and his subsequent treatment in Paris, sparked considerable debate at that time about the differences between humans and animals.

https://youtu.be/yddJBd6D2lo

The film demonstrates the instructional procedures that Itard used to socialize the boy, instruct him in basic skills, and teach him language. Although Itard did not have the benefits of knowing research-based practices, he implemented many strategies that have since been validated—positive reinforcement, contingent and systematic instruction—setting the foundation for many proven practices used today.

–Steve Smith

Edouard Seguin brought Itard's legacy of education and concepts of fair treatment of individuals with intellectual disabilities to the United States in 1844. Seguin is considered the father of special education in America. Soon thereafter, in 1848, Samuel Gridley Howe introduced the idea of separate, residential schools for children with intellectual disabilities to the United States. However, he predicted that institutions could become shameful segregated settings, breeding fear, mistrust, and abuse. His predictions proved true. As the timeline below illustrates, shifts to more positive attitudes and care were inconsistent for more than a century to come, and negative, even cruel, responses to this disability persisted. People with intellectual disabilities were victims of great abuse, bias, and discrimination. They were exterminated in the German Holocaust and, worldwide, were denied schooling and shunned from society. In Europe and the United States, this group of individuals was segregated in institutions, where they were subjected to inhumane treatment.

Education and Supports for Individuals with Intellectual Disabilities Timeline

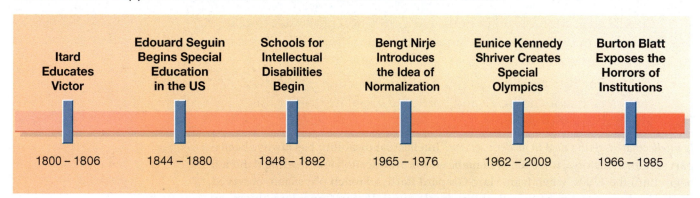

Itard Educates Victor	Edouard Seguin Begins Special Education in the US	Schools for Intellectual Disabilities Begin	Bengt Nirje Introduces the Idea of Normalization	Eunice Kennedy Shriver Creates Special Olympics	Burton Blatt Exposes the Horrors of Institutions
1800 – 1806	1844 – 1880	1848 – 1892	1965 – 1976	1962 – 2009	1966 – 1985

Have the concepts of social justice and fair treatment for individuals with intellectual disabilities changed across time? The seeds of bias and discrimination are planted deep in the history of people with intellectual disabilities, which may explain why social justice remains an important issue even today. Perhaps a short background about the treatment these individuals have experienced over time would be helpful in understanding why perceptions, language, and attitudes are so important to this group. The often fictional and much embellished stories about the negative influence this group has on society go back 140 years. In 1877, Richard Dugdale, a sociologist and volunteer inspector for the New York Prison Association, wrote about the criminal activities, lack of employment, and other negative aspects of several generations of the Jukes family. He wanted to illustrate that people with cognitive disabilities were a danger to society—the source of crime, poverty, and other social ills plaguing the country at that time—and that, to protect society, they should be institutionalized and sterilized to prevent them from producing more people like themselves. However, more recent genealogical research has shown that Dugdale focused on only a portion of the Jukes family tree, and failed to include other members who were successful and well-respected members of their community. He was not the only one to inflate stories about individuals with intellectual disabilities. In 1912, Henry Goddard released the story of Deborah Kallikak, who came from a family of "feebleminded" people prone to criminal activity. Goddard claimed that intellectual disability was passed on by heredity, so nothing could be done to correct the situation. Goddard's conclusion, like Dugdale's, was that such people should be removed from society and their population controlled. This movement, regarding the purposeful planning or prevention of reproduction to improve the human race, is referred to as **eugenics**. By 1917, all but four states had institutions where babies with intellectual disabilities were routinely sent, most of which were large and segregated. They were no longer boarding schools where children could thrive and learn, but instead had become awful places of abuse and neglect. For more about the history of all disabilities go to the Disability Social History Project, www.disabilityhistory.org.

The 1960s and 1970s were a time of great change in attitudes and practices. Researchers and program developers proved that students with intellectual disabilities could learn more than anyone had previously thought, in the areas of both daily living skills and language development. Bengt Nirje, from Sweden, first introduced the concept of **normalization**, which would become fundamental to current thinking about these individuals. Nirje put forth the belief that all citizens should be provided the same opportunities and conditions for everyday living. Those with intellectual disabilities should have opportunities, like people without disabilities, to live a normal life in the community. Wolf Wolfensburger brought Nirje's ideas to the United States, where they were developed and expanded. As a result, most individuals with intellectual disabilities were brought out of institutions and into the community with dreams and hopes of typical lives, working with colleagues, and enjoying time with friends and families. Burton Blatt, a special education advocate, called for the closure of *all* institutions and continued to develop ideas about community living and family social services.

Today, people with intellectual disabilities are still fighting for their place in society and in the community, but progress is being made. They are becoming a real part of daily life in American communities. They go to school, some attend special college programs, some find good work, and most live in the community. More than ever before, these individuals believe that their hopes and dreams can become realities.

Topic 9.11 Personal Stories

- The changes in language over the years reflect changes in society's attitudes toward individuals with intellectual disabilities.
- Commitment and advocacy by the families of individuals with intellectual disabilities have had positive effects on the lives of many others.

Is society becoming more respectful of people with intellectual disabilities? Across time, individuals with this disability have faced segregation, discrimination, and disrespect. However, it does appear that the situation is improving. In recent years, growing

President Obama, Rosa Marcellino, and her family celebrate the passage of Rosa's Law, which stripped the term *mental retardation* from all federal language.

attention has been paid to the language used when talking about all people with disabilities (see again the section on people-first language in Topic 1.8). The words we use are important because language is a reflection of perceptions. What we say sends a clear message about dignity and respect. This is the reason why in 2007, AAIDD, the oldest professional organization concerned with individuals with disabilities, changed the term *mental retardation* to *intellectual disability*. It is also why Congress passed Rosa's Law in 2010, which retroactively replaced the term *mental retardation* with *intellectual disability* in all federal laws and regulations. Since then, the Special Olympics organization and many advocates have spearheaded a campaign to eliminate the "R word" from everyone's speech. They are calling for an end to the use of the term *retard*, regardless of the situation.

Can we document the power of advocacy on the lives of people with intellectual disabilities? Absolutely! The Kennedy family's advocacy for individuals with intellectual disabilities, which spans two generations, cannot be overstated. Rosemary Kennedy, born in 1918, had an intellectual disability and lived in a segregated setting away from family and friends for most of her adult life. Rosemary's brothers and sister initiated a family commitment to social justice, advocacy, and the development of landmark service agencies that model dignity and respect for all people with disabilities, particularly those with cognitive challenges. Rosemary's sister, Eunice Kennedy Shriver, started Camp Shriver in her backyard in 1962 so children and youth with cognitive disabilities could have a means for athletic development and competition. This backyard camp evolved into Special Olympics, now serving 4.2 million athletes worldwide. Rosemary's brother, Robert Kennedy, stimulated the deinstitutionalization movement when he called attention to the horrific abuses at Willowbrook, an institution in New York. His actions encouraged Burton Blatt, then a professor at Boston University, to expose the horrors of such residential facilities in his 1966 photo-essay, *Christmas in Purgatory,* which is freely available online.

The following video shows the discovery of the horrors of Willowbrook and Robert Kennedy's influence.

▶ **Willowbrook: The Last Disgrace**

https://youtu.be/lWDt5IE8RPI

Another of Rosemary's brothers, President John F. Kennedy (JFK), started efforts to establish a national committee to study necessary improvements in education, research, and teacher training for all students with disabilities, but with a special focus on intellectual disability. President Lyndon Johnson actually formed this committee after Kennedy's assassination, and the committee is still active today. A third brother, Senator Ted Kennedy, was instrumental in creating the first IDEA law in 1975 and the ADA law in 1990.

The next generation of Kennedys—particularly Eunice Kennedy Shriver's children—have carried on the family's commitment to individuals with disabilities. Anthony Kennedy Shriver founded Best Buddies International while he was a student at Georgetown University. The organization connects university students as volunteers to provide supports to people with intellectual disabilities. His brother, Tim Shriver, is the current chairman of Special Olympics and a major spokesperson in the movement to ban the "R word" and eliminate bias and discrimination experienced by many people with intellectual disabilities.

The children of Joe and Rose Kennedy established a legacy of advocacy on behalf of individuals with disabilities. Rosemary (third from left), their oldest daughter had intellectual disabilities. Rosemary's brother, President John F. Kennedy (second from left), was instrumental in stimulating many federal programs that initiated research, teacher training, and demonstration projects that benefit students with disabilities even today. Her sister Eunice started Special Olympics, her sister Jean began Very Special Arts, and brother Teddy authored considerable legislation guaranteeing the rights of individuals with disabilities to education and access to the community.

Their sister, Maria Shriver, is a journalist, producer, and author. She is also the former first lady of California, a disability advocate, and a sponsor of many charitable events benefiting individuals with intellectual disabilities. She also authored the book *What's Wrong with Timmy*, which focuses on the friendship of two children who, despite their differences, prove to have much in common.

The story of the Kennedy family is one of dedication and advocacy. Collectively, they have made, and continue to make, a difference in the lives of so many. We can all learn a lot about the power of activism from the examples they set.

Check Your Understanding 9.3

Click here to gauge your understanding of the concepts in this section.

Future Perspectives

Learning Outcome

Explain how preventive measures can reduce the incidence of intellectual disability, discuss how inaccurate public information threatens the implementation of preventive measures, explain how technology can benefit individuals with intellectual disabilities, particularly in areas of independent living.

Topic 9.12 Prevention: Environmental Protections

- Environmental toxins and child abuse are two preventable causes of intellectual disability.

- Inaccurate public information threatens the implementation of preventive measures.

Topic 9.13 Technology: Connecting and Scheduling

- Technology can connect individuals with intellectual disabilities to people within their systems or networks of support.

- Technology can help improve skills that contribute to independence and lead to an improved community presence.

Courtesy of Prentke Romich Company, Wooster, OH.

Future advances in technology have the potential to improve everyone's lives, but the possibilities for those with disabilities seem without limits.

Topic 9.12 Prevention: Environmental Protections

- Environmental toxins and child abuse are two preventable causes of intellectual disability.
- Inaccurate public information threatens the implementation of preventive measures.

Does a clear link exist between the identification of specific causes of intellectual disability and the development and implementation of preventive measures? When a cause is identified, ways to prevent debilitating effects often follow soon after. Yet, even with this knowledge, preventive actions are not always taken. As responsible citizens, we need to understand the cause-and-effect relationships between inaction and harm to children. Let's look at some examples.

Everyone should be on the alert for toxins lurking in the environment that have the potential to cause great harm to children.

pzAxe/Fotolia

Toxins abound in the environment. Exposure to environmental toxins—such as lead—is a major cause of intellectual disability, but it is preventable through better regulations and a cleaner environment. The link between lead poisoning and intellectual disability in children is clear. Fortunately, the incidence of elevated levels of lead in the blood of children has decreased since the late 1990s because lead has been banned in many products for decades. However, some 4.3% of children under the age of six have moderately elevated levels. Children at higher risk are those from low-income families who encounter lead on the walls of older apartments and houses that had been painted years ago with lead-based paint. These children and their families are also more likely to live in neighborhoods where long-closed factories are located. These factories operated in an era without protective regulations, contaminating the areas surrounding them. The Exide battery recycling plant in Los Angeles County is a tragic example of such a case. For years, children living in the area have been exposed to high levels of lead. Their families cannot afford to move, and the area remains toxic. Further, lead still lingers in the soil and along sections of old freeways where residues remain from leaded gasoline (which is now banned). Lead is still found in today's jet fuel, and, unfortunately, sometimes in children's toys because they are not routinely checked for the presence of lead paint. Sadly, lead poisoning is not a thing of the past.

In Chapter 3, we mentioned the lead-contaminated water in Flint, MI. The CNN news story below highlights the health issues the Flint residents now face as a result.

▶ **The Effects of Flint's Lead Poisoning Disaster**

https://youtu.be/hqnaq2Vn-CA

In addition to removing toxins, here are two other examples of how better preventive measures can make a difference. Child abuse causes devastating harm to children, including brain damage and resulting problems with cognition. Think about this startling statistic: each day in America 1,837 children are victims of abuse or neglect. Clearly, child abuse is preventable, children can be better protected from abusive family members, and the penalties for hurting children could be more severe.

On another front, some 40,000 babies are born each year with symptoms of prenatal alcohol exposure. Not all babies are equally affected, for the damage depends on the amount of alcohol consumed by the expectant mother and the point during the pregnancy and length of time (first, second, third, or all trimesters) she drinks. Many children with fetal alcohol spectrum disorders (FASDs) need special education services when in school. Few of those with fetal alcohol syndrome (FAS), the most serious end of this spectrum of disorders, are able to live independently as adults because of very significant cognitive, behavioral, and often physical disabilities. The cost of each case of FAS is estimated to be at least $2 million. Beyond monetary costs, the damage done to these babies is tragic, and it is preventable. Because of the tragic and long-term impacts of prenatal drinking on children, the American Academy of Pediatrics released a report in 2015 emphasizing that there is no safe amount of alcohol consumption, nor is there any time during pregnancy when women can safely drink.

How can the dangers of public misinformation put all children at risk for illness and disability? The importance of immunization programs to protect children and their mothers from disease cannot be overemphasized. The incidence of intellectual disability has been greatly reduced through immunizations against Rh blood incompatibility and viruses such as those causing rubella, meningitis, and measles. In 1944, doctors discovered the dangerous outcomes when pregnant women did not share the same Rh factor as their babies. Until a vaccine was developed, 10,000 deaths occurred every year, in addition to many more children born with severe disabilities.

Rubella, or the German measles, has devastating effects on unborn children, particularly for those whose mothers are infected during the first trimester. In the mid-1960s, no vaccine was available to protect people from this disease. The epidemic of 1964–1965 resulted in tens of thousands of neonatal deaths and miscarriages. Of the 20,000 infants born who had been infected, 11,600 had profound deafness,

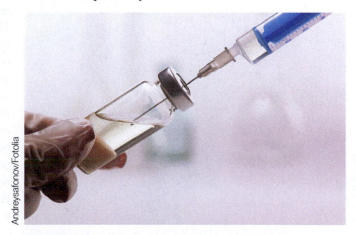

Andreysafonov/Fotolia

3,580 had visual disabilities, and 1,800 had intellectual disability. After the development and widespread use of the rubella vaccine, this disease has been practically eliminated. The same is true for measles, which has been almost completely eradicated in the United States. According to the Centers for Disease Control and Prevention, in 2000 no cases of measles were reported in the United States. Unfortunately, alarming increases were noted in 2014 and 2015: a multi-state outbreak of measles was linked to unvaccinated people visiting Disneyland in 2015. The disease spread rapidly, causing the closure of daycare centers and schools. Although some of the affected children were too young for vaccinations (under the age of one) or too vulnerable due to various health conditions, others became sick because their parents purposely chose not to vaccinate them.

The Children's Defense Fund reports that among the world's industrialized nations the United States ranks 26th for immunization rates. Why are parents withholding vaccines from children? The most common reason is public misinformation about the dangers of unprotected children and inaccurately blaming vaccines as a cause of disabilities. For example, while no proven connection between the measles vaccine and autism spectrum disorders exists, beliefs still persist about such a relationship (see Chapter 8 for an example of the dangers of misinformation and how the public still engages in risky behavior because they are leaving their children unprotected from diseases).

Topic 9.13 Technology: Connecting and Scheduling

- Technology can connect individuals with intellectual disabilities to people within their systems or networks of support.
- Technology can help improve skills that contribute to independence and lead to an improved community presence.

Is today's technology too sophisticated for people with intellectual disabilities? The answer to that question is simple: absolutely not! The benefits of current technology and the explosion of software applications are important for students and adults with intellectual disabilities. Many of us spend increasing portions of our day on computers, tablets, and smartphones. These devices help us coordinate our lives, prepare papers, monitor our budgets, provide access to information, maintain friendships, and even assist us when we are lost or in trouble. However, because of costs, access to these technologies can be challenging and prohibitively expensive, particularly for those who typically have difficulty finding and holding jobs, let alone high-paying jobs.

It seems that everyone stays in touch with friends through email, social media, and smartphones. Until recently, students with intellectual disabilities were often excluded from this exchange. But thanks to **e-Buddies**, one of seven programs offered by Best Buddies International, email is now an important part of school and daily life for students with intellectual disabilities. This program pairs people who have intellectual disabilities with peer volunteers without disabilities. They email each other at least once a week for a minimum of a year and are matched on interests, age, and gender. The pairs are not from the same state or province and are not permitted to meet in person. E-Buddies does everything possible to ensure safety, privacy, and an excellent experience for every pair. All e-Buddies applicants are screened, and the email system used goes through a central e-Buddies mailbox, which does not reveal personal email addresses. One of this program's many benefits is that it motivates students with intellectual disabilities to use computers and systems of communication. Click here to learn more about e-Buddies: www.e-buddies.org

Technology connects us to friends everywhere.

Javieratael/Fotolia

How can technology support self-determination skills? People with all types of disabilities—including intellectual disability—who use the Internet report a sense of empowerment and liberation because of the capacity to purchase things online, communicate with others, and search the Internet for information. Both apps available to the general public and those developed specifically for people with disabilities can be helpful. For example, many of us use apps that pinpoint our current location, guide us to our destinations, or send news alerts about current events. We also use them to connect with family and business colleagues by way of software and applications that allow for voice activation and video conferencing.

Most tablets and smartphones have universal access features that can be used by individuals who face complex challenges. For students who cannot read, text-to-speech technology removes print barriers. Picture icons provide illustrations in apps that then "speak" thousands of words. Built-in calendar programs help to keep track of important appointments, daily schedules, and even leisure-time activities. Now available are special apps, like the one shown in the figure below, that combine daily calendars with icons to prompt users as they follow a daily schedule (e.g., get ready for the day, leave for school or work, have lunch). Like the one in the accompanying illustration, some of these apps actually guide the individual throughout the day.

Specially designed daily organizers can prompt the successful following of a daily routine. An alarm can be used not only to wake up on time but also to assist being on time throughout the day. Of course, such programs can be more or less sophisticated, but regardless, they can provide structure to the entire day.

Example of a Daily Organizer App

The possibilities are endless, but here is how technology might work for a high school student with an intellectual disability assigned to a new job in the community. The entire week's schedule is entered into the daily organizer by the individual, with the assistance of a teacher or mentor. The time to take the bus to work is entered into the calendar, with an alarm set as a reminder. Directions on how to get to work using the city bus are entered in, as are the names of the job coach, co-workers, and supervisor. The time schedule for breaks, lunch, and end of day are also entered. Finally, the individual enters the schedule for the return bus route to complete the day's agenda. Those who also use a GPS navigational system can get additional assistance in finding the location of a new work site and their way home.

This technology explosion opens vistas and opportunities unimaginable only a few years ago. However, learning how to use technology—both hardware and software—can be challenging. Explicit instruction on how to use a computer, assistance in buying one, help with setting up the computer's devices (e.g., hooking up cameras, activating microphones), and support in using accessible software could well become an important part of this century's functional curricula. The opportunities are limitless, with greater results for access and a community presence.

Check Your Understanding 9.4

Click here to gauge your understanding of the concepts in this section.

Summary

Intellectual Disability Described

Intellectual disability results from significantly impaired cognitive functioning (e.g., remembering, reasoning, transferring learning from one task to another), problems with adaptive skills (e.g., social skills, living independently, holding a job), and the need for supports. Intellectual disability emerges during the developmental period, between birth and age 18.

- Intellectual disability ranges from profound and severe to mild; however, over 95% of all cases are in the mild range.

- Two of the most common causes of intellectual disability, fragile X syndrome and Down syndrome, have a genetic basis; the third most common cause, fetal alcohol spectrum disorders (FASDs), results from alcohol intake by pregnant women and is preventable.

- While other students with disabilities have experienced increasingly greater levels of inclusive education, students with intellectual disabilities still have less access to the general education classroom and curriculum because they often receive their education in more restrictive settings.

Special Education

While students with intellectual disabilities should not be denied access to the general education curriculum, many of them need a functional curriculum in which they learn the skills necessary to live and work in the community as adults.

- While the need for supports is a characteristic of intellectual disability, networks of supports and assistance from family, friends, co-workers, and social service agencies also are solutions to the challenges posed by this disability.

- Accommodations must reflect students' individual needs. All students with intellectual disabilities might benefit from instructional and testing accommodations, but students with the most signficant cognitive problems might also need adaptations such as alternate academic achievement standards along with alternate assessments.

- High-quality preschool services provide an important beginning to educational programs that have lifelong benefits.

- A functional curriculum focuses on practical and adaptive skills needed to have a community presence, hold a job, have friends, and live independently.

- Self-determination, the ability to make choices and advocate for one's needs and desires, is an important collection of skills necessary to live independently.

- Being college- and career-ready are important transition goals so that employment and independent living outcomes improve.

- Supported employment that often includes job coaches, help from co-workers, and concessions from employers not only provides opportunities for competitive employment but also is cost effective.

People and Situations

Possibly more than any other group of people with disabilities, those with intellectual disabilities have faced bias and discrimination since the beginning of history. Today, using people-first language, expressing dignity and respect in the words we choose, welcoming people with intellectual disabilities, and providing opportunities for community participation help reduce the stigma associated with this disability.

- Special education began in France in 1798, when farmers found a wild boy in the woods in Avignon and brought him to Dr. Itard in Paris for care and treatment.

- Today, children and adults are no longer sent to spend their lives in isolated, residential institutions, but they do need to be better prepared to live independently and have jobs in the community.

- Many individuals, families, advocacy groups, and organizations make a real difference in the lives of individuals with intellectual disabilities who are seeking their places in society and a community presence.

Future Perspectives

Government, policy makers, and individuals can reduce the severity and even lower the number of cases of intellectual disability through preventive actions. Increased access to commonly available technology can improve these individuals' participation in daily American life.

- Substantially more actions (e.g., removing lead from the environment, ensuring all children are vaccinated, increasing access to health care, convincing pregnant mothers to not drink alcohol) could be taken to reduce the incidence of this disability.

- Computer technology can be used to connect individuals who have intellectual disabilities with others who can provide supports and to help them structure and organize their day.

Addressing CEC Standards

Council for Exceptional Children (CEC) knowledge standards addressed in this chapter: 6.2, 1.0, 5.1, 5.7, 4.2, 7.0.

See the Appendix for the complete CEC Initial Level Special Educator Preparation Standards.

Chapter 10
Emotional and Behavioral Disorders

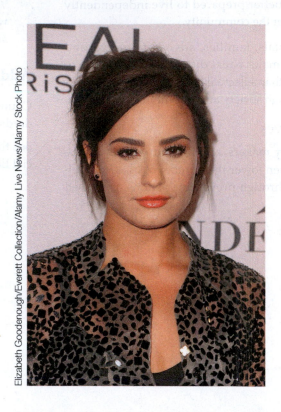

Elizabeth Goodenough/Everett Collection/Alamy Live News/Alamy Stock Photo

Singer/actress Demi Lovato was bullied as a child for being overweight, which led to an eating disorder—bulimia—at a very young age. Despite getting professional help for that condition, she started cutting herself, a form of self-mutilation, at age 11. In an interview with Robin Roberts, she explained that, "It [cutting] was a way of expressing my own shame of myself on my own body. And there were some times where my emotions were just so built up, I didn't know what to do. The only way I could get instant gratification was through an immediate release on myself. I don't think I was ever trying to kill myself, but I knew that if I had ever gone too far, that I wouldn't care." Although she continued to receive professional help, and even with a rise to superstardom thanks to Disney movies, a hit TV show, and a chart-topping album, her mental health issues eventually spiraled out of control. After admitting herself to a residential treatment facility for substance abuse, she received yet another diagnosis: bipolar disorder.

As an adult, Demi has worked to raise awareness about mental illness and the need for better mental health services. Among her many speeches, interviews, and recognitions, she was a featured speaker at the National Alliance on Mental Illness (NAMI) national convention and was honored by the U.S. Substance Abuse and Mental Health Services Administration for her work as a mentor to young adults with mental illness and substance abuse. She wrote a book, *Staying Strong 365 Days a Year*, which provides an open and honest look at her struggles, along with lessons, reflections, and daily goals to help others who face similar challenges. She continues to be a mental health advocate while maintaining a successful musical career.

As with the other disabilities we have discussed in this text, mental health issues are lifelong conditions. Yet, with proper supports—as Demi has shown—individuals with these disorders can lead happy, productive, independent lives.

To watch the full interview with Robin Roberts, in which Demi discusses living with bullying, bulimia, cutting, depression, and bipolar disorder (all by the age of 18), go to https://youtu.be/bNBiNnyIu74

 ## Learning Outcomes

Emotional and Behavioral Disorders Described

Define emotional and behavioral disorders (EBD), describe the different types of EBD, recognize the characteristics of students with EBD, and understand prevalence and placement data for students with EBD.

Special Education

Explain the ways in which EBD can impact personal relationships and academic skills, describe accommodations that can lessen these challenges, understand methods that parents and classroom teachers can use to reduce challenges associated with EBD, and describe supports to help students with EBD transition to post-secondary options such as school, work, and independent living.

People and Situations

Describe the history of treatment for individuals with EBD, explain some current concerns in the field, and identify reputable organizations that provide reliable information for individuals with EBD and their families.

Future Perspectives

Describe some of the concerns regarding appropriate identification of EBD and access to mental health services, and understand how new technology can support mental health services for individuals with EBD.

Emotional and Behavioral Disorders Described[1]

Learning Outcome

Define emotional and behavioral disorders (EBD), describe the different types of EBD, recognize the characteristics of students with EBD, and understand prevalence and placement data for students with EBD.

Topic 10.1 Emotional and Behavioral Disorders Defined

- Students with emotional and behavioral disorders display problem behaviors to an excessive degree.
- Despite problems with the IDEA definition of emotional disturbance, it must be used to qualify students for special education services.

---

[1]References for Chapter 10 are found at the end of this text.

Topic 10.2 Types of Emotional and Behavioral Disorders

- Emotional and behavioral disorders can be divided into externalizing behaviors, internalizing behaviors, and low-incidence conditions.

- Even though internalizing behaviors are less disruptive to school environments, they can be extremely serious.

Topic 10.3 Characteristics

- Students with externalizing behaviors often exhibit aggression, hyperactivity, impulsivity, noncompliance, and delinquency.

- Characteristics of internalizing behaviors—withdrawal, depression, and anxiety—are harder to detect.

Topic 10.4 Prevalence and Placement

- EBD is considered a high-incidence disability, although these students are placed in more restrictive settings than many students with other high-incidence disabilities.

- IDEA has specific disciplinary procedures for violations directly resulting from a student's disability.

Prudkov/Fotolia

Many people associate aggressive or destructive behaviors with emotional and behavioral disorders. As a result, conditions like anxiety disorders or depression often go undetected.

Topic 10.1 Emotional and Behavioral Disorders Defined

- Students with emotional and behavioral disorders display problem behaviors to an excessive degree.

- Despite problems with the IDEA definition of emotional disturbance, it must be used to qualify students for special education services.

Who are students with emotional and behavioral disorders? Students with **emotional and behavioral disorders (EBD)** exhibit severe, chronic, and pervasive problem behaviors. These individuals may have one or more mental health conditions. In education, teachers and other professionals must abide by the IDEA definition, which uses the term **emotional disturbance**. Not all students with EBD require special education services. Only those whose behavior problems are so extreme that they adversely influence educational performance are eligible (see the following table).

Definitions of Emotional and Behavioral Disorders

Term	Definition	Source
Emotional disturbance	Emotional disturbance means a condition exhibiting one or more of the following characteristics over a long period of time and to a marked degree that adversely affects a child's educational performance: (A) An inability to learn that cannot be explained by intellectual, sensory, or health factors. (B) An inability to build or maintain satisfactory interpersonal relationships with peers and teachers. (C) Inappropriate types of behavior or feelings under normal circumstances. (D) A general pervasive mood of unhappiness or depression. (E) A tendency to develop physical symptoms related to fears associated with personal or school problems. (ii) Emotional disturbance includes schizophrenia. The term does not apply to children who are socially maladjusted, unless it is determined that they have an emotional disturbance [as defined by IDEA].	IDEA '04, U.S. Department of Education
Mental health condition Mental illness	A condition that impacts a person's thinking, feeling or mood and may affect his or her ability to relate to others and function on a daily basis.	National Alliance on Mental Illness
Mental illness	Collectively all diagnosable mental disorders; health conditions that are characterized by alterations in thinking, mood, or behavior (or some combination thereof) associated with distress and/or impaired functioning	Centers for Disease Control and Prevention

SOURCES: From 34 CFR Parts 300 and 303, *Assistance to States for the Education of Children with Disabilities and the Early Intervention Program for Infants and Toddlers with Disabilities; Final Regulations* (p. 1262), U.S. Department of Education, 2006, *Federal Register*, Washington, DC; "*Mental Health Conditions.*" National Alliance on Mental Illness, retrieved from http://www.nami.org/Learn-More/Mental-Health-Conditions http://www.cdc.gov/mentalhealth/basics.htm; and "*Mental Illness.*" Centers for Disease Control and Prevention, retrieved from http://www.cdc.gov/mentalhealth/basics.htm

It is important to recognize that most people experience mild maladjustment for short periods at some point in their lives, so, to qualify for special education services, a child must exhibit the characteristics for a long time and to a marked degree or significant level of intensity. In addition to the intensity, frequency, and duration of problem behaviors, professionals must consider other factors (e.g., age-appropriateness) to determine whether they are of concern. The problem behavior of a 2-year-old who screams and cries when asked to take a nap is perceived very differently from that of a 12-year-old who screams and cries when asked to complete a math worksheet. Clearly, the second child's behavior is inappropriate and some type of intervention or support is needed. However, determining the appropriateness of less visible behaviors or conditions, such as depression, can be difficult. Further, education, mental health, and research communities often use job- or field-specific terms to refer to similar types of behaviors, which can be confusing. Those in mental health professions often refer to the *Diagnostic and Statistical Manual of Mental Disorders,* fifth edition (*DSM-5*), which does not have an overarching definition of emotional and behavioral disorders. Instead, the *DSM-5* contains highly specific diagnostic criteria for separate, distinct conditions and disorders, some of which are included later in this chapter.

Cultural Considerations

In addition to the information above, professionals should also consider a student's cultural norms and expectations. Misperceptions can occur when behavioral expectations are different at home than in school. For example, a teacher may have concerns about a student who seems reluctant to answer questions or who seems to avoid interpersonal interactions with her. Although she may think he is overly withdrawn, the student may actually feel that he is showing the teacher an appropriate amount of respect, based on his cultural background. Here is another situation: a teacher interprets a student's assertive behavior as aggression. After talking to the parents, the teacher discovers that the family spent six months in an overcrowded refugee camp in Europe before family members were able raise the funds to bring them

to the United States. During their time in the camp, the parents believed their daughter needed to be able to stand up for herself. Because conditions in the classroom differ from those in the camp, the parents and teacher are able work together to ensure the student's assertive behaviors—which include many positive aspects of self-advocacy—are appropriate. The teacher is also able to connect the student and the family with appropriate school and community supports, including mental health services, to help them all deal with the trauma associated with their refugee and relocation experiences. As this situation demonstrates, teachers need as much information as possible about their students to avoid misconceptions. Further, ongoing home-school communication is critical for student success.

What are the concerns with the IDEA definition? This definition has received many criticisms from professionals who feel that:

- The term *emotional disturbance* excludes students whose disability is purely behavioral.

- The reference to *educational performance* can be narrowly interpreted to mean only academic performance and thus exclude other aspects of education such as school-related social skills, life skills, or vocational skills.

- The exclusion of students who exhibit signs of **social maladjustment** leaves many without needed supports.

Despite the attention given to social maladjustment, particularly regarding discipline and violence in schools, these students are *not* eligible for special education services unless they also have another qualifying condition. Some interpret the term *socially maladjusted* as a reference to students with **conduct disorders**, which cannot be used alone as a qualification for special services. Yet, as is evident from the description of conduct disorder in the following table, which uses criteria from the *DSM-5* definition, students with this condition need intensive supports and services. Educators, policy makers, and advocates continue to debate these issues with, as yet, no resolution. Although alternate definitions have been developed, none have been universally accepted.

Summary of Conduct Disorder Characteristics

Required Standards	Essential Problem Areas	Applications
Individual must display at least three behaviors.	• Bullies, threatens, or intimidates • Initiates physical fights • Causes serious physical harm using a weapon • Engages in physical cruelty to people • Engages in physical cruelty to animals • Steals with confrontation • Steals without confrontation • Forces sexual activity on someone • Sets fire with intent to cause damage • Deliberately destroys property • Breaks into a house, building, or car • Lies to obtain or avoid something • Stays out all night (begins prior to age 13) • Runs away from home • Commits truancy (begins prior to age 13)	Jonas (12 years old): • Skips school (10 times this quarter). • Shoplifts. • Vandalizes. • Was arrested during a home invasion (last week).
Behaviors must be repetitive and persistent, and must violate others' basic rights or societal norms/rules.	• At least three criteria occurring in the previous 12 months • At least one criterion occurring in the previous six months	Ten instances of truancy constitute repetitive and persistent behavior. Three criteria (truancy, theft, and vandalism) have occurred within the past year. The home invasion was within the past six months.
Behaviors impair other activities significantly.	Creates problems: • Socially • Educationally • Vocationally	Jonas has few friends, is failing school, and was fired from a part-time job as a dog walker because he tried to start dogfights.

Topic 10.2 Types of Emotional and Behavioral Disorders

- Emotional and behavioral disorders can be divided into externalizing behaviors, internalizing behaviors, and low-incidence conditions.

- Even though internalizing behaviors are less disruptive to school environments, they can be extremely serious.

What are the different types of EBD? Emotional and behavioral disorders can be classified into three different types: externalizing behaviors, internalizing behaviors, and low-incidence conditions. **Externalizing behaviors** include actions like aggression, hyperactivity, impulsivity, noncompliance, or delinquency. **Aggression** (verbal or physical) involves an observable behavior with intended harm to someone or something. Aggression in very young children (particularly boys) is predictive of future violence, delinquency, and school dropout. We discussed **hyperactivity** and **impulsivity** in Chapter 7 as common characteristics of ADHD. Remember that ADHD and EBD often occur in combination, so it shouldn't be surprising that students with EBD often exhibit these two features. **Noncompliance**, the refusal to comply with or follow rules or instructions, is a commonly voiced frustration of teachers. **Delinquency** refers to a juvenile's engagement in illegal acts, such as theft or assault. Although some children who are delinquent also have EBD, many do not. Similarly, not all children with EBD are also delinquent. Regardless, be aware that many of these youth are at risk for criminal justice system involvement.

What are some of the less-recognized emotional or behavioral disorders? In contrast to externalizing behaviors, **internalizing behaviors** are less obvious, characterized by withdrawn actions, and can include conditions such as anorexia or bulimia, anxiety, and depression. **Anorexia** and **bulimia** are life-threatening eating disorders tied to a preoccupation with weight and body image and most prevalent among teenage girls. Symptoms of **anxiety disorders** can include extreme apprehension when the individual is separated from family, friends, or familiar environments; excessive avoidance of strangers; or unfocused, excessive worry and fear. **Depression** is more than just feeling sad; it is a serious condition that can include persistent feelings of hopelessness, worthlessness, lethargy, loss of appetite, lack of interest in previously enjoyable activities, and suicidal thoughts. Depression interferes with a person's ability to engage in or complete daily activities. Teenagers exhibit symptoms similar to those of adults; however, depression is often difficult to recognize in children, as their symptoms are much different and tend to vary by age. As a result, a child's symptoms may be overlooked or misinterpreted. For example, a depressed child might attempt to harm himself by running into a busy street, but adults might think the child is just being reckless. Because internalizing behaviors are typically not disruptive, they often do not receive sufficient attention from education professionals.

Childhood Depression: Warning Signs

Preschoolers	Ages 6–8	Ages 9–12	Teenagers
• Anger • Trouble sleeping • Eating problems • Separation anxiety	• Frequent accidents • Attention-seeking behaviors • School problems	• Lethargy • Low self-esteem • Self-destructive behavior • Suicidal thoughts	• Changes in eating and/or sleeping patterns • Low energy, apathy, withdrawal • Physical complaints (headache, stomachache) • Difficulty concentrating or making decisions • Rebelliousness • Substance abuse • Preoccupation with death

Some conditions occur infrequently (low-incidence) in school-age children, but are quite serious when they do occur. **Schizophrenia**, one such condition, involves bizarre delusions (e.g., believing police are controlling one's thoughts), hallucinations (e.g., voices telling one what to do), extreme disorganization, passive or unresponsive behavior, lack of emotional responsiveness, and incoherence. Schizophrenia is most prevalent between the ages of 15 and 45; however, when it does occur in children, the effects on a family are devastating. Children with schizophrenia require IEPs that involve collaboration of multidisciplinary team members from medical and mental health fields.

This fact sheet, from the Parent Center for Information and Resources, provides information on different types of emotional and behavioral disorders and specific conditions that fall within each.

▶ **Emotional Disturbance**

http://www.parentcenterhub.org/wp-content/uploads/repo_items/fs5.pdf

Topic 10.3 Characteristics

- Students with externalizing behaviors often exhibit aggression, hyperactivity, impulsivity, noncompliance, and delinquency.

- Characteristics of internalizing behaviors—withdrawal, depression, and anxiety—are harder to detect.

What types of characteristics do students with externalizing behaviors display? As we mentioned in the previous topic, students with externalizing behaviors exhibit verbal and physical aggression, hyperactivity, impulsivity, noncompliance, and delinquency to a marked and excessive degree. **Oppositional defiant disorder (ODD)** includes many of these behaviors. The following table summarizes some key diagnostic criteria for ODD from the *DSM-5*. Imagine how the characteristics associated with ODD would affect a student's social interactions, personal relationships, success at school, and acceptance in the community.

Oppositional Defiant Disorder Characteristics

Required Standards	Symptoms	Applications
Displays at least four symptoms.	• Loses temper • Is easily annoyed • Is angry or resentful • Argues with authority figures or adults • Refuses to comply with requests or rules • Deliberately annoys others • Blames others for mistakes • Displays spitefulness or vindictiveness	Nine-year-old Arturo gets impatient and then angry because Brandon is taking too long on the computer. He yells at Brandon, refusing to sit down at his teacher's request. Instead, he argues with her, saying that if Brandon were faster, then he (Arturo) wouldn't have to get so mad. He continues to blame Brandon and his teacher on his way to the principal's office and later tears pages out of Brandon's math book to "get back at him for all the problems he caused."
Symptoms must be persistent and frequent, and occur in interactions with more than one person.	• For young children (under five), almost daily • For older children (five and older), at least once per week • Lasting at least six months	Arturo exhibits these behaviors one to two times per week, with different classmates. He has displayed these behaviors for the past two years.
Symptoms are inconsistent with expected behavioral norms.	Uncharacteristic for • Age • Developmental level • Gender • Culture	Arturo's behaviors are atypical for boys his age, from his cultural background.
Behaviors impair other activities significantly.	Creates problems: • Socially • Educationally • Vocationally	Arturo's classmates shun him. He is unable to focus or concentrate for extended periods before having an outburst, resulting in academic failure.

What types of characteristics do students with internalizing behaviors display? In contrast to the overt behaviors described above, internalizing behaviors are less often noticed and reported by teachers. For example, a student with an anxiety disorder feels anxious in anticipation of an event perceived as threatening. Associated characteristics of an anxiety disorder include muscle tension and cautious or avoidant behaviors, which are not easily observable to parents, teachers, or other adults. The following table summarizes some of the key diagnostic criteria for social anxiety disorder from the *DSM-5*. People with social anxiety disorder have a marked fear or anxiety about one or more social situations in which the individual is exposed to possible scrutiny by others. Social situations can include social interactions (conversing with someone, meeting new people), being in places where one can be observed (when eating or drinking), or performing. The average age of onset for social anxiety disorder is 13, although the range is 8 to 15 years of age. Do you think these behaviors, exhibited by a child, would gain your attention if you hadn't read this section?

Social Anxiety Disorder

Required Standards	Symptoms	Applications
Fear of displaying anxiety or acting in a way that others will perceive negatively.	Fears of • humiliation and • embarrassment that would subsequently lead to rejection by or offense to others	Twelve-year-old Asa has two fears: being called on in class by the teacher and being asked a question by a peer. She fears embarrassment if she cannot answer correctly and worries that the other students will shun her.
The social situations usually provoke fear or anxiety.	In children, these may be expressed through: • Crying. • Tantrums. • Immobility. • Clinging. • Shrinking. • An inability to speak.	Many days, she feels paralyzed by her fear during class, unable to move. If a peer asks her a simple question ("Which textbook page are we supposed to be reading?"), she can't respond. She spends many lunch periods crying in the restroom, afraid that her peers don't like her.
The social situations are avoided, or endured with intense fear or anxiety.	The fear or anxiety is disproportionate to the actual threat posed by the situation.	Although Asa has never experienced either of the situations she fears, she tries to stay home from school every day.
The fear, worry, or avoidance is persistent (six months or longer) and causes clinically significant distress or impairment.	Affects areas of functioning: • Social • Occupational • Other	Asa is so preoccupied with her fears that she cannot pay attention during class or take notes. As a result, she is failing three classes.
The fear, anxiety, or avoidance cannot be attributed to other factors.	Cannot be attributed to: • Physiological effects of drugs or medications • A medical condition • Another mental disorder (e.g., panic disorder, ASD)	Asa has no other conditions that could be contributing to her fears.

As you can see, the characteristics of internalizing behaviors are much different from those of externalizing behaviors. The following table summarizes some of the most common characteristics of these two conditions.

Examples of Externalizing and Internalizing Behaviors

Externalizing Behaviors	Internalizing Behaviors
Violates basic rights of others	Exhibits painful shyness
Violates societal norms or rules (e.g., stealing)	Is depressed
Causes property loss or damage	Has an eating disorder (anorexia or bulimia)
Demonstrates hostility and/or defiance	Is socially withdrawn
Argues or has tantrums	Has unfounded fears and phobias
Is physically aggressive	Verbalizes feelings of low self-esteem
Ignores teachers' reprimands	Has excessive worries
Demonstrates obsessive/compulsive behaviors	Panics
Causes or threatens physical harm to people or animals	Exhibits self-destructive behavior
Uses lewd or obscene gestures	Entertains ideas of suicide

Topic 10.4 Prevalence and Placement

• EBD is considered a high-incidence disability, although these students are placed in more restrictive settings than many students with other disabilities.

• IDEA has specific disciplinary procedures for violations directly resulting from a student's disability.

Is EBD a high- or low-incidence disability? It is a high-incidence disability, the last to be covered in this text (Chapters 11 through 14 address low-incidence disabilities). However, fewer students are served under the IDEA category of emotional disturbance than in any of the other high-incidence categories. The following pie chart compares the percentages of students with EBD to those served in the other high-incidence disability categories.

Disability Prevalence: 2014–2015 School Year

SOURCE: U.S. Department of Education. (2015). *Students Ages 6 through 21 under IDEA, Part B, as a Percentage of Population, by Disability Category and State.* [IDEA Section 618 Data Products: Static Tables, 2014–2015 Part B *Child Count and Educational Environments*]. Retrieved from http://www2.ed.gov/programs/osepidea/618-data/static-tables/index.html

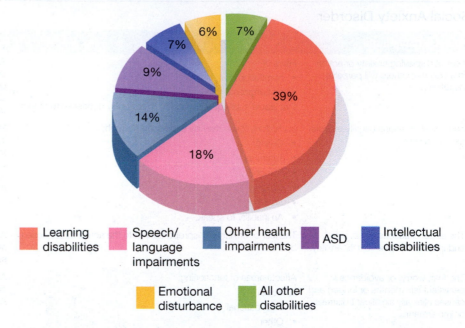

Although many people think that students with EBD receive their education in self-contained or segregated settings, their education actually takes place in a variety of settings: general education classrooms, resource rooms, separate special education classrooms, special schools, juvenile correctional facilities, residential institutions, and hospitals. As following chart indicates, the largest percentage of students with EBD spend most of their day in general education settings. However, despite the movement toward inclusion, significantly more students with EBD are placed in the most restrictive settings (i.e., homebound/hospital, residential facility, correctional facility) compared to their peers with other disabilities.

Educational Placements for Students with EBD, Ages 6–21

SOURCE: U.S. Department of Education. (2015). *Number and Percent of Students Ages 6 through 21 Served under IDEA, Part B, by Educational Environment and State.* [IDEA Section 618 Data Products: Static Tables, 2014–2015 Part B *Child Count and Educational Environments*]. Retrieved from http://www2.ed.gov/programs/osepidea/618-data/static-tables/index.html

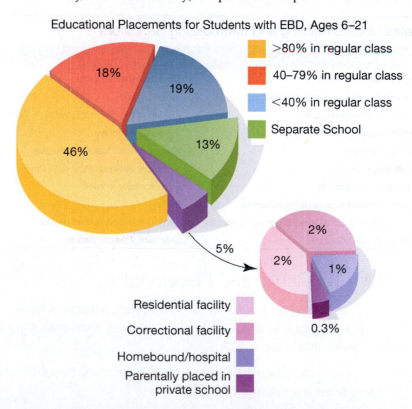

Educational Placements for Students with EBD, Ages 6–21

How do suspension and expulsion procedures differ for students with EBD, and how do they affect placement decisions? To answer this question, let's think about a fictional student who violates his school's code of conduct and is suspended. One immediate problem is that the student is no longer being educated; instead, he may be sitting at home watching TV or playing video games. A second problem is that when our fictional student is not in school, he is more likely to get into trouble—vandalism, shoplifting, and other delinquent acts. Although school personnel may think suspension is a good solution because it prevents the student from causing further disruption in school, it's probably not too helpful for the student. If our fictional student has a disability, a third problem arises: he is no longer receiving a free appropriate public education (FAPE, see Topic 4.3) to which he is entitled, nor is he receiving the special education services outlined in his IEP. Because he is no longer in school or in the setting delineated in his IEP, a change of placement has occurred. Finally, if our student has EBD, and the actions that resulted in suspension were caused by that disability (referred to as **manifestation determination** in IDEA), then he is essentially being suspended as a result of his disability. A loose analogy would be a situation in which a student with a learning disability was suspended for failing a test, or a student with a language disorder was suspended for not understanding a teacher's directions. None of these situations would be acceptable or appropriate.

IDEA regulations provide specific guidance on implementing school discipline policies for students with disabilities. To gain a better understanding of this process, first read through the outlined procedures and then view the flowchart that follows.

1. Violations of codes of conduct can result in removal from the current setting to **Interim Alternative Educational Settings (IAES)**, another setting, or suspension for up to 10 school days to the same extent that such alternatives are applied to students without disabilities.

2. Students removed from their current placements must continue to receive educational services in order to make progress toward achieving their IEP goals.

3. Within 10 school days of a change-of-placement decision, the IEP team must determine whether the behavior was the result of either

   • the disability or
   • poor implementation of the IEP.

4. If either of these applies (i.e., manifestation determination), the team must

   • conduct a functional behavioral assessment,
   • implement a behavior intervention, and
   • return the child to the original placement.

5. If the behavior occurred while a **behavior intervention plan (BIP)** was in effect, the team must review and modify the plan as necessary.

6. Regardless of manifestation determination, students may be removed to an IAES for up to 45 school days for violations involving weapons, drugs, or infliction of serious bodily injury.

IDEA Disciplinary Procedures Flowchart

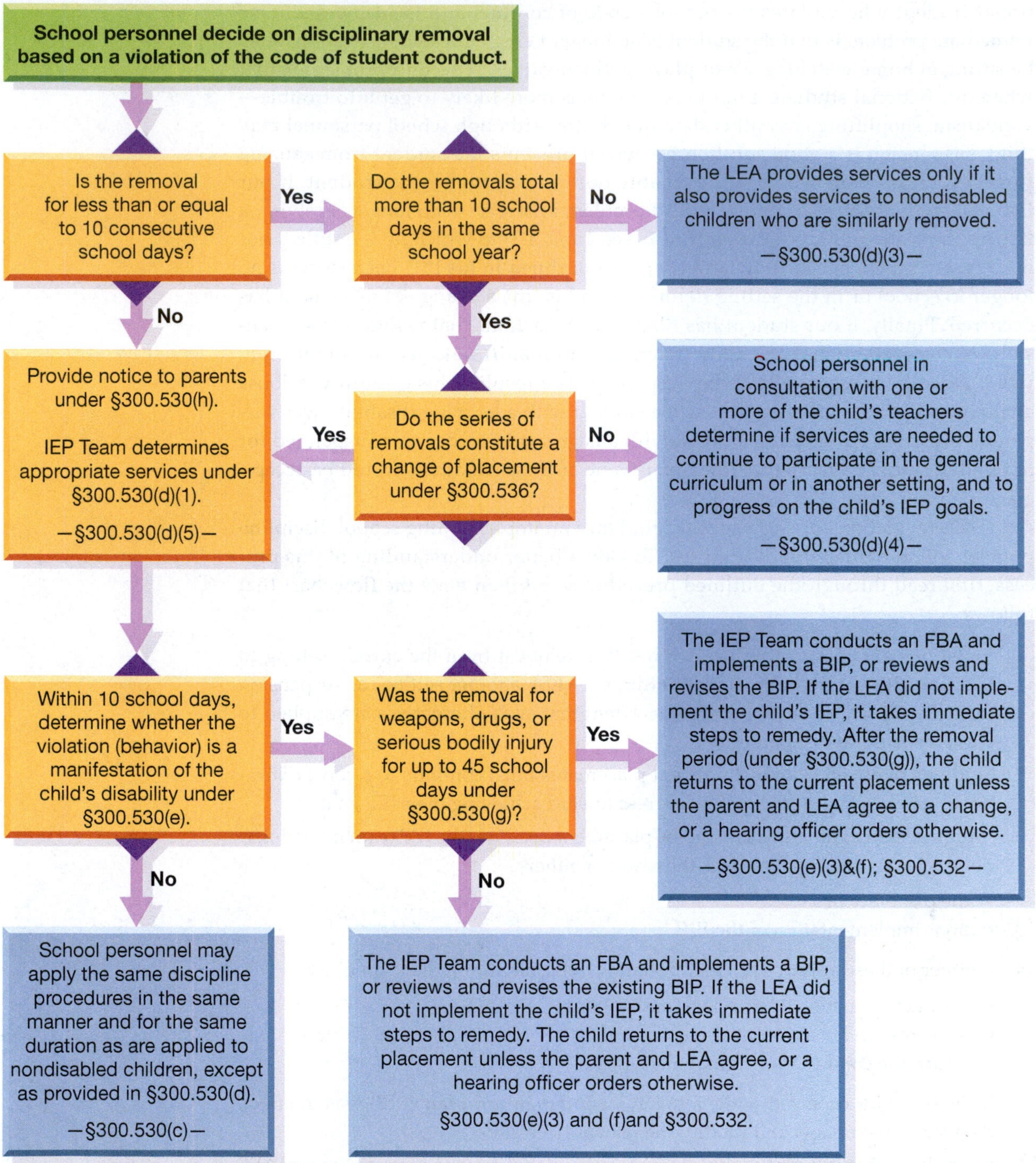

School personnel decide on disciplinary removal based on a violation of the code of student conduct.

Is the removal for less than or equal to 10 consecutive school days?

— Yes →

Do the removals total more than 10 school days in the same school year?

— No →

The LEA provides services only if it also provides services to nondisabled children who are similarly removed.

—§300.530(d)(3)—

No ↓ (from first box)

Yes ↓ (from second box)

Provide notice to parents under §300.530(h).

IEP Team determines appropriate services under §300.530(d)(1).

—§300.530(d)(5)—

← Yes —

Do the series of removals constitute a change of placement under §300.536?

— No →

School personnel in consultation with one or more of the child's teachers determine if services are needed to continue to participate in the general curriculum or in another setting, and to progress on the child's IEP goals.

—§300.530(d)(4)—

Within 10 school days, determine whether the violation (behavior) is a manifestation of the child's disability under §300.530(e).

— Yes →

Was the removal for weapons, drugs, or serious bodily injury for up to 45 school days under §300.530(g)?

— Yes →

The IEP Team conducts an FBA and implements a BIP, or reviews and revises the BIP. If the LEA did not implement the child's IEP, it takes immediate steps to remedy. After the removal period (under §300.530(g)), the child returns to the current placement unless the parent and LEA agree to a change, or a hearing officer orders otherwise.

—§300.530(e)(3)&(f); §300.532—

No ↓ (from manifestation box)

No ↓ (from weapons box)

School personnel may apply the same discipline procedures in the same manner and for the same duration as are applied to nondisabled children, except as provided in §300.530(d).

—§300.530(c)—

The IEP Team conducts an FBA and implements a BIP, or reviews and revises the existing BIP. If the LEA did not implement the child's IEP, it takes immediate steps to remedy. The child returns to the current placement unless the parent and LEA agree, or a hearing officer orders otherwise.

§300.530(e)(3) and (f)and §300.532.

SOURCE: Center for Parent Information and Resources. *Building the Legacy: Training Curriculum on IDEA 2004; Module 19: Key Issues in Discipline,* written by Renee Bradley, Office of Special Education Programs, U.S. Department of Education, in partnership with NICHCY Handout E-17, p. 53E. Retrieved from http://www.parentcenterhub.org/wp-content/uploads/repo_items/legacy/E-handouts.pdf

Note: The Center for Parent Information and Resources provides more information on IDEA's disciplinary procedures at http://www.parentcenterhub.org/repository/disciplineplacements/

Check Your Understanding 10.1

Click here to gauge your understanding of the concepts in this section.

Special Education

Learning Outcome

Explain the ways in which EBD can impact personal relationships and academic skills, describe accommodations that can lessen these challenges, understand methods that parents and classroom teachers can use to reduce challenges associated with EBD, and describe supports to help students with EBD transition to post-secondary options such as school, work, and independent living.

Topic 10.5 Challenges and Their Solutions

- In addition to behavioral challenges, students with EBD also struggle with social skills and academics.

- Explicit instruction in social skills and academics—within a PBIS framework—can address some challenges; however, many students with EBD also require mental health services or pharmacological intervention.

Topic 10.6 Accommodations

- Some students with EBD may benefit from accommodations that target externalizing behaviors, such as hyperactivity and noncompliance.

- Other students who exhibit internalizing behaviors may benefit from accommodations that address anxiety and depression.

Topic 10.7 Early Intervention

- The causes of EBD in young children usually include multiple, overlapping risk factors.

- When very young children exhibit signs of EBD, effective early intervention programs can eliminate or reduce problem behaviors.

Topic 10.8 School Years

- The PBIS approach establishes a framework for providing behavior supports to all students.

- Functional behavioral assessments and behavioral intervention plans can be used to address more serious behaviors.

Topic 10.9 Transition

- The long-term outcomes for students with EBD are worse than those for students with other types of disabilities.

- Teachers, counselors, transition specialists, and other professionals can take positive steps to increase the future educational and employment success of students with EBD.

The interventions and supports needed for a child with EBD to become a successful adult must begin early.

Topic 10.5 Challenges and Their Solutions

- In addition to behavioral challenges, students with EBD also struggle with social skills and academics.

- Explicit instruction in social skills and academics—within a PBIS framework—can address some challenges; however, many students with EBD also require mental health services or pharmacological intervention.

In addition to the characteristics associated with externalizing and internalizing behaviors, do students with EBD face other challenges? Compared to any other group of students, those with or without disabilities, current data indicate that students with EBD have some of the poorest social and academic outcomes. Their challenging behaviors and limited social skills often demand teachers' attention, interfere with instruction, lead to strained personal relationships, and negatively impact the learning environment.

Being socially competent can mean a number of things: exercising self-control during conflicts, cooperating with others, or expressing one's needs appropriately. However, in situations where these skills are necessary, students with EBD often demonstrate one of the following:

- *Skill deficits*—can't do something
- *Performance deficits*—won't do something
- *Fluency problems*—hasn't had enough practice to perform something well or with automaticity

Let's look at some examples of these deficits in the following scenario.

Social Skills Scenario

After lunch, a group of middle schoolers starts an impromptu game of Frisbee Keep-Away, boys versus girls. Sage, who has strong social skills, joins in the game easily by waving his hand and calling, "Over here!" to a classmate, who throws him the Frisbee. In contrast, Sorrell doesn't know how to enter the game appropriately (skill deficit), so he tackles the girl who has the Frisbee, earning him a visit to the principal's office and the ire of his classmates. Heather wants to join the game, knows how to do so effectively, but chooses not to because of the anxiety it causes her (performance deficit). Instead, she hovers around the periphery of the game, finally leaving to sit unhappily alone. Rosemary also knows how to appropriately join the group; however, she is uncomfortable doing so because she has little experience joining in a social game activity such as this (fluency deficit). To mask her insecurity, she joins a group of older students who are smoking cigarettes behind the school gym (a behavior in which, unfortunately, she has no skill, performance, or fluency deficits).

In addition to the challenges described above, students with EBD also react differently to social situations. Several examples are provided in the table below.

Examples of Social Skills Deficits

Students with externalizing behaviors are more likely to:	Students with internalizing behaviors may:
• Misinterpret a neutral interaction as having a hostile intent (e.g., when accidentally bumped in the hallway, they assume the peer is starting a fight).	• Avoid peer interactions (e.g., sit alone at recess or lunch in a place where other students are less likely to initiate interactions).
• Use aggressive strategies to get what they want (e.g., using intimidation or physical violence rather than talking or negotiating).	• Display odd or distracting behaviors (e.g., vocalizations, facial tics) in response to stress or anxiety.

Many students with EBD also demonstrate poor academic performance. They are more likely to fail a grade or be suspended or expelled from school. Their behaviors often interfere with the ability to learn requisite skills. These students typically have low levels of academic engagement and act out to escape work that is unpleasant, unappealing, or too difficult. As a result, they often lack basic skills (e.g., reading, writing, and math) and fall behind academically. Many of them have more significant academic problems than their general education peers and show greater academic deficits than many students with other disabilities. In fact, some research data indicate that a good number of students with EBD exhibit academic deficits as severe as those of students with learning disabilities. At best, these academic difficulties appear to remain stable; at worst, they deteriorate over time. The more severe the EBD symptoms, the more the academic performance is affected, which increases the likelihood for school failure, dropout, and juvenile delinquency. In fact, students with EBD are retained more often and have higher school dropout rates than students in any other disability category. Students who end up in the juvenile justice system are even less likely to receive services and supports specified in their IEPs.

Emotional and Behavioral Disorders: Challenges

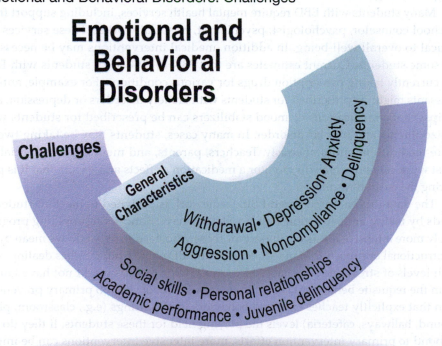

What are some solutions to the challenges listed above? Often, students with EBD require a comprehensive set of **wraparound supports** that include strong academic instruction, social skills training, individualized behavioral interventions, and, in many cases, mental health services and medical interventions. **Positive Behavioral Interventions and Supports (PBIS)**, which you learned about in Chapter 2, provide a multi-tiered system of supports for all students, but particularly for those in need of more intensive and individualized supports. We discuss each of these solutions briefly below.

The single most effective technique for preventing problem behaviors is to teach well. Students who are academically engaged have fewer opportunities to be disruptive and are less likely to try and avoid academic tasks by acting out. Teachers must use evidence-based practices that are actively engaging and also designed for students' varying skill levels (review UDL and differentiated instruction in Topic 2.3 and Topic 2.4). When students demonstrate academic skills that are significantly below grade level, many strategies for students with learning disabilities are effective, particularly when combined with explicit instruction in deficit areas.

Social skills should be explicitly taught to students with social skills deficits. Social skills instruction should include (1) teaching, (2) demonstrating, (3) practicing, and (4) doing. In this approach, skills that are not in the students' behavioral repertoire—"can't do" problems (skill deficits) rather than "won't do" problems (performance deficits)—are taught. Key components of effective social skills programs include:

- Initiating instruction as early as possible.
- Training for teachers and parents in the use of positive discipline techniques.
- Embedding the social skills instruction within the general education curriculum.
- Providing numerous practice opportunities to promote generalization and maintenance.
- Using peer supports.

Long-term follow-up data on social skills instruction show extremely positive results; children who participate in these programs early (e.g., first grade) are significantly less likely to commit violent crimes, drink heavily, become pregnant, or contribute to a pregnancy in their later teen years.

Many students with EBD require mental health services, including support from a school counselor, psychologist, psychiatrist, or social worker. These services are critical to overall well-being. In addition, medical interventions may be necessary for some students. Current estimates are that 38% to 79% of all students with EBD are currently taking prescription drugs for various conditions. For example, antidepressants might be prescribed for students with anxiety disorders or depression, and antipsychotic medications or mood stabilizers can be prescribed for students with schizophrenia and bipolar disorder. In many cases, students may be taking two or more medications simultaneously. Teachers, parents, and mental health specialists must work collaboratively to monitor a medication's effects and ensure that it is producing the desired results.

The data-driven, three-tiered PBIS framework is designed to meet all students' needs by taking an instructional approach to behavior and then providing progressively more intensive levels of support for those who need it. What do we mean by an "instructional approach"? Many students with EBD come from families dealing with high levels of stress and/or chaos. As a result, their parents might not have taught them the requisite behavioral skills for success in school. A PBIS primary prevention plan that explicitly teaches expected behaviors in all settings (e.g., classroom, playground, hallways, cafeteria) levels the playing field for these students. If they do not respond to primary intervention efforts, more intensive interventions can be implemented. We provide examples of specific interventions for each tier of the PBIS framework in Topic 10.8.

Emotional and Behavioral Disorders: Solutions

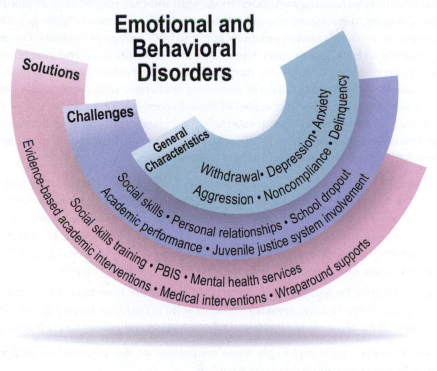

Topic 10.6 Accommodations

- Some students with EBD may benefit from accommodations that target externalizing behaviors, such as hyperactivity and noncompliance.

- Other students who exhibit internalizing behaviors may benefit from accommodations that address anxiety and depression.

What types of accommodations best address the needs of students with externalizing behaviors? Recall that students with EBD who exhibit externalizing behaviors may be verbally or physically aggressive and noncompliant. One accommodation that can be easily implemented, and works for many students in addition to those with EBD, is to establish clearly stated rules with consequences that are consistently applied, which helps students understand the outcomes of their behavior. As you learned earlier, a large number of these students also have ADHD, so they are hyperactive and impulsive. Such students will likely benefit from accommodations outlined in Topic 7.6, such as reduced noise and distractions, brief assignments, and frequent breaks. Following are two other accommodations that might help students with externalizing behaviors.

- *Providing options*—Students with externalizing behaviors often enter into power struggles with authority figures, such as teachers. This may occur when a student is asked to comply with a request or complete a task. Providing students with options ("Would you like to finish your essay now or start your math assignment?") instead of giving them commands allows them to feel a sense of control over a situation.

- *Small-group instruction*—This accommodation is often recommended for students with emotional and behavioral disorders, as well as those with ADHD, who have trouble maintaining focus or controlling their behavior. When providing instruction in small groups, a teacher has the ability to more closely monitor student behavior, offer support, and provide feedback.

How do accommodations differ for students who exhibit internalizing behaviors? Like students with externalizing behaviors, those with internalizing behaviors (anorexia, bulimia, anxiety, depression) also experience academic and social challenges. Therefore, some of the same recommendations apply to both groups of students. For example, students in both groups may have difficulty concentrating and consequently benefit from prompts, note takers, frequent breaks, and alternate testing locations. Also, students in both groups often demonstrate challenges with organization, setting goals, and completing tasks. A checklist of steps to complete or a planner can be helpful. However, unlike students with externalizing behaviors, those with internalizing behaviors often experience high levels of stress. Following are a couple of accommodations teachers may want to consider for these students.

- *Preferential seating*—In this case, preferential seating may mean placing a student near a doorway (as opposed to near a teacher for students with behavioral concerns, or near the board for those with visual impairments). This allows a student who is feeling stressed and overwhelmed to take frequent breaks by leaving the classroom without disrupting instruction or peers. It may also enable a student to avoid sitting near classmates who increase his or her anxiety levels.

- *Extended time for tests and assignments*—Giving more time to complete a test or assignment can reduce stress for students who experience anxiety. It can also be beneficial for those with depression, whose moods and energy levels fluctuate.

The following table highlights some commonly used accommodations for students with emotional and behavioral disorders.

Examples of Frequently Used Accommodations for Students with EBD

Presentation	Setting	Response	Scheduling or Timing
• Verbal or visual cues	• Separate room for testing	• Providing options	• Extended time for tests
• Prompts	• Reduced noise/distractions	• Alternate response modes	• Frequent breaks
• Note takers	• Preferential seating	• Computer software	• Shorter, more frequent study periods
• Recorded lectures	• Checklist of steps/planner		• Brief assignments (or broken into parts)
• Textbooks and syllabus prior to class	• Small-group or one-on-one instruction		

The Center for Adolescent Research in Schools (CARS)

CARS is a center funded by the U.S. Department of Education's Institute of Education Sciences to develop and evaluate interventions for high school students with EBD. The center created the *Classroom-Based Interventions Manual*, which includes information on **Check & Connect** and a number of effective classroom interventions, including accommodations.

The manual contains an entire section, as well as a worksheet, to help school personnel select and implement accommodations that best address each student's specific academic and behavioral concerns. To learn more about CARS and to access the manual, visit http://coe.lehigh.edu/cars.

Topic 10.7 Early Intervention

- The causes of EBD in young children usually include multiple, overlapping risk factors.

- When very young children exhibit signs of EBD, effective early intervention programs can eliminate or reduce problem behaviors.

What causes EBD in young children? The causes can be difficult to identify and may result from several co-occurring factors. For example, research suggests a relationship between prenatal drug exposure and childhood EBD: 53% of drug-exposed children in Head Start preschool programs are identified as having a disability by kindergarten. Of course, we can't discount the effects of the home environment on these statistics: a pregnant woman who takes illegal drugs probably also lacks key parenting skills that will affect her child's mental health (e.g., the child may receive poor supervision, punitive or inconsistent discipline, few positive interactions). While a single negative experience does not necessarily lead to emotional problems, multiple risk factors (e.g., poverty, abuse, neglect, parental stress, exposure to violence, inconsistent expectations and rules, turmoil) over extended periods can contribute to the development of such problems. When children come from high-risk backgrounds, they often:

- Learn problem behaviors through imitation of those around them.
- Develop problem behaviors as coping mechanisms.
- Develop mental illnesses, triggered by psychological trauma.

The following figure illustrates how exposure to social risk factors can lead to long-term negative outcomes. On the other hand, it also depicts how exposure to early interventions can result in long-term positive outcomes.

The Path to Long-Term Negative Outcomes for At-Risk Children and Youth

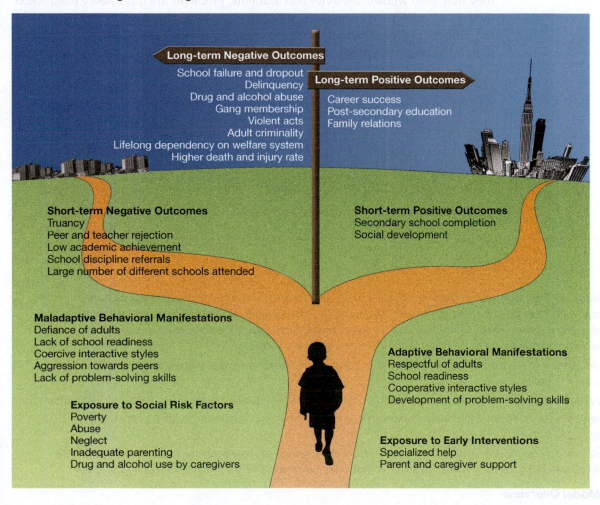

What are some early warning signs of EBD? Very young children are usually not able to verbally express their feelings, emotions, and thoughts. Therefore, many early indications of mental health conditions in young children are behaviorally based. Here are a few:

- Displays extreme anxiety
- Worries excessively
- Exhibits hyperactivity
- Has frequent nightmares
- Displays aggression
- Is disobedient
- Has frequent temper tantrums

Because young children will probably not be able to verbalize emotions such as anxiety or worry, their feelings may be evident in other ways: refusal to go to bed or engage in other activities that cause them anxiety; whimpering or crying when presented with stress-inducing events; or changes in appetite or sleep habits.

While internalizing behavior problems can be challenging to identify in young children, extreme externalizing behaviors are often obvious by age three. Indeed, 15% of preschoolers engage daily in three or more acts of overt aggressive behavior (e.g., hitting and kicking, pushing), and 10% exhibit daily episodes of serious antisocial behavior (e.g., calling names, playing mean tricks). Without proper intervention, severe problem behaviors seen in preschoolers tend to be very stable over time. In other words, they do not go away as children get older. Without necessary supports, they may even worsen. Behavior and academic problems are most easily fixed when they are identified at a young age. As the graphic above illustrates, early intervention can address problems before they grow more serious or become firmly entrenched patterns. Intervention needs to involve both the child *and* the family in order to break what has usually developed into a predictable and negative sequence. This can help avoid the need for more intensive interventions later in the child's life.

Effective early intervention programs often have the following components:

- Active parental involvement
- Teaching, through examples, about the relationship between behavior and its consequences
- Instruction on appropriate behaviors for different settings (setting demands)
- Instruction on how to make and keep friendships (e.g., social skills training)

The *Pyramid Model*

The *Pyramid Model for Promoting Young Children's Social-Emotional Competence* is a multi-tiered framework, similar to the PBIS framework, developed for young children. The goal of the *Pyramid Model* is to promote the social-emotional competence of young children as well as to address challenging behavior. Evidence-based practices appropriate for young children's developmental stages are incorporated within the framework, which contains:

- *Universal practices*—These focus on the development of nurturing and responsive relationships and high-quality supportive environments.
- *Secondary practices*—Explicit instruction is provided in social-emotional skill acquisition, fluency, generalization, and maintenance.
- *Tertiary interventions*—Intensive, individualized interventions are implemented to address the most persistent and challenging behaviors.

Young children in classrooms that utilize the *Pyramid Model* demonstrate stronger social skills and fewer challenging behaviors than children in typical early childhood settings. The video below explains the *Pyramid Model* in more detail.

▶ *Pyramid Model* **Overview**
https://www.youtube.com/watch?v=xYYOUtMHHJs

Topic 10.8 School Years

- The PBIS approach establishes a framework for providing behavior supports to all students.

- Functional behavioral assessments and behavioral intervention plans can be used to address more serious behaviors.

What can educators do to increase positive behavior while reducing problem behaviors? Teachers need to teach well, use an effective classroom behavior management system, and be responsive to their students' individual needs. A teacher who is unskilled in managing the classroom or individual students' differences may unintentionally create an environment where students become frustrated or withdrawn. In some cases, a teacher can escalate a situation when he or she responds inappropriately to a student's behavior. In many schools, a small number of teachers—often those with poor behavior management skills—make the majority of office and special education referrals. Further, students placed in poorly managed classrooms display significantly higher rates of problem behaviors and aggression than their peers in well-managed classrooms.

As mentioned earlier, PBIS provides a framework for schoolwide and classwide behavior management and help for students who need additional supports. Primary prevention involves establishing schoolwide expectations for all key areas. Expectations are clear, concise, and simple (e.g., "Follow directions," "Be respectful," "Be prepared"), with detailed examples of how to behave in different settings. Students are given opportunities to practice, and teachers provide reinforcement when students meet expectations. Effective classroom behavior management systems—which provide clear guidance for a student's behavior in the form of classroom rules, procedures, and consequences for both compliance and noncompliance—provide a solid foundation. Teachers can further prevent problem behaviors by engaging in effective teaching behaviors like:

- Having all materials ready and within reach before beginning a lesson.

- Beginning instruction promptly.

- Gaining students' attention and providing advance organizers.

- Maintaining an appropriately brisk instructional pace to maintain students' attention and providing adequate **opportunities to respond (OTRs)**.

- Giving **specific praise** for both academic and behavioral responses.

- Providing scaffolding, corrective feedback, or redirection when needed.

- Assessing student performance regularly, through both formal and informal measures.

- Providing **active supervision**.

The PBIS Pyramid Model

Tertiary Interventions:
Students with high-risk behaviors
Focus: Reduce behavior intensity/severity
Specialized, individualized supports
Needed for 1–5% of students

Secondary Interventions:
At-risk students
Focus: Reduce problem behaviors
Small group supports
Needed for 5–10% of students

Primary or Universal Prevention:
All students
Focus: Prevention
Effective with 80–90% of students

SOURCE: Adapted from "Graphic: PBIS Pyramid Model," in PBIS Website graphic Item #4 Continuum of School-Wide Instruction & Positive Behavior Support, © 09-17-12.

Two practices—opportunities to respond (OTR) to academic questions, tasks, or commands and specific praise—are described in more detail in the following table. They are simple, easy to implement, and complementary to effective instructional practices that can be used with all students at the primary or universal tier to produce large gains in appropriate behavior. Unfortunately, despite research validating the positive effects of increased OTR, teachers are *less* likely to engage students with EBD for fear of triggering disruptive behaviors. Similarly, students with EBD are *less* likely to receive specific praise than their classmates. So this group of students, whose disruptive behaviors put them most in need of OTR and specific praise, are the least likely to get it!

OTR and Specific Praise

	Opportunities to Respond (OTR)	Specific Praise
Description	Providing students with multiple chances to answer questions, complete tasks, or follow directions: • 4–6 times/minute for new material. • 8–12 times/minute for previously learned material. Techniques such as choral responding (where students answer in unison) or visual responses (thumbs up/thumbs down) are helpful in achieving these high OTR rates because teachers can assess many student responses at once rather than asking students one by one.	Providing immediate, specific, positive feedback when a student does something well or complies with instructions or classroom rules (e.g., "I like the way you got started on your seatwork right away," rather than a vague "Good job").
Research findings	Higher rates of OTR are associated with increased: • Academic outcomes. • Student engagement.	Higher rates of teacher praise are associated with increases in: • Following directions. • Academic engagement. • On-task behavior. • Compliance.

The **Good Behavior Game** is another example of an evidence-based behavioral intervention that can increase positive student behaviors.

The Good Behavior Game

The Good Behavior Game rewards students for following classroom rules and engaging in positive behaviors during set periods during the day. Here's how it works:

- The teacher divides students into teams.
- If any member of a team engages in disruptive or noncompliant behavior during the specified time, the entire team gets a checkmark.
- The entire team wins if their total number of checkmarks remains below a pre-set number (often four).
- All teams can win as long as they do not exceed the pre-established number of checkmarks.
- Team prizes gradually move from the tangible (e.g., stickers) to the more abstract or intrinsic (e.g., teacher praise, self-satisfaction).

Teachers should reinforce positive behaviors exhibited by team members. They should also ensure that all teams have the ability to win, and should not use the Good Behavior Game when one or more students in the class are unable to control their behavior adequately. This situation could cause friction between team members or harassment of the offending student.

Over 40 years of research validates the Good Behavior Game as a way to improve and maintain positive classroom conduct and to decrease disruptive and aggressive behaviors, particularly among male students initially rated by their teachers as displaying excessive behaviors of this kind. Even better, longitudinal research has shown that students who played the Good Behavior Game in elementary school exhibited, as young adults, significantly lower rates of drug and alcohol abuse, delinquency, and incarceration for violent crimes.

Gagliardilmages/Shutterstock

Here are two resources that provide more in-depth information about effective behavior supports for classroom teachers at the primary prevention level:

- The Center for Positive Behavioral Interventions and Supports offers a free document, *Supporting and Responding to Behavior: Evidence-Based Classroom Strategies for Teachers*. This document can be downloaded at http://www.pbis.org/common/cms/files/pbisresources/Supporting%20and%20Responding%20to%20Behavior.pdf
- The Academic and Behavioral Response to Intervention Project at the University of Louisville has an entire library of videos that demonstrate many of the evidence-based practices and interventions that can be used within the PBIS framework, as well as effective teaching behaviors such as those listed above (e.g., OTR, specific praise, active supervision). This video library can be accessed at http://louisville.edu/education/abri/training.html

What about students who need more supports? For those who need more than primary prevention efforts, secondary interventions are then provided. These are targeted, small-group or individual interventions such as social skills instruction or the Check-In/Check-Out (CICO) approach.

Social Skills Instruction and Check-In/Check-Out

	Social Skills Instruction	CICO
Description	Providing explicit instruction to improve skill deficits in areas such as: • Peer relations (interacting with friends) • Self-management (controlling temper) • Compliance (following teachers' directions) • Assertion (asking for help) • Academics (working independently)	Providing students with frequent access to positive reinforcement for appropriate behavior via five components: 1. Morning check-in with a specified teacher or other relevant adult (counselor) 2. Daily behavior point card, which is carried to every class 3. Structured teacher feedback on identified behavioral expectations, documented on the card 4. Afternoon check-out and review of point card with specified teacher/adult 5. Home-school communication via the point card, signed by parent
Research findings	Associated with increases in: • Social interaction skills (inviting a peer to play, sharing) • Social communication skills (asking and answering questions, paying a compliment)	More effective when implemented with: • Individual students rather than with small groups • Students with attention-seeking behaviors rather than those with avoidance behaviors

Tertiary interventions are reserved for students with the most intensive needs. To address the most severe, chronic, and pervasive behaviors, a **functional behavioral assessment (FBA)** can be conducted to determine the cause of the problem behavior. A function-based intervention is then designed based on this information. The FBA process and the development of a subsequent behavior intervention plan (BIP) (discussed previously in Topic 4.7) are explained in the box below. FBA-based interventions have been shown to reduce problem behaviors by 70% and are effective for students with a wide range of disabilities and problem behaviors.

A Closer Look at Evidence-Based Practices

Functional Behavioral Assessments (FBAs) and Behavior Intervention Plans (BIPs)

Many students misbehave in an attempt to either obtain or avoid something. To determine why a student engages in a problematic behavior (i.e., the function of the behavior), school personnel can conduct a functional behavioral assessment (FBA). This involves:

1. *Identifying and defining the problem behavior and the desired behavior:* The problem and desired behaviors should be defined in precise and measurable terms, as opposed to ambiguous or vague terms, so that they can be easily recognized and recorded. For example, *Gregor screams profanities at the teacher* is more easily observed and measured than *Gregor is disrespectful to the teacher.*

2. *Collecting data:* Data are collected on when and where the behavior occurs, the frequency (how often it occurs) or duration (how long it lasts) of the behavior, antecedent conditions (what happens right before the behavior that might have triggered it), and consequences (what happens right after the behavior that might be reinforcing it). These data can be gathered by interviewing parents, teachers, and the student; by asking them to complete a form containing questions about the student's behavior; or by observing the student.

3. *Determining the function of the behavior and testing the hypothesis:* A hypothetical function for the behavior is determined on the basis of the data: *Gregor yells profanities at the teacher to avoid doing class work that is too difficult.* Next, the probable cause of the behavior should be tested to confirm the function: *The teacher gives Gregor work that is at his academic skill level. Gregor no longer screams profanities.*

   The teacher gives Gregor work that is slightly harder, and he screams profanities. The hypothesis appears to be correct.

4. *Developing a behavior intervention plan:* An intervention that teaches the student a replacement for the problem behavior is developed. The replacement behavior (or desired behavior) gives the student a better way of fulfilling the same need: *When the work is too hard, Gregor will raise his hand to get teacher assistance.*

5. *Implementing the intervention:* All steps in the behavior intervention plan should be implemented. The teacher will continue to collect data and will provide positive reinforcement to the student when he engages in the desired replacement behavior.

6. *Evaluating the intervention:* These data are reviewed and evaluated to determine if the intervention is effective and the student's behavior is improving; adjustments or modifications are made as necessary.

The OSEP Technical Assistance Center on Positive Behavioral Interventions & Supports has a sample behavior intervention plan template, available at https://www.pbis.org/resource/804/behavior-support-plan-template

We should note that although an FBA is a standard tertiary intervention, it can be used to analyze the function of any type of behavior, in settings in and out of the classroom, for people with and without disabilities, of all ages. In a non-academic example, a teenager might ask, "Why does my little brother always have to go to the bathroom right after dinner?" FBA data might indicate that he does so to avoid his evening chores (clearing the table and doing the dishes). His bathroom behavior might even be reinforced when his mother gets tired of waiting for him to return and makes an older sibling do the dishes!

For more information on conducting a functional behavioral assessment and developing a behavior intervention plan, and to view examples of each, visit the following IRIS Module. After working through the module, you can try using your newly acquired skills to analyze and modify the behaviors of roommates, friends, siblings, and significant others.

▶ IRIS Module: Functional Behavioral Assessment: Identifying the Reasons for Problem Behavior and Developing a Behavior Plan
http://iris.peabody.vanderbilt.edu/module/fba/

All of these interventions fall within the multi-tiered PBIS framework, which provides the flexibility to help all students: those who need minimal supports, others who benefit from targeted interventions, and those who require intensive, individualized interventions. The following box highlights some of the positive results occurring in schools nationwide that have adopted this framework.

PBIS Outcomes

Nationwide, over 9,000 schools are implementing PBIS. The outcomes are exciting and include reduced:

- Discipline referrals
- Vandalism
- Delinquency
- Tobacco, alcohol, and illicit drug use
- Problems in non-instructional settings (playgrounds, hallways, buses)

Further, students with EBD show improved academic achievement and school engagement, and students at risk for EBD or who are developing problem behaviors are identified and receive intervention earlier. For more resources on PBIS, visit the Technical Assistance Center on Positive Behavioral Interventions & Supports (http://www.pbis.org).

Topic 10.9 Transition

- The long-term outcomes for students with EBD are worse than those for students with other types of disabilities.

- Teachers, counselors, transition specialists, and other professionals can take positive steps to increase the future educational and employment success of students with EBD.

How do students with EBD fare during and after high school? Unfortunately, these students have very poor outcomes. While in school, they have the highest rates of disciplinary actions (63%) and suspensions and expulsions (73%) of all students with disabilities. The high school completion rate for all students with disabilities is 72%; students with EBD have the lowest rate (56%). As expected, without a high school diploma, these students have low rates of college attendance and high rates of unemployment and

Sascha Burkard/Alamy Stock Photo

With proper services and supports, this young man's delinquency and arrest might have been prevented.

under-employment. When they are employed, their social and behavioral challenges negatively affect their work experiences, causing high job turnover. They frequently have poor interpersonal relationships and a high need for mental health services. Longitudinal data show that up to two-thirds of youth with EBD, many of whom have a history of delinquency that starts at a young age, eventually have some involvement with the criminal justice system.

How can we improve long-term outcomes for these students? The data above depict a bleak picture for students with EBD. However, interventions that address key predictors of post-school success can be used to improve these outcomes:

- Social skills instruction
- Inclusion in general education classes
- High school completion or graduation
- Instruction in self-advocacy
- Provision of career-awareness activities
- Exposure to a variety of job experiences through shadowing, internships, and work-study
- Interagency collaboration
- Social network development

Some of these should be familiar to you because we covered them in earlier chapters. However, teachers, counselors, and transition specialists need to make some modifications to typical procedures or interventions in order to meet the needs of students with EBD. Let's look at a few examples.

The type of social skills instruction that adolescents require for success as adults differs greatly from the instruction needed in early childhood or during the school years. For instance, to prevent high job turnover, social skills instruction should focus on the positive social interactions needed not only to get a job but also to keep it once hired. Practice opportunities must be provided for common work situations, such as dealing with an angry customer or a difficult co-worker, or handling disagreements with a supervisor (a situation in which strong self-advocacy skills are also needed). Many of these students come from home environments in which they do not see effective social or communication skills modeled, so they require explicit instruction in areas that many of us might assume are common-sense behaviors: calling in when sick or late for work rather than simply not showing up; limiting the number of days that one calls in late or sick; requesting a change in schedule; or providing plenty of notice when days off are needed. These students also need help thinking through more unique scenarios, such as whether or not to disclose their disability to an employer, or explaining issues related to their involvement in the juvenile justice system.

During career-awareness activities, students should learn to identify careers that align with their strengths while also recognizing careers that might best be avoided. For example, a career in customer service or human resources might not be the optimal choice for a student with social anxiety disorder. Students who have challenging behaviors or anger management issues should select vocations and work environments that have few or none of the triggers for those behaviors.

We discussed interagency collaboration in earlier chapters, in which school personnel and those from agencies such as vocational rehabilitation work together to support postsecondary and vocational goals. When necessary, these partners also work to ensure a smooth transition from student to adult disability services. For students with EBD, additional agencies might be involved, such as child welfare or child protective services, behavioral or mental health programs, treatment programs for substance abuse, and the juvenile justice system. When these agencies are part of the collaborative effort, IEP team members may include social workers, counselors, and probation officers.

Many adolescents with EBD have social networks that are not always conducive to positive or productive lifestyles. Helping these students develop supportive, positive social networks can reinforce the types of behaviors that will lead to more successful long-term outcomes. Transition personnel can work with adolescents to encourage the cultivation of healthy and constructive friendships. They can also help students participate in rewarding activities such as community sports and leisure-time events or working with service-oriented organizations. Through these activities, they are more likely to encounter positive peer and adult role models. The use of peer mentors, adolescents who have successfully dealt with similar challenges and received training on how to support their mentees, is a strategy that has also supported adolescents with EBD during their transition to increased independence.

The National Technical Assistance Center on Transition (NTACT) is funded by the U.S. Department of Education to help professionals in state agencies and local school districts provide evidence-based transition services to students with disabilities in order to improve their long-term outcomes in postsecondary education and employment. The NTACT Website (http://transitionta.org) has resources on topics such as transition planning, graduation, and post-school success.

Check Your Understanding 10.2

Click here to gauge your understanding of the concepts in this section.

People and Situations

Learning Outcome

Describe the history of treatment for individuals with EBD, explain some current concerns in the field, and identify reputable organizations that provide reliable information for individuals with EBD and their families.

Topic 10.10 Origins and History

- Historically, the care and treatment of people with mental health issues has been poor, cruel, and abusive.

- Across time, examples of positive and humane treatment of these individuals do exist, and hopeful signs indicate a kinder and more positive future for those with EBD.

Topic 10.11 Personal Stories

- There are many successful adults with EBD, a large number of whom will require lifelong supports.

- The Center for Parent Information and Resources, the National Alliance on Mental Illness, and the PACER Center are some of the reputable organizations that provide reliable information and supports for individuals with EBD and their families.

Photograph by Disability Rights California

The seclusion of students in tiny, windowless, locked rooms such as this is a negative, sometimes dangerous, practice that is still being used far too often.

St. Mary of Bethlehem, also known as Bethlem Royal Hospital or Bedlam, in London was the first institution for people with mental illness; it was a dreadful and disgraceful place of confinement.

Topic 10.10 Origins and History

- Historically, the care and treatment of people with mental health issues has been poor, cruel, and abusive.

- Across time, examples of positive and humane treatment of these individuals do exist, and hopeful signs indicate a kinder and more positive future for those with EBD.

How have individuals with EBD typically been treated across time? Unfortunately, the answer is that they were treated horribly. The roots and reasons for mistreatment are deeply established and hard to overcome. It is important to know this history, to prevent such mistreatment from recurring. Everyone must be alert to instances of cruelty and abuse so that social justice and fairness can become a guarantee for this group of people.

In many ancient cultures, it was commonly believed that people who did not follow behavioral conventions, who acted differently, were possessed by the devil. These were people whom society was expected to shun and fear. Some believed that personality disorders and atypical behavior patterns were contagious and that the general public needed protection from "catching" such conditions. As a result, people with EBD were removed from the community.

Treatment during the Middle Ages was particularly harsh. Those with EBD were commonly imprisoned or confined in poorhouses where they were beaten, put in chains or straitjackets, and even tortured. In 1547, St. Mary of Bethlehem was established in London as the first institution for people with mental disorders. An awful place, it came to be called Bedlam, a term now used to refer to noise and chaos. The conditions at Bedlam were intolerable—residents were chained, beaten, and starved. The public not only was aware of these deplorable conditions but also encouraged them; a popular form of entertainment at the time was to take the family for an outing to view the "lunatics" at Bedlam. No public outrage arose over the situation, nor were any calls made for humane care or treatment.

As you learned in the previous chapter, the history of institutions in America for people with intellectual disabilities was horrific. The facilities were initiated with good intentions but became places where people were warehoused to live in deplorable conditions. The same is true for institutions or asylums for people with EBD. By and large, the closure of these segregated, residential institutions was an important step in developing better outcomes and a community presence for people with intellectual disabilities. However, the same is not the case for people with mental illness.

In the 1970s, large, congregate institutions were closed, with the admirably intentioned goal of replacing them with well-funded community-based programs. Unfortunately, insufficient funding was allocated for the alternative programs, and too few were available to address the needs of those who were released. The result was a national tragedy. Left without appropriate services, many individuals with mental illness ended up on the streets, creating a homeless problem that continues to plague cities and communities across the nation today.

The homeless population in America is rising at alarming rates. According to the U.S. Housing and Urban Development Department, many cities are dealing with problems of chronic homelessness. In Los Angeles, which tops the nation in this area, the homeless population has increased by 55% since 2013. Some 254,000 men, women, and children experience homelessness at some point during the year, and on any given night approximately 82,000 people are homeless. In 2015, 10% of the county's homeless were military veterans, 20% had physical disabilities, and 30% had some type of mental illness. People with disabilities are disproportionately represented in this terrible situation. Between 42% and 77% of the overall homeless population do not receive the public benefits to which they are entitled. It is common for homeless people, particularly those with mental illness, to spend nights in the city jail because they have no other place to go. Police officers report they are unprepared to deal with the complex problems these people present to themselves and the community.

Ruben Sanchez @lostintv/Moment/Getty Images

Too many people in today's society live without adequate housing. About a third of them have mental illness.

Individuals with EBD face other negative situations. For example, schoolchildren with EBD experience more punitive interventions than other students. Many states still allow the use of **corporal punishment** (paddling, spanking, rapping hands), despite its negative effects and the lack of research to support its use. Those most vulnerable to its application are students with disabilities (not just those with EBD), students from low-income backgrounds, and culturally and linguistically diverse boys (particularly African Americans). The use of **restraint** has become a topic of controversy, as incidents have come to light in which students were bruised, injured, and even killed while being restrained. Types of restraint used in schools have included:

- *Physical restraint*—A student is immobilized with a reduced ability to move the torso, arms, legs, or head freely. Prone restraint, in which a student is held face-down on the floor, can be lethal.

- *Mechanical restraint*—A student is immobilized through the use of a device or piece of equipment that restricts freedom of movement.

Investigations by the National Disability Rights Network and the U.S. Government Accountability Office found instances in which restraint caused lacerations, abrasions, dehydration, broken bones, dislocated joints, and death. In many cases, restraint was used by inexperienced, poorly trained staff, and initiated for relatively minor infractions. **Seclusion** is the process by which a student is involuntarily confined to a room or area from which he or she is physically prevented from leaving; in such cases, a door may be locked or blocked. Abuses of this practice include locking students in very small (e.g., 4-foot by 4-foot) rooms, sometimes without adequate ventilation or with no lighting, for hours at a time; forcing students to sit in their own urine because they were not allowed to use the restroom; and failing to monitor students with self-injurious behavior. In a few tragic cases, students have committed suicide while locked up.

The U.S. Department of Education has released a set of guidelines discouraging the use of physical restraint and seclusion, except in extreme cases, as a last resort, and with appropriate training and supervision of school personnel (summarized in the box below). In addition, the Department of Education encourages the use of PBIS and other preventive techniques to control student behavior. Clearly, we can do a better job of protecting our children from harm at the hands of their own teachers. The full set of Department of Education recommendations, *Restraint and Seclusion: A Resource Document*, can be downloaded at http://www2.ed.gov/policy/seclusion/restraints-and-seclusion-resources.pdf.

Are there examples across history when individuals with EBD were treated well? Yes, although not consistent across time, people with mental illness were not always treated poorly. For example, in ancient Egypt, mental and physical illnesses were thought of as one problem and were not treated with different methods. Physicians and priests used positive remedies for all sicknesses.

Although it took centuries, the negative attitudes, beliefs, and fears of the Middle Ages eventually changed. In 1792, the French psychiatrist Philippe Pinel called for kinder treatment (i.e., unchaining) of patients at Salt-pêtrière, a Paris asylum for the "insane." Around the same time, Benjamin Rush, the father of American psychiatry, proposed more humane methods of diagnosing and treating individuals with mental illness. Upon return from England and exposure to the "lunatic reform movement," Dorothea Dix documented the abuse of "insane persons" who were housed in cages, chained, and beaten while forced to live in the Massachusetts mental hospital in Worcester. In 1843, she published the results of her study in a book, *Memorial*, which is credited with improved services for individuals with mental disorders. In response, a national movement began, and asylums for those with mental illness were established in almost every state. By the mid-1800s, the Association of Medical Superintendents of American Institutions for the Insane (now the American Psychiatric Association) was founded. While these early institutions were positive and generated hope, conditions and treatment deteriorated over time, eventually leading to their closures.

The development of positive programs for children began after Leo Kanner's book *Child Psychiatry* was published in 1935. Kanner (a psychiatrist whose work with students with autism spectrum disorder was highlighted in Topic 8.10) brought the development of services for children in America to the forefront. He founded the first pediatric psychiatry department at Johns Hopkins University Hospital and raised awareness about the need for positive mental health services for children. During the 1960s and 1970s, researchers, scholars, and educators created new ways to teach students with EBD. In 1962, Norris Haring and Lakin Phillips published *Educating Emotionally Disturbed Children*, a book that documented their experimental work in schools using behavioral principles, a structured environment, and collaboration between the home and school environments. That same year, Eli Bower published a definition of behavioral disorders that serves as the foundation for the current federal definition of emotional disturbance. In the 1960s, Nicholas Hobbs introduced Project Re-Ed, a landmark effort demonstrating the effectiveness of an ecological approach that included home and community environments. Frank Hewett's Santa Monica Project developed the engineered classroom, in which structure, consistency, and behavior management proved effective. In 1964, a classic study about the positive effects of the teacher's attention on a preschooler's social interactions with his peers during playtime was published. This study, which emphasized applied behavioral analysis (ABA) techniques, sparked new interest in the importance of how the environment can influence people's actions.

In the 1980s, University of Oregon researchers Rob Horner and George Sugai undertook work that ran counter to typical school disciplinary procedures. Instead of focusing on reactive, punitive consequences, they began to investigate the effects of preventive, positive behavioral supports. Their work resulted in the development of the PBIS framework.

Today, we may be on the verge of another positive cycle in the history of individuals with EBD. With regard to the homelessness issue discussed earlier, Los Angeles may provide an example of how to turn this problem around. Proposals are being made for sweeping reforms in housing, services, and other approaches that will help people move off the streets. No longer would city jails function as places of crisis intervention. Although such ambitious plans will take years to implement, what is exceptionally important is the change in public opinion. Conversations are taking place about the best approaches to solve these complex problems. Consensus is building that the time for positive action is now.

Topic 10.11 Personal Stories

- There are many successful adults with EBD, a large number of whom will require lifelong supports.

- The Center for Parent Information and Resources, the National Alliance on Mental Illness, and the PACER Center are some of the reputable organizations that provide reliable information and supports for individuals with EBD and their families.

Are there positive stories about individuals who have EBD? Many successful adults fall into this category. Demi Lovato, whom you learned about in the chapter opening vignette, is one such person. The late Carrie Fisher, best known as Princess Leia Organa from the *Star Wars* movies, also had bipolar disorder. She openly shared her struggles and was often commended for her efforts to eliminate the stigma associated with mental illness. When Omaze—a fundraising company—partnered with the cast of *Star Wars: The Force Awakens* to raise money for their favorite charities, Fisher selected the PACER Center's Children's Mental Health and Emotional and Behavioral Disorders Project, which we discuss in more detail below.

David Edwards/Media Punch/Alamy Live News/Alamy Stock Photo

Carrie Fisher at a book signing for *The Princess Diarist* in November, 2016, just a few weeks before her death.

However, even with Demi Lovato's current success, it is possible that future news stories about her will contain reports of relapses. Why do we say this? Most disabilities, including mental health disorders, are lifelong conditions. Like everyone, those who face the challenges associated with these disorders have good days and bad. And for some, years of success can be punctuated by periods of intense struggles. Here is an all-too-common scenario. An individual with schizophrenia or bipolar disorder will see improvements—feel better, have fewer or no symptoms—after receiving intervention (i.e., prescription drugs, counseling, therapy). Because of this, he may decide after a while that he no longer needs medication and stops taking it, which causes the symptoms to return and the challenges to start anew. In another case, biological changes—growth, weight gain, hormonal changes—might affect the individual's reaction to a medication, making it less effective and causing symptom recurrence and behavioral regressions. When relapses do occur, it is important for individuals in that person's support group, whether teachers, family members, friends, or co-workers, to continue providing assistance and support.

In the box below, you'll learn about a high school student named Kelsey. Her story of success depicts the real-life challenges, struggles, and incredibly hard work of a team of school personnel as they provide the wraparound supports that Kelsey needs. In *On the Screen*, we highlight a fictional story about several individuals dealing with different mental health conditions.

Who Cares About Kelsey?

Dan Habib/whocaresaboutkelsey.com

"I have a lot of anger issues. 'Cuz when I get mad like, I don't think, I just do. Boys called me mean names so I had a habit of punching them in the face. I beat people up. I'm not nice. I don't know. I'm just a bitch. I believe in safety pins, jeans, piercings, and tattoos. Not Barbies and glitter. Most people don't understand my attitude and sense of humor, my hyperness. My family doesn't understand any of that. Obviously if you spent a little bit more time with me talking about how I am you'd understand that yeah, I've had a really crappy life and a little bit of caring will take me a long, long way."

—Kelsey Carroll

Kelsey Carroll, a 19-year-old high-school senior with an emotional and behavioral disorder, was the subject of the 2012 documentary *Who Cares About Kelsey?* The film followed her through her senior year and chronicled the many potential causes of her disability (abuse, neglect, homelessness), the challenges that she faced (anger management, self-mutilation, academic failure), and the supports and interventions that her school put in place to help her cope and earn enough credits to graduate. One of the schoolwide supports implemented at Somersville High School was the PBIS framework, which reduced discipline referrals by 60% and dropout rates by 70%. Students like Kelsey received intensive services, which included academic tutoring and personal and career counseling, from a team of caring adults.

Now in her mid-twenties, Kelsey is confident and independent, and has made dozens of presentations on behalf of the film at professional conferences.

SOURCE FOR QUOTE: Habib, D. (2012). *Who Cares About Kelsey?* Retrieved from http://www.whocaresaboutkelsey.com

On the Screen: *Silver Linings Playbook*

https://www.youtube.com/watch?v=Lj5_FhLaaQQ

Nominated for eight Academy Awards, including a win for Jennifer Lawrence in the Best Performance by an Actress in a Leading Role category, this film provides a candid look at the daily successes and failures of two people with different mental health conditions. Several other characters in the film, including the main character's father, also have challenging behaviors, which lends to discussions of contributing causes and factors. Issues discussed in this chapter, such as social skills deficits and medication, are also addressed in the film.

What organizations are available to support children and adolescents with EBD and their families? A number of organizations provide valuable information and offer support. We highlight three of them here.

- The Center for Parent Information and Resources (http://www.parentcenterhub. org)—This national center, funded by the U.S. Department of Education, represents a network of technical assistance and dissemination centers that provide information and services to families of children with disabilities. Each state has at least one Parent Training and Information Center that can help parents through online, phone, or face-to-face interactions. The Website for the national network contains resources on many relevant topics, including disability, behavior, and mental health.

- The National Alliance on Mental Illness (NAMI)—This organization, through its Website (www.nami.org), provides information on various mental health conditions, warning signs, and treatments, and offers support targeted toward specific groups: family members, adolescents, college students, veterans and active military, diverse communities, LGBTQ, and those in the law enforcement and faith communities. NAMI also offers a number of options for active involvement through advocacy and awareness activities, and provides a place on its Website for people to share their personal stories.

- PACER Center—A parent training and information center, PACER provides families of children who have disabilities with information, support, workshops, and referrals to other relevant agencies and organizations. The Children's Mental Health and Emotional and Behavioral Disorders Project (http://www.pacer.org/cmh/), one component of PACER's work, supplies resources on topics as diverse as dealing with biting behaviors to planning for school IEP meetings. Like NAMI, PACER has a place on its Website for individuals and families to share their stories. PACER's National Bullying Prevention Center (http://www.pacer.org/bullying/) offers many types of resources that address bullying. Additionally, PACER has an extensive video library that includes public service announcements filmed by various celebrities, including Demi Lovato, who was PACER's 2010 spokesperson.

Check Your Understanding 10.3

Click here to gauge your understanding of the concepts in this section.

Future Perspectives

Learning Outcome

Describe some of the concerns regarding appropriate identification of EBD and access to mental health services, and understand how new technology can support mental health services for individuals with EBD.

Topic 10.12 Prevention: Appropriate Access to Mental Health Services

- Compared to their peers, males and African American students are disproportionately identified as having EBD, receive more severe disciplinary procedures, and have higher rates of contact with the juvenile justice system.

- To improve long-term outcomes, parents, teachers, and other adults must recognize the warning signs of EBD and ensure students get the appropriate mental health services.

Topic 10.13 Technology: Current Considerations and Future Possibilities

- Technology use for people with EBD has some unique advantages, but applications should be selected carefully.

- Future technology innovations hold promise for both research and mental health interventions.

Carballo/Fotolia

Many apps can now provide immediate help and support to individuals who are struggling with mental health conditions by putting them in touch with their social support networks, contacting a counselor or therapist, or even helping them regulate their breathing when they feel anxious.

Topic 10.12 Prevention: Appropriate Access to Mental Health Services

- Compared to their peers, males and African American students are disproportionately identified as having EBD, receive more severe disciplinary procedures, and have higher rates of contact with the juvenile justice system.

- To improve long-term outcomes, parents, teachers, and other adults must recognize the warning signs of EBD and ensure students get the appropriate mental health services

How disproportionate is the identification of students with EBD? We must do a better job of properly identifying students with EBD. At present, clear gender and racial differences are evident in the EBD category. Males are far more likely to be identified than females. The over-representation of African American boys is also of concern. In addition to disproportionate placements in the EBD category, African American youths:

- Are three times more likely than White or Asian/Pacific Islander students to be suspended.

- Are three times more likely than students from other groups to be arrested for a violent offense.

- Are two to four times more likely to end up in residential placements (compared to White and Hispanic students, respectively).

- Represent 17% of the youth population but make up 62% of youths prosecuted in adult court.

These data hint at a worrisome progression: suspended students are more likely to be involved in delinquent acts and to be arrested, prosecuted, and incarcerated. Ironically, the average yearly expenditure to incarcerate one youth in the United States is $146,302—more than 13 times *greater* than the average per-pupil expenditure ($10,700).

As you learned in Chapter 3, disproportionality is a problem when students are incorrectly identified as having disabilities. Particularly in the case of EBD, students are subjected to the segregation, negative perceptions, and poor outcomes associated with this disability category. It benefits everyone to implement positive approaches to school behavior (such as PBIS), utilize equitable and fair disciplinary procedures, appropriately identify students who have EBD, and provide behavioral and mental health supports for those who truly need them.

Given the disproportionality data, are we over-identifying students with EBD? No. In fact, most students who have EBD are not receiving appropriate services. Less than 1% (i.e., 0.51%) of all school-age children are provided with special education services under the IDEA category of emotional disturbance. However, some experts believe that the actual prevalence is closer to 3% to 6% of all students. Why is there such a discrepancy between those who have EBD and those who are given services? Many students with EBD do not receive services because:

- The IDEA definition remains unclear and subjective.
- School personnel are reluctant to give a child the stigmatizing label of EBD.
- Few or limited services are available in many districts, or funding constraints limit the number of students identified.
- Confusion exists regarding the exclusion of students who are socially maladjusted.
- Students with internalizing behaviors are under-identified.
- Only those with severe problems are identified, while those with mild or moderate impairments are overlooked.

The information in the last bulleted entry raises concerns that large numbers of students exhibit symptoms that have not yet reached the chronic, severe, or persistent level required to make a diagnosis of mental illness, but they clearly need help. According to the CDC, suicide is the third leading cause of death among children and adolescents between the ages of 10 and 14. Among high school students, the data are truly worrisome: 17% report having seriously considered suicide in the past 12 months; 14% made a suicide plan; and 8% attempted suicide one or more times. Yet, most of these children and adolescents are not students identified with EBD, which highlights the need for more accurate recognition of mental health conditions in *all* students.

Throughout the first sections of this chapter, we provided symptoms of specific mental health conditions; below we highlight some general warning signs that parents, teachers, and other adults should be trained to recognize. When students exhibit these signs, they should receive immediate mental health supports (e.g., referrals, counseling). Some of the most common symptoms include:

- Excessive worrying, fear, or sadness.
- Confused thinking, difficulty concentrating or learning.
- Extreme moodiness or mood swings.
- Unusually strong or prolonged feelings of irritability or anger.
- Changes in sleep habits, tiredness, and little energy.
- Increases or decreases in appetite or changes in eating habits.
- Altered perceptions of reality.
- Physical ailments such as headaches, stomachaches, or general achiness.
- Reclusiveness or avoidance of social activities and/or family and friends.
- Substance abuse.
- Talk of suicide or giving away favorite items.

An Under-Identified and Under-Served Population

The National Institutes of Mental Health and the Centers for Disease Control conducted a three-year study of the health and well-being of American children—the National Health and Nutrition Examination Study (NHANES). After surveying over 3,000 children, they found that 13% had some type of emotional or behavioral disorder. Yet nearly half had *not* sought treatment from a mental health professional, and only one-third of those with anxiety disorders were receiving treatment. The results of this study confirm that students with EBD are not appropriately identified, nor do they receive adequate intervention or treatment.

Topic 10.13 Technology: Current Considerations and Future Possibilities

- Technology use for people with EBD has some unique advantages, but applications should be selected carefully.

- Future technology innovations hold promise for both research and mental health interventions.

Is it possible to address some mental health needs through technology? Yes, the use of technology has opened up some interesting and exciting options for supporting the mental health needs of people with EBD. Apps are now available with a variety of relevant uses: self-management for anxiety attacks, medication reminders, or training techniques and videos for dealing with social situations. In other cases, apps serve the simple function of keeping users connected with their social support group members, such as therapists, family members, friends, and peer mentors. As with many of the technology devices and apps that we have discussed in previous chapters, users should evaluate any app carefully, read the reviews, and determine whether its features match his or her needs. The following table summarizes some benefits and questions to consider when selecting apps for individuals with EBD.

Apps for Mental Health: Benefits and Additional Considerations

Benefits	Additional Considerations
• Convenience of treatment at any time, in any location	• Does it provide scientifically validated treatment?
• Low cost or free	• For which mental health symptoms or conditions was it designed?
• Allow for anonymity	• Does it protect confidential information?
• Less intimidating for those who are reluctant to seek therapy	• Does it deliver everything it advertises?

NAMI *AIR* (Anonymous. Inspiring. Relatable) is an example of an app designed specifically for individuals with mental health conditions and their family members. Developed by the National Alliance on Mental Illness, NAMI *AIR* provides a social network through which users can share stories and receive positive feedback (responders can send users a "like" or a "hug") or hear from others who have gone through something similar ("me too!"). The app can also connect them with the NAMI Helpline or access other information for help. More information about this free app can be found on the NAMI Website: https://www.nami.org/Find-Support/ Breathe-Easy-with-NAMI-AIR

What are some future possibilities regarding technology and EBD? In an innovative study on the use of apps to treat depression, research participants were recruited, screened, enrolled, treated, and evaluated with the use of their smartphones.

Researchers recruited study participants from all around the country, including very rural areas; and the racial and ethnic demographics of the participants mirrored those of the general population. In fact, researchers were able to recruit, screen, and select participants in a fraction of the time and for a portion of the cost of typical studies. Final results of the study are not yet available, though preliminary data show mixed findings. Participants appeared to have a slightly higher dropout rate than those who receive traditional therapy; however, all three apps tested seem to have a significant positive effect on mood and disability.

Current technology applications already use the sensors in phones and watches to collect data on health characteristics (heart rate), movement patterns, and social interactions (texts, phone calls), as well as to predict future actions (e.g., "Traffic is normal. If you leave now, it will take you 13 minutes to get to work."). Future apps may be able to combine these data with those on vocal inflections, breathing rates, and other identifiers to determine when a user is experiencing stress, a manic episode, or depression. Several apps may even work in concert; more sophisticated ones might provide multiple levels of support. For example, when one app detects that the user is experiencing anxiety, a second one opens that supports coping or self-management skills, while sending the user a query regarding whether he would like to contact a member of his support group.

Check Your Understanding 10.4

Click here to gauge your understanding of the concepts in this section.

Summary

Emotional and Behavioral Disorders Described

Students with emotional and behavioral disorders (EBD) display problem behaviors to an excessive degree.

- Students with EBD qualify for special education services under the IDEA category of emotional disturbance.

- Emotional and behavioral disorders can be divided into externalizing behaviors, internalizing behaviors, and low-incidence conditions.

- Students with externalizing behaviors often exhibit aggression, hyperactivity, impulsivity, noncompliance, and delinquency; students with internalizing behaviors—withdrawal, depression, and anxiety—often go unnoticed.

- EBD is considered a high-incidence disability, although these students are placed in more restrictive settings than many students with other high-incidence disabilities.

- IDEA has specific disciplinary procedures for violations directly resulting from a student's disability, which can affect his or her placement.

Special Education

Emotional and behavioral disorders create challenges in many areas: academics, social skills, and behavior.

- Explicit instruction in social skills and academics—within a PBIS framework—can address some challenges; however, many students with EBD also require mental health services or pharmacological intervention.

- Some students with emotional and behavioral disorders may benefit from accommodations that target externalizing behaviors, such as hyperactivity and noncompliance. Other students who exhibit internalizing behaviors may benefit from accommodations that address anxiety and depression.

- The causes of EBD in young children usually include multiple, overlapping risk factors. Effective early intervention programs can eliminate or reduce problem behaviors.

- The PBIS approach establishes a framework for providing behavior supports to all students. Within that framework, functional behavioral assessments (FBAs) and behavioral intervention plans (BIPs) can be used to address more serious behaviors.

- Teachers, counselors, transition specialists, and other professionals can take positive steps to increase chances for future educational and employment success for students with EBD.

People and Situations

Historically, the care and treatment of people with mental health issues has been poor, cruel, and abusive.

- Although treatment of individuals with EBD has improved over time, negative practices such as corporal punishment, restraint, and seclusion are still used in schools today.
- The Center for Parent Information and Resources, the National Alliance on Mental Illness, and the PACER Center are some of the reputable organizations that provide reliable information and supports for individuals with EBD and their families.

Future Perspectives

To improve long-term outcomes, parents, teachers, and other adults must recognize the warning signs of EBD and

ensure students get the appropriate mental health services. Technology may provide innovative ways to offer some of these services.

- At present, males and African American students are disproportionately identified as having EBD, receive more severe disciplinary procedures, and have higher rates of contact with the juvenile justice system.
- Technology use for people with EBD has some unique advantages, but applications should be selected carefully.

Addressing CEC Standards

Council for Exceptional Children (CEC) knowledge standards addressed in this chapter: 6.2, 1.0, BD1K1, BD1K3, BD2K1, BD4S1, BD8S2.

See the Appendix for the complete CEC Initial Level Special Educator Preparation Standards.

Chapter 11
Physical and Health Disabilities

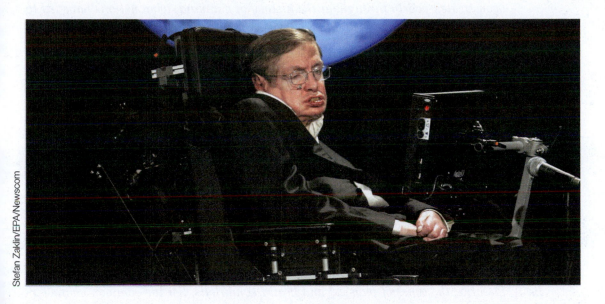

Stephen Hawking is the author of *A Brief History of Time*, a researcher, a member of the Royal Society, and a member of the U.S. National Academy of Sciences. A former mathematics professor at Cambridge University and regarded as one of the most brilliant scientists in the world, Hawking has been theorizing about the origins of the universe, challenging commonly accepted models, and proposing groundbreaking research. His abilities allow him to understand, publicly recognize, and counsel us all to acknowledge the contributions of imperfection as humanity strives to understand the universe in which we live.

Dr. Hawking is also a person with a physical disability. He was diagnosed with amyotrophic lateral sclerosis (ALS), a debilitating disease, right after his 21st birthday. Today, he uses a motorized wheelchair for mobility and a computerized speech synthesizer to communicate. He has three children and three grandchildren, continues an active schedule of travel and public speaking tours, and still hopes to travel into space in the future. The movie about his life is featured in this chapter's *On the Screen* found in Topic 11.11.

⌄ Learning Outcomes

Physical and Health Disabilities Described

Describe the types of physical and health conditions, list the common characteristics of these disabilities, and provide details about why the precise prevalence of those that require special education services is unknown.

Special Education

Describe ways that the challenges posed by physical and health disabilities can be addressed by adjustments to the physical environments found in school settings, and explain how teachers can be responsive to the unique and individual needs of students with these conditions.

People and Situations

Provide examples of how individuals with physical and health disabilities have been treated poorly throughout the history of mankind, what actions have led to improvements in how they are treated, and how their participation in American life can still be improved.

Future Perspectives

Explain how emerging technologies have made and will make a difference in the ways in which these individuals participate at school and in daily life.

Physical and Health Disabilities Described[1]

Learning Outcome

Describe the types of physical and health conditions, list the common characteristics of these disabilities, and provide details about why the precise prevalence of those that require special education services is unknown.

Topic 11.1 **Physical and Health Disabilities Defined**

- Physical and health disabilities arise from many different conditions that restrict movement or require specialized health care.

- Students whose disabilities do not negatively affect their educational performance are not eligible for special education services.

Topic 11.2 **Types of Physical and Health Disabilities**

- Physical disabilities comprise two major groups of conditions— neuromotor impairments and muscular/skeletal conditions.

- Health disabilities comprise two major groups of conditions— chronic illnesses and infectious diseases.

Topic 11.3 **Characteristics**

- Physical and health disabilities comprise many different conditions, each with its own set of characteristics.

- Characteristics come together in unique patterns, requiring an individualized response to each student.

---

[1]References for Chapter 11 are found at the end of this text.

Topic 11.4 Prevalence and Placement

- Because states do not report students served through IDEA by separate conditions, the prevalence of each physical or health condition is unknown.

- Students with physical or health disabilities use all special education placement options called out in IDEA.

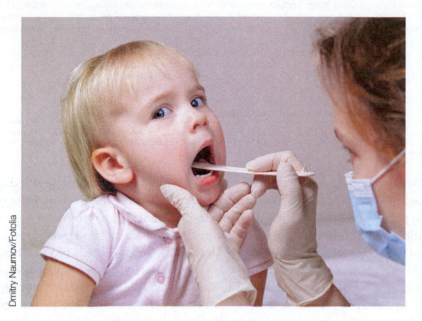

Access to health care with routine well-child checkups, along with visits to the doctor when a child is ill, can ensure both prevention and early treatment when necessary.

Topic 11.1 Physical and Health Disabilities Defined

- Physical and health disabilities arise from many different conditions that restrict movement or require specialized health care.

- Students whose disabilities do not negatively affect their educational performance are not eligible for special education services.

What are physical and health disabilities that require special education? The federal government considers **physical disabilities** and **health disabilities** as separate special education categories. The IDEA definitions for these disabilities are found in the following table.[2]

---

[2] Note that IDEA lists ADHD under the health disabilities category. As you learned in Chapter 7, we devoted a separate chapter to ADHD because its prevalence is much greater than that of most other health conditions and because its nature is so different from that of the others in this category.

Definitions of Physical and Health Disabilities

Term	Definition	Source
Orthopedic impairment (physical disability)	Orthopedic impairment means a severe orthopedic impairment that adversely affects a child's educational performance. The term includes impairments caused by a congenital anomaly, impairments caused by disease (e.g., poliomyelitis, bone tuberculosis), and impairments from other causes (e.g., cerebral palsy, amputations, and fractures or burns that cause contractures).	IDEA '04, U.S. Department of Education
Other health impairment (health disability)	Other health impairment means having limited strength, vitality, or alertness, including a heightened alertness to environmental stimuli, that results in limited alertness with respect to the educational environment, that— 1. is due to chronic or acute health problems such as asthma, attention deficit disorder or attention deficit hyperactivity disorder, diabetes, epilepsy, a heart condition, hemophilia, lead poisoning, leukemia, nephritis, rheumatic fever, sickle cell anemia, and Tourette syndrome, and 2. adversely affects a child's educational performance.	IDEA '04, U.S. Department of Education

SOURCE: From 34 CFR Parts 300 and 301, *Assistance to States for the Education of Children with Disabilities and Preschool Grants for Children with Disabilities;* Final Rule (pp. 1263–1264), U.S. Department of Education, August 14, 2006, *Federal Register*, Washington, DC.

The two special education categories of physical disabilities and health disabilities are not as separate or discrete as their definitions make them seem. Some conditions typically grouped under **orthopedic impairments** (also referred to as physical disabilities) can result in long-term health problems and vice versa. For example, one student with cerebral palsy may face physical challenges and need considerable assistance from a physical therapist (PT) to learn how to control movement for speech and walking, and yet have no special health care needs. Another student with cerebral palsy may have physical limitations, seizures, and serious health care issues. Possibly more than any other group, students with physical or health problems need accommodations to the learning and physical environments required by Section 504 of the Rehabilitation Act so they can participate fully in general education or inclusive educational environments. Although many students with physical and health disabilities need accommodations, they do not always require special education services.

How do physical and health disabilities relate to special education? First, not all physical disabilities require a special education response. When determining whether a student qualifies for special education services, the key consideration is the impact of the condition on the student. The orthopedic impairment *must* meet two important criteria:

Because they can't always attend school, some children with physical or health disabilities need the school to come to them so they can maintain their academic progress.

- Be severe

- Affect educational performance adversely

Although not all students with physical disabilities require or receive special education services, they may need some special accommodations (see also Topic 11.6), such as providing more space in the classroom to store bulky equipment or allowing wheelchairs to pass freely in the classroom.

Second, as with physical disabilities, not all health disabilities require a special education response. Again, the impact of the condition is key when determining whether the student qualifies for special education services. The health impairment *must* meet three important criteria:

- Result in limited strength, vitality, or alertness

- Be due to chronic or acute health problems

- Affect educational performance adversely

Sonya Etchison/Shutterstock

The impact of health conditions can affect children's lives in different ways. Teachers should know that some health conditions are lifelong, but their impact might change from day to day. In contrast, other health conditions are temporary and last only a short time. Further, some conditions do not impact educational performance and do not require special services. In such cases, the appropriate response may be as simple as ensuring that the student does not miss important instruction while sick at home or in the hospital. For example, asthma is the most common reason for school absenteeism. Teachers can help these students by removing as many allergens (e.g., classroom pets, chalk dust) from the classroom as possible and by making sure that homework and in-class assignments are sent to the affected student at home, possibly via email or a classmate. No such actions require special education services. However, for students whose status is considered **medically fragile**, there may be periods when special education services bring school to them, either at their homes or in the hospital.

Topic 11.2 Types of Physical and Health Disabilities

- Physical disabilities comprise two major groups of conditions—neuromotor impairments and muscular/skeletal conditions.

- Health disabilities comprise two major groups of conditions—chronic illnesses and infectious diseases.

What are the major physical disabilities seen in children, and how are these conditions grouped? Students with physical disabilities, which IDEA calls orthopedic impairments, have problems with the structure or functioning of their bodies that are significant enough to impact their educational performance. For many such students, their physical challenges do not affect educational performance, but they do require physical environments that do not limit access to classrooms and schools. For example, some children with cerebral palsy have very restricted **mobility** and use a wheelchair, but they do not require special education services to address academic performance. However, other students with the same condition have more complex issues that affect their academic performance. Those students both need and qualify for special education services.

Physical disabilities result from many different conditions, which are divided into two groups: **neuromotor impairments** and **muscular/skeletal conditions**. Conditions classified under each grouping are listed in the following figure.

Conditions of Physical Disabilities

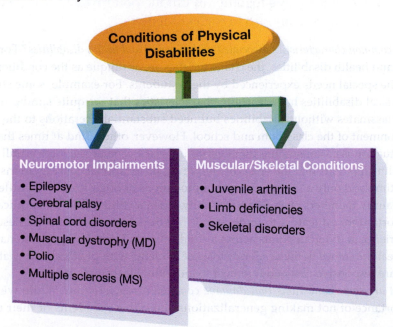

Conditions of Physical Disabilities

Neuromotor Impairments
- Epilepsy
- Cerebral palsy
- Spinal cord disorders
- Muscular dystrophy (MD)
- Polio
- Multiple sclerosis (MS)

Muscular/Skeletal Conditions
- Juvenile arthritis
- Limb deficiencies
- Skeletal disorders

What major health disabilities are seen in children, and how are these conditions grouped? Many students with health disabilities or **special health care needs** have precarious health situations that compromise their ability to learn, which results in the need for special education services. The federal government, through IDEA, uses the term **other health impairment** to describe a condition or disease that creates a special health care need or health disability for a student. As shown in the following figure, health conditions are divided into two groups: **chronic illnesses** and **infectious diseases**.

Conditions of Health Disabilities

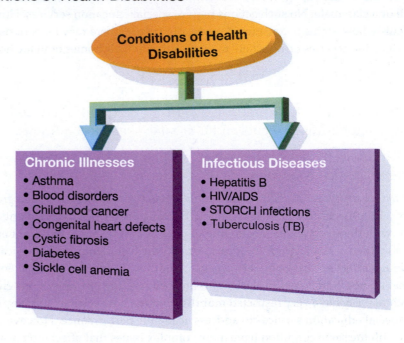

Topic 11.3 Characteristics

- Physical and health disabilities comprise many different conditions, each with its own set of characteristics.

- Characteristics come together in unique patterns, requiring an individualized response to each student.

Are there common characteristics associated with physical and health disabilities? For many physical and health disabilities, the characteristics are as unique as the conditions that created the special needs experienced by these students. For example, some students with physical disabilities have learning characteristics that are quite similar to those of their classmates without disabilities but need substantial alterations to the physical environment of the classroom and school. However, others find at times that their health situation is so consuming that everything else becomes secondary. Still others have health situations that are episodic, requiring many special considerations at one point in time and only a few special accommodations at other times. Regardless, the lives of family members change dramatically when a child becomes chronically ill. It is important for educators to understand the stress and concerns that these families experience at different points across a child's illness. Education professionals who make a real difference in the academic lives of students with physical and health disabilities are responsive first and foremost to individual learning needs.

What are some conditions that do have common characteristics? While we stress the importance of not making generalizations about these students or their unique disabilities, some conditions do have specific features, several of which are included throughout the chapter. In this section, we discuss characteristics associated with **cerebral palsy**, **sickle cell disease**, and **diabetes**—three of the more common, though still low-incidence, conditions seen at schools. In Topic 11.8 we discuss, in some detail, managing seizures caused by epilepsy.

Cerebral palsy is a neurological condition that occurs during infancy or early childhood and is irreversible. Its severity depends on the precise location of brain damage, the degree of brain damage, and the extent of involvement of the central nervous system. Many individuals with cerebral palsy have impaired mobility and poor muscle development. Those with cerebral palsy whose **motor functioning** is affected show the following characteristics, either alone or in combination: jerky movements, spasms, involuntary movements, and lack of muscle tone. In such situations, assistive devices to help with mobility or other daily activities and accommodations (e.g., peer note taker) can be most helpful.

For many with cerebral palsy, poor muscle tone and difficulties in motor functioning create problems with producing intelligible speech. Unfortunately, many people misinterpret the speech difficulties as a sign of intellectual disability. Although some degree of intellectual disability is present in about half of children with cerebral palsy, others are intellectually gifted. It is a tragic mistake to assume that cerebral palsy and intellectual disability always occur in combination.

Some diseases strike one group of students more than others. For example, sickle cell disease is a hereditary, life-threatening blood disorder, and 95% of all cases occur among African Americans. This condition causes the red blood cells to become rigid and take on a crescent, or sickle, shape. During what is called a "sickling crisis," these rigid, crescent-shaped cells can clog small blood vessels, depriving some tissues of oxygen and resulting in extreme pain, swollen joints, high fever, and even strokes. For many individuals, these sickling crises are episodic, resulting in long periods away from school.

Diabetes is a life-threatening and debilitating disease. **Type 1 diabetes** (formerly referred to as juvenile diabetes) occurs when the body stops producing insulin, subsequently impairing the ability to break down glucose into energy. Type 1 diabetes is rare and is usually diagnosed during childhood or early adulthood. **Type 2 diabetes** occurs when the body does not use insulin properly, causing blood glucose levels to rise. Although the incidence of both types of diabetes is on the rise, the increase in type 2 diabetes is proportionately related to the number of American children and youth who are overweight. Particularly when blood glucose levels are out of balance (e.g., hypoglycemia, or low blood glucose; hyperglycemia, or high blood glucose), students can experience clumsiness, speech difficulties, blurred vision, confusion, inattention, headache, seizures, or loss of consciousness.

Topic 11.4 Prevalence and Placement

- Because states do not report students served through IDEA by separate conditions, the prevalence of each physical or health condition is unknown.

- Students with physical or health disabilities use all special education placement options called out in IDEA.

Is it possible to determine the exact prevalence of each condition of physical and health disabilities that result in a need for special education? The answer to this question is "No." The primary reason is that the federal government uses two categories for these disabilities and does not require states to report the specific conditions that result in these disabilities. Therefore, we do not know the specific number or percentage for each of the physical and health conditions producing special needs. Here are a few other reasons:

- No national or state-based registries are kept for specific health or physical conditions that require special education services.

- Many health and physical conditions do not result in the need for special education services because the condition does not affect educational performance, so the overall number of children with physical and health disabilities is higher than the number served through IDEA.

- Because some individuals have multiple conditions, they may be reported in other special education categories.

All health conditions in children require careful monitoring by professionals.

When thinking about children with physical and health impairments, keep other factors in mind. Look again at the figure in Topic 1.2. Notice that only 1% of all schoolchildren fall within the physical disabilities category, one of the smallest disability categories. The health disabilities category is much larger, serving some 12% of all students with disabilities; however, this category includes students with ADHD, a more common condition. Between 1997 (when students with ADHD were added to the health disabilities category) and 2010, the size of this group grew by over 284%! And, these rates continue to rise. Data comparing the 2008 and 2012 prevalence rates showed a 20% increase. Remember, many different conditions can cause health disabilities and most of these are rare. If ADHD were not included in this category, it would be a low-incidence group, like physical disabilities.

Most conditions that cause physical and health disabilities are rare in children. In other words, few are affected. Some specific databases do keep records on the prevalence of these conditions in children. The more common ones are listed in the following table. However, remember that these statistics give the total prevalence, including children who do not need special education services. Asthma is a good example; it affects many students, but very few qualify or need special education services to succeed at school. So, the percentages in this table are much larger than the percentages of these students served through IDEA and special education.

Prevalence by Condition

Condition	Estimated Prevalence in U.S. Children	Important Points for Teachers
Asthma	8%	• Most common chronic condition among children • Results in severe difficulty in breathing; chronic coughing • Leading cause of absenteeism (14 million school days per year)
Type 1 diabetes	0.25%	• The majority of cases of diabetes in children are type 1. • This condition requires constant management. • School personnel may need to assist with diabetes management (e.g., administering insulin, checking blood glucose, selecting appropriate food).
Epilepsy (children who have two or more seizures)	0.3%	• More than 300,000 children under age 15 are affected. • Seizures in 70% of those affected can be controlled by medication.
Cerebral palsy	0.3%	• Not a disease • Not progressive (i.e., it does not worsen over time)
Sickle cell disease	0.02% of all children; 0.2% of African American children	• Genetic blood disorder • Now screened for at birth • Requires careful medical management

Where do students with physical and health disabilities receive their education? More than other groups of students with disabilities, students with health and some physical disabilities who qualify for special education use the full range of placement options available under IDEA. Over half (55%) of all students with physical disabilities attend their local neighborhood schools and participate in inclusive general education classes more than 80% of every school day. Over 64% of students with health disabilities participate in general education classes more than 80% of the school day. Although the number is small, some students with physical and health disabilities receive their education at home or in hospital settings. For example, slightly less than 4% of all students with health impairments have chronic illnesses so severe that their education needs to be delivered in separate classrooms, at their homes, or in hospitals.

Check Your Understanding 11.1

Click here to gauge your understanding of the concepts in this section.

Special Education

Learning Outcome

Describe ways that the challenges posed by physical and health disabilities can be addressed by adjustments to the physical environments found in school settings, and explain how teachers can be responsive to the unique and individual needs of students with these conditions.

Topic 11.5 Challenges and Their Solutions

- Students with physical and health disabilities often face challenges associated with physical abilities, mobility, health, fatigue, absenteeism, and episodic health crises.

- Responsive supports such as assistive technology, peer assistance, distance learning, Universal Design for Learning, and the provision of related services can mitigate the effects of such challenges.

Topic 11.6 Accommodations

- Many accommodations used by students with physical and health disabilities, such as technology, flexible schedules, service animals, and word processing software, allow for continued access to classmates and the general education curriculum.

- Teachers can reduce barriers caused by inaccessible school environments through careful thought, adjusting furniture, providing space for storage, and placing visual information at everyone's eye level.

Topic 11.7 Early Intervention

- Advances in newborn screening now allow for early identification of many conditions.

- Early identification enables the delivery of treatment and services at crucial points in a child's life, which can prevent or reduce the impact of disabilities.

Topic 11.8 School Years: Managing Health Emergencies, Including Seizures

- Health emergencies at school require the quick action of teachers who know the procedures and protocols of their schools.

- Each type of seizure requires a different response; regardless, it is important for teachers to stay calm, keep the child safe, and reassure classmates.

Topic 11.9 Related Services: Collaboration with School Nurses, Physical Therapists, and Occupational Therapists

- Different related service providers, each with a unique role, collaborate with teachers to help students with physical and health disabilities overcome challenges presented by their conditions.

- Multidisciplinary teams are individually determined to meet the unique needs of each student.

The ability to play outside and move independently is a joyful part of life for all children.

Topic 11.5 Challenges and Their Solutions

- Students with physical and health disabilities often face challenges associated with physical abilities, mobility, health, fatigue, absenteeism, and episodic health crises.

- Responsive supports such as assistive technology, peer assistance, distance learning, Universal Design for Learning, and the provision of related services can mitigate the effects of such challenges.

Are there common challenges faced by students with health and physical disabilities? In Topic 11.3, we discussed many of the characteristics these disabilities present while underscoring that each condition has a unique combination of features and that each child's situation must be individually considered. In general, common characteristics are limitations in physical abilities, impaired motor functioning, poor heath, and episodic health crises. These can lead to a myriad of challenges, which can affect classroom performance. For example, physical limitations result in impaired or restricted mobility. Some students use wheelchairs or walkers to help them move about more freely. For these individuals, access to the physical environment requires special attention from school personnel.

Impaired motor functioning limits or prevents some students from being able to use a pencil, turn a page in a book, or even speak clearly. Whether they have physical or health disabilities, many of these students also experience great fatigue. All of the extra effort it takes to engage in school activities can result in being tired and seemingly disengaged. Many students with health problems experience high levels of absenteeism, either because of frequent visits to the doctor or because they are too sick to go to school. Educators must address such issues so that lack of participation and of access to peers and the curriculum, as much as possible, does not impair learning.

Challenges: Physical and Health Disabilities

Physical and Health Disabilities

How can educators provide solutions to the challenges presented by these disabilities? Many challenges can be overcome with simple adjustments to the classroom environment, while others require the work of teams of experts who can provide special services to teachers, students, and families. In the next topic, we outline a number of accommodations that specifically address these special needs. Here, we briefly present some specific supports that can help resolve some of the issues faced by students.

Many students with physical disabilities experience limited mobility. Even if they can walk, their efforts may be marked by such exertion and inefficiency that they require assistive technology (e.g., cane, crutches, wheelchair) to get around. Students with cerebral palsy may also need braces to help support the affected limbs and increase functionality or to prevent **contractures**, which would eventually lead to bone deformities and additional mobility limitations. Further, the principles of Universal Design for Learning (UDL; see Topic 2.3 for a review) have many applications for students with physical disabilities. For example, students with limited motor functioning often have difficulties writing, so allowing other options for expressing or demonstrating their learning (e.g., a verbal report) can be effective.

Students with health disabilities can face multiple challenges that require unique supports. Although not all supports will provide total solutions, many do resolve or lessen the disability's impact. For example, related service providers help to implement accommodations and facilitate the use of assistive technology devices in instructional settings. To address frequent absenteeism, teachers can use a variety of technologies, such as **distance education** (also known as **distance learning**), video chatting (e.g., Skype, FaceTime), and virtual meetings, to connect the student to the classroom. Peers can take notes for students who are away from the classroom or who have problems taking notes in the classroom due to motor limitations or excessive fatigue.

Teachers can help students with physical and health disabilities in so many ways. The examples in the Tips for Teaching Students with Sickle Cell Disease box show how many different responses can be combined to improve educational outcomes for these students, who face serious and long-term special health care needs.

Tips for Teachers of Students with Sickle Cell Disease

1. Be sure students stay hydrated and drink plenty of water across the entire school day. Allow students to have a bottle of water handy and encourage frequent sips of water rather than drinking large amounts all at once.

2. Permit frequent trips to the bathroom because this condition causes a greater need. Having a permanent special pass reduces interruption to instruction and minimizes attention on the student.

3. Because extreme heat or cold can trigger an episode, avoid seating the student near a drafty location or an air conditioner vent, or in front of fans. Encourage the student to have extra layers of clothing in order to adjust their body temperature as needed.

4. Allow for accommodations during recess and physical education to reduce strenuous activities, while still permitting moderate exercise and maximum involvement (e.g., scorekeeper, teacher's assistant, referee).

5. Take special precautions in case of injuries. Do not place a cold pack on an injury. Do apply pressure to a wound, elevate a limb, and call for medical attention.

6. Watch for signs of a stroke. Be sure to know and have readily available the students' **Individualized Healthcare Plan (IHP)**. Be prepared to act quickly.

7. Be attuned to the student's emotional well-being. These students may be teased by their peers, causing them to withdraw and isolate themselves. Create as many opportunities for them to work and play with as many different classmates as possible.

8. Continually communicate with parents. Arrange for an easy and fluid communication system, which may be emailing, texting, telephoning, or sending notes back and forth between home and school.

SOURCE: Adapted from Centers for Disease Control and Prevention. (2015). *Tips for Supporting Students with Sickle Cell Disease.* Retrieved from http://www.cdc.gov/ncbddd/sicklecell/documents/tipsheet_supporting_students_with_scd.pdf

The figure below summarizes some available solutions to address the challenges faced by students with physical and health disabilities.

Solutions: Physical and Health Disabilities

Physical and Health Disabilities

Solutions · Challenges · General Characteristics

Physical limitations · Impaired motor functioning · Episodic health crises · Poor general health

Mobility · Speech · Access · Fatigue · Participation · Absenteeism

Accommodations · Universal Design for Learning · Assistive technology · Peer assistance · Distance education · Related services

Topic 11.6 Accommodations

- Many accommodations used by students with physical and health disabilities, such as technology, flexible schedules, service animals, and word processing software, allow for continued access to classmates and the general education curriculum.

- Teachers can reduce barriers caused by inaccessible school environments through careful thought, adjusting furniture, providing space for storage, and placing visual information at everyone's eye level.

In what ways can teachers help students with physical and health disabilities access the curriculum more easily and demonstrate their learning more effectively? Possibly more than any other group, students with physical or health problems use accommodations to enable full participation in general education or inclusive educational environments. Recall that Section 504 of the Rehabilitation Act requires the availability of accommodations. However, teachers must remember that not all students with physical or health conditions require or receive special education services.

Although students with health impairments might require different accommodations than those with physical disabilities, students in both disability categories often face challenges with stamina, hospital visits, and illnesses. For these reasons, some of the following accommodations and supports might help in providing an appropriate education:

- Distance education—For some students with fragile health, school does not exist in a single place. When students are too sick to attend school, their education may take place at home or in the hospital. They may continue to access the general education curriculum by using technology. Many schools are already using online learning management systems (e.g., Schoology), which provide options for posting assignments, uploading completed homework, discussion boards, blogs, and more. These systems are perfect for students who cannot attend school regularly. Teachers can post videos of class lectures; students can participate in class discussions via video chatting, collaborate on joint documents, and form **communities of practice**. In other cases, students may need online course options, which allow them to work through course content at their own pace.

- Digital textbooks—Textbooks often present a problem: they are too heavy to carry and the pages can be difficult to manipulate. Standard texts can be replaced with e-texts that are easily delivered to a laptop or mobile device. Students with IEPs can order e-books at no charge through Bookshare, an accessible online library, at www.Bookshare.org.

The following IRIS Module explains how to obtain textbooks, other instructional materials, and text-reader software at no cost.

▶ **IRIS Module: Bookshare: Providing Accessible Materials for Students with Print Disabilities**
http://iris.peabody.vanderbilt.edu/module/bs/

Many students with health conditions or physical disabilities experience periods when they are exceptionally tired, do not have sufficient energy to sustain working for long periods, or do not have the muscle strength necessary to keep up with their peers. Accommodations can include supports like:

- *Flexible schedules*—For example, scheduling harder classes in the morning for a student whose health condition causes overwhelming fatigue in the afternoon or extending due dates for complex assignments may be all that is needed.

- *Word processing software*—This enables students who cannot write as fast and efficiently as others to keep up with classmates while producing readable documents.
- *Service animals*—These highly trained assistants can help individuals who have poor dexterity or lack the physical strength to perform tasks such as opening cupboard doors or carrying heavy books. Additionally, service animals can alert an individual that a seizure is imminent and protect an individual who is having one. Note that when these dogs accompany a student to school, peers must understand that the animals are working and cannot be distracted from their jobs. Because the ongoing care and handling of service dogs require a certain level of maturity and commitment, many organizations have minimum age requirements for owners, ranging from 12 to 16 years of age. Older classroom peers, once educated about a service dog's responsibilities, are less likely to treat it like a pet or get distracted by the animal in class.

Watch the following video to learn the story of Ricochet and Patrick, the amazing surfing team.

▶ **From Service dog to SURFice dog: Turning disappointment into a joyful new direction**

https://www.youtube.com/watch?v=BGODurRfVv4

Service animals, like dogs and monkeys, can be helpful at school, at home, and in the community by assisting people with disabilities with many tasks, such as getting items off a shelf, lifting heavy objects, and even turning pages in a book.

The following table highlights a number of accommodations that might benefit students with health and physical impairments. Again, when determining appropriate accommodations, the IEP team must consider the student's functional ability and needs.

Presentation, Setting, Response, and Scheduling Accommodations for Students with Physical and Health Disabilities

Presentation	Setting	Response	Scheduling or Timing
• Note takers	• Accessible location	• Scribes	• Extended time
• Digital texts	• Accessible workstation (e.g., adjustable desk)	• Computer	• Breaks
• Positioning tools (e.g., book stand)	• Distance education	• Word prediction software	• Flexible schedule
• Securing materials to work area	• Working with a peer or in a group	• Voice-to-text software	• Shorter assignments

What can teachers do to reduce barriers to the physical environment? Although students with physical disabilities might receive a number of accommodations throughout the school day, they often find the school building and the classroom inaccessible. In particular, older schools were not designed with wheelchairs or mobility issues in mind. Similarly, teachers often set up their classrooms for instructional efficiency without considering the needs of students who have physical limitations. However, modifications to the physical environment are critical for reducing barriers for students with physical disabilities. Teachers can start creating a more welcoming and friendly classroom environment for students with mobility issues by:

- Removing hazards and barriers to movement.
- Improving classroom traffic patterns.
- Creating flexible seating arrangements.
- Providing safe and secure space to store assistive technology devices.
- Creating more space in the classroom to store bulky equipment or to allow wheelchairs to pass freely in the classroom.
- Adjusting tables, desks, and other furniture.
- Placing visual information (e.g., graphs, posters, charts) at a height that can be viewed from a wheelchair.
- Placing supplies in locations that are accessible.

E.D. Torial/Alamy Stock Photo

Even in the best of situations, negotiating large, motorized wheelchairs in tight classroom situations can require everyone's cooperation.

Topic 11.7 Early Intervention

- Advances in newborn screening now allow for early identification of many conditions.

- Early identification enables the delivery of treatment and services at crucial points in a child's life, which can prevent or reduce the impact of disabilities.

Can diseases and conditions be identified early in children's lives? Until recently, the incidence of many major health and physical disabilities could not be reduced or prevented because they were not identified early enough. Now, **newborn screening** is saving lives and preventing disabilities. The idea of newborn screening was first introduced in the 1960s to identify babies who were unable to process a protein in milk, a condition known as phenylketonuria (PKU), which, with repeated exposure, can cause intellectual disabilities. Identifying PKU in infancy and informing families allowed them to refrain from giving milk and other foods high in protein to their babies with PKU. Since that pioneering effort, an increasing number of newborn screening tests have been developed. For example, some 30 metabolic disorders can now be identified from blood panels taken from infants even before they leave the hospital. These tests detect disorders such as congenital hypothyroidism (CH), congenital toxoplasmosis, cystic fibrosis (CF), PKU, sickle cell disease, and many others.

Other types of screenings help identify infants with different physical or health conditions. For example, all 50 states have some sort of compliance programs for Early Hearing Detection and Intervention (EHDI) to help identify babies with severe hearing impairments or deafness (which will be discussed in more detail in Chapter 12).

What is the role of newborn screening in preventing disabilities or reducing their impact? While some newborns may initially appear healthy, very serious conditions such as congenital heart defects, deafness, or blood conditions may be present. Newborn screenings aim for early identification and treatment, which can be critical in bringing the child and family life-saving techniques. These tests are usually conducted in the hospital before the baby leaves or, for those not born in hospitals, shortly after birth at a nearby doctor's office, hospital, or clinic.

Sometimes these tests provide **false-positive results**, which then require further testing. However, when newborns do show signs of critical conditions, steps can often be taken to help prevent serious problems such as brain damage, organ damage, and even death. Sometimes corrective actions may be as simple as changing the baby's diet. For example, in cases of PKU, protein-rich foods and some sweeteners build up in the baby's body. Placing the baby on a special diet can prevent brain damage. Other conditions, like hypothyroidism, require early treatment with medications to avoid slow growth and brain damage. By detecting sickle cell disease early, proper treatment can be administered and preventive measures instituted so that serious illness will not develop. Detecting congenital heart defects allows correction of the problem with surgery; early interventionists can then help the family prepare a physical environment in which normal development can take place. Early identification of other conditions allows for preventive actions and places the family and doctors on alert so measures can be taken quickly if serious symptoms arise. Each year more states routinely test for an increasing number of genetic, endocrine, and metabolic conditions before babies leave the hospital. These advances in medical technology lead to better outcomes for children otherwise at risk for lifelong disabilities.

Newborn screening allows for the identification of conditions that can result in disabilities and brings early intervention services to the infant and family as soon as possible.

Topic 11.8 School Years: Managing Health Emergencies, Including Seizures

- Health emergencies at school require the quick action of teachers who know the procedures and protocols of their schools.

- Each type of seizure requires a different response; regardless, it is important for teachers to stay calm, keep the child safe, and reassure classmates.

Do teachers have a role in caring for and helping students with medical emergencies? Yes, teachers' responsibilities extend beyond instruction, and when medical crises occur at school, teachers have important roles to play in getting help to students. Children's health emergencies and accidents can and do happen anywhere. They are usually unpredictable and require the quick response of an adult to minimize negative outcomes. Many school personnel know what actions to take when a student falls and breaks an arm, has an injury on the practice field, or shows signs of fever. For more severe medical emergencies, many schools have a clear set of procedures to follow. It is important that all teachers and on-site school administrators are well versed in the school's procedures.

Because children spend a considerable portion of their day at school, it is not surprising that an estimated 10% to 20% of childhood injuries occur there. Further, as more and more children with chronic health care needs attend their neighborhood schools, the incidence of medical emergencies at school has increased. At the same time, a school nurse is rarely assigned to a single school anymore; most provide itinerant medical coverage to multiple schools, rotating throughout the week. As a result, the teacher is often on the front line of dealing with medications, emergencies, and injuries. Clearly, emergency plans and protocols need to be in place for events such as seizures, choking, bleeding, head traumas, allergic reactions, and sports accidents. In addition, every school should have medical supplies readily on hand, as well as procedures in place for when and how to contact emergency medical services.

Teachers should be aware of every student who has a special health care need. Many of them have an Individualized Healthcare Plan (IHP) that contains important information about medication, activity levels, dietary needs, equipment, transportation, accommodations, and emergency procedures (including contact information for parents and medical personnel). For students who receive special education services, these plans are part of their IEPs. The IHPs need to be up-to-date and easily accessible to all relevant school personnel.

What should teachers do when a student has a seizure at school? **Seizures**, an abnormal burst of electrical energy in the brain that interrupts normal function, are more common than most of us think. Here are a few important facts. First, it is estimated that 4% to 6% of all children have one seizure. Second, a child who has only one seizure does not have epilepsy. Third, **epilepsy** is a neuromotor impairment in which a person has two or more seizures; however, only 1% of all children have this condition. And fourth, of the 1% who have had two or more seizures, 70% to 80% do *not* develop a lifelong condition. The majority of students who have epilepsy successfully control their seizures with medication. Researchers are investigating treatment options that will prevent the occurrence of continuing seizures.

Although uncontrolled epilepsy is very rare, seizure events are more common. We highlight them here because what can happen during a seizure can be puzzling, even frightening to others. The student may lose consciousness and may experience involuntary actions such as uncontrolled eye movements, body jerks, quick loss of muscle control, and sudden falls to the floor. Cool heads must prevail, and students and teachers must remain calm. Quick actions from teachers are important to ensure both the safety of the student involved and that of his or her classmates. To prevent injuries if he or she falls or hits objects in the area, it is important not to leave the student until the episode is over. The following box provides additional tips for teachers.

It is important for all school personnel to recognize the signs of a seizure quickly and also to respond appropriately bringing safety and calmness to the situation.

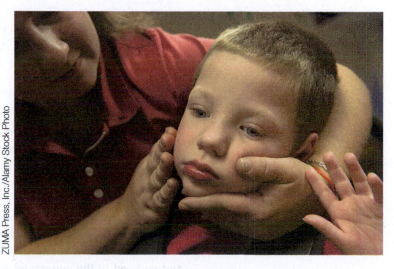

ZUMA Press, Inc./Alamy Stock Photo

Tips for Teachers: Understanding and Managing Seizures at School

1. *Absence seizure:* momentary loss of awareness, sometimes accompanied by blinking or movements of the face or arms; may be frequent; fully aware after an episode
   - Be sure key parts of the lesson are not missed once the episode is over.

2. *Simple partial seizure:* consciousness not lost; unable to control body movements; experiences feelings, visions, sounds, and smells that are not real
   - Comfort and reassure if the child is frightened.

3. *Complex partial seizure:* consciousness clouded, unresponsive to instructions, inappropriate and undirected behaviors, sleepwalking appearance, of short duration (a minute or two); prolonged confusion after an episode, no recall of seizure
   - Gently guide child back to seat.
   - Speak softly.
   - Ensure child's safety.
   - Ignore uncontrollable behaviors.

   - Ensure full consciousness before changing locations.
   - Help child sort out confusions.

4. *Generalized tonic-clonic seizure:* body stiffens and jerks; may fall, lose consciousness, lose bladder control, have erratic breathing; lasts several minutes; child can be confused, weary, or belligerent afterward
   - Remain calm.
   - Reassure classmates.
   - Ease child to floor.
   - Clear area.
   - Rest head on a pillow.
   - Turn on side.
   - Do not put anything in child's mouth.
   - Do not restrain.
   - Let rest after jerking ceases.
   - Re-engage in class participation.

SOURCE: Adapted from *Seizure First Aid* by the Epilepsy Foundation (2014). Retrieved from www.epilepsyfoundation.org

When a seizure occurs, teachers have dual responsibilities. They must be certain that precautions are taken so the student receives proper medical attention after the incident and must be prepared in case of another seizure episode. They also need to dispel the fears of classmates who may have been frightened by their classmate's behavior and welcome the student who has had a seizure back to the classroom much as they would a student with any other health impairment.

Topic 11.9 Related Services: Collaboration with School Nurses, Physical Therapists, and Occupational Therapists

- Different related service providers, each with a unique role, collaborate with teachers to help students with physical and health disabilities overcome challenges presented by their conditions.

- Multidisciplinary teams are individually determined to meet the unique needs of each student.

Which related services are used most often to support students with physical and health disabilities? School nursing, physical therapy, and occupational therapy are the three most common related services used by students with physical and health disabilities. It is natural, and often correct, to associate **school nurses** with students with health disabilities. For students with chronic and long-term illness, school nurses often fill the role of **case manager**. They coordinate the implementation of specific accommodations and modifications spelled out in each student's IHP.

Most students with health disabilities require very few accommodations to access and succeed in the general education curriculum. However, some students may be too sick to attend their neighborhood schools. In these cases, instruction may need to be delivered at their homes or even in hospital settings. When these students are well enough to transition back to neighborhood schools, they initially do so on a part-time basis, gradually increasing time spent at school. During this transition period, school nurses provide invaluable services by coordinating with other medical personnel, teachers, and family members to ensure a seamless coordination of health care services.

The following IRIS Module helps school nurses and other education professionals understand their roles in working with students with disabilities when participating in 504 plan and IEP meetings, advocating for students with health care needs, promoting their services, collaborating with others, and establishing support networks.

▶ **IRIS Module: School Nurses: Roles and Responsibilities in School Settings**
http://iris.peabody.vanderbilt.edu/module/nur01-personnel/

Physical therapists (PTs) evaluate the quality of students' movement and teach them how to compensate for and change inefficient motor patterns. Most students with physical disabilities need help to overcome the challenges of controlling their muscles and moving freely, whether for walking or writing a paper. This often requires a physical therapist to first assess the student's skills and then provide therapy to the student and consultation with the teacher.

Occupational therapists (OTs) assess and work to improve upper-body movement, fine motor skills, and other skills used in daily living activities. Together, PTs and OTs analyze a student's physical abilities and then determine which assistive devices will be beneficial (often in conjunction with assistive technology specialists). Once they have evaluated a student's physical abilities, occupational therapists can help teachers with issues like:

- Knowing which accommodations they should provide.
- Understanding proper positioning so a student with a physical challenge can sit comfortably when taking notes during a lecture.
- Arranging a classroom so a wheelchair will be able to pass freely.

Because these professionals know effective ways to adapt pencils, computer keyboards, or desks and chairs, they can also help identify devices that will assist students who have limited strength to transport heavy book bags from class to class.

How are related services combined for students with these disabilities? While school nursing, physical therapy, and occupational therapy are the most commonly used related services for these students, many others are utilized as well (see Topic 4.10 for a review of the related services offered through IDEA). Remember, the types and complexity of students' conditions vary widely. It is important not to associate a particular set of related services with either physical disabilities or health disabilities. During an IEP meeting, members of an individually determined multidisciplinary team (e.g., educators, school nurses, physical therapists, occupational therapists, school psychologists) are brought together to meet the needs of a student. Although each related service provider has specialized expertise, the combined comprehensive knowledge of the team can result in greater success for the student when participating in activities at school, at home, and in the community.

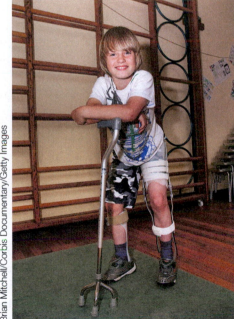

Brian Mitchell/Corbis Documentary/Getty Images

Students with physical disabilities must often consider other aspects of school besides their academic classwork. This student works with a physical therapist to improve his strength and balance in order to increase his mobility.

Check Your Understanding 11.2

Click here to gauge your understanding of the concepts in this section.

People and Situations

Learning Outcome

Provide examples of how individuals with physical and health disabilities have been treated poorly throughout the history of mankind, what actions have led to improvements in how they are treated, and how their participation in American life can still be improved.

Topic 11.10 Origins and History

- Since the beginning of human history, individuals with physical and health disabilities have been treated poorly, subjected to cruel and inhumane treatment.

- Activists, many of whom have physical and health disabilities, are responsible for today's changes in access, attitudes, and participation.

Topic 11.11 Personal Stories

- American society holds values that liken physical perfection with desirability and popularity; students with physical disabilities can feel left out or isolated.

- Increased exposure and awareness can change attitudes toward individuals with physical and health disabilities, as reflected in the media.

Topic 11.10 Origins and History

- Since the beginning of human history, individuals with physical and health disabilities have been treated poorly, subjected to cruel and inhumane treatment.

- Activists, many of whom have physical and health disabilities, are responsible for today's changes in access, attitudes, and participation.

Has the treatment of people with physical and health disabilities been fair and just across time? The answer is, "No." The history of physical and health disabilities is as old as the history of the human race. Unfortunately, many of the stories about these individuals and their conditions are terrible—fraught with misconceptions, abuse, and tragedy. However, history does tell us that some treatment was well meaning, even though it seems strange to us today, given our current knowledge. For example, evidence of care for spinal cord injuries goes back to prehistoric times. The earliest documented treatment was to apply meat and honey to the neck!

Around 400 BC, Hippocrates, a doctor in Greece, changed the way physical and health conditions were considered. Many of his treatments, like stretching a person's body on a rack to correct neck and body deformities, were not successful. Some of his ideas, like thinking that epilepsy was caused by sitting in the sun too long, were misguided. Regardless, Hippocrates insisted that scientific methods be applied to medicine. He tried to remove superstitious perceptions of illnesses and other individual differences. Contrary to some of the thinking of that time, he was convinced that the gods' anger over something or someone was not the reason for human suffering.

Unfortunately, although such superstitious ideas have their roots in centuries-old myths, they still linger today in some cultures.

Across the centuries, people with disabilities have been treated differently than everyone else. At times, royalty and wealthy families kept people with disabilities for entertainment purposes. Many court jesters were people with physical disabilities. In some cultures during the Middle Ages, infants born with obvious physical differences were left to die. Horrible treatment is not relegated to ancient history, however. In the 1930s and 1940s, during World War II, people considered inadequate according to standards of health and beauty were victims of Hitler's Holocaust.

During the twentieth century in the United States, many students with physical and health disabilities attended separate schools, which often had the latest physical therapy equipment available, including therapeutic swimming pools. The best thinking of the time was to bring experts from many disciplines and a wide range of services to students with these special needs. However, the result was isolation and segregation. Because their education was separate from that of their siblings and neighborhood friends, many former students with physical disabilities worked successfully to close these schools.

What was the role of people with disabilities in the guarantee of their civil rights, and what major changes increased their access to mainstream society? In the 1960s, the denial of civil rights to African Americans came to the public's attention. Issues of discrimination and bias were brought to the courts and to Congress, and laws were passed to protect these individuals' basic rights. Not long after, people with disabilities followed a similar pattern of advocacy and legislation to gain their civil rights and attain social justice. People with disabilities became civil rights activists who demanded access to everyday life. Many of these early advocates had physical and health disabilities caused by polio, and they were graduates of separate, segregated special education schools. They argued that separate was not equal in any situation. Ed Roberts and Judy Heumann, who were introduced in Topic 1.5, were two such advocates who fought for rights guaranteeing that people with disabilities could participate fully in daily life. They orchestrated wheelchair sit-ins and demonstrations, lobbied Congress, and filed lawsuits. More information on the history of people with physical and health disabilities can be found in this chapter's timeline.

Timeline: Progress In Health And Access Across Time

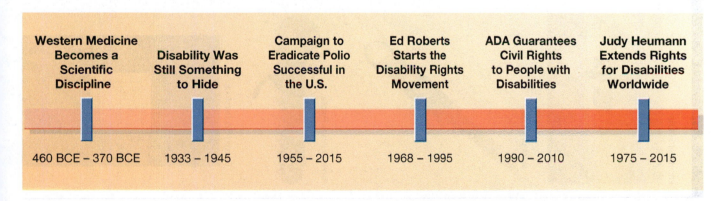

Western Medicine Becomes a Scientific Discipline	Disability Was Still Something to Hide	Campaign to Eradicate Polio Successful in the U.S.	Ed Roberts Starts the Disability Rights Movement	ADA Guarantees Civil Rights to People with Disabilities	Judy Heumann Extends Rights for Disabilities Worldwide
460 BCE – 370 BCE	1933 – 1945	1955 – 2015	1968 – 1995	1990 – 2010	1975 – 2015

Such actions from members of the disability community prompted the passage of Section 504 of the Rehabilitation Act (prohibiting discrimination) in 1973 and later,

Naomi Tyler

Even when labeled inappropriately (the elevator does not have a disability), elevators help to overcome impossible barriers that restrict important access.

in 1990, the creation of the Americans with Disabilities Act (ADA), which requires removal of physical barriers in public buildings and restaurants (you can review these laws in Topic 4.1). The ADA has made a big difference in the lives of individuals who face challenges with mobility that restrict their ability to participate in typical activities at school, in the community, or at work. For example, while elevators do not replace inaccessible stairways, they offer a convenient alternative.

Not only does the ADA law guarantee people with disabilities access and reduced discrimination and bias, but also its implementation has shown that everyone benefits when the environment is simpler to negotiate. For example, door levers provide easier access than doorknobs for those with full hands. Curb cuts, the ramps that are at almost every sidewalk crossing, are helpful for people pushing strollers on sidewalks, customers pushing grocery carts in parking lots, and passengers with luggage at airports. Accessible park trails allow more of us to enjoy the outdoors. Sidewalks, trails, buildings, and even appliances are now designed with principles of **universal design** in mind (see the box), which is the foundation for the educational concept of **Universal Design for Learning (UDL)** that you learned about in Chapter 2.

Universal Design

For years, many buildings were not accessible for individuals with physical impairments. Some multi-story buildings, including schools, were not equipped with elevators, which made access impossible for individuals in wheelchairs. The Americans with Disabilities Act, passed in 1990, required that all public buildings and services be completely accessible to individuals with disabilities. In response, architects developed universal design principles that went beyond the stipulations in this law and provided guidelines for the development of new buildings that would be accessible to as many people as possible, including those with disabilities. These principles, which now apply to more than buildings, strive to improve on the original conceptual design while including options for equitable, flexible, simple, and intuitive use that requires little physical effort. For example, doorframes in universally designed homes are slightly wider for wheelchairs and walkers, sinks and countertops are lower (or can even be electronically adjusted to higher or lower heights), and innovative designs for oven doors allow them to be pulled open and then slid out of the way, making it safer to reach into a hot oven. Universal design can also be applied to products like kitchen gadgets and tools. Innovator Sam Farber designed a potato peeler with a wide handle for his wife, who had arthritis. That potato peeler became the first of over 1,000 products created by OXO, a company that develops items for use by as many people as possible. View some common household items below. You might have a universally designed product in your home and not even realize it!

kocetoilief/Fotolia

aleks-p/Fotolia

Jaimie Duplass/Fotolia

Doomu/Shutterstock

The ADA also alerted businesses to the fact that developing specific services for people with disabilities could be profitable. Today, some cruises cater to individuals with fragile health, allowing everyone to enjoy a holiday. Special skiing, sailing, and camping programs are now available for children with physical and health disabilities.

Until 1988, children with chronic health disabilities had no access to camping experiences. The Hole in the Wall Gang camps, founded by the late actor Paul Newman, have specially designed environments that allow children with very serious health conditions to enjoy sports and activities they would otherwise not be able to participate in. Visit the Website to learn more about what is offered at the Hole in the Wall Gang Camp: http://www.holeinthewallgang.org/.

The Hole in the Wall Gang Camp

The opportunity to go to camp is no longer denied to children with special health care needs because of the creative and generous efforts of all involved with the Hole in the Wall Gang Camps, which have locations across the nation.

Topic 11.11 Personal Stories

- American society holds values that liken physical perfection with desirability and popularity; students with physical disabilities can feel left out or isolated.

- Increased exposure and awareness can change attitudes toward individuals with physical and health disabilities, as reflected in the media.

The tradition of placing stone heads of scary creatures on buildings began in ancient times, becoming popular features on churches during the 1100s to invoke fear and to reinforce the importance of protecting the church. High on the northwest tower of the National Cathedral in Washington, DC, a sculpture of Darth Vader joins other gargoyles that serve as drainpipes to keep water away from the stone walls of the cathedral.

In what ways are individuals with physical and health impairments treated poorly in society?   Youth, beauty, and physical fitness are obsessions of modern American society. Through celebrities and athletes, the entertainment and advertising industries project images of beauty and fitness that are often unrealistic. Have you noticed messages about physical perfection in television shows, commercials, music videos, and movies? Have you or your friends ever assigned ratings to others on the basis of physical appearance (such as ranking them on a scale of 1 to 10)? In stories, physical attractiveness or strength is often associated with virtue or goodness, and imperfection and "deformities" with evil. For example, Darth Vader, whose infamous labored breathing is recognized across generations worldwide, is the evil nemesis in the *Star Wars* films. This kind of negative symbolism has been repeated in many books and movies, including *The Hunchback of Notre Dame*, *The Dark Crystal*, *The Lion King*, and *The Wizard of Oz*.

Students with physical and health disabilities are not always included in peer activities. Young children whose physical conditions prevent them from engaging in typical playground activities may be ignored or left out of games during recess; playground equipment may be inaccessible. Students may find it difficult to participate in after-school clubs, sports, or other activities. As they get older,

Sculpture and photograph by Jay Hall Carpenter

teenagers with physical and health conditions may likewise be excluded from typical adolescent activities when wheelchairs or electric scooters can't fit into friends' cars or when health conditions limit their ability to hang out on weekends or spend the night away from home. Although many teenagers worry about dating, that they won't be seen as attractive by potential boyfriends or girlfriends, these feelings can be intensified for adolescents with physical and health disabilities. And, sadly, students of all ages with physical and health disabilities experience higher rates of bullying than the general student population. Children whose disability affects their physical appearances report being called derogatory names in reference to their disability. For students with severe allergies, bullying can include purposely exposing them to items that will trigger a reaction.

How are some of these attitudes changing? As individuals with disabilities become more visible in society, this exposure increases awareness and acceptance. Acceptance engenders more positive attitudes, which translates into more proactive measures for inclusion. For example, although we still have a long way to go, a greater number of playgrounds are being built according to universal design principles, improving access for all children. Accommodations are being made in many more areas outside the typical school day. Peers push their friends in wheelchairs during high school marching band performances, plan leisure activities at accessible venues, and pool gas money to contribute to the friend with the car trunk large enough to carry a wheelchair. Additionally, friends learn to watch for signs of fatigue and change activities when necessary.

Media portrayals are also becoming more positive. For example, you might have noticed more commercials that feature individuals with disabilities, a recent development. The movie *Soul Surfer* depicts the story of Bethany Hamilton, the young surfing champion who lost her arm to a shark, and illustrates the importance of family, faith, and fortitude. The British reality television series *Britain's Missing Top Model* challenged the fashion industry's standards of the ideal woman. Shown on BBC America, eight models, each with disabilities, competed for a large prize by taking on difficult assignments. Although as outrageous as many other reality shows, it raised awareness by telling the stories of young women with disabilities striving to advance their careers in the fashion and entertainment industry. And, in an exciting step towards more positive inclusion of people with disabilities, the television show *Speechless* features Micah Fowler, an actor with cerebral palsy, in a leading role. To further demonstrate how the portrayal of individuals with disabilities has changed, this chapter's *On the Screen* features *A Brief History of Time*, the story of Stephen Hawking, whom you read about earlier in the chapter opening vignette.

On the Screen: *A Brief History of Time*

https://youtu.be/5_y13Pbo4qs

This film depicts the life of the brilliant theorist Stephen Hawking (see chapter opener), who, despite his physical and health disabilities, contributes to human understanding of the origins of the universe. The film shows the overwhelming personal and professional challenges he faced and overcame. This very human story illustrates the joys and tragedies of his personal life, but it also centers on his great achievements and the respect he received from the public and the academic community.

Check Your Understanding 11.3

Click here to gauge your understanding of the concepts in this section.

Future Perspectives

Learning Outcome

Explain how emerging technologies have made and will make a difference in the ways in which these individuals participate at school and in daily life.

Topic 11.12 Prevention: Accidents and Disease

- Understanding what causes the conditions resulting in physical and health disabilities can lead to the development of preventive measures.

- Advances in medicine, access to health care, and increased public awareness may hold the key to reduced impact of physical and health disabilities.

Topic 11.13 Technology: Prosthetics and Robotics

- Emerging technologies, like prosthetic devices that enable people with missing arms and legs to move independently, will allow freedom of movement barely imagined a decade ago.

- Robotics engineers are developing technologies that will permit an individual to use his or her mind to control the movements of an artificial limb or to use a robot to assist with daily living, hinting at a future that is almost unimaginable.

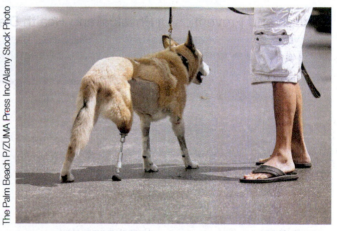

The meaning of participation has been taken to a whole new level.

Topic 11.12 Prevention: Accidents and Disease

- Understanding what causes the conditions resulting in physical and health disabilities can lead to the development of preventive measures.

- Advances in medicine, access to health care, and increased public awareness may hold the key to reduced impact of physical and health disabilities.

Can the incidence of physical and health disabilities be reduced? Yes, the future holds great promise that the incidence of both physical and health disabilities will be reduced. As researchers successfully determine causes for more disabilities, preventive solutions

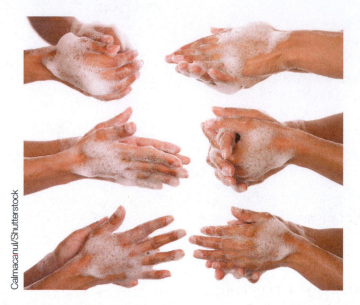

Simple preventive techniques, like frequent hand washing, can halt the spread of illness, even in crowded school settings.

are often close behind. Too often, physical disabilities result from preventable accidents and injuries. Whether from accidents or child abuse, injuries can lead to cerebral palsy, seizure disorders, spinal cord injuries, brain damage, and even death. Engineers are continually designing more effective child safety seats, air bags, seat belts, and other protective devices to safeguard children from spinal cord injuries. Older children must understand the importance of using safety equipment like helmets, knee pads, and other protective gear when riding a bicycle, playing football, skiing, riding in a car, or skateboarding. In general, disabilities can be reduced when the public is better informed and engages in the precautions and protections that prevent the terrible consequences of accidents at school, at home, and in the community. Additionally, future medical advances will provide more vaccines, therapies, and other interventions to help prevent and treat today's illnesses.

Although we know a lot about how diseases are transmitted, we have not yet ensured that **universal health care precautions** are standard practices in classrooms. Most of these practices are simple, like washing hands frequently, using hand sanitizers often, and being certain that classrooms are clean. These procedures can protect students with compromised immune systems and help to prevent illnesses and subsequent absences. Sadly, such universal precautions are not in place in most classrooms.

Causes and Prevention of Physical and Health Disabilities

Physical Disabilities		Health Disabilities	
Causes	**Prevention**	**Causes**	**Prevention**
Motor vehicle accidents	Child restraints Safety belts Auto air bags Motorcycle helmets Following driving rules	Infections and disease	Vaccinations Access to health care Frequent hand washing Use of disposable gloves Good hygiene
Water and diving accidents	Diving safety Swimming safety	Asthma	Removal of allergens
Gunshot wounds	Gun control Weapons training Ammunition locked away	Poisoning/toxins	Safe storage First aid
Sports injuries	Protective equipment Headgear Conditioning/training	Premature birth	Prenatal care Access to health care
Child abuse	Family support services Alert teachers Parent training	Human immunodeficiency virus (HIV) infection	Abstinence or safe sex Avoidance of drugs Use of gloves around blood

What are other ways to reduce the impact of physical and health disabilities? Scientists are working hard to discover new treatments for many diseases and health conditions. As with many cases of physical disabilities, the incidence of health disabilities will diminish as new medical procedures, vaccines, and other preventive measures are developed. However, medical advances are useless if families and their children do not have access to quality health care. This access is a key ingredient in the prevention of many disabilities; for those that cannot be avoided, their impact can be lessened. Prenatal checkups can ensure access to intensive medical care for the mother and infant if problems occur; provide diagnosis and treatment for maternal illnesses that can damage the developing infant; and help prevent fetal exposure to infections, viruses, drugs, alcohol, and other toxins. Providing prenatal care to all pregnant women is well worth the expense. In exchange, long-term health costs are reduced and the personal costs of disabilities are avoided. Access to health care in childhood also safeguards children from long-term effects of infectious diseases, saving billions of dollars in long-term health care costs and preventing disability-related complications in millions of lives.

As with the prevention of physical disabilities, enhanced public awareness is important. Recall the discussion about the importance of vaccines in Chapter 8. Parents can help prevent the spread of infections by vaccinating their children against diseases such as mumps, measles, and chickenpox. Parents should not withhold such measures because of faulty information, such as the media reports that blamed childhood vaccines for the rise in cases of autism spectrum disorder (ASD).

Topic 11.13 Technology: Prosthetics and Robotics

- Emerging technologies, like prosthetic devices that enable people with missing arms and legs to move independently, will allow freedom of movement barely imagined a decade ago.

- Robotics engineers are developing technologies that will permit an individual to use his or her mind to control the movements of an artificial limb or to use a robot to assist with daily living, hinting at a future that is unimaginable.

Will emerging technologies change the lives of people with physical disabilities? Possibly for more than any other group of individuals with disabilities, the developing science in **prosthetics** and robotics will benefit those who face physical challenges. Innovations in prosthetics are leveling the playing field for many people who require artificial limbs to walk and run like everyone else. Special limbs are being designed and developed for different purposes. They allow people to enjoy a skiing holiday, take a morning jog, hike in the mountains, or stroll through the mall.

New technology is allowing for flexibility and dexterity never thought possible. Notice how this boy can even pick up a block with his prosthetic hand!

Prosthetic hands are exceptionally versatile and allow those without hands to type, use dinnerware, write with a pencil or pen, and grasp objects otherwise not possible to hold. Newer models are exceptionally flexible, are lightweight, have great strength, and are capable of many functions. Some are encased in rubber foam that resembles human skin, giving the appearance of a real hand. Futuristic products that help their users feel things are under development or just coming on the market.

In the following video, Nicki Ashwell of the United Kingdom demonstrates the many fine motor tasks she can accomplish with her bionic hand (pictured above). It is considered the most lifelike hand developed so far, not because of its appearance, but because of the dexterity it provides.

▶ **Bionic Hand**

https://www.youtube.com/watch?v=wJL5AT3IFhE

Britta60/Fotolia

Imagine a world where no one has to use a wheelchair!

How can robotics contribute to the lives of individuals with physical and health disabilities? The field of **robotics**, the science and technology that develops computer-controlled mechanical devices, provides a promising new frontier for research, development, and innovation. Although rapid advancement in this area is due to the tragic cases of soldiers returning from war with missing limbs, this technology will benefit those with physical disabilities whose limbs are unusable because of birth defects, childhood accidents, and sports injuries. Some of these advances utilize current-day computer technology and software, like the iPad and other tablets. High school and college students who compete in robot competitions are honing their skills in developments that will benefit us all in the future. The applications are almost beyond imagination, except, of course, by screenwriters who created film characters like RoboCop or The Bionic Woman for television shows!

The wheelchairs many people use to participate in everyday life have drawbacks. A big disadvantage is the inability to stand up, look someone in the eye, and have a conversation on their level. Such challenges may be relegated to the past. In 2014, the U.S. Food and Drug Administration approved the marketing and sale of the first wearable, motorized device that helps people with spinal cord injuries walk again. ReWalk is a **powered exoskeleton** that includes a metal brace to support the individual's legs and upper body; a tilt sensor; a battery-operated motor that supplies movement; and a wireless remote control that commands the device to stand, walk, and sit down. The individual wears a backpack containing the computer and power supply and uses crutches for extra stability. High school senior Justin Covarrubias, who was paralyzed in 2014 from a motor-cross accident, is now walking again with the help of this new device. ReWalk signals a future with more independence for so many with restricted mobility.

To see the ReWalk exoskeleton in action, look at the following video.

▶ **ReWalk Exoskeleton**

https://www.youtube.com/watch?v=cBzwbbTPJg0

Check Your Understanding 11.4

Click here to gauge your understanding of the concepts in this section.

Summary

Physical and Health Disabilities Described

Physical and health disabilities are caused by many different conditions that restrict mobility and result in special health care needs; all require unique responses to limit their impact on the individuals affected.

- Not all students with physical disabilities or health impairments require special education services.

- Almost all of these students, however, require help from teams of education and related service professionals to receive the accommodations and adjustments to the environment that they need to succeed.

- Health disabilities that require special education responses, except ADHD, are rare among children, although a precise count is not available.

- A special group of students with health disabilities are considered medically fragile. Often, throughout their education, these students' educational needs might be met in separate classrooms, at home, or in hospitals.

Special Education

Teachers have important roles to play in the lives of children with physical and health disabilities, whether they require special services or not.

- Teachers can assist greatly by helping to manage health disabilities that occur at school.

- Simple accommodations to the learning and physical environments help these students access the curriculum, assessments, their peers, and the school culture.

- Collaboration among related service providers, general and special educators, the family, and students with physical and health disabilities can support the attainment of everyone's goals.

People and Situations

Despite challenges faced in daily life and with the long-term historic biases they are striving to overcome, people with health and physical disabilities are assuming their places in modern society.

- Advocates, many of whom have disabilities themselves, are responsible for changes in attitudes and legal protections that have improved access and acceptance.

- Improved acceptance is evident as more positive portrayals of individuals with physical and health disabilities are appearing in the media (i.e., film and television).

Future Perspectives

Today's scientific knowledge and technology advances can prevent injuries and illnesses that lead to disabilities and can lessen their impact when they do occur.

- The transfer of diseases from one student to another can often be prevented through vaccinations and by using simple universal health care precautions, such as washing hands frequently and using hand sanitizers often.

- Safety precautions and well-engineered devices, such as car seats and protective gear, prevent serious injuries.

- Research and development currently underway is bringing robotic engineering to new levels; amazing prosthetics and artificial limbs are now available, and the future will offer robots, as well as arms and legs with movement, controlled by the person's thoughts.

Addressing CEC Standards

Council for Exceptional Children (CEC) knowledge standards addressed in this chapter: 6.2, 1.0, PH1K1, PH1K2, PH2K1, PH2K2, PH4K1, PH4S1, PH5K1, PH8S3, PH10K1, PH10S5.

See the Appendix for the complete CEC Initial Level Special Educator Preparation Standards.

Chapter 12
Deafness and Hard of Hearing

Hemant Mehta/Getty Images

The introduction to this chapter is a little different from those in previous chapters. Instead of reading about a person with a hearing impairment, we want you to watch a video, and then think about the questions posed below.

▶ **SCOTUS Chief Justice John Roberts Used ASL Today at the Supreme Court**

https://youtu.be/XV_TGrZheOU

How much of the information presented by the news anchor were you able to comprehend? What cues helped you understand the information? What additional supports did you want, and how easy would they have been to provide? Finally, how much of the video were you able to attend to before you "tuned out"?

The vast majority of us take the process of hearing for granted; we don't think about how remarkable and effortless it is to be able to turn sounds into meaning, or how they can make us feel. We are warmed by the sound of an old friend's voice, startled by a loud clap of thunder, lulled by the sounds of ocean waves, excited by the roar of a crowd, or moved by musical melodies. Our interactions with others and personal growth are also affected by the hearing process, as we expand our knowledge, share ideas, express emotions, and communicate at work and in social situations. Yet, as you just experienced, we miss out on a lot when information is conveyed in a way that we cannot access. Keep this in mind as you read this chapter. Consider the types of supports that would have helped you understand the video better; students with hearing loss in inclusive settings also require supports and accommodations, many of which are relatively easy to provide. Finally, keep in mind that the video you watched was less than three minutes long. Imagine how hard it would be to pay attention for an entire class period, much less an entire day, if you could not easily understand what your teacher was saying.

Learning Outcomes

Deafness and Hard of Hearing Described

Understand the differences in the definitions for hearing impairments *and* deafness, *be familiar with the types of hearing screenings and be able to make sense of information on an audiogram, recognize the characteristics of students who are deaf or hard of hearing, and understand the various settings in which these students receive education.*

Special Education

Explain the ways in which hearing loss can impact communication, interpersonal, and academic skills; describe accommodations that can lessen these challenges; understand methods that parents and classroom teachers can use to reduce challenges associated with hearing loss; and describe supports to help students who are deaf or hard of hearing transition to post-secondary options such as school, work, and independent living.

People and Situations

Describe the history of instruction for students with hearing impairments and share some positive examples of inclusion.

Future Perspectives

Describe the benefits of early intervention and prevention, and identify technological advances in the treatment of hearing loss.

Deafness and Hard of Hearing Described[1]

Learning Outcome

Understand the differences in the definitions for hearing impairments *and* deafness, *be familiar with the types of hearing screenings and be able to make sense of information on an audiogram, recognize the characteristics of students who are deaf or hard of hearing, and understand the various settings in which these students receive education.*

Topic 12.1 Deafness and Hard of Hearing Defined

- The normal process of hearing involves many steps that convert sounds into meaningful information.

- IDEA uses the term *deafness* to refer to the most severe type of hearing loss and *hearing impairment* to refer to all other types.

Topic 12.2 Types of Hearing Loss

- Audiologists use air and bone conduction methods to test hearing abilities and chart the results on audiograms.

- Hearing loss can be categorized by type, severity, or the age at which the hearing loss occurred.

---

[1]References for Chapter 12 are found at the end of this text.

Topic 12.3 Characteristics

- Students with conductive losses show different types of impairments in their hearing than those those who have sensorineural losses.
- The degree of hearing loss does not always accurately represent the individual's functional or residual hearing abilities.

Topic 12.4 Prevalence and Placement

- In relation to other disabilities, very few students are deaf or hard of hearing.
- Many students with profound hearing loss, those who consider themselves Deaf, attend separate classrooms or separate schools.

The girl on the left uses hearing aids; the boy on the right has a cochlear implant. When provided with appropriate accommodations and assistive technology, students with hearing loss can perform as well as their hearing classmates and also feel fully included in school activities.

Topic 12.1 Deafness and Hard of Hearing Defined

- The normal process of hearing involves many steps that convert sounds into meaningful information.
- IDEA uses the term *deafness* to refer to the most severe type of hearing loss and *hearing impairment* to refer to all other types.

How does the hearing process work? The hearing process is truly amazing, and involves the three parts of the ear:

- *Outer ear*—the **pinna** and **auditory canal**
- *Middle ear*—the **eardrum**, **eustachian tube**, and **ossicles** (hammer, anvil, and stirrup)
- *Inner ear*—the **cochlea**, its membranes and hair cells, and the semicircular canals

When sound waves pass through air, water, or some other medium, they cause the eardrum, also known as the **tympanic membrane**, to vibrate. These vibrations are carried to the inner ear, where they pass through receptor cells that send impulses to the brain. The brain translates these impulses into meaningful sound. Hearing loss can occur due to obstructions or damage anywhere along the path from the outer ear, through the middle ear, to the inner ear, on to the auditory nerve, and then to the brain.

The following figure traces the process of normal hearing as sound moves from the outer ear through the middle ear and then to the inner ear, where it is translated into electrochemical signals and transmitted to the brain via the auditory nerve.

The Structure of the Human Ear

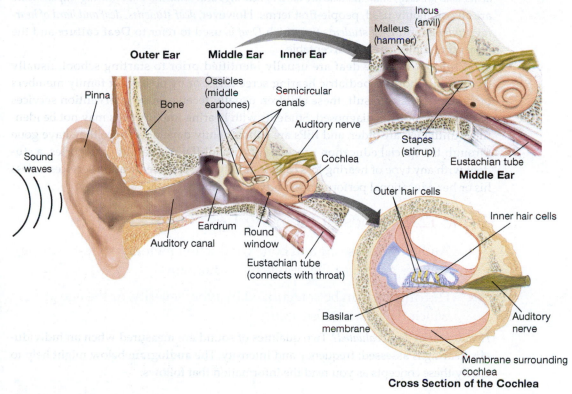

SOURCE: *"Physiology of Behavior"* with Neuroscience Animations and Student Study Guide CD-ROM (8th ed.), by Neil R. Carlson, 2004, Upper Saddle River, NJ: Pearson Education, Inc. Reprinted and electronically reproduced by permission of Pearson Education, Inc., Upper Saddle River, New Jersey.

The U.S. National Library of Medicine has the following animated video of the hearing process on its Website. Note the multiple options for viewers: typical view, view with closed captions (for viewers with hearing loss), and view with audio descriptions (for viewers with vision loss).

▶ **Hearing and the Cochlea**

www.nlm.nih.gov/medlineplus/ency/anatomyvideos/000063.htm

How does IDEA define different types of hearing loss? In general, people with **hearing impairments** have limited use of hearing. The type and amount of functional hearing these individuals have vary greatly. Hearing impairments are typically categorized into two groups: **hard of hearing** and **deafness**. These are considered separate disability categories in IDEA, though with slightly different terminology. Deafness refers to the most severe type of hearing loss while hearing impairment refers to all other types. The IDEA definitions for deafness and for hearing impairments are provided in the following table.

Definitions of Deafness and Hearing Impairments

Term	Definition	Source
Deafness	Deafness means a hearing impairment that is so severe that the child is impaired in processing linguistic information through hearing, with or without amplification, that adversely affects a child's educational performance.	IDEA '04, U.S. Department of Education
Hearing impairment	Hearing impairment means an impairment in hearing, whether permanent or fluctuating, that adversely affects a child's educational performance but that is not included under the definition of deafness.	IDEA '04, U.S. Department of Education

SOURCES: From 34 CFR Parts 300 and 303, *Assistance to States for the Education of Children with Disabilities and the Early Intervention Program for Infants and Toddlers with Disabilities; Final Regulations* (pp. 1261, 1262), U.S. Department of Education, 2006, *Federal Register*, Washington, DC.

Many terms are applied to this group of students. *Students with hearing loss, students who are deaf, students who are hard of hearing,* and *students with hearing impairments* are all commonly used, people-first terms. However, *deaf students, deaf and hard of hearing students,* and *Deaf students* (in which *Deaf* is used to refer to **Deaf culture** and the Deaf community) are also acceptable.

Children who are deaf are usually identified prior to starting school, usually through newborn or pediatric hearing screenings, or by observant family members or caregivers. As a result, these children usually receive early intervention services once the disability is diagnosed. Students with hearing impairments may not be identified until they are older, and IEPs are subsequently developed once they have gone through the special education process. As with all IDEA disability categories, a student with any type of hearing loss cannot qualify for special education services unless his or her educational performance is adversely affected.

Topic 12.2 Types of Hearing Loss

- Audiologists use air and bone conduction methods to test hearing abilities and chart the results on audiograms.

- Hearing loss can be categorized by type, severity, or the age at which the hearing loss occurred.

How is hearing loss evaluated? Two qualities of sound are measured when an individual's hearing is assessed: frequency and intensity. The **audiogram** below might help to clarify these concepts as you read the information that follows.

Common Sounds in Decibels and Hertz

Frequency levels (Hz) are represented by the vertical lines in the chart, while intensity, or loudness, (dB) levels are indicated by the horizontal lines in the chart.

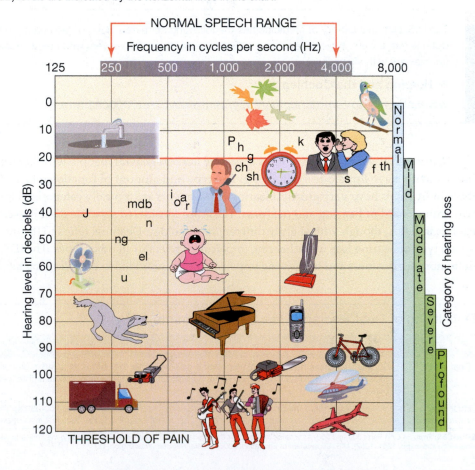

The **frequency of sound** is the number of vibrations per second. High frequencies are perceived through our ears as high pitch or tone; low frequencies, as low pitch or deep sounds. **Hertz (Hz)** is the unit in which frequency is measured. The normal ear hears sounds that range from approximately 20 Hz to 20,000 Hz; speech sounds fall approximately in the middle of the human hearing range (between 250 Hz and 4,000 Hz). If you have some knowledge of music, it might help to know that the frequency of middle C on the piano is approximately 250 Hz. The next vertical line on the audiogram, 500 Hz, is approximately one octave above middle C; 1,000 is two octaves above middle C; and so on.

The second sound quality assessed is **sound intensity**, or loudness. **Decibels (dB)** are the units that measure the intensity of sounds. Softer, quieter sounds have lower decibel measurements; louder sounds have higher ones. A decibel level of 125 or greater is painful to the average person. Sounds ranging from 0 to 120 dB are used to test how well an individual can hear different frequencies; a child with normal hearing should be able to perceive sounds at 0 dB. As you can see in the figure, speech sounds and noises in the environment have various frequencies (Hz) and intensities (dB). Regardless of our hearing abilities, humans cannot perceive all sounds. For example, some dog whistles use high frequencies that are beyond the hearing range of humans.

Audiologists, specialists in hearing abilities, conduct assessments that determine whether an individual's hearing is normal. For children and adults, audiologists use **pure sounds**—sound waves of specific frequencies—at various combinations of hertz and decibels and also at various bands of pitch and loudness. They use special equipment, such as an **audiometer**, an instrument that produces sounds at precise frequencies and intensities. The results of these audiology assessments are plotted on an audiogram, which is a grid or graph like the figure above. Each ear is tested separately and the results are marked on the chart with different symbols. A hearing threshold is determined by noting when the person first perceives the softest sound at each frequency level. The audiometer is set to indicate that a person has no hearing loss at 0 dB for various hertz levels. Scores falling below the 20-dB line represent some degree of hearing loss.

Most children's hearing is assessed by the **air conduction audiometry method**, which uses pure-tone sounds generated by an audiometer. Earphones are placed over the child's ears, and the child raises his or her hand upon hearing a sound. Such testing is usually done by a pediatrician at a well-child checkup or by a school nurse. When a hearing loss is suspected, an audiologist continues testing by using the **bone conduction audiometry method**, which involves placing a vibrator on the forehead so that sound can bypass the outer and middle ear and go directly to the inner ear.

Are there different types of hearing loss? Yes, hearing loss is often categorized by type, severity, and age of onset. Let's first consider the types of hearing loss, which are often broken down in the following way:

1. **Conductive hearing loss**—This occurs in the outer or middle ear and prevents sound waves from traveling (being conducted) to the inner ear. It is often temporary or correctable. You may have experienced a conductive hearing loss at some point, caused by a change in air pressure when flying in an airplane or riding in a car in the mountains. Audiologists can determine conductive hearing losses by using the bone conduction assessment method discussed above. When the bone conduction thresholds are normal (near 0 dB) and the air conduction thresholds are abnormal, the hearing loss is conductive.

This student is having her hearing evaluated by the air conduction audiometry method during a yearly pediatric exam. She raises her hand every time she hears a tone.

Naomi Tyler

2. **Sensorineural hearing loss**—This is caused by damage to the inner ear, the hair cells, or the auditory nerve. This type of hearing loss is sometimes referred to as *nerve deafness*; greater damage to the hair cells results in more severe hearing loss. This kind of loss is common among older adults but not in children. Sensorineural hearing losses are much more difficult to correct than conductive hearing losses.

3. **Mixed hearing loss**—This is the result of both conductive and sensorineural hearing losses.

4. **Auditory neuropathy spectrum disorder**—Sound enters the ear normally, but a problem with or damage to the inner ear or the auditory nerve does not allow sound to organize in way that can be understood by the brain.

Another way to categorize hearing loss is by the degree of loss or severity, which is important regardless of the type of hearing loss. Severity of hearing loss is divided into the following levels:

- *Mild hearing loss (21–40 dB)*—This represents typical hearing except for an inability to hear or understand speech that is soft or produced at a distance.
- *Moderate hearing loss (41–55 dB)*—Typical conversational speech is hard to follow.
- *Moderately severe hearing loss (56–70 dB)*—Only loud speech can be heard.
- *Severe hearing loss (71–90 dB)*—Even loud speech is hard to understand.
- *Profound hearing loss (91 dB)*—Only assistive listening devices enable the individual to understand information presented orally.

Typically, losses in the mild to moderate range are categorized as hard of hearing. Severe and profound hearing losses are categorized as deafness.

There are also ways to categorize hearing loss using the age of onset:

- **Congenital** hearing loss—This occurs at or before birth.
- **Adventitious** hearing loss—This occurs after birth.
- **Prelingual deafness**—This occurs before a child has learned to speak and understand language. The child's deafness is congenital or occurs during infancy.
- **Postlingual deafness**—This occurs after the child has learned to speak and understand language. Although this type of hearing loss is severe or profound, many of these individuals are able to retain their abilities to use speech and to communicate with others orally.

The Centers for Disease Control and Prevention (CDC) Website www.cdc.gov /ncbddd/hearingloss/types.html provides excellent information about hearing loss, screening and diagnosis, data and statistics, and more.

Topic 12.3 Characteristics

- Students with conductive losses show different types of impairments in their hearing than those who have sensorineural losses.

- The type of hearing loss does not always accurately represent the individual's functional or residual hearing abilities.

How do different types of hearing loss impact a student? The most common hearing loss in children is caused by a head cold; sinus infection; or ear infection, such as **otitis media**. The resulting conductive hearing loss is usually temporary. On any given day, it is likely that 20% of elementary school students have a mild conductive hearing loss. Also, some 80% of all children experience a conductive hearing loss at some time during their elementary school years. Difficulties from such hearing losses disappear once the ear infection clears up. Other conductive hearing losses that are not temporary can usually be corrected with hearing aids, through surgery, or by other medical techniques.

We have included an audiogram below for a student named Travis, who has a conductive hearing loss. We also show again the audiogram from Topic 12.2 so you can compare Travis's hearing levels with those needed to hear common sounds. Look at both of these as you read the information about Travis's audiogram.

Travis's Audiogram: Conductive Hearing Loss

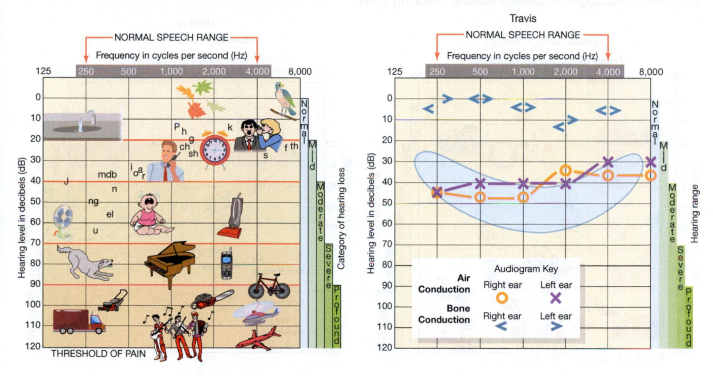

Each ear is tested separately, as indicated by the codes: O for the right ear and X for the left ear for the air conduction test; < for the right ear and > for the left ear for the bone conduction test. Travis's hearing threshold—the point at which he can first perceive sound—is marked on the audiogram for each ear. His hearing loss, of about 40 dB, is in the mild range. When his hearing threshold falls below a picture of a common sound, he is unable to perceive that sound. For example, Travis cannot hear sounds like dripping water, rustling leaves, or people whispering. The light blue shaded area on this audiogram (sometimes called the speech banana because of its shape) marks the area where speech sounds fall. Travis's audiogram indicates that he can perceive only a few speech sounds (/ng/, /el/, and /u/). Also note the differences in the profiles is for Travis's air conduction and bone conduction tests. The bone conduction test reveals that, when the middle ear is bypassed, his hearing is much closer to 0 dB. Travis's hearing loss either is temporary or can be corrected through surgery or other medical treatment. Most children with normal hearing have auditory thresholds at approximately 0 dB; Travis's thresholds are considerably below 0.

Unlike those with conductive hearing losses, students affected by a sensorineural loss are able to hear different frequencies at different intensities. Heredity and genetics, diseases such as meningitis, and **noise-induced hearing loss (NIHL)** are the primary causes of sensorineural hearing loss in young children and teenagers. For these students, hearing aids can have mixed results. The audiogram for Heather, below, indicates that she has a 30-dB sensorineural hearing loss. Note the similarity between her scores from the air conduction and bone conduction tests. Heather's hearing was also tested with her hearing aids on, as denoted by the *A* symbol on the audiogram. With the use of aids, Heather's hearing loss is not as serious; it is now at a mild functional level. Because Heather's hearing abilities, when she uses her hearing aids, lie above the blue area, Heather can hear speech sounds at the sound intensities measured during the hearing assessment.

Heather's Audiogram: Sensorineural Hearing Loss

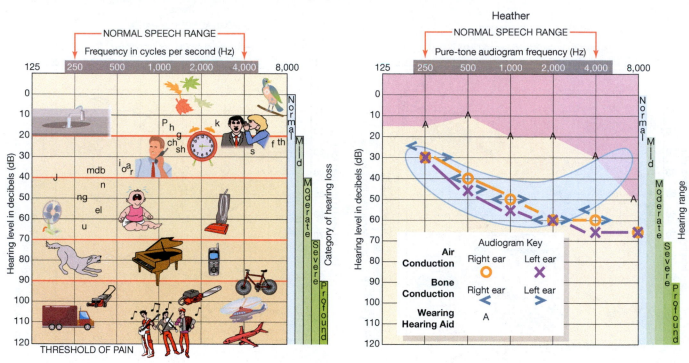

Does the type of hearing loss affect how well a person can hear? Teachers should not make assumptions about a student's ability to hear or process auditory information based on the type or degree of hearing loss. Such information does not always accurately represent the individual's ability to hear, nor does it automatically indicate the type of accommodations the individual will need. Why might this be so? The answer rests partly in the amount and type of **residual hearing**—how much functional hearing—the person has. When using a functional organizational system, hearing impairments are often divided into two categories:

- Hard of hearing—Information can be processed from sound, usually with the help of a hearing aid.
- Deafness—Limited sound can be perceived, but hearing is not the primary means of gaining information.

If the hearing loss falls in the mild range, the individual can hear nearly all speech sounds and most conversations. If the amount of loss is moderate and predominantly in the sound ranges for speech, using oral communication and developing good speech abilities are more difficult. At the other end of the continuum are those whose abilities provide them with little serviceable hearing even when they use hearing aids. People who are deaf have little, if any, residual hearing. Their ability to communicate with others and to learn academic subjects is seriously affected.

Topic 12.4 Prevalence and Placement

- In relation to other disabilities, very few students are deaf or hard of hearing.

- Many students with profound hearing loss, those who consider themselves Deaf, attend separate classrooms or separate schools.

How many students are hard of hearing or deaf? Hard of hearing and deafness are low-incidence conditions, so relatively few children have hearing loss. As the chart below shows, the percentage of students with hearing impairments is significantly smaller than the percentage of those with high-incidence disabilities. The CDC's most recent data indicate roughly 5,000 infants are born with hearing loss each year. However, the prevalence of hearing impairments is great among older Americans; estimates are that almost half of people over the age of 70 have hearing loss.

Disability Prevalence, 2014–2015 School Year

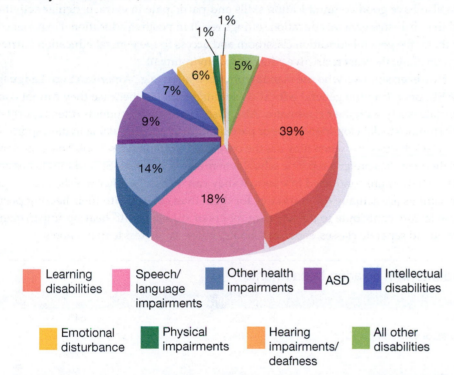

■ Learning disabilities	■ Speech/ language impairments	■ Other health impairments	■ ASD	■ Intellectual disabilities
■ Emotional disturbance	■ Physical impairments	■ Hearing impairments/ deafness	■ All other disabilities	

SOURCE: U.S. Department of Education. (2015). *Child Count and Educational Environments: Number and Percent of Students Ages 6 Through 21 Served Under IDEA, Part B, by Educational Environment and State.* Retrieved from http://www2.ed.gov/programs/osepidea/618-data/static-tables/index.html

Roughly 1% of students with disabilities receive special education services through IDEA's hearing impairments and deafness categories. However, these data do not reflect the actual percentage of students with hearing loss. One reason is that in reporting to the federal government, states can place students in only one category. About 40% of students with hearing impairments have additional disabilities, and they are often placed in another special education category. Some specific conditions have an increased likelihood of hearing impairments. For example, 75% of individuals with Down syndrome have a conductive hearing loss. However, these students are usually reported in the intellectual disabilities category. Many students with a hearing loss and another disability are reported in the multiple disabilities category, and students who are deaf and blind are assigned to the deaf-blindness category. To get a better idea of the prevalence of hearing impairments, with or without other disabilities, the following Websites contain additional statistics and demographics:

- Gallaudet Research Institute—http://research.gallaudet.edu/Demographics/
- Centers for Disease Control and Prevention—http://www.cdc.gov/ncbddd/hearingloss/data.html.

Where do students with hearing loss receive their education? The placement or rate of inclusion in the general education setting is somewhat masked by the data shown in the accompanying table. When comparing students with hearing loss to all students with disabilities who attend general education classes for some portion of the day, the percentages are slightly lower for those with hearing loss (see the first three rows in the table below). However, they are greater for special classes and separate schools. The reasons for these differences rest in the two distinct groups of students with hearing loss. Substantially more students have mild to moderate hearing loss than profound hearing loss. The interpretation of least restrictive environment (LRE) is very different for these two groups of students and their families. Students with mild to moderate hearing loss who also have good communication skills and participate in extracurricular activities find that inclusive general education settings result in positive educational experiences. For them, the general education classroom and access to the general education curriculum constitute the least restrictive educational environment.

However, students who use manual communication (e.g., **American Sign Language** or **ASL**) often find the general education setting restrictive because they cannot communicate easily with their classmates. Also, Deaf high school students often report few opportunities to develop friendships or participate in extracurricular activities, sports, or even class discussions when they are the only Deaf student at a school. These students and their families prefer a separate school where everyone uses ASL and the classes and other activities are conducted in a format they can access. In other words, these separate settings are actually *less* restrictive for them than classes with their hearing peers. These factors contribute to the larger numbers of students with hearing impairments who attend separate classes, separate schools, and separate residential schools.

Educational Environments for Students with Hearing Impairments[2]

Environment	Hearing Impairments	All Disabilities
Inside regular education class ≥ 80% of school day	60%	64%
Inside regular education class between 40% and 79% of school day	18%	20%
Inside regular class ≤ 39% of school day	9%	12%
Separate school	9%	3%
Residential facility	3%	0.4%
Homebound/hospital	0.2%	0.4%
Correctional facility	0.04%	0.2%
Parentally placed in private school	2%	1%

SOURCE: U.S. Department of Education. (2015). *Number and Percent of Students Ages 6 through 21 Served under IDEA, Part B, by Educational Environment and State.* [IDEA Section 618 Data Products: Static Tables, 2014-2015 Part B Child Count and Educational Environments]. Retrieved from http://www2.ed.gov/programs/osepidea/618-data/static-tables/index.html

Among the highest percentages of students with disabilities who graduate from high school with a regular diploma are those with hearing loss. Compared to students with other disabilities, this group (along with students who have visual impairments, about whom you will learn in the next chapter) has a fairly decent graduation rate (above 70%). In comparison, slightly more than 60% of students with learning disabilities and less than 45% of those with emotional or behavioral disorders earn standard high school diplomas.

[2]Percentages total to greater than 100% due to rounding.

Check Your Understanding 12.1

Click here to gauge your understanding of the concepts in this section.

Special Education

Learning Outcome

Explain the ways in which hearing loss can impact communication, interpersonal, and academic skills; describe accommodations that can lessen these challenges; understand methods that parents and classroom teachers can use to reduce challenges associated with hearing loss; and describe supports to help students who are deaf or hard of hearing transition to post-secondary options such as school, work, and independent living.

Topic 12.5 Challenges and Their Solutions

- Common challenges associated with hearing loss include language development, communication, academic achievement, interpersonal interactions, and social-emotional development.

- Solutions that can lessen the effects of hearing loss include early intervention, speech therapy, accommodations, American Sign Language, and assistive technology.

Topic 12.6 Accommodations

- Even students with mild to moderate hearing loss require accommodations to access content presented in class.

- Students who are deaf require accommodations to access information presented orally and, often, to communicate with others.

Topic 12.7 Early Intervention

- Nearly all newborns undergo otoacoustic emissions (OAE) hearing screening before leaving the hospital; early warning signs for infants and toddlers can help identify those who develop hearing loss later.

- Early intervention services result in strong long-term outcomes for children with hearing impairments.

Topic 12.8 School Years

- Teachers should consider adjusting certain aspects of the classroom routines, instruction, and environment to meet the needs of students with hearing loss.

- Most students with hearing loss use only speech to communicate, but almost half additionally use some form of manual communication.

Topic 12.9 Transition

- Many more postsecondary options exist now for students with hearing impairments than in the past.

- *Map It: What Comes Next?* is a series of free online training modules designed to help adolescents with hearing loss navigate the transition process.

Although some type of sign language is used by deaf individuals worldwide, each country's version of sign language is unique.

Topic 12.5 Challenges and Their Solutions

- Common challenges associated with hearing loss include language development, communication, academic achievement, interpersonal interactions, and social-emotional development.

- Solutions that can lessen the effects of hearing loss include early intervention, speech therapy, accommodations, American Sign Language, and assistive technology.

What challenges does hearing loss create? Humans learn and communicate by listening, speaking, observing, and reading. For most people, oral language is a substantial component of the communication process. Those who cannot hear or speak using oral language have a more restricted ability to communicate—a difference that shapes the way these students interact with others, the methods through which they are taught, the content of their curricula, and the related services they require for an appropriate education.

Issues differ widely across groups of students with hearing loss. For example, those who fall into the hard of hearing group—those with mild to moderate hearing loss—profit from assistive listening devices, like hearing aids, and may not qualify for special education services. Unfortunately, their needs may be overlooked because teachers assume that assistive devices fully compensate for the disability. In many cases, however, these students still have difficulties comprehending sounds in the environment, understanding speech, and engaging in oral communication. Those who were born deaf or whose deafness occurred in early childhood find it difficult to develop oral speech and to gain information through auditory means without substantial assistance. These individuals cannot understand sounds with or without hearing aids.

Key challenges faced by these children start with communication difficulties. Infants and toddlers who cannot hear speech sounds or words do not mimic them by babbling or imitating words; consequently, they often have delayed language development. The ability to hear is also related to speech intelligibility. As a general rule of thumb, intelligibility decreases as the degree of hearing loss increases, even with speech therapy.

These students often struggle in school. Language skills are the foundation for most subjects, so language delays affect their ability to learn academic content. Low academic achievement in reading is of particular concern. The attainment of strong reading skills is important because students must be able to read captions for television, videos, and movies, and they often communicate through written formats (texting, email) rather than by phone. And, students in middle school and high school learn as much from reading content area texts as through lectures, so the reading demands only intensify as students get older. They have further challenges if they miss key oral information during class. Many teachers are unaware of how significant even a small hearing loss can be. For example, in a noisy classroom, a loss of 16 dB (just within the range of what is considered normal hearing) can cause a student to miss up to 10% of what a teacher says, even when standing a mere three feet away. Without amplification through assistive technology, students with losses of 35 to 40 dB—clearly in the range of a mild hearing loss—may miss 50% of what the teacher or classmates say during discussions.

Interpersonal interactions and relationships can be affected if hard of hearing students miss pieces of oral conversations, instructions, or verbal communications during play ("I'm open!" during a basketball game), or even some non-verbal signals or cues (e.g., heavy sigh, throat clearing). When classmates cannot sign, Deaf students who use American Sign Language (ASL) can feel excluded. As a result, their social-emotional development can be affected.

Deafness and Hard of Hearing: Challenges

How can the challenges of hearing loss be lessened or overcome? One of the first steps is early identification and intervention. As you'll learn in Topic 12.7, universal infant hearing screenings allow babies only a few months old to be fitted with hearing aids and enable parents to start ASL immediately. It also permits parents to make decisions about **cochlear implants** and other types of surgical interventions while a child is very young.

Speech therapy is an important related service for children whose parents decide on an oral approach to communication. High levels of intelligible speech do not come automatically to children who are deaf or hard of hearing, even for those who wear hearing aids or have cochlear implants. Years of speech therapy are often warranted.

Accommodations, which you will read about in the next topic, are key to success in school. These students should receive support with many visuals (e.g., pictures, graphs, charts, and written notes), as well as with special seating arrangements so that they can see everyone who is taking turns speaking.

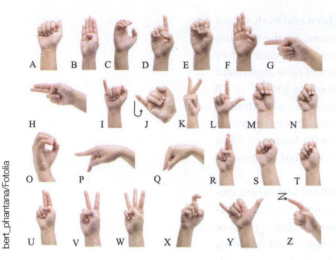

Although ASL generally uses signs that represent entire words or concepts, the individual letters of a word are manually spelled when no sign exists for a word or name. Use the photo above to sign the letters in your name.

For deaf students, ASL is an alternate means of communication. It is a complete and complex language and is not merely a translation of English. In fact, ASL is the fifth-most commonly studied foreign language on college campuses across the country! ASL has its own rules for grammar, punctuation, and sentence order. Further, it is not a universal language; each country's version of sign language is different. For example, British Sign Language (BSL) is very different from ASL.

Improvements in assistive technology now help individuals with hearing loss in many ways. For some, technology allows them to hear sounds. For others, technology enables them to compensate for significant hearing losses. Some of these technological supports are discussed in Topic 12.6.

Deaf Culture

Members of the Deaf community—note the capital D, which denotes a separate group from the overall deaf population—consider themselves a minority group, much like ethnic and racial minorities in this country. To them, deafness is not a disability but rather an aspect of their culture, rich in history and language, that unites them. Deaf communities around the world consistently report a sense of empowerment, belonging, and optimism.

The language of the American Deaf community is ASL, used in all aspects of their culture. For many Americans who are Deaf, ASL is a second language they learn later in life, often at residential schools where they also learn about Deaf

culture. A very small percentage of Deaf people learn ASL from birth. Typically, these individuals have at least one Deaf parent and are called **Deaf of Deaf** (being born Deaf of Deaf parents). They and their hearing siblings—who are called **CODAs** (Child of a Deaf Adult)—are typically proud of their Deaf heritage. Although these individuals clearly represent a minority within a minority, life can be substantially easier for them. They learn sign language as their native language, which they develop naturally and within typical milestone timeframes, just as hearing babies develop oral language. For these individuals, their deafness is a language difference, not a disability.

Deafness and Hard of Hearing: Solutions

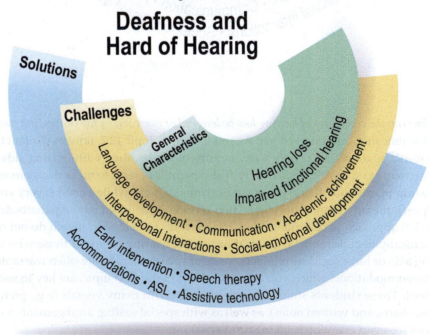

Deafness and Hard of Hearing

Solutions

Challenges

General Characteristics

Hearing loss • Impaired functional hearing

Language development • Communication • Academic achievement

Interpersonal interactions • Social-emotional development

Early intervention • Speech therapy

Accommodations • ASL • Assistive technology

Topic 12.6 Accommodations

- Even students with mild to moderate hearing loss require accommodations to access content presented in class.

- Students who are deaf require accommodations to access information presented orally and, often, to communicate with others.

Does every student with a hearing loss need accommodations to participate fully in the general education curriculum? Even a mild hearing loss in one ear can cause a student to struggle academically. One reason may be the extra effort required to listen carefully to the teacher, take notes, and process what is being presented. These students should be supported with many visuals and may benefit from a note taker. Classroom peers who are willing to be note takers can take a free online class—offered by Pepnet 2, a center funded by the U.S. Department of Education—that provides key information about hearing loss and describes effective note-taking strategies. To learn more, visit http://www.pepnet.org/training/notetaker. When not having to con-

Courtesy of FrontRow

This teacher, using an FM listening device, is providing an accommodation for a student with a moderate hearing impairment during whole-group instruction in his general education classroom. Some versions of this device have replaced the headset with a small microphone that clips to the teacher's collar.

centrate simultaneously on both understanding lectures and class discussion and also taking notes, students can focus fully on the instruction being presented. They may also benefit from accommodations such as preferential seating, which can place them closer to speakers or farther from noisy areas (e.g., doorways, pencil sharpeners, air vents). For class instruction and discussions, a U-shaped seating arrangement in which the student with the hearing impairment is sitting at either end (depending on which ear has the better hearing) is most effective for hearing and seeing the teacher and peers.

Another reason that students may struggle is that even a slight difference in hearing ability can make a big difference in what is understood. Recall that in a noisy classroom, a student with a slight hearing loss can miss up to 10% of what a teacher says even if he or she is close by, and those with mild hearing loss may miss 50% of what of being said in class. Even those students with cochlear implants or hearing aids—which often do not sufficiently eliminate background sounds in classroom settings, lecture halls, auditoriums, and other large, noisy environments—miss important information. **Assistive listening devices**, such as the two options highlighted below, can help prevent students from missing content that is presented orally. In fact, about 45% of students with hearing impairments use such devices.

- **FM (frequency-modulated) transmission device**—This wireless assistive listening device allows both teacher and student freedom of movement. The teacher speaks into a small microphone, and the student receives sound through a small receiver connected directly to his or her hearing aids. Background noise is reduced, and the teacher is free to move around the classroom without the worry of always needing to be in full view of all students.

- **Induction** or **hearing loops**—These inexpensive assistive listening devices amplify sound and reduce background noise in large rooms such as school auditoriums, concert halls, and theaters. As illustrated in the diagram below, these devices route sound from its source through an induction loop, where sound is passed directly to the listener's ear by means of a t-coil, a standard part of most hearing aids. An added benefit is that they do not require users with hearing aids to obtain additional specialized equipment to use the system.

Diagram of an Inductive or Hearing Loop System

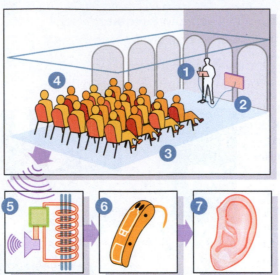

1. **Audio Inputs:** (e.g., existing PA system, dedicated microphone) feed audio signal to induction loop amplifier.

2. **Induction Loop Amplifier:** current is driven into audio loop or loops.

3. **Audio Loop or Loops:** current flowing through the cable creates a drop- and dead-free zone.

4. **Magnetic Field:** magnetic field signal comes to an individual's hearing aid.

5. **Hearing Aid:** equipped with a telecoil.

6. **Telecoil:** signal is amplified into high-quality audio signal and delivered directly to the individual's ear.

7. **Ear**

SOURCE: *Ampetronic: Listen to the Difference. How Do Induction Loops Work?* Retrieved from www.ampetronic.com/basics_how.asp. Source information and image Copyright © Ampetronic 2000–2012. All rights reserved.

What types of accommodations can teachers provide to help deaf students access the curriculum? Think about how much classroom time is allotted to providing oral instructions, describing processes, lecturing, and discussions. These components account for a large part of classroom instruction, and students who are deaf cannot process them. Even those who read lips miss a lot of information because they are unable to see the speaker's lips or are attending to other tasks such as taking notes. To help students access oral information, teachers can use visual aids, such as pictures, charts, visual cues, advance organizers, and written notes about the topic of discussion. In addition to missing information presented orally, these students may have very limited, if any, speech. Interpreters may be an effective accommodation for addressing both of these issues: They can translate oral information as well as communicate the student's thoughts and ideas to teachers and peers.

To assist students in accessing classroom content and curriculum that is presented orally, teachers can also present the material as printed text. One way to do this is by captioning, which can be accomplished in a variety of ways.

With real-time captioning, a transcriptionist is transcribing a lecture, which is projected on the screen so that students can access it as it is being delivered.

- Captioned videos—Through the same type of captioning that many individuals rely on to access information on news and TV programs when in a busy airport or working out, deaf students can access instructional content presented in educational videos. These captions—which may be **open captions** or **closed captions**—are a direct translation of what is being said.

- **Real-time captioning (RTC)**, also referred to as **Communication Access Real-time Translation (CART)**, involves a transcriptionist using a stenotype machine and special software to transcribe what is being said (e.g., in a lecture, speech, class discussion). Within two seconds the text is available for the student to read on his or her laptop computer, a screen, or a monitor.

The video below provides a demonstration of how CART services work.

▶ **Communication Access Realtime Translation: CART Services for Deaf and Hard-of-Hearing People**
https://youtu.be/qn4B0gyDosA

As with all students with disabilities, those with hearing impairments benefit from accommodations that meet their individualized needs. The following table lists some accommodations often used for students who are deaf or hard of hearing.

Examples of Frequently Used Accommodations for Students with Hearing Impairments

Presentation	Setting	Response	Scheduling or Timing
• Real-time captioning • Visual cues and prompts • Visual aids • Advance organizers • Captioning • Assistive listening devices	• Reduced noise • Reduced visual distractions • Preferential seating • Special lighting	• Note takers • Interpreters • Text-to-speech software	• Extended time to complete assignments • Breaks to reduce auditory and visual overload

Topic 12.7 Early Intervention

- Nearly all newborns undergo otoacoustic emissions (OAE) hearing screening before leaving the hospital; early warning signs for infants and toddlers can help identify those who develop hearing loss later.

- Early intervention services result in strong long-term outcomes for children with hearing impairments.

How is hearing loss detected in infants and young children? Most states have adopted universal hearing screening for infants, most of which happen at their birth hospital, allowing for early identification. Because infants cannot follow instructions or raise their hands in response to a sound, the air conduction audiometry method is not a valid assessment tool for newborns. Recall from Topic 12.1 that hair cells in the cochlea vibrate during the hearing process. When these hair cells vibrate, they create very low-level sounds called **otoacoustic emissions (OAEs)**. These emissions make it possible to screen newborns for hearing loss. In an OAE hearing screening, a small probe is placed in the child's ear canal and produces a low-volume sound. In response to the sound, the cochlea produces OAEs, which travel from the middle ear to the ear canal and then are picked up by a tiny microphone on the probe. The OAEs are analyzed within 30 seconds by a hand-held screening unit that indicates whether the infant passed the screening or should be referred for further testing.

The Early Childhood Hearing Outreach (ECHO) Initiative has a brief video that demonstrates the OAE hearing screening process.

▶ **How Otoacoustic Emissions (OAE) Hearing Screening Works**

http://www.infanthearing.org/flashplayer/echo-video-player-hd.htm?file=http://www.infanthearing.org/flashvideos/Hear%20and%20Now/Introduction%20to%20the%20OAE%20Procedure.mp4

Young children who initially pass OAE hearing screenings may develop a hearing impairment later due to factors such as **noise-induced hearing loss** or hereditary conditions. Parents and teachers should be alert to early warning signs of hearing loss, as indicated in the following table.

Early Warning Signs of Hearing Loss

Infants	Young Children
• Does not startle at loud noises • Fails to turn head toward sounds after 6 months of age • Is not speaking single words by 12 months of age • Turns toward visual cues (walking by, waving) but not auditory cues (calling his or her name) • Appears to hear sounds sporadically	• Has delayed speech or language • Has unclear or unintelligible speech • Has difficulty following directions (mistakenly attributed to lack of attention) • Responds to others' speech with questions ("What?") • Has TV or music volume up too high • Speaks in an excessively loud voice

How do early intervention services help infants and toddlers who are deaf and hard of hearing? Early intervention positively affects the lifelong outcomes of deaf and hard of hearing children. With early identification, young children can have IFSPs and receive family-centered early intervention services, which includes related services and assistive technology. Early intervention positively affects the speech, language, and achievement of these young children in the following ways:

- Allows children to be fitted with hearing aids as young as four weeks of age, or receive cochlear implants (which can now occur before their first birthday)

- Results in better reading achievement and speech abilities in later years, especially when initiated prior to the age of six months

- Supports the acquisition of language skills during the appropriate developmental periods through related services and high-quality preschool programs

- Helps families better understand and meet the unique needs of their children

Not all infants with hearing loss will have delayed language development. Deaf children of Deaf parents learn sign language during their infancy as their native language. They "babble" with their hands at about the same time that hearing infants make verbal babbling sounds. They produce two-word utterances in ASL at about the same time as their peers who do not have hearing losses. These Deaf children learn English as a second language. By the time they reach school age, most of them are reading two grade levels above deaf children of hearing parents.

Because this baby is learning ASL as his first language, he will probably meet all of his language developmental milestones.

Huntstock, Inc/Alamy

Topic 12.8 School Years

- Teachers should consider adjusting certain aspects of the classroom routines, instruction, and environment to meet the needs of students with hearing loss.

- Most students with hearing loss use only speech to communicate, but almost half additionally use some form of manual communication.

What do teachers need to know about working with deaf and hard of hearing students in the general education classroom? One of the most important things to keep in mind is that these students should be held to the same high standards as the rest of the class. Their hearing loss is a separate issue from their ability to learn the material, and one that can be adjusted for or worked around. The following box provides some general tips for teachers regarding recommended adjustments, many of which are applicable or helpful to *all* students.

Tips for Teachers: Adjusting Classroom Routines, Instruction, and Environments

Teacher Communications

- Articulate clearly, but do not talk louder unless you have an unusually soft voice.
- Speak more slowly, but avoid exaggerated lip movements.
- Say the student's name first, to ensure having his or her attention, before asking a question.
- Do not chew gum or cover your mouth when talking.
- Do not turn your back to the class when speaking.
- When moving around the classroom, be aware of how this may affect a student's ability to hear your voice or read your lips.
- Repeat information by paraphrasing.
- Instead of a whiteboard/chalkboard, use an overhead projector or computer projection system so the speaker can face the class when talking. Be sure there is no glare obstructing the projection.
- Do not stand with direct light behind you.

Additional Student Support

- Reduce background noise as much as possible.
- Alert student to shifts in content and topics of instruction.
- Provide handouts to support important information from lectures, guest speakers, field trips, and instructional media.

- Restate other students' questions if they cannot be clearly heard or seen by the student.
- For class discussions, make sure the student knows who is about to speak, and ensure that he or she can see each individual who is talking. Arranging students' chairs in a circle or U shape allows the student to see each classmate's face.
- Spend time talking with the student so each can be familiar with the other's speech.
- Remind the student to check the batteries for technology daily.

Assistance from Classmates

- Recruit classmates as note takers.
- Set up a buddy system: one classmate per class, unit, or topic.

Collaboration with Others

- Seek advice and information about the student's hearing status from the student and family members.
- Keep a file about settings for hearing aids or cochlear implants.
- Become aware and informed about the proper use of the student's technology; know how to troubleshoot.

What do teachers need to know about communication options for deaf students? Students with profound and severe hearing losses, who represent some 40% of all students with hearing loss, use a number of different communication systems, including manual communication or ASL, oral speech, or a simultaneous communication method, in which manual signs are produced at the same time as spoken words. The method of communication a student uses significantly impacts how instruction is delivered.

A number of methods combine sign and speech. For example, **cued speech** uses hand signals to help the student know what word was said when reading lips. Some words, like *pan* or *bat*, look alike when they are spoken, and cues can help indicate which word was actually said. **Signed English** is a form of manual communication that uses **finger spelling** to translate English. In this method each letter of the alphabet is assigned a sign and used to translate English: words are spelled out, but the rules of grammar and language are the same as for English speech. Another method, the **total communication approach**, uses a combination of oral speech and finger spelling. The student uses whatever communication mode is easiest and most effective. Most students who have cochlear implants use this method. Students who use forms of manual communication often are provided an interpreter, a valuable resource to the classroom teacher. Keep in mind, however, that interpreters are *not* teachers or educational assistants. Their job is not to teach students but to translate information that the teacher is conveying.

Tips for Teachers: Working with Interpreters

Planning and Organization

- Interpreters and teachers set up standard meeting times.
- They have established clear roles for working together during instruction.
- All meetings regarding the student are scheduled when the student's interpreter can attend.
- Storage and working space are designated for the interpreter.
- Lesson plans and supporting materials are shared days before the instructional activity.
- Teachers and interpreters have time to meet before the instructional activity to clarify vocabulary and content.

Classroom Organization and Management

- The interpreter and the student are able to see the teacher and each other.

- Placement for the interpreter is not distracting to other students in the class.
- Glare and other visual obstructions are eliminated.

Courtesy and Social Conventions

- Everyone talks directly to the student, not to the interpreter.
- Eye contact is with the student, not with the interpreter (even when the interpreter is speaking and translating manual communication for the student).
- The interpreter is not an academic tutor or classroom manager who resolves disruption.
- The interpreter translates everything that is spoken (e.g., students' comments), not just the teacher's lectures.

Topic 12.9 Transition

- Many more postsecondary options exist now for students with hearing impairments than in the past.

- *Map It: What Comes Next?* is a series of free online training modules designed to help adolescents with hearing loss navigate the transition process.

What types of postsecondary options are available for students with hearing impairments? Several decades ago, deaf students had few postsecondary options, and those few existed primarily because of funding from the federal government. College options have increased for deaf and hard of hearing students over the years. Today, Gallaudet University serves both undergraduate and graduate students and is the nation's only liberal arts university primarily for deaf students. The National Technical Institute for the Deaf (NTID) at the Rochester Institute of Technology in New York offers technical and vocational degrees. Other colleges and universities (e.g., California State University–Northridge, St. Paul College) provide two-year and four-year degrees. These are just a few of the postsecondary schools that welcome deaf and hard of hearing students.

IDEA does not have authority over colleges and universities; however, many of the accommodations that students received during their elementary and high school careers are now available to them in college. Most colleges and universities provide an array of accommodations: note takers, interpreting services, and assistive listening devices. Such readily available supports allow students with hearing loss to choose from many different schools.

What types of transition supports are available for students with hearing impairments? Like all students with disabilities, those who are deaf or hard of hearing should begin transition planning early and have individualized transition plans included in their IEPs. In addition to the different types of transition supports that you have learned about in earlier chapters (transition specialists, job coaches, vocational rehabilitation counselors), adolescents with hearing loss and their families can access help and support through Pepnet 2, a federally funded technical assistance center. The center's mission is to increase the education, career, and lifetime choices available to individuals who are deaf or hard of hearing. Technical assistance is provided through live, one-on-one support offered in a variety of communication modes, through in-person and online training, and via the project's Website (http://www.pepnet.org). One of the center's unique services is *Map It: What Comes Next?*—a series of free online interactive training modules to help adolescents navigate the transition process. The training is based on three questions: Who am I? What do I want? How do I get there? Students work through a series of video vignettes (signed in ASL with spoken English and captions), self-assessments, and sets of interactive questions that help them identify goals and the steps necessary to achieve them. Their work is saved in an electronic portfolio. More information on *Map It* can be found at http://www.pepnet .org/training/mapit.

Check Your Understanding 12.2

Click here to gauge your understanding of the concepts in this section.

People and Situations

Learning Outcome

Describe the history of instruction for students with hearing impairments and share some positive examples of inclusion.

Topic 12.10 Origins and History

- Across time, sign language has become the language of the Deaf, though not without some discord.

- The Deaf community, like all other minority groups, has had to fight for civil rights and social justice.

Topic 12.11 Personal Stories

- Individuals with hearing loss are experiencing greater inclusion in society than ever before.

- Some organizations that provide support and resources for individuals with hearing loss and their families are: the Laurent Clerc National Deaf Education Center, Pepnet 2, the Alexander Graham Bell Association for the Deaf and Hard of Hearing, and the National Institute on Deafness and Other Communication Disorders (NIDCD).

(left) In 1924, Dorothy Brett, born into British nobility, moved to New Mexico with D. H. Lawrence, a famous writer and artist of the time. She became a well-regarded painter and member of the Taos Artists. Brett was hard of hearing and used a hearing trumpet, which she called Toby, to help her hear. (right) An early hearing aid, which was called a hearing trumpet.

Topic 12.10 Origins and History

- Across time, sign language has become the language of the Deaf, though not without some discord.

- The Deaf community, like all other minority groups, has had to fight for civil rights and social justice.

How did the use of sign language become established in the Deaf community? Unlike other groups of individuals with disabilities, those with hearing loss have had access to specialized education for centuries. Typically, special programs were delivered separately, most often in separate schools. History tells us that specialized education for those with substantial hearing loss began in the 1500s. It was then that a Spanish monk, Pedro Ponce de León, demonstrated that deaf students could learn to read, write, and speak. Credited with being the first teacher of the deaf, de León taught his students through a combination of manual communication and writing. In the 1600s, William Holder and John Wallis began programs for deaf students in England. They adopted the teaching methods of de León and used both manual communication and writing in their instruction. All of these early programs were located in separate schools; typically, they were residential. By the 1700s, schools for the deaf had been established in England, Scotland, France, and Germany.

Thomas Hopkins Gallaudet, a young divinity student, started the first special school for the deaf in the United States. Because he was impressed with the manual communication techniques being used in France, he brought Laurent Clerc, a deaf Frenchman now regarded as the father of Deaf culture in America, to the United States. Together, in 1817, Clerc and Gallaudet began the first American school for deaf students in Hartford, Connecticut. There ASL formed its roots. It became the language of the Deaf in the United States and a symbol of Deaf culture in America.

However, segregated schools for the deaf and the use of manual communication became controversial. Edward Gallaudet, Thomas Gallaudet's son, and Alexander Graham Bell began what is now referred to as the "Hundred Years War." Each of these men had a deaf mother and a highly successful father. Bell invented the telephone and the audiometer and worked on the phonograph. Gallaudet was the president of the nation's college for the deaf, now named after him, and was a renowned legal scholar. These two men clashed over methods of communication. Bell believed that residential schools and the use of sign language fostered segregation and would lead to more marriages between deaf people. He thought a deaf variety of the human race would eventually result. Therefore, he proposed legislation to prohibit two deaf adults from marrying, eliminate residential schools, ban the use of manual communication, and prevent people who were deaf from becoming teachers. Gallaudet strongly opposed Bell's positions, and he won support from Congress for the manual approach, along with national funding specifically for deaf students at the postsecondary level. The resulting national network of schools for the deaf advanced the use of ASL, developed a tight-knit community of Deaf people, fostered Deaf culture, and supported advocacy for the rights of Deaf individuals.

Courtesy of the Museum of disABILITY

Frymire Archive/Alamy Stock Photo

Alexander Graham Bell and Edward Gallaudet each led camps that strongly disagreed about separate schools, separate language, separate culture, and separate lives for deaf people.

Has the path to social justice been easy for people with hearing impairments? Throughout time, this group of individuals has been surrounded by controversy as they have sought fair treatment and social justice. We already mentioned the Hundred Years War, during which contentious debates raged about deafness, humanity, segregation, and dignity. Bell and his followers believed that deafness was not a positive experience in the lives of people. However, those in the Deaf advocacy movement often refer to the Deaf who lived on Martha's Vineyard during the 1800s as a positive example of a fully inclusive society. You can read more about this extraordinary community in the following box.

Deaf Citizens of Martha's Vineyard

The seventeenth century settlers of Martha's Vineyard came from Kent, England. These settlers carried a recessive gene for deafness. As a result, many used sign language. The hearing residents of the island were bilingual, learning both oral and sign language skills early in life. For generations, over 25% of the island's residents could not hear. Because deafness occurred at such a high rate and in nearly every family, these deaf individuals were treated differently than deaf residents on the mainland. Those living on Martha's Vineyard had a real community presence and were included in all aspects of work, play, and church life. Unlike their counterparts on the mainland, they were free to marry whomever they wished. According to tax records, they generally earned average or above average incomes, with some becoming quite wealthy. Deaf individuals had some advantages over their hearing neighbors and family members. They were literate and better educated than the general population because they received tuition assistance to attend the school for the Deaf in Connecticut. As a result, many were leaders in their communities. There are numerous accounts about hearing people asking their Deaf neighbors to read something to them or write a letter for them. For more than 200 years, life in this relatively isolated environment was much the same for those with and without hearing loss. These citizens demonstrated that a disability does not have to be a handicap. Their story is often used when the abilities of Deaf people and their civil rights are questioned. To learn more about this fascinating story, go to https://www.verywell.com/deaf-history-marthas-vineyard-1046546

As you learned in Topic 1.5, Deaf pride has united the Deaf community since the 1980s and has been a catalyst for the group's advocacy for civil rights. In 1988, Gallaudet University's Board of Trustees appointed a hearing president who did not know ASL. Protests from Deaf Gallaudet students and the Deaf community erupted and the crisis was dubbed "Deaf President Now Movement." The campus was closed and the students marched on Washington, DC. The results were that I. King Jordan became the first Deaf college president and the Deaf advocacy movement gained solidarity.

Sarah L. Voisin/Washington Post/Getty Images

I. King Jordan served as Gallaudet's eighth president, from 1988 to 2006. He served on various committees and commissions under three former U.S. Presidents—H.W. Bush, Bill Clinton, and Barack Obama—and raised international awareness about deafness and hard of hearing issues.

Topic 12.11 Personal Stories

- Individuals with hearing loss are experiencing greater inclusion in society than ever before.

- Some organizations that provide support and resources for individuals with hearing loss and their families are: the Laurent Clerc National Deaf Education Center, Pepnet 2, the Alexander Graham Bell Association for the Deaf and Hard of Hearing, and the National Institute on Deafness and Other Communication Disorders (NIDCD).

How inclusive is society for individuals with hearing loss? Awareness and support for individuals with hearing loss continues to improve. Earlier in this chapter, you learned about Deaf culture. This community provides a sense of inclusion and acceptance for those who are deaf, with all events and activities not only accessible but also designed with deafness as the primary consideration. Deaf West Theatre, a theater group based in Los Angeles, includes both hearing and deaf actors in its shows. Deaf West's plays are written in ASL or have been translated into ASL. They recently received national attention after earning three 2016 Tony nominations for the musical *Spring Awakening*: Best Revival of a Musical, Best Director of a Musical, and Best Lighting Design of a Musical. They performed a scene from that show at the 70th Annual Tony Awards, which you can view at the following link: https://youtu.be/CSagsMcak4Q

In contrast to Deaf culture and groups like Deaf West Theatre, organizations like No Limits (http://nolimitsfordeafchildren.org/) help children with hearing impairments feel more comfortable using speech by improving their communication skills and self-esteem through theater-based and educational programs. Plays produced by No Limits are original and are written specifically for children who are deaf or hard of hearing, with the goal of improving their interactions with peers and increasing their abilities to express themselves.

Kids with No Limits

You can learn more about No Limits and hear from some of their students and families in this video: https://youtu.be/lhuT_2P5t3s

Although Deaf individuals have a strong community, they can feel isolated from those who only communicate orally. As a result, Deaf people can face communication challenges at work or in activities of daily life (e.g., shopping). Yet, common uses of technology, such as texting or email, can make communication easier.

As the video below shows, when hearing individuals are willing to learn different ways to communicate, Deaf individuals feel less isolated and more included.

▶ **Barista Learns Sign Language for Customer**

https://youtu.be/6-pMZBQrjcU

On the Screen: *Switched at Birth*

The television series *Switched at Birth* focuses on two fictional families whose teenage daughters—one of whom is Deaf—were switched at birth. The characters use ASL, and the show provides a glimpse into Deaf culture and the lives of Deaf people and their families. In particular, one episode—which focused on the impending closure of the school for Deaf students and their transfer to neighborhood schools—was conducted entirely in ASL. The episode addressed the sense of security and belonging they feel with classmates who are Deaf and some of their concerns about attending school with hearing classmates.

https://youtu.be/qp_MQWHMo9s

What organizations or agencies are available to support children and adolescents with hearing loss and their families? A number of organizations and agencies provide valuable information and offer support. We highlight several of them here.

- The Laurent Clerc National Deaf Education Center (http://www.gallaudet.edu/clerc-center/about-us/mission.html) is a federally funded center on deaf education, located at Gallaudet University in Washington, DC. It maintains two demonstration schools (birth through eighth grade, high school) and develops, evaluates, and disseminates school curricula, materials, and information on instructional techniques and strategies. The center's Website contains a wealth of information on many topics: ASL, assistive technology, Deaf culture, early intervention, family resources, hearing aids, and more.

- Pepnet 2 (http://pepnet.org/), mentioned earlier in the chapter, is a federally funded center that supports the postsecondary education, training, and employment of individuals who are deaf and hard of hearing. In addition to resources on these topics, the center also provides information in many areas: technology, communication options, accommodations, and co-existing disabilities. To increase career awareness, the center has a video library that features deaf and hard of hearing adults in many different professions (veterinarian, pediatrician, optometrist, certified financial planner, lawyer).

- The Alexander Graham Bell Association for the Deaf and Hard of Hearing (www.agbell.org) promotes oral language development, early intervention, and early diagnosis. It also promotes total communication and other methods to ensure that deaf and hard of hearing students begin learning to communicate as early as possible. The organization provides considerable support and information for parents.

- The National Institute on Deafness and Other Communication Disorders (NIDCD) (https://www.nidcd.nih.gov/health/hearing-ear-infections-deafness), part of the National Institutes of Health, has current data and statistics on deafness and hearing loss as well as information on a broad range of subjects (e.g., noise-induced hearing loss, ASL, assistive devices, captions). The agency also offers material specifically for parents and health professionals.

Check Your Understanding 12.3

Click here to gauge your understanding of the concepts in this section.

Future Perspectives

Learning Outcome

Describe the benefits of early intervention and prevention, and identify technological advances in the treatment of hearing loss.

Topic 12.12 Prevention: Universal Screenings and Exposure to Environmental Noise

- Universal hearing screenings of infants allow for both early diagnosis and treatment and better chances for strong language development and communication skills.

- Noise-induced hearing loss (NIHL) can be prevented by avoiding prolonged exposure to common sounds in the environment.

Topic 12.13 Technology: Improved Devices and Medical Advances

- There are different types of hearing aids; those worn by children often do not provide the same level of sound quality as the more expensive versions worn by adults.

- Cochlear implants and auditory brainstem implants are surgical options for individuals with sensorineural hearing loss.

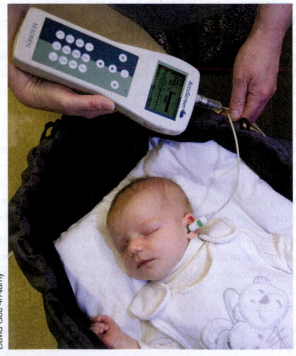

This newborn is getting an OAE (otoacoustic emissions) hearing screening through the Early Hearing Detection and Intervention program.

Topic 12.12 Prevention: Universal Screenings and Exposure to Environmental Noise

- Universal hearing screenings of infants allow for both early diagnosis and treatment and better chances for strong language development and communication skills.

- Noise-induced hearing loss (NIHL) can be prevented by avoiding prolonged exposure to common sounds in the environment.

How have advances in early detection technologies improved outcomes for infants and toddlers with hearing loss? Two factors allow children with severe and profound hearing impairments and their families to receive important early intervention services during infancy:

1. The discovery of otoacoustic emissions (OAEs), the low-level sounds made when hair cells in the inner ear vibrate (mentioned in Topic 12.7)

2. State laws that now mandate **universal newborn hearing screening**

The development of special equipment that can recognize OAEs makes it possible to diagnose deafness in newborns and then implement critical early intervention services. In 1993, only 11 hospitals nationwide screened the majority of their newborns. At the same time, some 70% of children with profound hearing loss were not identified until their preschool years. Today, *every* state has established an Early Hearing Detection and Intervention program and 97% of all infants are screened during the first few months of life. Infants with permanent hearing loss are identified before the age of three months, usually before they leave the hospital after birth, and they receive early intervention services before the age of six months. Early recognition is important because it allows babies with hearing loss to be fitted with hearing aids and be given early language development interventions. Otherwise, these children would not develop language and communication skills during key developmental periods, which would impact them throughout their lives.

What types of hearing loss can be prevented? Noise-induced hearing loss (NIHL) is almost 100% preventable, but it is not well understood by the public. NIHL is the reason for hearing loss in over 22 million teenagers and adults. It usually occurs slowly, across years of exposure, without any pain or awareness, but it can lead to deafness. While the one-time sound of an explosion can result in immediate deafness, exposure to noise of 85 dB for sustained periods can also damage the ear's hair cells and cause sensorineural hearing loss.

Medical professionals have noted an alarming increase in NIHL among young adults; recent studies show that one in five teenagers has some type of hearing loss. In fact, the World Health Organization (WHO) now estimates that 1.1 billion young people worldwide are at risk for hearing loss from unsafe listening levels on personal devices and in entertainment venues (e.g., concerts, clubs). The popularity of earbuds and headphones is largely to blame. Because earbuds are inserted into the ear canal and are closer to the eardrum, the volume of whatever is being listened to (e.g., music, movie, telephone conversation) can be increased by nearly 10 dB—the difference between the relatively safe noise levels of an alarm clock (90 dB) to the unsafe levels of a motorcycle (100 dB). When the earbuds do not form a tight seal in the ear, users turn up the volume even more to drown out background noise. Exposure to music at 100 dB for more than 15 minutes is also unsafe, yet common for young adults at clubs and concerts. To avoid NIHL associated with earbuds and headphones, consider these precautions:

- Use the 60/60 rule—Listen at no more than 60% of a device's maximum volume, for no more than 60 minutes per day.

It is rather shocking to realize that these tiny devices threaten the hearing abilities of a large proportion of the world's population!

- What can others hear?—Determine whether those around you can hear what you are listening to. If they can, even if it's muffled, the volume is loud enough to cause permanent damage.

- Use noise-canceling headphones—Although these still pose a risk if used at high volumes for extended periods, they reduce or eliminate background noise and thus can be used at lower volumes.

- Use parental controls—Many devices now come with parental controls that can limit or lock volume levels.

When engaged in any activities with probable dangerous noise levels (e.g., going to a club, riding a motorcycle, mowing the lawn), wear earplugs. Parents should also carry earplugs for young children, even for events such as football or basketball games, where the noise from the crowd, opening ceremonies (e.g., cannon fire, jet fly-overs), or celebrations (e.g., fireworks at the end of a game) can cause damage. Other NIHL risks, such as listening to loud music in the car, can be reduced by simply turning down the volume.

Many other causes of childhood hearing loss are preventable. For example, maternal rubella (German measles) was once a major cause of deafness in newborns; in 1972, it was responsible for almost 11% of known cases of deafness. Today the incidence rate is negligible because almost everyone is protected from the disease through vaccinations. Also available are vaccines to prevent meningitis, another cause of hearing problems (and other disabilities). Many colleges and universities require students to get this vaccine prior to living in the dorms.

Topic 12.13 Technology: Improved Devices and Medical Advances

- There are different types of hearing aids; those worn by children often do not provide the same level of sound quality as the more expensive versions worn by adults.

- Cochlear implants and auditory brainstem implants are surgical options for individuals with sensorineural hearing loss.

What are the different types of hearing aids? As you learned in Topic 12.6, *Accommodations*, most deaf and hard of hearing students use some sort of assistive listening device, such as hearing aids. These devices pick up sound through a microphone, amplify it, and then deliver it to the ear through a speaker. Since the development of small batteries in the 1950s, hearing aid technology has advanced rapidly and now audiologists can fit infants as young as four weeks old with hearing aids, providing them with better access to sounds and improving their language and learning potential. Hearing aids are of two types:

- Behind-the-ear (BTE)—A plastic case that contains the electrical components of the aid, worn behind the ear, is connected to an ear mold in the outer ear. The sound travels from the aid through the mold and then into the ear.

- In-the-ear (ITE)—A plastic case that holds the electronic components fits inside the outer ear. Variations of this type are in-the-canal (ITC) hearing aids, which are molded to fit the person's ear canal, and completely-in-canal (CIC), which is barely visible in the ear.

Types of Hearing Aids

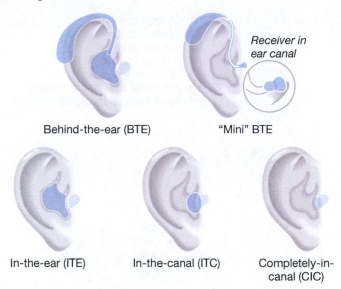

Behind-the-ear (BTE)

"Mini" BTE

Receiver in ear canal

In-the-ear (ITE)

In-the-canal (ITC)

Completely-in-canal (CIC)

Styles of hearing aids

Source: NIH/NIDCD

For several reasons, BTE hearing aids are recommended for small children. First, the size of the ear canal changes as children grow, causing them to outgrow ITE hearing aids on a regular basis. Second, the ITE cases are made of hard plastic which, if damaged, can cut a child's ear canal during typical childhood play activities. Third, ITC and CIC aids are extremely small; young children, whose fine motor skills are not fully developed, have difficulty adjusting and removing these types of aids. Finally, the small size of the ITE aids makes them easier to lose, and their higher price makes them more expensive to replace.

Many hearing aids can now be programmed for different environments; the user can select and adjust the settings accordingly. Moreover, digital hearing aids can be programmed to amplify certain frequencies more than others. Even so, teachers should be aware that the types of hearing aids worn by most students will not have the degrees of selectivity of those worn by adults. In general, a child's hearing aid is more likely to amplify *all* sounds. So, while the sound of the teacher's voice is magnified, so is the background noise in the classroom (e.g., foot or pencil tapping, whispering). Also, sounds that are farther away from the student become muffled. As a result, a teacher's voice could sound relatively clear at a distance of three feet but sound muted at a distance of 10 feet. Some frequencies are harder to amplify than others. A student with a hearing aid may be able to understand the speech of her female teachers, but have difficulty deciphering that of a male teacher with a particularly deep voice. Finally, be aware that children may take their hearing aids out or turn them off; in some cases a student might simply need an auditory break.

What types of medical innovations are available for individuals with hearing loss? Cochlear implants work very differently from hearing aids. They are surgically implanted and help those with sensorineural losses. These devices have four important parts:

- Microphone—picks up sound from the environment

- Speech processor—selects and organizes sounds from the microphone

- Transmitter/receiver/stimulator—receives signals from the processor and converts them to electrical impulses

- Electrode array—collects impulses and sends them to regions of the auditory nerve

The following figure shows a typical cochlear implant.

Cochlear Implant

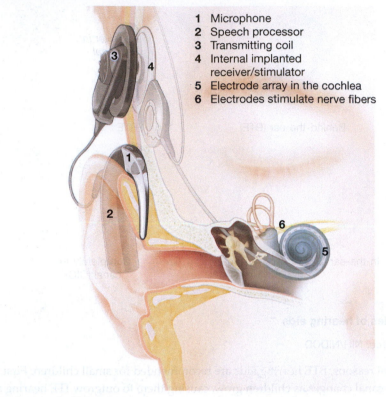

1 Microphone
2 Speech processor
3 Transmitting coil
4 Internal implanted receiver/stimulator
5 Electrode array in the cochlea
6 Electrodes stimulate nerve fibers

SOURCE: Courtesy Cochlear Ltd.

The following video shows the process of how a cochlear implant works in more detail.

▶ **How a Cochlear Implant Works**

https://youtu.be/zeg4qTnYOpw

Because the implant relays electrical signals rather than sounds, people who receive cochlear implants must learn to interpret the signals, which usually requires therapy provided by an audiologist. Additional speech and language therapy is usually warranted to improve speech production. Data indicate that speech and oral language outcomes are better when children with profound deafness receive implants as infants, so children are increasingly receiving cochlear implants before their first birthday. The government estimates that some 38,000 children and 58,000 adults now have these implants. Bilateral cochlear implants, in which an individual has a cochlear implant in each ear, are becoming more common.

Outcomes for those with cochlear implants vary depending on the type of hearing loss. For those who have postlingual deafness, cochlear implants allow them to hear and understand sounds once again. For them, the turnaround from silence to hearing is almost miraculous. However, speech production after surgery is difficult for children who never had functional hearing to begin with and, therefore, had never learned to interpret environmental sounds. Although many children who received implants as infants do develop understandable speech, it can take 10 years of intensive speech therapy to achieve this goal. As a result, many of those who receive cochlear implants during early childhood rely on *both* sign language and oral speech to communicate with others. Although some develop remarkable oral speech abilities, many do not. Finally, the use of cochlear implants is disputed in the Deaf community, whose members feel that an infant or child with hearing loss should be accepted and celebrated rather than subjected to an operation that permanently destroys the cochlea.

Auditory Brainstem Implant

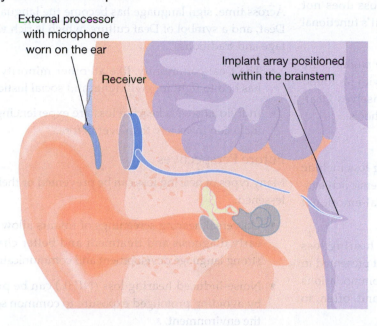

External processor with microphone worn on the ear

Receiver

Implant array positioned within the brainstem

The **auditory brainstem implant** is a more recent medical advance that builds on cochlear implant technology. With an auditory brainstem implant, a surgically implanted device bypasses the cochlea and auditory nerve and stimulates the part of the brain that processes sound. The auditory brainstem implant has two parts:

- External component—a processor that is worn on the ear, through which sound is received by a microphone, translated from a sound wave to an electrical signal, and then transmitted to the internal component

- Internal component—a device, placed just below the skin near the ear, that contains a receiver that picks up information from the external component and relays it to an implant array that is implanted in the brainstem

This type of device is an option for individuals for whom a cochlear implant is not possible because their auditory nerves do not work or have been removed due to other medical conditions (e.g., a tumor).

Check Your Understanding 12.4

Click here to gauge your understanding of the concepts in this section.

Summary

Deafness and Hard of Hearing Described

The normal process of hearing involves many steps and allows us to turn sounds into meaningful information.

- IDEA uses the term *deafness* to refer to the most severe type of hearing loss and *hearing impairment* to refer to all other types.

- Audiologists use air and bone conduction methods to test hearing abilities and chart the results on audiograms.

- Hearing loss can be categorized by type, severity, or the age at which the hearing loss occurred.

- Hearing loss, whether temporary or permanent, has many causes. The degree of hearing loss does not always accurately represent an individual's functional or residual hearing abilities.

- In relation to other disabilities, very few students are deaf or hard of hearing. Many students with profound hearing loss, those who consider themselves Deaf, attend separate classrooms or separate schools.

Special Education

Common challenges associated with hearing loss include language development, communication, academic achievement, interpersonal interactions, and social-emotional development.

- Even students with mild to moderate hearing loss require accommodations to access content presented in class. Students who are deaf require accommodations to access information presented orally and, often, to communicate with others.

- Nearly all newborns undergo otoacoustic emission (OAE) hearing screening before leaving the hospital; early warning signs for infants and toddlers can help identify those who develop hearing loss as they grow older, and early intervention services can then be put into place.

- Teachers should consider adjusting certain aspects of the classroom routines, instruction, and environment to meet the needs of students with hearing loss.

- Most students with hearing loss use only speech to communicate, but almost half additionally use some form of manual communication.

- Many more postsecondary options exist now than in the past for students with hearing impairments. To help them plan their futures, *Map It: What Comes Next?*—a series of free online training modules—can help adolescents with hearing loss navigate the transition process.

People and Situations

Across time, sign language has become the language of the Deaf, and a symbol of Deaf culture, which is rich with heritage and traditions.

- The Deaf community, like all other minority groups, has had to fight for civil rights and social justice.

- Individuals with hearing loss are experiencing greater inclusion in society than ever before.

Future Perspectives

Many types of hearing loss can be prevented or their impact lessened.

- Universal hearing screenings of infants allow for both early diagnosis and treatment and better chances for strong language development and communication skills.

- Noise-induced hearing loss (NIHL) can be prevented by avoiding prolonged exposure to common sounds in the environment.

- There are different types of hearing aids; those worn by children often do not provide the same level of sound quality as the more expensive versions worn by adults.

- Cochlear implants and auditory brainstem implants are surgical options for individuals with sensorineural hearing loss.

Addressing CEC Standards

Council for Exceptional Children (CEC) knowledge standards addressed in this chapter: 6.2, 1.0, D&HH1K1, D&HH1K2, D&HH1K3, D&HH2K2, D&HH5S5, D&HH7K1, D&HH8S1, D&HH10K1, D&HH10S1.

See the Appendix for the complete CEC Initial Level Special Educator Preparation Standards.

Chapter 13
Visual Disabilities: Low Vision and Blindness

Photograph of the artist courtesy of Laurie and Michae Naranjo.

"I don't know if I would have been a better sculptor if I could see. My work might be somewhat different or the same. I don't know, but one thing is for sure: I don't think that I am disabled. I don't have time to have a disability because I am working too much, too hard, and I'm having too much fun doing what I'm doing."

After he was wounded in the Vietnam War and lost his sight, Michael Naranjo was sent to a school for blind students and told to learn to make wallets. He refused. After much negotiating, he was finally allowed to carve a piece of wood. Michael writes, "For the next month I carved a fish jumping out of water. I don't know if anyone looking at the piece would have known what it was, but *I* knew." He continued to hone his skills, and now his works are found in important collections around the world, including those in the Vatican and in the White House. He and his wife, Laurie, contribute their time and expertise to Very Special Arts, a program for young artists with disabilities. They have also established numerous tactile art exhibits at museums and gardens across the country. Yet, had Michael not fought against the low expectations that his instructor held for him, his influence in the art world—and on all of the young artists with whom he has worked—would have been lost.

—Quotations courtesy of Michael Naranjo

Learning Outcomes

Low Vision and Blindness Described

Explain the different definitions for visual disabilities and the purposes of each, understand the functions of vision screenings and assessments, recognize the characteristics of students with visual disabilities, and understand the various settings in which these students receive their education.

Special Education

Explain how visual disabilities can impact all areas of a student's school experience; describe how specialized instruction, accommodations, and assistive technology can reduce the challenges of vision loss; and describe steps that parents, caregivers, and teachers can take to help compensate for vision loss in the early years, address additional curricular needs in the school years, and reduce poor employment outcomes during adulthood.

People and Situations

Explain how the education of students with visual disabilities has changed over time and describe how accommodations and assistive technology can support the attainment of life goals.

Future Perspectives

Explain how the effects of vision loss are being reduced or eliminated through medical and technological advances.

Low Vision and Blindness Described[1]

Learning Outcome

Explain the different definitions for visual disabilities and the purposes of each, understand the functions of vision screenings and assessments, recognize the characteristics of students with visual disabilities, and understand the various settings in which these students receive their education.

Topic 13.1 Low Vision and Blindness Defined

- The vision process is complex and involves many optical components.

- Some definitions of visual disabilities distinguish between conditions—such as *low vision* and *blindness*—while other definitions indicate the age of onset or are used to qualify for government services.

Topic 13.2 Types of Low Vision and Blindness

- Vision screenings identify potential vision problems, while comprehensive vision assessments, conducted by specialists, identify and treat various types of visual conditions.

---

[1]References for Chapter 13 are found at the end of this text.

- Visual disabilities can be caused by damage to optical components, disruption to the visual process, or interference with the brain's ability to interpret visual stimuli.

Topic 13.3 Characteristics

- Students might display certain physical and learning characteristics that can alert teachers to the presence of a visual disability.

- Play behaviors and social skills of children with visual impairments may be different from those of their sighted peers.

Topic 13.4 Prevalence and Placement

- Visual disabilities are a low-incidence disability, with very few schoolchildren receiving services through this IDEA category.

- Most students with visual disabilities receive their education in general education settings with the support of vision specialists.

Vision screenings, which include a brief observation of a child and her eyes, often provide the first indication of vision problems.

gwimages/Fotolia

Topic 13.1 Low Vision and Blindness Defined

- The vision process is complex and involves many optical components.

- Some definitions of visual disabilities distinguish between conditions—such as *low vision* and *blindness*—while other definitions indicate the age of onset or are used to qualify for government services.

How does the vision process work? The vision process is complicated and involves both optical and neurological components. When people have normal vision, four elements must be present and operating:

1. Light
2. Something that reflects light
3. An eye processing the reflected image into electrical impulses
4. A brain receiving and giving meaning to these impulses

Structure of the Human Eye

The eye is a very complicated mechanism. Vision loss occurs when this mechanism is damaged or obstructed in such a way that objects in the environment cannot be perceived or understood. Damage to any part of the eye can result in serious limitations to an individual's abilities to see and process visual information.

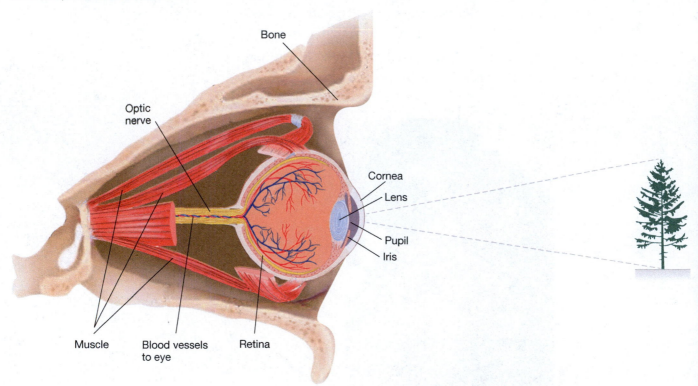

How are visual disabilities defined? People with **visual disabilities**, also referred to as visual impairments, have limited use of their sight. The functional sight they have varies greatly in type and amount. Visual disabilities are often divided into two categories:

1. Low vision—Students with **low vision** have some functional sight, but the ability to perform daily activities is affected. In these cases, **residual vision** can be further developed for use in many school activities, including reading. You may be surprised to learn that the majority of students with visual disabilities use vision as their primary method of learning.
2. Blindness—Students who are **blind** have no functional vision and may perceive only shadows or movement. These students must be educated through other sensory channels, such as touch and hearing.

There are numerous definitions of visual impairments, some of which were developed for specific purposes. For example, the federal government uses multiple classification systems for visual impairments, depending on the purpose of the designation. For special education eligibility, the IDEA definition of *visual disabilities* includes both *partial sight* (what we refer to as low vision) and *blindness*. For non-educational purposes, the federal government uses the terms *low vision* and **legally blind** to identify individuals who are eligible for special benefits. The following table compares some of these terms and definitions, including those from various federal agencies, from professional organizations, and within the visual disabilities field.

Definitions of Visual Disabilities

Term	Definition	Source
Visual impairment	Visual impairment, including blindness, means an impairment in vision that, even with correction, adversely affects a child's educational performance. The term includes both partial sight and blindness. (Note: used to qualify for special education services)	IDEA '04, U.S. Department of Education
Vision impairment	Visual acuity less than 20/40 with the best possible correction in the better-seeing eye, and excluding those whose vision loss categorizes them as *blind*.	Centers for Disease Control
Low vision	Vision problems alone, or combined with other health problems, that prevent an individual from working. (Note: used to qualify for Social Security Disability Insurance and/or the Supplemental Security Income (SSI) programs)	Social Security Administration
	A level of vision which, with standard correction, hinders an individual in the planning and/or execution of a task, but which permits enhancement of the functional vision through the use of optical or nonoptical devices, environmental modifications and/or techniques.	Anne Corn, education professional, researcher
Legally blind	Vision that cannot be corrected to better than 20/200 in the better eye or a visual field of 20 degrees or less in the better eye. (Note: used to qualify for Social Security Disability Insurance and/or the Supplemental Security Income (SSI) programs)	Social Security Administration
	Central visual acuity of 20/200 or less in the better eye, with best correction, and/or a visual field of 20 degrees or less.	American Foundation for the Blind and Centers for Disease Control

SOURCES: From 34 CFR Parts 300 and 303, *Assistance to States for the Education of Children With Disabilities and the Early Intervention Program for Infants and Toddlers With Disabilities; Final Regulations* (p. 1265), U.S. Department of Education, 2006, *Federal Register*, Washington, DC; American Foundation for the Blind, 2017, *School Experience for Children and Youth with Vision Loss*, retrieved from www.afb.org/section.aspx?FolderID=2&SectionID=15&TopicID=411&DocumentID=4897; Centers for Disease Control and Prevention, 2011, *Blindness and Vision Impairment*, retrieved from http://www.cdc.gov/healthcommunication/ToolsTemplates/EntertainmentEd/Tips/Blindness.html; *Instruction in the Use of Vision for Children and Adults with Low Vision: A Proposed Program Model*, by Anne L. Corn, Spring 1989, Education Resources Information Center (ERIC), *Review, 21*(1), pp. 26–28; Social Security Administration, 2015, *If You're Blind or Have Low Vision—How We Can Help*, retrieved from http://www.ssa.gov/pubs/EN-05-10052.pdf.

Another way to define visual disabilities is by **age of onset**. Individuals who are **congenitally blind** have been blind since birth or infancy. Those who lost their sight after the age of two are **adventitiously blind**. This distinction is important because people who lose their sight after age two have some memory of what things look like. The later the disability occurs, the more they remember. Visual memory is an important factor in learning, for it can influence one's understanding of visual concepts. To gain a better understanding of how difficult it can be to grasp some visual concepts, look at the picture next to this text. Now, imagine that you have never had any sight. How could someone help you understand concepts like *beautiful, blue, reflection,* or *cloud* to describe this ocean scene?

Iakov Kalinin/Fotolia

Topic 13.2 Types of Low Vision and Blindness

- Vision screenings identify potential vision problems, while comprehensive vision assessments, conducted by specialists, identify and treat various types of visual conditions.

- Visual disabilities can be caused by damage to optical components, disruption to the visual process, or interference with the brain's ability to interpret visual stimuli.

How are visual disabilities identified? In most states, vision screenings are recommended for school-age children. During a screening, students typically receive a cursory test of their visual acuity using a **Snellen chart**. The chart comes in two versions: one version uses the letter E placed in various positions in different sizes; the other uses rows of alphabet letters in different sizes.

The Snellen chart was originally developed by a Dutch ophthalmologist in 1862.

Ideally, the vision screener—often a trained volunteer, a school nurse, or a pediatrician—also briefly observes the child for any problem indicators (e.g., an awkward head tilt, watery or unfocused eyes). It is also helpful to include teachers' observations about classroom behaviors and performance, such as whether a child complains about scratchy eyes or headaches, rubs his or her eyes excessively, or has difficulty discriminating letters or symbols when completing classroom assignments.

Once a screening identifies possible eye or vision problems, the student is then referred for further diagnosis and treatment to an eye specialist:

- **Ophthalmologist**—a medical doctor who specializes in eye disorders, conducts physical examinations of the eye, prescribes corrective lenses and medicines, prescribes drugs, and performs surgery

- **Optometrist**—a professional who measures vision, prescribes corrective lenses, and makes functional recommendations

- **Optician**—a specialist who fills the ophthalmologist's or optometrist's prescription for glasses or corrective lenses

In a comprehensive eye exam, visual acuity is more precisely assessed. Normal visual acuity, which is measured by how accurately a person can see an object or image 20 feet away, is defined as 20/20. A person whose vision is measured at 20/40 sees at 20 feet what people who do not need visual correction (glasses or contact lenses) can see at 40 feet away. Although states and school districts vary in the criteria they use to determine eligibility for special education services, people with visual acuity measuring 20/70 to 20/200 in the better eye, with correction, are typically considered to have low vision. Acuity below 20/200 classifies an individual as legally blind.

The eye specialist will also assess **field of vision**, which is measured in degrees. Normal field of vision is about 160 to 180 degrees horizontally and includes both central vision and peripheral vision. You may have heard the term **tunnel vision**, which refers to a severely restricted field of vision in which the individual has central vision but limited peripheral vision.

Visual Acuity and Field of Vision

As the photos below illustrate, an impaired visual field is different from decreased visual acuity, yet they may occur simultaneously. The visual field is the area one can see when looking straight ahead, typically 160 to 180 degrees wide. When a person's visual field is reduced to 20 degrees or less, he or she is considered legally blind.

Normal acuity

Normal visual field

Impaired lower visual field

Impaired acuity

Impaired peripheral fields

"Blind spots" in the visual field

SOURCE: Photos courtesy of the IRIS Center, Peabody College, Vanderbilt University.

What are the different types of visual disabilities, and how do they occur? The following table lists conditions that affect various parts of the eye.

Common Eye Conditions

Type	Definition
Conditions of the Eye	
Myopia	Nearsightedness; allows focus on objects close but not at a distance.
Hyperopia	Farsightedness; allows focus on objects at a distance but not close.
Astigmatism	An eye disorder that produces images on the retina that are not equally in focus.
Amblyopia	"Lazy eye"; reduced vision in one eye due to inadequate use during early childhood.
Strabismus	Improper alignment of the eyes, which can cause one or both eyes to turn in (crossed) or out.
Nystagmus	Rapid, involuntary movements of the eye that interfere with bringing objects into focus.
Conditions of the Cornea, Iris, and Lens	
Glaucoma	Fluid in the eye is restricted, causing pressure to build up and damage the retina.
Aniridia	Undeveloped iris due to lack of pigment (albinism); results in extreme sensitivity to light.
Cataract (opacity of the crystalline lens)	A cloudy film covering the lens of the eye.
Conditions of the Retina	
Diabetic retinopathy	Changes in the eye's blood vessels caused by diabetes.
Macular degeneration	Damage to a small area near the center of the retina; results in restricted central vision and difficulties in reading and writing.
Retinopathy of prematurity (ROP)	Retinal damage in premature infants caused by abnormal blood vessel growth.
Retinal detachment	Detachment of the retina; interrupts transmission of visual information to the brain.
Retinitis pigmentosa	Genetic eye disease; leads progressively to blindness; night blindness is the first symptom.
Retinoblastoma	A tumor that impairs vision.
Condition of the Optic Nerve	
Atrophy	Reduced function of the optic nerve.

The most common eye problems in children are **myopia** (nearsightedness), **strabismus** (crossed eyes), and **amblyopia** ("lazy eye"), although these conditions do not result in vision loss severe enough to require special education services. With both amblyopia and strabismus, the misalignment of the eyes usually results from the inability of the eye muscles to work together. Glasses, surgery, and eye exercises are all successful treatment options for these conditions, so special education is rarely required. The severity of many of the other disorders can be reduced by corrective lenses and advances in medical technology.

As you'll learn in Topic 13.4, the number of children who require special education services because of visual impairments is exceptionally low—less than 0.06% of the total public school population. So, while some of the conditions in the table above are common causes of visual impairments, many are relatively rare in the general population. One such example is **retinopathy of prematurity (ROP)**, a condition that affects premature infants. In ROP, premature retinal blood vessels fail to grow toward the edge of the retina, instead growing in the wrong direction. In severe cases, scar tissue develops and can cause retinal detachment. Hereditary

Teap/E+/Getty Images

This child has amblyopia. Treatment often involves covering the strong eye, forcing development of the weaker eye's muscles.

conditions (e.g., **albinism**) can also produce visual disabilities. **Congenital cataracts**, another common reason for childhood blindness, can affect newborns through factors like maternal infection or reactions to antibiotics given for those infections. In older children, trauma to the eye through accidents, household mishaps, and sports injuries can cause vision loss.

Jen Pham/Alamy Stock Photo

Many of the childhood accidents that cause vision loss or blindness can be prevented through proper adult supervision or protective sports gear.

Topic 13.3 Characteristics

- Students might display certain physical and learning characteristics that can alert teachers to the presence of a visual disability.

- Play behaviors and social skills of children with visual impairments may be different from those of their sighted peers.

What characteristics do students with visual disabilities display? As you have learned throughout this text, a disability does not affect any two individuals in exactly the same way. The same is true for visual disabilities, which can influence aspects of behavior, physical activity, social skills, and academic performance differently for each child. Teachers must be alert to subtle cues that suggest a vision problem. An observant child care provider or teacher who notices signs such as those listed in the following table can refer the child for screening or further assessment.

Possible Signs of Vision Problems

Appearance of the Eyes	Problems with Schoolwork	Behavior and Movement
The student's eyes	The student has difficulty	The student
• water excessively	• reading small print	• appears clumsy
• are red or continually inflamed	• identifying details in pictures	• bumps or trips over objects
• appear crusty	• discriminating letters	• displays eye–hand coordination problems (e.g., catching a ball)
• seem dull, wrinkled, or cloudy	• doing close work	• covers an eye while reading
• are swollen		• tilts head
• look gray or white (one or both pupils)		• holds an object close to an eye to view it
• are not aligned		• complains of headache after working on an assignment

Some characteristics of visual disabilities are tied to **visual efficiency**—how well an individual can use his or her sight. A student with very poor acuity might lean forward and squint at a teacher in an attempt to improve vision. A child with a restricted field of vision might look at a teacher from an angle, placing the teacher in the portion of her visual field that she can access best. In contrast, a blind student might not train her eyes on the teacher at all, instead turning or tilting her head to the side to create optimal listening conditions.

For students who have some sight, visual efficiency can be influenced by many factors: time of day, setting, or lighting levels. Types of font and color contrast can also affect how well visual text can be viewed. For example, look at each of the following font samples and answer the following questions: Which font was easiest to read? What characteristics made it easiest to read (size, font type, contrast between font color and background)? Which option(s) do you think would be better to use with a student who has a visual impairment?

Once upon a time...	12-point Calibri font
Once upon a time…	12-point Times New Roman font
Once upon a time...	*12-point Handwriting-Caflisch Script font*
Once upon a time...	16-point Calibri font, bold, black on white contrast
Once upon a time...	16-point Calibri font, bold, white on black contrast
Once upon a time...	16-point Calibri font, bold, black on blue color contrast
Once upon a time...	16-point Calibri font, bold, dark green on light green color contrast
Once upon a time...	16-point Calibri font, bold, yellow on light bue color contrast

How are non-academic areas affected by vision loss? Children with visual disabilities might exhibit delays in areas involving gross motor skills that are dependent on sight. They may also show preferences for activities that differ from those of their peers, or they may not display certain common behaviors at all. Let's look at two areas in which these delays are often evident, play skills and social skills, and how educators can promote the development or improvement of these skills.

PLAY SKILLS   Play, an important part of human development, promotes exploration and the development of motor, social, and language skills. Children with visual disabilities typically demonstrate a two-year lag in the development of play skills. Teachers might observe that these children play very differently from others in that they:

- Engage in high rates of solitary play.
- Seek out adults rather than other children.

- Avoid spontaneous play.
- Prefer noisy play activities to abstract or symbolic ones.
- Become disoriented by quick, unpredictable movements of sighted peers.
- Select only toys that are concrete, familiar items.

Although children at this age usually run and play, this child may prefer to remain in one spot due to the visual challenges associated with navigating through the playground, its equipment, or the fast-paced requirements of many group games.

Sighted children might not understand these behaviors and thus prefer sighted playmates. Simply putting children together—whether for parent-coordinated play dates or during recess at school—will not guarantee voluntary play between sighted children and those who are blind. To ensure positive interactions, adults may need to provide explicit instruction to both sighted children and those with visual impairments.

SOCIAL SKILLS   Recall that a child who is congenitally or adventitiously blind has little or no memory of how the world looks. This child does not respond to her mother's smile or to a wave from a friend, so she has fewer opportunities for indirect social learning. While sighted children begin learning social skills in infancy, often through typical interactions, many young children with visual disabilities need explicit instruction to learn them. For example, looking at someone's face when he or she speaks is an expected behavior during conversations, yet it could be considered irrelevant by a child with severely limited sight. Nevertheless, students with visual impairments might need explicit instruction on facing someone who is speaking in order to not appear rude or to increase comfort levels for sighted individuals who are not used to listeners turned in other directions.

Social skills develop further during childhood, so inappropriate or immature social behaviors can inhibit a child's ability to make friends, join in games, or resolve conflicts. Students with visual disabilities may:

- Ask too many irrelevant questions.
- Not understand conversational expectations like taking turns or facing the speaker.
- Stand too close (i.e., invade personal space).
- Engage in inappropriate acts of affection.
- Be less assertive than their sighted peers.

Teachers, peers, and family members can help children gain social competence. Instructors can teach the explicit and implicit rules of games and social interactions. Peers can be taught to model appropriate social skills, to prompt their classmate when these skills should be applied, and to provide feedback. And parents can organize play dates and give feedback to their child about his or her interpersonal interactions. The following box provides examples of how teachers can promote positive social interactions in their classrooms.

TIPS for Promoting Positive Social Interactions

For the student with low vision or blindness

- Provide instruction and practice in everyday social conventions (turning toward the speaker).
- Prompt and reinforce students when they display appropriate body language.
- Teach appropriate methods for initiating conversations and activities with others.
- Teach and monitor appropriate eating etiquette (e.g., chewing with your mouth closed), and explain why improper manners might irritate peers.
- Provide instruction on nonverbal cues, such as tone of voice, to interpret another person's emotional state or reaction.

For classroom peers

- Explain the nature of the student's visual impairment (if the student is comfortable with this).
- Provide examples of what the student can and cannot see (e.g., "Shaquan can tell that a shadow approaching is a person, but he can't identify which person it is.").
- Coach them to call the student's name when they want his attention, rather than simply starting a conversation (in which the student may not realize he is expected to participate).
- Encourage them to identify themselves to the student when initiating contact.
- Explain why a student might engage in a certain behavior that they find annoying (e.g., holding on to a peer's clothing when going out to recess) and discuss positive ways to communicate how they would prefer the student to behave.

Topic 13.4 Prevalence and Placement

- Visual disabilities are a low-incidence disability, with very few schoolchildren receiving services through this IDEA category.

- Most students with visual disabilities receive their education in general education settings with the support of vision specialists.

How many students have visual disabilities? Due to factors associated with aging, the vast majority of people with visual disabilities are over the age of 65. In contrast, the incidence of low vision and blindness among children is exceptionally small. Although approximately one-fourth of all school-age children have impaired vision, the use of eyeglasses or contacts can correct the majority of these issues. Most do not need special education because their vision can be improved sufficiently to avoid a negative effect on educational performance. Nationally, only 25,491 students with visual disabilities between the ages of 6 and 21, the majority of whom have low vision, are receiving special education services. It is important to understand that nearly two-thirds of children with visual disabilities have more than one disability, and that they are not counted in the visual disabilities category. If a student also has a hearing impairment, he or she will most likely be counted in the deaf-blind category (see Chapter 14). If a child has impaired vision and moderate or severe intellectual disabilities, the child will likely be included in the multiple disabilities category (also in Chapter 14). Yet, even with the various combinations of disability categories taken into consideration, only a small fraction (0.06% to 0.1%) of all schoolchildren have visual disabilities requiring special education services, a clear indication that visual impairments are a low-incidence disability.

Where do students with visual disabilities receive their education? The following figure depicts the educational placements for students with visual disabilities in the United States. Most attend neighborhood schools with the support of vision specialists, whom you'll learn about in Topic 13.8. These students participate in the general education curriculum alongside their sighted peers—with whom they will eventually compete for employment as adults—thus underscoring the need for teachers to hold them to the same high expectations.

Educational Environments for Students Ages 6–21

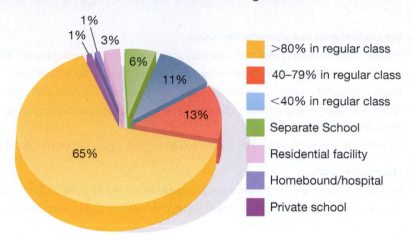

Legend:
- >80% in regular class
- 40–79% in regular class
- <40% in regular class
- Separate School
- Residential facility
- Homebound/hospital
- Private school

65%, 13%, 11%, 6%, 3%, 1%, 1%

Although most students with visual disabilities attend neighborhood schools, it is important to recognize that specialized schools (e.g., residential or separate schools for the blind) play a vital role in the educational system. Remember that IDEA requires students to have an array of educational placement options that meet their individual needs; specialized schools are part of that continuum. The faculty and staff have expertise and training in visual disabilities, and the facilities are often state-the-art, designed with visual accommodations as a primary consideration rather than as an afterthought. Students can be part of a community where they do not feel different. Because all instruction and school activities are conducted with the necessary supports in place, students have more opportunities to participate in extracurricular activities, clubs, and sports. In addition to providing services to students in their own schools, over 80% of specialized schools provide outreach services to public school students with visual disabilities, including direct instruction by **teachers of students with visual impairments (TVIs)** and **orientation and mobility (O&M) instructors**. Specialized school staff members also provide consultation services and conduct inservice and professional development activities for general educators so that they are better able to provide instruction to these students.

Check Your Understanding 13.1

Click here to gauge your understanding of the concepts in this section.

Special Education

Learning Outcome

Explain how visual disabilities can impact all areas of a student's school experience; describe how specialized instruction, accommodations, and assistive technology can reduce the challenges of vision loss; and describe steps that parents, caregivers, and teachers can take to help compensate for vision loss in the early years, address additional curricular needs in the school years, and reduce poor employment outcomes during adulthood.

Topic 13.5 Challenges and Their Solutions

- In addition to academic skills, visual disabilities can affect other areas of a student's school experience, such as navigating the school building or interacting with others.

- Solutions that can lessen the effects of visual disabilities include specialized education, accommodations, and assistive technology.

Topic 13.6 Accommodations

- Students with low vision often require different accommodations than students with blindness.

- Teachers can make simple changes to the classroom environment to make it safer and easier to navigate for students with visual disabilities.

Topic 13.7 Early Intervention: Motor and Concept Development

- Parents and caregivers can creatively engage infants and toddlers with visual disabilities in activities that will support early motor development.

- Infants and toddlers with vision loss require extra instruction to learn concepts their sighted peers learn through observation.

Topic 13.8 School Years: The Expanded Core Curriculum

- Blind students must learn specialized skills not covered in the general education curriculum.

- Instruction in orientation and mobility must begin early and can include the use of canes and guide dogs.

- IEP teams must take multiple factors into account when considering braille use.

Topic 13.9 Transition

- Adults with visual disabilities face challenges in finding full-time employment, starting with misperceptions held by hiring managers and human resources personnel.

- Improved employment outcomes for adults with visual disabilities start with increased career awareness in the early years, part-time jobs during adolescence, development of job-related skills as part of the expanded core curriculum, and the use of assistive technology.

siraanamwong/Fotolia

Can you see the number 7 in this picture? If not, you may have a color vision defect (color blindness). Most people with color blindness have trouble distinguishing colors in the red-green spectrum.

Topic 13.5 Challenges and Their Solutions

- In addition to academic skills, visual disabilities can affect other areas of a student's school experience, such as navigating the school building or interacting with others.

- Solutions that can lessen the effects of visual disabilities include specialized education, accommodations, and assistive technology.

What challenges do visual disabilities create? In the first part of this chapter, we discussed various types of vision loss and how they affect functional vision. That vision loss, depending on the degree of severity, results in a number of challenges (see the following figure).

Visual Disabilities: Challenges

Visual Disabilities

Challenges

General Characteristics

Visual acuity challenges
Impaired visual field
Poor or no functional vision

Gross motor skills • Abstract concepts • Play skills • Social skills • Independent movement • Sight-dependent academic tasks

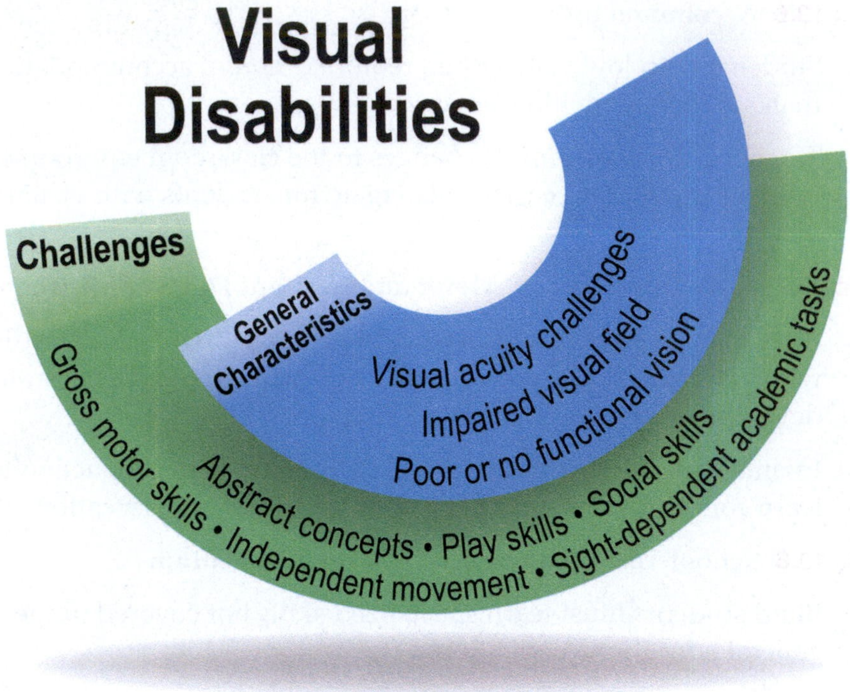

Classroom teachers may tend to focus on academic challenges and how the visual impairment affects a student's ability to see the board, read from a textbook, or watch a video. Remember, however, that a large part of the school day requires a student to move independently from one place to another: finding one's way from a desk to the small-group area; walking from the classroom to the cafeteria and proceeding through the lunch line; traveling from the cafeteria to the playground, gym, or wherever one's friends are hanging out; or successfully navigating playground equipment or playing in games with peers. Further, these same activities (among many others) require skills in social interactions: working well with others in small groups, conversing with friends at lunch, or exhibiting good team sportsmanship. Comprehension of even small communicative gestures (e.g., rolling eyes, shrugging shoulders) or subtle moments (e.g., the class falls silent when the principal appears in the doorway) is dependent on the ability to see. Without cues or prompts from others, children with visual impairments can miss nuances that result in embarrassment, misunderstandings, or more.

How can the challenges of visual disabilities be lessened or overcome? Because visual impairments can affect so many facets of life, these students may require extra instruction in areas that their sighted peers do not: braille skills as an alternative to reading print; orientation and mobility skills to assist navigation through their environment; and training on new assistive technologies that can help compensate for vision loss. Further, this extra training requires that education personnel not only work on the skills needed by the child at a particular time, but also plan ahead for the skills the child may need in a few months, in a few years, or even as an adult. Classroom teachers and specialists must coordinate efforts so that students can practice their skills and use assistive technology successfully in general education settings, in leisure settings with their peers, or in independent activities of their choosing.

The next section of this chapter focuses on accommodations, educational interventions, and other solutions to challenges faced by students with visual impairments (see the figure below). Keep in mind that many of these practices, while introduced or discussed in one section or for one age group, often span several. For example, although we discuss issues tied to concept development in Topic 13.7, all students—those with visual disabilities as well as their sighted peers—will be introduced to both concrete and abstract concepts throughout their entire school careers. We discuss the use of **braille** and the **expanded core curriculum** in Topic 13.8, yet a child's introduction to braille and many other skills begins much earlier and continues through graduation.

Visual Disabilities: Solutions

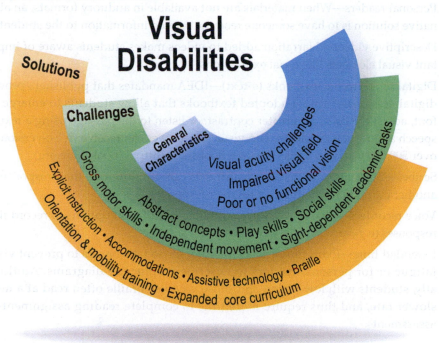

Topic 13.6 Accommodations

- Students with low vision often require different accommodations than students with blindness.

- Teachers can make simple changes to the classroom environment to make it safer and easier to navigate for students with visual disabilities.

What types of accommodations do students with low vision and blindness require? Because the needs of students who have low vision differ from those who are blind, different accommodations might be required, although some accommodations are beneficial for all students with visual impairments. Remember that teachers must adjust their approach to working with a student based on his or her individual needs and the demands of each situation. Additionally, students with visual disabilities often must use assistive devices for success at school. Some of these are discussed below; others will be covered in Topic 13.13.

This student is using a common hand-held magnifier to view the small details on a globe.

ACCOMMODATIONS FOR ALL STUDENTS WITH VISUAL IMPAIRMENTS For students with visual impairments, accessing information presented in books or by the classroom teacher can be challenging. Completing classroom assignments or assessments can also be difficult, especially if a handwritten response is required. To help students with visual disabilities overcome some of these barriers, the teacher can provide accommodations, such as:

- Recorded books and texts—Many books and texts are available on CDs or as electronic files. To access these auditory formats, students will need equipment to play the recorded books (e.g., CD player).

- Personal readers—When materials are not available in auditory formats, an alternative solution is to have someone read the printed information to the student.

- Descriptive videos—Narration added to videos makes students aware of important visual elements like facial expressions.

- Digital or electronic textbooks (e-text)—IDEA mandates that publishers provide digital versions of school-adopted textbooks that allow students to enlarge the font, adjust the color for greater contrast, or listen to the passage using a text-to-speech application. Students with visual disabilities can receive free e-versions of over 500,000 texts and books through Bookshare (http://bookshare.org).

- Scribes—Students with visual impairments can communicate their responses to another individual who then writes their responses.

- Voice recorders—Students can use a number of different options to record their responses (e.g., recording devices, computer software).

- Extended time—Extra time allows for students to take breaks to prevent visual fatigue or for personal readers to describe graphics or diagrams. Additionally, students with low vision and those who use braille often read at a much slower rate, and thus require more time to complete reading assignments or assessments.

ACCOMMODATIONS FOR STUDENTS WITH LOW VISION Recall that the majority of students with visual impairments use vision as their primary method of learning. Many students with low vision are able to read the standard 12-point font used in elementary and high school textbooks, although they may need to hold books closer to their eyes than their peers to adjust for varying type and print styles. For those not able to access standard print in textbooks or when visual information is presented in other formats, students may benefit from the following accommodations:

- **Enlarged print**—Many standard publications (e.g., dictionaries, *Reader's Digest*) are readily available in enlarged print. If the larger version is not available, teachers can enlarge print by using copiers, scanners, and computers.

- **Magnification devices**—Students can use magnifiers to enlarge print in books or worksheets. When reading from a distance (e.g., text on a whiteboard), these students might require a hand-held telescope.

- **Visual cues**—Using boldface print or highlighting items in the text can draw attention to items of importance.

- **Preferential seating**—The location of the student's desk can affect how well he or she accesses information. For example, a student might need to sit closer to the board or away from a window that produces problematic glare.

The video below shows a demonstration of several devices that students with low vision can use to enlarge print. The video incorporates the use of **audio description**, another type of accommodation for students with visual disabilities.

▶ **CCTV Caption DVO**

https://www.youtube.com/watch?v=A7rOabs5HUo

ACCOMMODATIONS FOR STUDENTS WHO ARE BLIND   Students who are blind differ greatly from students with low vision. Many don't read print, but instead have text materials translated into other formats. In addition to the audio recordings and text-to-speech (e.g., digital books) options mentioned above, students who are blind might benefit from the following accommodations:

- **Tactile materials**—To make visual information such as graphs, charts, figures, or diagrams accessible, teachers can provide representations adapted for touch. The Perkins School for the Blind has demonstration videos for teachers on how to adapt physical environments, make science lessons accessible, and develop tactile graphics: http://www.perkinselearning.org/

- **Braille**—Braille is a method of representing letters, numbers, punctuation marks, and words through the use of raised dots that can be read with one's fingers.

Alsu/Shutterstock

Braille books are an accommodation for students who do not have enough residual vision to read regular or enlarged print.

Stevie Wonder's Grammy Pitch for Greater Accessibility

After performing at the 2016 Grammy Awards, Stevie Wonder presented the award for the Song of the Year category. Before announcing the winners (Ed Sheeran and Amy Wadge for "Thinking Out Loud"), he joked with audience members about their inability to read the envelope, which was in braille. He then went on to acknowledge the need for accessibility for all people in all activities of life.

https://www.youtube.com/watch?v=Hta9F0OrQ7U

The following table highlights a number of accommodations that benefit students with visual disabilities. Some of these accommodations are used for all students with visual impairments, while others are more commonly used for those who have low vision (LV) or those who are blind (B).

Frequently Used Accommodations for Students with Visual Impairments

Presentation	Setting	Response	Scheduling or Timing
Recorded books and texts	More physical space for materials or equipment	Scribes	Extended time
Personal readers	Small-group administration	Voice recorders	Breaks
Descriptive videos	Preferential seating (LV)	Writing answers on a computer	Testing across multiple days
Digital or electronic textbooks	Reduced glare (LV)	Electronic note taker	
Enlarged print (LV)	Direct lighting (LV)	Recording answers in the test	
Magnification devices (LV)	Minimized visual distractions (LV)	booklet (LV)	
Visual cues (LV)		Brailler (B)	
Tactile graphics (B)			
Braille (B)			
Talking calculator (B)			

What types of accommodations can teachers make to the classroom environment? In addition to providing instructional accommodations, teachers can make simple changes to the classroom's physical environment, such as those listed in the following box.

Accommodations to the Classroom Environment

Modifying the Physical Environment

Make the Classroom Safe

- Open or close doors fully (a half-open door can be a dangerous obstacle).
- Teach students to push chairs under desks.
- Familiarize students with potential problem areas such as low obstacles (trash cans), protruding objects (pencil sharpeners), and changes in floor elevation (steps).
- Secure rugs or mats firmly to the floor.

Arrange the Furniture Carefully

- Eliminate clutter (e.g., electrical cords), particularly in aisles.
- Keep frequently used furniture and materials in consistent places.
- Place coat cubbies or stands near classroom entrance; position other storage areas to be easily accessible.
- Provide larger desks and storage areas to accommodate technology devices.

Consider Lighting Needs

- Use window shades with adjustable blinds to allow for increase or reduction of light.
- Seat the student where glare is minimized.
- Use glare-resistant computer screens.
- Use floor or desk lamps to provide additional lighting if necessary.
- Avoid placing equipment in front of windows.

Use Contrasting Colors

- Cover the student's desk with brightly colored paper to help him or her locate it easily.
- Attach high-contrast, colorful shapes to drawers, cupboards, and other frequently used materials.
- Use dark letters on pale backgrounds for bulletin boards.

SOURCE: IRIS Center (2006a). http://iris.peabody.vanderbilt.edu/v01_clearview/challenge.htm

Learn more about accommodations for students with visual impairments by visiting the following IRIS Module.

▶ **IRIS Module: Instructional Accommodations: Making the Learning Environment Accessible to Students with Visual Disabilities**
http://iris.peabody.vanderbilt.edu/module/v02-successsight/

Topic 13.7 Early Intervention: Motor and Concept Development

- Parents and caregivers can creatively engage infants and toddlers with visual disabilities in activities that will support early motor development.

- Infants and toddlers with vision loss require extra instruction to learn concepts their sighted peers learn through observation.

How is early motor development affected by vision loss? The sense of sight contributes to achievement of the most basic infant and toddler developmental milestones, beginning with simple movements such as reaching for and touching objects they see. Sighted infants who are placed on their stomachs will lift their heads to observe their environments, then later use their arms to push upward to get a better view of their surroundings. In doing so, they develop their head and neck muscles first, then those in their arms and torsos. These initial activities prepare them for later stages of physical movement in which they learn to propel their little bodies toward objects of interest by rolling, scooting, crawling, and eventually walking—a milestone usually achieved around the age of 12 months.

In contrast, infants with visual impairments do not see tantalizing objects in their environments, so they have less motivation to reach for things, to raise their bodies off the ground, or to move to another location. This lack of physical activity results in delayed **gross motor** development. These infants often learn to walk after age two, frequently skipping the creeping and crawling stages, and continue to have gross motor delays and problems with eye-hand coordination throughout their preschool years.

Because the home is a baby's natural environment, most programs for blind infants include home-based instruction with considerable family involvement. Family members and caregivers can support motor development by attending to subtle cues and responding through auditory and tactile means. For example, infants and toddlers with vision loss or blindness will lean toward an object of interest—one that has bright colors or flashing lights, or that makes appealing sounds. Adults can respond by bringing the object to the child's hands for tactile exploration, and then providing verbal descriptions as the child explores. Later, objects can be moved slightly out of reach, encouraging the child to move toward the object, gradually increasing the space between the child and the desired item. Family members and caregivers can also support the development of muscle control and strength by playing games that require movement or exploration; even seemingly simple actions like rocking to the beat of music can contribute to head or torso muscle development. One of the hardest, yet most important, undertakings for parents is to encourage independence. To this end, they must allow their infants and toddlers to explore the environment, knowing that they will get the same bumps and bruises as young children without vision loss. Parents can even encourage early mobility training using typical play items such as toy lawn mowers and other push toys that can support walking. These toys also provide a safety measure; because the toy is pushed in front of the child, it will bump into furniture and walls first, signaling obstacles to be avoided.

What strategies can support concept development for children with visual disabilities? For typically developing young children, many new words and concepts are introduced visually: a mother points to an illustration in a picture book and labels it "elephant"; or a sibling gestures toward the sky and says, "Wow, look at the moon!" Parents and caregivers must make extra efforts to support concept development for young children with visual disabilities by providing opportunities to touch items that other children learn about through sight, and that might not be part of normal tactile experiences (e.g., cupboards, ceilings, curtains, car steering wheels).

Children with visual disabilities can benefit from having books read to them when simple adjustments are made. Adults can describe the pictures in a book in more detail than they would normally, providing extra explanation when the picture displays information critical to the story. Some companies produce tactile picture books specifically for infants and toddlers with visual disabilities and, with the advent of

Boca/Fotolia

This infant is pulling himself across the floor to get to the brightly colored ball that has captured his attention.

Casey A. Cass/University of Colorado

These are examples of some of the 3-D book pages that the Tactile Children's Book Project develops. Children with visual disabilities can feel the items in the illustrations of a story.

three-dimensional (3D) printing, even more options could soon be available (see the Tactile Children's Book Project for pictures: http://www.tactilepicturebooks.org).

In other cases, caregivers can adapt books they already have by tracing around the outlines or details of pictures using a hot glue gun or tactile craft supplies. Children can then feel the unique characteristics of objects in the book that they probably would not get the opportunity to touch in real life—an elephant's trunk or tusks, a barn's silo, or the many shapes of the moon.

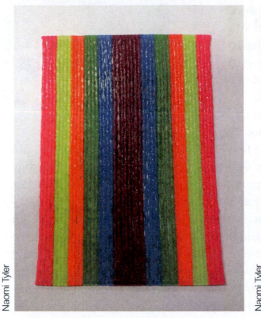 

In this children's book, key features of the prince's wardrobe (crown, pendant) and ceremonial objects (scepter, orb) have been outlined using WikkiStix®.

Other concepts are learned indirectly, as in the case of a child who figures out what *bright* is after hearing repeated uses of the word on sunny days, under football stadium lights, and in reference to a flashlight. Because young children with visual disabilities cannot visually observe all of the activities going on around them, adults must also explicitly explain and describe what is happening: "Goldie [the dog] is using her front paw to scratch behind her ear. The jingling noise is from the tags on her collar. Her paw keeps hitting them." This description can be aided through tactile means. It might be hard for the child to touch the dog's paw while she's scratching, but the adult could move the child's hand to his or her own ear, simulate the scratching motion, and say, "This is what Goldie is doing." The important point to remember is that parents, family members, and caregivers need to find alternate ways to communicate anything that would normally be observed through sight; otherwise, the child's grasp of concepts and ideas will be diminished.

Topic 13.8 School Years: The Expanded Core Curriculum

- Blind students must learn specialized skills not covered in the general education curriculum.

- Instruction in orientation and mobility must begin early and can include the use of canes and guide dogs.

- IEP teams must take multiple factors into account when considering braille use.

What extra skills must blind students acquire? Many students with low vision can have their educational needs met through the accommodations you learned about earlier, and through assistive technology. Yet even with accommodations, students who are blind require additional supports. They typically use aids like canes or service dogs to move around independently. Many students can't read print, but instead have text materials translated into other formats: audio recording, print to speech, or braille. And, as discussed in the previous section, learning how to socialize and interact with others may not occur naturally. Therefore, these students (and some students with low vision) require an expanded core curriculum (ECC) that covers:

Stockbyte/Getty Images

- Orientation and mobility.

- Compensatory or functional skills, including options for accessing information (braille, large print, audio).

- Social skills.

- Independent living (e.g., self-care, food preparation, money management).

- Recreation and leisure.

- Vocational and career preparation.

- Assistive technology.

Using their sense of touch, these young children can distinguish between an elephant and a zebra. For children with visual impairments, adults need to provide additional explanations about their colors (gray vs. black and white stripes), the way the animals move (elephants lumber while swaying their head from side to side; zebras gallop), the way a tail swishes to bat away flies, and so on. Even concepts like stripes, lumber, gallop, and swish will need additional explanation.

The expanded core curriculum addresses highly specialized skills, so experts in visual disabilities—teachers of students with visual impairments (TVIs) and orientation and mobility (O&M) instructors—typically provide instruction in these areas. Additional time must be allocated for learning these critical skills, which means that students will occasionally be pulled from the general education class. As a result, professionals must collaborate to ensure that students master necessary skills from both the general education and the expanded core curriculum.

Teachers of Students with Visual Impairments

A TVI specializes in visual impairments and serves as a resource to other educators, parents, and students. A TVI also has expertise in instructional and assessment practices as well as knowledge of other agencies that provide supports for students with visual disabilities. He or she may work directly with the student and may also provide consultative services and support to the general education teacher and other professionals at the child's school. Specifically, the TVI can:

Wavebreak Media ltd/Alamy Stock Photo

- Provide instruction in disability-specific skills, such as braille.

- Reinforce concepts from the core academic subjects.

- Teach components of the expanded core curriculum.

- Conduct assessments to determine a student's abilities, needs, and necessary accommodations.

- Provide information on implementing accommodations.

- Work with appropriate organizations and agencies to access instructional materials (e.g., digital texts available through Bookshare®, braille, books on tape).

- Create materials to support academic success (e.g., braille labels for classroom items, print copies of a student's braille work, or braille versions of classroom handouts).

- Help general educators structure the physical and academic environments.

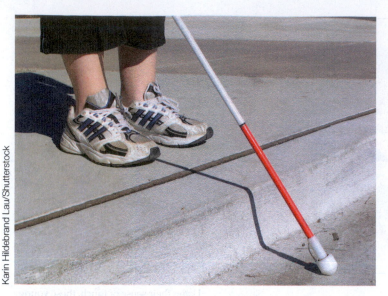

As she walks, this woman's cane drops from sidewalk level to street level, signaling where the sidewalk ends and alerting her to step down. Some canes, whose white color indicates the user is blind, also have a red section on the end, to increase their visibility to others. Most states have laws requiring drivers to stop and/or yield to pedestrians who are blind.

How do students learn orientation and mobility skills? Instruction in orientation and mobility needs to begin early, between the ages of two and six. Canes and guide dogs assist with orientation and mobility. How does a cane help with mobility? While a person is walking, the cane is tapped on the ground and makes a sound. That sound, combined with physical contact at the end of the cane, helps the user know when a hallway ends, when stairs begin and end, or when obstacles are in his or her path. Proficient use of a long cane requires years of instruction and practice. Orientation and mobility instructors can work with parents and the child to determine the best device for the child at each developmental level. Cane length should be appropriate for a child's size or height. Sometimes called kiddie canes or pre-canes, small canes are lightweight so that young children can handle them easily. They have a groove on the handle to encourage correct finger placement and a wrist strap so children can't easily drop them. The tips are rounded for easy gliding action.

Guide dogs are trained to lead a person safely from one location to another. They receive extensive training to automatically stop at curbs and stairs, maintain a direct route (no chasing after other dogs!), avoid obstacles, lead their owners to an elevator's buttons and—perhaps most importantly—to ignore any command from their owners that would place them in danger.

Stephanie's Guide Dog

Stephanie Zundel is a student at Vanderbilt University, majoring in child studies with a minor in sociology. In the video below, she explains how guide dogs are trained and demonstrates some basic commands with her dog, Marley.

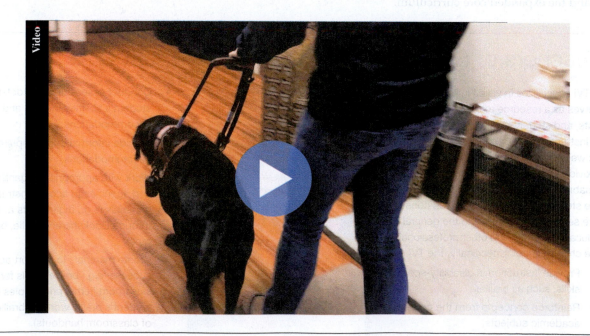

Orientation and Mobility Instructors

Orientation and mobility (O&M) instructors—who are considered related service providers by IDEA—teach students the skills necessary to independently navigate their classroom, school, home, and community. Students studying orientation skills learn to identify where they are, determine where they want to go, and come up with a plan to arrive there, using auditory cues and landmarks to help them. Mobility skills allow students to travel from one location to another. An O&M instructor may:

- Evaluate each student's functional vision to determine its use in O&M activities.
- Assess students' O&M skills as well as their progress in the expanded core curriculum.

Spencer Grant/PhotoEdit

- Provide instruction in various low-vision and mobility devices.
- Help students orient themselves in various environments.
- Teach students specific routes from one location to another.
- Consult with family members and relevant school professionals on environmental design, reinforcing O&M skills, services, and equipment.
- Provide information on additional resources (e.g., recreational opportunities, guide dog facilities).

What should teachers know about braille? Another component of the expanded core curriculum is the use of braille. As mentioned earlier, braille uses combinations of raised dots that can be read with one's fingers to represent letters, numbers, punctuation marks, and words. This method consists of a system of six dots, arranged in two vertical lines contained in a cell. Each dot within a cell has a corresponding number: the left vertical dots are numbered from top to bottom (1, 2, 3); the right vertical dots, also starting from the top, are numbered 4, 5, and 6.

Although braille is an effective alternative to visual reading, the number of braille users is declining because:

- Reading can be cumbersome and slow.
- Becoming even minimally proficient takes extensive training and practice.
- Additional codes for different symbols, such as those in math and music, make it difficult for students with cognitive impairments to master the system completely.
- Few teachers know how to use or teach braille.

Because of concerns regarding the literacy rates of blind students and braille, Congress addressed concerns about braille use in IDEA, which are summarized in the following box.

Braille Alphabet
punctuation and numbers

a b c d e f g h i j

k l m n o p q r s t

u v w x y z à è ù é

ç â ê î ô û ë ï ü ì

1 2 3 4 5 6 7 8 9 0

> < , ; : . ? ! " "

( ) * / √ √ x + − @

Alexander Kaludov/Fotolia

Every letter, number, and punctuation mark is identified by a combination of raised dots within a cell. Dot 1 represents the letter *a*, the combination of dots 1, 4, and 5 represents the letter *d*, and so on.

What IDEA Says About . . .

Braille and Its Use

The IEP team for each student with a visual disability must consider special factors about each child's method of reading.

- IEPs must address the issue of braille instruction and the use of braille in classroom settings.

- The child's reading and writing skills, educational needs, and future need for instruction in braille or use of braille must be evaluated.

- If that method is deemed appropriate for the student, instruction should be provided in braille and the student should be allowed to use braille.

- The decision whether to use braille cannot be based on factors such as the availability of alternative reading methods or of braille instruction.

- Once the decision is made, services and materials must be delivered without undue delay.

SOURCE: U.S. Department of Education (2006).

Topic 13.9 Transition

- Adults with visual disabilities face challenges to finding full-time employment, starting with misperceptions held by hiring managers and human resources personnel.

- Improved employment outcomes for adults with visual disabilities start with increased career awareness in the early years, part-time jobs during adolescence, development of job-related skills as part of the expanded core curriculum, and the use of assistive technology.

How is the world of work different for adults with visual disabilities than for their sighted peers? Among adults with disabilities, those with visual impairments have some of the highest college attendance rates; 26% attend two-year colleges, and 43% attend four-year colleges. Unfortunately, they have much lower employment rates. Recent data indicate that, while the labor force participation rate of all U.S. adults was 73%, the rate for those with visual disabilities was only 36%. The data tell a partial story; only 24% of employed adults with visual disabilities indicated that they were employed full-time. Even worse, during a four-year period of economic recession, the labor force participation rate decreased by only 2% for the U.S. adult population overall, but by double that amount (4%) for adults with visual impairments, indicating that this group not only experiences inequity in employment but also is at a greater disadvantage during times of economic instability.

One factor contributing to this problem is that many human resources personnel—those in charge of recruiting and hiring for companies—hold misperceptions about employees with visual disabilities. Some of these misperceptions are:

- Blind employees are capable of doing very few jobs in their company.

- Accommodations for workers who are blind are very expensive.

- Blind employees need someone to help them do their job.

- ADA regulations make it difficult to fire an employee who is blind.

Given these misconceptions, it is not surprising that adults with visual disabilities have difficulty finding full-time employment. The resulting lack of income subsequently affects their ability to engage in other independent living activities like renting an apartment, socializing with friends, or participating in recreational and leisure activities.

What factors contribute to postsecondary school success for students with visual disabilities? Consider how young children implicitly develop **career awareness** as they observe their surroundings. They see that many vocations require a uniform (police, firefighters, nurses), some may require suits or dresses (lawyers, business executives), while others may have more casual dress expectations (child care workers, personal trainers). These children also recognize vehicles that align with some careers (fire engine, ambulance), as well as special equipment, accessories, or gear used (stethoscope, briefcase); and they observe the locations in which these people work (child care center, office, park). Because this information is often transmitted visually, individuals with visual impairments have gaps in their career knowledge base that may go unnoticed by others. These gaps may continue to grow throughout the middle school years and beyond, as students progress from career awareness to career exploration, preparation, and placement. As with other areas we have discussed, teachers and family members need to fill in the gaps in the career knowledge base of students with visual disabilities by explicitly describing everyday sights, allowing students to tactilely explore job-related items (when appropriate), and explaining what might otherwise be considered common knowledge (e.g., "In the lab, the scientists wear long lab coats to protect their clothing, latex gloves to protect their hands, and goggles over their eyes. Would you like to hold some of these things or try them on?").

Research shows that managers who know someone with a visual disability are more likely to hire employees who are blind or have low vision. As employers become more knowledgeable, the employment opportunities for adults with visual disabilities can improve.

Chances are you immediately recognize this person's vocation. What are the identifying aspects of his uniform that provide these clues? You probably also recognize which vehicle he drives. Again, what are the key identifying features? These are all pieces of career-awareness information—probably obtained when you were very young—that must be explicitly explained to children with visual disabilities.

Career exploration, the next stage in the career education process, can sometimes be difficult for students with visual impairments, as training and practice in the expanded core curriculum may take up time during evenings, weekends, or summers—time during which their sighted peers are holding part-time jobs. Teachers and family members should not discount the importance of these first jobs, as they teach important employability skills, such as the ability to plan and organize; to problem solve; to interact appropriately with co-workers, supervisors, or customers; and to work and contribute as a team member. Many of these skills are developed incrementally over time. For students with visual disabilities, some of these skills must be explicitly taught.

Expanded core curriculum skill areas needed for college life and adult independence—vocational and career preparation, independent living (which includes self-care, food preparation, and money management), and recreation and leisure—take on greater significance as students get older and enter the career preparation stage. O&M skills become critical for independence. In fact, recent research findings indicate that two predictors of post-school employment are:

- The ability to travel independently outside the home, use public transportation, and arrange train or plane trips.
- High outcome expectations (e.g., an adult's positive self-perceptions about his or her ability to obtain employment, financial self-sufficiency, and independent living).

Recall that assistive technology is considered a related service for all disabilities, but is explicitly identified as a component of the expanded core curriculum for students with visual disabilities. Adults who have access to appropriate assistive technology can function more independently and experience greater success than those who do not have these supports.

In each of the videos below, Stephanie demonstrates some of the assistive technology that she uses for school and for functioning independently on campus and in the community.

JAWS and Refreshable Braille Display

In this video Stephanie explains JAWS, a screen reader, and how it works together with a refreshable braille display.

Braille Writer

In this video, Stephanie explains how a Braille writer works.

Color Scanner

In this video Stephanie demonstrates how a color scanner can help the blind choose clothing, by scanning a garment and alerting the user audibly.

Money Scanner

In this video, Stephanie shows how a money scanner works, which scans a bill and alerts the user of its dollar amount.

The following IRIS Module provides additional information on setting up a classroom for students with visual disabilities, including considerations and planning for some of the AT devices demonstrated earlier.

▶ **IRIS Module: Accommodations to the Physical Environment: Setting Up a Classroom for Students with Visual Disabilities**
http://iris.peabody.vanderbilt.edu/module/v01-clearview/#content

As they transition into college or work settings, older students with visual disabilities may receive support from several entities: school districts, adult service agencies, or community rehabilitation providers. At times, confusion may arise when one agency assumes another is addressing certain aspects of the individual's program or providing required supports. In these cases, supports and services may be omitted or dropped. When multiple entities collaborate to clearly define roles and responsibilities, students with visual disabilities are more likely to receive the services and supports they need for a successful transition to an independent, adult life.

Check Your Understanding 13.2

Click here to gauge your understanding of the concepts in this section.

People and Situations

Learning Outcome

Explain how the education of students with visual disabilities has changed over time and describe how accommodations and assistive technology can support the attainment of life goals.

Topic 13.10 Origins and History

- The education of children with visual disabilities started in the 1700s, with many changes occurring over the centuries.

- Several events in the mid-1900s caused many students to move from specialized schools to their neighborhood schools.

Topic 13.11 Personal Stories

- Individuals with visual disabilities can fully participate in life's activities with the support of assistive technology and appropriate accommodations.

These blind runners are competing in a men's 100-meter race, tethered to sighted runners who guide them. With proper accommodations, people with visual disabilities can engage in the same leisure activities as their sighted friends and family members.

Topic 13.10 Origins and History

- The education of children with visual disabilities started in the 1700s, with many changes occurring over the centuries.

- Several events in the mid-1900s caused many students to move from specialized schools to their neighborhood schools.

When did the education of students with visual disabilities begin? Educational programs for blind students started in France in the late eighteenth century. In contrast to the history of other disabilities you've learned about, institutions for individuals with visual disabilities were established to provide specialized instruction rather than to separate them from society. In 1784, Valentin Haüy opened the first school for the blind in Paris, the Institution for Blind Youth. Haüy conceived a written system of raised letters, but his work ended in 1789, when the French Revolution broke out. In the early 1800s, Louis Braille, also French, developed his famous tactile system for reading and writing, the embossed six-dot cell system. Braille, who lost his sight at age 3 due to an accident in his father's workshop, was only 15 years old when he developed the braille system (an indication that he should also be considered gifted and talented, see Chapter 15). In 1821, Samuel Gridley Howe opened the first U.S. school for blind students, the New England Asylum for the Blind (now the Perkins School for the Blind). Around 1832, two private boarding schools were founded to serve children from wealthy families, the New York Institute for the Blind and the Pennsylvania Institution for the Instruction of the Blind. These schools were originally established in what were rural areas at the time. As communities developed in the areas around the schools, many of them began providing day classes to local students who did not need residential services. Now these schools are referred to as specialized, rather than residential, schools.

The first mainstreaming occurred in 1900, when Frank Hall, the Illinois School for the Blind superintendent, successfully advocated for blind students to attend neighborhood schools in Chicago. These students attended general education classes and had a special education teacher who taught braille and supported their participation in the general education curriculum. (On a side note, Hall also developed the first mechanical braille writer, a small, portable machine for writing and taking notes in braille.)

In 1913, Edward Allen taught the first class for students with low vision in Boston; later that year, Robert Irwin started a class in Cleveland. These programs were

In 1844, Louis Braille and his students conducted a public demonstration of braille. One student dictated to a second, who transcribed his words in braille. A third student then entered the room and read the notes aloud. A member of the audience, thinking it was a trick, heckled the students. The heckler was finally convinced when they repeated the demonstration and used a theater ticket taken from his own pocket.

modeled after classes in England, where students participated in general education whenever possible, but schoolwork was almost exclusively oral. Reading and writing tasks were kept to a minimum in a misinformed attempt to preserve any remaining sight. This method was popular for almost 50 years, until research on visual efficiency by Natalie Barraga in 1964 showed that vision can worsen if not used consistently.

Are students with visual disabilities still educated in separate, specialized schools today? As you learned in Topic 13.4, less than 10% of students with visual impairments currently attend the specialized schools that were popular during the early twentieth century. What led to this shift in educational placements? During the 1950s and 1960s, two events caused a dramatic increase in the number of students with visual disabilities:

1. Premature infants were given extra oxygen to survive; ironically, this resulted in retinopathy of prematurity (ROP), which you learned about earlier.
2. A rubella (German measles) epidemic left many children with multiple disabilities, often including visual disabilities.

The increased student numbers strained the capacity of specialized schools, which had previously served 85% of all students with visual disabilities. Simultaneously, the mainstreaming movement that began several decades earlier had taken hold, and parents advocated for their children to attend local public schools. As a result, many students eventually moved out of residential schools and back to neighborhood schools. With the passage of IDEA in 1975, this trend continued and now most students live at home and attend local public schools, though many receive outreach services provided by staff from specialized schools. In turn, the enrollment at specialized schools now reflects the availability of supports and services for students who have visual impairments and other co-existing disabilities (e.g., intellectual disabilities).

Topic 13.11 Personal Stories

- Individuals with visual disabilities can fully participate in life's activities with the support of assistive technology and appropriate accommodations.

What can individuals with visual disabilities accomplish? When provided with proper accommodations, individuals with visual disabilities can achieve the same accomplishments as their sighted peers. In many cases, however, significant challenges must be addressed to achieve success, as shown in the following box.

On the Screen: *Ray*

The film *Ray* chronicles not only the life and talents of music legend Ray Charles but also the many challenges he faced—and overcame—as a blind African American living in a time when the guarantees of IDEA, the ADA, and the civil rights movement had not yet been established. Many of those challenges were created by people who held low or negative perceptions of him based on his disability, his race, or both.

Jamie Foxx won an Academy Award for his outstanding portrayal of Ray Charles. As with the other *On the Screen* films you have read about throughout this text, *Ray* features a character with a disability played by an actor without a disability—something that you learned about in Topic 1.4.

https://youtu.be/X1rJvSF3l6k

As illustrated in this chapter's *On the Screen*, public misconceptions tend to focus on fallacies of what blind people *can't* do. Instead, we'd like to show you what individuals who have low vision or blindness *can* do. Let's take a look at an adventurer; a scientist; and an organization for runners.

You may have heard of Erik Weihenmayer, the mountain climber. While few sighted individuals have ever scaled Mount Everest, Erik did it as part of his quest to scale the Seven Summits—the highest mountains on each continent. Of the approximately 350 climbers to ever achieve that feat, Erik is the only one who is blind. More recently, Erik kayaked 277 miles solo through the Colorado River in the Grand Canyon—an exploit never before attempted by a blind athlete, much less accomplished by one. Erik utilizes an array of assistive technology in concert with unique accommodations to support his many adventures. When paragliding, he uses a radio system to communicate with his instructor (assistive technology) and hangs a heavy bell from a long rope tied to his leg to assist with landing (accommodation). How does the bell help? When it hits the ground, the sound signals to Erik to begin landing maneuvers.

To support others through adventure-based activities, Erik co-founded No Barriers, a non-profit organization dedicated to helping people reach their full potential by tackling personal challenges. No Barriers, whose slogan is "What's within you is stronger than what's in your way," includes activities for young people (No Barriers Youth) and for veterans (No Barriers Warriors). You can learn more about Erik and view videos of his various adventures on his *Touch the Top* Website, http://www.touchthetop.com.

Erik Weihenmayer

Dr. Joshua Miele, a scientist at the Smith-Kettlewell Eye Research Institute, earned his bachelor's degree in physics and his Ph.D. in psychoacoustics. His research focuses on using technology to overcome typical access barriers for individuals with visual disabilities; using geographic information system (GIS) data to create tactile maps; and developing tools that allow blind individuals to use a Livescribe Smartpen™ to access items like a talking braille periodic table. His latest work is the Descriptive Video Exchange, a crowd-sourcing service that lets people record descriptions of what they see in a video or movie. The narrations, along with timing information, are stored in audio files on a server that blind individuals can access and listen to while they watch a video or movie. YouDescribe, an offshoot of the Descriptive Video Exchange, allows contributors to record audio descriptions for YouTube videos. You can learn more about Dr. Miele's pioneering research at http://www.mielelab.org/ and add audio descriptions to videos at www.youdescribe.org.

Achilles International (http://www.achillesinternational.org) is an organization that pairs volunteers and athletes with disabilities for recreational running. Many of the athletes train for competitive events that range from 5K runs to the New York City Marathon. Achilles members are quick to explain that they use the term *running* to refer to any type of forward locomotion such as running, walking, or using a scooter, wheelchair, or handcycle. The organization also has several specialized programs: Achilles Kids for children with disabilities and the Achilles Freedom Team for U.S. military veterans.

Dr. Joshua Miele

The following video provides an overview of the Achilles program and philosophy. Watch carefully; you should recognize one of the Achilles athletes!

▶ **Achilles Nashville and Hope & Possibility® Race 2016**

https://youtu.be/I6lcCfogC28

Check Your Understanding 13.3

Click here to gauge your understanding of the concepts in this section.

Future Perspectives

Learning Outcomes

Explain how the effects of vision loss are being reduced or eliminated through medical and technological advances.

Topic 13.12 Prevention: Medical Advances

- Advances in medical treatments can prevent some types of vision loss and treat other conditions early enough to prevent permanent damage.

- New technological advances have the potential to enhance or replace damaged components of the visual system.

Topic 13.13 Technology: Assistive Technology, Apps, and Software

- Assistive technology (AT) devices can support access to or generation of information.

- New technology, software, and applications are improving the daily lives of individuals with visual disabilities.

Naomi Tyler

This charging station, located at an airport gate waiting area, reminds us that some of the most basic items in our lives need to be accessible to everyone.

Topic 13.12 Prevention: Medical Advances

- Advances in medical treatments can prevent some types of vision loss and treat other conditions early enough to prevent permanent damage.

- New technological advances have the potential to enhance or replace damaged components of the visual system.

How are medical advances helping to prevent visual disabilities? Advances in medical research are helping to identify specific causes of disabilities, leading to a number of preventive measures and medical interventions. For example, a vaccine now prevents rubella, a former cause of visual impairments and of multiple disabilities. In addition, precautions are now taken to prevent high levels of oxygen use, one cause of retinopathy of prematurity (ROP), in premature infants. Another preventive measure for ROP was discovered in a recent clinical study, which found that severe ROP could be detected early through retinal scans in premature infants. The findings of this study hold promise for early surgical treatment of ROP.

The video below from the National Eye Institute explains retinopathy of prematurity (ROP), advances in diagnostic assessments, and early treatment options.

▶ **NEI: Retinopathy of Prematurity**
https://youtu.be/BVYwo-RmDNE

Researchers are also working to identify genes that are responsible for some forms of blindness. Through this research, the gene that causes retinitis pigmentosa has been located and isolated, and there is hope for a cure in the near future. Also, gene replacement therapy has been used successfully to restore partial vision to people with Leber congenital amaurosis, a hereditary condition. Researchers aim to develop similar treatments for other genetically based vision disorders, hoping to begin therapy with infants as young as six months, before any permanent vision damage can occur. In another area of medical research, stem-cell treatments have been used successfully to replenish certain cells in the retina, improving vision for people with Stargardt's disease or age-related macular degeneration. New medical therapies—laser treatment, surgery, and corneal implants—also help to reduce the incidence or lessen the severity of visual disabilities among children.

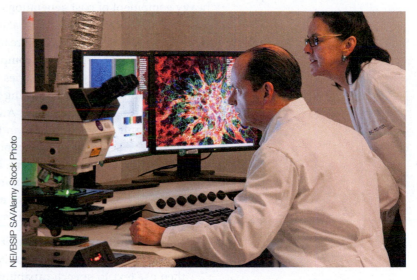

NEI/BSIP SA/Alamy Stock Photo

Researchers strive to determine more effective prevention, early detection, and treatment options for vision loss.

What kinds of technological advances in medicine can help people with visual disabilities? New medical technology is signaling a wave of very science fiction–like advances. For instance, prototypical contact lenses can detect changes in eye fluid buildup for patients with glaucoma. By measuring the pressure within the eye over a 24-hour period, doctors can gauge medication and treatment options accordingly. Better yet, contacts that can deliver medication directly onto the eye are now being tested and refined. Some other developments on the horizon include:

- Retinal microchip implants that restore limited sight to individuals with retinitis pigmentosa or macular degeneration.

- Contact lenses with biochemical sensors that can monitor glucose levels (an indicator of diabetes); cholesterol, sodium, potassium, and lithium levels; and body temperature. The contacts would change color to indicate biochemical levels.

- Electrical stimulation to the brain's visual cortex that can create images—shapes, colors, and contrasts. Stimulating more neurons results in a wider visual field, while increasing the electrical current improves visual acuity.

With the rapid pace of technological innovations, we can anticipate that the negative effects of many types of visual disabilities will be reduced and, in some cases, completely eliminated in the future.

Topic 13.13 Technology: Assistive Technology, Apps, and Software

- Assistive technology (AT) devices can support access to or generation of information.

- New technology, software, and applications are improving the daily lives of individuals with visual disabilities.

How can assistive technology (AT) devices support students with visual disabilities? Most of these students require assistive technology (AT) devices or services, which allow them to access information using visual, audio, or tactile methods. In the 1970s, the first print-to-voice translator, the Kurzweil Reader, enabled immediate access to all printed information. While a breakthrough at the time, it only hinted at the remarkable innovations to come. AT devices are now more accessible and easier to use than the large, heavy equipment of past generations.

What are some of the new innovations that are making life more accessible for individuals with visual disabilities? Screen readers (software programs) provide audio output of text, allowing access to most computer-based activities, including surfing the Web. Apple's™ Accessibility Technologies department has developed standard accessibility features for its products, earning Apple the American Foundation for the Blind's 2015 Helen Keller Achievement Award. For example, the Zoom™ feature allows users to magnify a specific area up to 20× and includes picture-in-picture display. Its VoiceOver™ screen reading technology translates text to speech, provides spoken descriptions of the screen's content, allows keyboard and gesture navigation, and is compatible with over 50 USB and refreshable braille displays.

Other technological advances allow access to information in ways that were unimaginable only a decade ago. Here are just a few:

- Mobile apps that scan U.S. paper currency and then "speak" (auditory output) to identify the bill; take photos of items like notes, memos, and store price tags and then use text-to-speech capabilities (auditory output) to read the information to the user; and identify the color(s) of a piece of clothing, allowing blind users to color-coordinate their outfits without help from roommates, spouses, or children.

- A virtual wireless braille keyboard that inputs finger strokes on any surface into an iPhone using VoiceOver™. This innovation was developed by Dr. Joshua Miele, whom you read about in Topic 13.11.

- The Brainport V100, just approved by the FDA, allows a user to "see" by interpreting electrical stimulations sent to the tongue via a small camera mounted on their sunglasses. The electrical stimulations, delivered through a lollipop-like gadget, provide a tingling sensation similar to that of carbonation bubbles. Users learn to translate these sensations into images. The Brainport V100 is not meant to be a substitute for sight, nor a replacement for Hoover canes or seeing-eye dogs. However, the new opportunities provided for blind individuals through this device are truly exciting.

In the video below, Erik Weihenmayer uses the Brainport to read written words and play tic-tac-toe with his daughter (who tries to trick him by claiming that she won). He is using an earlier model of the device in which the camera is larger and worn via a headmount, rather than the newer, smaller sunglasses model.

▶ **Brainport Vision Device**

https://youtu.be/xNkw28fz9u0

With the prospect of even more new and innovative inventions on the horizon, the future is full of expanding possibilities for individuals with visual disabilities.

Check Your Understanding 13.4

Click here to gauge your understanding of the concepts in this section.

Summary

Low Vision and Blindness Described

The characteristics of children with visual disabilities vary greatly, depending on the condition that caused the impairment and the severity of vision loss. Most children with visual disabilities have some functional vision.

- Although various terms and definitions exist, visual disabilities can be divided into two subgroups: low vision (some functional sight but daily functioning is affected) and blindness (no functional sight).

- A visual disability occurs when there is damage to any optical component (e.g., retina, optic nerve) or to the brain's ability to interpret visual stimuli.

- Teachers should be alert to warning signs that a child may have a visual impairment, and recognize that students with visual disabilities might prefer different types of play activities and exhibit social behaviors different from those of their sighted peers.

- Only 0.06% to 0.1% of all schoolchildren have visual disabilities and receive special education services, most of which are provided in general education settings.

Special Education

Special education services can provide the supports needed for students with disabilities to achieve success in school.

- Students with visual impairments face some challenges, but these can be lessened or overcome through accommodations, assistive technology, and some specialized instruction.

- Academic accommodations allow students with visual disabilities to access content presented in books or in class and to complete assignments or tests, while accommodations to the physical environment make the classroom accessible and safe.

- Vision loss can impede the early development of gross motor skills and the understanding of abstract concepts, resulting in the need for early and ongoing intervention in these areas.

- In addition to instructional accommodations, students with visual disabilities often require an expanded core curriculum, which includes skills taught by specialists (e.g., orientation and mobility, braille).

- Some areas of the expanded core curriculum (e.g., vocational and career preparation, independent living) take on greater significance as students prepare to transition to independent adult life.

People and Situations

The history of education for individuals with visual disabilities is more positive than that of many other disabilities.

- Residential schools focused on providing specialized instruction rather than separating these individuals from society.

- People with visual disabilities can engage in activities and achieve accomplishments commensurate with those of their sighted peers when appropriate accommodations and supports are provided.

Future Perspectives

Medical advances strive to prevent or repair vision loss, while innovations in technology are improving the lives of individuals with visual disabilities.

- Groundbreaking medical advances aim to enhance or replace damaged components of the visual system to improve vision.

- New assistive technology tools, software programs, and applications make it easier to read, write, work on computers, and conduct other activities of daily living.

Addressing CEC Standards

Council for Exceptional Children (CEC) knowledge standards addressed in this chapter: 6.2, 1.0, B&VI1K2, B&VI1K3, B&VI2K1, B&VI2K5, B&VI4K1, B&VI4S1, B&VI5S1, B&VI8S3, B&VI10K2.

See the Appendix for the complete CEC Initial Level Special Educator Preparation Standards.

Chapter 14
Other Low-Incidence Disabilities

Multiple Disabilities, Deaf-Blindness,
Traumatic Brain Injury

Pete Souza

During the 25th anniversary celebration of IDEA, President Obama types a message to Haben Girma. Her device receives his message and translates it into braille, which she reads on a refreshable braille display.

Haben Girma is a graduate of Lewis and Clark College and Harvard Law School, an attorney for Disability Rights Advocates, and a person who is deaf and blind, a condition known as deaf-blindness. In a recent TED Talk, she described how a college cafeteria experience sparked her interest in law and in disability rights advocacy.

"The cafeteria had about five different food stations, and there was a menu at the door, and people would read the menu and choose what they wanted to eat. Blind students like myself couldn't read the menu. The staff at the cafeteria offered to read me the menu, but I couldn't hear it. As a blind student, my first choice would be to read the menu in braille. Braille takes time to produce, so we compromised. The staff agreed to email me the menu at the start of each meal, and I would be able to read it on my computer using a screenreader. It was a great idea, but the cafeteria constantly forgot to email the menus. Since I couldn't read the menu, and I couldn't hear the staff in the cafeteria, I couldn't choose what I was going to eat. So after classes, I would pick a station at random, I would go up and take whatever was served by the staff behind the counter, I would take it to the table, and only then would I realize what I was going to eat. There were some unhappy surprises.

"As a busy student with classes and preparing for exams and writing papers, the last thing I needed was this added frustration. But sometimes they did remember to send the menus, and when they did, I was thrilled to have choices. For example, if the menu said, "Station 3, tortellini with smoked gouda cheese," I would know to skip stations 1 and 2 and go straight to station 3. When they remembered to send the menus, life was delicious. But they regularly forgot to send the menus.

"And there's that decision, do you just deal and let it go, or do you do something about it? And those menus, at that cafeteria, was a pivotal moment for me when I decided I should do something, for myself, and for future blind students who came to that college. Or anyone else who needed menus in alternative formats. So I explained to the manager at the cafeteria that I paid to eat at the cafeteria and like all the other students, I deserved access to the menus so I could take advantage of these services. The manager told me, they're very busy, he's doing me a big favor, and I needed to stop complaining and be more appreciative. I don't know about you, but if there's chocolate cake at station 4 and no one tells me, I'm not feeling appreciative. So, after several incidences of missed chocolate cake, I had enough, I tried something new."

A lack of access to cafeteria menus is probably not something most college students think about. Yet, for students like Haben, this is a common challenge encountered in school or college cafeterias. To solve this problem, Haben taught the cafeteria staff about the Americans with Disabilities Act (ADA), which you learned about in Chapters 1 and 4. As a result, they consistently provided her with accessible menus, and her passion for advocacy was kindled. You will learn more about Haben later in this chapter. Until then, you can view her full speech, and several others, on her Website: https://habengirma.com

This chapter is organized somewhat differently from previous chapters because we present information about three distinct special education categories: multiple disabilities, traumatic brain injury, and deaf-blindness. Each is considered a low-incidence disability because relatively few students receive special services through these categories. In most cases, these disabilities are very significant and present complex learning profiles, requiring substantial and intensive accommodations, modifications, supports, instruction, and special education services. Because the impact of the disabilities is so severe, affected students are also referred to as *students with the most significant disabilities* or *students with severe disabilities.*

These disabilities share some characteristics and challenges with many disabilities you have already learned about. For example, students with multiple disabilities have at least two disabilities in combination. In many cases, these students have intellectual disabilities, which we discussed in Chapter 9, along with another disability, such as a physical or health impairment (Chapter 11), and many also have speech and language impairments (Chapter 5). Students with traumatic brain injury (TBI) often present characteristics similar to those with learning disabilities (Chapter 6), attention deficit hyperactivity disorder (Chapter 7), and speech and language impairments (Chapter 5). When we discuss individuals who have deaf-blindness, we will build on information you learned about deafness and hearing loss (Chapter 12) and visual disabilities (Chapter 13).

Although each of these low-incidence disabilities has a unique definition and criteria for identification, students with these disabilities often have common goals like gaining independence, finding meaningful employment, and living as independently as possible. So in this chapter we combine some discussions and review key information presented separately in other chapters in order to address the special nature of these disabilities.

Learning Outcomes

Other Low-Incidence Disabilities Described

Understand the definitions and characteristics of multiple disabilities, traumatic brain injury, and deaf-blindness; be familiar with their prevalence rates; and understand the various settings in which these students receive their education.

Special Education

Describe different accommodations that can lessen challenges associated with multiple disabilities, TBI, and deaf-blindness; understand methods that parents and classroom teachers can use to reduce challenges associated with these disabilities; and describe supports to help students transition to postsecondary options and independence.

People and Situations

Describe two turning points in the history of people with multiple disabilities, TBI, and deaf-blindness, identify some ways in which these individuals can experience more community inclusion and involvement, and list reputable organizations that provide reliable information for these individuals and their families.

Future Perspectives

Describe the benefits of prevention and immediate medical intervention for TBI, and identify helpful assistive technology for individuals with the most significant disabilities.

Other Low-Incidence Disabilities Described[1]

Learning Outcome

Understand the definitions and characteristics of multiple disabilities, traumatic brain injury, and deaf-blindness; be familiar with their prevalence rates; and understand the various settings in which these students receive their education.

Topic 14.1 Multiple Disabilities

- Students with multiple disabilities have at least two complex disabilities.
- Multiple disabilities usually result in serious, multi-faceted challenges, often unique across individuals.

Topic 14.2 Traumatic Brain Injury (TBI)

- Traumatic brain injury results from a head injury caused by physical force.
- Resulting challenges are usually severe and can affect speech, balance, mobility, and cognition.

---

[1]References for Chapter 14 are found at the end of this text.

Topic 14.3 Deaf-Blindness

- Some individuals with deaf-blindness have no functional vision or hearing; however, most have some use of either their hearing or their vision, or both.

- Each individual's disabilities combine in unique ways; therefore, no assumptions should be made about the person's abilities or the educational programs needed.

Topic 14.4 Prevalence and Placement

- Multiple disabilities, TBI, and deaf-blindness have a combined prevalence rate of much less than 1% of all public school students.

- The vast majority of students with multiple disabilities and deaf-blindness receive their education in separate classes, in special schools, at home, or in hospital settings.

The combined effects of several disabilities give each student a unique learning profile. High expectations set by educators and family members ensure that these students achieve their full potential.

Topic 14.1 Multiple Disabilities

- Students with multiple disabilities have at least two complex disabilities.

- Multiple disabilities usually result in serious, multi-faceted challenges, often unique across individuals.

What are multiple disabilities, and how are they defined? Individuals with **multiple disabilities** have more than one disability, and the effects are such that the individual requires **extremely intensive, sustained, individualized instruction and supports**. For many of these students, one of their disabilities is an intellectual disability that is usually *not* in the mild range. IDEA's definition of multiple disabilities is outlined in the following table.

Definition of Multiple Disabilities

Term	Definition	Source
Multiple Disabilities	Multiple disabilities means concomitant impairments (such as intellectual disability–blindness or intellectual disability–orthopedic impairment), the combination of which causes such severe educational needs that they cannot be accommodated in special education programs solely for one of the impairments. Multiple disabilities does not include deaf-blindness.	IDEA '04, U.S. Department of Education

SOURCE: From 34 CFR Parts 300 and 301, *Assistance to States for the Education of Children with Disabilities and Preschool Grants for Children with Disabilities; Final Rule* (pp. 1261, 1263, 1265), U.S. Department of Education, August 14, 2006, *Federal Register*, Washington, DC.

What are some of the characteristics associated with multiple disabilities? Individuals with multiple disabilities display a range of skills, abilities, and problem areas. This group of individuals tends to share common challenges:

- Very limited communication abilities (understanding others and expressing themselves)

- Movement or mobility issues

- Difficulties with memory

- Problems transferring or generalizing learning from one situation, setting, or skill to another

- Need for supports for many of life's major activities (daily living, leisure, community participation, employment)

- Need for services from many different professionals and disciplines

These characteristics are not consistent across every individual. Some may need supports in only one area, but others require numerous supports for access to and participation in society. For example, an individual with a significant cognitive disability might need to live with someone who will assist with transportation to and from work and supports for activities of daily living, such as shopping for food and preparing healthy meals. If that individual also has a moderate hearing loss, he might need additional help, like an interpreter at work or at other events (e.g., doctor or dentist appointment).

Topic 14.2 Traumatic Brain Injury (TBI)

- Traumatic brain injury results from a head injury caused by physical force.

- Resulting challenges are usually severe and can affect speech, balance, mobility, and cognition.

What is traumatic brain injury, and how is it defined? **Traumatic brain injury (TBI)** became a separate disability category in the 1990 reauthorization of IDEA. Educators need to know that TBI *is not* a condition present at birth, nor is it due to a stroke, a brain tumor, or other internally caused brain damage. However, it is also important for educators to understand that TBI:

- Can be due to a concussion or head injury, possibly from an accident or child abuse.

- Is not always apparent or visible.

- May or may not result in loss of consciousness.

Definitions of Traumatic Brain Injury (TBI)

Term	Definition	Source
Traumatic brain injury	Traumatic brain injury means an acquired injury to the brain caused by an external physical force, resulting in total or partial functional disability or psychosocial impairment, or both, that adversely affects a child's educational performance. Traumatic brain injury applies to open or closed head injuries resulting in impairments in one or more areas, such as cognition; language; memory; attention; reasoning; abstract thinking; judgment; problem solving; sensory, perceptual, and motor abilities; psychosocial behavior; physical functions; information processing; and speech. The term does not apply to brain injuries that are congenital or degenerative, or to brain injuries induced by birth trauma.	IDEA '04, U.S. Department of Education
Traumatic brain injury	Traumatic brain injury (TBI), a form of acquired brain injury, occurs when a sudden trauma causes damage to the brain. TBI can result when the head suddenly and violently hits an object, or when an object pierces the skull and enters brain tissue.	National Institute of Neurological Disorders and Stroke, National Institutes of Health
Traumatic brain injury	A TBI is caused by a bump, blow, or jolt to the head or a penetrating head injury that disrupts the normal function of the brain. Not all blows or jolts to the head result in a TBI. The severity of a TBI may range from "mild" (i.e., a brief change in mental status or consciousness) to "severe" (i.e., an extended period of unconsciousness or memory loss after the injury). Most TBIs that occur each year are mild, commonly called concussions.	Centers for Disease Control and Prevention (CDC)

SOURCES: From 34 CFR Parts 300 and 301, *Assistance to States for the Education of Children with Disabilities and Preschool Grants for Children with Disabilities;* Final Rule (pp. 1261, 1263, 1265), U.S. Department of Education, August 14, 2006, *Federal Register,* Washington, DC; National Institute of Neurological Disorders and Stroke (2016, February 11), retrieved from http://www.ninds.nih.gov/disorders/tbi/tbi.htm; and Centers for Disease Control and Prevention (2016, January 22), retrieved from http://www.cdc.gov/traumaticbraininjury/get_the_facts.html

What are some of the characteristics associated with TBI? Problems resulting from head injuries can last for a very short time or for years or can result in lifelong problems. Additionally, the features of TBI range from mild to severe. Youth with moderate to severe injuries often experience physical effects, as well as dramatic changes in cognitive, behavioral, and academic skills.

Frequent Characteristics of TBI

Physical	Cognitive	Social/Emotional	Educational
Dizziness	Short-term memory problems	Mood swings or irritability	Difficulty with multi-step tasks
Headaches	Long-term memory problems	Anxiety	Problems remembering routines or schedules
Fatigue	Attention deficits	Depression	Distractibility
Blurred vision	Disorganization	Restlessness	Difficulty with long assignments
Insomnia	Non-sequential thinking	Lack of motivation	Difficulty learning new skills

SOURCE: Adapted from Center for Parent Information and Resources (n.d.), *Traumatic Brain Injury.* NICHCY Disability Fact Sheet 18, retrieved from http://www.parentcenterhub.org/repository/tbi/

In severe cases, students with TBI may experience balance problems, may have difficulty walking or performing other gross motor activities, or may lose their ability to walk entirely. These students may also lose speech capabilities and have to re-learn how to talk. In these situations, it is common for students to experience depression or withdrawal because they remember their prior skills and abilities and struggle to deal with their current physical and/or cognitive situations.

Prior to the 1960s, most children with TBI died soon after the trauma. Changes in emergency treatment, imaging technology, and surgical treatments now result in a 95% survival rate. After the medical emergencies are over, however, intensive special services and ongoing medical supports are often needed, as illustrated in the video below.

Dylan Rizzo was injured in a car crash. The video follows Dylan through several years of recovery facilitated by many types of therapy and medical interventions to address his TBI. Notice the progress that Dylan makes across time, particularly the degree to which he can move his arms and lift objects, his ability to walk, and his speech and language capabilities.

▶ **Back to Life**

https://youtu.be/LlQhfMCVPE4

Topic 14.3 Deaf-Blindness[2]

- Some individuals with deaf-blindness have no functional vision or hearing; however, most have some use of either their hearing or their vision, or both.

- Each individual's disabilities combine in unique ways; therefore, no assumptions should be made about the person's abilities or the educational programs needed.

What is deaf-blindness, and how is it defined? When you think of **deaf-blindness**, you probably think of someone who has no vision or hearing ability whatsoever. Although this is true for some individuals, most of those with deaf-blindness have some residual hearing and/or vision. However, the combination of vision and hearing loss produces unique challenges for this group of individuals. When hearing and vision both fall into the ranges of severe or profound losses, the immediate world may well end at one's fingertips and be exceptionally restricted.

We provide two definitions of deaf-blindness below: (1) the IDEA definition and (2) a functional definition from the National Center on Deaf-Blindness, a technical assistance and dissemination center funded by the U.S. Department of Education's Office of Special Education Programs.

Definitions of Deaf-Blindness

Term	Definition	Source
Deaf-blindness	Deaf-blindness means concomitant hearing and visual impairments, the combination of which causes such severe communication and other developmental and learning needs that the person cannot be appropriately educated in special education programs solely for children with deafness or children with blindness.	IDEA '04, U.S. Department of Education
Deaf-blind	Children are considered to be deaf-blind when the combination of their hearing and vision loss causes such severe communication and other developmental and educational needs that they require significant and unique adaptations in their educational programs.	National Center on Deaf-Blindness

SOURCES: From 34 CFR Parts 300 and 301, *Assistance to States for the Education of Children with Disabilities and Preschool Grants for Children with Disabilities*; Final Rule (pp. 1261, 1263, 1265), U.S. Department of Education, August 14, 2006, *Federal Register*, Washington, DC; and National Center on Deaf-Blindness (n.d.), *What Is Deaf-Blindness?* retrieved from https://nationaldb.org/library/list/3

What characteristics are associated with deaf-blindness? Almost half of students with deaf-blindness have enough residual vision to allow them to read enlarged print, see sign language, move about in their environment, and recognize friends and family. Some have sufficient hearing to understand certain speech sounds or hear loud noises; some can develop intelligible speech. But others have such limited vision and hearing that they profit little from either sense. The combination of hearing and vision loss presents three important challenges:

- Feelings of isolation—The inability to see or hear others around them reduces typical opportunities for human interaction. Teachers and family members must make extra efforts to include students in daily interactions (e.g., group discussions in class, family conversations at home) and also encourage these students to seek out others and initiate interactions.

---

[2]Like many people with vision and hearing loss, many of these individuals do not always use people-first language when referring to themselves and prefer *deaf-blind individuals* or *people who are deaf-blind*. Because there are also those who prefer people-first language, we alternate terms (people-first vs. disability-first) throughout this chapter.

- Problems with communication—These students often use some type of tactile communication system, which we will discuss further in Topic 14.6. Communication opportunities are limited, or breakdowns occur, when family members, teachers, and peers are not proficient in the communication method. Further, these students miss visual or auditory cues (e.g, eye rolling, laughter) that convey common messages.

- Problems with mobility—Most individuals who are deaf-blind need considerable supports and a highly individualized educational program to be safe and find the environment accessible. The components of purposeful movement—awareness of their environment and the ability to change locations, to seek protection from danger, and to make decisions about when to move—are goals for many of these students.

The following table shows the levels or severity of vision and hearing loss of individuals reported in the most recent deaf-blind child count, as well as the types of additional disabilities these individuals have. The majority of students with deaf-blindness (63%) have some functional vision that can be utilized for learning and in everyday activities. Similarly, nearly half of all deaf-blind individuals have adequate residual hearing. In addition to vision and hearing losses, it is estimated that some 90% of these individuals have additional disabilities (e.g., intellectual disability), making certain aspects of their educational programs similar to those of students with multiple disabilities.

Levels of Severity and Additional Disabilities Among Students with Deaf-Blindness

Vision Loss	Hearing Loss	Additional Disabilities[3]
• 5% are totally blind	• 11% have severe to profound hearing loss	• 75% have speech or language impairments
• 6% have light perception only	• 15% have moderately severe hearing loss	• 67% have cognitive disabilities
• 26% are legally blind	• 19% have moderate hearing loss	• 60% have physical disabilities

SOURCE: *The 2014 National Child Count of Children and Youth Who Are Deaf-Blind*, 2014 Census Tables, retrieved from https://nationaldb.org/library/page/2199

Topic 14.4 Prevalence and Placement

- Multiple disabilities, TBI, and deaf-blindness have a combined prevalence rate of much less than 1% of all public school students.

- The vast majority of students with multiple disabilities and deaf-blindness receive their education in separate classes, in special schools, at home, or in hospital settings.

What are the prevalence rates for these low-incidence disabilities? These three special education categories have very different prevalence rates, as illustrated in the following chart. Yet, when combined, they total only 2.42% of students with disabilities and far less than 1% of all public school students.

---

[3]Does not total to 100% due to overlapping conditions (e.g., a student may have speech and language impairments and a cognitive disability).

Disability Prevalence: 2014–2015 School Year[4]

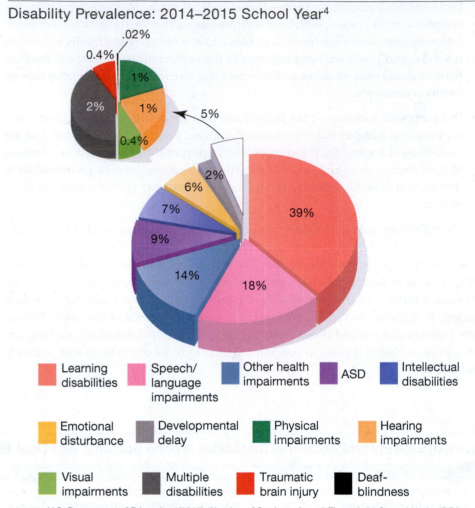

Learning disabilities — 39%
Speech/language impairments — 18%
Other health impairments — 14%
ASD — 9%
Intellectual disabilities — 7%
Emotional disturbance — 6%
Developmental delay — 2%
Physical impairments — 0.4%
Hearing impairments — 1%
Visual impairments — 1%
Multiple disabilities — 2%
Traumatic brain injury — 0.4%
Deaf-blindness — .02%
5%

Learning disabilities	Speech/ language impairments	Other health impairments	ASD	Intellectual disabilities
Emotional disturbance	Developmental delay	Physical impairments	Hearing impairments	
Visual impairments	Multiple disabilities	Traumatic brain injury	Deaf-blindness	

SOURCE: U.S. Department of Education. (2015). *Number of Students Ages 6 Through 21 Served Under IDEA, Part B, by Disability and State: 2014–2015.* [IDEA Section 618 Data Products: Static Tables, 2014-2015 Part B *Child Count and Educational Environments*]. Retrieved from http://www2.ed.gov/programs/osepidea/618-data/static-tables/index.html#part-b

According to the U.S. Department of Education, only 125,305 students ages 6 to 21 are included in the federal special education category of multiple disabilities. Depending on how states include individuals in one category or another, these numbers and percentages fluctuate state by state. For example, some states report students with an intellectual disability and also a mild visual disability in the multiple disabilities category, while others report these students in the intellectual disabilities category. For this reason, precise numbers about the national prevalence of multiple disabilities cannot be provided.

Relatively few students receive special education services because of TBI. Across the nation, 25,408 students or 0.4% of students with disabilities are included in this category. Unlike students with multiple disabilities and deaf-blindness, many of those with TBI receive special education services for the limited time that they are recovering from their injuries. Although some sustain lifelong disabilities, others recover and can return to the lives they had before their accident. Some may receive special education services or accommodations through Section 504 for a limited period. Others, particularly those with milder injuries, are never identified; their disabilities are not recognized and they do not receive special education services at all.

Two different databases are used to record the number of students with deaf-blindness. One is referred to as the National Deaf-Blind Census and includes deaf-blind

---

[4]Note that the IDEA category of *developmental delay* is included in this chart. Recall that students, ages three to nine, can be served in this category without being identified with a specific disability.

students who also have other disabilities. The other database, maintained by the U.S. Department of Education, Office of Special Education Programs (OSEP), includes only students with a combination of hearing and vision impairments. According to the National Deaf-Blind Census, some 9,384 students—ages 6 to 21—are identified as having deaf-blindness. In contrast, the federal government reports that only 1,237 students were included in this category across the entire nation, a number so small that it represents 0.0025% of all U.S. students. The following map shows the number of deaf-blind students in each state according to the National Center on Deaf-Blindness.

National Deaf-Blind Child Count Map

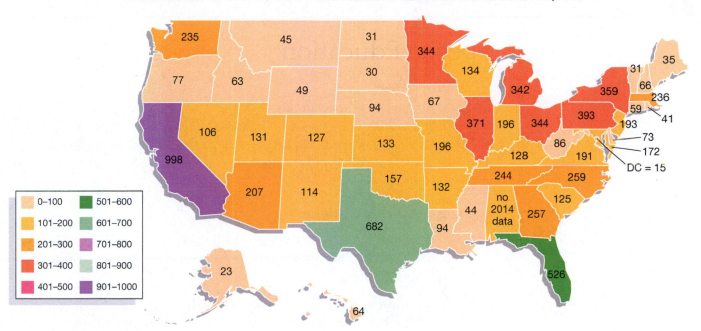

Total Number of U.S. Children and Students with Deaf-Blindness = 9,384

Legend:
- 0–100
- 101–200
- 201–300
- 301–400
- 401–500
- 501–600
- 601–700
- 701–800
- 801–900
- 901–1000

SOURCE: National Center on Deaf-Blindness (2016), National Deaf-Blind Child Count Maps, 2014, retrieved from https://nationaldb.org/childcount

Where do students with these disabilities receive their education? Participation in general education varies across these three special education categories. Students with less significant needs spend more time in general education settings than those whose complex needs require more intensive or individualized services.

Educational Environments for Students with Multiple Disabilities, TBI, and Deaf-Blindness

Environment	Multiple Disabilities	TBI	Deaf-Blindness
Inside regular education class ≥ 80% of school day	13%	50%	23%
Inside regular education class between 40% and 79% of school day	16%	22%	13%
Inside regular class < 40% of school day	46%	20%	35%
Separate school	19%	5%	18%
Residential facility	1.4%	0.5%	7%
Homebound/hospital	3%	2%	3%
Correctional facilities	0.1%	0.09%	0%
Parentally placed in private schools	0.5%	0.9%	0.6%

SOURCE: U.S. Department of Education. (2015). *Child Count and Educational Environments* [IDEA Section 618 Data Products: State Level Data Files, 2014-2015 Part B]. Retrieved from http://www2.ed.gov/programs/osepidea/618-data/state-level-data-files/index.html#part-b

Students with TBI have the highest rate of inclusion in general education. Of those between the ages of 6 and 21, about 50% attend general education classes for 80% or more of the school day. According to the federal government, students with deaf-blindness have a much lower participation rate; only 23% of them learn alongside students without disabilities for 80% or more of the school day. Some databases provide a slightly different picture of the inclusive education rates for students with deaf-blindness. According to the National Center on Deaf-Blindness (NCDB), only 13% of these students (some 994) attend general education classes more than 80% or more of the school day.

Check Your Understanding 14.1

Click here to gauge your understanding of the concepts in this section.

Special Education

Learning Outcome

Describe different accommodations that can lessen challenges associated with multiple disabilities, TBI, and deaf-blindness; understand methods that parents and classroom teachers can use to reduce challenges associated with these disabilities; and describe supports to help students transition to postsecondary options and independence.

Topic 14.5 Accommodations

- Although the needs of students with multiple disabilities, TBI, and deaf-blindness vary greatly, these students can all benefit from accommodations.

- In addition to accommodations, some students with the most significant disabilities may require a modified curriculum.

Topic 14.6 Early Intervention

- Because of the severity of their conditions, infants with the most significant disabilities are often identified at birth or soon thereafter.

- These young children have IFSPs through which they receive needed therapies, and their parents also receive training.

Topic 14.7 School Years

- Many of the academic and behavioral interventions effective with other disabilities are appropriate for students with multiple disabilities, TBI, or deaf-blindness.

- Many of these students require special curricula and instructional topics that are not part of the general education curriculum.

Topic 14.8 Transition

- Individualized transition plans for students with multiple disabilities, TBI, and deaf-blindness contain some of the same kinds of goals as those for students with other types of disabilities.

- Community-based instruction (CBI) is an evidence-based practice for teaching many skills, including those necessary for independent living.

Allsorts Stock Photo/Alamy Stock Photo

This man works at a telephone helpline. With proper supports and accommodations, many adults with the most significant disabilities can be employed.

Topic 14.5 Accommodations

- Although the needs of students with multiple disabilities, TBI, and deaf-blindness vary greatly, these students can all benefit from accommodations.

- In addition to accommodations, some students with the most significant disabilities may require a modified curriculum.

What types of accommodations benefit students with these low-incidence disabilities? Because the needs of these students, and the barriers they face when accessing the curriculum, vary so greatly, each group will be discussed separately. Keep in mind that although we will highlight accommodations to address some common barriers for each group, these services should be determined on an individual basis. When identifying appropriate instructional and testing accommodations and supports for a student, the type of disability(ies), the severity of the disability(ies), and the impact of the disability(ies) on educational performance should be considered.

Because students with multiple disabilities can have a multitude of disability combinations, ranging from mild to severe, their ability levels vary greatly. This makes it almost impossible to discuss general accommodations that can be used with this group of students. However, as you learned in Topic 14.1, these students often have difficulty with cognitive functioning, communication skills, and functional life skills. Additionally, they often have impaired motor skills and sensory functions. A few supports that may be beneficial for many of these students are:

- Hand-held computers.
- Augmentative and alternative communication (AAC).
- Peer buddy supports.

Students with TBI have impairments that range from mild to severe, but many have problems with remembering information, staying focused, finding the right word(s) to express an idea, and performing tasks with multiple steps. Because their characteristics are similar to those of students with learning disabilities and ADHD, they may benefit from accommodations for these disabilities (see Topic 6.6 and Topic 7.6). A few are listed below.

- Advance organizers
- Repeating instructions
- Reduced noise/distractions
- Verbal or visual cues
- Checklist of needed items
- Graphic organizers
- Calculator
- Note takers
- Word processor
- Extended time for assignments and tests

Additionally, these students often experience reduced stamina, seizures, headaches, hearing loss, and vision problems. While they are still recovering, they may benefit from flexible scheduling for class work, homework, and assessments so they can demonstrate their actual learning.

As you learned earlier, a great percentage of students with deaf-blindness have some residual hearing and/or vision. They may benefit from accommodations for students with hearing impairments (see Topic 12.6) and for those with visual impairments (see Topic 13.6). Others have limited hearing and vision and may not benefit from many of these accommodations because those recommended for hearing impairments often rely on visual accommodations and those used for visual impairments are often auditory in nature. It is also important to keep in mind that about 90% of these students have additional impairments, such as speech language impairments, intellectual disabilities, physical health impairments, and complex health issues. This may make identifying potentially beneficial supports even more difficult. Still, a number of supports are suitable for this group of students:

- Large print text
- Braille materials
- Audio books
- CCTV
- Note takers
- Readers
- Interpreters
- Assistive listening devices
- Manual communication

Are accommodations adequate to help these students access the general education curriculum and demonstrate their knowledge? Typically, students with TBI can successfully access the general education curriculum with accommodations that are adjusted as their health status and medical conditions improve across time. However, this is not usually the case for students with multiple disabilities or those with deaf-blindness. Because these students often have significant cognitive impairments, they might require more substantial adaptations. Recall from Topic 9.6 that students with the most significant cognitive impairments (less than 1% of all students with disabilities) can receive instruction based on **alternate achievement standards**. These are achievement standards linked to the grade-level content; however, the content usually differs in breadth, depth, and complexity. By simplifying the content or reducing the amount or depth of information covered, students have more time to grasp the targeted content and skills.

As with all students, most of those with disabilities participate in standard state- or district-wide assessments, using a variety of accommodations (e.g., braille, extra time). Even those with the most significant cognitive impairments are assessed for accountability purposes. Students whose instruction is based on alternate achievement standards are administered **alternate assessments** instead of the state assessments given to the general school population. These tests are sometimes referred to as *alternative assessments based on alternate achievement standards* (AA-AAS). As you learned earlier, these tests are related to grade-level content, but they assess only a portion of the content or a more simplified version of the content. The major objective of including these students in tests that assess grade-level content is to ensure high expectations for these students. Although in past years, many of these students received instruction only in life skills, educators are now beginning to understand that these students can learn and can benefit from grade-level academic content.

At present, the federal government allows no more than 1% of all students being tested to use alternate assessments. That is why sometimes these tests are referred to as the *1% assessment*. Unfortunately, students who take these tests are sometimes referred to by terms such as the *1% kids*. Although these terms have taken hold among many educators, it is unfair to label students in this way, simply because they use alternate curricula or have adjusted standards. Just as it is important to use people-first language, it is also important not to refer to individuals with disabilities in a stigmatizing way. For up-to-date information about each state's accountability system and policies about alternative assessments and accommodations, visit the Website maintained by the National Center on Educational Outcomes at https://nceo.info

Topic 14.6 Early Intervention

- Because of the severity of their conditions, infants with the most significant disabilities are often identified at birth or soon thereafter.

- These young children have IFSPs through which they receive needed therapies, and their parents also receive training.

How are infants and toddlers with multiple disabilities, TBI, or deaf-blindness identified? Many factors, or a combination of factors, can cause the conditions associated with multiple disabilities or deaf-blindness, including heredity, complications during pregnancy, or problems during birth. Because of the severity of the disabilities, most of these children are identified at, or shortly after, birth. Hospital doctors and nurses often recognize early warning signs that alert them to disabilities in newborns, and universal newborn screening procedures identify infants with hearing and vision problems. Other infants are identified when they do not meet typical infant and toddler developmental milestones. It is rare for a child with multiple disabilities or with deaf-blindness to make it to kindergarten without being identified, although some of these students may start receiving services under the IDEA category of developmental delay until the exact nature of their disability can be ascertained.

Usher syndrome, a genetic condition that causes deaf-blindness, is one of the few exceptions in which children are usually identified at older ages. Individuals with Usher syndrome have congenital deafness, progressive blindness, and intellectual disabilities. These children are born deaf and then, across time, lose their ability to see. In addition, many people with Usher syndrome have problems with walking, balance, and other motor activities. This recessive, X-linked genetic syndrome is rare, affecting roughly 4 of every 100,000 people. However, its prevalence varies by locale. For example, in Louisiana some 15% to 20% of students with deaf-blindness have Usher syndrome, and 30% of all deaf individuals in three parishes (counties) have the syndrome. By comparison, nationally only 3% to 6% of students with deaf-blindness have Usher syndrome. Why the concentration in Louisiana? Remember the story of the Deaf on Martha's Vineyard who came to America from Kent, England, carrying a gene for congenital deafness? A similar situation occurred in Louisiana where the Cajun people, who emigrated from Nova Scotia, carried the gene responsible for Usher syndrome. Because the Cajun communities are small and less mobile, the prevalence is higher.

The identification process for children with TBI also involves medical professionals. Infants and toddlers can experience TBI through falls, accidents, or **shaken baby syndrome**. Symptoms of TBI for very young children can include lack of consciousness, lethargy, breathing difficulties, pale or bluish skin color, difficulty eating, vomiting, and convulsions. A severe TBI may be identified rather quickly for children treated in emergency rooms. Other cases might not be recognized immediately, such as when a toddler, walking on wobbly legs, falls when an adult is not looking. Later, as the toddler is uncharacteristically lethargic, unresponsive, or not interested in eating, a pediatrician may be the first to determine that a TBI has occurred.

What types of early intervention services do these children receive? For children with the most significant disabilities, high-quality early intervention and preschool services have strong, positive, long-term outcomes. The presence or absence of these services affects the number and intensity of supports needed as adults, level of independence, level of community presence, and quality of life. As a result, it is critical that infants and toddlers with significant needs receive the extra interventions and supports that will help them learn, grow, and prepare for school and eventually life as an adult.

These children have individualized family service plans (IFSPs) and usually receive early intervention services in their homes. Such services often include a combination of therapies (e.g., occupational, physical, speech and language). In addition to services through IDEA, some infants also require medical interventions (e.g., surgery to address heart defects), oxygen therapy for those with lung problems, or special (soft) diets for those whose digestive systems cannot assimilate solid foods.

Family members also receive services to help them interact in positive and supportive ways with their infants (e.g., how to reinforce therapies during daily routines). For example, a toddler who has had multiple surgeries may avoid moving his arms and legs because of painful post-surgery memories. Parents can learn how to encourage and reinforce his limb movement, which is necessary to develop subsequent reaching, grasping, rolling over, crawling, and walking skills. Family members are also taught how to support knowledge and concept development. In Chapter 13, you learned some of the challenges of teaching abstract concepts to a young child with visual disabilities. Those challenges can be compounded when the child also has a hearing loss. Incidental learning, particularly that which occurs through visual and auditory means, is impaired, and parents must learn different ways of providing information to a child through tactile methods.

These infants usually need early intervention in communication skills. Speech and language therapy can improve speech communication skills for some students with significant disabilities. The use of augmentative and alternative communication (AAC) devices, discussed in further detail in Topic 14.12, can also start at a very young age. Some deaf-blind children have enough functional vision to use ASL; some have enough residual hearing to learn to speak (such as Haben Girma, who was featured in the chapter opening vignette).

In some cases, early intervention professionals will teach the child to communicate through tactile methods or a combination of methods, as is illustrated in the video below. Lacy uses both oral language and ASL to answer her mother's questions.

▶ **Lacy Talks With Her Mom—Module 8**
https://youtu.be/uQp0Eihw2WA

Although infants and toddlers often receive early intervention services in their homes, older children—those between the ages of three and five—usually receive special education services in preschool programs. Many of these programs are fully inclusive; children with and without disabilities play, learn, and grow together. Students without disabilities, who show typical developmental patterns, are role models for language, social behavior, and motor skills. In turn, they learn from a very young age to accept and accommodate for all types of differences among their friends.

Topic 14.7 School Years

- Many of the academic and behavioral interventions effective with other disabilities are appropriate for students with multiple disabilities, TBI, and deaf-blindness.

- Many of these students require special curricula and instructional topics that are not part of the general education curriculum.

What types of interventions are effective with students with multiple disabilities, TBI, or deaf-blindness? In many cases, academic and behavioral interventions that we have discussed in previous chapters are appropriate for these students. For example, students with multiple disabilities often have intellectual disabilities, speech and language impairments, and physical or health impairments, so evidence-based practices for those disabilities can be used. Students with TBI often have learning characteristics similar to those of their classmates with learning disabilities or with ADHD, such as memory deficits, attention problems, language impairments, and academic difficulties, so the evidence-based practices discussed in those chapters are often applicable. Many of the techniques and interventions appropriate for students with hearing loss or visual impairments can be used with deaf-blind students, depending on the amount of functional hearing or vision they have. When selecting interventions, the key is to recognize the ways in which a disability, or combination of disabilities, affects each child and address those needs on an individual basis. The following table summarizes the disabilities, evidence-based practices, and related services that you have learned about in previous chapters that may be effective for students with multiple disabilities, TBI, or deaf-blindness.

Summary of Evidence-Based Practices

Disability	Evidence-Based Practice/ Related Service	Recommended for All Students with Disabilities
Speech or language impairment	• Speech/language therapy • AAC devices • Graphic organizers	UDL Differentiated instruction Accommodations Assistive technology Self-determination Self-advocacy
Learning disability	• Explicit instruction • Learning strategies • Study skills instruction	
ADHD	• Self-regulation strategies • Behavior therapy • Organization and time management instruction	
ASD	• ABA • PECS	
Intellectual disability	• Functional curriculum • Community-based instruction	
EBD	• Counseling/mental health services • FBA • Wraparound supports	
Physical/health impairment	• Physical therapy • Occupational therapy • School nursing services	
Hearing impairment	• Manual communication (ASL) • Interpreters	
Visual disability	• Braille • Orientation and mobility training • Expanded core curriculum	

How is instruction for students with the most significant disabilities different from that of students with other disabilities? As with blind students, some students with deaf-blindness need to learn skills from the expanded core curriculum, such as braille and orientation and mobility. Some require services from specialized personnel. For example, many deaf-blind students benefit from the aid of an **intervener** to facilitate communication and as a bridge to interacting with other people, objects, or information in the environment. These professionals provide services similar to those of an interpreter for Deaf students. However, instead of only giving translations of oral speech, interveners also work with teachers to provide and facilitate instruction. The following table supplies more information on the role of the intervener.

The Role of the Intervener

Information Access	Communication Access	Social-Emotional Access
Presents information in formats that student can access	Facilitates development of communication skills	Develops a trusted relationship with the student
Connects student to people and objects in the environment	Responds to student's communication	Reduces the student's sense of isolation
Helps student learn incidental concepts and information	Provides opportunities for communication with others	Supports development of self-determination skills

SOURCE: Adapted from *A Family's Guide to Interveners for Children with Combined Vision and Hearing Loss,* by L. Alsop, C. Berg, V. Hartman, M. Knapp, C. Levasseur, M. Prouty, & S. Prouty, 2012, Logan, UT: Utah State University SKI-HI Institute. Retrieved from http://intervener.org/wp-content/uploads/2012/06/A-Familys-Guide-to-Interveners.pdf

For those interested in learning more about interveners, we have included links to two videos. In the first video, two interveners talk briefly about their roles, and one demonstrates how he works with a student with deaf-blindness. In the second video, several interveners work with students to introduce new concepts, practice academic skills, and engage in activities of daily living (combing hair and brushing teeth). You'll notice that two of the interveners consistently keep their own hands under the hands of the students to help them learn through touch. This type of communication is sometimes referred to as the *hand under hand* method.

▶ **Luis and Gloria: Intervener Take Aways**

https://www.youtube.com/watch?v=UnSU3YpxUa8

▶ **Interveners and Students Working Together – Module 3**

https://www.youtube.com/watch?v=aKIXMD3NQIA

Students with the most significant disabilities may require more comprehensive systems of support than students with a single disability, particularly when the combination of disabilities produces complex and severe learning needs. For those who require significant time and intensive interventions to learn skills related to independent living, a functional curriculum or **alternate curriculum**, which focuses on instructional areas related to a person's daily needs, is appropriate. In each case, the IEP team members make decisions regarding the curriculum the student should follow based on his or her individual needs and abilities. Team members must take care not to let stereotypes or low expectations influence their decisions; as Haben Girma in the chapter opening vignette shows us, individuals with multiple challenges can excel when provided appropriate accommodations, assistive technology, and supports.

When an IEP team determines that a student will not be able to learn academic skills or knowledge from the general education curriculum (e.g., biology, algebra) at a level that would be useful in daily life, team members will then develop goals and objectives for a functional curriculum. Reading instruction within a functional curriculum focuses on learning practical words, such as those found on menus or traffic signs, or recognizing those important for personal safety (e.g., *warning, danger, poison, caution*). Examples of functional mathematics skills are those needed to successfully handle money or measure ingredients in a recipe. Functional skills in other areas—transportation, recreation and leisure, personal care—are taught so that the individual has as much independence as possible. The accountability for progress on these skills then occurs through an alternate assessment (see Topic 14.5).

Topic 14.8 Transition

- Individualized transition plans for students with multiple disabilities, TBI, and deaf-blindness contain some of the same kinds of goals as those for students with other types of disabilities.

- Community-based instruction (CBI) is an evidence-based practice for teaching many skills, including those necessary for independent living.

What kinds of transition goals are included in IEPs for students with multiple disabilities, TBI, or deaf-blindness? These students usually have individualized transition plans (ITPs) as part of their IEPs. Because their disabilities are so severe, many continue to receive special education services through the age of 21, as allowed under IDEA. For those who plan to attend college, the extra years may be needed to amass the number of high school course credits required for graduation. Why might this be so? These students might not be able to take full course loads every year. Students with multiple disabilities or TBI who have medical and health concerns may miss a lot of school, requiring them to re-take classes or to take a reduced class load. Students with deaf-blindness may need to spend several periods per day learning braille or orientation and mobility skills, which also reduces their course completion rate.

Regardless of whether students are planning for college or postsecondary vocational training or jobs, IEP team members—including the student—must carefully plan for the appropriate option, considering factors and skill development discussed in previous chapters:

- Study skills
- Time management
- Organizational skills
- High school graduation requirements
- College admissions requirements
- College disability services
- Pre-vocational opportunities (e.g., job shadowing, internships)
- Vocational training
- Independent living skills

Person-centered planning involves the individual with disabilities and the family in decisions about services needed, jobs to be supported, living arrangements, and related preferences. The IEP team must also incorporate the student's preferences and interests when developing goals related to future educational options, living arrangements, and employment opportunities. Therefore, the promotion of individual choice, self-determination, and self-advocacy skills are important components of transition planning. Think back to the chapter opening vignette, when Haben Girma discussed her cafeteria dilemma. Most of us don't realize the importance of something as simple as being able to choose our own meals—until that choice is taken away. Imagine how frustrating it would be to spend four years without choice-making opportunities during mealtime, which is what Haben's college experience would have been like had she not used her self-determination and self-advocacy skills to change that situation. Not only did she improve her own situation, but also she improved the attitudes and perceptions of the cafeteria staff as well as the mealtime options for future students with visual disabilities. Something as simple as providing choices, which includes the consideration of the student's preferences in the decision-making process, can produce positive results in far-reaching areas of the student's life, such as employment and style of living.

Make no assumptions about what people can accomplish! College graduation is a personal goal for many students with multiple disabilities, TBI, or deaf-blindness. Sadly, some students never have a chance to attend college because someone in a position of power (e.g., transition coordinator, college admissions officer, professor) has negative perceptions or low expectations for people with disabilities.

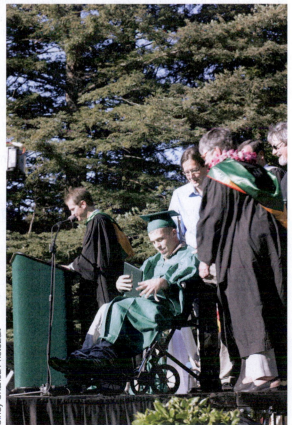

Cindy Charles/PhotoEdit

What are ways in which functional skills are taught? For many students with the most significant disabilities, the last few years of school are guided by overall aspirations for independent living and community presence. Their ITPs often reflect goals related to employment, community participation, recreation and leisure, continuing education, independent living, and self-determination. These goals require carefully orchestrated instruction and guided experiences within the community, which often take years of work and planning by the students, family members, and teams of professionals from different agencies and organizations. These guided experiences often begin early in their school careers. For example, during elementary and middle school, students should be introduced to sports and recreational activities in school and in the community. When in high school, they should participate in school sports and extracurricular activities when appropriate. Added benefits of early exposure to recreation and leisure include the development of skills needed to make friends and participate in social activities. Similarly, opportunities to learn functional skills need to occur in the community, or **natural settings**. **Community-based instruction (CBI)**, explained in more detail in the accompanying box and video, is an evidence-based practice used to teach these skills in a natural setting and has been shown to improve success and inclusion in typical daily life activities and lead to competitive employment opportunities.

Community-Based Instruction (CBI)

For students under age 14, education and training in functional skills can consist of simulations that occur in the classroom or other school locations. After age 14, when allowable by child labor laws, learning should happen in authentic, or natural, settings that reflect the student's interests and preferences. Instruction is systematic, designed for success, and delivered by special education personnel, job coaches, or vocation specialists.

Steps to Follow

1. Assess the student's preferences and interests.
   - Determine the student's job preferences and interests.
   - Involve the student in determining the type of job and employment site.
   - Practice at school before placing the student at a job site or pairing with an employee.
2. Establish community-based training sites.
   - Develop a list of work site opportunities (e.g., types and size of businesses, work opportunities).
   - Identify and analyze job appropriateness (e.g., interest, age appropriateness, skill requirements) and match with the student.
   - Be sure the site is welcoming; interview the boss and co-workers.
   - Select job sites within feasible distances for transportation from school and home.
   - Establish open communication pathways between the school and work site.
   - Develop job site evaluation criteria.

3. Ensure the student knows implicit and explicit rules of the site and can meet skill expectations. Teach the student to:
   - Use transportation to travel from school, arrive at work on time, and independently return home.
   - Dress appropriately, take breaks properly, and execute the work tasks correctly.
   - Seek help when necessary, work well with a mentor or job coach, interact appropriately with co-workers, and find natural supports in the workplace.

Example of a Transportation Map

This visual, developed by a high school student, provides a guide to get from work to home using public transportation.

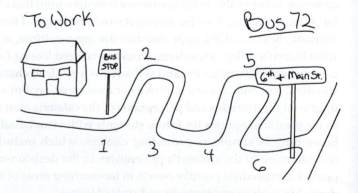

The video below highlights some key features of community-based instruction and shows a number of students in various community settings learning vocational and independent life skills. It also highlights some of the non-academic skills (e.g., social, behavioral) that students need for success in the community.

▶ **Why CBI? Community-Based Instruction**

https://youtu.be/i__gP3ZzQDA

Check Your Understanding 14.2

Click here to gauge your understanding of the concepts in this section.

People and Situations

Learning Outcome

Describe two turning points in the history of people with multiple disabilities, TBI, and deaf-blindness, identify some ways in which these individuals can experience more community inclusion and involvement, and list reputable organizations that provide reliable information for these individuals and their families.

Topic 14.9 Origins and History

- The accomplishments of one or two people can influence the treatment and education of countless individuals with disabilities.

- Single events can inspire innovations that prevent some disabilities or spur the development of services to support those who have them.

Topic 14.10 Personal Stories

- Sometimes creative individuals develop programs and opportunities that make a remarkable difference in recreation and leisure experiences for many people.

- A number of reputable organizations provide reliable information and supports for individuals with disabilities and their families.

These adults are enjoying a vacation that was arranged by Sprout, an organization that coordinates over 100 trips per year for adults with disabilities.

Courtesy of GoSprout.org http://www.gosprout.org

Topic 14.9 Origins and History

- The accomplishments of one or two people can influence the treatment and education of countless individuals with significant disabilities.

- Single events can inspire innovations that prevent some disabilities or spur the development of services to support those who have them.

Are there examples of successful individuals with significant disabilities in our history? Stories of success can often inspire others to think and behave in more positive ways. Although Helen Keller is probably the world's most famous deaf-blind person, she would have accomplished none of her celebrated achievements without her teacher, Anne Sullivan, who had low vision. Here is their interesting story, some of which overlaps with history that you learned in Chapter 13 and that illustrates Helen Keller's noteworthy "family tree." As you may recall from Topic 13.10, Samuel Gridley Howe was the founder of the Perkins School for the Blind. Located in Boston, it was the first school in the United States for blind students. One of Howe's pupils was Laura Dewey Bridgman, who had deaf-blindness. Laura communicated with other people by tapping letters and using a manual alphabet, and she used braille for reading. Laura eventually became a teacher at Perkins, and one of her students was Anne Sullivan.

At the age of 20, Anne moved to Alabama to teach Helen Keller, a six-year-old who had been born with normal vision and hearing but who became deaf and blind after a serious illness when she was 19 months old. Anne brought a gift, the doll shown in the photo below, that the students at the Perkins School for the Blind made for Helen. As Helen held the doll, Anne would spell "d-o-l-l" into her hand to help her connect manual letters with concrete objects. In the end, the link between water and "w-a-t-e-r" enabled Helen to make this connection, and her education took off. Anne taught Helen throughout her school years and remained with Helen when she attended Radcliffe College, struggling through the heavy reading requirements with failing vision while manually signing everything she read to Helen. Helen graduated from Radcliffe in 1904, a remarkable achievement for a woman of her time. The two women remained lifelong companions until Anne's death in 1936, at which time Polly Thomson, who had been their secretary, assumed Anne's responsibilities. Helen had a long career as a writer and social activist, traveling the globe and meeting with many world leaders. Her successes helped people recognize the accomplishments that individuals with disabilities could achieve with determination, hard work, appropriate accommodations, and meaningful supports.

What is an example of a key turning point in history that has affected individuals with the most significant disabilities? Sometimes, unfortunately, a tragic event calls attention to a problem, which forces people to generate solutions. For instance, prior to the 1960s, there was no vaccine for rubella, so the disease could not be prevented. Between 1962 and 1965, a rubella epidemic swept the nation. The aftermath was devastating, particularly for children whose mothers contracted the disease while pregnant. These children were born with disabilities, particularly blindness, deafness, and deaf-blindness. Before the epidemic, the prevalence had been exceptionally low—only 20 deaf-blind people were reported in the 1920 census and 160 people in 1930. Even with the recognition that Helen Keller had received by that time, very few services were available for this extremely small population. Then the epidemic of the 1960s occurred and resulted in some 2,500 babies born with deaf-blindness and many others with serious vision and hearing problems. Although IDEA was not yet a reality, Congress

Helen Keller (left), holding the doll given to her by Anne Sullivan (right).

recognized the importance of getting services to these children and their families. In 1967, Congress established the Helen Keller National Center to provide rehabilitation services to deaf-blind individuals. Since then, development of technical assistance and other services has continued and been expanded.

Revisiting the Vaccination Controversy

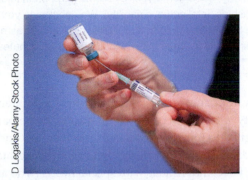

D Legakis/Alamy Stock Photo

Recall from Topic 8.10 that Andrew Wakefield's fraudulent claims of an ASD-vaccination link have caused many parents to postpone or deny the measles, mumps, and rubella (MMR) vaccination for their children. After reading about the devastating results of the rubella epidemic of the 1960s, you now understand why it is important for all children to be protected.

Topic 14.10 Personal Stories

- Sometimes creative individuals develop programs and opportunities that make a remarkable difference in recreation and leisure experiences for many people.

- A number of reputable organizations provide reliable information and supports for individuals with disabilities and their families.

What are some examples of community participation and inclusion for individuals with the most significant disabilities? Students and adults with multiple disabilities, TBI, or deaf-blindness have low rates of participation in the community. These individuals often find that travel and recreational activities are not available to them. Even family outings can present challenges that most of us cannot anticipate. However, thanks to the creativity and ingenuity of some individuals, the opportunities for participation are expanding in many settings. We provide two examples below.

In 1979, Anthony Di Salvo created Sprout (http://gosprout.org), one of the first vacation programs designed specifically for people who have disabilities and could not otherwise take vacations. Today, the company offers over 100 trips, domestic and international, every year. In addition, Sprout offers programs for individuals with disabilities who live in New York City, such as evening and weekend recreational and cultural activities for adults, or school vacation programs for adolescents and young adults between the ages of 14 and 21. Sprout has grown and expanded over the years to include other activities such as Sproutstock, an annual music and video festival; Make-a-Movie Program, which produces films with actors who have developmental disabilities in the main roles; and the Sprout Film Festival, which features films and videos related to the lives of individuals with intellectual and developmental disabilities.

Anthony Di Salvo/Sproutflix

Anthony Di Salvo, founder of Sprout

On the Screen

Rather than focus on a single film in this chapter, we introduce you to an entire collection of movies. Sproutflix, another one of Anthony Di Salvo's innovative ideas, is an offshoot of Sprout that distributes films featuring individuals with intellectual and developmental disabilities, with the goal to inspire, inform, and spark change. All Sproutflix films have passed a committee selection process and have been screened at the Sprout Film Festival, an annual event in New York City that is followed by a year-long tour. Together, Sproutflix and the Sprout Film Festival strive to

use film to promote social change, celebrate the lives of individuals with intellectual and developmental disabilities, challenge assumptions, and vanquish stereotypes.

Like other film and video services, Sprout films can be accessed by livestream, download, or DVD. Viewers can sort through the Sproutflix library of films by genre (e.g, action, comedy, documentary) or by theme (e.g., brain injury, relationships, intellectual disability). We encourage you to visit the Sproutflix site (http://sproutflix.org/) and stream one of their free films, many of which are under 20 minutes long.

Morgan's Wonderland (www.MorgansWonderland.com) offers a different type of recreation and leisure opportunity: a totally-accessible, non-profit theme park in San Antonio, Texas. The park is designed to improve inclusive opportunities and interactions for those with and without disabilities, from all socioeconomic backgrounds, and of all ages (e.g., "Senior Fridays"). Here, individuals with special needs (who are admitted for free), their families, and friends can engage in all sorts of fun activities: access a Sensory Village, play wheelchair basketball and other sports, explore specially designed slides and other equipment on a fully accessible playground, and ride a wheelchair-accessible train (Wonderland Express). The park also has a Ferris wheel, a carousel, and Off-Road Adventure ride, all of which are fully accessible for people in wheelchairs. The park's designers didn't just plan for physical inclusiveness, but for emotional acceptance as well. For example, the Ferris wheel staff members load the gondolas according to the needs of the riders, not according to a pre-set, timed schedule. So families don't feel stress or pressure from staffers or other riders if it takes them a few minutes to enter and get themselves and their equipment situated. The park emphasizes quality rather than quantity, so huge crowds are not a problem. Family members can wear special computerized bracelets to help them keep track of each other.

The video below introduces you to Morgan Hartman, the inspiration for the park, her family, and their dream for a fully inclusive environment.

▶ **The Story of Morgan's Wonderland**
https://youtu.be/5WkuKJxwmOk

What organizations or agencies are available to support students with the most significant disabilities and their families? A number of organizations and agencies provide valuable information and offer support. We highlight several of them here.

- *TASH* (www.tash.org) seeks to promote full inclusion of students with the most significant disabilities at school, in the community, and in daily life. The organization works to foster social justice and advocates for equity, opportunities, and human rights.

- The *Brain Injury Association of America* (www.biausa.org) seeks to raise awareness and understanding about TBI. It has a network of state and local affiliates, and together they are working to ensure that more health and social services are available to individuals affected.

- The *National Institute of Neurological Disorders and Stroke* (https://www.ninds.nih.gov/Disorders/All-Disorders/Traumatic-Brain-Injury-Information-Page) is part of the National Institutes for Health and provides reliable information about TBI.

- *The National Center on Deaf-Blindness* (NCDB) (www.nationaldb.org) is funded by the U.S. Department of Education to provide technical assistance to the states about deaf-blind children and youth. It provides the largest collection of information related to deaf-blindness in the world.

- *The American Association of Deaf-Blind* (AADB) (www.aadb.org) is an organization "of, by, and for deaf-blind Americans and their supporters." The organization maintains an information clearinghouse. The group is currently focusing on how to improve services and also to make technology more accessible and less expensive for deaf-blind people.

Check Your Understanding 14.3

Click here to gauge your understanding of the concepts in this section.

Future Perspectives

Learning Outcome

Describe the benefits of prevention and immediate medical intervention for TBI, and identify helpful assistive technology for individuals with the most significant disabilities.

Topic 14.11 Prevention: TBI

- Although the cause of TBI is unknown in many cases, motor vehicle accidents and falls are leading factors.

- Simple preventive actions and parent training can prevent many cases of TBI.

Topic 14.12 Technology: Improving Access

- Switches are devices that can enhance the functionality of many types of assistive technology.

- Advancements in technology allow individuals with the most significant disabilities to gain more access to the community than ever before.

Andy Mead/Icon SMI/Getty Images

As a society, we are now more knowledgeable about the dangers of repeated head injuries and concussions. Observant teachers may be the first to recognize the signs of a TBI and alert medical professionals and families so that further damage can be prevented.

Topic 14.11 Prevention: TBI

- Although the cause of TBI is unknown in many cases, motor vehicle accidents and falls are leading factors.

- Simple preventive actions and parent training can prevent many cases of TBI.

What are the leading causes of TBI? In most cases, we need to understand the causes of a condition or disability in order to enact preventive measures. The following charts show the leading causes of TBI for young people but depict the data in two different ways. The first shows the leading causes of TBI overall; the second breaks those data out by age groups.

Leading Causes of TBI Resulting in Hospitalization: Ages Birth Through Age 24

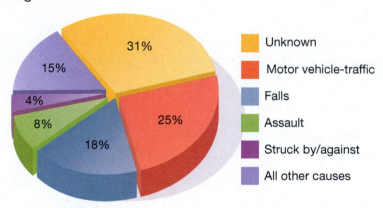

SOURCE: Centers for Disease Control and Prevention (CDC), *Percent Distributions of TBI-Related Hospitalizations by Age Group and Injury Mechanism — United States, 2006–2010*, retrieved from http://www.cdc.gov/traumaticbraininjury/data/dist_hosp.html

Leading Causes of TBI Resulting in Hospitalization: By Age Group

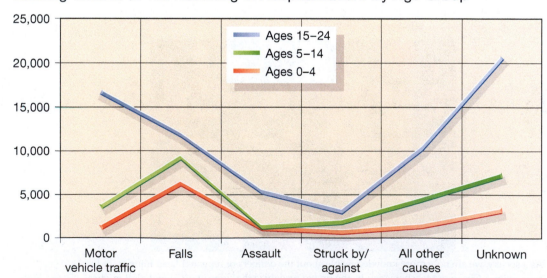

SOURCE: Centers for Disease Control and Prevention (CDC), *Percent Distributions of TBI-Related Hospitalizations by Age Group and Injury Mechanism — United States, 2006–2010*, retrieved from http://www.cdc.gov/traumaticbraininjury/data/dist_hosp.html

As you can see from the first chart, unknown causes account for the largest portion of TBI cases in the United States. Of those for which the origin is known, motor vehicle accidents are the leading cause, followed by falls. However, the numbers look very different when compared across age groups. Individuals in the 15- to 24-year age group have the highest number of cases, accounting for the majority of the unknown and motor vehicle instances. In contrast, falls are the leading cause of TBI for the younger age groups, with a much lower incidence of TBIs caused by motor vehicle accidents.

Instances of TBI resulting from sports and recreation injuries can fall under the "struck by/against" category. These injuries typically occur among older children, particularly teenage boys who participate in contact sports or who do not take safety precautions (i.e., wearing helmets) while engaged in activities such as bicycling, skateboarding, or riding in all-terrain vehicles (ATVs). In fact, the rate of TBIs among males is two to three times higher than the rate of females, depending on the age group. The most recent data regarding sports-related TBIs are illustrated in the following graph.

Sports-Related Causes of TBI Among People Age 19 or Younger

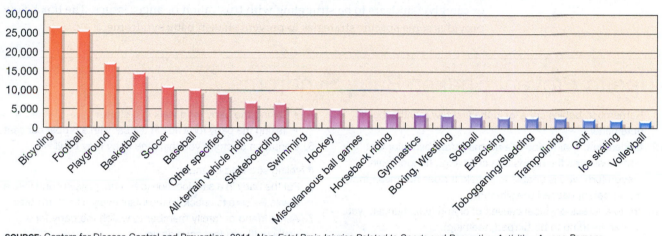

SOURCE: Centers for Disease Control and Prevention, 2011, *Non-Fatal Brain Injuries Related to Sports and Recreation Activities Among Persons Aged ≤19 years–United States*, 2001–2009, retrieved from www.cdc.gov/mmwr/preview/mmwrhtml/mm6039a1.htm?s_cid=mm6039a1_w#tab2

Earlier in the chapter we mentioned shaken baby syndrome, a cause of TBI in infants. Most of these abuse cases are caused by male parents and caregivers (fathers, stepfathers, mothers' boyfriends) who become frustrated by an infant's excessive crying and respond with physical force. Sadly, assault is the leading cause of TBI-related deaths for children under the age of four.

How can TBI be prevented? Many TBI cases can be prevented or the injuries minimized through common sense measures. Recall that motor vehicle accidents are a leading cause for those between the ages of 15 and 24. Many of these accidents can be prevented through typical safety measures: wearing seat belts and refraining from dangerous or reckless driving behaviors (speeding, texting or distracted driving activities, driving under the influence of alcohol or drugs). Wearing helmets when bicycling, skateboarding, or playing contact sports can reduce the possibility of TBIs as well. Avoiding high-risk behaviors can prevent tragic accidents, but when they do occur, immediate medical attention can reduce the severity of the damage. Although access to health care is critical, some children try to hide their injuries from parents and teachers because they don't want to get in trouble for breaking rules or are embarrassed that they behaved irresponsibly. In other cases, they may not remember the injury, understand its seriousness, or realize the symptoms they are experiencing indicate head trauma. Consequently, they fail to mention the symptoms to an adult. To recognize when an injury has occurred and to get immediate medical help, teachers and parents must be alert to these symptoms.

All concussions are serious, even those that are not considered TBIs or that do not result in a loss of consciousness or hospitalization. It is important to follow concussion protocols to prevent further brain injury, which then can turn into a TBI. Injured athletes should not return to play until cleared by a neurologist or physician who is trained in or specializes in concussion evaluations, as pediatricians may not have the expertise required to properly evaluate a brain injury. Injured brains require complete rest, so students recovering from a concussion should avoid even the most common tasks: reading and writing—which includes texting, not just schoolwork—driving, watching television, playing video games, or talking on the phone. This can be difficult for parents to enforce, as most children and teenagers have a difficult time sitting quietly without engaging in any activities. However, until the concussion issues have been resolved and the student has been cleared by the appropriate medical personnel, these actions can protect the brain and prevent more serious consequences later.

Finally, parent and community training on shaken baby syndrome can teach parents better ways of dealing with a crying infant. Increased public awareness can also provide community members with ways to recognize and intervene when a parent or caregiver appears to be struggling with frustration or anger issues. The box below provides some specific strategies to prevent shaken baby syndrome.

Tips to Prevent Shaken Baby Syndrome

1. Remember, babies cry a lot in the first few months, but it gets better.
2. Understand that crying is a normal infant behavior that communicates the needs of a child (e.g., hunger, pain, discomfort) who is unable to speak. It does not mean that a bad parent caused the situation.
3. Try to address physical causes of crying (e.g., hunger, wet diaper, needing to be burped, teething).
4. Try other means to calm the baby, such as
   - Rubbing the child's back
   - Gently rocking the child
   - Offering a pacifier to the child
   - Singing or talking softly
   - Taking the baby for a walk in a stroller
   - Taking the baby for a ride in the car with a proper car seat
5. Contact a doctor if you think the baby may be ill.

If feeling stressed or angry:
6. Put the baby in a safe location (e.g., crib, playpen) and take a break. Be sure to check on the infant every 5 to 10 minutes.
7. Ask a friend or family member to watch the baby for a while until you feel calm again.
8. Seek help from counselors or other health care professionals for ongoing feelings of anger.

SOURCE: Adapted from Centers for Disease Control and Prevention (CDC), *A Journalist's Guide to Shaken Baby Syndrome: A Preventable Tragedy,* retrieved from https://stacks.cdc.gov/view/cdc/5865/Email

Topic 14.12 Technology: Improving Access

- Switches are devices that can enhance the functionality of many types of assistive technology.

- Advancements in technology allow individuals with the most significant disabilities to gain more access to the community than ever before.

What are some technology options for individuals with multiple disabilities, TBI, or deafblindness? You learned in Chapter 5 about **augmentative and alternative communication (AAC) devices**, which allow for communication that would not otherwise be possible for many individuals with significant disabilities. Use of AAC is a documented proven practice that supplements or replaces spoken communication. As you learned, AAC devices or systems can be very simple, like **communication boards** that allow individuals to use pictures to make their needs known, express their feelings, or interact with others. They can also be high-tech and include devices and systems like speech synthesizers that produce spoken words for the individual. In many of these systems, the individual touches symbols on a touchscreen; the device then converts the message to speech.

However, some people with disabilities do not have the physical strength or motor skills necessary to perform a seemingly simple action such as pointing to a picture or symbol. In other cases, the individual has significant cognitive disabilities that prohibit the use of AAC systems that require reading, that entail understanding print symbols, or that would be difficult for the person to understand and use. In yet other cases, the communicative goal is to convey the simplest of messages, such as "yes" rather than "no," or to indicate a preference for juice over milk at lunch. In such situations, the use of **switches** can be helpful. A switch—any type of electrical tool that activates a second device—can be connected to many different types of devices, creating an assistive technology "bundle" that can meet the needs of an individual.

An example of how switches and other forms of technology can be combined is provided in the video below. In this video, Jared, who has cerebral palsy and extremely limited physical abilities, uses simple switches, in combination with other technologies, to perform complicated functions as he runs his own graphic and Website design business.

▶ **AT in Action: Meet Jared!**

https://youtu.be/muWTCmZTbYk

As the video illustrates, switches can be used for other purposes besides communication. In Jared's case, switches help him to maneuver his wheelchair, conduct the activities of his business, and play computer games. Switches can also help individuals with disabilities have some level of autonomy over daily activities: turning on music to listen to favorite songs or artists, activating the TV, or turning off lights. Switches come in a variety of styles that address different functions and user abilities:

- Activation options—touch, proximity (e.g., identifies movement within a set distance from the device), infrared, sip and puff

- Type of feedback—tactile, auditory, visual

- Size—small, medium, or large surface areas

- Amount of force or pressure required to activate

Technological innovations for people with disabilities are being created at a rapid pace, and it can present a challenge to keep up with the latest advances. The U.S. Department of Education's Center on Technology and Disability (http://www.ctdinstitute.org) provides assistive technology information and services to students with disabilities and their families. The center also offers helpful information and training (e.g., Webinars) for teachers, researchers, service providers, and state and local leaders.

Costs for such technology can be prohibitive, particularly because few individuals with multiple disabilities, TBI, or deaf-blindness have high-paying jobs and their general living costs are often high due to medical expenses, the need for additional supports, and so on. For those who have deaf-blindness, however, financial support is available. Congress established the National Deaf-Blind Equipment Distribution Program in 2011, which gives most deaf-blind individuals access to recently developed communication services. The costs for purchasing and maintaining both specialized and "off the shelf" equipment are now covered. This law allows people in need to have and use devices that open doors to society and eliminate isolation from their daily lives.

What are some other examples of technologies that enhance access for people with multiple disabilities, TBI, or deaf-blindness? Examples of helpful technology are so plentiful that it would be impossible to include them all in this text. Further, technology changes so quickly that even those innovations we have highlighted in our chapters will have been improved upon or upgraded between the time this text goes online and the time you read it! Many technologies developed for individuals with disabilities now have a demand among all consumers, while other devices and apps designed for everyday use have benefits for those with disabilities. We think that a presentation by Haben Girma, whom you met in the chapter opening vignette, explains these benefits better than we can. In her speech, she demonstrates ways in which assistive technology can be used in conjunction with "regular" technology to provide access to the same types of everyday activities and communications that most people use. Haben gave this speech at Apple's 2016 Worldwide Developers Conference (WWDC) to demonstrate how she uses technology (some of which you learned about in Chapter 13) while exhorting developers to continue to push the innovative envelopes necessary to improve access for everyone. In her speech, she also discusses many of the other themes we have addressed throughout this text: the concept of a societal handicap vs. a disability, the benefits of UDL for everyone, and the need for high expectations.

Although we highly recommend watching Haben Girma's entire speech, we realize that you may not be able to view the entire 26-minute speech, so we have included the times for key parts of the presentation. If you choose to watch the entire video, you'll see Haben dancing (salsa), view pictures of her surfing and climbing a multi-story rope jungle gym, and hear a little bit about her experiences in an unfamiliar hotel during a visit to China—all examples of the active and inclusive lifestyle that can be achieved through a combination of societal acceptance, high expectations, a strong education, and appropriate supports and accommodations.

Here are timeframes for sections of Haben's speech:

- Explanation of her vision and hearing capabilities and Facebook friendships—01:08 to 03:50
- Communicating with President Obama and forms of communication—03:51 to 06:35
- Dancing and deafness—06:36 to 08:08
- Helen Keller and societal handicaps—08:08 to 11:17
- Technology demonstration—11:18 to 13:47
- Helpful technology features and the need for accessible apps—13:47 to 15:25
- Visit to China and "Why do blind people need a camera app?"—15:26 to 17:04
- Planning for accessibility and benefits to businesses—17:05 to 20:45
- Disability-based innovations that have crossed over to mainstream use—20:46 to 22:44
- Innovation and exploration, jungle gyms, and surfing—22:45 to 25:55

▶ **Disability & Innovation: The Universal Benefits of Accessible Design, by Haben Girma @ WWDC 2016**
https://youtu.be/_bC7Mvy7Vn4

Check Your Understanding 14.4

Click here to gauge your understanding of the concepts in this section.

Summary

Other Low-Incidence Disabilities Described

Three types of low-incidence disabilities require complex and very individualized educational responses: multiple disabilities, traumatic brain injury (TBI), and deaf-blindness

- Students with multiple disabilities have at least two complex disabilities that result in serious, multi-faceted challenges, unique across individuals.

- TBI results from a head injury produced by physical force; this injury presents serious challenges and can affect areas such as speech, balance, mobility, and cognition.

- Some individuals with deaf-blindness have no functional vision or hearing; however, most have some use of either their hearing or vision, or both.

- Multiple disabilities, TBI, and deaf-blindness have a combined prevalence rate of much less than 1% of all public school students; many of these students receive their education in more restrictive settings than other students with disabilities.

Special Education

Students with multiple disabilities, TBI, and deaf-blindness require a highly individualized and specially designed education to meet the unique challenges presented by their disabilities.

- Although the needs of students with multiple disabilities, TBI, and deaf-blindness vary greatly, these students can all benefit from accommodations.

- Some students with these disabilities may require a modified curriculum.

- Because of the severity of their conditions, infants with the most significant disabilities are often identified at birth or soon thereafter. These young children have IFSPs through which they receive needed therapies, and their parents also receive training.

- Many of the academic and behavioral interventions effective with other disabilities are appropriate for students with multiple disabilities, TBI, and deaf-blindness. However, many of these students require special curricula and instructional topics that are not part of the general education curriculum.

- Individualized transition plans (ITPs) for students with multiple disabilities, TBI, and deaf-blindness contain some of the same kinds of goals as those for students with other types of disabilities. In addition, community-based instruction (CBI) is an evidence-based practice that can be used to teach many skills, including those necessary for independent living.

People and Situations

The accomplishments of one or two people can influence the treatment and education of countless individuals with disabilities.

- Single events can inspire innovations that prevent some disabilities or spur the development of services to support those who have them.

- Sometimes creative individuals develop programs and opportunities that make a remarkable difference in recreation and leisure experiences for many people.

Future Perspectives

Of the three types of disabilities discussed in this chapter, TBI has the highest potential for successful preventive measures. Technological advances, however, can improve the daily lives of individuals with all of these disabilities.

- Although the cause of TBI is unknown in many cases, motor vehicle accidents and falls are leading factors. As a result, simple preventive actions and parent training can prevent many cases of TBI.

- Switches are devices that can enhance the functionality of many types of assistive technology.

- Advancements in technology allow individuals with the most significant disabilities to have more access to the community than ever before.

Addressing CEC Standards

Council for Exceptional Children (CEC) knowledge standards addressed in this chapter: 6.2, 1.0, 5.1, 3.0, 4.2, 7.0, DBI1K1, DBI1K2, DBI4S7, DBI10S1.

See the Appendix for the complete CEC Initial Level Special Educator Preparation Standards.

Chapter 15
Gifted and Talented

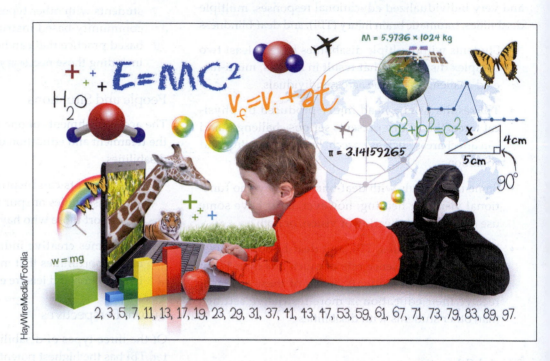

HayWireMedia/Fotolia

Yesterday my son, after spending 10 minutes sitting alone in deep concentration, with a calculator, paper, and pen, suddenly jumped up, screaming, "That's it! That's right! Point nine, nine, nine, repeating to infinity, equals one! It's true! It definitely equals one!" My son is 3 years old!

I didn't know what to say as he leaped on top of me excitedly, unable to stop talking about his eureka moment. So, after composing myself, I said, "Maybe .9999 repeating is just almost equal to 1?" He looked at me oddly. Then I said, "Point nine is how much less than 1?" He said, "One tenth." I asked, "How much less than 1 is 0.999999?" He said, "One one-millionth." "So," I finished, "maybe 0.9999 repeating to infinity is always missing some little piece."

He immediately countered with this: "One-third equals 0.3333 repeating to infinity, and two-thirds is 0.6666 repeating to infinity." He finished with, "One-third plus two-thirds equals one. And 0.3333 repeating plus 0.6666 repeating equals 0.9999 repeating . . . so, 0.9999 equals 1!" Then he ran around screaming with glee.

I have had so many jaw-dropping moments with this child, starting with hearing words come out of his mouth at 3 months of age, that I have become somewhat immune to his uniqueness. I look at him at night, clad in a diaper, sleeping calmly, with the remnants of the day's smiles still on his face, and wonder how it is that I am so lucky. And then, as I clean up, picking up from the floor math books aimed at kids 10 years his senior; shutting down a PowerPoint presentation he created that day, which includes an illustrated story he wrote; and tripping over scads of real 3-year-old toys, I start to worry about everything.

—Father of a highly gifted child, as cited in *Education of the Gifted and Talented* (6th ed.), by Gary A. Davis, Sylvia B. Rimm, and Del Siegle, © 2011, Upper Saddle River, NJ: Pearson Education. Reprinted and electronically reproduced by permission of Pearson Education, Inc., Upper Saddle River, NJ.

Learning Outcomes

Gifted and Talented Described

Define gifted and talented, describe the different types of giftedness, recognize the characteristics of gifted students, and understand prevalence and placement data for these students.

Special Education

Explain the academic and social challenges that gifted students encounter at school, describe accommodations that can address these challenges, understand practices and strategies that early childhood and classroom teachers can use to challenge gifted students and meet their unique needs, and describe factors to consider during the high school years to promote a successful transition to college.

People and Situations

Describe the history of gifted education and identify resources for gifted students and their parents.

Future Perspectives

Explain why many gifted and talented students do not receive educational supports and services that meet their learning needs, understand that certain groups of students are underrepresented in gifted programs, identify online learning sources that can be used to differentiate instruction and provide enrichment opportunities, and recognize that distance learning opportunities can help accommodate the needs of gifted students.

Gifted and Talented Described[1]

Learning Outcome

Define gifted and talented, describe the different types of giftedness, recognize the characteristics of gifted students, and understand prevalence and placement data for these students.

Topic 15.1 Gifted and Talented Defined

- Gifted and talented children have outstanding abilities and talents.

- Identification of gifted and talented students often rests on the results of intelligence or achievement test scores, but it should consider information from multiple sources.

Topic 15.2 Types of Giftedness

- Gifted students may be categorized using different constructs.

- Gifted students with disabilities are referred to as *twice-exceptional*.

---

[1]References for Chapter 15 are found at the end of this text.

Topic 15.3 Characteristics

- Even though gifted and talented students can display exceptional abilities in many areas, they often have common characteristics.

- These students tend to be socially and emotionally well-adjusted.

Topic 15.4 Prevalence and Placement

- Each state's definition and identification criteria influence the prevalence rate of students who are eligible for gifted and talented services or programs.

- The types of services provided to students vary based on grade level.

"Creativity is just connecting things. When you ask creative people how they did something, they feel a little guilty because they didn't really do it, they just saw something. It seemed obvious."—Steve Jobs, founder of Apple, Inc., inventor.
(Quote from "Steve Jobs: The Next Insanely Great Thing," by Gary Wolfe, *WIRED Magazine*, February 1996.)

Topic 15.1 Gifted and Talented Defined

- Gifted and talented children have outstanding abilities and talents.

- Identification of gifted and talented students often rests on the results of intelligence or achievement test scores, but it should consider information from multiple sources.

What does it mean to have special gifts and talents? Concepts and definitions of **gifted** and **talented** have evolved over the years. Across time, the definitions of giftedness have ranged from a narrow view based exclusively on cognition, reasoning, and the score a person receives on an intelligence test to a multi-dimensional view of intelligence, aptitudes, abilities, creativity, and talents.

Definitions of giftedness are used to identify students who are eligible for special programs. Although these programs are designed to meet the needs of gifted and talented students, they are not the same as special education programs to which other students with exceptionalities are entitled. As you will learn later in this chapter, gifted programs are not mandated by IDEA and are not provided in all states or districts. The following table provides three definitions commonly used to describe students who are considered gifted or talented. The first is the U.S. Department of Education's definition of giftedness, which gained national prominence in 1972 with the release of the Marland Report to Congress. Because this report on gifted education was crafted by Sidney Marland, the U.S. Commissioner of Education in 1972, it is sometimes referred to as the "Marland definition." With the passage of the Jacob K. Javits Gifted and Talented Students Education Act of 1988 (PL 100-297), a broader perspective on the education of the gifted and development of talent emerged, and that basic definition has been retained in every reauthorization of the Elementary and Secondary Education Act. The third definition is that of the National Association for Gifted Children, an organization devoted to helping educators, parents, and policy makers develop the abilities and talents of gifted children.

Definitions of Gifted and Talented

Term	Definition	Source
Gifted and talented children	Gifted and talented children are those identified by professionally qualified persons who by virtue of outstanding abilities are capable of high performance. These are children who require differentiated educational programs and services beyond those normally provided by the regular school program in order to realize their contributions to self and society. Children capable of high performance include those with demonstrated achievement and/or potential in any of the following areas: 1. General intellectual ability 2. Specific academic aptitude 3. Creative or productive thinking 4. Leadership ability 5. Visual or performing arts 6. Psychomotor ability It can be assumed that utilization of these criteria for identification of the gifted and talented will encompass a minimum of 3 to 5 percent of the school population.	U.S. Department of Education (The Marland Definition)
Gifted and talented	. . . (S)tudents, children, or youth who give evidence of high achievement capability in areas such as intellectual, creative, artistic, or leadership capacity, or in specific academic fields, and who need services or activities not ordinarily provided by the school in order to fully develop those capabilities.	Elementary and Secondary Education Act (2002), PL 107-110, Definition 22, as reauthorized in the Every Student Succeeds Act (2015)
Gifted individuals	Gifted individuals are those who demonstrate outstanding levels of aptitude (defined as an exceptional ability to reason and learn) or competence (documented performance or achievement in top 10% or rarer) in one or more domains. Domains include any structured area of activity with its own symbol system (e.g., mathematics, music, language) and/or set of sensorimotor skills (e.g., painting, dance, sports).	National Association for Gifted Children

SOURCES: U.S. Department of Education, *The Marland Report (The Marland Definition)* (pp. 10–11), Washington, DC, U.S. Government Printing Office, 1972; Elementary & Secondary Education Title IX—General Provisions, SEC. 9101; U.S. Department of Education, *Definitions*, National Association for Gifted Children, retrieved from https://www.nagc.org/resources-publications/resources/definitions-giftedness

Although there are two federal definitions of gifted and talented (listed in the table above), each state is allowed to develop its own definition; some include characteristics such as special talents and exceptional **creativity**. However, the federal definitions serve as the basis for most states' current definitions. A listing of every state's definition of giftedness is available at the National Association for Gifted Children's (NAGC) Website: www.nagc.org/uploadedFiles/Advocacy/State%20definitions%20(8-24-10).pdf

How are gifted and talented students identified? Identification of gifted children often happens early. They express their uniqueness almost from birth. These infants and toddlers master developmental milestones earlier than their typically developing peers and stay ahead of their age-mates across the early childhood period. They walk independently well before they are one year old; they talk in complete sentences before they are two. It is common to see these babies turning pages in books by the time they are six months old and reading books well before they start kindergarten. When parents, pediatricians, or child care providers notice that children are reaching developmental milestones earlier than expected, they can refer them for special programs or for early entrance to kindergarten.

Parents are usually the first to notice their child's gifts and alert the teacher. Unfortunately, teachers often do not recognize gifted behaviors and may fail to refer students for initial testing. Regardless, teachers are usually involved in the initial step in the assessment process, which is to refer students for screening or testing. Assessment is typically the gatekeeper to education for the gifted, but identification methods vary, reflecting the priorities of a school, district, or state. For example, if intelligence is the primary consideration, then IQ scores are given preference (e.g., at least two standard deviations above the norm, a score of 130 or higher). If academic achievement is the priority, then the criteria may focus on achievement scores (e.g., the top 3% to 5% of students, or those scoring in the 95th percentile or higher). However, these methods don't always identify culturally or linguistically diverse students or those from low-income backgrounds, as their intelligence and achievement test scores are often not indicative of their true potential. The methods also do not recognize students who exhibit exceptional creativity. For these reasons, among others, it is important to use multiple sources of information to identify gifted students.

The Talent Pool system of identification considers a broader range of characteristics and multiple sources of data in an attempt to find all students who exhibit giftedness and creativity. The procedures for identifying students are based on Renzulli's three-ring conception of giftedness, which considers three gifted traits: above average ability, creativity, and **task commitment**.

Renzulli's Three-Ring Conception of Giftedness

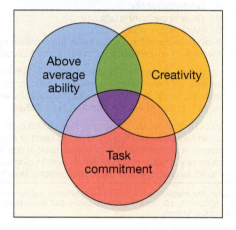

Rather than depending on IQ or achievement tests, teachers are encouraged to consider students who display outstanding skills in different areas (e.g., verbal and non-verbal reasoning, leadership, academics, art, creative writing, oral language). The multi-step process of the Talent Pool incorporates many identification measures:

- Intelligence tests (including non-verbal measures)
- Achievement tests
- Tests of creativity
- Teacher nominations
- Parent nominations
- Peer nominations
- Self-nominations
- Product samples or portfolios
- Performances (e.g., music, theater)

Talent Pool Identification System

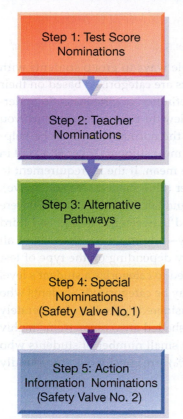

Step 1: Test Score Nominations	• Students in the 92nd percentile or higher are admitted. • These students will represent roughly half of the talent pool.
Step 2: Teacher Nominations	• Teachers nominate additional students using criteria like exceptional creativity, motivation, talents, performance, or potential.
Step 3: Alternative Pathways	• Other students are considered via parent-, peer -, or self-nominations, special testing (creative writing, mechanical ability), product or portfolio reviews, etc. • Admission is determined by a screening or selection committee.
Step 4: Special Nominations (Safety Valve No.1)	• The list of students from steps 1–3 is sent to all teachers, who may then nominate additional students. • This allows recommendations from resource room teachers, previous-year teachers, and others who may recognize special gifts and talents.
Step 5: Action Information Nominations (Safety Valve No. 2)	• Students who have exceptional interests about a certain topic or a desire to study it independently are included.

SOURCE: Adapted from *A Practical System for Identifying Gifted and Talented Students,* by J. Renzulli, NEAG Center for Gifted Education & Talent Development.

The Talent Pool system is beneficial for identifying those who are at risk of not being included, like those from diverse or high-poverty backgrounds or gifted under-achievers (more on these groups in Topic 15.12). Other advantages are that the Talent Pool Identification System allows more students to participate in gifted programming, eliminates problems associated with teacher bias or over- and under-referrals, and is not seen as elitist or exclusionary.

The National Association for Gifted Children provides a summary of research-based practices for identifying gifted students in *The Role of Assessments in the Identification of Gifted Students.* You can access this position paper at www.nagc.org/uploadedFiles/assessment%20pos%20paper%20final.pdf

Talent Searches and Above-Level Testing

The **talent search** concept was originally developed by Julian Stanley, a psychologist at Johns Hopkins University. Stanley used the Scholastic Aptitude Test (SAT)—a college admissions test—to assess a middle school student's mathematical ability because his skills were more advanced than the grade-level test could determine. Today, talent searches use grade-level and **above-level testing** to qualify students for their programs, which then provide additional talent development opportunities: accelerated weekend or summer programs, mentorships, and career counseling. Researchers tout the ability of above-level testing to detect discrete differences in top-performing students (e.g., to discriminate between those who are in the

top 0.01% of ability levels). The outcomes of the programs' participants are outstanding: higher grades, early graduation, admission to competitive colleges, and outstanding career achievements. To learn more about talent search opportunities, visit http://www.davidsongifted.org/db/Articles_id_10260.aspx

Concerns with the programs center on the demographics of the participants, many of whom are predominately White students from middle- and upper-income backgrounds. There are costs associated with the programs, as they are not school district–led initiatives, so efforts to provide talent search opportunities to students from low-income families—many of whom are culturally and linguistically diverse—are important.

Topic 15.2 Types of Giftedness

- Gifted students may be categorized using different constructs.
- Gifted students with disabilities are referred to as *twice-exceptional*.

How are gifted students categorized? There are multiple ways to group students with exceptional abilities and talents. Sometimes, students are categorized based on their IQ, which is implied or called out in almost every definition of giftedness. To understand the different IQ categorizations, let's briefly review the normal curve, which you learned about in Topic 9.2. The following figure of the normal curve may be helpful as you read this section. Recall that the scores of most students (over 68%) fall in the middle, within one standard deviation from the mean. If the IQ requirement to qualify for gifted programs is a score of 124 or higher (blue shaded area and above), then 6% of all children would be identified as gifted and talented. If an IQ of 130 were used as the minimum score, then anyone who scored between the second and third standard deviations above the mean would qualify—slightly more than 2% of all students (green shaded area and above). Scores vary depending on the type of test used and sometimes different cut-off scores are applied to categorize a student's level of giftedness. Following is one way that students may be categorized: Students who fall between 130 and 145 (green shaded area) are considered "gifted" to "moderately gifted;" those who fall between 145 and 160 (purple shaded area) range from "highly gifted" to "exceptionally gifted;" and the extremely small number of students who score beyond 160 (only about 1 in 30,000, or 0.0003%), are considered "profoundly gifted."

IQ Scores Distributed Along a Normal Curve

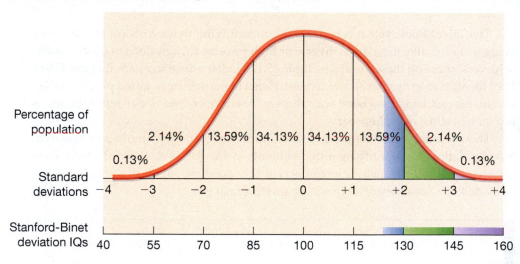

However, no standard exists for how high a student must score to be identified as gifted. For this reason, a student in some schools, districts, or states may be considered gifted if his IQ score is at least 124, while another student may not be considered gifted unless her score is at least 130.

You can view a short video that explains more about the normal curve, IQ scores, and giftedness at

▶ **IQ Tests and Gifted Children**
https://youtu.be/K3VEaNFtojM

Another way to think about categorizing gifted students is Howard Gardner's theory of **multiple intelligences**. This theory offers a broader view of giftedness and talents than that which can be captured by an intelligence test score. Gardner theorizes that intelligence has many dimensions, which all people possess, but to different degrees, and an individual may excel in one or more areas, but not necessarily all of them. Gardner first proposed seven dimensions of intelligence, but he and his colleagues now include eight areas of intelligence.

Gardner's Multiple Intelligences

Intelligence	Explanation	Adult Outcomes
1. Linguistic	The ability to think in words and use language in complex ways	Lawyer, poet, public speaker, writer
2. Logical-mathematical	The ability to calculate, quantify, and hypothesize and to recognize patterns	Engineer, mathematician, scientist
3. Spatial	The capacity to think three dimensionally	Architect, artist, pilot, surgeon
4. Body-kinesthetic	The ability to use the body and hands skillfully	Choreographer, rock climber, skilled artisan
5. Musical	Sensitivity to rhythm, pitch, melody, and tone	Acoustic engineer, composer, musician
6. Interpersonal	The ability to understand and act productively on others' actions and motivations	Actor, political leader, salesperson, teacher, therapist
7. Intrapersonal	The ability to understand one's own feelings and capabilities	Autobiographer, sensitive individual, good decision maker
8. Naturalist	The ingenuity to observe patterns, create classifications, and develop and understand systems	Archeologist, farmer, hunter, landscape architect

SOURCE: Based on multiple sources and *Frames of Mind: Theory of Multiple Intelligences*, by H. Gardner, 1983, New York, NY: Basic Books.

Gardner has considered adding a ninth intelligence area, existential intelligence (also called spirituality). It refers to heightened awareness of the human condition and global issues and interest in the meaning of such concepts as life, death, and love. Those who possess this type of intelligence include philosophers, theologians, religious leaders, artists, and writers. They are people such as Mother Teresa and Martin Luther King, Jr.—who dedicated their lives to the greater good of society—and Socrates, who explored the ethical behavior of mankind. Although this type of intelligence has gained a lot of attention in recent years, Gardner has not yet added it to his list because it does not meet every criterion he set forth for inclusion.

Can students who are gifted and talented also have disabilities? Of course they can. While there are no systems that track the number of gifted students with disabilities, experts estimate that disabilities occur within the gifted population at the same rate as in the general population. So, gifted students can have co-existing learning disabilities, autism, emotional or behavioral disorders, and more. This unique group of learners is referred to as **twice-exceptional** students, although some people and organizations use the term specifically for gifted students with learning disabilities.

If you were asked to think of people with disabilities who are also gifted or who have outstanding talents, you might think of these people, many of whom were mentioned in earlier chapters: Stephen Hawking (physical disability), Ludwig van Beethoven (deafness), Thomas Edison (learning disability), Helen Keller (deaf-blindness), Franklin D. Roosevelt (physical disability), Charles Schwab (learning disability), and Michael Phelps (ADHD). In Chapter 5, you met Sara Solomon. Recall

Courtesy of Sara Solomon

Sara Solomon is a twice-exceptional student: she is gifted and has a physical disability.

that she has cerebral palsy (CP), but that has not stopped her from racking up quite a notable list of achievements (e.g., recognitions from President George W. Bush, *Black Enterprise Magazine*, and the Institute of Entrepreneurship). These people have achieved great things, made major contributions to their respective fields, and received considerable recognition, proving that *anyone* can have exceptional abilities, talents, or creativity.

Attention to gifted students with disabilities is relatively new. During the 1970s, June Maker drew the profession's attention to the needs of a particular subgroup of learners: gifted students with learning disabilities. In 1977, she published the results of her research, shedding light on this previously unrecognized group of students and stressing the importance of providing them with a unique educational experience. Even today, twice-exceptional students are not always identified. This is often because they are:

- Identified as gifted but not as having a disability because the giftedness masks the disability.
- Identified as having a disability but not as gifted because the disability masks the giftedness.
- Not identified at all, as each condition masks the other.

Twice-exceptional students present a conundrum. For instance, if a gifted student has a learning disability, which characteristic should the teacher address? The answer is *both*. If a student has ADHD, are the behavioral issues a reflection of the disability or is the student bored with the academic content and not being challenged? The teacher must systematically determine the answer by collecting data. (Remember functional behavioral assessment, which you learned about in Chapters 8 and 10.) Experts recommend that the student should first be thought of as a gifted student who needs special supports, rather than as a student with a disability who has special talents. This keeps the focus on the student's strengths and avoids instructional programming that dwells on the student's academic or behavioral deficits. The National Education Association (NEA) has five recommendations for working with these students:

1. Make accommodations for their academic strengths and gifts.
2. Make accommodations for their academic weaknesses or disabilities.
3. Provide direct instruction to promote classroom success.
4. Address the students' social/emotional needs.
5. Address the students' behavioral needs.[2]

The following Tips for Teachers box provides more specific suggestions within these five areas that teachers can follow. Notice that many of these tips reflect practices that you learned about in previous chapters.

[2]"The Twice-Exceptional Dilemma" ed. 1, © 2006, National Education Association. Retrieved from www.nea.org/assets/docs/twiceexceptional.pdf

Tips for Teachers

Make accommodations for academic strengths and gifts

- Provide gifted education services (e.g., acceleration, differentiation) whenever appropriate.
- Provide enrichment programs and activities.
- Use student strengths, interests, and passions to pique student interest, teach material, and assess understanding.

Make accommodations for academic weaknesses or disabilities

- Use technology (e.g., speech-to-text programs, audio books, Bookshare™) to compensate for disability areas.
- Use validated practices, such as hands-on learning, graphic organizers, study skills training, and learning strategy instruction.
- Teach students to self-advocate for their needs.
- Provide testing accommodations (e.g., extended time, alternate locations).

Provide explicit instruction to promote classroom success

- Provide explicit instruction in skill areas affected by the disability (e.g., reading, writing, mathematics).

Address the students' social/emotional needs

- Promote a safe learning environment.
- Give students opportunities to talk (in small groups or with professionals) about stress and stress-relieving techniques.
- Provide opportunities to interact with other twice-exceptional students.
- Set up mentorships with successful twice-exceptional adults.

Address the students' behavioral needs

- Maintain a well-structured, consistent classroom environment (by implementing a behavior management system).
- Provide positive behavioral supports to promote appropriate actions.
- Conduct a functional behavioral assessment when necessary to determine a behavior's function.
- Teach positive behaviors to replace unwanted or negative behaviors.

"The Twice-Exceptional Dilemma" ed. 1, ©2006, National Education Association. Accessed at www.nea.org/assets/docs/twiceexceptional.pdf

To learn more, view the NAGC's position statement on twice-exceptional students at http://www.nagc.org/sites/default/files/Position%20Statement/twice%20exceptional.pdf

Topic 15.3 Characteristics

- Even though gifted and talented students can display exceptional abilities in many areas, they often have common characteristics.

- These students tend to be socially and emotionally well-adjusted.

Do any commonalities exist among gifted and talented students? Experts agree that gifted students share some common characteristics that set them apart from their peers. As you may recall, Joseph Renzulli includes task commitment as one of his three dimensions of gifted behavior (along with above average ability and creativity). His conceptualization of task commitment is reflected in the gifted student who is extremely motivated, focused, or task-oriented, or who demonstrates great perseverance—key traits in high achievers. Additionally, gifted students often demonstrate remarkable talent, and perhaps exceptional dedication and commitment, in one or more of the following six areas:

- Intellectual ability (e.g., reasons abstractly, learns quickly)
- Academic aptitude (e.g., remembers large amounts of information, focuses extensively on a topic)
- Creativity or productive thinking (e.g., exhibits individualism, sense of humor)

- Leadership ability (e.g., makes good decisions, possesses self-confidence)
- Visual and performing arts talents (e.g., expresses feelings through dance)
- Psychomotor ability (e.g., is energetic, makes precise movements)

Within each of these broad areas lie more specific domains in which a student may excel. For example, within the *academic aptitude* area, students may show particular strengths in science or mathematics. Others who exhibit exceptional talent in the area of *visual and performing arts* may do so through dance or music. As with all other students with exceptionalities, it is important to keep in mind that gifted students constitute a heterogeneous group. Even though they often display common characteristics, these students are unique and have individual needs that must be considered when planning programs and providing services.

Although not exhaustive, the following table lists a number of characteristics common to gifted students. Notice that some of these map to the six areas listed above. Take a moment to consider how other characteristics in the table are associated with these areas.

Common Characteristics of Gifted Students

Intellectual/Academic	Social/Emotional
Reasons abstractly	Criticizes self
Conceptualizes and synthesizes	Empathizes
Manages and processes information quickly and meaningfully	Plays with older friends
Solves difficult problems	Persists
Learns quickly	Is intense
Shows intellectual curiosity	Exhibits individualism
Has wide interests	Has strength of character
Dislikes drill and routine	Demonstrates leadership abilities
Generalizes learning	Is concerned about ethical Issues
Remembers great amounts of material	Takes risks
Displays strong verbal skills	Is independent and autonomous
Prefers learning in a quiet environment	Is highly sensitive to others and self
Adapts to new learning situations	Has mature sense of humor
Applies varied reasoning and thinking skills	Is nonconforming
Is highly motivated by academic tasks	Uses different modes of expression
Focuses and concentrates on a topic or idea for long periods of time	Experiences great stress from failure
Makes good decisions	Possesses self-confidence
Is highly organized	Is liked by peers
Creates and invents	Has high expectations for self and others
Is self-motivated	Expresses feelings and ideas fluently
Has a large vocabulary	Strives for perfection

How do these students compare to their peers in the area of social-emotional development or skills? Researchers have been trying to answer this question for decades. In 1921, Lewis Terman (about whom you will learn more in Topic 15.10) began tracking over 1,500 students with high IQs. After decades of collecting data on their psychological well-being, he concluded that gifted students experience fewer psychological problems than their typically developing peers. Since that time researchers have conducted a number of studies and have found mixed results regarding the psychological well-being of gifted students. However, in a recent review of 18 studies, the overwhelming finding was that gifted students are more socially and emotionally adjusted than their non-gifted peers. More specifically, as a group they have fewer problems with anxiety, depression, and externalizing behaviors and greater self-esteem and social skills. Furthermore, two recent studies have shown that, as a whole, these students are as psychologically well adjusted as their typically developing peers. And this was the case from early childhood well into adulthood—one study examined students in first and second grades, and another was a longitudinal study that identified students at age 13 and followed them for 40 years. Moreover, the longitudinal study revealed that these adults at midlife reported high ratings in regard to positive feelings and satisfaction with life, career direction, and relationships.

Although on average these students fare well socially and emotionally, it is important to understand that within this group (as within any group) there will be students who experience social and emotional issues. In particular, the following subgroups have been shown to have more psychological problems.

- Underachieving students and those demonstrating creative talents may experience more psychological issues, such as lower self-concept and internalizing and externalizing behaviors. However, this is not necessarily tied to their giftedness per se but rather to lack of appropriate and challenging coursework.

- Highly gifted students have been found to display more behavioral problems than their peers, and these issues may increase in proportion to the level of giftedness. Think about what it would be like to spend hours every day being "taught" information that you already know and may have learned years ago. It is easy to see how this could lead to boredom and frustration and, consequently, acting-out behaviors.

- Students with perfectionistic tendencies may experience higher levels of anxiety.

Also, some gifted students may have difficulty connecting with peers of the same age because they have advanced communication skills, are often socially mature, and have very different interests. This does not mean that these students are socially inept but rather that they may have trouble fitting in with same-age peers. As a result, these students often prefer engaging with older children who are more intellectually similar. In fact, most students who attend classes with older students and have the opportunity to interact with more like-minded peers are socially and emotionally well-adjusted.

Topic 15.4 Prevalence and Placement

- Each state's definition and identification criteria influence the number of students who are eligible for gifted and talented services or programs as well as the types of services they receive.

- The types of services provided to students vary based on grade level.

How many gifted and talented students are in our nation's schools? Because the education of gifted or talented students is neither mandated nor funded by IDEA, states do not include prevalence information about these students in their reports to the federal government about students with disabilities. However, the National Association for Gifted Children (NAGC) estimates that approximately 3 to 5 million students are currently identified as gifted or talented in American elementary and secondary schools. Considerable variation occurs across the states in regard to the number of students who are considered gifted and talented. While the national average is between 6% and 10%, the Davidson Institute reported that for the 2014–2015 school year, 3.8% of all students in Maine were identified as gifted and talented, while 16.4% of all students in Maryland were so identified. Children in Maryland are probably not smarter and more talented than those who live in Maine. Rather, the way that each state defines giftedness differs drastically. The more restrictive the criteria (e.g., requiring an IQ score of 130 or higher versus a score of 124 or higher), the fewer students are recognized and served. Further, many states identify students but do not mandate special programs, so gifted education might be offered at some schools but not others. (Topic 15.12 will explore the differences in state policies and support in greater detail.) Without national guidelines, such inconsistencies will continue, leaving many students without the educational opportunities they deserve and require.

You also learned earlier that talent pools identify many students whose gifts or talents are not readily evident through IQ or achievement scores. These students may be discovered through other gifts or talents—creativity, leadership, and artistic abilities. As a result, districts and states that use these broader definitions of gifted or talented will have larger numbers of gifted and talented students (as in Maryland's case).

Where do most gifted students receive services? The general education classroom is still one of the most commonly used settings across all grade levels for delivering gifted services. However, service delivery options usually vary depending on the age of the student and the district in which the student attends school. For elementary students, services are often provided in a resource classroom for 1 to 4 hours each week, or the students are served in the general education classroom where the teacher uses **cluster grouping** to differentiate instruction (which will be discussed in more detail in Topic 15.8). Middle school students are likely to receive instruction in special classes designed for gifted students, in advanced or **honors classes** that group students by ability, or through differentiated instructional activities in the regular classroom. In high school, these students are typically served in Advanced Placement (AP) classes, dual enrollment classes, or honors classes—classes available to any high-achieving student, not just those who are gifted. As with elementary students, middle and high school students are most likely to receive only 1 to 4 hours of gifted services per week. The rest of their time is typically spent in the general education classroom, where they receive the same level of instruction as their peers. As a result, these students spend a large portion of their day not being challenged. This is unfortunate because longitudinal research on mathematically gifted students suggests that the amount of time, or the dose, of STEM (Science, Technology, Engineering, and Mathematics) educational opportunities prior to college is directly related to STEM accomplishments later in life: those experiencing more opportunities during their school years have more remarkable STEM achievements as adults. Additionally, although gifted students have a range of learning needs, they all typically receive the same services within a given school without regard to their strengths, learning preferences, or interests. In other words, this "one size fits all" approach does not address individual needs.

Grouping practices, such as those mentioned above (e.g., honors classes, special classes for gifted students), allow students to receive specialized instruction with peers of similar abilities and offer a solution to the boredom and frustration that gifted students often experience in typical classrooms. Grouping practices range from full-time programs (e.g., magnet or special schools for gifted students) to part-time or temporary programs (e.g., pull-out programs, special interest clubs). Although research consistently shows improved academic benefits when gifted students are grouped for specialized instruction, grouping has been unfairly criticized by individuals who lack a clear understanding of these practices. Some erroneously claim that they are elitist or that they promote student arrogance; in fact, research has shown that students in these programs are *less* arrogant thanks to exposure to other children whose abilities are commensurate with their own. Other critics worry that grouping equates with **tracking**; yet grouping practices seek to enhance instruction, while tracking prevents higher achievement for some students, particularly those assigned to a less rigorous track. As we look to the future, we must offer better programs for gifted students. We must do a better job of preventing underachievement and of enhancing—rather than stifling—creativity, giftedness, and other talents.

Special Education

Learning Outcome

Explain the academic and social challenges that gifted students encounter at school, describe accommodations that can address these challenges, understand practices and strategies that early childhood and classroom teachers can use to challenge gifted students and meet their unique needs, and describe factors to consider during the high school years to promote a successful transition to college.

Topic 15.5 Challenges and Their Solutions

- Gifted students encounter a number of challenges at school, many of which are often overlooked.

- Solutions to these challenges include early intervention, acceleration, differentiated instruction, and enrichment.

Topic 15.6 Accommodations

- Accommodations for gifted students differ slightly from those for students with disabilities.

- Acceleration is an effective method of accommodating the academic needs of gifted students.

Topic 15.7 Early Intervention

- Early intervention is critical for the cognitive and social-emotional development of young gifted children.

- Early intervention strategies for gifted children include early entrance to kindergarten or first grade and classroom strategies that address the unique learning needs of the child.

Topic 15.8 School Years

- General education teachers can address the unique learning needs of their gifted students by differentiating instruction.

- Enrichment programs offer special opportunities, often outside the standard school day.

Topic 15.9 Transition

- Gifted and talented students often require support to transition successfully from high school to college.

- Transition services should begin in middle school and address skills to help students plan for and succeed in college.

"There Once Was a Girl Who Could Soar . . ."

The four limericks below were written by New Jersey teacher Nancy Karsner, about her experiences—and those of some classmates—growing up gifted in a school with no gifted programs. These limericks illustrate what gifted students experience when they are not provided challenging curriculum and learning opportunities.

There once was a girl who could soar.
Couldn't wait to see what was in store.
With no program in place
She gave in to the pace
And accepted that school was a bore.

Smart Linda wanted to learn.
But soon realized it "wasn't her turn."
Some kids couldn't read
They were the ones with the "need"
More knowledge she continued to yearn.

There was a small child named Sue.
She imagined things that were fancy and new.
Teachers made her teach Steven
Until things became even,
'Cause new lessons for her were so few.

"Challenge me" she begged and she pleaded.
"You're already smart!" they all bleated.
"But, I want to know more!"
"Just go wait by the door"
So high school she never completed.

SOURCE: Nancy Karsner, Ocean City, N.J., Teacher of Gifted and Talented Students.

Topic 15.5 Challenges and Their Solutions

- Gifted students encounter a number of challenges at school, many of which are often overlooked.

- Solutions to these challenges include early intervention, acceleration, differentiated instruction, and enrichment.

What types of challenges do gifted students encounter? Perhaps one of the biggest obstacles facing gifted and talented students is overcoming the assumption that they do not experience challenges and therefore do not need special attention or unique educational programs to reach their full potential and develop their talents. This attitude is often reflected in classrooms where instruction targets the typically developing student and any additional time and effort is spent on remediation. It is also reflected in the actions of federal policy makers who tend to allocate little, if any, funding for gifted programs and services. The Jacob K. Javits Gifted and Talented Students Education Act, a national law pertaining to the education of gifted students, does not include guarantees or full protections for these students. It does not mandate states to provide special programs or services, and, as you will learn in Topic 15.10, it is often under-funded or not funded at all. Once we acknowledge that gifted students have unique challenges, the next step is to explore these challenges so that we can recognize and address them. Here we will discuss five challenges often encountered by these students: being underchallenged, **underachievement**, not being identified for creative abilities, **asynchrony**, and bullying and teasing.

Perhaps the most common challenge is being in an environment that does not address the gifted students' learning needs by offering stimulating and demanding curriculum or faster-paced instruction. Gifted students typically spend 80% of their day in the general education classroom working on the same content and skills as their typically developing classmates, yet they have already mastered 40% to 50% of that instruction. These students, then, are not academically engaged for a good portion of the day, resulting in missed opportunities to develop intellectually. Students may experience even more time non-engaged if the teacher repeats information to help other students learn the content or if behavioral disruptions occur. Because of this lack of academic engagement, students often experience boredom, frustration, and poor motivation. Additionally, they come to believe that they can succeed with little to no effort and consequently do not develop good work habits. Although this may be the case during the early years of school, many of these students are consequently unprepared to tackle advanced courses and difficult tasks in high school and beyond. After years of near-perfect performance, the inability to maintain high levels of performance with little effort, combined with their expectations to maintain exceptional grades or achievement, causes them to falter or withdraw.

Being underchallenged often prevents students from achieving their fullest potential. Some experts estimate that half of all gifted students do not perform commensurate with their potential. Because their classroom achievement may be only average, teachers fail to recognize their gifted behaviors or to refer them for screening or assessment, so these students are often not identified as being gifted. Gifted students may also underachieve because they lack motivation or have poor self-efficacy or self-regulation skills. A third cause of underachievement is the presence of a disability (twice-exceptional) that affects achievement. Not only does underachievement lead to failure to reach academic potential, but also it often precipitates school dropout by gifted students. Surprisingly, estimates project that up to one-fourth of all high school dropouts are gifted students. Unfortunately, gifted dropouts experience the same types of negative outcomes as other dropouts: lower wages, unemployment, health issues, and reliance on government assistance.

Gifted Underachievers May Display

Nonconformity
- Teacher defiance or resistance
- Impulsivity
- Indifference to rules

Low or variable self-esteem
- Higher self-esteem in areas of strength
- Lower self-esteem in non-strength areas
- Difficulty living up to expectations of being gifted
- Learned helplessness

Avoidance behaviors
- Lack of effort tied to fear of being average or of failure
- Dependency
- Hostility
- Pass up competitive activities unless they perceive they can win
- Quit activities in which they are not the best

Another challenge is that students with creative abilities and talents are often not identified as being gifted and, therefore, do not receive services and supports that develop their talents. Experts believe this creative stifling begins early in life. For example, many parents allow toddlers to watch hours of mind-numbing television each day. Children play with dolls and action figures that "speak" a limited number of pre-programmed phrases, discouraging the most basic forms of creativity. Many popular video games are achievement-oriented (accomplish a mission, acquire a prize) but do not encourage creative thinking or problem solving. In school, teachers favor highly intelligent students who do well academically, but they do not always appreciate divergent, independent, or imaginative behavior. Accountability systems (e.g., high-stakes testing) focus on content standards and create pressure to ensure that an entire class attains a standard level of achievement. Many teachers feel challenged to address everything in the standard curriculum, with little time left for more in-depth study or coverage of additional topics of interest. Less time is allotted for activities that focus on thinking skills, art, music, or creativity. Some students, locked into inflexible curricula and classrooms, never even realize they have gifted or creative behaviors. The cumulative result of these factors is that highly capable students tune out, shut down, or drop out.

Gifted students may also experience uneven intellectual, social, and physical development, which is referred to as *asynchronous development* or *asynchrony*. This is not uncommon for this population of students and often occurs to a greater degree for highly gifted students. For example, students may be intellectually advanced but their fine motor development or social skills have not kept pace, or a student may excel greatly in one subject but not in another. Because they often are more advanced cognitively and have very different interests, they may have difficulty relating to same-age peers.

A final challenge is that in some environments, a social stigma is associated with being gifted or excelling academically. Such students stand out as being different from their peers and are often bullied and teased, especially during middle school. This may be even more problematic when students are singled out to receive separate services in a pull-out program. In response, some students withdraw, while others attempt to mask their talents. Additionally, students who are members of certain cultural and racial groups face peer pressure and lack of acceptance when they achieve to high standards.

Gifted and Talented: Challenges

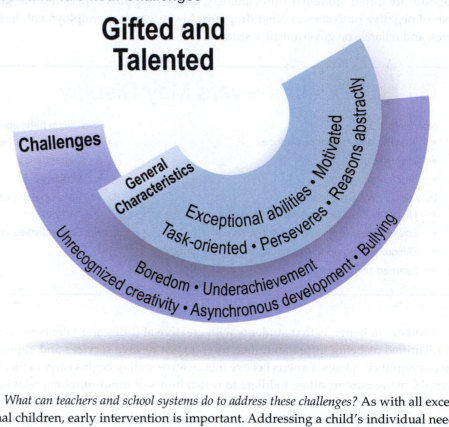

Gifted and Talented

Challenges

General Characteristics

Exceptional abilities • Motivated • Reasons abstractly
Task-oriented • Perseveres

Boredom • Underachievement • Asynchronous development • Bullying
Unrecognized creativity

What can teachers and school systems do to address these challenges? As with all exceptional children, early intervention is important. Addressing a child's individual needs in preschool can prevent boredom and help to develop gifts and talents to the fullest potential. When students enter school, it is important for teachers to meet their individual needs by providing challenging curriculum, fast-paced instruction, and opportunities to explore topics of interest. However, research suggests that gifted dropouts become frustrated as early as elementary school and begin to disengage at school. One factor to consider is whether 1 to 4 hours of instruction in a resource classroom each week, the only form of specialized instruction that many gifted elementary students experience, is enough to keep these students engaged.

One of the most effective ways to meet the needs of young students as well as those in middle and high school is through **acceleration**, which allows students to move through the content at a quicker pace or at a younger age than their peers. Numerous types of acceleration options that expose students to more advanced or challenging curriculum will be explored in-depth in Topic 15.6. General education and special education teachers can also provide more advanced learning opportunities for gifted students by differentiating instruction and offering enrichment opportunities, both of which will be discussed in Topic 15.8.

Gifted and Talented: Solutions

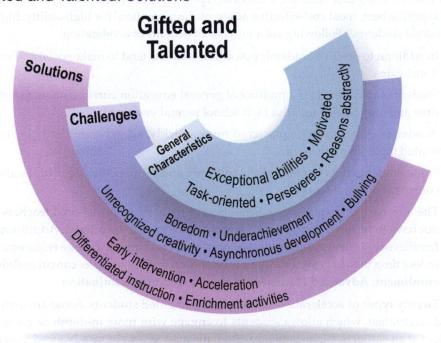

Topic 15.6 Accommodations

- Accommodations for gifted students differ slightly from those for students with disabilities.

- Acceleration is an effective method of accommodating the academic needs of gifted students.

If gifted students excel academically, why do they need accommodations? First, it is important to understand the difference between accommodations for students with disabilities and those for gifted students. As you've learned throughout this book, accommodations are changes to *how* a student accesses instructional content and demonstrates learning. For students with disabilities, accommodations remove barriers to learning so they can access the general education curriculum and keep pace with peers without disabilities. Accommodations for gifted students, on the other hand, remove barriers that prevent students from learning at a pace and level commensurate with their own unique learning needs. Recall that gifted students learn more quickly, think more abstractly, and like to explore topics in greater depth or complexity than their peers. To achieve their highest potential, gifted students must be able to access the curriculum *at their own level* and they must be intellectually and academically challenged. Without appropriate accommodations and academic strategies that enhance their learning, gifted students often experience negative outcomes: they are frustrated and bored, become disenchanted with school, fail to achieve their fullest potential, and sometimes drop out of school.

How can gifted students be intellectually and academically challenged? This can be accomplished through additional instruction or opportunities beyond what is available to typical learners in general education classes. Acceleration is an effective option that allows students to move through the curriculum more rapidly or at a younger age than their same-age peers. In either case, acceleration speeds up the pace of instruction and exposes students to a challenging curriculum. Acceleration is well researched and has been shown to have positive effects on student learning. In fact, according to the authors of *A Nation Empowered: Evidence Trumps the Excuses Holding Back America's Brightest Students*, a national report on acceleration, research indicates that it is "the best, most cost-effective academic 'intervention' for high-ability, highly motivated students." Following are a number of benefits of acceleration.

- In addition to positive academic outcomes, students tend to make social and emotional gains.

- Students can complete the traditional general education curriculum in a shorter time and may be able to finish high school several years early.

- Academic content can be mastered more quickly, allowing students to study related topics in more depth.

- Some students develop better self-concepts and more positive attitudes about course content and school.

- The approach is cost-effective. Schools save money because special teachers do not have to be hired and special courses do not have to be offered. Additionally, families save college tuition costs because students complete college requirements in less time than is typical through acceleration options such as **concurrent/dual enrollment**, **Advanced Placement (AP)**, and **credit by examination**.

Twenty types of acceleration can be offered to gifted students. Some are *content-based acceleration*, which allows students to engage with more in-depth or complex content at an earlier age than is typical. Students may receive more advanced material in their grade-level classroom, or they may receive instruction in a different classroom with older students for a portion of the day, often for a single subject in which they excel. With content-based acceleration, gifted students remain with their age-level peers for a portion, if not all, of the day. Other types of acceleration options are categorized as *grade-based acceleration*, which reduces the number of years a student attends K–12 classes. The following box lists the different types of acceleration. Following the box, you will learn about prominent acceleration options for preschoolers, elementary students, and secondary students.

Types of Acceleration

Content-Based Acceleration

Continuous progress
Self-paced instruction
Subject-matter acceleration/Partial acceleration
Curriculum compacting
Mentoring
Extracurricular programs
Distance learning courses
Concurrent/dual enrollment
Advanced Placement
International Baccalaureate (IB) program
Accelerated/honors high school or residential high school
Credit by examination
Acceleration in college

Grade-Based Acceleration

Early admission to kindergarten
Early admission to first grade
Grade-skipping
Combined classes
Telescoping curriculum
Early entrance into middle school, high school, or college
Early graduation from high school or college

Adapted from Assouline, S. G., Colangelo, N., & VanTassel-Baska, J. (2015). *A nation empowered: Evidence trumps the excuses holding back America's brightest students* (Vol. 2). Iowa City, IA: The Belin-Blank Center.

For preschool students, one of the most common types of acceleration is early admission to kindergarten or even first grade. This option should be considered when a child's giftedness is apparent during the toddler or preschool years. The approach has several advantages: children can skip a year of foundational content they have already mastered, they will not experience a disruption in academic content or social relationships that students already in school might experience when skipping a grade, and parents save on the cost of preschool. To determine eligibility for early admission to kindergarten, children should be tested to ensure they are cognitively, academically, and socially ready. Children who enter school early based on the results of this type of testing typically perform well academically and socially. This option will be discussed in more detail in Topic 15.7.

Once students are in elementary school, they may be eligible for grade-skipping (sometimes referred to as double promotion or whole-grade acceleration). With this approach, students advance to a grade ahead of their same-age classmates. Although research demonstrates the effectiveness of this option, less than 1.5% of all students skip a grade or enter school early. This is unfortunate because the outcomes for students who skip a grade tend to be very positive, as discussed in the following box.

Long-Term Benefits of Grade-Skipping

The benefits of acceleration—specifically, grade-skipping—are not only evident for gifted students, but for society as a whole. Consider longitudinal data from the Study of Mathematically Precocious Youth (SMPY). Researchers compared the adult professional achievements of individuals from the SMPY who had skipped grades to those who had not. The grade-skippers were more likely to pursue advanced degrees in STEM fields, earn those degrees at an earlier age, and publish more highly cited STEM–related research than the non–grade-skippers. Why does this matter? Acceleration (i.e., grade-skipping) allowed these gifted individuals to reduce their time in school, which then provided them with more time in their respective fields, resulting in more scientific discoveries and advances. These individuals—both grade-skippers and non–grade-skippers—had already been identified as the top 1% of mathematically talented youth. Yet the simple provision of grade-skipping made a significant difference in their contributions to society.

SOURCE: From "When Less Is More: Effects of Grade Skipping on Adult STEM Productivity Among Mathematically Precocious Adolescents," by G. Park, D. Lubinski, and C. P. Benbow, August 13, 2012. APA, adapted with permission.

Another option to consider for this age group and beyond is curriculum compacting. The general education teacher can reduce (or even eliminate) coverage of topics by skipping introductory lessons and spending less time on concepts or information that the student masters quickly. This can result in the student reading 40% to 50% less of the grade-level reading curriculum. Saved time can then be re-allocated to other activities (e.g., independent study, internships, advanced study).

In high school, students can take Advanced Placement (AP) courses. These college-level courses, taken in the high school setting, allow students to earn college credit. Although not developed specifically for gifted students, AP courses provide an option for more challenging and in-depth learning in specific areas of study. AP courses are the fastest-growing acceleration option: the number of students taking these courses has greatly increased in the past decade. This is in part due to technology, which allows students in small, rural districts who previously did not have access to AP courses to take advantage of this acceleration option. A benefit of earning college credit is that students do not have to take these courses again in college. Long-term effects also accrue: college students who take AP courses in high school are more likely than their college peers to earn bachelor's and master's degrees.

Regardless of the evidence on the positive effects of acceleration, which demonstrates that this option is the most effective intervention for gifted students, only nine states have policies pertaining to acceleration. It is often under-utilized due

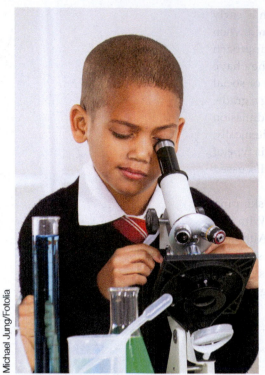

Because of curriculum compacting, this student has the opportunity to explore science topics that are of interest to him.

Michael Jung/Fotolia

to negative perceptions. Many educators and parents are resistant or opposed because they believe that students will struggle socially. However, research has shown that students who are accelerated do as well or better socially and emotionally as their peers who have not been, in regard to self-confidence, social relationships, and involvement in extra-curricular activities. In fact, most of these students have communication skills that are more aligned with those of older students and prefer to interact with them. Another misconception about acceleration is that children will not gain a true understanding of content that is learned at a fast pace. In fact, research has shown that high school students can still recall the information in graduate school. To help determine whether a student is likely to succeed when accelerated, teachers can use the *Iowa Acceleration Scale*, an effective tool to help make informed decisions. This tool guides educators and parents in gathering information in a number of domains such as academic ability, academic achievement, social skills, maturity, and motivation. Educators can also use an online tool, the IDEAL Solutions® for STEM Acceleration (http://www.idealsolutionsmath .com), to determine if acceleration in STEM subjects is a good option for elementary and middle school students. After entering a student's standardized test scores (e.g., ACT scores), the program provides guidance on how to proceed.

To learn more about acceleration and its benefits, you can visit the Acceleration Institute at http://www.accelerationinstitute.org. You can also read the latest research findings on acceleration in *A Nation Empowered: Evidence Trumps the Excuses Holding Back America's Brightest Students*, a national report that can be downloaded for free at the Belin-Blank IDEAL Solutions for STEM Acceleration Website (http://www.idealsolutionsmath.com/Ecomm/Product/Default.aspx).

Topic 15.7 Early Intervention

- Early intervention is critical for the cognitive and social-emotional development of young gifted children.

- Early intervention strategies for gifted children include early entrance to kindergarten or first grade and classroom strategies that address the unique learning needs of the child.

If gifted children are already academically advanced, why do they require early intervention? As you learned in previous chapters, early intervention is critical for students with disabilities and can often mitigate the challenges posed by their disabilities. This is also the case for gifted students. Some researchers suggest that services for these students should start even earlier if possible because they move through developmental milestones (e.g., talking, walking, reading) at a much younger age than typically developing children or those with delays or disabilities. Providing engaging and enriched environments in the preschool years can support cognitive and emotional development. Early intervention also results in other positive outcomes for gifted students: an eagerness to learn, greater self-confidence, acceptance of oneself, and better adjustment to the academic and social demands of school. Additionally, early intervention can prevent underachievement, which you learned in Topic 15.5 is a barrier to reaching full potential for many of these children.

Even though early intervention is critical, many students in preschool have yet to be identified, so they do not receive appropriate supports. Preschool teachers typically do not receive training on how to spot children with high potential and often do not recognize the characteristics. Although parents are often the first to suspect that their child is gifted, they often are not confident in their evaluation and are hesitant to discuss their child's gifts or talents with the teacher. This may be especially true for parents whose children display undesired behaviors in class (e.g., acting out, not following directions, focusing on something of interest instead of the classroom activity).

Even if children are identified during preschool, few communities have programs for gifted preschoolers. Further, few preschool teachers know how to make appropriate accommodations for gifted children in their programs, nor do they have access to the types of advanced materials that would benefit these children. Although these barriers can impede the cognitive growth of all gifted students, this lack of support during the preschool years can have a much greater negative impact on the cognitive development of children from underrepresented groups or those living in poverty. Middle- and upper-income families often provide enrichment materials and experiences for their children, something that families from low-income backgrounds are often unable to offer.

What types of early intervention strategies are effective for gifted preschoolers? Although limited research exists on effective strategies for young gifted children, evidence does reveal that early entrance to kindergarten or first grade can provide a stimulating learning environment and result in positive outcomes for some gifted students. When considering this option, it is important that children are carefully screened to make sure they are intellectually, academically, and socially ready to advance to a formal school setting. This includes making sure that the child has: advanced cognitive skills; necessary academic abilities (for early entrance to kindergarten, an interest in learning how to read and perform mathematics calculations; for early entrance to first grade, a minimum of first grade level reading comprehension and mathematics reasoning skills); classroom readiness and learning skills (e.g., following routines, interacting in a small group); fine motor skills and hand-eye coordination; and social-emotional maturity. Although many teachers have concerns about the social maturity of these students, a large number of gifted students are socially mature for their age, often demonstrating advanced social and communication skills and preferring to interact with older children. Overall, children who are carefully selected to advance to kindergarten or first grade are very successful, performing as well as, and often better than, their grade-level peers. Unfortunately, almost 40% of states (including Puerto Rico) do not allow early entrance into kindergarten. The remaining states are fairly equally split between permitting early entrance into kindergarten, leaving the decision up to the local education agency, and having no policy in place to address early school entrance. When considering early school entry, it is important to understand that states have different policies pertaining to kindergarten attendance: only about one-third of all states require students to attend kindergarten, a majority requires districts to offer half-day programs, and about one-fourth require districts to offer full-day programs.

Grade acceleration is not a suitable option for all gifted children. However, all gifted children should be challenged so that they reach their full potential. The National Association for Gifted Children recommends "providing engaging, responsive learning environments in which young learners' interests, strengths, and skills are identified, developed, and used to guide individualized learning experiences." Following are several strategies or practices teachers can implement that align with this recommendation.

- Implement student-centered activities that are responsive to the student's academic needs and interests. Challenging and engaging learning activities may reduce or eliminate undesirable behaviors displayed by children whose educational needs have previously not been met.

When grade acceleration is not a viable option, preschool teachers can challenge gifted children by providing resources that meet their instructional needs.

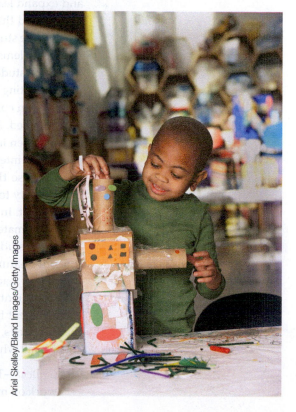

Ariel Skelley/Blend Images/Getty Images

- Provide instruction at the child's **zone of proximal development**—slightly above the student's current performance level so that it is challenging. Keep in mind that a child may not excel in all areas and, therefore, may need advanced instruction only in targeted areas.

- Provide books, games, and other educational resources that are more advanced than the typical resources found in the classroom.

- Provide opportunities for these children to play and interact with older children.

- Differentiate instruction for children with varying interests, strengths, and skills by developing interest centers that contain resources at different levels of difficulty and by using flexible grouping to work with students who have the same strengths or interests.

- Collaborate with families. Parents are great sources of information regarding their child's interests and strengths and should be partners in the identification process and the planning of learning environments.

Topic 15.8 School Years

- General education teachers can address the unique learning needs of their gifted students by differentiating instruction.

- Enrichment programs offer special opportunities, often outside the standard school day.

How can differentiated instruction address the needs of gifted students? Today, most gifted students receive instruction in general education classrooms. Teachers can address the needs of all learners, including gifted students, by implementing differentiated instruction in response to students' academic readiness, learning profiles, and interests. As you learned in previous chapters, teachers differentiate instruction for students with disabilities so that they can more easily access and learn the content and then demonstrate learning. For gifted learners, however, the concept is used to extend and expand learning of the basic curriculum and content standards. It is important to understand that this means providing students with challenging content. Too often, when these students complete an activity or assignment quickly, they are simply given more problems of the same level. If they have mastered the content or skill, this only frustrates students and sometimes seems like punishment. Also vital to know is that differentiating instruction for gifted students does not mean having them help classmates learn content but rather providing opportunities for these students to grow in areas of need. Another factor to keep in mind is that differentiating instruction should be used even in gifted classes or programs because students' abilities, learning preferences, and interests occupy a wide range.

Because these students learn content and skills more quickly, they need the opportunity to work at a faster pace, explore complex topics, and delve deeper into the content. In addition, they often have interests that are far different from those of their classmates, and they should be allowed to explore these topics in depth. Given that these students will be working at a different level and pace than their classmates, it is only natural they will need alternate methods of demonstrating their learning. Recall that teachers can differentiate instruction by modifying three instructional elements: content, process, and product. Following are a few strategies for differentiating each element for gifted students. As you read through these strategies, keep in mind that the needs, strengths, and interests of each gifted student are unique and should be considered when differentiating instruction.

- *Content*—Teachers can provide higher-level materials that allow these students to work on more complex concepts and skills. They can also offer advanced learning opportunities for students to integrate ideas and make connections to other concepts as well as to apply the information and skills they have learned. Teachers can also differentiate content by implementing some of the content-based acceleration options presented in Topic 15.6. These include curriculum compacting and self-paced instruction.

- *Process*—Teachers should provide activities that require students not only to learn and recall information but also to analyze, synthesize, and evaluate the content. They can also engage these higher-level thinking skills by asking students open-ended questions rather than factual questions. The goal is to get students thinking more deeply and abstractly about the content. Teachers can also use flexible grouping strategies that permit higher-ability students or students with similar interests to work together.

- *Product*—Instead of requiring students to demonstrate learning through summarizing content, teachers should provide assessment options that allow them to synthesize the information learned.

To gain a better understanding of how to modify instruction to meet the needs of gifted students, compare typical assignments to those differentiated for advanced learners in the following box.

A Comparison of Traditional and Differentiated Assignments

General Education Assignment

1. Discuss plot, setting, and characters in the novel *The Pearl* by John Steinbeck.

2. Charles invested $10,000 in stock in January. When he sold it in December, the price was up 10 percent from his purchase price. What was his profit on this stock?

3. Pretend you are a newscaster studying World War II. Select one of the following to complete, based on your role:

   a. Write a news report that outlines a significant event in the war.

   b. Re-create a significant event and describe how that event was critical to the outcome of the war.

   c. Design a flyer based on a significant event.

Differentiated Assignment

1. Compare and contrast the plot, setting, characters, motivation, theme, and climax of *The Pearl* with *Of Mice and Men*, two novels by John Steinbeck. How would you characterize the author's style?

2. Which would you rather choose?

   a. Eighty percent profit in year 1, and 50% loss in year 2.

   b. Five percent profit in year 1, and 5% profit in year 2.

   Explain your reasoning in writing, and share your thinking with the class.

3. Using a medium of your choice (song, dance, poster, PowerPoint presentation, flowchart, etc.), illustrate the cause-and-effect relationships among the precipitating events of World War II.

Recall that in Topic 15.4 you learned that elementary school teachers typically use cluster grouping to differentiate instruction in the general education classroom.

The video below highlights a school district that uses schoolwide clustering and illustrates how gifted students are served in mixed-ability classrooms.

▶ **The Schoolwide Cluster Grouping Model**

https://youtu.be/JESnt-CFX1Q

To learn more about differentiating instruction, view the following IRIS Module, which explains different strategies that can be used to differentiate content, process, and product. It also examines students' traits (e.g., interest, learning profile) that influence learning.

▶ **IRIS Module: Differentiated Instruction: Maximizing the Learning of All Students**
http://iris.peabody.vanderbilt.edu/di/

What is enrichment, and how does it differ from differentiated instruction? Unlike differentiated instruction, which modifies instruction, **enrichment** is a method of offering activities or opportunities that supplement the grade-level curriculum or that are unrelated to the curriculum. However, the definitions of enrichment programs vary, and some consider it a form of differentiation that meets the educational needs of both high achievers and gifted students. Broadly speaking, this approach expands the breadth and depth of the general education curriculum or allows for the exploration of additional topics. The goal of enrichment is to encourage higher-level thinking and creativity on a given topic or in a subject area. Students can work independently on special assignments (e.g., preparing an in-depth report on the period being studied in the social studies text, gathering additional information from the Internet about a scientific topic) or in groups (e.g., clubs). Examples of enrichment activities include:

- Independent study
- Field trips
- Academic competitions
- Learning or interest centers
- Saturday programs
- Summer programs (e.g., **Governor's School programs**, study abroad, programs hosted by universities, camps)
- Mentorships/internships
- Programs that connect students across the country and world (e.g., *Future Problem Solving, Odyssey of the Mind, Destination ImagiNation, MATHCOUNTS, Junior Great Books*)

One popular and long-standing enrichment model is the **Schoolwide Enrichment Model (SEM)**. It seeks to develop the talent of and provide advanced learning opportunities for all students in the school as well as to offer additional opportunities for students based on their strengths and interests. Students "revolve" into and out of different levels of their program, which includes three types of enrichment activities:

- *Type 1 Exploratory Activities* expose students to new and exciting content typically not covered in class (e.g., topics, occupations, events); they are carried out through a variety of instructional approaches (e.g., speakers, field trips, demonstrations, videos and films, interest centers).

- *Type 2 Group Training Activities* encourage students to develop their cognitive and affective abilities, including critical thinking and problem solving, through their own expressive skills (e.g., writing a play, doing a pen-and-ink sketch, using equipment).

- *Type 3 Individual and Small Group Investigations of Real Problems* allow students who show great interest in and are motivated by particular topics, issues, or ideas to pursue them. They are provided with specialized instruction and activities and are encouraged to apply advanced investigative and creative skills.

For more on the SEM, go to http://gifted.uconn.edu/schoolwide-enrichment-model/sem3rd/

Topic 15.9 Transition

- Gifted and talented students often require support to transition successfully from high school to college.

- Transition services should begin in middle school and address skills to help students plan for and succeed in college.

Why do gifted and talented students need transition services? These students excel academically, and often in other areas as well, so school personnel might assume that they will make a seamless transition from high school to college. However, in addition to the typical assistance provided to all college-bound students, some gifted students require additional supports for this transition. For example, economically disadvantaged students, as well as those from diverse families, may need help selecting appropriate courses that will prepare them for college (e.g., AP courses, honors programs). Some students may need guidance in making sure they have met the requirements for selective universities and in selecting schools that are a good fit for their academic and social needs and interests. This type of preparation and forethought could help address college dropout rates among gifted students. Also, students who are considering early entrance into college, and their parents, may need support as they research the positive and negative aspects of this option. An unsuccessful transition to college can have negative outcomes: poor academic performance, psychological symptoms that interfere with daily activities, and even dropping out of college.

In addition to dealing with typical challenges that students face before and after transitioning from high school to college (e.g., selecting a college, homesickness, doing laundry and daily chores, the temptations of alcohol), gifted students face unique problems, which are related to their:

- *Multiple talents*—Some of these students excel in many areas, making it difficult for them to narrow their focus and choose a career.

- *Awareness of expectations*—Expectations for gifted students are often very high, whether self-imposed or imposed by others. This can result in actions such as making decisions to please others, avoiding classes or activities in which success is not certain, procrastinating indefinitely, and not planning for life after high school.

- *Perfectionism*—Gifted students are often perfectionists who set very high standards for themselves. As tasks get more challenging, these students may experience stress and frustration when their outcome does not meet their expectations or that of others. Many such students will never have received a grade lower than an A until they enter college, and the first time this occurs can be devastating.

- *Lack of study skills*—It is not unusual for many gifted students to breeze through high school academics. Because of this, they never acquired the study skills they will need to meet the demands of college.

- *Limited experience with competition*—These students may have experienced little or no academic competition in high school, always making the highest grades. For many, college is the first time they encounter academic competition. They are often unprepared for this, and their belief in their own academic abilities declines. It is difficult to shift from thinking they have to be the brightest student in the class to learning content that can put them on the path to a rewarding career.

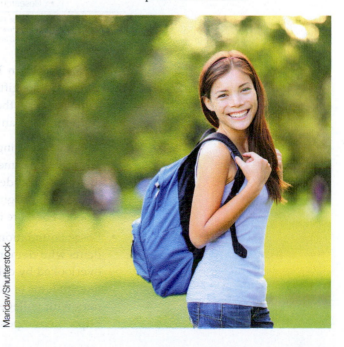

Although this student is prepared for the academic challenges of college, imagine the social challenges she may encounter in an environment where all peers are much older.

Maridav/Shutterstock

- *Asynchrony*—Recall that it is not unusual for gifted students' intellectual development to surpass their social and emotional development. For this reason, some students may have difficulty establishing social relationships with peers, making decisions, or setting goals. These issues can be even more problematic if a student has skipped grades and enters college at an early age. Although the student may be intellectually prepared for this stimulating environment, he or she may not be socially and emotionally ready for the more independent setting.

When should transition services be provided, and what should they include? To help prepare students, school personnel should begin transition planning four to six years before students graduate from high school. These services not only address skills that students will need but also help them navigate the college selection and admission process. The following table outlines skills and activities that should be addressed or explored at different grade levels.

Transition Activities

Grades	Skills or Activities
7th–8th	• Self-awareness • Time management • Study skills • Career awareness • Decision making • Develop an academic plan that includes advanced courses and those required by colleges • Participate in regional talent searches
9th–10th	• Self-awareness and decision making (continued) • Set goals • Pursue interests • Begin to differentiate potential career interests from hobbies • Make connections between academic talents, values, and interests and potential careers • Create a list of academic and non-academic awards and recognitions • Prepare for college entrance tests (e.g., take practice tests) • Engage in meaningful activities (e.g., volunteer experiences, extracurricular activities, leadership opportunities)
11th–12th	• Procure an internship • Arrange for a mentor • Begin the college application and selection process • Take college entrance exams • Research financial aid options and complete scholarship applications

SOURCE: Adapted from *College Planning for Gifted Students* (2nd ed.), by S. L. Berger, 1998, Reston, VA: The Council for Exceptional Children, retrieved from ERIC database. (ED439566); and *College Planning for Gifted Students* (4th ed.), by S. L. Berger, 2014, Waco, TX: Prufrock Press, Inc.

As mentioned in Topic 15.5, students from diverse backgrounds are often underrepresented in the gifted and talented category. For these students who demonstrate academic promise, there are a number of programs that promote academic success and support their transition to college, such as:

- GEAR UP (Gaining Early Awareness and Readiness for Undergraduate Programs)—The U.S. Department of Education funds states and partnerships to provide services to groups of students in high-poverty middle and high schools for a six- to seven-year period (beginning no later than seventh grade and extending through high school). For more information, visit http://www.edpartnerships.org/gear-up

- Posse Foundation—This private non-profit organization offers support to students who demonstrate great academic and leadership potential but are often overlooked by colleges; the foundation places them in a small diverse group of like students (a Posse) who support each other's individual growth. Posse partners with colleges to provide scholarships for these students. Learn more at https://www.possefoundation.org

Check Your Understanding 15.2

Click here to gauge your understanding of the concepts in this section.

People and Situations

Learning Outcome

Describe the history of gifted education and identify resources for gifted students and their parents.

Topic 15.10 Origins and History

- Individuals with special gifts and talents have long been recognized, but it was not until the twentieth century that we witnessed growth in educational services for these students in the United States.

- Public support for special programs and gifted education has wavered across time.

Topic 15.11 Personal Stories

- Gifted and talented individuals are found in all walks of life and have the ability to change the world around us.

- Organizations such as the National Association for Gifted Children, Davidson Institute, and Duke TIP provide support to gifted students, their families, and their educators.

Westend61/Getty Images

Without public support and funding for gifted programming, students often do not receive the services they need to meet their potential but instead experience frustration and boredom at school.

Topic 15.10 Origins and History

- Individuals with special gifts and talents have long been recognized, but it was not until the twentieth century that we witnessed growth in educational services for these students in the United States.

- Public support for special programs and gifted education has wavered across time.

When did gifted and talented students begin receiving special attention and services? As early as 3000 BC, the Egyptians sent the best students (along with royalty) to court schools or assigned mentors to work with them in intensive internships to develop their special talents. Around 500 BC, Confucius, a Chinese philosopher, proposed special education for gifted children, and by AD 618, gifted and talented children were brought to the Chinese imperial court for a superior education. Much later, in 1869, Francis Galton proposed that genius was genetically determined and that eminence was due only to two factors: (1) an internal motivation to excel and (2) intellect. Several decades later, in 1905, Alfred Binet developed the first intelligence test. Although it was not originally created to identify gifted students, this test nonetheless marks the beginning, in this country, of interest in such individuals and is still heavily relied upon today to identify gifted students. Leta Hollingworth, one of the early pioneers in the field of education of the gifted, who joined the faculty at Teachers College, Columbia University, in 1916, taught the first course and wrote the first textbook in this area. Soon after, in the 1920s educational services for these individuals expanded. One of Hollingworth's major contributions to the field was her theory that giftedness is affected by *both* heredity and environment, a concept widely held today. In 1925, Lewis Terman began a 50-year longitudinal study of 1,528 children with exceptionally high cognitive aptitude—those with IQ scores over 135 (most over 140). Terman's narrow view of giftedness associated high intelligence with high academic achievement. Terman also believed intelligence to be a fixed characteristic—one that people are born with and that does not increase or decrease across time. Today's professionals are much less confident than Terman in the results of standardized tests. They now recognize that such tests can be inherently biased against individuals who are not from the dominant American culture or who have not received a strong and traditional educational foundation. They also understand that intelligence, like any other trait, is influenced by both genetics and environment. It is not a fixed characteristic, nor is it signaled only by a high IQ score. Today, much broader views of exceptional intelligence, aptitude, creativity, and talents are considered when defining giftedness.

The Termites

The students in Terman's famous longitudinal study—known as "Termites"—not only had high IQs, but were deemed to be psychologically, physically, and socially superior to their peers. Many went on to great achievements in their respective fields. However, two eventual Nobel Prize winners, Luis Alvarez and William B. Shockley, did not have sufficiently high IQ scores and were subsequently excluded from Terman's study. As their example indicates, there is clearly more to giftedness than just high intelligence.

Why do supports for students who are gifted or talented vary across time? Americans have demonstrated a wavering commitment to gifted and talented students. Negative attitudes about gifted education are deeply rooted in ideas about equity and social justice. Further, many hold the mistaken assumption that these students will thrive without special programs, that they can make it on their own. Quite sadly, this is simply untrue. Gifted individuals often do not reach their potential because their educational programs did not meet their needs.

During the eighteenth century, many of our nation's leaders viewed education as best for the elite. Thomas Jefferson, however, argued against elitism, believing that the purpose of education was to foster democracy. During the nineteenth century, egalitarianism—the notion that no one should get special treatment—became popular. The egalitarian position held that no individual should be considered better than anyone else, regardless of innate abilities, status, or education. As a result, education for gifted children was considered undemocratic, elitist, unnecessary, and wasteful.

When security, national pride, or position in the global economy is perceived to be at stake, attitudes tend to change. For example, in 1957, Russia launched *Sputnik*, the first space satellite. This launch was viewed as a risk to U.S. national security and a blow to national pride. U.S. leaders vowed to catch up and surpass the competition. Federal funding was appropriated to develop methods to identify high-achieving students (particularly in math and science), establish special programs, and conduct research on effective instruction for these learners. Gifted students were seen as a great national resource: the people who would make the United States a world leader once again. Such attention paid off. Americans were the first to land on the moon—winning the "space race"—and developed remarkable innovations in science and technology. This focus on developing the potential of gifted students was short-lived. As the 1960s gave rise to the civil rights movement, gifted education was again seen as elitist and separate. This attitude remained prominent into the next decade and, as a result, when IDEA was passed in 1975, students with disabilities were guaranteed special and unique educational services but gifted and talented students were not included in those guarantees.

However, in 1988, Congress passed the Jacob K. Javits Gifted and Talented Students Education Act, a separate national law supporting gifted education. The Javits Act funded:

- Grants to states and districts for gifted education program implementation and enhancement.

- Grants to colleges, state education agencies, and local districts to develop and expand models to serve underrepresented gifted students.

- The National Research Center on the Gifted and Talented, which provides information on validated practices in gifted education.[3]

Unlike IDEA, which guarantees full protections for students with disabilities, the Javits Act does not do so for gifted students. Additionally, it does not include a national mandate requiring states to provide special programs or services to gifted and talented students. Further, the Javits Act has been historically under-funded. In 2005, the U.S. House of Representatives voted for zero funding for gifted education programs, although the U.S. Senate reinstated some of the funds in that year's appropriations budget. To further illustrate the wavering commitment to gifted education, funding for the Javits Act was completely eliminated in 2011. Three years later, in 2014, it was partially restored at $5 million and increased to $10 million in 2015. Review the information in the following table, noting the marked differences in 2015 funding levels for gifted students compared to IDEA funding for infants and toddlers (Part C funding) and preschoolers, children, youth, and adolescents (Part B funding).

---

[3] Jacob K. Javits Gifted and Talented Students Education Program, U.S. Department of Education.

A Comparison of Funding Levels (2015)

Programs	2015 Federal Appropriations
IDEA Part B (School Age)	$11.5 billion
IDEA Part B (Preschool)	$353 million
IDEA Part C (Infants & Toddlers)	$439 million
Jacob Javits Act (Gifted)	$10 million

SOURCE: *Federal Outlook for Exceptional Children: Fiscal Year 2016.* Arlington, VA: Council for Exceptional Children (2015, June).

It appears as though gifted education may again be gaining more favor. The reauthorization of the Elementary and Secondary Education Act in 2015—now referred to as the Every Student Succeeds Act—includes more provisions to support gifted students. This revision clearly indicates that Title 1 funds can be used to identify and support these students. Also, funding allocated to the Javits Act for the 2017 fiscal year budget has increased to $12 million.

Topic 15.11 Personal Stories

- Gifted and talented individuals are found in all walks of life and have the ability to change the world around us.

- Organizations such as the National Association for Gifted Children, Davidson Institute, and Duke TIP provide support to gifted students, their families, and their educators.

How have gifted individuals touched our daily lives? Our world has been greatly influenced by gifted individuals. For instance, think about the electronic devices and software you use every day. How many of them are Apple products (e.g., iPhone, iPad, Mac computers)? How often do you use Microsoft products (e.g., Word, Excel)? Do you check your social media accounts (e.g., Facebook) multiple times per day? For most people, these products or services are part of our everyday lives, all developed by gifted individuals. Notice that the developers of these products and services are listed in the following table. Now, think about what you do for enjoyment (e.g., reading, listening to music, watching movies). Look for the artistic individuals in the table. Not only have those listed had incredible success, but also they began experiencing such success at a young age. In addition, as you review the table, note that many of these individuals graduated from high school or college early. This lends further proof to what the research says about the positive benefits of acceleration. Moreover, observe that several experienced boredom and frustration, and a few dropped out of college. Again, this illustrates what you learned earlier in the chapter about gifted students and the negative feelings they sometimes experience in school. Finally, you will see that gifted students flourish in many areas (e.g., technology, music, acting, science, politics, human rights).

Gifted Individuals and Their Accomplishments

Albert Einstein	• Renowned physicist who developed the theory of relativity; wrote his first major physics paper as a teenager; won a Nobel Prize for physics • Felt alienated in elementary school
Martin Luther King, Jr.	• A leader of the civil rights movement and a Nobel Prize winner • Entered college at age 15 and graduated with a B.A. at 19
Yo-Yo Ma	• World-class cellist; first performed at Carnegie Hall at 15 • Graduated from high school at age 15
Sandra Day O'Connor	• First woman to serve on the Supreme Court • Graduated from high school at 16 and from Stanford University at age 20 with a B.A.
Condoleezza Rice	• First African American woman to serve as provost of Stanford University, a U.S. National Security Advisor, and the U.S. Secretary of State (2005–2009) • Graduated from high school at age 15 and college at age 20; received a master's degree at age 21
Michael Kearney	• Began teaching at Vanderbilt University at age 16 • Graduated from college with a B.A. at age 10 and received a master's degree in biochemistry by 14
Christopher Paolini	• Wrote *Eragon*, the first of four books in the *Inheritance Cycle* series, at age 15 • Homeschooled for his early years and completed an accredited correspondence course to graduate high school at age 15
Mark Zuckerberg	• Co-founder and CEO of Facebook • Dropped out of Harvard after his sophomore year to devote his time to Facebook
Steve Jobs	• Co-founder of Apple, Inc. • School administrators suggested grade acceleration, but his parents were opposed; dropped out of college after one semester
Bill Gates	• Co-founder of Microsoft • Parents moved him to a preparatory school at age 13 because he was bored and withdrawn in public school; at age 15, he and his business partner sold their first computer program
Whoopi Goldberg	• Award-winning actress and comedian • Twice-exceptional: gifted and dyslexic • Dropped out of school at age 17
Will Smith	• Actor and musician; first rap album made him a millionaire at age 17
Taylor Swift	• Grammy award–winning singer and songwriter; first top 10 single at age 16

On the Screen: *Steve Jobs* and *Straight Outta Compton*

We have selected two films for this chapter that feature gifted and talented individuals with exceptional creative abilities. *Steve Jobs* details the life of the iconic tech innovator across a 14-year time span, depicted through backstage events during three different Apple™ product launches. In his uncompromising quest for quality and perfection, there are scenes in which his harsh treatment of Apple team members, friends, and family is inexplicable, reminding us that even gifted individuals face challenges with social, emotional, and behavioral issues. Yet, his brilliance and creativity are clearly evident as he envisions technological devices that transform the way society lives, works, and plays. Further, his young daughter's giftedness becomes apparent in conversations, and disagreements, with her father.

https://youtu.be/aEr6K1bwlVs

Because we have discussed the under-representation of students of color and those from poor backgrounds—among others—in programs for gifted and talented youth, we wanted to include *Straight Outta Compton* in this feature. This film showcases the talents and creativity of the members of N.W.A, a hip hop group that rose to fame in the 1980s. Despite their obvious skills in writing, music, and even business entrepreneurship, their talents were mostly unrecognized while they were in school. The group's members faced challenges of crime, poverty, and racism, which they included in their controversial "reality rap" lyrics.

https://youtu.be/-F5WcFPDzko

An interesting link exists between two of the individuals featured in these films. Andre Young (Dr. Dre), a member of N.W.A. and co-founder of Beats (maker of the popular headphones, speakers, and other audio products), sold his company to Steve Job's Apple in 2014 for roughly $3 billion, the biggest deal in Apple's history at that time.

What organizations provide support for gifted students, their families, and educators? A number of organizations provide valuable information and offer support, such as:

- National Association for Gifted Children—This organization not only supports research and professional development that benefit gifted children but also advocates for these students by developing policies and practices that target their needs. The Website includes a wealth of resources for administrators, educators, and parents; offers information on a number of educational practices that benefit gifted students; and provides information about each state's gifted education policies and statistics. To access this information, visit http://www.nagc.org

- Davidson Institute for Talent Development—This privately funded foundation offers programs, services, and resources that support the development of profoundly gifted students (those scoring in the 99.9th percentile on achievement or IQ tests) ages 18 and under. Services include: Davidson Young Scholars, a free program offered to families of children ages 5 to 18 to help support the development of their child's gifts; Think Summer Institute, a three-week residential program in which 13- to 16-year-old students take college-level courses on campus; and the Davidson Gifted Database, which offers a wealth of information for students as well as educators. To learn more about what Davidson Institute has to offer, visit http://www.davidsongifted .org. You can read personal success stories of students and their families who have benefited from Davidson Young Scholars at http://www.davidsongifted.org/Young-Scholars/Success-Stories

- Duke University Talent Identification Program (Duke TIP)—This non-profit organization serves academically gifted and talented students in grades 4 through 12. The mission of this organization is to identify gifted students and provide challenging programs and opportunities that will develop their talents and gifts. In addition to an abundance of resources on gifted students, the Website provides information for students, families, and educators about the talent search process, weekend and summer programs, online learning opportunities, and much more. For additional information, visit https://tip.duke.edu

Check Your Understanding 15.3

Click here to gauge your understanding of the concepts in this section.

Future Perspectives

Learning Outcome

Explain why many gifted and talented students do not receive educational supports and services that meet their learning needs, understand that certain groups of students are underrepresented in gifted programs, identify online learning sources that can be used to differentiate instruction and provide enrichment opportunities, and recognize that distance learning opportunities can help accommodate the needs of gifted students.

Topic 15.12 Issues to Resolve

- Because educational programming for gifted and talented students is not federally mandated, these students often do not receive instructional services that meet their needs.

- Girls, culturally and linguistically diverse students, those from low-income backgrounds, and twice-exceptional students are under-represented in gifted programs.

Topic 15.13 Technology: Expanding Options

- Online learning can support differentiation and enrichment opportunities by providing access to in-depth information on topics of interest.

- Distance learning can provide acceleration opportunities that might be unavailable in a student's school or district.

DragonImages/Fotolia

Through advances in technology, teachers have greater options for differentiating instruction and providing enrichment opportunities for gifted students.

Topic 15.12 Issues to Resolve

- Because educational programming for gifted and talented students is not federally mandated, these students often do not receive instructional services that meet their needs.

- Girls, culturally and linguistically diverse students, those from low-income backgrounds, and twice-exceptional students are underrepresented in gifted programs.

Why is there such variability in programs for students who are gifted and talented? Perhaps one of the biggest challenges facing gifted and talented students is overcoming the assumption that they do not need special attention or unique educational programs to reach their full potential and develop their talents. As you have read, negative attitudes about gifted education are deeply rooted in America's concept of equity and also stem from myths about gifted and talented students. Assumptions seem to be that these individuals will thrive without special programs—that they can make it on their own. Quite sadly, this is simply untrue: gifted individuals often do not reach their potential because their educational programs did not meet their needs.

As you learned in Topic 15.10, Congress passed a national law, the Jacob K. Javits Gifted and Talented Students Education Act, in 1988 to support gifted education. Recall that this law does not include guarantees or full protections for gifted students, as IDEA does for students with disabilities, and consequently does not mandate states to provide special programs or services to gifted and talented students. Because no national mandate exists, every state has a different policy regarding gifted education. Additionally, individual state-level support for gifted programs differs greatly. On top of this, states can change their policies and funding levels across time. In the past several years, four states that had mandated gifted education have reversed their policy, now not requiring any services for these students. Another three states that had partial funding for gifted education have eliminated their state funding for such programs. This again points to the wavering commitment to gifted education, reflecting what has occurred at the federal level. Without consistent funding, the limited services available for gifted and talented students are in jeopardy. In the following figure, note that:

- Only 4 states mandate gifted education and fully fund services for these students.
- 23 states mandate support and provide partial funding for services.
- 8 states mandate gifted education but allocate no funding for services.
- 15 states as well as the District of Columbia—over 30% of the states—do not mandate gifted education.

A Comparison of Gifted Education Policies Across the U.S.

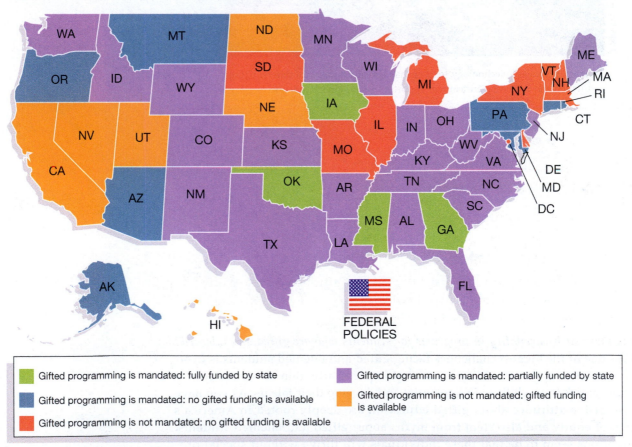

SOURCE: *Gifted Education Policies*, Davidson Institute for Talent Development, retrieved from www.davidsongifted.org/db/StatePolicy.aspx

Which groups face unique obstacles to participation in gifted education? Although gifted and talented students in general are an under-served population, four groups of gifted students face particular challenges in achieving their potential: females, diverse students, low-income students, and twice-exceptional students.

Differences between the academic achievement of males and females have been noted since the 1920s, when giftedness first came to educators' attention. Ironically, although many of his research associates were women with highly productive academic careers, Lewis Terman included few women in his study of gifted individuals. Today, gender differences—particularly girls' poor representation and achievement in STEM fields—are still troubling. Consider that women earn 45% of all doctoral degrees, but less than one-third of these are in chemistry, computer sciences, mathematics, physics, or engineering. Additionally, half of all women are in the workforce, but only 26% have careers in science or engineering. Some believe these disparities are due to girls' lower self-esteem and lack of confidence in STEM subjects, unfortunately often reinforced by teachers and parents who overlook their strengths or fail to consider them for higher-level or advanced courses. Yet, researchers have also found that gifted girls with high mathematics aptitude often have equally high verbal skills, which widens their career options, and they tend to prefer people-oriented fields like medicine or law, in which they still excel. Still, given the current national emphasis, and future dependence, on STEM fields, we must ensure that every capable student is provided with sufficient opportunities to achieve in these areas.

African American, Native American, and Hispanic students participate in special programs for gifted and talented students at rates substantially below what their percentages in the school population would predict (see the following figure). Notice that African American participation in gifted programs is approximately 50% less than that for all students, and the participation of Hispanic students is about 40% less. As mentioned earlier, lower academic achievement levels and lower performance on intelligence and achievement tests may cause teachers to overlook them for gifted programs. For Hispanic students, the effects of second-language acquisition may mask their giftedness or creativity. Students from diverse backgrounds, particularly African Americans, are less likely to attend schools that offer gifted services. When gifted programs are available, these students often do not want to participate. They may face peer rejection or ridicule if they do well in school, and sometimes their families are unsupportive of, or less aware of, identification for gifted education. Further, many diverse students are taught by teachers of a different racial and cultural background. Because of a lack of cultural knowledge or factors tied to cross-cultural dissonance, these teachers may not recognize their students' giftedness (which is not necessarily tied to achievement), have biases, or have lower expectations for diverse students. Additionally, students may perform differently when taught by a teacher of the same racial or cultural background (e.g., more comfortable displaying some of their gifted behaviors), and parents may feel more comfortable discussing their child's unique abilities with a teacher of the same race. Because gifted programming is not always culturally responsive and directed at the specific needs of these students, some who do enter these programs feel unwelcomed by the teachers and drop out. Clearly, educators must do a better job of identifying gifted and talented students from diverse backgrounds and then retaining them in the programs. You can learn more about identifying and serving this population of students by reading *Including Diverse Learners in Gifted Education Programs and Services* at https://www.nagc.org/resources-publications/resources/timely-topics/including-diverse-learners-gifted-education-programs.

Percentage of Gifted and Talented Students by Race/Ethnicity

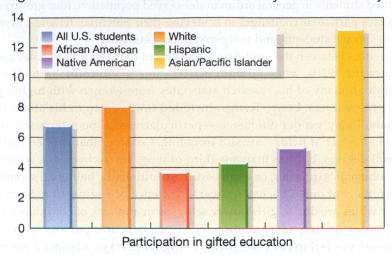

NOTE: While 13.1% of Asian/Pacific Islander students are identified, some particular subgroups of these students are more likely to live in poverty (e.g., Samoans, Hmong) and are less likely to be identified for gifted education.

SOURCE: Snyder, T.D., de Brey, C., and Dillow, S.A. (2016). *Digest of Education Statistics 2014* (NCES 2016-006). National Center for Education Statistics, Institute of Education Sciences, U.S. Department of Education. Washington, DC. Retrieved from https://nces.ed.gov/pubs2016/2016006.pdf

Gifted students who are poor are often under-served because their schools (both urban and rural) have fewer instructional resources, more uncertified and inexperienced teachers who cannot recognize or address signs of giftedness or creativity, and a lack of basic courses, such as algebra or geometry. Moreover, they offer fewer honors classes, AP courses, enrichment activities, or accelerated programs. Why might this be so? Sadly, perceptions still exist that poor children cannot perform as well as middle- or upper-income students, so there is no need for these programs. Even if AP courses are available, low-income students are often underrepresented. Results of a recent study indicated that economically advantaged students were three times more likely to be enrolled in AP courses and International Baccalaureate programs than low-income students. In addition to low expectations on the part of school personnel, these students may be underrepresented because they are under-achieving or because their parents (who are less likely to have a high school or college education than parents of more economically advantaged students) may not encourage them to take advanced courses. Just think of all the talent that is squandered, the achievements that are lost, when we do not provide the necessary supports for these students.

As you learned in Topic 15.2, twice-exceptional students are not always identified because the disability masks the giftedness. If identified, many students receive services that address their giftedness or disability, but not both. Additionally, many schools have implemented a response-to-intervention process, which replaces the traditionally used comprehensive assessment method, to discover students with learning disabilities. Gifted students with learning disabilities (the largest proportion of twice-exceptional students) are often not recognized as being gifted or having a disability through this process because they are able to compensate for any academic weaknesses and yet do not excel academically. Such cases frequently require a comprehensive assessment. Although identification and service delivery require a more concerted and collaborative effort among school professionals with expertise in both areas, it is important for educators to meet the learning needs of each student. With the appropriate services, these students can achieve their high potential.

Potential and Loss

"... failure to help the gifted child reach his potential is a societal tragedy, the extent of which is difficult to measure but what is surely great. How can we measure the sonata unwritten, the curative drug undiscovered, the absence of political insight? They are the difference between what we are and what we could be as a society."

—James Gallagher, Summer 1994
Delta Kappa Gamma, as cited in *The Twice-Exceptional Dilemma*, National Education Association (2006).

Topic 15.13 Technology: Expanding Options

- Online learning can support differentiation and enrichment opportunities by providing access to in-depth information on topics of interest.

- Distance learning can provide acceleration opportunities that might be unavailable in a student's school or district.

Can technology and online learning solve some of the educational programming problems in gifted education? Yes, technology can be a tool, an inspiration, and a means to independent learning. For students who are bored with slow-paced instruction or frustrated at having to sit through lessons on content they have already mastered, technology can enable them to study advanced topics in greater depth. Now available are many online learning opportunities that allow teachers to differentiate content and instruction and that provide enrichment opportunities for advanced learners. For example, NASA's Jet Propulsion Laboratory (JPL) Website includes apps that students can download to engage in simulations or other learning opportunities. One app allows students to view a three-dimensional image of Earth and monitor activities such as sea level rise and volcanic eruptions by using specialized tools and maps. Another allows students to work with scientists and mission planners to analyze real Mars mission data and assume exploration topic responsibilities (e.g., polar caps, volcanic regions). In the arts, students can take a virtual tour of the Louvre in Paris and inspect masterpieces in closer detail than would ever be allowed if they were there in person. The Smithsonian has virtual tours, online collections, and interactive games and apps that provide hundreds—if not thousands—of hours of study in art, history, and more.

Learning games are also an effective resource for targeting the individual needs of students. These games incorporate learning new content or a skill as well as practice opportunities with feedback. Students who interact with content in an online game format not only tend to be engaged and motivated by the task but also show substantial gains in achievement. Numerous games are available, but as with all educational resources, teachers need to review them to make sure they live up to their claims of addressing educational content. The following table lists several online learning sites (including those listed above) and online learning games that can be used to differentiate learning and provide enrichment opportunities for gifted students.

Online Learning Resources and Apps

NASA's Jet Propulsion Laboratory (JPL) http://www.jpl.nasa.gov	Provides interactive activities on a number of STEM-related topics
Smithsonian http://www.si.edu	Offers virtual tours, online collections, and interactive games and apps in areas such as art, history, and air and space
Louvre http://www.louvre.fr/en	Allows close examination of art exhibits and collections
Gizmos https://www.explorelearning.com	Provides over 400 simulations in which students engage in mathematical and scientific exploration (e.g., manipulating variables, analyzing data)
GarageBand https://itunes.apple.com/us/app/garageband/id682658836?mt=12	Allows students to create and record their own music

In the video below, learn how a teacher is using an online learning project, with virtual worlds, to provide enriching and engaging learning activities for her gifted students.

▶ **Using Virtual Worlds to Engage Gifted Learners**

https://youtu.be/j7FOOmKKVhg

What technology options are available for accelerating a student's learning? Advances in distance education technology, often used in college courses, can have great benefits for gifted students. Distance education can provide acceleration opportunities for those who do not have advanced courses available at their local schools or for those who want to explore topics not covered at school, and students can take online courses for credit from anywhere in the nation. For example, one student can work through an online tutorial in chemistry or physics while a classmate learns the computer programming needed to develop an environmental monitoring and control system. Distance education can also be used to facilitate differentiation and enrichment, particularly for those who live in rural and remote areas. Additionally, through the use of technology, students can participate in important conversations about current events and issues with others worldwide. For example, UNICEF "assembles" students around the world to discuss important topics like environmental issues and hunger.

Some distance education offerings are designed for and used exclusively by students participating in gifted education, while others are available to anyone but typically target older students or adults. The following table provides a list of distance learning opportunities offered by universities and other programs.

Distance Learning Opportunities

Stanford University's Educational Program for Gifted Youth (EPGY) http://epgy.stanford.edu	Provides special online courses for high school students who want to study specific content in more depth
Johns Hopkins' Center for Talented Youth http://cty.jhu.edu	Offers multimedia courses in math and science, some of which are designed for elementary students
Duke University's Talent Identification Program (Duke TIP) www.tip.duke.edu	Makes coursework available in a variety of subjects (e.g., social psychology, history of the ancient world, anatomy and physiology) and includes online discussions to support its distance learning opportunities
Northwestern Center for Talent Development http://www.ctd.northwestern.edu/program_type/online-programs	Offers online courses, enrichment opportunities, and more for K–12 gifted students
Khan Academy https://www.khanacademy.org	Offers instruction on a number of topics such as mathematics, science, computer programming, and history through instructional videos and practice opportunities
Alcumus http://www.artofproblemsolving.com/alcumus	Includes over 13,000 mathematical problems, many of which are from national math competitions, and adjusts learning based on student performance; targets high-achieving students
Massive Open Online Courses (MOOC)	Makes available free college-level courses, but they do not count toward a degree; offered by many universities (e.g., Duke, MIT, Yale, Carnegie Mellon, UC Berkeley)

Despite all the advantages of online learning, the completion rates of gifted students are disappointing—well below 80%. Students' interests must be matched with the course offerings, and the independent study skills necessary for success must be in place. With careful selection and implementation, the benefits of distance delivery options outweigh concerns. Online learning can provide the missing educational ingredient for many gifted students, removing the limits imposed by traditional education systems and allowing exploration of virtually any topic in the world.

Technology Considerations

Technology is only a solution to a lack of gifted programming if students have access to it. Unfortunately, the very students who could most benefit from technological advances may have the least access. Students in high-poverty schools—which have few AP, honors, or enrichment options—also tend to have antiquated technology infrastructures. They may have older computers that lack necessary software or have limited Internet connections. Further, these schools may lack instructional technology staff or support, which means that broken computers are not fixed or replaced or that systems or software problems go unresolved.

Another issue centers on typical online safety considerations. Even though students are gifted, they are still subject to the same online dangers as their peers. So teachers must be sure to address safety issues (e.g., giving out personal information) and personal behaviors (e.g., netiquette, sexting) that may arise, particularly when students are engaged in collaborative work with teens and adults in locations nationwide and worldwide.

Check Your Understanding 15.4

Click here to gauge your understanding of the concepts in this section.

Summary

Gifted and Talented Described

Gifted children have outstanding abilities and talents in one or more areas (e.g., intellectual, creative, artistic, leadership), and their giftedness is usually evident at a very early age.

- Gifted and talented students are often identified through intelligence or achievement test scores, but information from multiple sources should be considered.

- Two methods used to categorize gifted students are IQ score ranges and Gardner's theory of multiple intelligences.

- Gifted students often share common characteristics such as abstract reasoning, persistence, learning information quickly, and strong verbal skills, and they tend to be socially and emotionally well adjusted.

- The services and supports that gifted students receive vary greatly from state to state because of the differences in state definitions and identification criteria.

Special Education

For gifted students to develop to their fullest potential, they should receive services and supports starting at a very early age.

- Many challenges that gifted students encounter at school can be addressed through early intervention, acceleration, differentiated instruction, and enrichment.

- Accommodations for gifted students remove barriers that prevent students from learning at a pace and level commensurate with their own unique learning needs.

- The unique needs of young gifted students can be met by providing engaging and enriching learning environments or by allowing early entrance to kindergarten or first grade.

- During the school years, the learning needs of gifted students can be addressed through differentiated instruction and enrichment opportunities and programs.

- Gifted and talented students often require transition services to help them navigate the college selection and admission process and to address skills that will be needed in college.

People and Situations

Although individuals with outstanding gifts and talents have been acknowledged for many centuries, the importance of providing educational supports and services to gifted students was not recognized in the United States until the twentieth century.

- Public support and funding for special programs and services for gifted students have been inconsistent across time.

- The contributions of gifted and talented individuals greatly impact the world, and organizations exist to support these students and to help them reach their fullest potential.

Future Perspectives

Because educational programming for gifted and talented students is not federally mandated, gifted students often do not receive the instructional services and supports they need to excel.

- Several groups are underrepresented in gifted programs: females, culturally and linguistically diverse students, those from low-income backgrounds, and twice-exceptional students.

- Because online learning allows for differentiation, enrichment activities, and acceleration opportunities, it is an effective way to meet the needs of gifted students.

Addressing CEC Standards

Council for Exceptional Children (CEC) knowledge standards addressed in this chapter: 6.2, 1.0, GT1K2, GT1K4, GT2K2, GT2K3, GT3K2, GT4S3, GT5S2, GT7K2, GT8K1, GT10S1.

See the Appendix for the complete CEC Initial Level Special Educator Preparation Standards.

Appendix
CEC Initial Level Special Educator Preparation Standards

Initial Preparation Standard 1: Learner Development and Individual Learning Differences	
1.0	Beginning special education professionals understand how exceptionalities may interact with development and learning and use this knowledge to provide meaningful and challenging learning experiences for individuals with exceptionalities.
Key Elements	
1.1	Beginning special education professionals understand how language, culture, and family background influence the learning of individuals with exceptionalities.
1.2	Beginning special education professionals use understanding of development and individual differences to respond to the needs of individuals with exceptionalities.

Supporting Explanation

Special educators place the learning needs of the individual at the center of special education instruction. Historically, *pedagogy* (or teaching skill) has been at the heart of special education. Whether helping individuals with exceptionalities master mathematics, vocational skills, independent living, or Philosophy, special educators alter instructional variables to optimize learning for individuals with exceptionalities. The raison d'être for special education lies in the specialized professional knowledge and skills to individualize access to learning in both specialized and general education curricula for individuals with exceptionalities. Development of expertise begins with a thorough understanding of and respect for similarities and differences in human growth and development. Like all educators, beginning special educators first respect individuals with exceptionalities within the context of human development and individual learning differences.

In addition, beginning special educators understand the characteristics between and among individuals with and without exceptionalities. They know exceptionalities can interact with multiple domains of human development to influence an individual's learning in school, community, and throughout life. Moreover, beginning special educators understand that the beliefs, traditions, and values across and within cultures can influence relationships among and between children and youth, their families, and the school community. Further, the experiences of individuals with exceptionalities can influence families, as well as the individual's ability to learn, interact socially, and live as fulfilled contributing members of the community.

However, beginning special educators' knowledge of human development goes beyond listing and ordering developmental milestones and reciting legal definitions of exceptionalities. Beginning special educators understand how exceptionalities can interact with development and learning, and modify developmentally appropriate learning environments to provide relevant, meaningful, and challenging learning experiences for individuals with exceptionalities. Beginning special educators are active and resourceful in seeking to understand how primary language, culture, and family interact with the exceptionality to influence the individual's academic and social abilities, attitudes, values, interests, and career and post-secondary options.

These learning differences and their interactions provide the foundation upon which beginning special educators individualize instruction to provide developmentally meaningful and challenging learning for individuals with exceptionalities.

Initial Preparation Standard 2: Learning Environments
2.0   Beginning special education professionals create safe, inclusive, culturally responsive learning environments so that individuals with exceptionalities become active and effective learners and develop emotional well being, positive social interactions, and self-determination.
Key Elements
2.1   Beginning special education professionals, through collaboration with general educators and other colleagues, create safe, inclusive, culturally responsive learning environments to engage individuals with exceptionalities in meaningful learning activities and social interactions.
2.2   Beginning special education professionals use motivational and instructional interventions to teach individuals with exceptionalities how to adapt to different environments.
2.3   Beginning special education professionals know how to intervene safely and appropriately with individuals with exceptionalities in crisis.

Supporting Explanation

Like all educators, beginning special educators develop safe, inclusive, culturally responsive learning environments for all children and youth. Beginning special educators also collaborate with education colleagues to include individuals with exceptionalities in general education environments and engage them in meaningful learning activities and social interactions.

Beginning special educators modify learning environments for individual needs. Knowledge regarding an individual's language, family, culture, and other significant contextual factors and how they interact with an individual's exceptionality guides the special educator in modifying learning environments and providing for the maintenance and generalization of acquired skills across environments and subjects.

Beginning special educators structure environments to encourage the independence, self-motivation, self-direction, personal empowerment, and self-advocacy of individuals with exceptionalities, and directly teach them to adapt to the expectations and demands of differing environments. Frequently, special educators safely intervene with individuals with exceptionalities in crisis. Special educators are also perceived as a resource in behavior management that includes the skills and knowledge to intervene safely and effectively before or when individuals with exceptionalities experience crisis (i.e., lose rational control over their behavior).

Initial Preparation Standard 3: Curricular Content Knowledge
3.0   Beginning special education professionals use knowledge of general and specialized curricula to individualize learning for individuals with exceptionalities.
Key Elements
3.1   Beginning special education professionals understand the central concepts, structures of the discipline, and tools of inquiry of the content areas they teach, and can organize this knowledge, integrate cross-disciplinary skills, and develop meaningful learning progressions for individuals with exceptionalities.
3.2   Beginning special education professionals understand and use general and specialized content knowledge for teaching across curricular content areas to individualize learning for individuals with exceptionalities.
3.3   Beginning special education professionals modify general and specialized curricula to make them accessible to individuals with exceptionalities.

Supporting Explanation

The professional knowledge base in general education has made clear that educators' understanding of the central concepts and structures of the discipline and the tools of inquiry related to the academic subject-matter content areas they teach makes a significant difference in student learning. There is good reason to generalize this conclusion to special educators.

Within the general education curricula, beginning special educators demonstrate in their planning and teaching a solid base of understanding of the central concepts, structures of the discipline, and tools of inquiry of the academic subject-matter content areas they teach so they are able to organize knowledge, integrate cross-disciplinary skills, develop meaningful learning progressions and collaborate with general educators in:

- Teaching or co-teaching the content of the general education curriculum to individuals with exceptionalities across a wide range of performance levels.

- Designing appropriate learning and performance accommodations and modifications for individuals with exceptionalities in academic subject matter content of the general education curriculum.

It should be noted that because of the significant role that content-specific subject-matter knowledge plays at the secondary school level, special education teachers routinely teach secondary level academic content area classes in consultation or collaboration with one or more general education teachers appropriately licensed in the respective content area. However, whenever special education teachers assume sole responsibility for teaching a general education curriculum academic subject matter course at the secondary level, they must possess a solid subject matter content knowledge base sufficient to ensure their students can meet state curriculum standards.

In addition, beginning special educators use a variety of specialized curricula (e.g., academic, strategic, social-emotional, independence curricula) to individualize meaningful and challenging learning for individuals with exceptionalities.

Initial Preparation Standard 4: Assessment	
4.0	Beginning special education professionals use multiple methods of assessment and data sources in making educational decisions.

Key Elements	
4.1	Beginning special education professionals select and use technically sound formal and informal assessments that minimize bias.
4.2	Beginning special education professionals use knowledge of measurement principles and practices to interpret assessment results and guide educational decisions for individuals with exceptionalities.
4.3	Beginning special education professionals, in collaboration with colleagues and families, use multiple types of assessment information in making decisions about individuals with exceptionalities.
4.4	Beginning special education professionals engage individuals with exceptionalities to work toward quality learning and performance and provide feedback to guide them.

Supporting Explanation

Like all educators, beginning special educators understand measurement theory and practice for addressing issues of validity, reliability, norms, bias, and interpretation of assessment results. Like their general education colleagues, beginning special educators regularly monitor the learning progress of individuals with exceptionalities in both general and specialized content and make instructional adjustments based on these data.

Beginning special educators also use assessment information to support a wide variety of decisions within special education. Beginning special educators understand the legal policies and ethical principles of measurement and assessment related to special education referral, eligibility, program planning, individualized instruction, learning, and placement for individuals with exceptionalities, including individuals from culturally and linguistically diverse backgrounds.

Beginning special educators understand the appropriate use and limitations of various types of assessments, and collaborate with families and other colleagues to assure nonbiased, meaningful assessments and decision making. They conduct formal and informal assessments of behavior, learning, achievement, and environments to individualize the learning experiences that support the growth and development of individuals with exceptionalities.

Beginning special educators make multiple types of assessment decisions including strategic adaptations and modifications in response to an individuals' constellation of social, linguistic, and learning factors in ways to minimize bias. Beginning special educators use assessment information to identify supports and adaptations required for individuals with exceptionalities to access the general education curricula and to participate in school, system, and statewide assessment programs.

Beginning special educators integrate the results of assessments to develop long-range individualized instructional plans anchored in both general and special education curricula, and translate these individualized plans into carefully selected shorter range goals and objectives. They also have a central role integrating the results of assessments in developing a variety of individualized plans, including family service plans, transition plans, behavior management plans, and so on.

Beginning special educators routinely use available technologies to support their assessments. With the rapid advance and use of technology, special educators use technologies to support and manage assessment of individuals with exceptionalities. The appropriate and efficient use of technology to support assessment tasks is an essential tool for special education professionals.

Initial Preparation Standard 5: Instructional Planning and Strategies	
5.0	Beginning special education professionals select, adapt, and use a repertoire of evidence-based instructional strategies to advance learning of individuals with exceptionalities.
Key Elements	
5.1	Beginning special education professionals consider individual abilities, interests, learning environments, and cultural and linguistic factors in the selection, development, and adaptation of learning experiences for individuals with exceptionalities.
5.2	Beginning special education professionals use technologies to support instructional assessment, planning, and delivery for individuals with exceptionalities.
5.3	Beginning special education professionals are familiar with augmentative and alternative communication systems and a variety of assistive technologies to support the communication and learning of individuals with exceptionalities.
5.4	Beginning special education professionals use strategies to enhance language development and communication skills of individuals with exceptionalities.
5.5	Beginning special education professionals develop and implement a variety of education and transition plans for individuals with exceptionalities across a wide range of settings and different learning experiences in collaboration with individuals, families, and teams.
5.6	Beginning special education professionals teach to mastery and promote generalization of learning.
5.7	Beginning special education professionals teach cross-disciplinary knowledge and skills such as critical thinking and problem solving to individuals with exceptionalities.

Supporting Explanation

Individualized decision making and individualized instruction are at the center of special education practice. In the selection, development, and adaptation of learning experiences for individuals with exceptionalities, beginning special educators consider an individual's abilities, interests, learning environments, and cultural and linguistic factors. The interactions of these factors with the implications of an individual's exceptionality guide the special educator's selection, adaptation, and use of a repertoire of evidence-based instructional strategies in promoting positive learning results in general and specialized curricula and in appropriately modifying learning environments for individuals with exceptionalities.

Beginning special educators teach personalized literacy and numeracy to individuals with exceptionalities who are often nonresponsive individuals in tiered intervention models. In their planning and teaching with these individuals, beginning special educators emphasize explicit instruction with modeling and guided practice to assure acquisition and fluency, as well as promote the development, maintenance, and generalization of knowledge and skills across environments, settings, and the life span through approaches such as cross-curricular lesson planning. Moreover, beginning special educators enhance 21st-century student outcomes such as critical thinking, creative problem solving, and collaboration skills for individuals with exceptionalities and increase their self-awareness and reliance, self-management and control, self-efficacy, and self-advocacy.

Beginning special educators provide effective language models and use communication strategies and resources to facilitate understanding of subject matter for individuals with exceptionalities whose primary language is not English. Beginning special educators match their communication methods to an individual's language proficiency and cultural and linguistic differences. Beginning special educators are familiar with augmentative and alternative communication systems and assistive technologies to support and enhance the language and communication of individuals with exceptionalities, and use individualized strategies to enhance language development and teach communication skills to individuals with exceptionalities.

Beginning special educators implement a variety of individualized learning plans across a wide range of settings and a range of different learning experiences, including individualized family service plans, individualized transition plans, and individualized behavior management plans. Transitions are specific points of potential difficulty for individuals with exceptionalities.

Beginning special educators develop a variety of individualized transition plans, such as for the transition from preschool to elementary school and from the secondary educational setting to various postsecondary work and learning contexts. For individuals with exceptionalities in early childhood, special educators focus the individualized instruction plan within the context of family services, taking into account the needs, priorities, and concerns of families as the primary providers of instruction.

Beginning special educators facilitate all personalized instructional planning within a collaborative context including the individuals with exceptionalities, families, professional colleagues, and personnel from other agencies as appropriate. Beginning special educators use technologies routinely to support all phases of instruction planning. With the rapid advance and use of technology, special educators use technologies to support and manage all phases of planning, implementing, and evaluating instruction.

Initial Preparation Standard 6: Professional Learning and Ethical Practice

6.0	Beginning special education professionals use foundational knowledge of the field and their professional ethical principles and practice standards to inform special education practice, to engage in lifelong learning, and to advance the profession.

Key Elements

6.1	Beginning special education professionals use professional ethical principles and professional practice standards to guide their practice.
6.2	Beginning special education professionals understand how foundational knowledge and current issues influence professional practice.
6.3	Beginning special education professionals understand that diversity is a part of families, cultures, and schools, and that complex human issues can interact with the delivery of special education services.
6.4	Beginning special education professionals understand the significance of lifelong learning and participate in professional activities and learning communities.
6.5	Beginning special education professionals advance the profession by engaging in activities such as advocacy and mentoring.
6.6	Beginning special education professionals provide guidance and direction to paraeducators, tutors, and volunteers.

Supporting Explanation

Beginning special educators practice in multiple roles and complex situations across wide age and developmental ranges that require ongoing attention to legal matters and consideration of serious professional and ethical issues. CEC's Code of Ethics and Standards for the Professional Practice guide beginning special education professionals. These principles and standards provide benchmarks by which special educators practice—and evaluate each other professionally.

Beginning special educators understand special education as an evolving and changing discipline based on philosophies, evidence-based principles and theories, policies, and historical points of view that continue to influence the field and the education of and services for individuals with exceptionalities and their families, in both school and society. Beginning special educators understand how these factors influence professional practice, including assessment, instructional planning, implementation, and program evaluation.

Beginning special educators are sensitive to the aspects of diversity with individuals with exceptionalities and their families; how human diversity can influence families, cultures, and schools; and how these complex issues can each interact with the delivery of special education services. Of special significance is the growth in the number and prevalence of English language learners (ELLs) and the provision of effective special education services for ELLs with exceptionalities and their families.

Beginning special educators understand the relationships of the organization of special education services to the organization of schools, school systems, and education-related agencies within the country and cultures in which they practice. Beginning special educators are aware of how their own and others' attitudes, behaviors, and ways of communicating can influence their practice, and use this knowledge as a foundation to inform their own personal understanding and philosophy of special education.

Beginning special educators engage in professional activities and participate actively in professional learning communities that benefit individuals with exceptionalities and their families, colleagues, and their own professional growth. Beginning special educators view themselves as lifelong learners, regularly reflect on and adjust their practice, and develop and use personalized professional development plans. Beginning special educators plan and engage in activities that foster their professional growth and keep them current with evidence-based practices. Beginning special educators also know how to recognize their own skill limits and practice within them.

There has been substantial growth in the use of special education paraeducators over the past few years, and beginning special educators frequently provide guidance and direction to paraeducators and others, such as classroom volunteers and tutors.

Initial Preparation Standard 7: Collaboration
7.0   Beginning special education professionals collaborate with families, other educators, related service providers, individuals with exceptionalities, and personnel from community agencies in culturally responsive ways to address the needs of individuals with exceptionalities across a range of learning experiences.

Key Elements
7.1   Beginning special education professionals use the theory and elements of effective collaboration.
7.2   Beginning special education professionals serve as a collaborative resource to colleagues.
7.3   Beginning special education professionals use collaboration to promote the well being of individuals with exceptionalities across a wide range of settings and collaborators.

Supporting Explanation

One of the significant changes in education over the past several decades is the rapid growth of collaborative educational teams to address the educational needs of students. The diversity of students, complexity of curricular demands, growing influence of technology, and rising targets for learner outcomes in the 21st century has created a demand for teams of educators collaborating together to ensure all students are effectively learning challenging curricula.

Special educators view general educators as possessing knowledge and expertise in curriculum, and general educators reciprocally view special educators as having knowledge and expertise in the education of individuals with exceptionalities. Beginning special educators embrace their role as a resource to colleagues and use the theory and elements of collaboration across a wide range of contexts and collaborators.

Beginning special educators collaborate with their general education colleagues to create learning environments that meaningfully include individuals with exceptionalities, and which foster cultural understanding, safety and emotional well being, positive social interaction, and active engagement. In addition, special educators use collaboration to facilitate personalized instruction planning and transitions of individuals with exceptionalities in promoting the learning and well-being of individuals with exceptionalities across a wide range of settings and different learning experiences.

Beginning special educators routinely collaborate with related-service providers, other educators (including special education paraeducators), personnel from community agencies, and others to address the needs of individuals with exceptionalities. Special educators have long recognized the positive significance of the active involvement of individuals with exceptionalities and their families in the education process, and special educators involve individuals with exceptionalities and their families collaboratively in all aspects of the education of individuals with exceptionalities.

Glossary

ABC analysis   A method for selecting interventions to modify behavior by identifying events that precede (antecedent) the inappropriate or target behavior, carefully describing the behavior, and identifying those events that follow (consequences) and that maintain or reinforce it

above-level testing   The process of administering a test intended for one group (e.g., ACT or SAT) to a gifted child who is younger or in a lower grade than the group for whom the test was designed; often given because grade-level tests cannot measure a gifted student's high ability level

accelerated high school   A high school program that serves only gifted students, offering advanced courses and opportunities to collaborate with mentors or to work as an intern; students often receive college, in addition to high school, credits for the courses they complete in these programs; also referred to as *honors high school*

acceleration   Moving students through a curriculum or year(s) of schooling, often for a particular subject, in a shorter period

accommodations   Services or supports that compensate for the challenges associated with a disability, enabling students with disabilities to access subject matter and demonstrate knowledge without altering assignment or test standards or expectations

achievement gap   The disparity in school and learning outcomes between students from certain backgrounds (e.g., racially/culturally/linguistically marginalized, low-income) and their dominant-society or higher-income peers

active supervision   A process in which the teacher moves around the room in relative proximity to the students, scanning to determine where additional instruction or feedback is needed

adaptive behavior   Performance of everyday life skills expected of adults; also referred to as *adaptive skills*

additive bilingualism   A framework for language acquisition in which a student adds a second language without losing his or her first language

advance organizers   Previews or organizational guides used to acquaint students with the content, structure, or importance of written material or a lecture

Advanced Placement (AP)   High school courses for which students can earn college credit after passing an exam

adventitious   Acquired, or occurring after birth

adventitiously blind   Blindness acquired after the age of two

age of onset   A medical term used to identify the age at which a person first acquires a condition or disorder, or when the symptoms of a disease first appear

aggression   Hostile and attacking behavior, which can include physical and verbal actions, directed toward self, others, or the physical environment

air conduction audiometry method   A method to test hearing that uses pure-tone sounds generated by an audiometer

albinism   A genetic disorder in which the body does not produce the normal amount of melanin (pigment), so the individual's eyes, skin, and hair have little or no color

alternate achievement standards   Achievement standards that are based on the grade-level content but for which the content has been simplified or the amount or depth of the content has been reduced

alternate assessments   Assessments administered to the 1% of students with the most significant cognitive disabilities; although related to grade-level content, these tests assess the student's knowledge of only a portion of the content or a more simplified version of the content

alternate curriculum   A curriculum designed for students with the most significant disabilities who cannot access the general education curriculum without significant modifications, or for whom the general education curriculum provides little or no benefit

amblyopia   "Lazy eye"; reduced vision in one eye due to inadequate use during early childhood

American Sign Language (ASL)   The language of Deaf Americans that uses manual communication; a signal of Deaf culture

anorexia   Condition characterized by intense fear of gaining weight, distorted body image, chronic absence of appetite or refusal to eat food; results in severe weight loss (e.g., at least 25% of body weight)

anxiety disorders   Conditions causing painful uneasiness, emotional tension, or emotional confusion

aphasia   The loss or impairment of language ability due to a brain injury

applied behavior analysis (ABA)   A process in which behavior is modified by altering the environment, including antecedents (what occurs before the behavior) and consequences (what occurs after the behavior); usually involves determining the function of the behavior; a validated approach to the treatment of ASD that uses the principles of reinforcement theory developed by B. F. Skinner and his colleagues

apprenticeship   A formal vocational arrangement in which a student learns trade-specific skills; can be time- or competency-based

Asperger's disorder/Asperger's syndrome   No longer considered a separate disorder within the autism spectrum; once defined as a type of autism spectrum disorder in which cognition is usually in the average or above average range (now referred to as Asperger syndrome)

assistive listening devices (ALDs)   Equipment (e.g., hearing aids, audio loops, FM transmission devices) that helps improve use of residual hearing

asynchrony   The uneven development of cognitive, emotional, and physical skills within gifted individuals; some skills (e.g., cognitive) develop far in advance of others (e.g., physical)

attention deficit hyperactivity disorder (ADHD)   A condition characterized by hyperactivity, impulsivity, and/or inattention; included in the *other health impairments* category

audio description   Verbal narration that describes key visual information in videos or movies that would not be available to viewers who are blind

audiogram   A grid or graph used to display a person's hearing abilities

audiologist   A related service provider who diagnoses hearing losses and auditory problems

audiometer   An instrument audiologists use to measure hearing

auditory brainstem implant   A surgical device that bypasses the cochlea and auditory nerve; for individuals who cannot benefit from a cochlear implant

auditory canal   A tube that connects the outer ear to the middle ear

auditory cue   Any sound that signals the beginning or end of a specified timeframe or activity

auditory neuropathy spectrum disorder   Condition caused by damage to the inner ear or auditory nerve, resulting in the inability of the brain to understand sounds

auditory processing   The way that the brain interprets, understands, or processes auditory information

auditory support   The use of a sound or words (e.g., bell, verbal instructions) to support the acquisition and demonstration of desired behaviors

augmentative and alternative communication (AAC)   Communication method that attempts to compensate for impairments in the ability to produce spoken language; can include using gestures, writing, pictures, or symbols, and often refers to assistive technology devices

augmentative and alternative communication (AAC) devices   Assistive technology that helps individuals communicate, including devices that produce simulated speech

autism   A term formerly used to refer to one of the conditions that fell under the autism spectrum disorder umbrella; still used in educational definitions (e.g., IDEA)

autism spectrum disorder (ASD)   A developmental disability characterized by significant delays and differences in social-communication skills and restrictive, repetitive behaviors; exists on a continuum of severity from mild to severe

autistic savant   An individual who displays behaviors associated with ASD, yet also possesses discrete abilities, unusual talents, and splinter skills

basic interpersonal conversation skills (BICS)   A term referring to social communication; the level of linguistic skill required for general or social communications but not necessarily for academic learning

behavior intervention plan (BIP)   Part of a student's IEP that includes a functional behavioral assessment (FBA) and procedures to prevent problem behaviors and intervene when they do occur

behavior modification   Systematic control of environmental events—particularly consequences—that produce specific changes in a student's observable responses; may include reinforcement, punishment, self-regulation, and other techniques for increasing or decreasing a student's behavioral response

behavior therapy   Technique that replaces specific, negative, undesirable behaviors with new, positive, appropriate behaviors

Best Buddies International   A worldwide volunteer organization that connects middle school, high school, and college students to people who have intellectual disabilities, with the purpose of forming friendships and providing supports

blind/blindness   A degree of vision loss in which the individual has no functional use of sight

Board Certified Behavior Analyst™ (BCBA)   An individual with demonstrated expertise in applying principles of behavior analysis to develop interventions for students with ASD and other disabilities; must have fulfilled national certification requirements

bone conduction audiometry method   A method to test for conductive hearing loss that uses a vibrator placed on a person's forehead so sound bypasses the outer and middle ear and goes directly to the inner ear

braille   A system of reading and writing that uses raised dots embossed on paper; a form of tactile reading created in 1824 by Louis Braille

bulimia   Condition characterized by chronically causing oneself to vomit or otherwise eliminate food that has already been consumed, to limit weight gain

bullying   Repeated, intentional, aggressive behavior that usually involves an imbalance of power and is meant to physically or emotionally hurt someone who is unable to effectively defend himself/herself

call-and-response   A type of back-and-forth communication in which a verbalization (call) from a speaker elicits a verbal or nonverbal response from the listener(s)

career awareness   Initial recognition of the world of work; first stage in career education

case manager   A professional who coordinates related services for individual students

catheter   A tube that is inserted into the body to either introduce or remove fluid.

cerebral palsy   Typically present at birth but often not diagnosed until the early childhood years, the neurological disorders included under this term are due to brain damage or infections and result in motor impairments

Check & Connect   An intervention approach in which a mentor monitors a student's academic and behavioral progress and links the student to appropriate interventions when the student demonstrates signs of disengagement; typically used with high school students

Check In/Check Out   A targeted intervention at the secondary prevention level of PBIS; student checks in with a teacher every morning to pick up a behavior card, which is marked by each period's teachers and then "checked out" by the morning teacher and by parents at home

Child Find   Requirement of IDEA to help identify, locate, and evaluate children and youth with disabilities

childhood disintegrative disorder (CDD)   Once considered a separate disorder within the autism spectrum; the child has typical development for at least two years and then experiences a significant loss of skills

chronic illnesses   Long-term or frequently recurring health conditions that can result in the need for special education services

cleft lip   A congenital condition in which the upper lip is not formed or connected properly to allow for correct articulation of sounds, resulting in a speech impairment

cleft palate   A congenital condition in which an opening in the roof of the mouth causes too much air to pass through the nasal cavity, resulting in a speech impairment

closed captions   Subtitles that can be seen when this option is selected

cluster grouping   Placing four to six gifted students in a mixed-ability classroom with a teacher who can differentiate instruction to meet these students' needs

cluttering   A type of dysfluency in an individual's speech pattern, often characterized by rapid, unorganized, or unintelligible speech containing omissions of sounds or word parts

co-teaching   An instructional model in which general and special educators teach as a team

cochlea   A structure of the inner ear that contains the organs of hearing

cochlear implant   Microprocessor that is surgically placed in the hearing mechanism to replace the cochlea so people with sensorineural hearing loss can perceive sounds

CODA   A child of a Deaf adult who may or may not be Deaf

cognition   Thinking skills

cognitive academic language proficiency (CALP)   A term referring to the ability to understand and engage in the advanced, complex language of classroom settings; academic language; the level of linguistic skill required to access the general education curriculum and profit from instruction

college- and career-readiness   A goal for high school graduates in which they have adequate knowledge and skills to be successful in post-secondary learning opportunities (e.g., two-year or four-year college, vocational training) without the need for remediation

combined classes A classroom arrangement consisting of multiple grade levels; younger students may have opportunities to interact with older students academically and socially

Communication Access Real-time Translation (CART) A computer-aided transcription service that provides immediate translation of the spoken word into print by using a stenotype machine, a laptop computer, and specialized software; also referred to as real-time captioning (RTC)

communication boards Low-tech assistive technology devices that display pictures or words that the individual can point to in order to communicate

communication disorder Disorder in speech, language, or hearing that impairs communications

communicative competence Proficiency in all aspects of communication in social and learning situations

communities of practice Groups of individuals working on mutual topics and connected through the Internet

community presence A goal of normalization; promotes ideals of independent living, working, social inclusion, and participation in the daily life of the community with or without supports

community-based instruction (CBI) A strategy that involves teaching functional and vocational skills in the environments in which they are needed

comorbidity Coexisting disabilities

comprehensible input Sheltered instruction method in which teachers provide instruction at a level just beyond the students' current level of language competence, while also providing supports necessary to understand the information, in order to improve language skills as well as content-area knowledge

concurrent enrollment An acceleration option that allows a student to take one class but earn credit for two separate but academically related classes, often at different institutions (e.g., a student takes a college-level English class in high school and simultaneously earns a high school and a college credit); also referred to as *dual enrollment*

conduct disorder A mental health condition that involves extreme externalizing, aggressive, and destructive behaviors; characteristics include lying, aggression, destruction of property, deceitfulness, rule violation, difficulty displaying socially acceptable behavior, and theft

conductive hearing loss Hearing impairment due to damage or obstruction to the outer or middle ear that blocks transfer of sound to the inner ear

congenital Occurring before or at birth

congenital cataracts Cataracts (a condition in which the eye's lens is cloudy instead of clear) that develop at birth or soon after; a major cause of childhood blindness

congenitally blind Blindness present at birth or occurring during early infancy

consulting teachers Special education teachers who serve as a resource to general education teachers

content (academic) The required knowledge or skills for a particular unit of study

content (language) An aspect of language that governs the intent and meaning of the message delivered in a communication

continuous progress A type of acceleration in which a student is provided new content as soon as he or she completes and masters the skill or concept being worked on

contracture Shortening, distortion, or hardening of tissue (e.g., muscle, tendon) that restricts movement

cornea The transparent, curved part of the front of the eye

corporal punishment A form of physical punishment that attempts to change behavior by inflicting pain (e.g., hitting, spanking)

creativity A group of traits such as inquisitiveness, imaginativeness, resourcefulness, and an ability to "think outside the box"; the ability to develop new or unique ideas

credit by examination Earning credit for a course by demonstrating mastery of the content on a test rather than by taking the course

cross-cultural dissonance A situation in which the home and school cultures are in conflict

cued speech Hand signals for speech sounds; assists with speech reading

cultural discontinuity A dissimilarity between home and school cultures that may result in conflict; see also *cross-cultural dissonance*

cultural pluralism All cultural groups are valued components of the society; language and traditions of each group are maintained

culturally competent Knowing and understanding the cultural standards of diverse communities

culturally diverse Being from a cultural group that is not Euro-centric or of mainstream America

culturally responsive instruction The inclusion of multiple perspectives, especially those of students in the classroom; the use of students' cultural knowledge, experiences, and learning histories to make learning more appropriate, relevant, and effective for them

curb cut A ramp created to reduce the drop from a sidewalk to the street

curriculum The plan that specifies the learning (i.e., knowledge, skills) to occur in classrooms in each grade and subject area

curriculum compacting A type of acceleration that involves eliminating or reducing introductory activities and redundant information in subjects or topics that the student can quickly and easily master; this allows students to study more advanced material or engage in enrichment activities

curriculum-based measurement (CBM) A type of progress monitoring; evaluates learning frequently (e.g., weekly, monthly) by collecting data directly on academic skills across an entire curriculum; also known as general outcome measure

data-based decision making The process of guiding or changing instruction based on the results of data gathered from students

Deaf culture Structures of social relationships, language (ASL), dance, theater, literature, and other cultural activities that bind the Deaf community

Deaf of Deaf Members of the Deaf community who are prelingually deaf and have at least one parent who is Deaf

deaf-blindness A disability involving both vision and hearing problems

deafness The most severe type of hearing impairment, usually with little or no functional hearing

decibels (dB) The unit of measure for intensity of sound

delinquency The act of engaging in illegal behaviors by juveniles

demographics Characteristics, such as race, ethnicity, socioeconomic state, age, or disability status of various groups of people

depression A state of despair and dejected mood

developmental disability An umbrella term that includes intellectual disability as well as other disabilities that occur in childhood, and are chronic and severe

diabetes A health condition resulting from inadequate insulin levels; long-term complications can include vision problems, nerve damage, skin infections

diagnostic assessment A type of assessment conducted before instruction to identify a student's areas of strength and the skills that are presenting difficulty

differentiated instruction An educational approach in which teachers adjust instruction to meet the needs of all students

discrete trials   An evidence-based intervention that uses teacher-directed activities, repetition of skills through practice, and careful application of rewards

disproportionate representation   Disparate proportion of group membership; over or underrepresentation

distance education or distance learning   Telecommunications technology used to deliver instruction to many different sites

distance learning courses   Courses that are typically offered online by colleges, universities, and organizations; students can take these courses during or outside school hours and are usually awarded credit

Down syndrome   A chromosomal disorder, with identifiable physical characteristics, that causes delays in physical and intellectual development

dual enrollment   An acceleration option that allows a student to take one class but earn credit for two separate but academically related classes, often at different institutions (e.g., a student takes a college-level English class in high school and simultaneously earns a high school and a college credit); also referred to as *concurrent enrollment*

dual language learner   Children who are learning two or more languages, either simultaneously (prior to age 3) or sequentially (additional language is learned after age 3)

due process   A non-court proceeding before an impartial hearing officer that can be used if parents and school personnel disagree on a special education issue

dysfluencies   Hesitations, prolongations, interruptions, or repetitions of sounds or words that interrupt a person's flow of speech; a speech disorder

e-Buddies   A program that creates email friendships between people with and without intellectual disability

eardrum   A structure of the middle ear, this vibrates with the presence of sound waves and stimulates the ossicles of the middle ear; also referred to as the *tympanic membrane*

early intervening   Providing explicit and intensive instruction to all struggling students to prevent compounding learning problems

early intervention services   Specialized services provided to infants and toddlers with disabilities or showing signs of developmental delays; services are provided from birth to age three (i.e., until the third birthday)

echolalia   Repeating words, sounds, or sound patterns with no communicative intent, meaning, or understanding

Education for All Handicapped Children Act (EAHCA or EHA)   Act of Congress passed in 1975 with many provisions for ensuring free appropriate public education for all students with disabilities; later renamed the Individuals with Disabilities Education Act

emotional and behavioral disorders (EBD)   A disability characterized by extreme behavioral or emotional responses that are very different from all norms and referent groups

emotional disturbance   The term used in IDEA for students with emotional and behavioral challenges that adversely affect educational performance

English language learner (ELL), English learner (EL)   Students learning English as their second language

enlarged print   Adjusted size of print so individuals with low vision can read

enrichment   Adding topics or skills to the curriculum; presenting a particular topic in more depth

epilepsy or seizure disorders   A condition characterized by a tendency to experience recurrent seizures resulting in convulsions; caused by abnormal discharges of neurons in the brain

equal education   All students receive the same education, resources, and opportunities

equitable education   All students receive the educational instruction, resources, supports, and opportunities necessary to achieve equal outcomes

eugenics   The promotion of selective breeding to improve the human race or protect society, in part by preventing reproduction by those who are deemed inadequate or different

eustachian tube   The part of the ear that equalizes pressure on both sides of the eardrum

evidence-based instructional practices   Skills, techniques, and strategies that research studies have proven to be effective and have produce desired outcomes

evidence-based practice   Instructional or behavioral techniques and interventions proven effective through rigorous research

excellence gaps   A situation in which a student's potential achievement is not reached because his or her academic needs are not met.

executive functions   The mental processes that control and coordinate activities related to learning, including processing information, retaining and recalling information, organizing materials and time, and using effective learning and study strategies

expanded core curriculum   A set of skills, supplemental to the general education curriculum, that address the disability-specific needs of students with visual impairments

explicit instruction   Directly teaching the desired instructional skills, goals, or target

expressive language   Used to convey thoughts, feelings, or information

externalizing behaviors   Behaviors directed toward others (e.g., aggressive behavior); these behaviors are usually easily observable

extracurricular programs   After-school or summer programs or courses that offer advanced instruction or enrichment opportunities

false positives   A result, usually from a test, that incorrectly indicates the presence of a condition (e.g., students without disabilities are mistakenly identified as having disabilities)

false-positive results   A situation that occurs when tests indicate positive signs of a condition but are proven inaccurate with further testing

fetal alcohol spectrum disorders (FASDs), including fetal alcohol syndrome (FAS)   Congenital conditions caused by the mother's drinking alcohol during pregnancy resulting in reduced intellectual functioning, behavior problems, and sometimes physical differences; FAS is the most severe condition on this spectrum

fidelity   See *fidelity of implementation*

fidelity of implementation   The implementation of an instructional technique or intervention that accurately follows the procedures under which it was validated

field of vision   The width of the area a person can see, measured in degrees

finger spelling   A manual communication system that uses the English alphabet

first/then board   A type of visual support that contains two pictures; the "first" picture is the behavior or action (often a non-preferred activity) required in order to receive the "then" picture (often a preferred item or activity)

504 Plan   A plan that specifies the accommodations and modifications necessary for a student with a disability in the general education setting; named for Section 504 of the Rehabilitation Act of 1973, which prohibits discrimination against individuals with disabilities, ensuring that children with disabilities have equal access to public education; students with 504 plans do not meet the eligibility requirements for special education under IDEA

fluency   The flow, smoothness, rate, or continuity of speech production

FM (frequency-modulated) transmission device   Assistive listening device that provides oral transmissions directly from the teacher to the student with a hearing loss

food insecurity   A condition caused when household income is insufficient to provide enough food for household members

form   The rule system of language; includes phonology, morphology, and syntax

formative assessment   A method of collecting data in an ongoing manner to gather feedback on student learning outcomes or skill acquisition; progress monitoring, including mastery measurement and general outcomes measures, are types of formative assessments

fragile X syndrome   The most common inherited reason for intellectual disability

free appropriate public education (FAPE)   Ensures that students with disabilities receive necessary education and services without cost to the family; one of IDEA's basic guarantees

frequency of sound   The number of vibrations per second of molecules through some medium like air, water, or wires, causing sound

full inclusion   A service delivery option in which all special services are provided in the general education classroom; see also *pull-in programming*

functional behavioral assessment (FBA)   A process in which data are collected to determine why a student engages in certain behaviors, with the goal of helping the student replace inappropriate behaviors with more acceptable ones

functional curriculum   Teaching skills needed for daily living; instruction in natural settings relating to life and vocational skills

general education curriculum   The same curriculum, based on the state's academic content standards, that is used with and expected of students without disabilities at that grade level

general outcome measure (GOM)   A type of formative assessment in which teachers test students on skills in one academic domain (e.g., mathematics, reading, writing) across the entire year's curriculum; often referred to as curriculum-based measurement (CBM)

generalization   The transfer of learned information or strategies from settings or instances where they were initially learned to other environments, people, times, or events

gifted   A term referring to individuals with high levels of intelligence, creativity, outstanding abilities, and potential for high performance; also referred to as *talented*

goal setting   Determining a pre-set criterion for desired academic or behavioral performance

Good Behavior Game   A behavior management strategy in which the teacher provides positive reinforcement to teams of students whose members all engage in a predetermined level of appropriate behavior

Governor's School programs   Summer residential programs for gifted and talented students; costs are state-supported (although not always in full)

grade-skipping   A form of acceleration; advances students to a grade ahead of their same-age peers

graphic organizers   Visual aids used to help students organize, understand, and remember academic content

gross motor   Use of the large muscles of the body, such as those needed for crawling, walking, and running

group home   Residence or center where a small number of individuals with disabilities live together in the community

grouping   Placing students with advanced abilities, potential, or performance levels in the same classes to receive appropriately challenging instruction; not to be confused with *tracking*

handicaps   Challenges and barriers imposed by others

hard of hearing   A mild to moderate hearing loss

health disabilities   Chronic or acute health problems resulting in limited strength, vitality, or alertness; other health impairments; special health care needs

hearing impairments   Any type of hearing loss that impairs understanding of sounds and communication; can be caused by damage to any of the components of the hearing process

hertz (Hz)   The unit of measure for sound frequency

heterogeneity   Variation among members in a group

high-incidence disabilities   Prevalence or occurrence in the general population is more common; special education categories with more students

high-tech device   A complex assistive technology device that typically uses electronics or computers

honors classes   Advanced classes for students who show high achievement in specific subject areas

honors high school   A high school program that serves only gifted students, offering advanced courses and opportunities to collaborate with mentors or to work as an intern; students often receive college, in addition to high school, credits for the courses they complete in these programs; also referred to as *accelerated high school*

hyperactivity   Extreme or excessive levels of physical activity; impaired ability to remain still for appropriate lengths of time

hyperresponsive   A heightened level of responsiveness to a stimulus (e.g., sound, touch); over-reaction

hyporesponsive   A diminished level of responsiveness to a stimulus (e.g., sound, touch); little or no reaction

IEP process   Eight steps used to identify students with disabilities and provide special education services for those who qualify

impulsivity   Impaired ability to control or inhibit one's own behavior

inattention   Inability to pay attention or focus

inclusion   Students with disabilities are educated in general education settings, access the general education curriculum, and learn alongside their peers without disabilities

individualized education program (IEP)   A written document that delineates the current levels of development, goals, individualized education, accommodations, modifications, and related services for children with disabilities, ages 3 to 21

individualized family service plan (IFSP)   Document that details individualized services, resources, and goals for infants and toddlers with disabilities (birth to age three) and their families

Individualized Healthcare Plans   Specific plans and services developed in response to an individual's health care needs; part of the IEP for students with special health care needs, the plan includes information about the student's medical needs and what nursing interventions will be implemented to address these needs

individualized transition plan (ITP)   Part of a high school student's IEP that outlines services required for a smooth transition from high school to post-secondary settings such as college or work; must be in place by the student's 16th birthday

Individuals with Disabilities Education Act (IDEA)   Name given in 1990 to the Education for All Handicapped Children Act (EHA) and used for all reauthorizations of the law; guarantees students with disabilities the right to a free appropriate public education in the least restrictive environment

induction or **hearing loop**   A listening device that directs sound from the source directly to the listener's ear through a specially designed hearing aid

infectious diseases   Contagious health conditions that can result in health disabilities, often short-term, which can lead to the need for special education services

instructional accommodations   Changes to instructional materials or to how classroom instruction is delivered, but do not change the expectations for the student

intellectual disability   A condition characterized by impaired intellectual functioning, limited adapted behavior, and need for supports; initial occurrence before age 18

intellectual functioning   Cognitive abilities

intensity   An aspect of voice referring to the loudness or softness of the sound produced while speaking

Interim Alternative Educational Setting (IAES)   Special education placement to ensure progress toward IEP goals; assigned when a serious behavioral infraction requires removal from current placement

internalizing behaviors   Behaviors directed inward toward oneself (e.g., withdrawal, anxiety, depression); more difficult to observe than externalizing behaviors

International Baccalaureate (IB) program   An academically challenging program offered at select schools; the high school program focuses on big ideas across content areas and applying knowledge; students who complete the program and pass the accompanying exam may be recognized by select universities

internship   A component of career exploration in which a student, through a formal agreement with an employer, learns and performs specified jobs during a predetermined timeframe; can be paid or unpaid

intervener   A related service provider who provides one-on-one translation and educational supports to students with deaf-blindness

IQ-achievement discrepancy   The traditional method used for learning disabilities identification, requiring a significant difference between potential or expected performance (based on a score on a test of intelligence [IQ] and a score from an achievement test)

iris   The colored part of the eye

job coach   A transition specialist who teaches vocational skills in the community and in actual job settings

job shadowing   A component of career exploration in which a student spends time in the workplace, observing an employee who performs daily work duties

joint attention   A social-communication activity in which two people focus attention on the same object or event; the use of gestures and eye movements (gaze) to coordinate mutual attention or interest, often between a child and an adult

language   Rule-based method used for communication

language delays   Slowed development of language skills; may or may not result in language impairments

language impairment   A disorder in which a difficulty or inability to master the various systems of rules in language interferes with communication

language minority students   In the United States, students who speak a language other than English

language-rich environments   Classrooms and other settings that encourage, foster, and support language development

language-sensitive environments   Classrooms where teachers are aware of the special linguistic needs of their students (e.g., language disorders, ELLs), adjust instruction accordingly, and provide appropriate supports and accommodations when needed

learned helplessness   Individuals become less willing to attempt tasks or do not understand how their actions affect success; usually due to repeated failure even after expending great effort, or to the over-involvement and control of others

learning centers   A specific area of the classroom that contains a variety of activities focused on a particular topic; students can work

independently, in pairs, or even in small groups to deepen their knowledge or build on or reinforce newly learned skills

learning disabilities (LD)   A disability in which students display unexpected underachievement and academic difficulties that are resistant to traditional instruction

learning menus   An aspect of differentiated instruction in which students are given a list (menu) of choices or options related to a learning objective

learning strategies   Type of instruction designed to help students learn, study, remember important concepts, and access difficult reading material in a strategic fashion

least restrictive environment (LRE)   A guarantee of the Individuals with Disabilities Education Act (IDEA) that, as much as possible and as appropriate, students with disabilities be educated with typical learners

legally blind   A category of blindness used to qualify for federal and state benefits

lens   The part of the eye located behind the iris that brings objects seen into focus

linguistically diverse   Having a home or native language other than English

low vision   A degree of vision loss in which vision is still useful for learning or for the execution of a task

low-incidence disabilities   Prevalence or occurrence in the general population is relatively uncommon; special education categories with few students

low-tech devices   Simple assistive technology devices such as communication boards

manifestation determination   A decision as to whether a student's disciplinary problems are due to his or her disability

mastery measurement (MM)   A type of assessment in which teachers test students on a single skill (e.g., double-digit addition)

mathematics disabilities   A condition in which a student's learning disability is most significant in areas of mathematics

mediation   Process through which a neutral party facilitates a meeting between parents and school officials to resolve disagreements about a student's individualized education program and questions about his or her placement and services

medically fragile   A term used to describe the status of some individuals with significant health disabilities

melting pot   Concept of a homogenized United States; cultural traditions and home languages are abandoned for the new American culture

mentoring   A type of acceleration that provides the opportunity for a student to work with a mentor, typically in an area or a field of interest, to learn more advanced content and skills or to learn them at a faster pace

metacognitive   That which is involved in the active processing of how one learns

misarticulations   Abnormal production of speech sounds

mixed hearing loss   Hearing impairment due to both conductive and sensorineural hearing losses

mnemonics   A learning strategy that promotes learning or remembering information (e.g., associating the first letters of items in a list with a word, sentence, or picture, such as HOMES for the Great Lakes)

mobility   The ability to move or be moved; usually refers to movement from place to place, although can also refer to movement of limbs or other body parts (e.g., limited joint mobility)

mobility skills   The ability to travel safely and efficiently from one place to another; a topic of instruction for students who are blind

modifications Changes to the instruction, curriculum, or assessments in which the requirements or demands are reduced and the expectations for the student are changed

morphology Rules that govern the structure and form of words and constitute the basic meaning of words

motor functioning The ability to perform precise or complex muscle movements; gross motor functions produce large movements like walking or running; small motor functions produce small movements like writing or unbuttoning a shirt

multi-tiered systems of support (MTSS) A framework that provides increasingly intensive levels of support and assistance for academic learning and behavior management

multicultural education Incorporates the cultures of all students into instruction

multiple disabilities A combination of more than one disability that has a complex, severe impact on the individual

multiple intelligences A multi-dimensional approach to intelligence; considers those who demonstrate exceptional abilities in any one of eight areas as gifted

muscular/skeletal conditions Conditions affecting muscles or bones and resulting in limited functioning

mutual accommodation Acceptance and use of students' language and culture within the classroom, while also teaching them the expectations and culture of the school

myopia Nearsightedness; one of the most common eye problems in children

nativism A strong opposition to immigration, which is seen as a threat to maintaining a country's dominant culture

natural environments Typical settings for infants and toddlers without disabilities; can include the home and community settings (e.g., child care, play groups)

natural settings Places where typical life events occur, such as locations in the community (e.g., stores, restaurants) or in the home

need for supports The degree to which someone needs assistance or help from friends, family, co-workers, classmates, or social service agencies

neuromotor impairments Conditions involving the nerves, muscles, and motor functioning

newborn screening Testing of newborns to determine the existence, or risk, of disability

noise-induced hearing loss (NIHL) Permanent hearing loss that occurs when loud sounds damage the hair cells in the inner ear; can be caused by a single extremely loud sound (e.g., explosion) or by continuous or long-term exposure to loud sounds (e.g., music)

noncompliance The refusal to comply with or follow rules or instructions

normal curve, or **bell-shaped curve** Theoretical construct of the typical distribution of human traits such as intelligence

normalization Making available ordinary patterns of life and conditions of everyday living

occupational therapist (OT) A professional who directs activities that help improve muscular control and develop self-help skills; a special education related service provider

open captions Subtitles or text tickers that are visible on the screen for everyone to read instead of, or in addition to, listening to spoken words

ophthalmologist A medical doctor who specializes in eye disorders

opportunities to respond (OTR) A practice in which students are actively engaged in learning activities by frequently answering questions, completing tasks, or following directions; can occur as frequently as 8–12 times per minute

opportunity gap The disparity in achievement between students who have basic or enhanced educational opportunities (e.g., homework help, summer enrichment camps) and those who don't

oppositional defiant disorder (ODD) A condition involving repeated acts of disobedience, hostility, or defiance toward authority figures

optic nerve A nerve that transmits visual information from the eye to the brain

optician A person who fills either the ophthalmologist's or optometrist's prescriptions for glasses or corrective lenses

optometrist A professional who measures vision and can prescribe corrective lenses (eyeglasses or contact lenses)

orientation and mobility (O&M) instructors Professionals who teach students who are blind to move freely through their environments and travel safely from place to place independently; O&M instructors are related service providers

orientation skills The mental map people use to move through environments; a topic of instruction for students who are blind

orthopedic impairment The term used in IDEA for physical disabilities resulting in special health care needs

ossicles Three tiny bones (hammer or malleus, anvil or incus, stirrup or stapes) in the middle ear that pass information to the cochlea

other health impairment The term used in IDEA for health disabilities; special health care needs

otitis media Middle ear infection, common in early childhood, that can interfere with normal language development

otoacoustic emissions (OAEs) The low level of sound produced when the hair cells inside the inner ear vibrate

overrepresentation Too many students from a diverse group participating in a special education category, beyond the level expected based on their proportion in the overall student population

paraprofessionals Educational assistants who help implement the IEPs of students with disabilities in the classroom, at school, for transportation needs, and in a variety of other settings

partial acceleration An acceleration option in which a student works on above grade-level content in one or more subject areas, either by attending a higher grade-level class for portions of the day or by working on above grade-level curriculum in the grade-level classroom; also referred to as *subject-matter acceleration*

people-first language Appropriate way to refer to most groups of people with disabilities; references the person before referencing the disability

person-centered planning A process in which an individual's personal strengths, preferences, interests, and vision for what they would like to do in the future is used to guide a team's efforts; used to help an individual with a disability develop the skills needed for adult life

pervasive developmental disorder–not otherwise specified (PDD-NOS) Once considered a separate disorder within the autism spectrum; a condition in which a person exhibits symptoms in at least one core area (e.g., social interaction, communication) but not all criteria for autism are met

phenylketonuria (PKU) A hereditary condition in which the amino acid phenylalanine is not properly metabolized; can cause intellectual disabilities if not diagnosed and regulated through diet shortly after birth

phonation An aspect of voice; the tone of the speech sounds that includes breathiness, hoarseness, or strained qualities

phonemic awareness The ability to listen to, identify, and manipulate phonemes—the smallest units of sounds that are combined to create words

phonological awareness Understanding, identifying, and applying sound-symbol relationships (letter sounds, rhyming); identifying, separating, or manipulating sound units of spoken language

phonology   The rules within a language used to govern the combination of speech sounds to form words and sentences

physical disabilities   Conditions related to a physical deformity or impairment of the skeletal system and associated motor function; physical impairments; orthopedic impairments

physical therapist (PT)   A professional who treats physical disabilities through many nonmedical means and works to improve motor skills; a special education related service provider

pica   A condition in which an individual eats non-food items (e.g., dirt, hair, paint, fabric)

picture communication boards   Low-tech assistive technology devices that display pictures the individual can point to in order to communicate

Picture Exchange Communication System (PECS)   A validated intervention for individuals with ASD with little or no verbal ability; pictures are used to communicate and express needs and desires

pinna   Outer structure of the ear

pitch   An aspect of voice; perceived high or low sound quality

placebo effect   A situation in which a patient who is given a non-medical treatment (e.g., a sugar pill) in place of an actual treatment (e.g., medicine) perceives his or her health or medical condition to have improved as a result; usually attributed to the patient's belief in the power of the treatment; placebos are often used in medical research

Positive Behavioral Interventions and Supports (PBIS)   A multi-tiered framework aimed at preventing problem behaviors and using evidence-based interventions to address existing problems

post-secondary education   Education after high school that can include college, university, community college, or vocational training

postlingual deafness   Having lost the ability to hear after developing language; acquired, or adventitious, deafness

powered exoskeleton   An outer framework that can be worn by a person to provide technology support for limb movement

pragmatics   The appropriate use of language in social contexts

pre-referral process   First step in the IEP process; strategies are used to address the student's needs to prevent unnecessary referrals to special education

prelingual deafness   Having lost the ability to hear before developing language

prevalence   Total number of cases at a given time

primary instruction   The first level in multi-tiered frameworks; refers to high-quality instruction in an RTI framework

primary prevention   See also *primary instruction*; refers to whole-school behavior management plans in a PBIS framework

probes   Short tests in one specific area (e.g., word identification fluency, math computation) that can be administered quickly (often in 5 minutes or less) and assess skills from across a portion of the curriculum

process   The way that a student accesses academic content or material

process/product debate   The argument about whether perceptual training or explicit instruction is more effective in teaching reading

product   The outcome or method through which a student demonstrates his or her learning

progress monitoring   A form of assessment that evaluates student learning on a frequent basis (e.g., monthly, weekly) to gather ongoing feedback on student learning or skill acquisition; general outcome measures (GOM), often referred to as curriculum-based measurement (CBM), and mastery measurement (MM) are types of progress monitoring

prosthetics   Artificial limbs

pull-in programming   Special education or related services delivered exclusively in the general education classroom; see also *full inclusion*

pull-out program   A service delivery option in which special education services are provided outside the general education classroom

pupil   The hole in the center of the iris that expands and contracts, admitting light to the eye

pure sounds   Pure-tone sound waves; used across specific frequencies to test an individual's hearing ability

randomized controlled trial   Study in which students are randomly assigned to either an intervention or a control group

rapid letter naming   Reading lists of alphabet letters and speaking them aloud as quickly as possible

reading disabilities   A condition in which a student's learning disability is most significant in reading

real-time captioning (RTC)   A computer-aided transcription service that provides immediate translation of the spoken word into print by using a stenotype machine, a laptop computer, and specialized software; also referred to as Communication Access Real-time Translation (CART)

receptive language   Understanding information that is received, through seeing, hearing, or touching (e.g., braille)

related services   Support services provided by professionals from a wide range of disciplines, necessary for a child with a disability to benefit from an individualized education

residential high school   A high school program for gifted students that is offered on a college campus; students simultaneously complete requirements for high school graduation and earn college credits

residual hearing   The amount of functional hearing a person has

residual vision   The amount and degree of functional vision that exists, despite a visual disability

resistant to treatment or **resistant to instruction**   A defining characteristic of learning disabilities in which validated methods typically used in general education settings are not effective enough to cause sufficient learning

resonance   An aspect of voice that involves excessive or insufficient nasality; gives the distinctive quality to each person's voice

resource room   Special education classroom where students receive a few hours of individualized instruction per day, or for blocks of time during the week. Although *resource room* is no longer the term used for IDEA reporting purposes, the term remains in the vernacular of both special and general education to refer to this placement option

response to intervention (RTI)   A multi-tiered framework of increasingly intensive interventions and supports, combined with progress monitoring, that is used to address academic difficulties and to identify students with learning disabilities

restraint   A method that restricts an individual's freedom of movement or physical activity

retina   The inside lining of the eye

retinopathy of prematurity (ROP)   A condition in which retinal damage occurs in premature infants who receive excess oxygen to help them breathe

Rett's disorder/Rett syndrome   Once considered a separate disorder within the autism spectrum; a disorder, affecting girls, in which a period of normal development is followed by loss of skills, lack of social engagement, impaired communication, and slowed head and brain growth

robotics   The science of using technology to create high-tech devices that can move and perform various tasks

scaffolded instruction   Instructional technique in which teachers provide support for new skill acquisition by systematically building on prior instruction, knowledge, and experiences

schizophrenia A disorder that includes bizarre delusions and dissociation with reality; very rare in children

school nurse A professional who assists with or delivers medical services at school, coordinates health services, and designs accommodations for students with special health care needs; a special education related service provider

Schoolwide Enrichment Model A schoolwide model for gifted education in which 15% to 20% of the school's students participate in activities to develop thinking skills, problem solving, and creativity

seclusion The act of involuntarily confining a student to a room or area, in isolation from others, from which he or she is physically prevented from leaving

secondary intervention The second level in multi-tiered frameworks; additional supports of moderate intensity provided to students who do not make adequate progress with primary prevention

secondary prevention See *secondary intervention*

Section 504 of the Rehabilitation Act of 1973 Federal law that outlines basic civil rights for people with disabilities; set the stage for both the Individuals with Disabilities Education Act, passed in 1975, and the Americans with Disabilities Act, passed in 1990

segregated settings A setting in which students with disabilities are completely removed from the general education setting, usually with little or no interaction with typically developing peers; see also *self-contained settings*

seizure Episodes of disturbed brain activity resulting in changes in behavior or attention

self-advocacy The act of promoting or speaking up for oneself and one's own best interests

self-contained settings A separate class—outside of the general education setting—exclusively for students with disabilities; see also *segregated settings*

self-determination A skill set that includes making decisions, choosing preferences, and exercising self-advocacy needed for independent living

self-injury Self-inflicted injuries (head banging, eye poking)

self-instruction Guiding oneself through an activity or a task with the use of self-induced statements; see also *self-talk*

self-management strategies Procedures that a student can use to modify his or her own behavior; include self-monitoring, self-instruction, goal setting, and self-reinforcement; see also *self-regulation strategies*

self-monitoring Tracking and recording one's own academic or behavioral performance

self-paced instruction A type of acceleration in which the student determines the pace of learning

self-regulation strategies Tactics that a student can use to modify his or her own behavior; include self-monitoring, self-instruction, goal setting, and self-reinforcement; see also *self-management strategies*

self-reinforcement Awarding a self-selected reinforcer or rewards to oneself upon completing a task or achieving a goal

self-talk Guiding oneself through an activity or a task with the use of self-induced statements; see also *self-instruction*

semantics The system within a language that governs content, intent, and meanings of spoken and written language

sensorineural hearing loss Hearing impairment due to damage to the inner ear or the auditory nerve

service animals Highly trained animals (e.g., dogs, monkeys) that provide assistance to individuals with disabilities

service coordinator The case manager who oversees the implementation and evaluation of an Individualized Family Service Plan (IFSP)

service learning Volunteer service in the community, often tied to objectives for a course or to the mission or priority of an organization or club

shaken baby syndrome A condition caused when an infant is violently shaken by an adult; results in traumatic brain injury and often death

Sheltered Instruction Observation Protocol (SIOP) A research-based model of sheltered instruction that provides a consistent framework for developing lessons and for reflecting on and improving instruction; includes both content and language objectives

sheltered instruction A method of instruction for English learners that supports the acquisition of content while they are learning English

sickle cell disease A genetic, life-threatening blood disorder in which red blood cells become hard and misshapen and can clog blood vessels, which interferes with the delivery of oxygen to areas of the body; 95% of the cases occur among African Americans

signed English Translation of English into a form of manual communication

single-case design Study in which an outcome (e.g., reading fluency) is measured repeatedly and systematically across multiple conditions or phases (e.g., prior to, during, and after the intervention); an individual or group of individuals can represent the "case," which serves as its own control

Snellen chart A chart used to test visual acuity, developed in 1862

social justice Toward an egalitarian society, based on principles of equality, fairness, and human rights; embraces the concept of dignity for every person

social maladjustment A term applied to students who do not act within society's norms but are not eligible for IDEA services as students with emotional disturbance

social story/social narrative A story that is read with a student to prepare him or her for commonly occurring situations (e.g., engaging with a peer) or an activity that is about to take place; it presents an anticipated social situation, the social or behavioral cues that a student should notice, and the desired appropriate response or behavior

socioeconomic level Also referred to as socioeconomic status (SES), a standard of economic and social position (of an individual or a family) calculated using income, education, and occupation

socioeconomic status An individual's or family's economic and social position in relation to others, based on income, education, and occupation

sound intensity Loudness

special health care needs A term sometimes used for health disabilities; chronic or acute health problems resulting in limited strength, vitality, or alertness; other health impairments

Special Olympics The world's largest sports organization specifically for individuals with intellectual disabilities

specific praise A positive, reinforcing statement that specifically and explicitly identifies the behavior that a student exhibited

speech Vocal production of language

speech impairment A disorder characterized by abnormal speech that is difficult to understand or interferes with communication

speech synthesizer Assistive technology device that creates a computer-generated voice or simulated speech sounds

speech-language pathologist (SLP) The professional who diagnoses and treats speech or language impairments; a related service provider

speech-language therapy A related service in which a student receives specialized instruction to improve speech (e.g., articulation) or language (e.g., expressive, receptive) skills

splinter skill   The ability to perform a task that is above an individual's age or typical functioning level and that does not generalize to other tasks

stereotypies   Non-productive behaviors (e.g., twirling, flapping hands, rocking) that an individual repeats at a high rate; also called stereotypical behaviors; commonly observed in individuals with autism spectrum disorder

stims   An abbreviated term for *self-stimulatory behaviors*; a repetitive behavior, thought to calm or stimulate an individual

stimulant medication   A class of psychoactive drugs that increases activity in the brain, resulting in temporary improvement

strabismus   Misalignment or crossing of the eyes; one of the most common eye problems in children

struggling learners   Students who have difficulty mastering academic content and who require additional or supplemental instructional supports

students of color   A broad term that encompasses students from African American, Hispanic, Asian American, or Native American backgrounds

study skills   Strategies for a systematic approach to studying; include aspects such as organization, listening, note taking, processing information, self-monitoring, and test taking

stuttering   The lack of fluency in an individual's speech pattern, often characterized by hesitations or repetitions of sounds or words

subject-matter acceleration   An acceleration option in which a student works on above grade-level content in one or more subject areas, either by attending a higher grade-level class for portions of the day or by working on above grade-level curriculum in the grade-level classroom; also referred to as *partial acceleration*

summative assessment   A method of measuring learning outcomes or skill acquisition, administered at the end of a unit or at the end of a school year

supported employment   A job-training strategy in which the student is placed in a paying job and receives significant assistance and support, and the employer is helped with the compensation

switch   A device that completes, breaks, or changes an electrical circuit connection; in assistive technology, used to activate other devices that enable a user to complete a task

symbol communication boards   Low-tech assistive technology devices that display symbols or words the individual can point to in order to communicate

syntax   Rules that govern word endings and order of words in phrases and sentences

systems or networks of supports   The constellation of services and assistance that address the need for supports, which is the third defining characteristic of intellectual disability

talent search   A method of identifying students with exceptional academic abilities by using above-level testing, which then qualifies them for additional talent development opportunities, such as accelerated weekend or summer programs, mentorships, and career counseling

talented   A term referring to individuals with high levels of intelligence, creativity, outstanding abilities, and potential for high performance; also referred to as *gifted*

task analysis   The process of breaking down activities or tasks into smaller, sequenced components; used to make the task easier to learn

task commitment   A group of traits such as perseverance, dedication, self-confidence, and high expectations for one's work; the capacity for high levels of interest and involvement in a given area

teachers of students with visual impairments (TVIs)   Specially trained and certified teachers who provide direct or consultative

special education services related to the effects of vision loss; TVIs are related service providers

telescoping curriculum   An acceleration option that involves providing instruction in a shorter span of time than usual (e.g., a semester instead of a year)

tertiary intervention   The third level in multi-tiered frameworks; intensive, individualized supports provided to students who do not respond adequately to secondary intervention

tertiary prevention   See *tertiary intervention*

testing accommodations   Changes to how a test is presented or to how the student is allowed to respond, but do not change the expectations for the student

tiered activities   Instructional tasks that are designed to teach and challenge students at different levels of readiness (low, middle, and high levels) for the same content or skills; tasks can differ in level of complexity, depth of information conveyed, or level of abstraction

tiered content   A process in which all students complete the same instructional activity, but the difficulty level of the content varies, based on student readiness levels

tiered products   Assessments that are designed to challenge students at different levels of readiness (low, middle, and high levels) as they demonstrate their knowledge of the same content or skills

time management   The ability to consciously plan and monitor the amount of time spent on specific activities, usually to increase efficiency, productivity, or educational outcomes

total communication approach   A method of instruction for students with hearing loss that employs any and all methods of communication (oral speech, manual communication, ASL, gestures)

tracking   A process in which students are sorted by achievement or performance levels, with little consideration for student interests, motivation, past accomplishments; heavily criticized for keeping some students (e.g., low-income) in low-ability tracks; not to be confused with *grouping*

transition specialist   Professional who collaborates with and acts as a liaison between numerous individuals and agencies to ensure that students with disabilities experience successful post-secondary transitions

traumatic brain injury (TBI)   A condition resulting from damage to the brain caused by blunt force trauma in which an object hits the head, or the head hits an object, with severe force

tunnel vision   Severe limitation in peripheral vision; limitations in the width of the visual field

twice-exceptional   Term used to describe a student who is gifted and also has a disability

tympanic membrane   A structure of the middle ear, this vibrates with the presence of sound waves and stimulates the ossicles of the middle ear; also referred to as the *eardrum*

type 1 diabetes   A health condition in which the body does not produce enough insulin; includes only 5% of all individuals with diabetes; formerly called *juvenile diabetes*

type 2 diabetes   A health condition in which the body does not use insulin properly, creating glucose buildup in the blood; includes 90% to 95% of all individuals with diabetes; associated with obesity

UNC TEACCH Autism Program (TEACCH) or **structured TEACCHing**   An instructional program developed for students with ASD in which visual aids are used to help students comprehend and structure their environments

underachievement   A discrepancy between an individual's high potential and his or her lower-than-expected performance

underrepresentation   Insufficient presence of individuals from a diverse group in a special education category; smaller numbers than would be predicted based on their proportion in the overall student population

unexpected underachievement   A defining characteristic of learning disabilities; poor school performance that cannot be explained by lack of effort, poor instruction, cultural or linguistic differences, or other extrinsic influences

Universal Design for Learning (UDL)   A research-based framework in which teachers incorporate flexible materials, techniques, and strategies to deliver instruction and students demonstrate their knowledge in a variety of ways; improves accessibility to the general education curriculum for all students; based on the premise of universal design in architecture

universal design   Barrier-free architectural and building designs that meet the needs of everyone, including people with physical challenges

universal health care precautions   Procedures used to prevent the spread of infectious diseases

universal newborn hearing screening   Testing of all newborns for hearing loss

universal screening   (academic) The first step in the RTI process; a brief test given at the beginning of the school year (and possibly one to two times later in the year) to identify students with inadequate skills who may be in need of assistance or more intensive instruction

use   The ability to apply language rules correctly in a variety of settings

verbal advance warning   A verbal statement that includes a timeframe and the activity that will occur when the timeframe has expired

video modeling/video priming   A video demonstration of desired skills or behaviors that is shown to the student immediately prior to a situation in which he or she will be expected to perform that skill

visual acuity   How clearly a person can see and distinguish subtle features at various distances

visual disabilities   Impairments in vision that, even with correction, affect educational performance, access to the community, and independence

visual efficiency   How well a person can use sight

visual processing   The way that the brain interprets, understands, or processes visual information

visual schedule   A schedule that contains words or pictures for ease of understanding

visual schedule   A type of visual support that explains upcoming or desired activities and the order in which they will occur

visual support   The use of a picture or other visually accessible item (e.g., symbol, label) to support communication or the acquisition and demonstration of desired behaviors

visual timer   Any type of time-keeping device that allows a person to see how much time has passed/is remaining

vocational rehabilitation agency   A state-level agency that provides resources and services to adults with disabilities; the agency's goal is to assist these individuals in obtaining gainful employment aligned with abilities, training, and education

voice problems   Abnormal spoken language production, characterized by unusual pitch, intensity, phonation, or resonance

wait time   A period of silence following a teacher-initiated question in which students are given time to ponder a response

well-baby visit   Routine medical checkup during infancy to monitor physical, cognitive, and emotional health and growth, administer vaccinations, and prevent other health risks (e.g., exposure to lead or second-hand smoke); older children have well-child visits

work sampling   A component of career exploration in which a student spends time in the workplace, learning selected aspects of potential jobs, without pay

working memory   A short-term memory system that holds information temporarily while a task—such as following directions, comprehending text, or solving a multi-step mathematics problem—is accomplished

wraparound supports   A service delivery model in which needs are met through collaboration between many agencies and systems (education, mental health, social services, community)

writing disabilities   A condition in which a student's learning disability is most significant in writing (including spelling)

Young Autism Program (YAP)   A validated treatment program for individuals with ASD that relies heavily on ABA principles; developed by Ivar Lovaas

zone of proximal development   Refers to a task or activity that is slightly above a student's current performance level so that it is challenging

References

Chapter 1

Albus, D., Lazarus, S. S., & Thurlow, M. L. (2015). *2012–13 publicly reported assessment results for students with disabilities and ELLs with disabilities* (Technical Report 70). Minneapolis, MN: University of Minnesota, National Center on Educational Outcomes.

Associated Press. (2010, May 15). *Spain: Court investigates charges of sexual abuse at center for disabled residents.* Retrieved from www.nytimes.com/2010/05/13/world/europe/web-briefs-abuse

Atwal, A. (2011, June 24). *Rising enrollments of students with disabilities at higher education institutions.* Retrieved from www.youthtoday.org/view_article.cfm?article_id=4860

Baglieri, S., Valle, J. W., Connor, D. J., & Gallagher, D. J. (2011). Disability studies in education: The need for a plurality of perspectives on disability. *Remedial and Special Education, 32,* 267–278.

Ballard, J., Ramirez, B. A., & Weintraub, F. J. (1982). *Special education in America: Its legal and governmental foundations.* Reston, VA: Council for Exceptional Children.

Blatt, B. (1965). *Christmas in purgatory: A photographic essay on mental retardation.* Syracuse, NY: Human Policy Press.

Branson, J., & Miller, D. (2002). *Damned for their difference: The cultural construction of deaf people as disabled.* Washington, DC: Gallaudet University Press.

Brown, L. (2015). Identity-first language. *Autistic Self Advocacy Network.* Retrieved from http://autisticadvocacy.org/home/about-asan/identity-first-language

Brown v. Board of Education, 347 U.S. 483 (1954).

Camarota, S. A. (2012, August). *Immigrants in the United States: A profile of America's foreign-born population.* Center for Immigration Studies. Retrieved from http://cis.org/2012-profile-of-americas-foreign-born-population

Center for Immigration Studies. (2015). Immigrants in the United States: A profile of America's foreign-born population. Retrieved from http://cis.org/node/3877

Center on Education Policy. (2009, November). *Has progress been made in raising achievement for students with disabilities? State test score trends through 2007–2008, Part 4.* Retrieved from www.cep-dc.org

Chamberlain, L. (2007, January 7). Design for everyone, disabled or not. *The New York Times, Real Estate.* Retrieved from www.nytimes.com

Cohen, J. S. (2010, August 18). *U. of I. opens state-of-the-art dorm for students with disabilities: Facility marks a new milestone for university, already a leader in disability services. Chicago Tribune.* Retrieved from www.chicagotribune.com/news/education/ct-met-u-of-i-disability-dorm20100818,0,796860.story

Cortiella, C., & Horowitz, S. H. (2014). *The state of learning disabilities: Facts, trends and emerging issues.* New York, NY: National Center for Learning Disabilities.

Dalton, B., Ingels, S.J., and Fritch, L. (2015). *High school longitudinal study of 2009 (HSLS:09) 2013 update and high school transcript study: A first look at fall 2009 ninth-graders in 2013 (NCES 2015-037).* U.S. Department of Education. Washington, DC: National Center for Education Statistics. Retrieved from http://nces.ed.gov/pubsearch

Deshler, D. D. (2003, May/June). A time for modern-day pioneers. *LDA Newsbriefs, 38,* 3–9, 24.

Deutsch, H. (2005). The body's moments: Visible disability, the essay and the limits of sympathy. *Prose Studies, 27,* 11–26.

Duncan, A. (2011, March 17). *Preparing students with disabilities for success: Secretary Duncan affirms commitment to students with disabilities.* Email received from White House Disability Group.

Easter Seals. (2011). *Writing about disability.* Retrieved from www.easterseals.com/site/PageServer?pagename=ntl_writedisability

Edgerton, R. B. (1967). *The cloak of competence: Stigma in the lives of the mentally retarded.* Berkeley, CA: University of California Press.

Eisenman, L. T., & Ferretti, R. P. (2010). Introduction to the special issue: Changing conceptions of special education. *Exceptional Children, 76,* 262–264.

Erevelles, N. (1996). Disability and the dialects of difference. *Disability & Society, 11,* 519–537.

Florian, L. (2007). Reimagining special education. In L. Florian (Ed.), *The Sage handbook of special education* (pp. 7–20). Thousand Oaks, CA: Sage Publications.

Florian, L., Hollenweger, J., Simeonsson, R. J., Wedell, K., Riddell, S., Terzi, L., & Holland, A. (2007). Cross-cultural perspectives on the classification of children with disabilities: Part 1. Issues in the classification of children with disabilities. *Journal of Special Education, 40,* 36–45.

Fuchs, D., Fuchs, L. S., & Stecker, P. M. (2010). The "blurring" of special education in a new continuum of general education placements and services. *Exceptional Children, 76,* 301–323.

Fuchs, D., Fuchs, L. S., & Vaughn, S. R. (Eds.). (2008). *Responsiveness to intervention.* Newark, DE: International Reading Association.

Fujiura, G. T. (2013). The demarcation of intellectual disability. *Intellectual and Developmental Disabilities, 51,* 83–85.

Gottlieb, J. (2010, June 7). Name change at agency to remove "retardation." *The New York Times, N.Y./Region.* Retrieved from www.nytimes.com/2010/06/08/nyregion/08name.html

Groce, N. E. (1985). *Everyone here spoke sign language: Hereditary deafness on Martha's Vineyard.* Cambridge, MA: Harvard University Press.

Heasley, S. (2015, June 2). Students with special needs face double-digit achievement gaps. *Disability Scoop.* Retrieved from www.disabilityscoop.com

Institute of Medicine (IOM). (2007). *The future of disability in America.* Washington, DC: The National Academies Press.

Ito, R. (2012, October 2). TCM shines a light on disabilities' roles: "The Project Image" explores the cinematic history of the disabled from 1927 to '87. *The Los Angeles Times,* p. D-4.

Kena, G., Musu-Gillette, L., Robinson, J., Wang, X., Rathbun, A., Zhang, J., Wilkinson-Flicker, S., Barmer, A., and Dunlop Velez, E. (2015). *The condition of education 2015 (NCES 2015-144).* U.S. Department of Education, National Center for Education Statistics. Washington, DC. Retrieved from http://nces.ed.gov/pubsearch.

Kena, G., Hussar W., McFarland J., de Brey C., Musu-Gillette, L., Wang, X., Zhang, J., Rathbun, A., Wilkinson-Flicker, S., Diliberti, M., Barmer, A., Bullock Mann, F., and Dunlop Velez, E. (2016). *The condition of education 2016 (NCES 2016-144).* U.S. Department of Education, National Center for Education Statistics. Washington, DC. Retrieved from http://nces.ed.gov/pubsearch

King, S. (2012, November 24). Right kids for these roles: Young actors with Down syndrome star in "Café de Flore" and Any Day Now. *The Los Angeles Times,* p. D-4.

Krogstad, J. M., & Fry, R. (2014). Dept. of Ed. projects public schools will be "majority-minority" this fall. *Pew Research Center.* Retrieved from http://www.pewresearch.org/fact-tank/2014/08/18/u-s-public-schools-expected-to-be-majority-minority-starting-this-fall/

Krogstad, J. M., Stepler, R., & Lopez, M. H. (2015, May 12). English proficiency on the rise among Latinos. *Pew Research Center.* Retrieved from http://www.pewhispanic.org/2015/05/12/english-proficiency-on-the-rise-among-latinos/

La Vor, M. L. (1976). Federal legislation for exceptional persons: A history. In F. J. Weintraub, A. Abeson, J. Ballard, & M. L. La Vor (Eds.), *Public policy and the education of exceptional children* (pp. 96–111). Reston, VA: Council for Exceptional Children.

Longmore, P. (2003). *Why I burned my book and other essays on disability.* Philadelphia, PA: Temple University Press.

McLaughlin, M. J. (2010). Evolving interpretations of educational equity and students with disabilities. *Exceptional Children, 76,* 265–278.

National Association for Gifted Children (NAGC). (2015). *Addressing excellence gaps in K-12 education. NAGC Position Statement.* Retrieved from http://www.nagc.org/sites/default/files/Position Statement/Excellence Gaps Position Statement.pdf

National Association for Gifted Children (NAGC). (2015). *NAGC praises senators for introducing bipartisan bill to support high-ability students.* Retrieved from www.nagc.org/about-nagc/media/press-releases/nacg-praises-senators-introducing-bipartisan-bill-support-high

National Center for Educational Statistics (NCES), U.S. Department of Education. (2015). *Fast facts: What are the new back to school statistics?* Retrieved from http://nces.ed.gov/fastfacts/display.asp?id=372

National Opinion Research Center (NORC) at the University of Chicago. (2010). *Doctorate-granting institution, race/ethnicity, time-to-degree, age, post doctoral plans, and post-doctoral mobility of doctoral recipients in special education: 2008.* Custom tabulation prepared under National Science Foundation Contract No. SRS-0754015.

National Science Foundation, National Center for Science and Engineering Statistics. (2013). *Doctorate recipients from U.S. universities: 2013.* Special Report NSF 15-304. Arlington, VA. Retrieved from http://www.nsf.gov/statistics/sed/2013/

Newman, L. A., & Madaus, J. W. (2015). An analysis of factors related to receipt of accommodations and services by postsecondary students with disabilities. *Remedial and Special Education, 36,* 208–219.

Newman, L., Wagner, M., Cameto, R., & Knokey, A. M. (2010). Comparisons across time of the outcomes of youth with disabilities up to 4 years after high school: A report of findings from the National Longitudinal Transition Study (NLTS) and the National Longitudinal Transition Study-2 (NLTS2) (NCSER 2010–3008). Menlo Park, CA: SRI International. Retrieved from http://ies.ed.gov/ncser/pubs/20103008/pdf/20103008.pdf

North, A. (2015, June 18). Making video games for everyone (not just the able-bodied). *The New York Times.* Retrieved from http://takingnote.blogs.nytimes.com/2015/06/18/making-video-games-for-everyone-not-just-the-able-bodied/?emc=edit_tnt_20150622&nlid=34601341&tntemail0=y&_r=0

Nussbaum, M. C. (2006). *Frontiers of justice: Disability, nationality, species membership.* Cambridge, MA: Belknap Press of Harvard University Press.

Plucker, J. A., Hardesty, J., & Burroughs, N. (2013). *Talent on the sidelines: Excellence gaps and America's persistent talent underclass.* Storrs, CT: Center for Education Policy Analysis, University of Connecticut. Retrieved from http://cepa.uconn.edu/mindthegap

Prabhala, A. (2007, February 20). *Mental retardation is no more: New name is intellectual and developmental disabilities.* Information from AAIDD. Retrieved from www.aamr.org

Raue, K., & Lewis, L. (2011). *Students with disabilities at degree-granting postsecondary institutions* (NCES 2011–018). U.S. Department of Education, National Center for Education Statistics. Washington, DC: U.S. Government Printing Office.

Rhoades, E. A. (2010). Commentary: Revisiting labels: "Hearing" or not? *The Volta Review, 110,* 55–67.

Rice, L. (2012, March 2). Actors with Down syndrome. *The EW Report, EW.com,* pp. 48–54.

Riddell, S. (2007). A sociology of special education. In L. Florian (Ed.), *The Sage handbook of special education* (pp. 34–45). Thousand Oaks, CA: Sage Publications.

Rioux, M. (2007). Disability rights in education. In L. Florian (Ed.), *The Sage handbook of special education* (pp. 107–116). Thousand Oaks, CA: Sage Publications.

Rodriguez, P. (2015). *Twice violated: Abuse and denial of sexual and reproductive rights of women with psychological disabilities.* Disability Rights International. Retrieved from http://www.driadvocacy.org/wp-content/uploads/Mexico-report-English-web.pdf

Roos, P. (1970). Trends and issues in special education for the mentally retarded. *Education and Training of the Mentally Retarded, 5,* 51–61.

Rosenthal, E., Jehn, E., & Galván, S. (2011, June). *Abandoned and disappeared: Mexico's segregation and abuse of children and adults with disabilities.* Washington, DC: Disability Rights International.

Safran, S. P. (1998). The first century of disability portrayal in film: An analysis of the literature. *Journal of Special Education, 31,* 467–479.

Safran, S. P. (2000). Using movies to teach students about disabilities. *Teaching Exceptional Children, 32,* 44–47.

Sandomierski, T., Kincaid, D., & Algozzine, B. (2008). Response to intervention and positive behavior support: Brothers from different mothers or sisters with different misters? *Positive Behavioral Interventions and Supports Newsletter, 4.* Retrieved from www.pbis.org/news/New/Newsletters/Newsletter4-2.aspz

Schalock, R. L., & Luckasson, R. (2013). What's at stake in the lives of people with intellectual disability? Part I: The power of naming, defining, diagnosing, classifying, and planning supports. *Intellectual and Developmental Disabilities, 51,* 86–93.

Science Daily. (2008, April 4). Rise in autism is related to changes in diagnosis, new study suggests. *Science News.* Retrieved from www.sciencedaily.com/releases/2008/04/080408112107.htm

Screen Actors Guild. (2011, September 28). *Study reveals continued lack of characters with disabilities on television.* Retrieved from www.sag.org/study-reveals-continued-lack-characters-disabilities-television

Screen Actors Guild–American Federation of Television and Radio Artists. (2015). *Performers with disabilities.* Retrieved from http://www.sagaftra.org/content/performers-with-disabilities

Shepard, K., West, J., & Wilson, C. (2015). *Overview of the federal investment in special education personnel preparation.* The Higher Education Consortium for Special Education (HECSE).

Siperstein, G. N., Parker R. C., Bardon, J. N., & Widaman, K. F. (2007). A national study of youth attitudes toward the inclusion of students with intellectual disabilities. *Exceptional Children, 73,* 435–455.

Siperstein, G. N., Pociask, S. E., & Collins, M. A. (2010). Sticks, stones, and stigma: A study of students' use of the derogatory term "retard." *Intellectual and Developmental Disabilities, 48,* 126–134.

Smith, J. D., & Lazaroff, K. (2006). "Uncle Sam needs you" or does he? Intellectual disabilities and lessons from the "Great Wars." *Mental Retardation, 44,* 433–437.

Snyder, T. D., & Dillow, S.A. (2015). *Digest of education statistics 2013* (NCES 2015-011). National Center for Education Statistics, Institute of Education Sciences, U.S. Department of Education. Washington, DC.

Taylor, S. J. (2006). Christmas in purgatory: A retrospective look. *Mental Retardation, 44,* 145–149.

Tassé, M. J. (2013). What's in a name? *Intellectual and Developmental Disabilities, 51,* 113–116.

U.S. Congress. Americans with Disabilities Act of 1990. Pub. L. No. 101-336, 104 STAT. 327.

U.S. Congress. Civil Rights Act of 1964. Pub. L. No. 82-352, 78 STAT. 241.

U.S. Congress. Individuals with Disabilities Education Act. Pub. L. No. 101-476.

U.S. Congress. Individuals with Disabilities Education Act. Pub. L. No. 105-17, 111 STAT. 37.

U.S. Congress. Individuals with Disabilities Education Improvement Act of 2004. Pub. L. No. 108-446.

U.S. Congress. No Child Left Behind Act of 2001. PL 107-110.

U.S. Congress. Rehabilitation Act of 1973, Section 504. 19 U.S.C. Section 794.

U.S. Department of Education. (1992). *Fifteenth annual report to Congress on the implementation of the Individuals with Disabilities Education Act.* Washington, DC: U.S. Government Printing Office.

U.S. Department of Education. (1995). *Seventeenth annual report to Congress on the implementation of the Individuals with Disabilities Education Act.* Washington, DC: U.S. Government Printing Office.

U.S. Department of Education. (2006). *Assistance to states for the education of children with disabilities program and the early intervention program for infants and toddlers with disabilities: Final rule.* Federal Register, 34 CFR Parts 300 and 301.

U.S. Department of Education. (2010). *Thirty-five years of progress in educating children with disabilities through IDEA.* Retrieved from www2.ed.gov/about/offices/list/osers/idea35/history/idea-35-history.pdf

U.S. Department of Education, Office of Special Education and Rehabilitative Services, Office of Special Education Programs. (2014). *Thirty-sixth annual report to Congress on the implementation of the*

Individuals with Disabilities Education Act, 2014. Washington, D.C.: Author.

Van Cleve, J. V. (Ed.). (2007). *The deaf history reader.* Washington, DC: Gallaudet University Press.

Watanabe, T., Vives, R., Jennings, A., & Panzar, J. (2015, July 10). Latino plurality points toward changes to come: Achievement gaps may shrink as population surges. *The Los Angeles Times,* pp. A-1, A-12.

Wehmeyer, M. L. (2013). Disability, disorder, and identity. *Intellectual and Developmental Disabilities, 51,* 122–126.

Winzer, M. A. (2007). Confronting difference: An excursion through the history of special education. In L. Florian (Ed.), *The Sage handbook of special education* (pp. 21–33). Thousand Oaks, CA: Sage Publications.

Chapter 2

Access Center. (n.d.). *Differentiated instruction for math.* Retrieved from www.k8accesscenter.org/training_resources/mathdifferentiation.asp

Adams, C., Pierce, R., & Dixon, F. (2007). *Tiered curriculum project.* Retrieved from www.doe.in.gov/exceptional/gt/tiered_curriculum/

Alliance for Excellent Education. (2010, September). *Fact sheet: High school dropouts in America.* Washington, DC: Alliance for Excellent Education. Retrieved from www.all4ed.org/files/GraduationRates_FactSheet.pdf

Al Otaiba, S., Folsom, J. S., Schatschneider, C., Wanzek, J., Greulich, L., Meadows, J., Li, Z., & Connor, C. M. (2011). Predicting first-grade reading performance from kindergarten response to tier 1 instruction. *Exceptional Children, 77,* 453–470.

American Academy of Child & Adolescent Psychiatry. (2011, March). *Facts for families: Bullying.* Retrieved from www.aacap.org/cs/root/facts_for_families/bullying

American Academy of Child & Adolescent Psychiatry. (2011, June). *Bullying.* Retrieved from www.aacap.org/galleries/default-file/Bullying_Fact_Sheet_2010.pdf

American Academy of Child & Adolescent Psychiatry, Task Force for the Prevention of Bullying. (2011, June). *Policy statement: Prevention of bullying related morbidity and mortality.* Retrieved from www.aacap.org/cs/root/policy_statements/policy_statement_prevention_of_bullying_related_morbidity_and_mortality

America's Promise Alliance. (2014). *Don't call them dropouts: Understanding the experiences of young people who leave high school before graduation.* Retrieved from http://gradnation.org/sites/default/files/DCTD%20Final%20Full_0.pdf

Batsche, G., Elliott, J., Graden, J. L., Grimes, J., Kovaleski, J. F., Prasse, D., et al. (2005). *Response to intervention: Policy considerations and implementation.* Virginia: National Association of State Directors of Special Education, Inc.

Bradley, R., Danielson, L., & Hallahan, D. P. (Eds.). (2002). *Identification of learning disabilities: Research to practice.* Mahwah, NJ: Erlbaum.

Bradshaw, C. P., Waasdorp, T. E., O'Brennan, L. M., & Gulemetova, M. (2011). *Findings from the National Education Association's nationwide study of bullying: Teachers' and education support professionals' perspectives.* Retrieved from www.nea.org/assets/img/content/Findings_from_NEAs_Nationwide_Study_of_Bullying.pdf

Bridgeland, J. M., DiIulio, J. J., & Morison, K. B. (2006, March). *The silent epidemic: Perspectives of high school dropouts.* Washington, DC: Civic Enterprises. Retrieved from www.ignitelearning.com/pdf/TheSilentEpidemic3-06FINAL.pdf

CAST. (2011). *Universal Design for Learning Guidelines version 2.0.* Wakefield, MA: Author.

Center for the Prevention of School-Aged Violence. (2010). *Statistics: Violence.* Retrieved from http://goodwin.drexel.edu/cposav/sav_stats.php

Chapman, C., Laird, J., Ifill, N., & KewalRamani, A. (2011). Trends in high school dropout and completion rates in the United States: 1972–2009. Washington, DC: U.S. Department of Education, National Center for Education Statistics. Retrieved from http://nces.ed.gov/pubs2012/2012006.pdf

Coalition for Evidence-Based Policy. (2003, December). *Identifying and implementing education practices supported by rigorous evidence: A user friendly guide.* Retrieved from www.ed.gov/rschstat/research/pubs/rigorousevid/rigorousevid.pdf

Council for Exceptional Children. (n.d.). *Differentiated instruction.* Retrieved from www.cec.sped.org/AM/Template.cfm?Section=Differentiated_Instruction&Template=/TaggedPage/TaggedPageDisplay.cfm&TPLID=

Council for Exceptional Children. (n.d.). *Why do students drop out of school?* Retrieved from www.cec.sped.org/AM/Template.cfm?Section=Home&TEMPLATE=/CM/ContentDisplay.cfm&CONTENTID=9279

Crevecoeur, Y. C., Sorenson, S. E., Mayorga, V. & Gonzalez, A. P. (2014). Universal Design for Learning in K-12 educational settings: A review of group comparison and single-subject intervention studies, *Journal of Special Education Apprenticeship, 3,* 1–23.

Davis, S., & Nixon, C. (2011). What students say about bullying. *Educational Leadership, 69,* 18–23.

Dynarski, M., Clarke, L., Cobb, B., Finn, J., Rumberger, R., & Smink, J. (2008). *Dropout prevention: A practice guide.* Washington, DC: National Center for Education Evaluation and Regional Assistance, Institute of Education Sciences, U.S. Department of Education. Retrieved from http://ies.ed.gov/ncee/wwc/pdf/practice_guides/dp_pg_090308.pdf

Fuchs, D., & Fuchs, L. S. (2005). Responsiveness to intervention: A blueprint for practitioners, policymakers, and parents. *Teaching Exceptional Children, 38*(1), 57–61.

Fuchs, D., Fuchs, L. S., & Compton, D. (2004). Identifying reading disabilities by responsiveness to instruction: Specifying measures and criteria. *Learning Disability Quarterly, 27,* 216–227.

Fuchs, D., Fuchs, L. S., McMaster, K. L., Yen, L., & Svenson, E. (2004). Non-responders: How to find them? How to help them? What do they mean for special education? *Teaching Exceptional Children, 36*(6), 72–77.

Fuchs, D., Mock, D., Morgan, P. L., & Young, C. L. (2003). Responsiveness to intervention: Definitions, evidence, and implications for the learning disabilities construct. *Learning Disabilities Research & Practice, 18*(3), 157–171.

Fuchs, L. S., Butterworth, J. R., & Fuchs, D. (1989). Effects of ongoing curriculum-based measurement on student awareness of goals and progress. *Education and Treatment of Children, 12,* 63–72.

Fuchs, L. S., & Fuchs, D. (2002a). Curriculum-based measurement: Describing competence, enhancing outcomes, evaluating treatment effects, and identifying treatment nonresponders. *Peabody Journal of Education, 77*(2), 64–84.

Fuchs, L. S., & Fuchs, D. (2002b). *What is scientifically-based research on progress monitoring?* National Center on Student Progress Monitoring. Retrieved from www.studentprogress.org/library/What_Is_Scientificall_%20Based_Research.pdf

Fuchs, L. S., & Fuchs, D. (2006). Implementing responsiveness to intervention to identify learning disabilities. *Perspectives, 32*(1), 39–43.

Fuchs, L. S., Fuchs, D., Hamlett, C. L., Phillips, N. B., & Bentz, J. (1994). Classwide curriculum-based measurement: Helping general educators meet the challenge of student diversity. *Exceptional Children, 60*(6), 518–537.

Fuchs, L. S., Fuchs, D., & Powell, S. (2004). *Using CBM for Progress Monitoring.* Washington, DC: American Institutes for Research.

Glass, D., Meyer, A., & Rose, D.H. (2013). Universal Design for Learning and the arts. *Harvard Educational Review, 83,* 98–119.

Hall, T. (2002). *Differentiated instruction.* Wakefield, MA: National Center on Accessing the General Curriculum.

Hall, T. E., Cohen, N., Vue, G., & Ganley, P. (2014). Addressing learning disabilities with UDL and technology: Strategic Reader. *Learning Disabilities Quarterly, 38,* 72–83.

Hammond, C., Linton, D., Smink, J., & Drew, S. (2007). *Dropout risk factors and exemplary programs.* Clemson, SC: National Dropout Prevention Center, Communities In Schools, Inc.

Heyvaert, M., Wendt, O., Van den Noortgate, W., & Onghena, P. (2015). Randomization and data-analysis items in quality standards for single-case experimental studies. *Journal of Special Education, 49,* 146–156.

"High school dropout crisis" continues in U.S., study says. (2009, May 5). *CNN.com*. Retrieved from http://articles.cnn.com/2009-05-05/us/dropout.rate.study_1_dropouts-enrollment-graduations?_s=PM:US

Horner, R., Sugai, G., Todd, A., Dickey, C. R., Anderson, C., Scott, T. (n.d.). Check in Check out: A targeted intervention. Retrieved from www.pbis.org/common/pbisresources/presentations/BEP_CICO_Anne.ppt

IRIS Center. (2004). *Classroom assessment (part 1): An introduction to monitoring academic achievement in the classroom*. Retrieved from http://iris.peabody.vanderbilt.edu/module/gpm/

IRIS Center. (2006). *RTI (part 1): An overview*. Retrieved from http://iris.peabody.vanderbilt.edu/module/rti01-overview/

IRIS Center. (2009). *Universal Design for Learning: Creating a learning environment that challenges and engages all students*. Retrieved from http://iris.peabody.vanderbilt.edu/module/gpm/

Kennedy, M. J., Thomas, C. N., Meyer, J. P., Alves, K. D., & Lloyd, J. W. (2014). Using evidence-based multimedia to improve vocabulary performance of adolescents with LD: A UDL approach. *Learning Disability Quarterly, 37*, 71–86.

King-Sears, M. (2009). Universal design for learning: Technology and pedagogy. *Learning Disability Quarterly, 32*, 199–201.

King-Sears, M. E., Johnson, T. M., Berkeley, S., Weiss, M. P., Peters-Burton, E. E., Evmenova, A. S., Menditto, A., & Hursh, J. C. (2014). An exploratory study of universal design for teaching chemistry to students with and without disabilities. *Learning Disability Quarterly, 38*, 84–96.

King-Sears, P. (2014). Introduction to *Learning Disability Quarterly* special series on Universal Design for Learning: Part one of two. *Learning Disability Quarterly, 37*, 68–70.

Mandlawitz, M. (2009, November/December). PBIS emerging as sibling to RTI. *LDA Newsbriefs*, 11.

Marino, M. T., Gotch, C. M., Israel, M., Vasquez E., III, Basham, J. D., & Becht, K. (2014). UDL in the middle school science classroom: Can video games and alternative text heighten engagement and learning for students with learning disabilities? *Learning Disability Quarterly, 37*, 87–99.

McFarland, J., Stark, P., & Cui, J. (2016). *Trends in High School Dropout and Completion Rates in the United States: 2013* (NCES 2016-117). U.S. Department of Education. Washington, DC: National Center for Education Statistics. Retrieved from http://nces.ed.gov/pubsearch

McQuarrie, L., McRae, P., & Stack-Cutler, H. (2008, February). *Differentiated instruction provincial research review: Choice, complexity, and creativity*. Alberta Initiative for School Improvement. Retrieved from http://education.alberta.ca/media/6412208/research_review_differentiated_instruction_2008.pdf

National Center for Education Statistics. (2016). *The Nation's Report Card: 2015 mathematics and reading assessments*. Institute of Education Sciences, U.S. Department of Education, Washington, DC. Retrieved from http://www.nationsreportcard.gov/reading_math_2015/#?grade=4

National Center for Education Statistics. (2016). Table 219.71: Population 16 to 24 years old and number of 16- to 24-year-old high school dropouts (status dropouts), by sex and race/ethnicity: 1970 through 2014. Institute of Education Sciences, U.S. Department of Education, Washington, DC. Retrieved from http://nces.ed.gov/programs/digest/d15/tables/dt15_219.71.asp?current=yes

Office of Management and Budget. (2015). *Fiscal Year 2015 budget of the U.S. government*. Washington, DC: U.S. Government Printing Office. Retrieved from www.whitehouse.gov/sites/default/files/omb/budget/fy2015/assets/budget.pdf

Reis, S. M., McCoach, D. B., Little, C. A., Muller, L. M., & Burcu Kaniskan, R. (2011). The effects of differentiated instruction and enrichment pedagogy on reading achievement in five elementary schools. *American Educational Research Journal, 48*(2), 462–501.

Rose, C. A., Monda-Amaya, L. E., & Espelage, D. L. (2011). Bullying perpetration and victimization in special education: A review of the literature. *Remedial and Special Education, 32*, 114–130.

Rose, D. H., & Gravel, J. W. (2010). *Technology and learning: Meeting special students' needs*. Wakefield, MA: National Center on Universal Design for Learning. Retrieved from www.udlcenter.org/sites/udlcenter.org/files/TechnologyandLearning.pdf

Rumberger, R., & Lim, S. A. (2008, October). *Why students drop out of school: A review of 25 years of research*. California Dropout Research Project Policy Brief 15. Retrieved from www.slocounty.ca.gov/Assets/CSN/PDF/Flyer+-+Why+students+drop+out.pdf

Safer, N., & Fleischman, S. (2005). Research matters: How student progress monitoring improves instruction. *Educational Leadership, 62*(5), 81–83.

Sandomierski, T., Loversky, T., & Jarot, N. (n.d.). Check-in/Check-out systems. Retrieved from www.pbis.org/common/cms/documents/Forum_09_Presentations/B6_CICO_Sandomierski.pdf

Schreier, A., Wolke, D., Thomas, K., Horwood, J., Hollis, C., Gunnell, D., Lewis, G., Thompson, A., Zammit, S., Duffy, L., Salvi, G., & Harrison, G. (2009). Prospective study of peer victimization in childhood and psychotic symptoms in a nonclinical population at age 12 years. *Archives of General Psychiatry, 66*, 527–536.

Seeley, K., Tombari, M. L., Bennett, L. J., & Dunkle, J. B. (2011, December). Bullying in schools: An overview. *OJJDP Juvenile Justice Bulletin*. Washington, DC: U.S. Department of Justice. Retrieved from www.ojjdp.gov/pubs/234205.pdf

Sherlock-Shangraw, R. (2013). Creating inclusive youth sports environments with the Universal Design for Learning. *Journal of Physical Education, Recreation, & Dance, 84*, 40–46.

Stavroula, V., Leonidas, K., & Koutselini, M. (2011). *Investigating the impact of differentiated instruction in mixed ability classrooms: Its impact on the quality and equity dimensions of education effectiveness*. Paper presented at the International Congress for School Effectiveness and Improvement, January, 2011. Retrieved from www.icsei.net/icsei2011/Full%20Papers/0155.pdf

Sum, A., Khatiwada, I., McLaughlin, J., & Palma, S. (2011). *High school dropouts in Chicago and Illinois: The growing labor market and income, civic, social and fiscal costs of dropping out of high school*. Northeastern University: Center for Labor Market Studies. Retrieved from www.northeastern.edu/clms/wp-content/uploads/High-School-Dropouts-in-Chicago-and-Illinois.pdf

Tomlinson, C. A., & Imbeau, M. B. (2010). Common sticking points about differentiation. *School Administrator, 69*, 18–22. Retrieved from www.aasa.org/content.aspx?id=23118

Tomlinson, C. A., & Imbeau, M. B. (2010). *Leading and managing a differentiated classroom*. Alexandria, VA: ASCD.

Tomlinson, C. A., & Murphy, M. (2015). *Leading for differentiation: Growing teachers who grow kids*. Alexandria, VA: ASCD.

U.S. Congress. *Elementary and Secondary Education Act of 2001*. PL No. 107-110.

U.S. Congress. *The Every Child Achieves Act of 2015*. S. 1177.

U.S. Congress. *Higher Education Opportunity Act of 2008*, PL No. 110-314.

U.S. Congress. *Individuals with Disabilities Education Improvement Act of 2004*. PL No. 108-446.

U.S. Congress. *The Student Success Act of 2015*, H.R. 5.

Vaughn Gross Center for Reading and Language Arts at The University of Texas at Austin. (2003). *Introduction to the 3-tier reading model: Reducing reading difficulties for kindergarten through third grade students* (4th ed.). Austin, TX: University of Texas System/Texas Education Agency.

Vaughn, S., Wexler, J., Barth, A. A., Cirino, P. T., Romain, M. A., Francis, D., Fletcher, J., & Denton, C. A. (2011). Effects of individualized and standardized instruction on middle school students with reading difficulties. *Exceptional Children, 77*, 391–407.

Vaughn, S. R., & Fuchs, L. S. (2003). Redefining learning disabilities as inadequate response to treatment: Rationale and assumptions. *Learning Disabilities Research & Practice, 18*(3), 137–146.

Yousafzai, Malala. (2013). *I am Malala*. New York: Little, Brown and Company.

Zumeta, R. (n.d.). Understanding types of assessment within an RTI framework. In *RTI Implementer Webinar Series*. National Center on Response to Intervention. Retrieved from http://www.rti4success.org/video/implementer-series-understanding-types-assessment-within-rti-framework

Chapter 3

Albrecht, S. F., Skiba, R. J., Losen, D. J., Chung, C. G., & Middelberg, L. (2012). Federal policy on disproportionality in special education: Is it moving us forward? *Journal of Disability Policy Studies, 23,* 14–25.

Artiles, A. J. (2003). Special education's changing identity: Paradoxes and dilemmas in views of culture and space. *Harvard Educational Review, 73,* 164–202.

Artiles, A. J. (2010). Re-framing disproportionality research: Outline of a cultural-historical paradigm. *Multiple Voices for Diverse Exceptional Learners, 11,* 24–37.

Artiles, A. J., & Bal, A. (2008). The next generation of disproportionality research: Toward a comparative model in the study of equity in ability differences. *Journal of Special Education, 42*(1), 4–14.

Artiles, A. J., Harry, B., Reschly, D. J., & Chinn, P. C. (2002). Over-identification of students of color in special education: A critical overview. *Multicultural Perspectives, 4,* 3–10.

Aud, S., Hussar, W., Johnson, F., Kena, G., Roth, E., Manning, E., Wang, X., & Zhang, J. (2012). *The condition of education 2012* (NCES 2012-045). Washington, DC: U.S. Department of Education, National Center for Education Statistics. Retrieved from http://nces.ed.gov/pubsearch

Baca, L. M., & Cervantes, H. T. (Eds.). (2004). *The bilingual special education interface* (4th ed.). Columbus, OH: Merrill.

Banks, J. A. (2006). *Cultural diversity and education: Foundations, curriculum, and teaching* (5th ed.). Boston, MA: Pearson Education, Inc.

Bernal, E. M. (2000). Three ways to achieve a more equitable representation of culturally and linguistically different students in GT programs. *Roeper Review, 24,* 82–88.

Bondy, E., Ross, D. D., Gallingane, C., & Hambacher, E. (2007). Creating environments of success and resilience: Culturally responsive classroom management and more. *Urban Education, 42*(4), 326–348.

Brice, A., & Rosa-Lugo, L. I. (2000). Code switching: A bridge or barrier between two languages? *Multiple Voices, 4,* 1–9.

Brown v. Board of Education, 347 U.S. 483 (1954).

Brown, M. R., Higgins, J., Pierce, R., Hong, E., & Thoma, C. (2003). Secondary students' perceptions of school life with regard to alienation: The effects of disability, gender, and race. *Learning Disability Quarterly, 26,* 227–238.

Bryant, D. P., Smith, D. S., & Bryant, B. R. (2008). *Teaching students with special needs in inclusive classrooms.* Boston, MA: Pearson Education, Inc.

Cartledge, G., & Kourea, L. (2008). Culturally responsive classrooms for culturally diverse students with and at risk for disabilities. *Exceptional Children, 74*(3), 351–371.

Cartledge, G., & Loe, S. A. (2001). Cultural diversity and social skill instruction. *Exceptionality, 9,* 33–46.

Castania, K. (2003). *The evolving language of diversity.* Ithaca, NY: Cornell Cooperative Extension, Cornell University.

Chapman, C., Laird, J., & KewalRamani, A. (2010). *Trends in high school dropout and completion rates in the United States: 1972–2008* (NCES 2011-012). Washington, DC: National Center for Education Statistics, Institute of Education Sciences, U.S. Department of Education. Retrieved from http://nces.ed.gov/pubsearch

Cheng, L. L. (1996). Beyond bilingualism: A quest for communication competence. *Topics in Language Disorders, 16,* 9–21.

Cheng, L. L. (1999). Moving beyond accent: Social and cultural realities of living with many tongues. *Topics in Language Disorders, 19,* 1–10.

Cheng, L. L., & Chang, J. (1995). Asian/Pacific Islander students in need of effective services. In L. L. Cheng (Ed.), *Integrating language and learning for inclusion: An Asian-Pacific focus* (pp. 3–59). San Diego, CA: Singular Publishing Group.

Coutinho, M. J., & Oswald, D. P. (2006). *Disproportionate representation of culturally and linguistically diverse students in special education: Measuring the problem.* Denver, CO: NCCRESt.

Cummins, J. (1984). *Bilingualism and special education: Issues in assessment and pedagogy.* San Diego, CA: College-Hill.

Cummins, J. (2010). Transformative multiliteracies pedagogy: School-based strategies for closing the achievement gap. *Multiple Voices for Diverse Exceptional Learners, 11,* 38–56.

D'Anguilli, A., Siegel, L. S., & Maggi, S. (2004). Literacy instruction, SES, and word-reading achievement in English-language learners and children with English as a first language: A longitudinal study. *Learning Disabilities Research & Practice, 19,* 202–213.

Davis, C., Brown, B., Bantz, J., & Manno, C. (2002). African American parents' involvement in their children's special education programs. *Multiple Voices, 5,* 13–27.

de Valenzuela, J. S., Copeland, S. R., Qi, C. H. (2006). Examining educational equity: Revisiting the disproportionate representation of minority students in special education. *Exceptional Children, 72*(4), 425–441.

Diana v. State Board of Education, No. C-70-37 Rfp (N.D. Calif. 1970).

Diaz, Y., Knight, L. A., & Chronis-Tuscano, A. (Winter, 2008). Adaptation and implementation of behavioral parent training for Latino families: Cultural considerations and treatment acceptability. *Report on Emotional and Behavioral Disorders in Youth, 8*(1), 2–8.

Donovan, M. Z., & Cross, C. T. (Eds.) (2002). *Minority students in special education and gifted education.* Committee on Minority Representation in Special Education. Washington, DC: National Academy Press.

Dresser, N. (2005). *Multicultural manners: Essential rules of etiquette for the 21st century.* Hoboken, NJ: John Wiley & Sons, Inc.

Dyson, A., & Gallannaugh, F. (2008). Disproportionality in special needs education in England. *Journal of Exceptional Children, 42*(1), 36–46.

Echevarría, J., & Graves, A. (2011). *Sheltered content instruction: Teaching English learners with diverse abilities.* Boston, MA: Pearson Education, Inc.

Echevarría, J., & Vogt, M. (2011). *Response to intervention (RTI) and English learners: Making it happen.* Boston, MA: Pearson Education, Inc.

Echevarría, J., Vogt, M., & Short, D.J. (2010). *Making content comprehensible for elementary English learners: The SIOP model.* Boston, MA: Allyn & Bacon.

Espinoza, R. (2011). *Pivotal moments.* Cambridge, MA: Harvard University Press.

Fletcher, T. V., Bos, C. S., & Johnson, L. M. (1999). Accommodating English language learners with language and learning disabilities in bilingual education classrooms. *Learning Disabilities Research & Practice, 14,* 80–91.

Ford, D. Y. (2012). Culturally different students in special education: Looking backward to move forward. *Exceptional Children, 78*(4), 391–405.

Ford, D. Y., Grantham, T. C., & Whiting, G. W. (2008). Culturally and linguistically diverse students in gifted education: Recruitment and retention issues. *Exceptional Children, 74*(3), 289–306.

Ford, D. Y., Howard, R. C., Harris, J. J., III, & Tyson, C. A. (2000). Creating culturally responsive classrooms for gifted African American students. *Journal for the Education of the Gifted, 23,* 397–427.

Fry, R. (2005). *The high schools Hispanics attend: Size and other key characteristics.* Washington, DC: Pew Hispanic Center.

Ganim, S., & Tran, L. (2016, January 13). How tap water became toxic in Flint, Michigan. *CNN.com.* Retrieved from http://www.cnn.com/2016/01/11/health/toxic-tap-water-flint-michigan/

Garcia, E. E. (2001). *Hispanic education in the United States.* New York, NY: Rowman & Littlefield.

Garrett, M. T., Bellon-Harn, M. L., Torres-Rivera, E., Garrett, J. T., & Roberts, L. C. (2003). Open hands, open hearts: Working with Native youth in the schools. *Intervention in School and Clinic, 38,* 225–235.

Gay, G. (2010). *Culturally responsive teaching: Theory, research, and practice* (2nd ed.). New York, NY: Teachers College Press, Columbia University.

Gay, G., & Kirkland, K. (2003). Developing cultural critical consciousness and self-reflection in preservice teacher education. *Theory Into Practice, 42*(3), 181–187.

Gollnick, D. M., & Chinn, P. C. (2013). *Multicultural education in a pluralistic society* (9th ed.). Boston, MA: Allyn & Bacon.

Good, T. L., & Nichols, S. L. (2001). Expectancy effects in the classroom: A special focus on improving the reading performance of minority students in first-grade classrooms. *Educational Psychologist, 36*(2), 113–126.

Goode, T. (2002, August). *Cultural competence.* Presentation to National Council on Disability, Cultural Diversity Committee, Washington, DC.

Harry, B. (2002). Trends and issues in serving culturally diverse families of children with disabilities. *Journal of Special Education, 36,* 131–138.

Harry, B. (2007). The disproportionate placement of ethnic minorities in special education. In Florian, L. (Ed.), *The Sage handbook of special education.* Thousand Oaks, CA: Sage Publications.

Harry, B. (2008). Collaboration with culturally and linguistically diverse families: Ideal versus reality. *Exceptional Children, 74*(3), 372–388.

Harry, B., & Klingner, J. (2006). *Why are so many minority students in special education? Understanding race and disability in schools.* New York, NY: Teachers College Press.

Harry, B., Arnaiz, P., Klingner, J., & Sturges, K. (2008). Schooling and the construction of identity among minority students in Spain and the United States. *Journal of Exceptional Children, 42*(1), 15–25.

Hart, J. E., Cramer, E. D., Harry, B., Klingner, J. K., & Sturges, K. M. (2010). The continuum of "troubling" to "troubled" behavior: Exploratory case studies of African American students in programs for emotional disturbance. *Remedial and Special Education, 31,* 148–162.

Herrera, S. C., & Murry, K. G. (2011). *Mastering ESL and bilingual methods: Differentiated instruction for culturally and linguistically diverse (CLD) students* (2nd ed.). Boston, MA: Pearson Education, Inc.

Holman, L. J. (1997). Working effectively with Hispanic immigrant families. *Phi Delta Kappan, 78,* 647–649.

Hosp, J. L., & Reschly, D. J. (2002). Predictors of restrictiveness of placement for African-American and Caucasian students. *Exceptional Children, 68,* 225–238.

Hosp, J. L., & Reschly, D. J. (2003). Referral rates for intervention or assessment: A meta-analysis of racial differences. *Journal of Special Education, 37,* 67–80.

IDEA Data Center (May, 2014). *Methods for assessing racial/ethnic disproportionality in special education: A technical assistance guide (revised).* Rockville, MD: Westat.

Ingersoll, R. (2001). *Teacher turnover, teacher shortages, and the organization of schools.* Seattle, WA: University of Washington, Center for the Study of Teaching and Policy.

Institute of Education Sciences. (2015). *Table 204.20: Number and percentage of public school students participating in programs for English language learners, by state: Selected years, 2002–03 through 2012–13.* Retrieved from http://nces.ed.gov/programs/digest/d14/tables/dt14_204.20.asp

Jairrels, V., Brazil, N., & Patton, J. R. (1999). Incorporating popular literature into the curriculum for diverse learners. *Intervention in School and Clinic, 34,* 303–306.

Jasper, A. D., & Bouch, E. C. (2013). Disproportionality among African American students at the secondary level: Examining the MID disability category. *Education and Training in Autism and Developmental Disabilities, 48,* 31–40.

Kalyanpur, M. (2008). The paradox of majority underrepresentation in special education in India. *Journal of Exceptional Children, 42*(1), 55–64.

Kea, C. D., & Utley, C. A. (1998). To teach me is to know me. *Journal of Special Education, 32,* 44–47.

Kena, G., Musu-Gillette, L., Robinson, J., Wang, X., Rathbun, A., Zhang, J., Wilkinson-Flicker, S., Barmer, A., & Dunlop Velez, E. (2015). *The condition of education 2015* (NCES 2015-144). Washington, DC: U.S. Department of Education, National Center for Education Statistics. Retrieved from http://nces.ed.gov/pubs2015/2015144.pdf

Kimble, M. (2012, April 26). Arizona immigration: SB 1070 took toll on state's reputation. *Los Angeles Times.* Retrieved from http://articles.latimes.com/2012/apr/26/nation/la-na-nn-arizona-immigration-20120425

Kishi, G. (2004). *Pihana Nā Mamo: Students of Hawaiian Ancestry.* Honolulu, HI: The Native Hawaiian Special Education Project, Hawaii Department of Education.

Klingner, J. K., Hoover, J. J., & Baca, L. M. (Eds.). (2008). *Why do English language learners struggle with reading? Distinguishing language acquisition from learning disabilities.* Thousand Oaks, CA: Corwin Press.

Kozol, J. (1991). *Savage inequalities: Children in America's schools.* New York, NY: Crown.

Kozol, J. (1995). *Amazing grace: The lives of children and the conscience of a nation.* New York, NY: Crown.

Kozleski, E. B., Sobel, D., & Taylor, S. V. (2003). Embracing and building culturally responsive practices. *Multiple Voices, 6,* 73–87.

Krause, M. (1992). Testimony to the Select Senate Committee on Indian Affairs on S. 2044, *Native American Languages Act of 1991,* to assist Native Americans in assuring the survival and continuing vitality of their languages, pp. 16–18.

Ladson-Billings, G. (2001). *Crossing over to Canaan: The journey of new teachers in diverse classrooms.* San Francisco, CA: Jossey Bass.

Lane, K. L., Pierson, M. R., Stang, K. K., & Carter, E. W. (2010). Teacher expectations of students' classroom behavior: Do expectations vary as a function of school risk? *Remedial and Special Education, 31,* 163–174.

Larry P. v. Riles, Civil Action No. C-70-37 (N.D. Calif. 1971).

Lau v. Nichols, 414 U.S. 563 (1974).

Lee, V. E., & Burkam, D. T. (2002). *Inequality at the starting gate.* Washington, DC: Economic Policy Institute.

Lessow-Hurley, J. (2005). *The foundations of dual language instruction.* Boston, MA: Pearson Education, Inc.

Lynch, E. W., & Hanson, M. J. (2004). *Developing cross-cultural competence: A guide for working with young children and their families* (3rd ed.). Baltimore, MD: Paul H. Brookes.

Mandell, D. S., Davis, J. K., Bevans, K., & Guevara, J. P. (2008). Ethnic disparities in special education labeling among children with attention-deficit/hyperactivity disorder. *Journal of Emotional and Behavioral Disorders, 16,* 42–51.

McCall, Z., & Skrtic, T. M. (2010). Intersectional needs politics: A policy frame for the wicked problem of disproportionality. *Multiple Voices for Diverse Exceptional Learners, 11,* 3–23.

Milner, H. R. (2012). *Start where you are, but don't stay there.* Cambridge, MA: Harvard University Press.

Montgomery, W. (2001, March/April). Creating culturally responsive, inclusive classrooms. *Teaching Exceptional Children 33,* 4–9.

Morgan, P. L., Farkas, G., Hellemeier, M. M., & Maczuga, S. (2012). Are minority children disproportionately represented in early intervention and early childhood special education? *Educational Researcher, 41,* 339–351.

Morgan, P. L., Farkas, G., Hellemeier, M. M., Mattison, R., Maczuga, S., Li, H., & Cook, M. (2015). Minorities are disproportionately underrepresented in special education: Longitudinal evidence across five disability conditions. *Educational Researcher, 44,* 278–292.

Morrier, M. J., & Hess, K. L. (2012). Ethnic differences in autism eligibility in the United States public schools. *Journal of Special Education, 46*(1), 49–63.

Moses, S. (2015, May 5). *Spending per student NYS school districts, 2015: Look up, compare any district, rank.* Retrieved from http://www.syracuse.com/schools/index.ssf/2015/05/spending_per_student_nys_school_districts_2015_lookup_compare_any_district_rank.html

National Center for Culturally Responsive Educational Systems. (NCCRESt, 2006). *Disproportionate representation of culturally and linguistically diverse students in special education: Measuring the problem.* Denver, CO: Author.

Neal, L. I., McCray, A. D., Webb-Johnson, G., & Bridgest, S. T. (2003). The effects of African American movement styles on teachers' perceptions and reactions. *Journal of Special Education, 37,* 49–57.

Nieto, S., & Bode, P. (2012). *Affirming diversity: The sociopolitical context of multicultural education* (6th ed.). Boston, MA: Pearson Education, Inc.

Obiakor, F. E. (1994). *The eight-step multicultural approach: Learning and teaching with a smile.* Dubuque, IA: Kendall/Hunt.

Ochoa, S. H., Robles-Pina, R., Garcia, S. B., & Breunig, N. (1999). School psychologists' perspectives on referrals of language minority students. *Multiple Voices, 3,* 1–14.

Office of English Language Acquisition. (2015). *Fast facts: Languages spoken by English Learners.* Washington, DC: Author.

Office of English Language Acquisition. (2015). *Fast facts: Profiles of English Learners.* Washington, DC: Author.

Ortiz, A. A. (1997). Learning disabilities occurring concomitantly with linguistic differences. *Journal of Learning Disabilities, 30,* 321–332.

Ortiz, A. A., Wilkinson, C. Y., Robertson-Courtney, P., & Kushner, M. I. (2006). Considerations in implementing intervention assistance teams to support English Language Learners. *Remedial and Special Education, 27*(1), 53–63.

Ortiz, A. A., & Yates, J. R. (2001). A framework for serving English language learners with disabilities. *Journal of Special Education, 14,* 72–80.

Parette, H. P., & Petch-Hogan, B. (2000, November/December). Approaching families: Facilitating culturally/linguistically diverse family involvement. *Teaching Exceptional Children, 33,* 4–10.

Patton, J. M., & Baytops, J. L. (1995). Identifying and transforming the potential of young gifted African Americans: A clarion call for action. In B. A. Ford, F. E. Obiakor, & J. M. Patton (Eds.), *Effective education of African American exceptional learners: New perspectives* (pp. 27–68). Austin, TX: Pro-Ed.

Phyler v. Doe, 102 S. Ct. 2382 (1982).

Reid, R., Casat, C. D., Norton, H. J., Anastopoulos, A. D., & Temple, E. P. (2001). Using behavior rating scales for ADHD across ethnic groups: The IOWA Conners. *Journal of Emotional and Behavioral Disorders, 9,* 210–218.

Reschly, D. J. (2002). Minority overrepresentation: The silent contributor to LD prevalence and diagnostic confusion. In R. Bradley, L. Danielson, & D. P. Hallahan (Eds.), *Identification of learning disabilities: Research to practice* (pp. 361–368). Mahwah, NJ: Erlbaum.

Robertson, C. (2011, September 28). Alabama wins in ruling on its immigration law. *The New York Times.* Retrieved from www.nytimes.com/2011/09/29/us/alabama-immigration-law-upheld.html

Rossell, C. (2004/2005). Teaching English through English. *Educational Leadership, 62,* 32–36.

Rothstein, R. (2004, May 19). Social class leaves its imprint. *Education Week,* 40–41.

Rueda, R., Lim, H. J., & Velasco, A. (2008). Cultural accommodations in the classroom: An instructional perspective. *Multiple Voices, 10*(1&2), 61–72.

Ruiz, N. (1995). The social construction of ability and disability: I. Profile types of Latino children identified as language learning disabled. *Journal of Learning Disabilities, 29,* 491–502.

Sadowsky, M. (2006, July/August). The school readiness gap. *Harvard Education Letter.* Cambridge, MA: Harvard Education Publishing Group. Retrieved from www.edletter.org/past/issues/2006-ja/readinessgap.shtml

Salend, S. J., & Salinas, A. (2003). Language differences or learning difficulties: The work of the multidisciplinary team. *Teaching Exceptional Children, 35,* 35–43.

Santos, R., Fowler, S., Corso, R., & Bruns, D. (2000). Acceptance, acknowledgement, and adaptability: Selecting culturally and linguistically appropriate early childhood materials. *Teaching Exceptional Children, 32,* 14–22.

Short, D., & Echevarria, J. (2004/2005). Teacher skills to support English language learners. *Educational Leadership, 62,* 9–13.

Skiba, R. J., Poloni-Staudinger, L., Simmons, A. B., Feggins-Azziz, L. R., & Chung, C. (2005). Unproven links: Can poverty explain ethnic disproportionality in special education? *Journal of Special Education, 39*(3), 130–144.

Skiba, R. J., Simmons, A. B., Ritter, S., Gibb, A. C., Rausch, M. K., Cuadrado, J., & Chung, C. (2008). Achieving equity in special education: History, status, and current challenges. *Exceptional Children, 74*(3), 264–288.

Stiefel, L., Schwartz, A. E., & Conger, D. (2003). *Language proficiency and home languages of students in New York City elementary and middle schools.* New York, NY: New York University, Taub Urban Research Center.

Sullivan, A. (2011). Disproportionality in special education identification and placement of English language learners. *Exceptional Children, 77,* 317–334.

Sweller, N., Graham, L. J., & Van Bergen, P. (2012). The minority report: Disproportionate representation in Australia's largest education system. *Exceptional Children, 79,* 107–125.

Thomas, W. P., & Collier, V. P. (1997). *School effectiveness for language minority students* (NCBE Resource Collection Series No. 9). Washington, DC: National Clearinghouse for English Language Acquisition. Retrieved from www.ncela.gwu.edu

Thorp, E. K. (1997). Increasing opportunities for partnership with culturally and linguistically diverse families. *Intervention in School and Clinic, 32,* 261–269.

Tiedt, P. L., & Tiedt, I. M. (2005). *Multicultural teaching: A handbook of activities, information, and resources* (7th ed.). Boston, MA: Allyn & Bacon.

Tornatzky, L. G., Pachon, H. P., & Torres, C. (2003). *Closing achievement gaps: Improving educational outcomes for Hispanic children.* Los Angeles, CA: The Center for Latino Educational Excellence, The Tomás Rivera Policy Institute, University of Southern California.

Tyler, N. T., Lopez-Reyna, N., & Yzquierdo, Z. (2004). The relationship between cultural diversity and the special education workforce. *Journal of Special Education, 38,* 22–38.

U.S. Census Bureau. (2011, March). *Overview of race and Hispanic origin: 2010.* Washington, DC: U.S. Department of Commerce. Retrieved from www.census.gov/prod/cen2010/briefs/c2010br-02.pdf

U.S. Census Bureau. (2013, July). *Race: About.* Retrieved from http://www.census.gov/topics/population/race/about.html

U.S. Census Bureau. (2015). *Public education finances: 2015.* Retrieved from http://www2.census.gov/govs/school/13f33pub.pdf

U.S. Department of Education. (2006). *Assistance to states for the Education of Children with Disabilities Program and the Early Intervention Program for Infants and Toddlers with Disabilities: Final rule.* Federal Register, 34 CFR Parts 300 and 301.

U.S. Department of Education. (2011). *30th annual report to Congress on the implementation of the Individuals with Disabilities Education Act, 2008.* Washington, DC: U.S. Government Printing Office.

U.S. Department of Education. (2014, July 7). New initiative to provide all students access to great educators. Retrieved from http://www.ed.gov/news/press-releases/new-initiative-provide-all-students-access-great-educators

U.S. Department of Education, Office for Civil Rights. (2014). *Fact sheet: Ensuring students have equal access to educational resources without regard to race, color, or national origin.* Retrieved from http://www2.ed.gov/about/offices/list/ocr/docs/dcl-factsheet-resourcecomp-201410.pdf

Vick, K. (2015, October 19). The great migration. *Time,* 38–49.

Weinstein, C. S., Tomlinson-Clarke, S., & Curran, M. (2004). Toward a conception of culturally responsive classroom management. *Journal of Teacher Education, 55*(1), 25–38.

Werning, R., Loser, J. M., & Urban, M. (2008). Cultural and social diversity: An analysis of minority groups in German schools. *Journal of Exceptional Children, 42*(1), 47–54.

Yates, J. R., Hill, J. L., & Hill, E. G. (2002, February). "A vision for change" but for who?: A "personal" response to the National Research Council report. *DDEL News, 11,* 4–5.

Zelasko, N., & Antunez, B. (2000). *If your child learns in two languages.* Washington, DC: National Clearinghouse for Bilingual Education, George Washington University.

Chapter 4

American Psychological Association. (2016). Individuals with Disabilities Education Act (IDEA). Retrieved from http://www.apa.org/about/gr/issues/disability/idea.aspx

Appl, D. J., Hoffman, B., & Hughes, M. A. (2015, July). Readiness skills that support toddlers' transition into preschool. *Young Exceptional Children.* Retrieved from http://yec.sagepub.com/content/early/2015/07/03/1096250615593328.full.pdf+html

Barnhill, G. P. (2005). Functional behavior assessment in schools. *Intervention in School and Clinic, 40,* 131–143.

Brown, M. R., Paulsen, K., & Higgins, K. (2003). Remove environmental barriers to student learning. *Intervention in School and Clinic, 39,* 109–112.

Brown-Chidsey, R. (2007). No more "waiting to fail." *Educational Leadership, 65,* 40–46.

Bruce, C. (2011, October 14). *Assistive technology as a related service and the data accountability system.* Personal communication.

Bryant, D. P., & Bryant, B. R. (2012). *Assistive technology for people with disabilities* (2nd ed.). Columbus, OH: Merrill/Pearson.

Bryant, D. P., Bryant, B. R., & Smith, D. D. (2017). *Teaching students with special needs in inclusive classrooms.* Thousand Oaks, CA: Sage Publications, Inc.

Center for Parent Information and Resources. (2014, April). *10 basic steps in special education.* Retrieved from http://www.parentcenterhub.org/repository/steps/

Centers for Disease Control. (2015, April 21). *Developmental milestones.* Retrieved from http://www.cdc.gov/ncbddd/actearly/milestones/index.html

Christensen, L. L., Braam, M., Scullin, S., & Thurlow, M. L. (2011). *2009 state policies on assessment participation and accommodations for students with disabilities* (Synthesis Report 83). Minneapolis, MN: University of Minnesota, National Center on Educational Outcomes. Retrieved from http://www.cehd.umn.edu/NCEO/onlinepubs/Synthesis83/default.htm

Council for Exceptional Children. (2002). *Understanding the differences between IDEA and Section 504.* Retrieved from http://www.ldonline.org/article/Understanding_the_Differences_Between_IDEA_and_Section_504

Council for Exceptional Children. (2008, August). *Higher Education Opportunity Act reauthorization: Summary of selected provisions for individuals with exceptionalities and the professionals who work on their behalf.* Retrieved from http://www.cec.sped.org/~/media/Files/Policy/Higher%20Education/HEA%20Comprehensive%20Summary.pdf

Council for Exceptional Children. (2008, August). *Higher Education Opportunity Act reauthorization, P.L.110-315. Summary of selected provisions for individuals with exceptionalities and the professionals who work on their behalf: Executive summary.* Retrieved from http://www.cec.sped.org/~/media/Files/Policy/Higher%20Education/HEA%20Executive%20Summary.pdf

Council for Exceptional Children. (2015, December 15). *CEC's summary of selected provisions in Every Student Succeeds Act (ESSA).* Retrieved from http://cecblog.typepad.com/files/cecs-summary-of-selected-issues-in-every-student-succeeds-act-essa-1.pdf

deBettencourt, L. (2002). Understanding the differences between IDEA and Section 504. *Teaching Exceptional Children, 34,* 16–23.

Families and Advocates Partnership for Education. (2001). *School accommodations and modifications.* Retrieved from http://www.wrightslaw.com/info/fape.accoms.mods.pdf

Fisher, D., & Frey, N. (2012). Accommodations & modifications with learning in mind. Insert to *The Special EDge,* i–iv.

Friend, M., & Cook, L. (2007). *Interactions: Collaboration skills for school professionals* (5th ed.). Boston, MA: Allyn & Bacon.

Fuchs, D., Fuchs, L. S., & Stecker, P. M. (2010). The "blurring" of special education in a new continuum of general education placements and services. *Exceptional Children, 76,* 301–323.

Gallo, C. (2011, January). Account for unique student variable during LRE analysis. *Special Education Report, 37,* 4.

Gallo, C. (2011, January). Push for LRE has gone too far, says leader of school for the deaf. *Special Education Report, 37,* 3.

Hall, D. (2007). *Graduation matters: Improving accountability for high school graduation.* Washington, DC: The Education Trust.

Harkin Honors 35th Anniversary of the Individuals with Disabilities Education Act, November 18, 2010, Press Files, Thomas R. Harkin Collection, Drake University Archives and Special Collections, Des Moines, Iowa.

Hang, Q., & Rabren, K. (2009). An examination of co-teaching: Perspectives and efficacy indicators. *Remedial and Special Education, 30,* 259–268.

Hong, B. S. S., Ivy, W. F., Gonzalez, H. R., & Ehrensberger, W. (2007). Preparing students for postsecondary education. *Teaching Exceptional Children, 40,* 32–38.

IRIS Center. (2010). *Accommodations: Instructional and testing supports for students with disabilities.* Retrieved from http://iris.peabody.vanderbilt.edu/acc/

IRIS Center. (2011). *Related Services: Common supports for students with disabilities.* Retrieved from http://iris.peabody.vanderbilt.edu/module/rs/

Lingo, A. S., Barton-Arwood, S. M., & Jolivette, K. (2011). Teachers working together: Improving learning outcomes in the inclusive classroom—practical strategies and examples. *Teaching Exceptional Children, 43,* 6–13.

Luckner, J. L., & Bowen, S. K. (2010). Teachers' use and perceptions of progress monitoring. *American Annals of the Deaf, 155,* 397–405.

Madaus, J. W., & Shaw, S. F. (2006). The impact of the IDEA 2004 on transition to college for students with learning disabilities. *Learning Disabilities Practice, 21,* 273–281.

Mazzotti, V. L., Test, D. W., & Mustian, A. L. (2014). Secondary transition evidence-based practices and predictors: Implications for policymakers. *Journal of Disability Policy Studies, 25,* 5–18.

Muller, E., & Burdette, P. (2007). Highly qualified teachers and special education: Several state approaches. *In Forum,* 1–10. Washington, DC: Project Forum, National Association of State Directors of Special Education.

National Dissemination Center for Children with Disabilities (NICHCY). (n.d.). *The basic special education process under IDEA 2004.* Retrieved from http://www.parentcenterhub.org/wp-content/uploads/repo_items/10steps.pdf

PEAK Parent Center. (n.d.). *Accommodations & modifications fact sheet.* Retrieved from https://www.osepideasthatwork.org/parentkit/peak_factsheet.asp

Ryder, R. (2016, February 1). *OSEP leadership update.* Presentation at the 2016 OSEP Virtual Leadership Conference.

Suter, J. C., & Giangreco, M. F. (2009). Numbers that count: Exploring special education and paraprofessional service delivery in inclusion-oriented schools. *Journal of Special Education, 43,* 81–93.

Test, D. W., Mazzotti, V. L., Mustian, A. L., Fowler, C. H., Kortering, L., & Kohler, P. (2009). Evidence-based secondary transition predictors for improving postschool outcomes for students with disabilities. *Career Development for Exceptional Individuals, 32,* 160–181.

Twachtman-Cullen, D., & Twachtman-Bassett, J. (2011). *The IEP from A to Z: How to create meaningful and measurable goals and objectives.* San Francisco, CA: Jossey-Bass.

U.S. Congress. *Americans with Disabilities Act of 1990.* Pub. L. No. 101-336, 104 STAT. 327.

U.S. Congress. *Assistive Technology Act of 2004.* Pub. L. No. 108-364, 118 STAT. 1707.

U.S. Congress. *Education for All Handicapped Children Act (EHA).* Pub. L. No. 94-142.

U.S. Congress. *Education for All Handicapped Children Act (EHA)* (reauthorized). Pub. L. No. 99-457.

U.S. Congress. *Elementary and Secondary Education Act.* Pub. L. No. 107-110.

U.S. Congress. *Every Student Succeeds Act.* Pub. L. No. 114-95.

U.S. Congress. *Higher Education Opportunity Act (HEOA).* Pub. L. No. 110-315.

U.S. Congress. *Individuals with Disabilities Education Act.* Pub. L. No. 101-476.

U.S. Congress. *Individuals with Disabilities Education Act.* Pub. L. No. 105-17, 111 STAT. 37.

U.S. Congress. *Individuals with Disabilities Education Improvement Act of 2004.* Pub. L. No. 108-446. 118 STAT. 2647.

U.S. Congress. *Rehabilitation Act of 1973, Section 504,* 19 U.S.C. section 794.

U.S. Department of Education. (2002). *The twenty-fourth annual report to Congress on the implementation of IDEA.* Washington, DC: U.S. Government Printing Office.

U.S. Department of Education. (2006, August 14). 34 CFR Parts 300 and 301, Assistance to States for the Education of Children with

Disabilities and Preschool Grants for Children with Disabilities: Final Rule (pp. 1263–1264), *Federal Register*, Washington, DC.

U.S. Department of Education, Office for Civil Rights. (2012). *Questions and answers on the ADA Amendments Act of 2008 for students with disabilities attending public elementary and secondary schools.* Retrieved from http://www2.ed.gov/about/offices/list/ocr/docs/dcl-504faq-201109.html

U.S. Department of Education, Office of Special Education Programs, Data Analysis System (DANS). (2012). *Children with disabilities receiving special education under Part B of the Individuals with Disabilities Education Act-2011.* Data updated as of July 15, 2012. Retrieved from www.ideadata.org

U.S. Department of Education, Office of Special Education and Rehabilitation Services. (2015, November 16). *Clarification of individualized education programs and state academic content standards.* (Departmental letter). Washington, DC: Author. Retrieved from http://www2.ed.gov/policy/speced/guid/idea/memosdcltrs/guidance-on-fape-11-17-2015.pdf

U.S. Department of Education, Office of Special Education and Rehabilitative Services, Office of Special Education Programs. (2015). *The thirty-seventh annual report to Congress on the implementation of the Individuals with Disabilities Education Act, 2015.* Washington, DC: U.S. Government Printing Office.

U.S. Department of Education, OSEP, Data Analysis Systems (DANS). (2012). *Implementation of FAPE requirements* 2011, OMB#1820-0517: Part B, IDEA. Retrieved from www.ideadata.org

U.S. Department of Health and Human Services & U.S. Department of Education. (2015, September 14). *Policy statement on the inclusion of children with disabilities in early childhood programs.* Washington, DC: Author. Retrieved from http://www2.ed.gov/policy/speced/guid/earlylearning/joint-statement-full-text.pdf

Wright, P., Wright, P., & O'Connor, S. (2010). *Wrightslaw: All about IEPs.* Hartfield, VA: Harbor House Law Press.

Zand, D. H., Pierce, K. J., Bultas, M. W., McMillin, S. E., Gott, R. M., & Wilmott, J. (2015). Accuracy of knowledge of child development in mothers of children receiving early intervention services. *Journal of Early Intervention, 37,* 226–240.

Zarate, M. E. (2007). *Understanding Latino parental involvement in education: Perceptions, expectations, and recommendations.* Los Angeles, CA: University of Southern California, Tomás Rivera Policy Institute.

Zirkel, P. (2015). Special education law: Illustrative basics and nuances of key IDEA components. *Teacher Education and Special Education, 38,* 263–275.

Chapter 5

Akamoglu, Y., & Dinnebeil, L. (2015). Coaching parents to use naturalistic language and communication strategies. *Young Exceptional Children.* 1–10. doi: 10.1177/1096250615598815

Allen, M. M., Ukrainetz, T. A., & Carswell, A. L. (2012). The narrative language performance of three types of at-risk first-grade readers. *Language, Speech, and Hearing Services in Schools, 43,* 205–221.

American Psychiatric Association. (2013). *Diagnostic and statistical manual of mental disorders* (5th ed.). Arlington, VA: American Psychiatric Association.

American Speech-Hearing-Language Association. (1993). Definitions of communication disorders and variations, *ASHA, 5* (Suppl. 10), 40–41.

American-Speech-Language-Hearing Association. (n.d.). *Stuttering: Causes and number.* Retrieved from www.asha.org/public/speech/disorders/StutteringCauses.htm

American-Speech-Language-Hearing Association. (n.d.). *Social language use (pragmatics).* Retrieved from www.asha.org/public/speech/development/Pragmatics/

American Speech-Hearing-Language Association (ASHA). (2008). *The ASHA leader online: Facts about cleft lip and palate.* Retrieved from www.asha.org

American Speech-Hearing-Language Association (ASHA). (2012). *Quick facts.* Retrieved from www.asha.org/quickfacts.htm

Anderson, N. B., & Shames, G. H. (2011). *Human communication disorders: An introduction* (8th ed.). Boston, MA: Pearson Education, Inc.

Bakken, J. P., & Whedon, C. K. (2002). Teaching text structure to improve reading comprehension. *Intervention in School and Clinic, 37,* 229–233.

Bauman-Waengler, J. (2012). *Articulatory and phonological impairments: A clinical focus* (4th ed.). Boston, MA: Pearson Education, Inc.

Bernthal, J. E., & Bankson, N. W. (2004). *Articulation and phonological disorders* (5th ed.). Boston, MA: Allyn & Bacon.

Blackorby, J., Wagner, M., Cadwallader, T., Cameto, R., Levine, P., & Marder, C., with Giacaione, P. (2002). *Behind the label: The functional implications of disability.* Menlo Park, CA: SEELS Project, SRI International.

Blank, M., Rose, S. A., & Berlin, L. J. (1978). *The language of learning: The preschool years.* New York, NY: Grune & Stratton.

Boulineau, T., Fore, C., III, Hagan-Burke, S., & Burke, M. D. (2004). Use of story-mapping to increase the story-grammar text comprehension of elementary students with learning disabilities. *Learning Disability Quarterly, 27,* 105–121.

Brandel, J., & Loeb, D. F. (2011). Program intensity and service delivery models in the schools: SLP survey results. *Language, Speech, and Hearing Services in Schools, 42,* 461–490.

Bremer, C. D., Vaughn, S., Clapper, A. T., & Kim, A. (2002). Collaborative strategic reading (CSR): Improving secondary students' reading comprehension skills. *Improving Secondary Education and Transition Services through Research, 1,* 1–7.

Brown, J. A., & Woods, J. J. (2016). Parent-implemented communication intervention: Sequential analysis of triadic relationships. *Topics in Early Childhood Special Education.* 1–10. doi: 10.1177/0271121416628200

Carbone, N. (2011, May 8). Life imitates art: Colin Firth struggles to shake *King's Speech* stammer. Retrieved from http://newsfeed.time.com/2011/05/08/life-imitates-art-colin-firth-struggles-to-shake-kings-speech-stammer/

Compton, D. L. (2002). The relationship between phonological processing, orthographic processing, and lexical development in reading-disabled children. *Journal of Special Education, 35,* 201–210.

Connor, D. J. (2012). Helping students with disabilities transition to college: 21 tips for students with LD and/or ADD/ADHD. *Teaching Exceptional Children, 44,* 17–25.

Conti-Ramsden, G., Durkin, K., Simkin, Z., & Knox, E. (2009). Specific language impairment and school outcomes. I: Identifying and explaining variability at the end of compulsory education. *International Journal of Language & Communication Disorders, 44,* 15–35.

Conture, E. G. (2001). Stuttering: Its nature, diagnosis, and treatment. Boston, MA: Allyn & Bacon.

Culatta, B., & Wiig, E. H. (2006). Language disabilities in school-age children and youth. In N. B. Anderson & G. H. Shames (Eds.), *Human communication disorders: An introduction* (7th ed., pp. 352–358). Boston, MA: Allyn & Bacon.

Dockrell, J. E., Lindsay, G., Connelly, V., & Mackie, C. (2007). Constraints in the production of written text in children with specific language impairments. *Exceptional Children, 73*(2), 147–164.

Durkin, K., Simkin, Z., Knox, E., & Conti-Ramsden, G. (2009). Specific language impairment and school outcomes. II: Educational context, student satisfaction, and post-compulsory progress. *International Journal of Language & Communication Disorders, 44,* 36–55.

Ely, R. (2005). Language and literacy in the schools. In J. B. Gleason (Ed.), *The development of language* (6th ed.). Boston, MA: Allyn & Bacon.

Falk-Ross, F. C. (2002). *Classroom-based language and literacy intervention: A programs and case studies approach.* Boston, MA: Allyn & Bacon.

Farnsworth, M. (2016). Differentiating second language acquisition from specific learning disability: An observational tool assessing dual language learners' pragmatic competence. *Young Exceptional Children.* 1–18. doi: 10.1177/1096250615621356

Fletcher, J. M., Lyon, G. R., Barnes, M., Stuebing, K. K., Francis, D. J., Olson, R. K., Shaywitz, S. E., & Shaywitz, B. A. (2002). Classifications of learning disabilities: An evidence-based evaluation. In R. Bradley, L. Danielson, & D. P. Hallahan (Eds.), *Identification of learning disabilities: Research to practice* (pp. 185–250). Mahwah, NJ: Erlbaum.

Fuchs, D., & Fuchs, L. S. (2005). *Response to intervention (RTI): Preventing and identifying LD.* Nashville, TN: Vanderbilt University, video conference presentation to the New York City School System.

Georgia Project for Assistive Technology. (n.d.). Supporting participation in typical classroom activities for students with disabilities through the use of accommodations, modifications, and assistive technology solutions. Retrieved from http://atto.buffalo.edu/registered/DecisionMaking/resourceroom-docs/GPATparticipation.pdf

Gerber, S., Brice, A., Capone, N., Fujiki, M., & Timler, G. (2012). Language use in social interactions of school-age children with language impairments: An evidence-based systematic review of treatment. *Language, Speech, and Hearing Services in Schools, 43,* 235–249.

Gleason, J. B. (2009). The development of language: An overview and a preview. In J. B. Gleason & N. B. Ratner (Eds.), *The development of language* (7th ed.). Boston, MA: Pearson Education, Inc.

Grames, L. M. (2008). Advancing Into the 21st century: Care for individuals with cleft palate or craniofacial differences. *The ASHA Leader, 13,* 10–13. Retrieved from http://leader.pubs.asha.org/article.aspx?articleid=2342996

Gregory, J. H., Campbell, J. H., Gregory, C. B., & Hill, D. G. (2003). Stuttering therapy: Rationale and procedures. Boston, MA: Allyn & Bacon.

Hager, E. M. (2012, July 25). For children who cannot speak, a true voice via technology. *New York Times.* Retrieved from www.nytimes.com/2012/07/26/technology/evolving-technology-gives-true-voices-to-children-who-cannot-speak.html?_r=1&emc=eta1

Hall, B. J., Oyer, J. J., & Haas, W. H. (2001). *Speech, language, and hearing disorders: A guide for the teacher* (3rd ed.). Boston, MA: Allyn & Bacon.

Harwood, L., Warren, S. F., & Yoder, P. (2002). The importance of responsivity in developing contingent exchanges with beginning communicators. In J. Reichle, D. R. Beukelman, & J. C. Light (Eds.), *Exemplary practices for beginning communicators: Implications for ACC* (pp. 59–96). Baltimore, MD: Paul H. Brookes.

Horton, S. V., Lovitt, T. C., & Bergerud, D. (1990). The effectiveness of graphic organizers for three classifications of secondary students in content area classes. *Journal of Learning Disabilities, 23,* 12–22, 29.

Inspiration Software, Inc. (© 2012). *Inspiration®.* Portland, OR: Author.

Inspiration Software, Inc. (© 2012). *Kidspiration®.* Portland, OR: Author.

IRIS Center for Training Enhancements. (2006). *Improving writing performance: A strategy for writing persuasive essays.* Retrieved from http://iris.peabody.vanderbilt.edu/module/pow/

IRIS Center. (2008). *CSR: A reading comprehension strategy.* Retrieved from http://iris.peabody.vanderbilt.edu/module/csr/

IRIS Center for Training Enhancements. (2011). *Related services: Common supports for students with disabilities.* Retrieved from http://iris.peabody.vanderbilt.edu/module/rs/

Ives, B., & Hoy, C. (2003). Graphic organizers applied to higher-level secondary mathematics. *Learning Disabilities Practice, 18,* 36–51.

Jenkins, J. R., & O'Connor, R. E. (2002). Early identification and intervention for young children with reading/learning disabilities. In R. Bradley, L. Danielson, & D. P. Hallahan (Eds.), *Identification of learning disabilities: Research to practice* (pp. 99–149). Mahwah, NJ: Erlbaum.

Justice, L. M. (2004). Creating language-rich preschool classroom environments. *Teaching Exceptional Children, 37,* 36–44.

Kaderavek, J. N. (2011). *Language disorders in children: Fundamental concepts of assessment and intervention.* Boston, MA: Pearson Education, Inc.

Kangas, K. A., & Lloyd, L. L. (2006). Augmentative and alternative communication. In G. H. Shames & N. B. Anderson (Eds.), *Human communication disorders: An introduction* (7th ed., pp. 436–470). Boston, MA: Allyn & Bacon.

Klingner, J., & Eppolito, A. M. (2014). *English language learners: Differentiating between language acquisition and learning disabilities.* Arlington, VA: Council for Exceptional Children.

Klingner, J. K., Vaughn, S., Hughes, M. T., Schumm, J. S., & Elbaum, B. (1998). Outcomes for students with and without learning disabilities in inclusive classrooms, *Learning Disabilities Research & Practice, 13*(3), 153–161.

Klingner, J. K., Vaughn, S., & Schumm, J. S. (1998). Collaborative strategic reading during social studies in heterogeneous fourth-grade classrooms. *Elementary School Journal, 99*(1), 3–22.

Kuder, J. S. (2008). *Teaching students with language and communication disabilities* (3rd ed.). Boston, MA: Pearson Education, Inc.

Lane, J. D., Gast, C. S., & Ledford, J. R. (2015). Including social opportunities during small group instruction of preschool children with social-communication delays. *Journal of Early Intervention.* 1–20. doi: 10.1177/1053815115588828

Lederer, S. H. (2015). Teaching children with language delays to say or sign more: Promises and potential pitfalls. *Young Exceptional Children.* 1–15. doi: 10.1177/1096250615621358

Lessow-Hurley, J. (2005). *The foundations of dual language instruction.* (4th ed.). Boston, MA: Pearson Education, Inc.

Levy, G. (2011, January 13). Stuttering versus cluttering: What's the difference? *ASHAsphere.* Retrieved from http://blog.asha.org/2011/01/13/stuttering-versus-cluttering-whats-the-difference/

Maugh, T. H., II. (1995, August 11). Study finds folic acid cuts risk of cleft palate. *Los Angeles Times,* A20.

Mazzotti, V. L., Test, D. W., & Mustian, A. L. (2014). Secondary transition evidence-based practices and predictors: Implications for policymakers. *Journal of Disability Policy Studies, 25,* 5–18.

McCormick, L. (2003). Language intervention and support. In L. McCormick, D. R. Loeb, & R. L. Schiefelbusch (Eds.), *Supporting children with communication difficulties in inclusive settings: School-based language intervention.* Boston, MA: Allyn & Bacon.

Melzi, G., & Ely, R. (2009). Language and literacy in the school years. In J. B. Gleason & N. B. Ratner (Eds.), *The development of language* (7th ed.). Boston, MA: Pearson Education, Inc.

Menn, L., & Stoel-Gammon, C. (2009). Phonological development: Learning sounds and sound patterns. In J. B. Gleason & N. B. Ratner (Eds.), *The development of language* (7th ed.). Boston, MA: Pearson Education, Inc.

Moore, G. P., & Kester, D. (1953). Historical notes on speech correction in the preassociation era. *Journal of Speech and Hearing Disorders, 18,* 48–53.

National Center on Educational Outcomes. (n.d.). *Reading and students with speech or language impairments.* Retrieved from http://www.cehd.umn.edu/NCEO/onlinepubs/PARA/readingandspeech/index.htm

National Secondary Transition Technical Assistance Center. (n.d.). *Improving post-school education outcomes: Evidence-based secondary transition predictors.* Retrieved from www.nsttac.org/sites/default/files/assets/pdf/FactSheetEducation081909.pdf

Nelson, N. W. (2010). *Language and literacy disorders: Infancy through adolescence.* Boston: Allyn & Bacon.

Nippold, M. A. (2012). Different service delivery models for different communication disorders. *Language, Speech, and Hearing Services in Schools, 43,* 117–120.

Norris, J. A., & Hoffman, P. R. (2002). Phonemic awareness: A complex developmental process. *Topics in Language Disorders, 22,* 1–34.

Olswang, L. B., Coggins, T. E., & Timler, G. R. (2001). Outcome measures for school-age children with social communication problems. *Topics in Language Disorders, 21,* 50–73.

Operation Smile. (n.d.). *Operation Smile: Global need & impact.* Retrieved from http://operationsmile.org/sites/default/files/Operation%20Smile%20Global%20Need%20%26%20Impact.pdf

Owens, R. E., Jr. (2006). Development of communication, language, and speech. In N. B. Anderson & G. H. Shames (Eds.), *Human communication disorders: An introduction* (7th ed., pp. 25–58). Boston, MA: Allyn & Bacon.

Owens, R. E., Jr., Metz, D. E., & Farinella, K. A. (2011). *Introduction to communication disorders: A life span evidence-based perspective* (4th ed.). Boston, MA: Pearson Education, Inc.

Pan, B. A. (2005). Semantic development: Learning the meanings of words. In J. B. Gleason (Ed.), *The development of language* (6th ed.). Boston, MA: Allyn & Bacon.

Paul, R., & Roth, F. P. (2011). Characterizing and predicting outcomes of communication delays in infants and toddlers: Implications for clinical practice. *Language, Speech, and Hearing Services in Schools, 42,* 331–340.

Payne, K. T., & Taylor, O. L. (2006). Multicultural influences on human communication. In N. B. Anderson and G. H. Shames (Eds.), *Human communication disorders: An introduction* (7th ed., pp. 93–125). Boston, MA: Allyn & Bacon.

Plante, E., & Beeson, P. M. (2008). *Communication and communication disorders: A clinical introduction* (3rd ed.). Boston, MA: Pearson Education, Inc.

Rahn, N. L., Coogle, C. G., & Storie, S. (2016). Preschool children's use of thematic vocabulary during dialogic reading and activity-based intervention. *Journal of Special Education. 1–11.* doi: 10.1177 /0022466915622202

Ramig, P. R., & Shames, G. H. (2006). Stuttering and other disorders of fluency. In N. B. Anderson and G. H. Shames (Eds.), *Human communication disorders: An introduction* (7th ed., pp. 183–221). Boston, MA: Allyn & Bacon.

Ratner, N. B. (2009). Atypical language development. In J. B. Gleason & N. B. Ratner (Eds.), *The development of language* (7th ed.). Boston, MA: Pearson Education, Inc.

Redmond, S. M. (2011). Peer victimization among students with specific language impairment, attention-deficit/hyperactivity disorder, and typical development. *Language, Speech, and Hearing Services in Schools, 42,* 520–535.

Reed, V. A. (2012). *An introduction to children with language disorders* (4th ed.). Boston, MA: Pearson Education, Inc.

Roberts, J. E., & Zeisel, S. A. (2002). *Ear infections and language development.* Washington, DC: U.S. Department of Education and American Speech-Language-Hearing Association.

Robinson, N. B. (2003). Families: The first communication partners. In L. McCormick, D. R. Loeb, & R. L. Schiefelbusch (Eds.), *Supporting children with communication difficulties in inclusive settings: School-based language intervention.* Boston, MA: Allyn & Bacon.

Rock, M. L. (2004). Graphic organizers: Tools to build behavioral literacy and foster emotional competency. *Intervention in School and Clinic, 40,* 10–18.

Roth, C., Magnus, P., Schjølberg, S., Stoltenberg, C., Surén, P., McKeague, I. W., Davey Smith, G., Reichborn-Kjennerud, T., & Susser, E. (2011). Folic acid supplements in pregnancy and severe language delay in children. *Journal of the American Medical Association, 306,* 1566–1573.

Salend, S. J. (2005). *Creating inclusive classrooms: Effective and reflective practices for all students* (5th ed.). Columbus, OH: Merrill/Prentice-Hall.

Salend, S. J., & Salinas, A. (2003). Language differences or learning difficulties: The work of the multidisciplinary team. *Teaching Exceptional Children, 35,* 35–43.

Sander, E. K. (1972). When are speech sounds learned? *Journal of Speech and Hearing Disorders, 37,* 62.

Small, L. H. (2005). *Fundamentals of phonetics: A practical guide for students* (2nd ed.). Boston, MA: Allyn & Bacon.

Stanton-Chapman, T. L., & Brown, T. S. (2015). Facilitating commenting and requesting skills in 3-year-old children with disabilities. *Journal of Early Intervention, 37,* 103–118.

Starling, J., Munro, N., Togher, L., & Arciuli, J. (2012). Training secondary school teachers in instructional language modification techniques to support adolescents with language impairment: A randomized controlled trial. *Language, Speech, and Hearing Services in Schools, 43,* 474–495.

Sunderland, L. C. (2004). Speech, language, and audiology services in public schools. *Intervention in School and Clinic, 39,* 209–217.

U.S. National Park Service. (n.d.). *A Trail of Tears Reading 3: "Every Cherokee man, woman, and child must be in motion …."* Retrieved from www.nps.gov/history/nr/twhp/wwwlps/lessons/118trail /118facts3.htm

U.S. Department of Education, Office of Special Education Programs, Data Analysis System (DANS). (2012). *Children with disabilities receiving special education under Part B of the Individuals with Disabilities Education Act-2011.* Data updated as of July 15, 2012. Retrieved from www.ideadata.org

U.S. Department of Education. (2015). *Child count and educational environments.* [IDEA Section 618 Data Products: State Level Data Files.] Retrieved from http://www2.ed.gov/programs/osepidea/618-data /state-level-data-files/index.html#bccee

Utley, C. A., & Obiakor, F. (Eds.). (2001). *Special education, multicultural education, and school reform: Components of quality education for learners with mild disabilities.* Springfield, IL: Charles C Thomas Publisher.

Van Riper, C., & Erickson, R. L. (1996). *Speech correction: An introduction to speech pathology and audiology* (9th ed.). Boston, MA: Allyn & Bacon.

Vaughn, S., Bos, C. S., & Schumm, J. S. (2007). *Teaching exceptional, diverse, and at-risk students in the general education classroom* (4th ed). Boston, MA: Pearson Education, Inc.

Vaughn, S., Klingner, J. K., & Bryant, D. (2001). Collaborative strategic reading as a means to enhance peer-mediated instruction for reading comprehension and content-area learning. *Remedial and Special Education, 22*(2), 66–74.

Vaughn, S., Klingner, J. K., Swanson, E. A., Boardman, A. G., Roberts, G., Mohammed, S. S., & Stillman-Spisak, S. J. (2011). Efficacy of Collaborative Strategic Reading strategy with middle school students. *American Educational Research Journal, 48,* 938–964.

Vaughn, S., & Linan-Thompson, S. (2004). *Research-based methods of reading instruction: Grades K–3.* Alexandria, VA: Association for Supervision and Curriculum Development.

Wagner, M., Newman, L., Cameto, R., Garza, N., & Levin, P. (2005). *After high school: A first look at the postschool experiences of youth with disabilities. A report from the National Longitudinal Transition Study-2* (NLTS2). Menlo Park, CA: SRI International.

Wellman, R. L., Lewis, B. A., Freebairn, L. A., Avrich, A. A., Hansen, A. J., & Stein, C. M. (2011). Narrative ability of children with speech sound disorders and the prediction of later literacy skills. *Language, Speech, and Hearing Services in Schools, 42,* 561–579.

Wetherby, A. M. (2002). Communication disorders in infants, toddlers, and preschool children. In G. H. Shames & N. B. Anderson (Eds.), *Human communication disorders: An introduction* (6th ed., pp. 186–217). Boston, MA: Allyn & Bacon.

Wright, C. A., & Kaiser, A. P. (2016). Teaching parents enhanced milieu teaching with words and signs using the Teach-Model-Coach-Review Model. *Topics in Early Childhood Special Education.* 1–13. doi: 10.1177 /0271121415621027

Chapter 6

Al Otaiba, S., Folsom, J. S., Schatschneider, C., Wanzek, J., Greulich, L., Meadows, J., Li, Z., & Connor C. M. (2011). Predicting first-grade reading performance from Kindergarten response to Tier 1 instruction. *Exceptional Children, 77,* 453–470.

American Psychiatric Association. (2013). *Diagnostic and statistical manual of mental disorders,* 5th ed. Arlington, VA: American Psychiatric Association.

Backenson, E. M., Holland, S. C., Kubas, H. A., Fitzer, K. R., Wilcox, G., Carmichael, J. A., Fraccaro, R. L., Smith, A. D., Macoun, S. J., Harrison, G. L., & Hale, J. B. (2015). Psychosocial and adaptive deficits associated with learning disability subtypes. *Journal of Learning Disabilities, 48,* 511–522.

Baker, S. K., Chard, D. J., Ketterlin-Geller, L. R., Apichatabutra, C., & Doabler, C. (2009). Teaching writing to at-risk students: The quality of evidence for self-regulated strategy development. *Exceptional Children, 75,* 303–318.

Boudah, D. J., & O'Neill, K. J. (1999). *Learning strategies.* Reston, VA: ERIC Clearinghouse of Disabilities and Gifted Education. (ERIC No. ED433669)

Bridges, M. S., & Catts, H. W. (2011). The use of a dynamic screening of phonological awareness to predict risk for reading disabilities in Kindergarten children. *Journal of Learning Disabilities, 44,* 330–338.

Brown, J. E., & Sanford, A. (2011, March). *RTI for English language learners: Appropriately using screening and progress monitoring tools to improve instructional outcomes.* Washington, DC: U.S. Department of Education, Office of Special Education Programs, National Center on Response to Intervention.

Bryan, T. (1974). Peer popularity of learning disabled children. *Journal of Learning Disabilities, 7,* 621–625.

Bryan, T., Burstein, K., & Ergul, C. (2004). The social-emotional side of learning disabilities: A science-based presentation of the state of the art. *Learning Disability Quarterly, 27*, 45–51.

Bryant, B. R., Bryant, D. P., Kethley, C., Kim, S. A., Pool, C., & Seo, Y.-U. (2008). Preventing mathematics difficulties in the primary grades: The critical features of instruction in textbooks as part of the equation. *Learning Disabilities Quarterly, 31*, 21–36.

Bryant, D. P. (2005). Commentary on early identification and intervention for students with mathematics disabilities. *Journal of Learning Disabilities, 38*, 340–345.

Bryant, D. P., & Bryant, B. R. (2008). Introduction to the special series: Mathematics and learning disabilities. *Learning Disabilities Quarterly, 31*, 3–8.

Bryant, D. P., Bryant, B. R., & Smith, D. D. (2017). *Teaching students with special needs in inclusive classrooms.* Thousand Oaks, CA: Sage Publications, Inc.

Bui, Y., Schumaker, J. B., & Deshler, D. D. (2006). The effects of a strategic writing program for students with and without learning disabilities in inclusive fifth-grade classes. *Learning Disabilities Research & Practice, 21*, 244–260.

Burr, E., Haas, E., & Ferriere, K. (2015). *Identifying and supporting English learner students with learning disabilities: Key issues in the literature and state practice* (REL 2015–086). Washington, DC: U.S. Department of Education, Institute of Education Sciences, National Center for Education Evaluation and Regional Assistance, Regional Educational Laboratory West. Retrieved from: http://ies.ed.gov/ncee/edlabs

Butterworth, B., Varma, S., & Laurillard, D. (2011, November 11). Dyscalculia: From brain to education (corrected version). *Science, 332*, 1049–1052.

Cavendish, W. (2013). Identification of learning disabilities: Implications of DSM-5 criteria for school-based assessment. *Journal of Learning Disabilities, 46*, 52–57.

Centers for Disease Control. (2014, April). *Alcohol use and pregnancy.* Retrieved from http://www.cdc.gov/ncbddd/fasd/alcohol-use.html

Centers for Disease Control. (2015, September). *Tobacco use and pregnancy.* Retrieved from http://www.cdc.gov/reproductivehealth/MaternalInfantHealth/TobaccoUsePregnancy/index.htm

Centers for Disease Control. (2015, December). *Pregnant women and influenza (flu).* Retrieved from http://www.cdc.gov/flu/protect/vaccine/pregnant.htm

Chard, D. J., Baker, S. K., Clarke, B., Jungjohann, K., Davis, K., & Smolkowski, K. (2008). Preventing early mathematics difficulties: The feasibility of a rigorous Kindergarten mathematics curriculum. *Learning Disabilities Quarterly, 31*, 11–20.

Clark, K. (2010, December 2). 8 steps for learning disabled students who want to go to college: Diligence, creativity, and resilience can help LD students succeed in college. *U.S. News & World Report.* Retrieved from www.usnews.com/articles/education/best-colleges/2010/12/02/8-steps-for-learning-disbled-students-who-want-to-go-to-college.html

Clemons, T., Igel, C., & Allen, J. (2010). Cues, questions, and advance organizers. In A. D. Beesley & H. S. Apthorp (Eds.), *Classroom instruction that works* (2nd ed., pp. 130–139). Denver, CO: Mid-continent Research for Education and Learning (McREL). Retrieved from ERIC database. (ED543521)

Compton, D. L., Fuchs, L. S., Fuchs, D., Lambert, W., & Hamlett, C. (2012). The cognitive and academic profiles of reading and mathematics learning disabilities. *Journal of Learning Disabilities, 45*, 79–95.

Correa, V. (2012). *Discussion of issues related to early childhood and learning disabilities.* Presentation to Education 605: Seminar in Learning Disabilities, Claremont Graduate University. October, 2012.

Cortiella, C. (2005). *No Child Left Behind: Determining appropriate assessment accommodations for students with disabilities.* New York, NY: National Center for Learning Disabilities. Retrieved from http://www.cehd.umn.edu/nceo/onlinepubs/NCLD/Accommodations.pdf.

Cortiella, C., & Horowitz, S. (2014). *The state of learning disabilities: Facts, trends, and emerging issues.* New York: National Center for Learning Disabilities.

Danforth, S. (2011). The actuarial turn in the science of learning disabilities. *Learning Disability Quarterly, 34*, 123–136.

Davidson, H. P. (1934). A study of reversals in young children. *Journal of Genetic Psychology, 45*, 452–465.

Davidson, H. P. (1935). A study of the confusing letters B, D, P, and Q. *Journal of Genetic Psychology, 46*, 458–468.

Davis, J. M., Christo, C., & Husted, D. (2009). Reading fluency and students with learning disabilities: The relationship to test accommodations. *Journal of Learning Disabilities, 15*, 105–120.

Deno, S., & Mirkin, P. (1974, Spring). Data-based instruction: A system for improving learning and preventing reading failure. *Manitoba Journal of Educational Research*, 1.

Deshler, D. (2005, January). A closer look: Closing the performance gap. *StrateNotes, 13*, 1–5.

Deshler, D. D., & Schumaker, J. B. (1986). Learning strategies: An instructional alternative for low-achieving adolescents. *Exceptional Children 52*(6), 583–590.

Dexter, D. D., & Hughes, C. A. (2011). Graphic organizers and students with learning disabilities: A meta-analysis. *Learning Disability Quarterly, 34*, 52–72.

Eaton, M., & Lovitt, T. C. (1972). Achievement tests vs. direct & daily measurement. In G. Semb (Ed.), *Behavior analysis and education: 1972.* Lawrence, KS: University of Kansas, Project Follow Through.

Engaging Technologies. (n.d.). *Livescribe Smartpens.* Retrieved from http://www.engaging-technologies.com/smartpens.html

Englert, C. S. (2009). Connecting the dots in a research program to develop, implement, and evaluate strategic literacy interventions for struggling readers and writers. *Learning Disabilities Research & Practice, 24*, 104–120.

Estell, D. B., Jones, M. H., Pearl, R., & Van Acker, R. (2009). Best friendships of students with and without learning disabilities across late elementary school. *Exceptional Children, 76*, 110–124.

Finn, C. E., Jr., Rotherham, A. J., & Hokanson, C. R. Jr. (Eds.). (2001). Conclusions and principles for reform. In C. E. Finn, Jr., A. J. Rotherham, & C. R. Hokanson, Jr. (Eds.), *Rethinking special education for a new century* (pp. 259–288). Washington, DC: Thomas B. Fordham Foundation and the Progressive Policy Institute.

Foegen, A., Jiban, C., & Deno, S. (2007). Progress monitoring in mathematics. *Journal of Special Education, 41*, 121–139.

Frostig, M. (1978). Five questions regarding my past and future and the past, present, and future of learning disabilities. *Journal of Learning Disabilities, 11*, 9–12.

Fuchs, D., & Deshler, D. D. (2007). What we need to know about responsiveness to intervention (and shouldn't be afraid to ask). *Learning Disabilities Research & Practice, 22*, 129–136.

Fuchs, D., & Young, C. L. (2006). On the irrelevance of intelligence in predicting responsiveness to reading instruction. *Exceptional Children, 73*, 8–30.

Fuchs, D., Fuchs, L. S., & Vaughn, S. R. (Eds.). (2008). *Responsiveness to intervention.* Newark, DE: International Reading Association.

Fuchs, L., Fuchs, D., & Hollenbeck, K. N. (2007). Extending responsiveness to intervention to mathematics at first and third grades. *Learning Disabilities Research & Practice, 22*, 13–24.

Fuchs, L. S., Fuchs, D., & Prentice, K. (2004). Responsiveness to mathematical problem-solving instruction: Comparing students at risk of mathematics disability with and without risk of reading disability. *Journal of Learning Disabilities, 37*, 293–306.

Geary, M. (2004). Mathematics and learning disabilities. *Journal of Learning Disabilities, 37*, 4–15.

Gerber, M. M. (2007). Globalization, human capital, and learning disabilities. *Learning Disabilities Research & Practice, 22*, 216–217.

Graham, S., & Harris, K. R. (2009). Almost 30 years of writing research: Making sense of it all with The Wrath of Khan. *Learning Disabilities Research, 24*, 58–68.

Graham, S., Harris, K. R., & Larsen, L. (2001). Prevention and intervention of writing difficulties for students with learning disabilities. *Learning Disabilities Research & Practice, 16*(2), 74–84.

Graney, S. B., Martinez, R. S., Missal, K. N., & Aricak, O. T. (2011). Universal screening of reading in late elementary school. *Remedial and Special Education, 31*, 368–377.

Graves, A. W., Brandon, R., Duesbery, L., McIntosh, A., & Pyle, N. B. (2011). The effects of tier 2 literacy instruction in sixth grade: Toward the development of a response-to-intervention model in middle school. *Learning Disability Quarterly, 34,* 73–86.

Gresham, F. M., Sugai, G., & Horner, R. H. (2001). Interpreting outcomes of social skills training for students with high-incidence disabilities. *Exceptional Children, 67,* 331–344.

Gresham, F. M., & Vellutino, F. R. (2010). What is the role of intelligence in the identification of specific learning disabilities? Issues and clarifications. *Learning Disabilities Research & Practice, 25,* 194–206.

Hallahan, D. P., Lloyd, J. W., Kauffman, J. M., Weiss, M. P., & Martinez, E. A. (2005). *Learning disabilities: Foundations, characteristics, and effective teaching* (3rd ed.). Boston, MA: Allyn & Bacon.

Hamblet, E. C. (2014). Nine strategies to improve college transition planning for students with disabilities. *Teaching Exceptional Children, 46,* 53–59.

Hammill, D. D. (1990). On defining learning disabilities: An emerging consensus. *Journal of Learning Disabilities, 23,* 74–84.

Hammill, D. D. (2004). What we know about the correlates of reading. *Exceptional Children, 70,* 453–468.

Hammill, D. D., & Larsen, S. (1974). The effectiveness of psycholinguistic abilities. *Exceptional Children, 41,* 5–14.

Haring, N. G. (1978). *The fourth R: Research in the classroom.* Columbus, OH: Merrill.

Harris, K. R., Graham, S., Mason, L., & Friedlander, B. (2008). *Every child can write: Educators' guide to powerful writing strategies.* Baltimore, MD: Brookes.

Hong, B. S. S., Ivy, F. W., Gonzalez, H. R., & Ehrensberger, W. (2007). Preparing students for postsecondary education. *Teaching Exceptional Children, 40,* 32–88.

Hott, B. L., Isbell, L., & Montani, T. O. (2014). *Strategies and interventions to support students with mathematics disabilities.* Council for Learning Disabilities. Retrieved from http://www.council-for-learning-disabilities.org/wp-content/uploads/2014/12/Math_Disabilities_Support.pdf

Impecoven-Lind, L. S., & Foegen, A. (2010). Teaching algebra to students with learning disabilities. *Intervention in School and Clinic, 46,* 31–37.

IRIS Center. (2006). *Improving writing performance: A strategy for writing persuasive essays.* Retrieved from http://iris.peabody.vanderbilt.edu/module/pow/

IRIS Center. (2008). *SRSD: Using learning strategies to enhance student learning.* Retrieved from http://iris.peabody.vanderbilt.edu/module/srs/

IRIS Center. (2009). *Universal design for learning: Creating a learning environment that challenges and engages all students.* Retrieved from http://iris.peabody.vanderbilt.edu/udl/

IRIS Center. (2013). *Study skills strategies (part 2): Strategies that improve students' academic performance.* Retrieved from http://iris.peabody.vanderbilt.edu/module/ss2/

Jamgochian, E. M., & Ketterlin-Geller, L. R. (2015). The 2% transition: Supporting access to state assessments for students with disabilities. *TEACHING Exceptional Children, 48*(1), 28–35.

Jenkins, J., & Terjeson, K. J. (2011). Monitoring reading growth: Goal setting, measurement frequency, and methods of evaluation. *Learning Disabilities Research & Practice, 26,* 28–35.

Johnson, D. R., Mellard, D. F., & Lancaster, P. (2007). Helping young adults with learning disabilities plan and prepare for employment. *Teaching Exceptional Children, 39,* 26–32.

Jones, D. (2003, November 10). Charles Schwab didn't let dyslexia stop him. *USA Today,* p. B-5.

Kato, M. M., Nulty, B. N., Olszewski, B. T., Doolittle, J., & Flannery, K. B. (2007). Helping students with disabilities transition to college. *Teaching Exceptional Children, 39,* 18–23.

Kavale, K. A. (2005). Effective intervention for students with specific learning disability: The nature of special education. *Learning Disabilities, 13,* 127–138.

Kavale, K. A., & Mostert, M. P. (2004). Social skills interventions for individuals with learning disabilities. *Learning Disability Quarterly, 27,* 31–43.

Kephart, N. (1960). *The slow learner in the classroom.* Columbus, OH: Merrill.

Kirk, S. A. (1977). Specific learning disabilities. *Journal of Clinical Child Psychology, 6,* 23–26.

Kirk, S. A., McCarthy, J. J., & Kirk, W. D. (1968). *Illinois test of psycholinguistic abilities* (ITPA). Champaign-Urbana, IL: University of Illinois Press.

Kovaleski, J. F., & Prasse, D. P. (2004). Response to instruction in the identification of learning disabilities: A guide for school teams. *Helping Children at Home and School II: Handouts for Families and Educators* (S8-159). Retrieved from www.nasponline.org

Lafay, A., St-Pierre, M., & Macoir, J. (2016). The mental number line in dyscalculia: Impaired number sense or access from symbolic numbers? *Journal of Learning Disabilities, 1–12.* doi: 10.1177/0022219416640783

Legere, E. J., & Conca, L. M. (2010). Response to intervention by a child with a severe reading disability: A case study. *Teaching Exceptional Children, 43,* 32–39.

Lienemann, T. O., Graham, S., Leader-Janssen, B., & Reid, R. (2006). Improving the writing performance of struggling writers in second grade. *Journal of Special Education, 40,* 66–78.

Lindsley, O. (1990). Precision teaching: By teachers for children. *Teaching Exceptional Children, 22,* 32–37.

Lindstrom, J. H. (2010). Mathematics assessment accommodations: Implications of differential boost for students with learning disabilities. *Intervention in School and Clinic 46*(1), 5–12. Retrieved from http://isc.sagepub.com/content/46/1/5.full.pdf

Lissner, S. L. (2006). *Transition to college: Strategic planning to ensure success for students with learning disabilities.* National Center for Learning Disabilities: Parent Policy Brief. Retrieved from www.LD.org

Lovitt, T. C. (1977). *In spite of my resistance: I've learned from children.* Columbus, OH: Merrill.

Lovitt, T. C. (2007). *Promoting school success* (3rd ed.). Austin, TX: Pro-Ed.

Lovitt, T. C. (2010). Tom Lovitt: Reflections on a career and the field of learning disabilities. *Intervention in School and Clinic, 46,* 54–59.

Lovitt, T. C., & Hansen, C. (1978). The use of contingent skipping and frilling to improve oral reading and comprehension. *Journal of Learning Disabilities, 9,* 481–487.

Lyon, G. R., Fletcher, J. M., Shaywitz, S. E., Shaywitz, B. A., Torgesen, J. K., Wood, F. B., Schulte, A., & Olson, R. (2001). Rethinking learning disabilities. In C. E. Finn, Jr., A. J. Rotherham, & C. R. Hokanson, Jr. (Eds.), *Rethinking special education for a new century* (pp. 259–288). Washington, DC: Thomas B. Fordham Foundation and the Progressive Policy Institute.

Madaus, J. W., & Shaw, S. F. (2006). The impact of the IDEA 2004 on transition to college for students with learning disabilities. *Learning Disabilities Research & Practice, 21,* 273–281.

Madaus, J. W., & Shaw, S. F. (2010). College as a realistic option for students with learning disabilities. Council for Learning Disabilities. Retrieved from http://www.council-for-learning-disabilities.org/college-as-a-realistic-option-for-students-with-learning-disabilities

Madaus, J. W., Zhao, J., & Ruban, L. (2008). Employment satisfaction of university graduates with learning disabilities. *Remedial and Special Education, 29,* 323–332.

McFarland, L., Williams, J., & Miciak, J. (2013). Ten years of research: A systematic review of three refereed LD journals. *Learning Disabilities Research & Practice, 28,* 60–69.

McLeskey, J., Kanders, E., Hoppey, D., & Williamson, P. (2011). Learning disabilities and the LRE mandate: An examination of national and state trends. *Learning Disabilities Research & Practice, 26,* 60–66.

McLeskey, J., & Waldron, N. L. (2011). Educational programs for elementary students with learning disabilities: Can they be both effective and inclusive? *Learning Disabilities Research & Practice, 26,* 48–57.

McMaster, K., & Espin, C. (2007). Technical features of curriculum-based measurement in writing: A literature review. *Journal of Special Education, 41,* 68–84.

Mellard, D., McKnight, M., & Jordan, J. (2010). RTI tier structures and instructional intensity. *Learning Disabilities Practice, 25,* 217–225.

Mellard, D., McKnight, M., & Woods, K. (2009). Response to intervention screening and progress-monitoring practices in 41 local schools. *Learning Disabilities Practice, 24,* 186–195.

Menzies, H. M., Mahdavi, J. N., & Lewis, J. L. (2008). Early intervention: From research to practice. *Remedial and Special Education, 29,* 67–77.

Moll, K., Göbel, S. M., Gooch, D., Landerl, K., & Snowling, M. J. (2016). Cognitive risk factors for specific learning disorder: Processing speed, temporal processing, and working memory. *Journal of Learning Disabilities, 49,* 272–281.

Moon, N. W., Todd, R. L., Morton, D. L., & Ivey, E. (2012). *Accommodating students with disabilities in science, technology, engineering, and mathematics (STEM): Findings from research and practice for middle grades through university education.* Atlanta, GA: Center for Assistive Technology and Environmental Access, College of Architecture, Georgia Institute of Technology. Retrieved from: http://www.catea.gatech.edu/scitrain/accommodating.pdf

Moran, A. (2014, March). *Inside the brain: What MRIs are teaching us.* Retrieved from https://www.understood.org/en/learning-attention-issues/getting-started/what-you-need-to-know/inside-the-brain-what-mris-are-teaching-us

National Center for Learning Disabilities. (2006). *Accommodations for students with LD.* Retrieved from http://www.ldonline.org/article/8022/

National Joint Committee on Learning Disabilities. (2011). Comprehensive assessment and evaluation of students with learning disabilities. *Learning Disability Quarterly, 34,* 3–16.

National Joint Committee on Learning Disabilities. (2011, March). *Learning disabilities: Implications for policy regarding research and practice.* Retrieved from www.ldonline.org/njcld

Nowicki, E. A. (2003). A meta-analysis of the social competence of children with learning disabilities compared to classmates of low and average to high achievement. *Learning Disability Quarterly, 26,* 171–188.

O'Connor, R. E., Bocian, K. M., Beach, K. D., Sanchez, V., & Flynn, L. J. (2016). Special education in a 4-year response to intervention (RtI) environment: Characteristics of students with learning disability and grade of identification. *Learning Disabilities Research & Practice, 28,* 98-112.

Ofiesh, N. S., Hughes, C., & Scott, S. S. (2004). Extended test time and postsecondary students with learning disabilities: A model for decision making. *Learning Disabilities Research & Practice, 19,* 57–70.

Orr, A. C., & Hammig, S. B. (2009). Inclusive postsecondary strategies for teaching students with learning disabilities: A review of the literature. *Learning Disability Quarterly, 32,* 181–196.

Pearl, R. (1982). LD children's attributions for success and failure: A replication with a labeled LD sample. *Learning Disabilities Quarterly, 5,* 173–176.

Peng, P., & Fuchs, D. (2016). A meta-analysis of working memory deficits in children with learning difficulties: Is there a difference between verbal domain and numerical domain? *Journal of Learning Disabilities, 49,* 3–20.

Reid, R., & Lienemann, T. O. (2006). Strategy instruction for students with learning disabilities. In K. R. Harris & S. Graham (Series Eds.), *What works for special-needs learners.* New York, NY: The Guilford Press.

Richards-Tutor, C., Baker, D. L., Gersten, R., Baker, S. K., & Smith, J. M. (2016). The effectiveness of reading interventions for English learners: A research synthesis. *Exceptional Children, 82,* 144–169.

Ritchey, K. D., & Goeke, J. L. (2006). Orton-Gillingham and Orton-Gillingham–based reading instruction: A review of the literature. *Journal of Special Education, 40,* 171–183.

Scanlon, D. (2013). Specific learning disability and its newest definition: Which is comprehensive? And which is insufficient? *Journal of Learning Disabilities, 46,* 26–33.

Schumaker, J. B., & Deshler, D. D. (2009). Adolescents with learning disabilities as writers: Are we selling them short? *Learning Disabilities Research & Practice, 24,* 81–92.

Scruggs, T. E., Mastropieri, M. A., Berkeley, S. L., & Marshak, L. (2010). Mnemonic strategies: Evidence-based practice and practice-based evidence. *Intervention in School and Clinic, 46,* 79–86.

Seethaler, P. M., & Fuchs, L. S. (2010). The predictive utility of Kindergarten screening for math difficulty. *Exceptional Children, 77,* 37–59.

Smith, G. W., & Riccomini, P. J. (2013). The effect of a noise reducing test accommodation on elementary students with learning disabilities. *Learning Disabilities Research & Practice, 28*(2), 89–95.

Strauss, A. A., & Lehtinen, L. (1947). *Psychology and education of the brain-injured child.* New York, NY: Grune & Stratton.

Sumner, E., Connelly, V., & Barnett, A. (2016). The influence of spelling ability on vocabulary choices when writing for children with dyslexia. *Journal of Learning Disabilities, 49,* 293–304.

Swanson, H. L. (2009). What about Bob or IQ and LD? *New times for DLD, 27,* 1–2.

Top Ten Reviews. (n.d.). *Digital pen review.* Retrieved from http://digital-pen-review.toptenreviews.com

Troia, G. (Ed.). (2008). *Writing instruction and assessment for struggling writers: From theory to evidence-based practices.* New York, NY: Guilford.

U.S. Department of Education. (1995). *The seventeenth annual report to Congress on the implementation of IDEA.* Washington, DC: U.S. Government Printing Office.

U.S. Department of Education. (2000). *Twenty-second annual report to Congress on the implementation of the Individuals with Disabilities Education Act.* Washington, DC: Government Printing Office. Retrieved from http://www2.ed.gov/about/reports/annual/osep/index.html

U.S. Department of Education (2001). *Twenty-third annual report to Congress on the implementation of the Individuals with Disabilities Education Act.* Washington, DC: Government Printing Office. Retrieved from http://www2.ed.gov/about/reports/annual/osep/index.html

U.S. Department of Education. (2002). *Twenty-fourth annual report to Congress on the implementation of the Individuals with Disabilities Education Act.* Washington, DC: Government Printing Office. Retrieved from http://www2.ed.gov/about/reports/annual/osep/index.html

U.S. Department of Education. (2003). *Twenty-fifth annual report to Congress on the implementation of the Individuals with Disabilities Education Act.* Washington, DC: Government Printing Office. Retrieved from http://www2.ed.gov/about/reports/annual/osep/index.html

U.S. Department of Education. (2004). *Twenty-sixth annual report to Congress on the implementation of the Individuals with Disabilities Education Act.* Washington, DC: Government Printing Office. Retrieved from http://www2.ed.gov/about/reports/annual/osep/index.html

U.S. Department of Education. (2005). *Number of children served under IDEA by disability and age group, 1994 through 2003.* Retrieved from www.ideadata.org

U.S. Department of Education. (2005). *Twenty-seventh annual report to Congress on the implementation of the Individuals with Disabilities Education Act.* Washington, DC: Government Printing Office. Retrieved from http://www2.ed.gov/about/reports/annual/osep/index.html

U.S. Department of Education. (2006). *Assistance to states for the education of children with disabilities program and the early intervention program for infants and toddlers with disabilities; Final rule.* Federal Register, 34 CFR Parts 300 and 301.

U.S. Department of Education. (2006). *Twenty-eighth annual report to Congress on the implementation of the Individuals with Disabilities Education Act.* Washington, DC: Government Printing Office. Retrieved from http://www2.ed.gov/about/reports/annual/osep/index.html

U.S. Department of Education. (2007). *Twenty-ninth annual report to Congress on the implementation of the Individuals with Disabilities Education Act.* Washington, DC: Government Printing Office. Retrieved from http://www2.ed.gov/about/reports/annual/osep/index.html

U.S. Department of Education. (2008). *Thirtieth annual report to Congress on the implementation of the Individuals with Disabilities Education Act.* Washington, DC: Government Printing Office. Retrieved from http://www2.ed.gov/about/reports/annual/osep/index.html

U.S. Department of Education. (2009). *Higher education and disability: Education needs a coordinated approach to improve its assistance to schools in supporting students. (GAO Report 10-33.)* Washington, DC: U.S. Government Accountability Office.

U.S. Department of Education. (2009). *Thirty-first annual report to Congress on the implementation of the Individuals with Disabilities Education Act.* Washington, DC: Government Printing Office. Retrieved from http://www2.ed.gov/about/reports/annual/osep/index.html

U.S. Department of Education. (2010). *Thirty-second annual report to Congress on the implementation of the Individuals with Disabilities Education Act.* Washington, DC: Government Printing Office. Retrieved from http://www2.ed.gov/about/reports/annual/osep/index.html

U.S. Department of Education. (2011). *Thirty-third annual report to Congress on the implementation of the Individuals with Disabilities Education Act.* Washington, DC: Government Printing Office. Retrieved from http://www2.ed.gov/about/reports/annual/osep/index.html

U.S. Department of Education. (2012). *Thirty-fourth annual report to Congress on the implementation of the Individuals with Disabilities Education Act.* Washington, DC: Government Printing Office. Retrieved from http://www2.ed.gov/about/reports/annual/osep/index.html

U.S. Department of Education. (2013). *Thirty-fifth annual report to Congress on the implementation of the Individuals with Disabilities Education Act.* Washington, DC: Government Printing Office. Retrieved from http://www2.ed.gov/about/reports/annual/osep/index.html

U.S. Department of Education. (2014). *Thirty-sixth annual report to Congress on the implementation of the Individuals with Disabilities Education Act.* Washington, DC: Government Printing Office. Retrieved from http://www2.ed.gov/about/reports/annual/osep/index.html

U.S. Department of Education. (2015). *2014 Child Count and Educational Environments, Part B* [IDEA Section 618 Data Products: State Level Data Files]. Retrieved from http://www2.ed.gov/programs/osepidea/618-data/state-level-data-files/index.html

U.S. Department of Education. (2015). *Thirty-seventh annual report to Congress on the implementation of the Individuals with Disabilities Education Act.* Washington, DC: Government Printing Office. Retrieved from http://www2.ed.gov/about/reports/annual/osep/index.html

U.S. Department of Education, Office of Special Education and Rehabilitation Services. (2015, October 23). *Policy guidance to clarify that there is nothing in the IDEA that would prohibit the use of the terms dyslexia, dyscalculia, and dysgraphia in IDEA evaluation, eligibility determinations or IEP documents.* (Departmental letter). Washington, DC: Author. Retrieved from http://www2.ed.gov/policy/speced/guid/idea/memosdcltrs/guidance-on-dyslexia-10-2015.pdf

U.S. Department of Education, Office of Special Education Programs (OSEP). (2005). *Number of children served under IDEA, by disability and age group (6–21), 1994 through 2003 (2003),* Data Table AA. Retrieved from www.ideadata.org

U.S. Department of Education, Office of Special Education Programs (OSEP), Data Accountability Center. (2012). *IDEA data: Analytic tool Part B Educational environments.* Retrieved from www.ideadata.org

U.S. Department of Education, Office of Special Education Programs (OSEP), Data Analysis System (DANS). (2011). *Children served under IDEA, Part B (2009),* Data Tables. Retrieved from www.ideadata.org

U.S. Department of Education, Office of Special Education Programs (OSEP), Data Analysis System (DANS). (2012). *Children with disabilities receiving special education under Part B of the Individuals with Disabilities Education Act-2011.* Data updated as of July 15, 2012. Retrieved from www.ideadata.org

Walker, M. A., & Stevens, E. A. (2016). Reading instruction for students with learning disabilities: An observation study synthesis (1980–2014). *Learning Disability Quarterly,* 1–12. doi: 10.1177/0731948716633868

Wallace, T., Espin, C. A., McMaster, K., Deno, S. L., & Foegen, A. (2007). CBM progress monitoring within a standards-based system: Introduction to the special series. *Journal of Special Education, 41,* 66–68.

Wanzek, J., & Vaughn, S. (2011). Is a three-tier reading intervention model associated with reduced placement in special education? *Remedial and Special Education, 32,* 167–175.

Wexler, J., Vaughn, S., Roberts, G., & Denton, C. A. (2010). The efficacy of repeated reading and wide reading practice for high school students with severe reading disabilities. *Learning Disabilities Research & Practice, 25,* 2–10.

Chapter 7

American Academy of Pediatrics. (2011). ADHD: Clinical practice guidelines for the diagnosis, evaluation, and treatment of attention-deficit/hyperactivity disorder in children and adolescents. *Pediatrics.* Retrieved from http://pediatrics.aappublications.org/content/pediatrics/early/2011/10/14/peds.2011-2654.full.pdf

American Psychiatric Association (APA). (2000). *Diagnostic and statistical manual of mental disorders, Fourth Edition, Text Revision (DSM-IV-TR)* (4th ed.). Washington, DC: Author.

American Psychiatric Association (APA). (2013). *Diagnostic and statistical manual of mental disorders, Fifth Edition, Text Revision (DSM-V)* (5th ed.). Washington, DC: Author.

Associated Press. (2009, February 7). Phelps: I "should get punished." *ESPN.* Retrieved from http://sports.espn.go.com/oly/swimming/news/story?id=3889527

Barkley, R. A. (2005). *Taking charge of ADHD: The complete, authoritative guide for parents.* New York, NY: The Guilford Press.

Barkley, R. A. (2006). *Attention-deficit hyperactivity disorder: A handbook for diagnosis and treatment* (3rd ed.). New York, NY: The Guilford Press.

Barkley, R. A. (2009a). History of adult ADHD pushed back to 1798! *ADHD Report, 17*(1), 1–5.

Barkley, R. A. (2009b). What is the role of atomoxetine in the management of ADHD? *ADHD Report, 17*(2), 1–11.

Beech, M. (2010). *Accommodations: Assisting students with disabilities* (3rd ed.). Tallahassee, FL: Florida Department of Education. Retrieved from www.fldoe.org/core/fileparse.php/7690accomm-educator.pdf

Biederman, J., Mick, E., & Garaone, S. V. (2000). Age-dependent decline of symptoms of attention deficit hyperactivity disorder: Impact of remission definition and symptom type. *American Journal of Psychiatry, 157,* 816–818.

Bouchard, M. F., Bellinger, D. C., Wright, R. O., & Weisskopf, M. G. (2010). Attention-deficit/hyperactivity disorder and urinary metabolites of organophosphate pesticides. *Pediatrics, 125*(6), 1270–1277.

Carbone, E. (2001). Arranging the classroom with an eye (and ear) to students with ADHD. *Teaching Exceptional Children, 34,* 72–81.

Carlson, C. L., Booth, J. E., Shin, M., & Canu, W. H. (2002). Parent-, teacher-, and self-rated motivational styles in ADHD subtypes. *Journal of Learning Disabilities, 35,* 103–113.

Cavendish, W. (2013). Identification of learning disabilities: Implications of DSM-5 criteria for school-based assessment. *Journal of Learning Disabilities, 46,* 52–57.

Centers for Disease Control and Prevention. (2014, December 10). *Key findings: Trends in the Parent-Report of Health Care Provider-Diagnosis and Medication Treatment for ADHD: United States, 2003–2011.* Retrieved from http://www.cdc.gov/ncbddd/adhd/features/key-findings-adhd72013.html

Centers for Disease Control and Prevention. (2016, April 26). *Behavior therapy first for young children with ADHD.* Retrieved from http://www.cdc.gov/features/adhd-awareness/index.html

Centers for Disease Control and Prevention. (2016, May 3). *ADHD in young children: Use recommended treatment first.* Retrieved from http://www.cdc.gov/vitalsigns/adhd/index.html

Cha, A. E. (2016, May 3). CDC warns that Americans may be overmedicating youngest children with ADHD. *The Washington Post.* Retrieved from https://www.washingtonpost.com/news/to-your-health/wp/2016/05/03/cdc-warns-that-americans-may-be-overmedicating-two-to-five-year-olds-with-adhd/

Children and Adults with Attention-Deficit/Hyperactivity Disorder (CHADD). (n.d.). *Mission and history.* Retrieved from www.chadd.org/Content/CHADD/AboutCHADD/Mission/default.htm

Children and Adults with Attention-Deficit/Hyperactivity Disorder (CHADD). (2007, November). *CHADD Statement: Research on AD/HD treatment misrepresented in media.* Retrieved from www.chadd.org/AM/Template.cfm?Section=CHADD_Public_Policy&Template=/CM/HTMLDisplay.cfm&ContentID=5174

Cortiella, C. (2005). *No Child Left Behind: Determining appropriate assessment accommodations for students with disabilities.* National Center for Learning Disabilities. Retrieved from http://www.cehd.umn.edu/nceo/onlinepubs/NCLD/Accommodations.pdf

Daly, P. M., & Ranalli, P. (2003). Using countoons to teach self-monitoring skills. *Teaching Exceptional Children, 35,* 30–35.

Dietz, S., & Montague, M. (2006). Attention deficit hyperactivity disorder comorbid with emotional and behavioral disorders and learning disabilities in adolescents. *Exceptionality, 14*(1), 19–33.

Dillon, R. F., & Osborne, S. S. (2006). Intelligence and behavior among individuals identified with attention deficit disorders. *Exceptionality, 14*(1), 3–18.

Duhaney, L. M. (2003). A practical approach to managing the behaviors of students with ADD. *Intervention in School and Clinic, 38,* 267–279.

DuPaul, G. J., Gormley, M. J., & Laracy, S. D. (2013). Comorbidity of LD and ADHD: Implications of *DSM-5* for assessment and treatment. *Journal of Learning Disabilities, 46,* 43–51.

DuPaul, G. J., Pinho, T. D., Pollack, B. L., Gormley, M. J., & Laracy, S. D. (2015). First-year college students with ADHD and/or LD: Differences in engagement, positive core self-evaluation, school preparation, and college expectations. *Journal of Learning Disabilities,* 1–14. doi: 10.1177/0022219415617164

DuPaul, G. J., & Stoner, G. (2014). *ADHD in the schools: Assessment and intervention strategies* (3rd ed.). New York: The Guilford Press.

Dutton, J. (2006, June). ADHD athletes: Inspiring sports starts with attention deficit. *ADDitude.* Retrieved from www.additudemag .com/adhd/article/989-4.html

Egeland, J., Johansen, S. N., & Ueland, T. (2011). Do low-effort learning strategies mediate impaired memory in ADHD? *Journal of Learning Disabilities, 43*(5), 430–440.

Elliott, S. N., & Marquart, A. M. (2004). Extended time as a testing accommodation: Its effects and perceived consequences. *Exceptional Children, 70,* 349–367.

Forness, S. R., & Kavale, K. A. (2001). Are school professionals missing their best chance to help troubled kids? *Emotional & Behavioral Disorders, 1,* 80–83.

Gantos, J. (1998). *Joey Pigza swallowed the key.* New York, NY: Farrar, Straus and Giroux.

Gay, G. (2002). Preparing for culturally responsive teaching. *Journal of Teacher Education, 53,* 106–116.

Gephart, H. R. (2003). Attention-deficit/hyperactivity disorder: Diagnosis and treatment through adulthood. *Primary Psychiatry, 10*(4), 27–28.

Gilbert, D. L., Isaacs, K. M., Augusta, M., MacNeil, L. K., & Mostofsky, S. H. (2011). Motor cortex inhibition: A marker of ADHD behavior and motor development in children. *Neurology, 76,* 615–622.

Gotsch, T. (2002, March). Medication issue could emerge in IDEA debate. *Special Education Report, 28,* 1–2.

Graham, S., Harris, K. R., & Olinghouse, N. (2007). Addressing executive function problems in writing: An example from the self-regulated strategy development model. In L. Meltzer (Ed.), *Executive function in education* (pp. 216–236). New York, NY: The Guilford Press.

Hale, J. B., Reddy, L. A., Semrud-Clikeman, M., Hain, L. A., Whitaker, J., Morley, J., Lawrence, K., Smith, A., & Jones, N. (2011). Executive impairment determines ADHD medication response: Implications for academic achievement. *Journal of Learning Disabilities, 44*(2), 196–212.

Hallahan, D. P., & Keogh, B. K. (2001). Introduction. In D. P. Hallahan & B. K. Keogh (Eds.), *Research and global perspectives in learning disabilities: Essays in honor of William Cruickshank* (pp. 1–12). Mahwah, NJ: Erlbaum.

Harris, K. R., Friedlander, B. D., Saddler, B., Frizzelle, R., & Graham, S. (2005). Self-monitoring of attention versus self-monitoring of academic performance: Effects among students with ADHD in the general education classroom. *The Journal of Special Education, 39*(3), 145–156.

Harrison, J. R., Bunford, N., Evans, S. W., & Owens, J. S. (2013). Educational accommodations for students with behavioral challenges: A systematic review of the literature. *Review of Educational Research,* 1–47.

Hoffman, B., Hartley, K., & Boone, R. (2005). Reaching accessibility: Guidelines for creating and refining digital learning materials. *Intervention in School and Clinic, 40,* 171–176.

Honos-Webb, L. (2005). *The gift of ADHD: How to transform your child's problems into strengths.* Oakland, CA: New Harbinger Publications, Inc.

Inspiration Software, Inc. (1998–2005). [Inspiration®]. Portland, OR: Author.

Inspiration Software, Inc. (1998–2005). [Kidspiration®]. Portland, OR: Author.

IRIS Center. (2013). *Study skills strategies (part 2): Strategies that improve students' academic performance.* Retrieved from http://iris.peabody .vanderbilt.edu/module/ss2/

IRIS Center. (2008). *SOS: Helping students become independent learners.* Retrieved from http://iris.peabody.vanderbilt.edu/module/sr/

Jacobson, L. T., & Reid, R. (2010). Improving the persuasive essay writing of high school students with ADHD. *Exceptional Children, 76*(2), 157–174.

Jensen, P. S. (2000). ADHD: Advances in understanding its causes, and best treatments. *Emotional and Behavioral Disorders in Youth, 1,* 9–10, 19.

Johnson, R. J., Gold, M. S., Johnson, D. R., Ishimoto, T., Lanaspa, M. A., Zahniser, N. R., & Avena, N. M. (2011). Attention-deficit/hyperactivity disorder: Is it time to reappraise the role of sugar consumption? *Postgraduate Medicine, 123*(5), 39–49. Retrieved from http://www.ncbi.nlm.nih.gov/pmc/articles/PMC3598008/pdf /nihms446714.pdf

Kim, Y., & Chang, H. (2011). Correlation between attention deficit hyperactivity disorder and sugar consumption, quality of diet, and dietary behavior in school children. *Nutrition Research and Practice, 5,* 236–245. Retrieved from http://www.ncbi.nlm.nih.gov/pmc /articles/PMC3133757/pdf/nrp-5-236.pdf

Krouse, K. (2009, February 1). Phelps apologizes for marijuana pipe photo. *New York Times.* Retrieved from www.nytimes.com/2009 /02/02/sports/othersports/02phelps.html

LDOnline. (1998). *Helping the student with ADHD in the classroom: Strategies for teachers.* Retrieved from http://www.ldonline.org/article /5911/

Lewandowski, L. J., Lovett, B. J., Parolin, R., Gordon, M., & Codding, R. S. (2007). Extended time accommodations and the mathematics performance of students with and without ADHD. *Journal of Psychoeducational Assessment, 25*(1), 17–28.

Loe, I. M., & Feldman, H. M. (2007). Academic and educational outcomes of children with ADHD. *Journal of Pediatric Psychology, 32*(6). Retrieved from http://jpepsy.oxfordjournals.org/content/32/6/643 .full.pdf+html

Low, K. (2011, October 19). *Adam Levine talks about ADHD.* Retrieved from http://add.about.com/od/famouspeoplewithadhd/a/Adam-Levine-Talks-About-Adhd.htm

Martin, D. (2010). Treatment for attention deficit disorder (ADHD). *Psych Central.* Retrieved from http://psychcentral.com/lib/2007 /treatment-for-attention-deficit-disorder-adhd/

McKinley, L. A., & Stormont, M. A. (2008). The school supports checklist: Identifying support needs and barriers for children with ADHD. *Teaching Exceptional Children, 41*(2), 14–19.

Merrell, K. W., & Boelter, E. (2001). An investigation of relationships between social behavior and ADHD in children and youth: Construct validity of the home and community social behavior scales. *Journal of Emotional and Behavioral Disorders, 9,* 260–269.

Millichap, J. G., & Yee, M. M. (2012). The diet factor in attention-deficit/hyperactivity disorder. *Pediatrics, 129*(1), 1–8.

Mink, J. W. (2011). Faulty brakes? Inhibitory processes in attention-deficit/hyperactivity disorder. *Neurology, 76,* 592–593.

Miranda, A., Jarque, S., & Tàrraga, R. (2006). Interventions in school settings for students with ADHD. *Exceptionality, 14*(1), 35–52.

Mount, I. (2004). America's 25 most fascinating entrepreneurs. David Neeleman, from JetBlue, for creating an airline fit for humans. *Inc.* Retrieved from www.inc.com/magazine/20040401/25neeleman.html

National Center for Health Statistics. (2011, December). *Summary health statistics for U.S. children: National Health Interview Survey, 2010.* (Vital Health Stat 10,250). Washington, DC: Author.

National Institute of Mental Health (NIMH). (2009, November). *The multimodal treatment of Attention Deficit Hyperactivity Disorder Study (MTA): Questions and answers.* Retrieved from www.nimh.nih .gov/trials/practical/mta/the-multimodal-treatment-of-attention-deficit-hyperactivity-disorder-study-mta-questions-and-answers .shtml

National Institutes of Health, National Institute of Neurological Disorders and Stroke. (2015, November 19). *Attention deficit-hyperactivity disorder information.* Retrieved from http://www.ninds.nih.gov /disorders/adhd/adhd.htm

National Resource Center on ADHD. (2015). *Psychosocial treatment for children and adolescents with ADHD.* Retrieved from http://www.chadd.org/Portals/0/Content/CHADD/NRC/Factsheets/Psychosocial%20Treatments%20for%20Children%20with%20ADHD.pdf

National Resource Center on ADHD. (2016a). *Managing medication for children and adolescents with ADHD.* Retrieved from http://www.chadd.org/Portals/0/Content/CHADD/NRC/Factsheets/medication.pdf

National Resource Center on ADHD. (2016b). *Treatment of teens with ADHD.* Retrieved from http://www.chadd.org/Understanding-ADHD/For-Parents-Caregivers/Teens/Treatment-of-Teens-with-ADHD.aspx

New York Times. (2011, January). *Attention deficit hyperactivity disorder (ADHD).* Retrieved from http://health.nytimes.com

Pappadopulos, E., & Jensen, P. S. (2001, Spring). What school professionals, counselors, and parents need to know about medication for emotional and behavioral disorders in kids. *Emotional & Behavioral Disorders in Youth, 35–37.*

Passell, L. (n.d.). Mom to live by: Debbie Phelps. *Parenting.* Retrieved from www.parenting.com/article/mom-to-live-by-debbie-phelps?page=0,1

Phelps, D. (2009). *A mother for all seasons.* New York, NY: Harper Collins Publishers.

Polanczyk, G., de Lima, M. S., Horta, B. L., Biederman, J., & Rohde, L. A. (2007). The worldwide prevalence of ADHD: A systematic review and metaregression analysis. *American Journal of Psychiatry, 164*(4), 942–948.

Rafferty, L. A. (2010). Step-by-step: Teaching students to self-monitor. *Teaching Exceptional Children, 43*(2), 50–58.

Re, A. M., Caeran, M., & Cornoldi, C. (2008). Improving expressive writing skills of children rated for ADHD symptoms. *Journal of Learning Disabilities, 41*(6), 535–544.

Reid, R., & Lienemen, T. O. (2006). *Strategy instruction for children with learning disabilities: What it is and how to do it.* New York, NY: The Guilford Press.

Reid, R., Trout, A. L., & Schartz, M. (2005). Self-regulation interventions for children with attention deficit/hyperactivity disorder. *Exceptional Children, 71*(4), 361–377.

Reynolds, C. R., & Fletcher-Janzen, E. (Eds.). (2002). Attention-deficit/hyperactivity disorder (ADHD). In *Concise encyclopedia of special education: A reference for the education of children, adolescents, and adults with disabilities and other exceptional individuals* (2nd ed., pp. 83–90). Hoboken, NJ: John Wiley & Sons, Inc.

Riordan, R. (n.d.). *An interview with Rick.* Retrieved from www.rickriordan.com/about-rick/an-interview-with-rick.aspx

Riordan, R. (2010, October 15). Rick Riordan on four ways to get kids with ADHD to read. *The Wall Street Journal.* Retrieved from http://blogs.wsj.com/speakeasy/2010/10/15/rick-riordan-on-four-ways-to-get-adhd-kids-to-read/

Salend, S. J., Elhoweris, H., & van Garderen, D. (2003). Educational interventions for students with ADD. *Intervention in School and Clinic, 38,* 280–288.

Salend, S. J., & Rohena, E. (2003). Students with attention deficit disorders: An overview. *Intervention in School and Clinic, 38,* 259–266.

Saey, T. H. (2011, September 10). ADHD linked to rare gene counts. *Science News, 10.*

Scanlon, D. (2013). Specific learning disability and its newest definition: Which is comprehensive? And which is insufficient? *Journal of Learning Disabilities, 46,* 26–33.

Schoenstadt, A. (2011, May). ADHD medications. *MedTV.* Retrieved from http://adhd.emedtv.com

Shaw, G., & Giambra, L. (1993). Task-unrelated thoughts of college students diagnosed as hyperactive in childhood. *Developmental Neuropsychology, 9,* 17–30.

Sibley, M. H., Waxmonsky, J. G., Robb, J. A., & Pelham, W. E. (2013). Implications of changes for the field: ADHD. *Journal of Learning Disabilities, 46,* 34–42.

Sing, A., Yeh, C. J., Verma, N., & Das, A. K. (2015). Overview of attention deficit hyperactivity disorder in young children. *Health Psychology Research 2015, 3,* 23–25. Retrieved from http://www.ncbi.nlm.nih.gov/pmc/articles/PMC4768532/pdf/hpr-2015-2-2115.pdf

Still, G. F. (1902). Some abnormal psychical conditions in children. *The Lancet, 1,* 1008–1012, 1077–1082, 1163–1168.

Strauss, A. A., & Lehtinen, L. (1947). *Psychology and education of the brain-injured child.* New York, NY: Grune & Stratton.

Strom, E. (2014). *Common modifications and accommodations.* Retrieved from https://www.understood.org/en/learning-attention-issues/treatments-approaches/educational-strategies/common-modifications-and-accommodations

Tannock, R. (2013). Rethinking ADHD and LD in *DSM-5*: Proposed changes in diagnostic criteria. *Journal of Learning Disabilities, 46,* 5–25.

U.S. Congress. *Individuals with Disabilities Education Improvement Act of 2004.* P.L. No. 108-446. 118 STAT. 2647.

U.S. Congress. *Rehabilitation Act of 1973, Section 504,* 19 U.S.C. Section 794.

U.S. Department of Education, Office of Special Education and Rehabilitative Services. (1991, September 16). *Joint Policy Memorandum.* Retrieved from http://www.wrightslaw.com/law/code_regs/OSEP_Memorandum_ADD_1991.html

U.S. Department of Education, Office of Special Education Programs, Data Analysis System (DANS). (2012). *Children with disabilities receiving special education under Part B of the Individuals with Disabilities Education Act-2011.* Data updated as of July 15, 2012. Retrieved from www.ideadata.org

U.S. Department of Health and Human Services. (n.d.). *Bullying and children and youth with disabilities and special health needs.* Retrieved from http://www.stopbullying.gov/at-risk/groups/special-needs/bullyingtipsheet.pdf

U.S. Department of Health and Human Services, National Institutes of Health (NIH). (2008). A*ttention deficit hyperactivity disorder (ADHD)* (NIH Publication No. 08-3572). Retrieved from http://www.nimh.nih.gov/health/publications/attention-deficit-hyperactivity-disorder/adhd_booklet.pdf

Van Kuren, L. (2003, November-December). Technology: The great equalizer. *CEC Today, 10,* 1, 5–6, 15.

Visser, S. N., Bitsko, R. H., Danielson, M. L., Perou, R., & Blumberg, S. J. (2010, November). Increasing prevalence of parent-reported attention-deficit/hyperactivity disorder among children–United States, 2003 and 2008. *Morbidity and Mortality Weekly Report, 59*(44), 1439–1443.

Visser, S. N., Zablotsky, B., Holbrook, J. R., Danielson, M. L., & Bitsko, R. H. (2015, September 3). Diagnostic experiences of children with attention-deficit/hyperactivity disorder. *National Health Statistical Reports, number 81.* Hyattsville, MD: National Center for Health Statistics. Retrieved from http://www.cdc.gov/nchs/data/nhsr/nhsr081.pdf

Volpe, R. J., DuPaul, G. J., Loney, J., & Salisbury, H. (1999). Alternative selection criteria for identifying children with ADHD: Observed behavior and self-reported internalizing symptoms. *Journal of Emotional and Behavioral Disorders, 7,* 103–109.

Waknine, Y. (2010, October 7). FDA approves extended-release Clonidine for pediatric ADHD. *Medscape Medical News.* Retrieved from www.medscape.com

Walker, C. (2014, December 19). Michael Phelps gets no jail time after entering guilty plea in DUI case. *The Baltimore Sun.* Retrieved from http://www.baltimoresun.com/sports/olympics/phelps/bal-michael-phelps-dui-trial-20141219-story.html

Ward, J., & Guyer, K. E. (2000). Medical management of ADHD. In B. P. Guyer (Ed.), *ADHD: Achieving success in school and life* (pp. 38–54). Boston, MA: Allyn & Bacon.

Weyandt, L. L. (2006). *An ADHD primer* (2nd ed.). Boston, MA: Allyn & Bacon.

Weyandt, L. L., Iwaszuk, W., Fulton, K., Ollerton, M., Beatty, N., Fouts, H., Schepman, S., & Greenlaw, C. (2003). The internal restlessness scale: Performance of college students with and without ADHD. *Journal of Learning Disabilities, 36*(4), 382–389.

Williams, S. (2010, February 5). Percy Jackson: My boy's own adventure. *The Guardian.* Retrieved from www.guardian.co.uk/lifeandstyle/2010/feb/08/percy-jackson-rick-riordan

Woodyard, C. (2002, October 8). JetBlue soars on CEO's creativity. *USA Today.* Retrieved from www.usatoday.com/educate/Entre9.pdf

Zambo, D. (2008). Looking at ADHD through multiple lenses: Identifying girls with the inattentive type. *Intervention in School and Clinic, 44*(1), 34–40.

Chapter 8

Alberto, P. A., & Troutman, A. C. (2009). *Applied behavior analysis for teachers* (8th ed.). Columbus, OH: Merrill/Pearson.

American Psychiatric Association (APA). (2003). *Diagnostic and statistical manual of mental disorders, Fourth Edition, Text Revision (DSM–IV–TR)* (4th ed.). Washington, DC: Author.

American Psychiatric Association (APA). (2013). *Diagnostic and statistical manual of mental disorders, Fifth Edition, Text Revision (DSM-V)* (5th ed.). Washington, DC: Author.

Asperger, H. (1944/1991). "Autistic psychopathy" in childhood (U. Frith, Trans. Annot.). In U. Frith (Ed.), *Autism and Asperger syndrome* (pp. 37–92). New York, NY: Cambridge University Press.

Autism Speaks (2012). *Applied behavior analysis (ABA)*. Retrieved from www.autismspeaks.org/what-autism/treatment/applied-behavior-analysis-aba

Autism Speaks. (2012). *Supporting learning in the student with autism.* Retrieved from https://www.autismspeaks.org/sites/default/files/sctk_supporting_learning.pdf

Autism Speaks. (2016). *What is autism? What is autism spectrum disorder?* Retrieved from https://www.autismspeaks.org/what-autism

Baer, D. M., Wolf, M. M., & Risley, T. R. (1968). Some current dimensions of applied behavior analysis. *Journal of Applied Behavior Analysis, 1,* 91–97.

Baron-Cohen, S. (2001). Theory of mind and autism: A review. In G. Lavaine Masters (Ed.), *International review of research in mental retardation.* New York, NY: Academic Press.

Begley, S., & Springen, K. (1996, May 13). Life in a parallel world: A bold new approach to the mystery of autism. *Newsweek,* p. 70.

Behavior Analyst Certification Board, Inc. (BACB). (2012). *Behavior analyst task list* (4th ed.). Retrieved from http://bacb.com/wp-content/uploads/2016/03/160101-BCBA-BCaBA-task-list-fourth-edition-english.pdf

Behavior Analyst Certification Board, Inc. (BACB). (2014). *Applied behavior analysis treatment of autism spectrum disorder: Practice guidelines for healthcare funders and managers* (2nd ed.). Retrieved from http://bacb.com/wp-content/uploads/2015/07/ABA_Guidelines_for_ASD.pdf

Bennett, K., Reichow, B., & Wolery, M. (2011). Effects of structured teaching on the behavior of young children with disabilities. *Focus on Autism and Other Developmental Disabilities, 26,* 143–153.

Bettelheim, B. (1967). *Infantile autism and the birth of self.* New York, NY: Free Press.

Blacher, J., & Christensen, L. (2011). Sowing the seeds of the autism field: Leo Kanner (1943). *Intellectual and Developmental Disabilities, 49,* 172–191.

Bondy, A., & Frost, L. (2002). *A picture's worth: PECS and other visual communication strategies in autism.* Bethesda, MD: Woodbine House.

Bondy, A., & Sulzer-Azaroff, B. (2002). *The Pyramid Approach to Education in autism.* Newark, DE: Pyramid Educational Products.

Boutot, E. A., & Hume, K. (2012). Beyond time out and table time: Today's applied behavior analysis for students with autism. *Education and Training in Autism and Developmental Disabilities, 47,* 23–38.

Boutot, E. A., & Myles, B. S. (2011). *Autism spectrum disorders: Foundations, characteristics, and effective strategies.* Columbus, OH: Merrill/Pearson.

Buescher, A. V. S., Cidav, Z., Knapp, M., & Mandell, D. S. (2014, August). Costs of autism spectrum disorders in the United Kingdom and the United States. *JAMA Pediatrics, 168,* 721–728. Retrieved from http://archpedi.jamanetwork.com/article.aspx?articleid=1879723

Cafiero, J. M. (2005). *Meaningful exchanges for people with autism: An introduction to augmentative & alternative communication.* Bethesda, MD: Woodbine House.

Cease-Cook, J., Fowler, C., & Test, D. W. (2015). Strategies for creating work-based learning experiences in schools for secondary students with disabilities. *Teaching Exceptional Children, 47,* 352–358.

Centers for Disease Control and Prevention (CDC). (2009). Prevalence of autism spectrum disorders–Autism and Developmental Disabilities Monitoring Network, United States, 2006. *MMWR Surveillance Summaries, 58*(SS10), 1–20. Retrieved from www.cdc.gov/mmwr/preview/mmwrhtml/ss5810a1.htm

Centers for Disease Control and Prevention (CDC). (2011, February 1). *Workshop on U.S. data to evaluate changes in the prevalence of autism spectrum disorders (ASDs): Executive summary.* Retrieved from www.cdc.gov/NCBDDD/autism/documents/EvaluatingChanges_ExecutiveSummary.pdf

Centers for Disease Control and Prevention (CDC). (2012). *Autism spectrum disorders (ASDs): Autism and Developmental Disabilities Monitoring (ADDM) Network.* Retrieved from www.cdc.gov/ncbddd/autism/addm.html

Centers for Disease Control and Prevention (CDC). (2012). *Autism spectrum disorders (ASDs): Data & statistics: Prevalence.* Retrieved from www.cdc.gov/ncbddd/autism/data.html

Centers for Disease Control and Prevention (CDC). (2012, March 30). Prevalence of autism spectrum disorders–Autism and Developmental Disabilities Monitoring Network, 14 sites, United States, 2008: Surveillance summaries, *Morbidity and Mortality Weekly Report (MMWR), 61*(SS03); 1–19. Retrieved from www.cdc.gov/mmwr/preview/mmwrhtml/ss6103a1.htm?s_cid=ss6103a1_w

Centers for Disease Control and Prevention (CDC). (2015, February 26). *Autism spectrum disorder: Signs and symptoms.* Retrieved from http://www.cdc.gov/ncbddd/autism/signs.html

Cihak, D. F., Smith, C. C., Cornett, A., & Coleman, M. B. (2012). The use of video modeling with the Picture Exchange Communication System to increase independent communicative initiations in preschoolers with autism and developmental delays. *Focus on Autism and Other Developmental Disabilities, 27,* 3–11.

Colvert, E., Tick, B., McEwen, F., Stewart, C., Curran, S. R., Woodhouse, E., Gillan, N., Hallett, V., Lietz, S., Garnett, T., Ronald, A., Plomin, R., Rijsdijk, F., Happé, F., & Bolton, P. (2015). Heritability of autism spectrum disorder in a UK population–based twin sample. *JAMA Psychiatry, 72,* 415–523.

Cooper, J. O., Heron, T. E., & Heward, B. L. (2007). *Applied behavior analysis* (2nd ed.). Columbus, OH: Merrill/Pearson.

Deer, B. (2011). Exposed: Andrew Wakefield and the MMR-autism fraud. Retrieved from http://briandeer.com/mmr/lancet-summary.htm

Deer, B. (2011, January 6). Secrets of the MMR scare: How the case against the MMR vaccine was fixed. *The BMJ.* doi: http://dx.doi.org/10.1136/bmj.c5347

DO-IT (Disabilities, Opportunities, Internetworking, and Technology). (2015). *What are typical challenges and accommodations for students with Asperger's Disorder and high-functioning Autism?* Retrieved from http://www.washington.edu/doit/what-are-typical-challenges-and-accommodations-students-aspergers-disorder-and-high-functioning

Freeman, R. D. (1967). Controversy over "patterning" as a treatment for brain damage in children. *Journal of the American Medical Association, 202,* 385–388.

Hall, L. J. (2013). *Autism spectrum disorders: From theory to practice* (2nd ed.). Columbus, OH: Merrill/Pearson.

Harris, S. L., LaRue, R. H., & Weiss, M. J. (2007). Programmatic issues: In P. Sturmey & A. Fitzer (Eds.), *Autism spectrum disorders: Applied behavior analysis, evidence, and practice* (pp. 232–264). Austin, TX: PRO-ED.

Hart, S. L., & Banda, D. R. (2010). Picture Exchange Communications System with individuals with developmental disabilities: A meta-analysis of single subject studies. *Remedial and Special Education, 31,* 476–488.

Hendricks, D. R., & Wehman, P. (2009). Transition from school to adulthood for youth with autism spectrum disorders. *Focus on Autism and Other Developmental Disabilities, 24,* 77–88.

Höfer, J., Hoffman, F., & Bachmann, C. (2016). Use of complementary and alternative medicine in children and adolescents with autism spectrum disorder: A systematic review. *Autism.* doi: 10.1177/1362361316646559

Hume, D., Boyd, B. A., Hamm, J. V., & Kucharczyk, S. (2014). Supporting independence in adolescents on the autism spectrum. *Remedial and Special Education, 35,* 102–113.

Hume, K., Sreckovic, M., Snyder, K., & Carnahan, C. R. (2014). Smooth transitions: Helping students with autism spectrum disorder navigate the school day. *Teaching Exceptional Children, 47,* 35–45.

Hurwitz, S. (2013). The gluten-free, casein-free diet and autism: Limited return on family investment. *Journal of Early Intervention, 35*, 3–19.

Hurwitz, S., & Watson, L. R. (2016). Joint attention revisited: Finding strengths among children with autism. *Autism, 20*, 538–550.

Hyman, S. L., Stewart, P. A., Foley, J., Cain, U., Peck, R., Morris, D. D., Wang, H., & Smith, T. (2016). The gluten-free/casein-free diet: A double-blind challenge trial in children with autism. *Journal of Autism and Developmental Disorders, 46*, 205–220.

IRIS Center. (2013). *Secondary transition: Helping students with disabilities plan for post-high school settings.* Retrieved from http://iris.peabody .vanderbilt.edu/module/tran/

IRIS Center. (2014). *Autism spectrum disorder: An overview for educators.* Retrieved from http://iris.peabody.vanderbilt.edu/module/asd1/

Kalkbrenner, A. E., Windham, G. C., Serre, M. L., Akita, Y., Wang, X., Hoffman, K., Thayer, B. P., & Daniels, J. L. (2015). Particulate matter exposure, prenatal and postnatal windows of susceptibility, and autism spectrum disorders. *Epidemiology, 26*, 30–42.

Kanner, L. (1943). Autistic disturbances of affective contact. *Nervous Child, 2*, 217–250.

Kellems, R. O., Grigal, M., Under, D. D., Simmons, T. J., Bauder, D., & Williams, C. (2015). Technology and transition in the 21st century. *Teaching Exceptional Children, 47*, 336–343.

Kennedy, C. H., & Horn, E. (2004). *Including students with severe disabilities.* Boston, MA: Allyn & Bacon.

Jones, K. B., Cottle, K., Bakian, A., Farlye, M., Bilder, D., Coon, H., & McMahon, W. M. (2010). A description of medical conditions in adults with autism spectrum disorder: A follow-up of the 1980s Utah/UCLA Autism Epidemiologic Study. *Autism, 20*, 551–561.

Lee, G. K., & Carter, E. W. (2012). Preparing transition-age students with high-functioning autism spectrum disorders for meaningful work. *Psychology in the Schools, 49.* doi: 10.1002/pits.21651

Lord, C., & Schopler, E. (1994). TEACCH services for preschool children. In S. Harris & J. Handleman (Eds.), *Preschool education programs for children with autism.* Austin, TX: PRO-ED.

Lovaas, O. I. (1987). Behavioral treatment and normal educational and intellectual functioning in young autistic children. *Journal of Consulting and Clinical Psychology, 55*, 3–9.

Lovaas, O. I. (1993). The development of a treatment-research project for developmentally disabled and autistic children. *Journal of Applied Behavior Analysis, 26*, 617–630.

Mazzotti, V., & Rowe, D. (2015). Meeting the transition needs of students with disabilities in the 21st century. *Teaching Exceptional Children, 47*, 298-300.

McCormick, C., Hepburn, S., Young, G. S., & Rogers, S. J. (2016). Sensory symptoms in children with autism spectrum disorder, other developmental disorders and typical development: A longitudinal study. *Autism, 20*, 572–579.

McCoy, K. M. (2011). *Autism from the teacher's perspective.* Denver, CO: Love Publishing Company.

Mesibov, G. B., & Shea, V. (2010). The TEACCH program in the era of evidence-based practice. *Journal of Autism and Developmental Disorders, 40*, 570–579.

Mesibov, G. B., & Shea, V. (2011). Evidence-based practices and autism. *Autism, 15*, 114–133.

Moon, N. W., Todd, R. L., Morton, D. L., & Ivey, E. (2012). *Accommodating students with disabilities in science, technology, engineering, and mathematics (STEM): Findings from research and practice for middle grades through university education.* Atlanta, GA: Center for Assistive Technology and Environmental Access, College of Architecture, Georgia Institute of Technology. Retrieved from http://www.catea .gatech.edu/scitrain/accommodating.pdf

National Institute of Child Health and Human Development, National Institutes of Health. (2001). *Autism and the MMR vaccine.* NIH Pub. No. 01-4963. Retrieved from www.nichd.nih.gov/publications /pubs/upload/autismMMR.pdf

National Institute of Child Health and Human Development, National Institutes of Health. (2012). *Definition of autism.* Retrieved from www.nichd.nih.gov/health/topics/asd.cfm

National Professional Development Center on Autism Spectrum Disorders. (2010). *Picture Exchange Communication System (PECS):*

Steps for implementation. Module: Picture Exchange Communication System (PECS). Retrieved from http://autismpdc.fpg.unc.edu /sites/autismpdc.fpg.unc.edu/files/PECS_Steps.pdf

Odom, S. L., Boyd, B. A., Hall, L. J., & Hume, K. (2010). Evaluation of comprehensive treatment models for individuals with autism spectrum disorders. *Journal of Autism and Developmental Disorders, 40*, 425–436.

Odom, S. L., & Wong, C. (2015). Connecting the dots: Supporting students with autism spectrum disorder. *American Educator,* Summer, 12–19, 44.

Offit, P. A. (2011). *Deadly choices: How the anti-vaccine movement threatens us all.* New York, NY: Basic Books.

Ontario Ministry of Education. (2007). *Effective educational practices for students with autism spectrum disorders.* Retrieved from http://www.edu.gov.on.ca/eng/general/elemsec/speced /autismSpecDis.pdf

Organization for Autism Research. (2012). *Life journey through autism: Navigating the special education system.* Retrieved from http://www .researchautism.org/resources/reading/documents/SPEDGuide.pdf

Organization for Autism Research & The Center on Secondary Education for Students with Autism Spectrum Disorders. (2013). *Understanding autism: A guide for secondary school teachers.* Retrieved from http://csesa.fpg.unc.edu/sites/csesa.fpg.unc.edu/files /UnderstandingAutismSecondaryTeachersGuide.pdf

Ott, J. N. (1976). Influence of fluorescent lights on hyperactivities and learning disabilities. *Journal of Learning Disabilities, 9*, 417–422.

PACER Center, Inc. (2014). *Day training and supported employment programs: Information for parents of students with developmental disabilities.* Minneapolis, MN: Author. Retrieved from http://www.pacer.org /parent/php/PHP-c199.pdf

Pantelis, P. C., & Kennedy, D. P. (2016). Estimation of the prevalence of autism spectrum disorder in South Korea, revisited. *Autism, 20*, 517–527.

Povenmire-Kirk, T. C., Bethune, L. K., Alverson, C. Y., & Kahn, L. G. (2015). A journey, not a destination: Developing cultural competence in secondary transition. *Teaching Exceptional Children, 47*, 319–328.

Pyramid Educational Consultants. (n.d.). *What is PECS?* Retrieved from http://www.pecsusa.com/pecs.php

Pyramid Educational Consultants. (2012). *PECS and the pyramid approach.* Retrieved from www.pecs.org.uk/general/documents /2011Infobrochure.pdf

Raz, R., Roberts, A. L., Lyall, K., Hart, J. E., Just, A. C., Laden, F., & Weisskopf, M. G. (2015). Autism spectrum disorder and particulate matter air pollution before, during, and after pregnancy: A nested case-control analysis within the Nurses' Health Study II cohort. *Environmental Health Perspectives, 123*, 264–270.

Roan, S. (2011, May 8). Autism rates may be higher than thought. *Los Angeles Times* HEALTH. Retrieved from http://articles.latimes .com/2011/may/08/health/la-he-autism-korea-20110509

Rowe, D. A., Mazzotti, V. L., Hirano, K., & Alverson, C. Y. (2015). Assessing transition skills in the 21st century. *Teaching Exceptional Children, 47*, 301–309.

Russa, M. B., Matthews, A. L., & Owen-DeSchryver, J. S. (2015). Expanding supports to improve the lives of families of children with autism spectrum disorder. *Journal of Positive Behavior Interventions, 17*, 95–104.

Ryan, J. B., Hughes, E. M., Katsiyannis, A., McDaniel, M., & Sprinkle, C. (2011). Research-based educational practices for students with autism spectrum disorders. *Exceptional Children, 43*, 56–64.

Sallows, G. O., & Graupner, T. D. (2005). Intensive behavioral treatment for children with autism: Four-year outcome and predictors. *American Journal on Mental Retardation, 110*, 417–438.

Schieve, L. A., Tian, L. H., Baio, J., Rankin, K., Rosenberg, D., Wiggins, L., Maenner, M. J., Yeargin-Allsopp, M., Durkin, M., Rice, C., King, L., Kirby, R. S., Wingate, M. S., & Devine, O. (2014). Population attributable fractions for three perinatal risk factors for autism spectrum disorders, 2002 and 2008 Autism and Developmental Disabilities Monitoring Network. *Annals of Epidemiology, 24*, 260–266.

Shogren, K. A., & Plotner, A. J. (2012). Transition planning for students with intellectual disability, autism, or other disabilities: Data from the National Longitudinal Transition Study–2. *Intellectual and Developmental Disabilities, 50,* 16–29.

Skinner, B. F. (1953). *Science and human behavior.* New York, NY: Macmillan Company.

Spencer, R. D., Petersen, D. B., & Gillam, S. L. (2008). Picture Exchange Communication System (PECS) or sign language: An evidence-based decision-making example. *Teaching Exceptional Children, 41,* 40–47.

Sturmey, P., & Sevin, J. A. (1994). Defining and assessing autism. In J. L. Matson (Ed.), *Autism in children and adults: Etiology, assessment, and intervention* (pp. 13–36). Pacific Grove, CA: Brooks/Cole.

Talay-Ongan, A., & Wood, K. (2000). Unusual sensory sensitivities in autism: A possible crossroads. *International Journal of Disability, Development and Education, 47,* 201–212.

Taylor, C. (2014, June 24). *Raising an autistic child: Coping with the costs.* Retrieved from http://time.com/money/2918134/cost-raising-autistic-child/

The Telegraph. (2012, March 22). *Number of children with autism soars by more than 50 per cent in five years.* Retrieved from www.telegraph.co.uk/news/9160322/Number-of-children-with-autism-soars-by-more-than-50-per-cent-in-five-years.html

Tincani, M. (2007). Beyond consumer advocacy: Autism spectrum disorders, effective instruction, and public schools. *Intervention in School & Clinic, 43,* 47–51.

Tincani, M., & Boutot, E. A. (2005). Autism and technology: Current practices and future directions. In D. L. Edyburn, K. Higgins, & R. Boone (Eds.), *The handbook of special education technology research and practice* (pp. 413–421). Whitefish Bay, WI: Knowledge by Design.

Tincani, M., Crozier, S., & Alazetta, L. (2006). The Picture Exchange Communication System: Effects on manding and speech development for school-aged children with autism. *Education & Training in Developmental Disabilities, 41,* 177–184.

Travers, J. C., Higgins, K., Pierce, T., Boone, R., Miller, S., & Tandy, R. (2011). Emergent literacy skills of preschool students with autism: A comparison of teacher-led and computer-assisted instruction. *Education and Training in Autism and Developmental Disabilities, 46,* 326–338.

U.S. Department of Education. (2006). Assistance to states for the education of children with disabilities program and the early intervention program for infants and toddlers with disabilities; Final rule. *Federal Register, 34* CFR Parts 300 and 301.

U.S. Department of Education, Office of Special Education Programs, Data Analysis System (DANS). (2012). *Children with disabilities receiving special education under Part B of the Individuals with Disabilities Education Act-2011.* Data updated as of July 15, 2012. Retrieved from www.ideadata.org

U.S. Department of Health and Human Services, Office of Head Start. *Head Start program performance standards, Federal Register version.* 45 CFR Part 1308, p. 178.

University of North Carolina School of Medicine. (2012). *TEACCH approach.* Retrieved from http://teacch.com/about-us-1/what-is-teacch

Volk, H. E., Kerin, T., Lurmann, F., Hertz-Picciotto, I., McConnell, R., & Campbell, D. B. (2014). Interaction of the MET receptor tyrosine kinase gene and air pollution exposure in autism spectrum disorder. *Epidemiology, 25,* 44–47.

Weng, O., Savage, M. N., & Bouck, E. C. (2014). iDIY: Video-based instruction using iPads. *Teaching Exceptional Children, 47,* 11–19.

Wing, L. (1989). Autistic adults. In C. Gillberg (Ed.), *Diagnosis and treatment of autism* (pp. 419–432). New York, NY: Plenum Press.

Chapter 9

Ability/Path.org. (2011, February 17). *"Disable bullying" campaign.* Retrieved from http://abcnews.go.com/Health/video/disable-bullying-campaing-12940890

Agran, M., & Wehmeyer, M. (2008). Person-centered career planning. In F. Rusch (Ed.), *Beyond high school: Preparing adolescents for tomorrow's challenges* (2nd ed., pp. 55–77). Columbus, OH: Merrill.

American Academy of Pediatrics. (2015, October 19). *AAP says no amount of alcohol should be considered safe during pregnancy.* Retrieved from https://www.aap.org/en-us/about-the-aap/aap-press-room/pages/AAP-Says-No-Amount-of-Alcohol-Should-be-Considered-Safe-During-Pregnancy.aspx

American Association on Intellectual and Developmental Disabilities (AAIDD). (2015). *Frequently asked questions on AAIDD's new diagnostic Adaptive Behavior Scale (DABS).* Retrieved from http://aaidd.org/intellectual-disability/diagnostic-adaptive-behavior-scale/faqs#WMxgsxi72Np8

American Association on Intellectual and Developmental Disabilities (AAIDD). (2015). *Frequently asked questions on intellectual disability.* Retrieved from http://aaidd.org/intellectual-disability/definition/faqs-on-intellectual-disability#.Vg7dT1ZwjFE

American Association on Intellectual and Developmental Disabilities (AAIDD) & The Arc. (2014, October 2). *Long term supports and services.* Retrieved from http://aaidd.org/news-policy/policy/position-statements/long-term-supports-and-services#.VgMUzem4DN4

Anderson, L., Larson, S. A., & Wuorio, A. (2011). *2010 FINDS national survey technical report part 1: Family caregiver survey.* Minneapolis: University of Minnesota, Research and Training Center on Community Living. Retrieved from http://www.thearc.org/document.doc?id=3673

Angell, M. E., Stoner, J. B., & Fulk, B. M. (2010). Advice from adults with physical disabilities on fostering self-determination during the school years. *TEACHING Exceptional Children, 42,* 64–75.

Arc, The. (2011). Still in the shadows with their future uncertain: *A report on Family and Individual Needs for Disability Supports (FINDS), 2011: Summary of key findings and a call to action.* Retrieved from www.thearc.org/document.doc?id=3140

Ayllon, T., & Azrin, N. H. (1964). Reinforcement and instructions with mental patients. *Journal of Experimental Analysis of Behavior, 7,* 327–331.

Bailey, D. B., Jr., Raspa, M., Holiday, D., Bishop, E., & Olmsted, M. (2009). Functional skills of individuals with fragile X syndrome: A lifespan cross-sectional analysis. *American Journal of Intellectual and Developmental Disabilities, 114,* 289–303.

Bakalar, N. (2011, January 3). Rh Factor, 1944. *The New York Times.* Retrieved from www.nytimes.com/2011/01/04/healthy/04first.html?_r=1&emc=tnt&tntemail0=y

Blatt, B. (1965). *Christmas in purgatory: A photographic essay on mental retardation.* Syracuse, NY: Human Policy Press.

Bouck, E. C., & Satsangi, R. (2014). Evidence-base of a functional curriculum for secondary students with mild intellectual disability: A historical perspective. *Education and Training in Autism and Developmental Disabilities, 49,* 478–486.

Bouck, E. C., & Satsangi, R. (2015). Is there really a difference? Distinguishing mild intellectual disability from *similar* disability categories. *Education and Training in Autism and Developmental Disabilities, 50,* 186–198.

Brown, I., & Radford, J. P. (2007). Historical overview of intellectual and developmental disabilities. In I. Brown and M. Percy (Eds.), *A comprehensive guide to intellectual and developmental disabilities.* Baltimore, MD: Paul Brookes Publishing.

Canella-Malone, H. I., Konrad, M., & Pennington, R. C. (2015). ACCESS! Teaching writing skills to students with intellectual disability. *TEACHING Exceptional Children, 47*(5), pp. 272–280.

Carter, E. W., Lane, K. L., Jenkins, A. B., Magill, L. Germer, K., & Greiner, S. M. (2015). Administrator views on providing self-determination instruction in elementary and secondary schools. *Journal of Special Education, 49,* 52–64.

Carter, E. W., Owens, L., Trainor, A. A., Sun, Y., & Swedeen, B. (2009). Self-determination of skills and opportunities of adolescents with severe intellectual and developmental disabilities. *American Journal on Intellectual and Developmental Disabilities, 114,* 179–192.

Cate, D., Diefendorf, M., McCullough, K., Peters, M. L., & Whaley, K. (Eds.). (2010). *Quality indicators of inclusive early childhood programs/practices: A compilation of selected resources.* Chapel Hill, NC: The University of North Carolina, FPG Child Development Institute, National Early Childhood Technical Assistance Center.

Cavkaytar, A. (2012). Teaching café waiter skills to adults with intellectual disability: A real setting study. *Education and Training in Autism and Developmental Disabilities, 47*(4), 426–437.

Centers for Disease Control and Prevention (CDC). (2010). *What would happen if we stopped vaccinations?* Retrieved from www.cdc.gov /vaccines/vac-gen/whatifstop.htm

Centers for Disease Control and Prevention (CDC). (2015). *Facts about FASD.* Retrieved from http://www.cdc.gov/ncbddd/fasd/facts.html

Centers for Disease Control and Prevention (CDC). (2015). *Fetal alcohol spectrum disorders (FASDs).* Retrieved from http://www.cdc.gov /ncbddd/fasd/facts.html

Centers for Disease Control and Prevention (CDC). (2015). *Measles cases and outbreaks.* Retrieved from http://www.cdc.gov/measles /cases-outbreaks.html

Children's Defense Fund. (2009, April 10). *Disparities in children's health and health coverage.* Retrieved from www.childrensdefense .org/child-research-data-publications/data/childrens-health-disparities-factsheet.pdf

Children's Defense Fund. (2014). *The state of America's children: Each day in America.* Retrieved from http://www.childrensdefense.org /library/state-of-americas-children/documents/2014-SOAC_each-day-in-America.pdf

Children's Defense Fund. (2015). *Ending child poverty now.* Retrieved from http://www.childrensdefense.org/newsroom/mediaresources /ending-child-poverty-now.pdf

Child Trends Databank. (2015). *Lead poisoning.* Retrieved from http://www.childtrends.org/?indicators=lead-poisoning

Christianson, S. (2003, Feb. 3). Bad seed or bad science? *New York Times.* Retrieved from http://www.nytimes.com/2003/02/08 /arts/bad-seed-or-bad-science.html?pagewanted=all

Cimera, R. E. (2010). National cost efficiency of supported employees with intellectual disabilities: 2002–2007. *American Journal of Intellectual and Developmental Disabilities, 115,* 19–29.

Cimera, R. E. (2012). The economics of supported employment: What new data tell us. *Journal of Vocational Rehabilitation, 37,* 109–117.

Correa, V. (2012). *Early childhood special education.* Presentation to ED 605, Claremont Graduate University, Teleconference, October 2012.

Eisenman, L. T. (2007). Self-determination interventions: Building a foundation for school completion. *Remedial and Special Education, 28,* 2–8.

Fujiura, G. T. (2013). The demarcation of intellectual disability. *Intellectual and Developmental Disabilities, 51,* 83–85.

Gelf, S. (1995). The beast in man: Degenerationism and mental retardation, 1900–1920. *Mental Retardation, 33,* 1–9.

Goode, D., Hill, D., Reiss, J., & Bronston, W. (2014). *A history and sociology of the Willowbrook State School.* Washington, DC: American Association on Intellectual and Developmental Disabilities.

Guralnick, M. J. (1998). Effectiveness of early intervention for vulnerable children: A developmental perspective. *American Journal on Mental Retardation, 102,* 319–345.

Harison, P., & Oakland, T. (2015). *Adaptive behavior assessment system (ABAS-3)* (3rd ed.). Torrance, CA: Western Psychological Services (WPS).

Hartman, M. A. (2009). Step by step: Creating a community-based transition program for students with intellectual disabilities. *TEACHING Exceptional Children, 42,* 6–58.

Heasley, S. (2015, January 20). Study finds postsecondary programs boost outcomes. *Disability Scoop.* Retrieved from http://www .disabilityscoop.com/2015/01/20/study-postsecondary-outcomes /19972/

Henry, L., & Winfield, J. (2010). Working memory and educational achievement in children with intellectual disabilities. *Journal of Intellectual Disability Research, 54*(4), 354–365.

Hewitt, A., Emerson, E., & Stansliffe, R. (2013). Introduction to the special issue: Community living and participation. *Intellectual and Developmental Disabilities, 51,* 293–297.

Hughes, C., Washington, B. H., & Brown, G. L. (2008). Supporting students in the transition from school to adult life. In F. Rusch (Ed.), *Beyond high school: Preparing adolescents for tomorrow's challenges* (2nd ed., pp. 266–287). Columbus, OH: Merrill.

Hunt, N., & Marshall, K. (2012). *Exceptional children and youth* (5th ed.). Belmont, CA: Wadsworth Cengage Learning.

Itard, J. M. G. (1806). *Wild boy of Aveyron.* (G. Humphrey and M. Humphrey, translators). (1962). Englewood Cliffs, NJ: Prentice-Hall. Originally published in Paris by Gouyon (1801).

Jirikowic, R., Gelo, J., & Astley, S. (2010). Children and youth with fetal alcohol spectrum disorders: Summary of intervention recommendations after clinical diagnosis. *Intellectual and Developmental Disabilities, 48,* 330–344.

Kauffman, J. M., & Payne, J. S. (1975). *Mental retardation: Introduction and personal perspectives.* Columbus, OH: Charles E. Merrill Publishing Company.

Kirk, S. A., & Johnson, G. O. (1952). *Educating the retarded child.* London, England: George G. Harrap & Co.

Larson, S. A., Lakin, K. C., Salmi, P., Scott, N., & Webster, A. (2010). Children and youth with intellectual or developmental disabilities living in congregate care settings (1977–2009): Healthy People 2010 Objective 6.7 outcomes. *Intellectual and Developmental Disabilities, 48,* 396–400.

Lee, S.-H., Wehmeyer, M. L., & Shogren, K. A. (2015). Effect of instruction with the self-determined learning model of instruction on students with disabilities: A meta-analysis. *Education and Training in Autism and Developmental Disabilities, 50,* 237–247.

Lent, J. R., & McLean, B. M. (1976). The trainable retarded: The technology of teaching. In N. G. Haring & R. L. Schiefelbush (Eds.), *Teaching special children* (pp. 197–223). New York, NY: McGraw-Hill.

Litvack, M. S., Ritchie, K. C., & Shore, B. M. (2011). High- and average-achieving students' perceptions of disabilities and of students with disabilities in inclusive classrooms. *Exceptional Children, 77,* 474–487.

Luckasson, R., Coulter, D. L., Polloway, E. A., Reis, S., Schalock, R. L., Snell, M. E., Spitalnik, D. M., & Stark, J. A. (1992). *Mental retardation: Definition, classification, and systems of supports.* Washington, DC: American Association on Mental Retardation (AAMR).

Martinez, D. C., & Queener, J. (2010). *Postsecondary education for students with intellectual disabilities.* Washington, DC: HEATH Resource Center, George Washington University.

Matheson, C., Olsen, R. J., & Weisner, T. (2007). A good friend is hard to find: Friendship among adolescents with disabilities. *American Journal on Mental Retardation, 112,* 319–329.

Moore, E. J., & Schelling, A. (2015). Postsecondary inclusion for individuals with an intellectual disability and its effects on employment. *Journal of Intellectual Disabilities, 19,* 130–148.

National Center on Educational Outcomes. (2013). *Alternate assessments for students with disabilities.* Retrieved from http://www.cehd.umn .edu/NCEO/TopicAreas/AlternateAssessments/altAssessTopic .htm

National Down Syndrome Society. (2010). *CDC study on the prevalence of Down syndrome.* Retrieved from www.ndss.org/index. php?option=com_content&view=article&id=153%3Aposition&limi tstart=2

National Fragile X Foundation. (2011). *Prevalence of fragile x syndrome.* Retrieved from www.fragilex.org/html/prevalence.htm

Newman, L., Wagner, M., Knokey, A.-M., Marder, C., Nagle, K., Shaver, D., Wei, X., with Cameto, R., Contreras, E., Ferguson, K., Greene, S., & Schwarting, M. (2011). *The post-high school outcomes of young adults with disabilities up to 8 years after high school: A report from the National Longitudinal Transition Study-2 (NLTS2)* (NCSER 2011-3005). Menlo Park, CA: SRI International.

Nirje, B. (1969). The normalization principle and its human management implications. In R. Kugel & W. Wolfensberger (Eds.), *Changing patterns in residential services for the mentally retarded* (pp. 179–195). Washington, DC: President's Committee on Mental Retardation.

Nirje, B. (1976). The normalization principle. In R. B. Kugel & A. Shearer (Eds.), *Changing patterns in residential services for the mentally retarded* (Rev. ed., pp. 231–240). Washington, DC: President's Committee on Mental Retardation.

Nonnemacher, S. L., & Bambara, L. M. (2011). "I'm supposed to be in charge": Self-advocates' perspectives on their self-determination support needs. *Intellectual and Developmental Disabilities, 49,* 327–340.

Oeseburg, B., Dijkstra, G. J., Groothoff, J. W., Reijneveld, S. A., & Jansen, D. E. (2011). Prevalence of chronic health conditions in children with intellectual disability: A systematic literature review. *Intellectual and Developmental Disabilities, 49,* 59–85.

Prabhalla, A. (2007, February 20). Mental retardation is no more—New name is intellectual and developmental disabilities. *AAIDD*

News. Washington, DC: American Association on Intellectual and Developmental Disabilities.

PubMed Health, National Center for Biotechnology Information (NCBI) at the U.S. National Library of Medicine (NLM). (2011). *Fetal alcohol syndrome.* Retrieved from www.ncbi.nlm.nih.gov/pubmedhealth /PMH0001909/

Rogan, P., & Rinne, S. (2011). National call for organizational change from sheltered to integrated employment. *Intellectual and Developmental Disabilities, 49,* 248–260.

Schalock, R. L., Borthwick-Duffy, S., Bradley, V. J., Buntinx, W. H. E., Coulter, D. L., Craig, E. M., Gomez, S. C., Lachapelle, Y., Luckasson, R., Reeve, A., Shogren, K. A., Snell, M. E., Spreat, S., Tassé, M. J., Thompson, J. R., Verdugo-Alonso, M. A., Wehmeyer, M. L., & Yeager, M. H. (2010). *Intellectual disability: Definition, classification, and systems of supports* (11th ed). Washington, DC: American Association on Intellectual and Developmental Disabilities (AAIDD).

Schalock, R. L., & Luckasson, R. (2013). What's at stake in the lives of people with intellectual disability? Part I: The power of naming, defining, diagnosing, classifying, and planning supports. *Intellectual and Developmental Disabilities, 51,* 86–93.

Schweinhart, L. J. (2005). *The High/Scope Perry Preschool study through age 40: Summary, conclusions, and frequently asked questions.* Ypsilanti, MI: High/Scope Educational Research Foundation. Retrieved from www.highscope.org

Sheppard, L., & Unsworth, C. (2011). Developing skills in everyday activities and self-determination in adolescents with intellectual and developmental disabilities. *Remedial and Special Education, 32,* 393–405.

Shogren, K. A., & Broussard, R. (2011). Exploring the perceptions of self-determination of individuals with intellectual disability. *Intellectual and Developmental Disabilities, 49,* 86–106.

Shogren, K. A., Wehmeyer, M. L., Palmer, S. B., Soukup, J. H., Little, T. D., Garner, N., & Lawrence, M. (2007). Examining individual and ecological predictors of self-determination of students with disabilities. *Exceptional Children, 73,* 488–509.

Shriver, T. (2011, March 30). Stop using the r-word. *The Colbert Report— 2011-30-03, Video Clip.* Comedy Central: www.colbertnation.com /video/tags/Tim%2BShriver

Siperstein, G. N., Pociask, S. E., & Collins, M. A. (2010). Sticks, stones, and stigma: A study of students' use of the derogatory term "retard." *Intellectual and Developmental Disabilities, 48,* 126–134.

Smith, J. D., & Wehmeyer, M. L. (2012). *Good blood, bad blood: Science, nature, and the myth of the Kallikaks.* Washington, DC: American Association on Intellectual and Developmental Disabilities.

Snell, M. E., & Luckasson, R. A., with Borthwick-Duffy, S., Bradley, V., Buntinx, W. H. E., Coulter, D. L., et al. (2009). The characteristics and needs of people with intellectual disability who have higher IQ scores. *Intellectual and Developmental Disabilities, 47,* 220–233.

Soukakou, E. P. (2010). *The Inclusive classroom profile.* Chapel Hill, NC: Frank Porter Graham Institute. Retrieved from http://build.fpg.unc .edu/sites/build.fpg.unc.edu/files/resources/Soukakou-Inclusive-Classroom-Profile-sample-9-2010-1.pdf

Soukakou E. P. (2012). Measuring quality in inclusive preschool classrooms: Development and validation of the Inclusive Classroom Profile (ICP). *Early Childhood Research Quarterly, 27(3),* 478–488.

Special Olympics (2009). *Rosa's Law.* Retrieved from www.specialolympics .org/PrintArticle.aspx?id=12302

Steere, D. E., & DiPipi-How, C. (2012). When you can't get out: Strategies for supporting community-based instruction. *TEACHING Exceptional Children, 45,* 60–67.

Talarico, L. (2011). *Teacher born with Down syndrome breaks stereotypes.* Retrieved from www.wltx.com/news/national/article/121995/2/ Teacher-Born-With-Down-Syndrome-Breaks-Stereotypes

Tassé, M. J. (2013). What's in a name? *Intellectual and Developmental Disabilities, 51,* 113–116.

Taylor, S. J. (2006). Christmas in purgatory: A retrospective look. *Mental Retardation, 44,* 145–149.

Timmons, J. C., Hall, A. C., Bose, J., Wolfe, A., & Winsor, J. (2011). Choosing employment: Factors that impact employment decisions for individuals with intellectual disability. *Intellectual and Developmental Disabilities, 49,* 285–299.

U.S. Congress. *Individuals with Disabilities Education Improvement Act of 2004.* Pub. L. No. 108-446. 118 STAT. 2647.

U.S. Department of Education. (1993). *Fifteenth annual report to Congress on the implementation of the Individuals with Disabilities Education Act.* Washington, DC: U.S. Government Printing Office.

U.S. Department of Education. (2001). *Twenty-third annual report to Congress on the implementation of the Individuals with Disabilities Education Act.* Washington, DC: U.S. Government Printing Office.

U.S. Department of Education. (2005). *Alternate achievement standards for students with the most significant cognitive disabilities* (Non-Regulatory Guidance). Retrieved from https://www2.ed.gov /policy/elsec/guid/altguidance.pdf

U.S. Department of Education. (2006, August 14). 34 CFR Parts 300 and 301, *Assistance to states for the education of children with disabilities and preschool grants for children with disabilities;* Final Rule (pp. 1263–1264), *Federal Register,* Washington, DC: Author.

U.S. Department of Education. (2011). *IDEA data: Data tables Part B child count (2010).* Retrieved from www.ideadata.org

U.S. Department of Education. (2012). *Individuals with Disabilities Education Act (IDEA), Part B, data collection history.* Retrieved from http://www2.ed.gov/programs/osepidea/618-data/collection-documentation/legacy-data-collection-information/data-history /b-datahistory.pdf

U.S. Department of Education. (2013). *Child count and settings.* [IDEA Section 618 State-Level Data File.] Retrieved from http://www2 .ed.gov/programs/osepidea/618-data/state-level-data-files /index.html#bccee

U.S. Department of Education. (2015). *Improving the academic achievement of the disadvantaged: Assistance to states for the education of children with disabilities,* 34 C.F.R. Parts 200 and 300.

U.S. Department of Education, Office of Special Education Programs, Data Analysis System (DANS). (2012). *Children with disabilities receiving special education under Part B of the Individuals with Disabilities Education Act-2011.* Data updated as of July 15, 2012. Retrieved from www.ideadata.org

U.S. Department of Education, Office of Special Education Programs, Data Analysis System (DANS). (2012). OMB #1820-0043: *Children with disabilities receiving special education under Part B of the Individuals with Disabilities Education Act 2011.* Data updated as of July 15, 2012. Retrieved from www.ideadata.org

U.S. Department of Education, Office of Special Education Programs (OSEP), Data Accountability Center. (2012). *IDEA data: Analytic tool Part B educational environments.* Retrieved from www.ideadata.org

U.S. Department of Education. (2013). *Child count and educational environments.* IDEA Section 618 Data Products: State Level Data Files. Retrieved from http://www2.ed.gov/programs/osepidea/618-data /state-level-data-files/index.html#bccee

U.S. Department of Education. (2014). *Child count and educational environments.* IDEA Section 618 Data Products: State Level Data Files. Retrieved from http://www2.ed.gov/programs/osepidea/618-data /state-level-data-files/index.html#bccee

U.S. Department of Education. (2015). *Child count and educational environments.* IDEA Section 618 Data Products: State Level Data Files. Retrieved from http://www2.ed.gov/programs/osepidea/618-data /state-level-data-files/index.html#bccee

U.S. Department of Health and Human Services, Substance Abuse and Mental Health Services Administration (2011, June 15). *The financial impact of fetal alcohol syndrome.* Retrieved from www .fasdcenter.samhsa.gov/publications/Cost.cfm

University of Iowa, College of Education. (2011). *REACH: Realizing Educational and Career Hopes: A college program for students with intellectual, cognitive, and learning disabilities.* Retrieved from www.education .uiowa.edu/services/reach/default/AboutREACH.aspx

Wehmeyer, M. L. (2007). *Promoting self-determination in students with developmental disabilities.* New York, NY: Guilford Press.

Wehmeyer, M. L. (2011). Presidential address 2011: Imagining the future: Establishing a new legacy for AAIDD. *Intellectual and Developmental Disabilities, 49,* 352–359.

Wehmeyer, M. L. (2013). Disability, disorder, and identity. *Intellectual and Developmental Disabilities, 51,* 122–126.

Wehmeyer, M. L., & Smith, J. D. (2006). Leaving the garden: Reconsidering Henry Herbert Goddard's exodus from the Vineland Training School. *Mental Retardation, 44,* 150–155.

Westling, D. L, Kelley, K. R., Cain, B., & Prohn, S. (2013). College students' attitudes about an inclusive postsecondary education program for individuals with intellectual disability. *Education and Training in Autism and Developmental Disabilities, 48,* 306–319.

Williams, J. F. & Smith, V. C. (2015). Fetal alcohol spectrum disorders. *Pediatrics, 136,* e1395–e1406.

Winton, P., Turnbull, A., & Blacher, J. (1984). *Selecting a preschool: A guide for parents of handicapped children.* Baltimore, MD: University Park Press.

Winzer, M. A. (1993). *The history of special education: From isolation to integration.* Washington, DC: Gallaudet University Press.

Wolfensberger, W. (1972). *The principle of normalization in human services.* Toronto: National Institute on Mental Retardation.

Wolfensberger, W. (2002). Social role valorization and, or versus, "empowerment." *Mental Retardation, 40,* 252–258.

Wright, P. W. D., & Wright, P. D. (2015, February). Transition, transition services, and transition planning. *Wrights Law.* Retrieved from http://www.wrightslaw.com/info/trans.index.htm

Chapter 10

Allen, K. M., Hart, B. M., Buell, J. S., Harris, F. R., & Wolf, M. M. (1964). Effects of social reinforcement on isolated behavior of a nursery school child. *Child Development, 35,* 511–518.

American Psychiatric Association. (2013). Conduct disorder. In *Diagnostic and statistical manual of mental disorders, Fifth Edition, Text Revision* (DSM–5) (5th ed.). Washington, DC: Author.

American Psychiatric Association (APA). (2013). *Diagnostic and statistical manual of mental disorders, Fifth Edition, Text Revision* (DSM-5) (5th ed.). Washington, DC: Author.

American Psychiatric Association. (2013). Oppositional defiant disorder. In *Diagnostic and statistical manual of mental disorders, Fifth Edition, Text Revision* (DSM-5) (5th ed.). Washington, DC: Author.

American Psychiatric Association (APA). (2013). Social anxiety disorder. In *Diagnostic and statistical manual of mental disorders, Fifth Edition, Text Revision* (DSM-5) (5th ed.). Washington, DC: Author.

Anderson, J. A., Kutash, K., & Duchnowski, A. J. (2001). A comparison of the academic progress of students with EBD and students with LD. *Journal of Emotional and Behavioral Disorders, 9,* 106–115.

Archwamety, T., & Katsiyannis, A. (2000). Academic remediation, parole violations, and recidivism rates among delinquent youth. *Remedial and Special Education, 21,* 161–170.

Axelrod, S., & Hall, R. V. (1999). *Behavior modification: Basic principles.* Austin, TX: PRO-ED.

Babyak, A. E., Koorland, M., & Mathes, P. G. (2000). The effects of story mapping instruction on the reading comprehension of students with behavioral disorders. *Behavioral Disorders, 25,* 239–258.

Babyak, A. E., Luze, G. J., & Kamps, D. M. (2000). The Good Student Game: Behavior management for diverse classrooms. *Intervention in School and Clinic, 35,* 216–223.

Barrish, H., Saunders, M., & Wolf, M. (1969). Good Behavior Game: Effects of individual contingencies for group consequences on disruptive behavior in a classroom. *Journal of Applied Behavior Analysis, 2,* 119–124.

Becker, S. P., Paternite, C. E., Evans, S. W., Andrews, C., Christensen, O. A., Kraan, E. M., & Weist, M. D. (2011). Eligibility, assessment, and educational placement issues for students classified with emotional disturbance: Federal and state-level analyses. *School Mental Health, 3,* 24–34.

Beech, M. (2010). *Accommodations: Assisting students with disabilities* (3rd ed.). Tallahassee, FL: Florida Department of Education. Retrieved from http://www.fldoe.org/core/fileparse.php/7690/urlt/0070069-accomm-educator.pdf

Bender, W. N., Shubert, T. H., & McLaughlin, P. J. (2001). Invisible kids: Preventing school violence by identifying kids in trouble. *Intervention in School and Clinic, 37,* 105–111.

Bower, E. M. (1960). *Early identification of emotionally disturbed children in school* (Rev. ed.). Springfield, IL: Thomas.

Bower, E. M. (1982). Defining emotional disturbance: Public policy and research. *Psychology in the Schools, 19,* 55–60.

Bower, E. M., & Lambert, N. M. (1962). *A process for in-school screening of children with emotional handicaps.* Princeton, NJ: Educational Testing Service.

Bowman-Perrott, L., Burke, M. D., Zaini, S., Zhang, N., & Vannest, K. (2015). Promoting positive behavior using the Good Behavior Game: A meta-analysis of single-case research. *Journal of Positive Behavior Interventions.* doi: 10.1177/1098300715592355.v

Bradley, A. (2007). *NICHCY's building the legacy training curriculum on IDEA 2004: Module 19: Key issues in discipline.* Washington, DC: National Dissemination Center for Children with Disabilities (NICHCY).

Bradshaw, C. P., Koth, C. W., Thornton, L. A., & Leaf, P. J. (2009). Altering school climate through school-wide Positive Behavioral Interventions and Supports: Findings from a group-randomized effectiveness trial. *Prevention Science, 10,* 100–115.

Bradshaw, C. P., Rodgers, C. R. R., Ghandour, L. A., & Garbarino, J. (2009). Social-cognitive mediators of the association between community violence exposure and aggressive behavior. *School Psychology Quarterly, 24,* 199–210.

Bradshaw, C. P., Schaeffer, C. M., Petras, H., & Ialongo, N. (2010). Predicting negative life outcomes from early aggressive-disruptive behavior trajectories: Gender differences in maladaptation across life domains. *Journal of Youth and Adolescence, 39,* 953–866.

Breeman, L. D., van Lier, P. A. C., Wubbels, T., Verhulst, F. C., van der Ende, J., Maras, A., Struiksma, A. J. C., Hopman, J. A. B., & Tick, N. T. (2015). Effects of the Good Behavior Game on the behavioral, emotional, and social problems of children with psychiatric disorders in special education settings. *Journal of Positive Behavior Interventions.* doi: 10.1177/1098300715593466

Brigham, A. (1847). The moral treatment of insanity. *American Journal of Insanity, 4,* 1–15.

Bullis, M., Walker, H. M., & Sprague, J. R. (2001). A promise unfulfilled: Social skills training with at-risk and antisocial children and youth. *Exceptionality, 9,* 67–90.

Bullis, M., & Yovanoff, P. (2006). Twenty-four months after high school: Paths taken by youth diagnosed with severe emotional and behavioral disorders. *Journal of Emotional and Behavioral Disorders, 14,* 99–107.

Carlson, G. A., & Kashani, J. H. (1988). Phenomenology of major depression from childhood through adulthood: Analysis of three studies. *American Journal of Psychiatry, 145,* 1222–1225.

Cartledge, G., Kea, C. D., & Ida, D. J. (2000). Anticipating differences, celebrating strengths: Providing culturally competent services for students with serious emotional disturbance. *TEACHING Exceptional Children, 32,* 30–37.

Cauce, A., Paradise, M., Ginzler, J., Embry, L., Morgan, C. J., Lohr, Y., & Theofelis, J. (2000). The characteristics and mental health of homeless adolescents: Age and gender differences. *Journal of Emotional and Behavioral Disorders, 8,* 230–239.

Center for Adolescent Research in Schools (2014). *The CARS classroom-based interventions manual.* Bethlehem, PA: Center for Adolescent Research in Schools, Lehigh University. Retrieved from https://coe.lehigh.edu/sites/coe.lehigh.edu/files/documents/CARS%20Classroom%20Manual%202-15.pdf

Centers for Disease Control and Prevention. (2013). *Mental health basics.* Atlanta, GA: Author. Retrieved from http://www.cdc.gov/mentalhealth/basics.htm

Centers for Disease Control and Prevention. (2015). *Suicide: Facts at a glance.* Atlanta, GA: Author.

Cheney, D., & Barringer, C. (1995). Teacher competence, student diversity, and staff training for the inclusion of middle school students with emotional and behavioral disorders. *Journal of Emotional and Behavioral Disorders, 3,* 174–182.

Children's and Adult Center for OCD and Anxiety. (n.d.). *Sample accommodations for anxious kids.* Retrieved from http://worrywisekids.org/node/40

Cochran, L., Feng, H., Cartledge, G., & Hamilton, S. (1993). The effects of cross-age tutoring on the academic achievement, social behaviors, and self-perceptions of low-achieving African-American males with behavioral disorders. *Behavioral Disorders, 18,* 292–302.

Conroy, M. A., Sutherland, K. S., Snyder, A. L., & Marsh, S. (2008). Classwide interventions: Effective instruction makes a difference. *TEACHING Exceptional Children, 40,* 24–30.

Costenbader, V., & Buntaine, R. (1999). Diagnostic discrimination between social maladjustment and emotional disturbance. *Journal of Emotional and Behavioral Disorders, 7,* 2–10.

Council for Children with Behavioral Disorders. (1989). Position Paper on definition and identification of students with behavioral disorders. *Behavioral Disorders, 15*(3) 180–189.

Council for Children with Behavioral Disorders. (2009, July 8). *CCBD's position summary on the use of physical restraint procedures in school settings.* Retrieved from www.cec.sped.org/Content/NavigationMenu/PolicyAdvocacy/CECPolicyResources/Restraint_and_Seclusion/default.htm

Council for Exceptional Children. (2009, September). *CEC's policy on physical restraint and seclusion procedures in school settings.* Arlington, VA: Author. Retrieved from www.cec.sped.org/AM/Template.cfm?Section=CEC_Professional_Policies&Template=/CM/ContentDisplay.cfm&ContentID=13030

Crundwell, R. M., & Killu, K. (2007). Understanding and accommodating students with depression in the classroom. *TEACHING Exceptional Children, 40*(1), 48–54.

Cruz, L., & Cullinan, D. (2001). Awarding points, using levels to help children improve behavior. *TEACHING Exceptional Children, 33,* 16–23.

Davis, C. A., Brady, M. P., Williams, R. E., & Hamilton, R. (1992). Effects of high-probability requests on the acquisition and generalization of responses to requests in young children and behavior disorders. *Journal of Applied Behavior Analysis, 25,* 905–916.

Dawson, L., Venn, M. L., & Gunter, P. L. (2000). The effects of teacher versus computer reading models. *Behavioral Disorders, 25,* 105–113.

Day, D. M., & Hunt, A. C. (1996). A multivariate assessment of a risk model for juvenile delinquency with an "under 12 offender" sample. *Journal of Emotional and Behavioral Disorders, 4,* 66–72.

Deutsch, A. (1949). *The mentally ill in America: A history of their care and treatment from colonial times* (2nd ed.). New York, NY: Columbia University Press.

Duckworth, S., Smith-Rex, S., Okey, S., Brookshire, M., Rawlinson, D., Rawlinson, R., Castillo, S., & Little, J. (2001). Wraparound services for young schoolchildren with emotional and behavioral disorders. *TEACHING Exceptional Children, 33,* 54–60.

Dunlap, G. & Fox, L. (2015, November). *The Pyramid Model: PBS in early childhood programs and its relation to school-wide PBIS.* The Pyramid Model Consortium. Retrieved from http://www.pyramidmodel.org/uploads/9/5/6/3/9563066/pbs_and_pyramid_model.pdf

Eber, L., Smith, C. R., Sugai, G., & Scott, T. M. (2002). Wraparound and positive behavioral supports in the schools. *Journal of Emotional and Behavioral Disorders, 10,* 171–180.

Edelsohn, G., Ialongo, N., Werthamer-Larsson, L., Crockett, I., & Kellam, S. (1992). Self-reported depressive symptoms in first-grade children: Developmentally transient phenomena. *Journal of the American Academy of Child and Adolescent Psychiatry, 31,* 282–290.

Elliott, S., & Gresham, F. M. (1991). *Social skills intervention guide.* Circle Pines, MN: American Guidance Service.

Ervin, R. A., DuPaul, G. J., Kern, L., & Friman, P. C. (1998). Classroom-based functional and adjunctive assessments: Proactive approaches to intervention selection for adolescents with attention deficit hyperactivity disorder. *Journal of Applied Behavior Analysis, 31,* 65–78.

Falk, K. B., & Wehby, J. H. (2001). The effects of peer-assisted learning strategies on the beginning reading skills of young children with emotional or behavioral disorders. *Behavioral Disorders, 26,* 344–359.

Feil, E. G., Walker, H. M., & Severson, H. H. (1995). The Early Screening Project for young children with behavior problems. *Journal of Emotional and Behavioral Disorders, 3,* 194–202.

Forness, S. R., & Kavale, K. A. (2001). Are school professionals missing their best chance to help troubled kids? *Emotional and Behavioral Disorders, 1,* 80–83.

Forness, S. R., & Knitzer, J. (1992). A new proposed definition and terminology to replace "serious emotional disturbance" in IDEA. *School Psychology Review, 21,* 12–20.

Fox, L., & Hemmeter, M. L. (2014). *Implementing Positive Behavioral Intervention and Support: The evidence-base of the Pyramid Model for supporting social emotional competence in infants and young children.* Pyramid Model Consortium. Retrieved from http://www.pyramidmodel.org/uploads/9/5/6/3/9563066/implementing_positive_behavioral_intervention_and_support.pdf

Franca, V. M., Kerr, M. M., Reitz, A. L., & Lambert, D. (1990). Peer tutoring among behaviorally disordered students: Academic and social benefits to tutor and tutee. *Education and Treatment of Children, 3,* 109–128.

Friesen, A., Hanson, M., & Martin, K. (2014). In the eyes of the beholder: Cultural considerations in interpreting children's behaviors. *Young Exceptional Children, 18,* 19–30.

Frey, K. S., Hirschstein, M. K., & Guzzo, B. A. (2000). Second step: Preventing aggression by promoting social competence. *Journal of Emotional and Behavioral Disorders, 8,* 102–112.

Gage, N. A., Lewis, T. J., & Stichter, J. P. (2012). Functional behavioral assessment-based interventions for students with or at risk for emotional and/or behavioral disorders in school: A hierarchical linear modeling meta-analysis. *Behavioral Disorders, 37,* 55–77.

Gersten, R., Fuchs, L. S., Compton, D., Coyne, M., Greenwood, C., & Innocenti, M. S. (2005). Quality indicators for group experimental and quasi-experimental research in special education. *Exceptional Children, 71,* 149–164.

Greenbaum, P. E., Dedrick, R. F., Friedman, R. M., Kutash, K., Brown, E. C., & Lardieri, S. P. (1996). National Adolescent and Child Treatment Study (NACTS): Outcomes for children with serious emotional and behavioral disturbance. *Journal of Emotional and Behavioral Disorders, 4,* 130–146.

Gresham, F. M. (2002). Social skills assessment and instruction for students with emotional and behavioral disorders. In K. L. Lane, F. M. Gresham, & T. E. O'Shaughnessy (Eds.), *Interventions for children with or at risk for emotional and behavioral disorders* (pp. 242–258). Boston, MA: Allyn & Bacon.

Gresham, F. M., Lane, K. L., MacMillan, D. L., & Bocian, K. M. (1999). Social and academic profiles of externalizing and internalizing groups: Risk factors for emotional and behavioral disorders. *Behavioral Disorders, 24,* 231–245.

Habib, D. (2012). *Who cares about Kelsey?* United States: DH Photography, LLC.

Harper, G. F., Mallette, B., Meheady, L., Bentley, A. E., & Moore, J. (1995). Retention and treatment failure in classwide peer tutoring: Implications for further research. *Journal of Behavioral Education, 5,* 399–414.

Harrison, J. R., Bunford, N., Evans, S. W., & Owens, J. S. (2013). Educational accommodations for students with behavioral challenges: A systematic review of the literature. *Review of Educational Research, 83*(4), 551–597.

Harry, B., & Klingner, J. (2006). *Why are so many minority students in special education? Understanding race and disability in schools.* New York, NY: Teachers College Press.

Hawkins, J. D., Catalano, R. F., Kosterman, R., Abbott, R., & Hill, K. G. (1999). Preventing adolescent health-risk behaviors by strengthening protection during childhood. *Archives of Pediatrics & Adolescent Medicine, 153,* 226–234.

Hemmeter, M. L., Fox, L., Snyder, P., & Algina, J. (2014, July). *A classroom-wide model for promoting social emotional development and addressing challenging behavior in preschool children.* The Pyramid Consortium. Retrieved from http://www.pyramidmodel.org/uploads/9/5/6/3/9563066/social_emotional_development__addressing_challenging_behavior_in_preschool_children.pdf

Hemmeter, M. L., Snyder, P., Fox, L., & Algina, J. (2016). Evaluating the implementation of the *Pyramid Model for Promoting Social-Emotional Competence* in early childhood classrooms. *Topics in Early Childhood Special Education,* 1–10. doi: 10.1177/0271121416653386

Hoagwood, K. (2001). Evidence-based practice in children's mental health services: What do we know? Why aren't we putting it to use? *Emotional and Behavioral Disorders in Youth, 1,* 84–87, 90.

Holland, G. (2015). L.A. tops nation in chronic homeless population. *LA Times*. Retrieved from www.latimes.com/local/california/la-me-homeless-national-numbers-20151120-story.html

Hollo, A., Wehby, J. H., & Oliver, R. M. (2014). Unidentified language deficits in children with emotional and behavioral disorders: A meta-analysis. *Exceptional Children, 80,* 169–186.

Horner, R. H., Carr, E. G., Halle, J., McGee, G., Odom, S., & Wolery, M. (2005). The use of single-subject research to identify evidence-based practice in special education. *Exceptional Children, 71,* 165–179.

Horner, R. H., & Sugai, G. (2002). *School-wide positive behavior support: Implementers' blueprint and self-assessment.* Eugene, OR: University of Oregon, OSEP Center on Positive Behavior Support.

Horner, R. H., Sugai, G., Lewis-Palmer, T., & Todd, A. W. (2001). Teaching school-wide behavioral expectations. *Emotional and Behavioral Expectations, 1,* 77–79, 93–95.

Hosp, J. L., & Reschly, D. J. (2002). Predictors of restrictiveness of placement for African-American and Caucasian students. *Exceptional Children, 68,* 225–238.

Hunter, L. (2001). The value of school-based mental health programs. *Emotional and Behavioral Disorders in Youth, 1,* 27–28, 46.

IDEA Practices. (2002). *Youth with disabilities in the juvenile justice system.* Retrieved from www.ideapractices.org

Institute for the Study of Homelessness & Poverty at Weingart Center. (2015). *Homelessness in Los Angeles County* Retrieved from www.laalmanac.com/social/so14.htm

IRIS Center. (2009). *Functional behavioral assessment: Identifying the reasons for problem behavior and developing a behavior plan.* Retrieved from http://iris.peabody.vanderbilt.edu/module/fba

Iwata, B. A., Dorsey, M. E., Slifer, K. J., Bauman, K. E., & Richman, G. S. (1982). Toward a functional analysis of self-injury. *Analysis and Intervention in Developmental Disabilities, 2,* 3–20.

Jamison, P., & Holland, G. (2016). Homeless measures take center stage in Mayor Garcetti's 2016 budget proposal. *LA Times*. Retrieved from www.latimes.comocal/lanow/la-me-in-garcetti-budget-20160420-story.html

Justice Policy Institute. (2015). *The tip of the iceberg: What taxpayers pay to incarcerate youth.* Retrieved from http://www.justicepolicy.org/uploads/justicepolicy/documents/factsheet_costs_of_confinement.pdf

Kamps, D., Kravits, T., Stolze, J., & Swaggart, B. (1999). Prevention strategies for at-risk students and students with EBD in urban elementary schools. *Journal of Emotional and Behavioral Disorders, 7,* 178–188.

Kanner, L. (1957). *Child psychiatry.* Springfield, IL: Thomas.

Kaslow, N. J., & Rehm, L. P. (1998). Childhood depression. In R. J. Morris and T. R. Kratochwill (Eds.), *The practice of child therapy* (3rd ed., pp. 48–90). Boston, MA: Allyn & Bacon.

Kauffman, J. M. (1999). How we prevent the prevention of emotional and behavioral disorders. *Exceptional Children, 65,* 448–468.

Kauffman, J. M., & Landrum, T. J. (2013). *Characteristics of behavioral disorders of children and youth* (10th ed.). Upper Saddle River, NJ: Merrill/Pearson Education.

Kazdin, A. (1987). Treatment of antisocial behavior in children: Current status and future directions. *Psychological Bulletin, 102,* 187–203.

Kellam, S. G., Mackenzie, A. C. L., Brown, C. H., Poduska, J. M., Wang, W., Petras, H., & Wilcox, H. C. (2011). The good behavior game and the future of prevention and treatment. *Addiction Science & Clinical Practice, 6,* 73–84.

Kern, L., Childs, K., Dunlap, G., Clarke, S., & Falk, G. (1994). Using assessment-based curricular intervention to improve the classroom behavior of a student with emotional and behavioral challenges. *Journal of Applied Behavior Analysis, 27,* 7–19.

Kern, L., Delaney, B., Clarke, S., Dunlap, G., & Childs, K. (2001). Improving the classroom behavior of students with emotional and behavioral disorders using individualized curricular modifications. *Journal of Emotional and Behavioral Disorders, 9,* 239–247.

Kern, L., & Wehby, J.H. (2014). Using data to intensify behavioral interventions for individual students. *TEACHING Exceptional Children, 46,* 45–53.

Klodnick, V. V., Sabella K., Brenner, C. J., Krzos, I. M., Ellison, M. L., Kaiser, S. M., Davis, M., & Fagan, M. (2015). Perspectives of young emerging adults with serious mental health conditions on vocational peer mentors. *Journal of Emotional and Behavioral Disorders, 23,* 226–237.

Landrum, T. J., Tankersley, M., & Kauffman, J. M. (2003). What is special about special education for students with emotional or behavioral disorders? *Journal of Special Education, 37,* 148–156.

Lane, K. L. (1999). Young students at risk for antisocial behavior: The utility of academic and social skills interventions. *Journal of Emotional and Behavioral Disorders, 7,* 211–223.

Lane, K. L. (2003). Identifying young students at risk for antisocial behavior: The utility of "teachers as tests." *Behavioral Disorders, 28,* 360–389.

Lane, K. L. (2004). Academic instruction and tutoring interventions for students with emotional/behavioral disorders: 1990 to present. In R. B. Rutherford, M. M. Quinn, & S. R. Mathur (Eds.), *Handbook of research in emotional and behavioral disorders* (pp. 462–486). New York, NY: Guilford Press.

Lane, K. L. (2007). Identifying and supporting students at risk for emotional and behavioral disorders within multi-level models: Data driven approaches to conducting secondary interventions with an academic emphasis. *Education and Treatment of Children, 30,* 135–164.

Lane, K. L., & Beebe-Frankenberger, M. E. (2004). *School-based interventions: The tools you need to succeed.* Boston, MA: Allyn & Bacon.

Lane, K. L., Gresham, F. M., & O'Shaughnessy, T. (2002). Identifying, assessing and intervening with children with or at-risk for behavior disorders: A look to the future. In K. L. Lane, F. M. Gresham, & T. E. O'Shaughnessy (Eds.), *Interventions for children with or at risk for emotional and behavioral disorders* (pp. 317–326). Boston, MA: Allyn & Bacon.

Lane, K. L., Harris, K., Graham, S., Weisenbach, J., Brindle, M., & Morphy, P. (2008). The effects of self-regulated strategy development on the writing performance of second grade students with behavioral and writing difficulties. *Journal of Special Education, 41,* 234–253.

Lane, K. L., Kalberg, J. R., & Edwards, C. (2008). An examination of school-wide interventions with primary level efforts conducted in elementary schools: Implications for school psychologists. In D. H. Molina (Ed.), *School psychology: 21st century issues and challenges.* (pp. 253–278). New York, NY: Nova Science.

Lane, K. L., Mahdavi, J. N., & Borthwick-Duffy, S. A. (2003). Teacher perceptions of the prereferral intervention process: A call for assistance with school-based interventions. *Preventing School Failure, 47,* 148–155.

Lane, K. L., O'Shaughnessy, T. E., Lambros, K. M., Gresham, F. M., & Beebe-Frankenberger, M. E. (2001). The efficacy of phonological awareness training with first-grade students who have behavioral problems and reading difficulties. *Journal of Emotional and Behavioral Disorders, 9,* 219–231.

Lane, K. L., Robertson, E. J., & Graham-Bailey, M. A. L. (2006). An examination of school-wide interventions with primary level efforts conducted in secondary schools: Methodological considerations. In T. E. Scruggs & M.A. Mastropieri (Eds.), *Applications of research methodology: Advances in learning and behavioral disabilities* (Vol. 19). Oxford, UK: Elsevier.

Lane, K. L., Wehby, J. H., Little, M. A., & Cooley, C. (2005). Students educated in self-contained classes and self-contained schools: Part II–How do they progress over time? *Behavioral Disorders, 30,* 363–374.

Lane, K. L., Wehby, J., Menzies, H. M., Doukas, G. L., Munton, S. M., & Gregg, R. M. (2003). Social skills instruction for students at risk for antisocial behavior: The effects of small-group instruction. *Behavioral Disorders, 28,* 229–248.

Lane, K. L., Wehby, J. H., Menzies, H. M., Gregg, R. M., Doukas, G. L., & Munton, S. M. (2002). Early literacy instruction for first-grade students at-risk for antisocial behavior. *Education and Treatment of Children, 25,* 438–458.

Lane, K. L., Weisenbach, J. L., Little, M. A., Phillips, A., & Wehby, J. (2006). Illustrations of function-based interventions implemented by general education teachers: Building capacity at the school site. *Education and Treatment of Children, 29,* 549–671.

Lee, H., Rojewski, J. W., Gregg, N., Jeong, S. (2015). Postsecondary education persistence of adolescents with specific learning disabilities or emotional/behavioral disorders. *Journal of Special Education, 49,* 77–88.

Lee, Y. Y., Sugai, G., & Horner, R. H. (1999). Using an instructional intervention to reduce problem and off-task behaviors. *Journal of Positive Behavior Interventions, 1*, 195–204.

Lewis, T. J., Jones, S. E. L., Horner, R. H., & Sugai, G. (2010). School-wide Positive Behavior Support and students with emotional /behavioral disorders: Implications for prevention, identification, and intervention. *Exceptionality, 18*, 82–93.

Lewis, T. J., & Sugai, G. (1999). Effective behavior support: A systems approach to proactive schoolwide management. *Exceptional Children, 31*, 1–24.

Little, L. (2002, Winter). In preschool classrooms: Linking research to practice. *Early Developments*, 7–9.

Lloyd, B. P., Torelli, J. N., & Symons, F. J. (2016). Issues in integrating psychotropic and intensive behavioral interventions for students with emotional and behavioral challenges in schools. *Journal of Emotional and Behavioral Disorders*, 1–11. doi: 10.1177/1063426616636346

Lynam, D. R. (1996). Early identification of chronic offenders: Who is the fledgling psychopath? *Psychological Bulletin, 120*, 209–234.

Maag, J. W. (2000). Managing resistance. *Intervention in Schools and Clinics, 35*, 131–140.

Maag, J. W. (2001). Rewarded by punishment: Reflections on the disuse of positive reinforcement in schools. *Exceptional Children, 67*, 173–186.

Maggin, D. M., Wehby, J. H., & Gilmour, A. F. (2016). Intensive academic interventions for students with emotional and behavioral disorders: An experimental framework. *Journal of Emotional and Behavioral Disorders*, 1–10. doi:10.1177/1063426616649162

Maggin, D. M., Wehby, J. H., Moore Partin, T. C., Robertson, R., & Oliver, R. G. (2011). A comparison of the instructional context for students with behavioral issues enrolled in self–contained and general education classrooms. *Behavioral Disorders, 36*, 84–99.

Maggin, D. M., Zurheide, J., Pickett, K. C., & Baillie, S. J. (2015). A systematic evidence review of the Check-in/Check-Out program for reducing student challenging behaviors. *Journal of Positive Behavior Interventions, 17*, 197–208.

Manley, R. S., Rickson, H., & Standeven, B. (2000). Children and adolescents with eating disorders: Strategies for teachers and school counselors. *Intervention in School and Clinic, 35*, 228–231.

Mattison, R. E., Hooper, S. R., & Glassberg, L. A. (2002). Three-year course of learning disorders in special education students classified as behavioral disorder. *Journal of the American Academy of Child & Adolescent Psychiatry, 41*, 1454–1461.

McConaughy, S. H., & Wadsworth, M. E. (2000). Life history reports of young adults previously referred for mental health services. *Journal of Emotional and Behavioral Disorders, 8*, 202–215.

Merikangas, K. R., He, J. P., Brody, D., Fisher, P. W., Bourdon, K., & Koretz, D. S. (2010). Prevalence and treatment of mental disorders among US children in the 2001–2004 NHANES. *Pediatrics, 125*, 75–81.

Miller, M. J., Lane, K. L., & Wehby, J. (2005). Social skills instruction for students with high incidence disabilities: An effective, efficient approach for addressing acquisition deficits. *Preventing School Failure, 49*, 27–40.

Miller-Johnson, S., Coie, J. E., Maumary-Gremaud, A., Lockman, J., & Terry, R. (1999). Relationship between childhood peer rejection and aggression and adolescent delinquency severity and type among African-American youth. *Journal of Emotional and Behavioral Disorders, 7*, 137–146.

Minnesota Association for Children's Mental Health. (n.d.). *Children's mental health disorder fact sheet for the classroom*. Retrieved from http://www.schoolmentalhealth.org/Resources/Educ /MHClassroomFactSheet.pdf

Moore, T. C., Wehby, J. H., Hollo, A., Robertson, R. E., & Maggin, D. M. (2014). Teacher reports of student health and its influence on students' school performance. *Journal of Positive Behavior Interventions, 16*, 112–122.

Moore Partin, T. C., Robertson, R. E., Maggin, D. M., Oliver, R. M., & Wehby, J. H. (2010). Using teacher praise and opportunities to respond to promote appropriate student behavior. *Preventing School Failure, 54*, 172–178.

Morris, R. J., Shah, K., & Morris, Y. P. (2002). Internalizing behavior disorders. In K. L. Lane, F. M. Gresham, & T. E. O'Shaughnessy (Eds.), *Interventions for children with or at risk for emotional and behavioral disorders* (pp. 223–241). Boston, MA: Allyn & Bacon.

Myles, B. S., & Simpson, R. L. (1998). Aggression and violence by school-age children and youth: Understanding the aggression cycle and prevention/intervention strategies. *Intervention in School and Clinic, 33*, 259–264.

National Alliance of Black School Educators & ILIAD Project. (2002). *Addressing over-representation of African American students in special education*. Arlington, VA: Council for Exceptional Children, and Washington, DC: National Alliance of Black School Educators.

National Disability Rights Network. (2009). *School is not supposed to hurt: Investigative report on abusive restraint and seclusion in schools*. Washington, DC: Author.

National Longitudinal Transition Study 2. (2005, November). *High school completion by youth with disabilities*. Menlo Park, CA: SRI International. Retrieved from http://www.nlts2.org/fact_sheets/nlts2_ fact_sheet_2005_11.pdf

National Longitudinal Transition Study 2. (2006, March). *School behavior and disciplinary experiences of youth with disabilities*. Menlo Park, CA: SRI International. Retrieved from http://www.nlts2.org/fact_ sheets/nlts2_fact_sheet_2006_03.pdf

Nelson, J. R., Benner, G. J., Lane, K., & Smith, B. W. (2004). An investigation of the academic achievement of K–12 students with emotional and behavioral disorders in public school settings. *Exceptional Children, 71*, 59–73.

Nelson, J. R., Johnson, A., & Marchand-Martella, N. (1996). Effects of direct instruction, cooperative learning, and independent learning practices on the classroom behavior of students with behavioral disorders: A comparative analysis. *Journal of Emotional and Behavioral Disorders, 4*, 53–62.

Newcomer, P. L. (1993). *Understanding and teaching emotionally disturbed children and adolescents* (2nd ed.). Austin, TX: PRO-ED.

Nichols, P. (2000). Role of cognition and affect in a functional behavioral analysis. *Exceptional Children, 66*, 393–402.

Norlin, J. W. (2012). *FBAs and BIPs: Meeting IDEA compliance obligations*. Palm Beach Gardens, FL: LRP Publications.

Office of Special Education and Rehabilitative Services, U.S. Department of Education. (2015). *Thirty-seventh annual report to Congress on the implementation of the Individuals with Disabilities Education Act, 2015*. Retrieved from http://www2.ed.gov/about/reports/annual /osep/2015/parts-b-c/37th-arc-for-idea.pdf

Pappadopulos, E., & Jensen, P. S. (2001). What school professionals, counselors, and parents need to know about medication for emotional and behavioral disorders in kids. *Emotional and Behavioral Disorders in Youth, 1*, 35–37.

Peacock Hill Working Group. (1991). Problems and promises in special education and related services for children and youth with emotional or behavioral disorders. *Behavioral Disorders, 16*, 299–313.

Quinn, S. R., & Poirier, J. M. (2004). Linking prevention research with policy: Examining the costs of the failure to prevent emotional and behavioral disorders. In R. B. Rutherford Jr., M. M. Quinn, & S. R. Mathur (Eds.), *Handbook of research in emotional and behavioral disorders* (pp. 78–97). New York, NY: Guilford Press.

Reid, J. B., & Patterson, G. R. (1991). Early prevention and intervention with conduct problems: A social interactional model for the integration of research and practice. In G. Stoner, M. R. Shinn, & H. M. Walker (Eds.), *Interventions for achievement and behavior problems* (pp. 715–740). Silver Spring, MD: National Association of School Principals.

Reid, R., Gonzalez, J. E., Nordness, A. T., Trout, A., & Epstein, M. H. (2004). A meta-analysis of the academic status of students with emotional/behavioral disturbance. *Journal of Special Education, 38*, 130–143.

Risley, T. (2005). Montrose M. Wolfe (1935–2004). *Journal of Applied Behavior Analysis, 38*, 279–287.

Robers, S., Zhang, J., & Truman, J. (2012). *Indicators of school crime and safety: 2011* (NCES 2012-002/NCJ 236021). Washington, DC: National Center for Education Statistics, U.S. Department of Education, and Bureau of Justice Statistics, Office of Justice Programs, U.S. Department of Justice.

Rudo, Z. H., Powell, D. S., & Dunlap, G. (1998). The effects of violence in the home on children's emotional, behavioral, and social functioning: A review of the literature. *Journal of Emotional and Behavioral Disorders, 6*, 94–113.

Scheuermann, B., Peterson, R., Ryan, J. B., & Billingsley, G. (2015). Professional practice and ethical issues related to physical restraint and seclusion in schools. *Journal of Disability Policy Studies*, 1–10. doi: 10.1177/1044207315604366

Schoenwald, S. K., & Hoagwood, K. (2001). Effectiveness and dissemination in research: Their mutual roles in improving mental health services for children and adolescents. *Emotional and Behavioral Disorders in Youth, 2*, 3–4, 18–20.

Scott, T. M., & Shearer-Lingo, A. (2002). The effects of reading fluency instruction on the academic and behavioral success of middle school students in a self-contained EBD classroom. *Preventing School Failure, 46*, 167–173.

Shores, R. E., Gunter, P. L., & Jack, S. L. (1993). Classroom management strategies: Are they setting events for coercion? *Behavioral Disorders, 18*, 92–102.

Sinclair, E. (1998). Head Start children at risk: Relationship of prenatal drug exposure to identification of special needs and subsequent special education kindergarten placement. *Behavioral Disorders, 23*, 125–133.

Sinclair, M. F., Christenson, S. L., Evelo, D. L., & Hurley, C. M. (1998). Dropout prevention for youth with disabilities: Efficacy of a sustained school engagement procedure. *Exceptional Children, 65*, 7–21.

Skiba, R. J., Chung, C., Trachok, M., Baker, T. L., Sheya, A., & Hughes, R. L. (2014). Parsing disciplinary disproportionality: Contributions of infraction, student, and school characteristics to out-of-school suspension and expulsion. *American Educational Research Journal, 51*, 640–670.

Souma, A. Rickerson, N., & Burgstahler, S. (2012). *Academic accommodations for students with psychiatric disabilities*. Retrieved from http://www.washington.edu/doit/sites/default/files/atoms/files/Academic_Accom_Psych.pdf

Stichter, J. P., Lewis, T. J., Richter, M., Johnson, N. W., & Bradley, L. (2006). Assessing antecedent variables: The effects of instructional variables on student outcomes through in-service and peer coaching professional development models. *Education and Treatment of Children, 29*, 665–692.

Strain, P. S., Steele, P., Ellis, R., & Timm, M. (1982). Long-term effects of oppositional child treatment with mothers as therapists and therapist trainers. *Journal of Applied Behavior Analysis, 15*, 163–169.

Sugai, G. (2011). *Maximizing impact of PBIS implementation at school and district levels*. University of Connecticut: OSEP Center on PBIS.

Sugai, G., & Horner, R. (2002). The evolution of discipline practices: School-wide positive behavior supports. *Child and Family Behavior Therapy, 24*, 23–50.

Sutherland, K. S., Adler, N., & Gunter, P. L. (2003). The effect of varying rates of opportunities to respond to academic requests on the classroom behavior of students with EBD. *Journal of Emotional and Behavioral Disorders, 11*, 239–248.

Sutherland, K. S., Wehby, J. H., & Yoder, P. J. (2001). An examination of the relation between teacher praise and students' with emotional/behavioral disorders opportunities to respond to academic requests. *Journal of Emotional and Behavioral Disorders, 10*, 5–14.

Talbott, E., & Thiede, K. (1999). Pathways to antisocial behavior among adolescent girls. *Journal of Emotional and Behavioral Disorders, 7*, 31–39.

Tobin, T. J., & Sugai, G. M. (1999). Using sixth-grade school records to predict school violence, chronic discipline problems, and high school outcomes. *Journal of Emotional and Behavioral Disorders, 7*, 40–53.

Tolan, P., Gorman-Smith, D., & Henry, D. (2001). New study to focus on efficacy of "whole school" prevention approaches. *Emotional and Behavioral Disorders in Youth, 2*, 22–23.

Torrey, E. F. (1997). *Out of the shadows: Confronting America's mental illness crisis*. New York, NY: John Wiley & Sons.

Townsend, B. L. (2000). The disproportionate discipline of African American learners: Reducing school suspensions and expulsions. *Exceptional Children, 66*, 381–391.

Trout, A. L., Nordness, P. D., Pierce, C. D., & Epstein, M. H. (2003). Research on the academic status of children with emotional and behavioral disorders: A review of the literature from 1961 to 2000. *Journal of Emotional and Behavioral Disorders, 11*, 198–210.

Umbreit, J., Ferro, J., Liaupsin, C., & Lane, K. (2007). *Functional behavioral assessment and function-based intervention: An effective, practical approach*. Upper Saddle River, NJ: Pearson Education.

Umbreit, J., Lane, K. L., & Dejud, C. (2004). Improving classroom behavior by modifying task difficulty: The effects of increasing the difficulty of too-easy tasks. *Journal of Positive Behavior Interventions, 6*, 13–20.

Unruh, D. K., & Murray, C. J. (2014). Improving transition outcomes for students with emotional and behavioral disorders. In H. M. Walker & F. M. Gresham (Eds.), *Handbook of evidence-based practices for emotional and behavioral disorders*. New York, NY: Guilford Press.

U.S. Census Bureau. (2015). *Per pupil spending varies heavily across the United States*. Retrieved from http://www.census.gov/newsroom/press-releases/2015/cb15-98.html

U.S. Congress. *Individuals with Disabilities Education Improvement Act of 2004*, 20 U.S.C. 1400 *et seq.* (2004) (reauthorization of Individuals with Disabilities Act 1990).

U.S. Department of Education. (1998). *Early warning, timely response: A guide to safe schools*. Washington, DC: Author. Retrieved from http://cecp.air.org/guide/guide.pdf

U.S. Department of Education. (2006, August 14*). Assistance to states for the education of children with disabilities and preschool grants for children with disabilities: Final rule. Federal Register, 34 CFR Parts 300 and 301*. Washington, DC: Author.

U.S. Department of Education. (2012). *Restraint and seclusion resource document*. Washington, DC: Author. Retrieved from http://www2.ed.gov/policy/seclusion/restraints-and-seclusion-resources.pdf

U.S. Department of Education. (2015). *Students ages 6 through 21 served under IDEA, Part B, as a percentage of population, by disability category and state*. [IDEA Section 618 Data Products: Static Tables, 2014–2015 Part B *Child Count and Educational Environments*]. Retrieved from http://www2.ed.gov/programs/osepidea/618-data/static-tables/index.html

U.S. Department of Education, Office for Civil Rights. (2016). *2013–2014 Civil Rights Data Collection: A first look*. Washington, DC: Author. Retrieved from http://www2.ed.gov/about/offices/list/ocr/docs/2013-14-first-look.pdf

U.S. Department of Health and Human Services, National Institute of Mental Health. (2011). *Depression*. Bethesda, MD: Author.

U.S. Department of Health and Human Services, National Institute of Mental Health. (2011). *Eating disorders*. Bethesda, MD: Author. Retrieved from www.nimh.nih.gov/health/publications/eating-disorders/eating-disorders.pdf

U.S. Department of Health and Human Services, National Institute of Mental Health. (2016, February 19). *A BRIGHT technological future for mental health trials: The BRIGHTEN study*. Retrieved from http://www.nimh.nih.gov/news/science-news/2016/a-bright-technological-future-for-mental-health-trials.shtml

U.S. Department of Health and Human Services, National Institute of Mental Health. (2016, May). *Technology and the future of mental health treatment*. Retrieved from http://www.nimh.nih.gov/health/topics/technology-and-the-future-of-mental-health-treatment/index.shtml

U.S. Senate, Health, Education, Labor, and Pensions Committee. (2014, February 12). *Dangerous use of seclusion and restraints in schools remains widespread and difficult to remedy: A review of ten cases*. Majority Committee Staff Report. Washington, DC: Author.

Vidair, H. B., Sauro, D., Blocher, J. B., Scudellari, L. A., & Hoagwood, K. E. (2014). Empirically supported school-based mental health programs targeting academic and mental health functioning: An update. In H. M. Walker & F. M. Gresham (Eds.), *Handbook of evidence-based practices for emotional and behavioral disorders*. New York, NY: Guilford Press.

Wagner, M., & Davis, M. (2006). How are we preparing students with emotional disturbances for the transition to young adulthood? Findings from the National Longitudinal Transition Study-2. *Journal of Emotional and Behavioral Disorders, 14*, 86–98.

Walker, H. M., Irvin, I. K., Noell, J., & Singer, G. H. S. (1992). A construct score approach to the assessment of social competence: Rationale, technological considerations, and anticipated outcomes. *Behavior Modification, 16*, 448–474.

Walker, H. M., Kavanagh, K., Stiller, B., Golly, A., Severson, H. H., & Feil, E. G. (1998). First step to success: An early intervention approach for preventing school antisocial behavior. *Journal of Emotional and Behavioral Disorders, 6*, 66–80.

Walker, H. M., Ramsey, E., & Gresham, F. M. (2004). *Antisocial behavior in school: Evidence-based practices* (2nd ed.). Belmont, CA: Wadsworth.

Walker, H. M., & Severson, H. H. (1992). *Systematic screening for behavior disorders (SSBD): User's guide and technical manual.* Longmont, CO: Sopris West.

Walker, H. M., & Sprague, J. (1999). The path to school failure, delinquency, and violence: Causal factors and potential solutions. *Intervention in School and Clinic, 35*, 67–73.

Walker, H. M., & Sprague, J. R. (2000). Intervention strategies for diverting at-risk children and youth from destructive outcomes. *Emotional and Behavioral Disorders in Youth, 1*, 5–8.

Wehby, J. H. & Kern, L. K. (2014). Intensive behavior intervention: What is it, what is its evidence base, and why do we need to implement now? *TEACHING Exceptional Children, 46*, 38–44.

Wehmeyer, M. L., Palmer, S. B., Agran, M., Mithaug, D. E., & Martin, J. E. (2000). Promoting causal agency: Self-determined learning model of instruction. *Exceptional Children, 66*, 439–453.

Wiley, A., & Siperstein, G. (2011). Seeing red, feeling blue: The impact of state political leaning on state identification rates for emotional disturbance. *Behavioral Disorders, 36*, 195–207.

World Health Organization (2016). *Depression.* Retrieved from http://www.who.int/mediacentre/factsheets/fs369/en/

Zigmond, N. (2006). Twenty-four months after high school: Paths taken by youth diagnosed with severe emotional and behavioral disorders. *Journal of Emotional and Behavioral Disorders, 14*, 99–107.

Zirkel, P. (1999). How to determine eligibility of students with problem behaviors. *The Special Educator, 17*, 7–8.

Chapter 11

American Association of Pediatrics. (2008). *Medical emergencies occurring at school.* Retrieved from http://pediatrics.aappublications.org/content/122/4/887

American Diabetes Association. (2011). *Safe at school.* Retrieved from http://www.diabetes.org/living-with-diabetes/parents-and-kids/diabetes-care-at-school/

American Diabetes Association. (2014). *Statistics about diabetes.* Retrieved from http://www.diabetes.org/diabetes-basics/statistics/

American Speech-Language-Hearing Association. (2015). *Early hearing detection and intervention (EHDI).* Retrieved from www.asha.org/Advocacy/federal/Early-Hearing-Detection-and-Intervention/

Ann & Robert H. Lurie Children's Hospital of Chicago. (n.d.). *Epilepsy in children.* Retrieved from https://www.luriechildrens.org/en-us/care-services/specialties-services/epilepsy/Pages/epilepsy-in-children.aspx

Asthma and Allergy Foundation of America (AAFA). (2015). *Asthma overview.* Retrieved from www.aafa.org/display.cfm?id=8&sub=42#fast

Beech, M. (2010). *Accommodations: Assisting students with disabilities* (3rd ed.). Tallahassee, FL: Florida Department of Education. Retrieved from http://www.fldoe.org/core/fileparse.php/7690/urlt/0070069-accomm-educator.pdf

Best, S. J., Heller, K. W., & Bigge, J. L. (2010). *Teaching individuals with physical or multiple disabilities.* Columbus, OH: Merrill.

Centers for Disease Control and Prevention. (2015). *Most recent asthma data.* Retrieved from http://www.cdc.gov/asthma/most_recent_data.htm

Centers for Disease Control and Prevention. (2015). *Newborn screening is important for your baby.* Retrieved from http://www.cdc.gov/Features/newborn-screening/

Centers for Disease Control and Prevention. (2015). *Sickle cell disease: Data and statistics.* Retrieved from http://www.cdc.gov/ncbddd/sicklecell/data.html

Centers for Disease Control and Prevention. (2015). *Tips for supporting students with sickle cell disease.* Retrieved from http://www.cdc.gov/ncbddd/sicklecell/documents/tipsheet_supporting_students_with_scd.pdf

Christensen, D., Van Naarden, B. K., Doernberg, N. S., Maenner, M. J., Arneson, C., L., Durkin, M. S., et al. (2014). Prevalence of cerebral palsy, co-occurring autism spectrum disorders, and motor functioning—Autism and Developmental Disabilities Monitoring Network, USA, 2008. *Developmental Medicine and Child Neurology, 56*, 59–65.

Coleman, M. B., & Heller, K. W. (2009). Assistive technology considerations. In K. W. Heller, P. E. Forney, P. A. Alberto, S. J. Best, & M. N. Schwartzman (Eds.), *Understanding physical, health, and multiple disabilities* (2nd ed., pp. 139–155). Columbus, OH: Merrill.

Crowe, J. (2011, June 19). Ankle transplant surgery gave former baseball star Robin Ventura a new lease on life. *Los Angeles Times, Sports.* Retrieved from www.latimes.com/sports/la-sp-crowes-nest-20110620,0,658672.column

DO-IT (Disabilities, Opportunities, Internetworking, and Technology) Center. (2015). *What is the difference between accessible, usable, and universal design?* Retrieved from http://www.washington.edu/doit/what-difference-between-accessible-usable-and-universal-design

Dolch, E. W. (1948). *Helping handicapped children in school.* Champaign, IL: Garrard Press.

Eberle, L. (1922). The maimed, the halt and the race. *Hospital Social Service, 6*, 59–63. Reprinted in R. H. Bremner (Ed.), (1970), *Children and youth in America, A documentary history: Vol. II, 1866–1932* (pp. 1026–1928). Cambridge, MA: Harvard University Press.

Epilepsy Foundation. (2014). *About epilepsy.* Retrieved from http://www.epilepsy.com/start-here/about-epilepsy-basics

Heller, K. W. (2009). Learning and behavioral characteristics of students with physical, health, or multiple disabilities. In K. W. Heller, P. E. Forney, P. A. Alberto, S. J. Best, & M. N. Schwartzman (Eds.), *Understanding physical, health, and multiple disabilities* (2nd ed., pp. 2–17). Columbus, OH: Merrill.

Heller, K. W., & Avant, M. J. T. (2009). Juvenile rheumatoid arthritis, arthrogryposis, and osteogenesis imperfecta. In K. W. Heller, P. E. Forney, P. A. Alberto, S. J. Best, & M. N. Schwartzman (Eds.), *Understanding physical, health, and multiple disabilities* (2nd ed., pp. 172–190). Columbus, OH: Merrill.

Heller, K. W., & Cohen, E. T. (2009). Seizures and epilepsy. In K. W. Heller, P. E. Forney, P. A. Alberto, S. J. Best, & M. N. Schwartzman (Eds.), *Understanding physical, health, and multiple disabilities* (2nd ed., pp. 294–315). Columbus, OH: Merrill.

Heller, K. W., & Coleman, M. B. (2009). Classroom adaptations for students with physical, health, and multiple disabilities. In K. W. Heller, P. E. Forney, P. A. Alberto, S. J. Best, & M. N. Schwartzman (Eds.), *Understanding physical, health, and multiple disabilities* (2nd ed., pp. 219–230). Columbus, OH: Merrill.

IRIS Center. (2007). *School nurses: Roles and responsibilities in the school setting.* Retrieved from http://iris.peabody.vanderbilt.edu

IRIS Center. (2009). *Universal Design for Learning: Creating a learning environment that challenges and engages all students.* Retrieved from http://iris.peabody.vanderbilt.edu/udl/

Jones, R. (Ed.). (1983). *Reflections on growing up disabled.* Reston, VA: Council for Exceptional Children.

La Vor, M. L. (1976). Federal legislation for exceptional persons: A history. In F. J. Weintraub, A. Abeson, J. Ballard, and M. L. La Vor (Eds.), *Public policy and the education of exceptional children* (pp. 96–111). Reston, VA: Council for Exceptional Children.

Longmore, P. (2003). *Why I burned my book and other essays on disability.* Philadelphia, PA: Temple University Press.

Maugh, T. H., III (2011, May 20). Small steps for paralyzed man, giant leaps for treating spinal cord injuries. *Los Angeles Times, Nation.* Retrieved from www.latimes.com/new/nationworld/nation/la-he-spinal-cord-20110520,0,6054699.story

Moon, N. W., Todd, R. L., Morton, D. L., Ivey, E. (2012). *Accommodating students with disabilities in science, technology, engineering, and mathematics (STEM): Findings from research and practice for middle grades through university education.* Atlanta, GA: Center for Assistive Technology and Environmental Access, College of Architecture, Georgia Institute of Technology. Retrieved from: http://www.catea.gatech.edu/scitrain/accommodating.pdf

National Diabetes Information Clearinghouse (NDIC). (2011). *National diabetes education program: Teens.* Retrieved from www.ndep.nih.gov /teens/index.aspx?redirect=true

National Institute of Neurological Disorders and Stroke (NINDS), National Institute of Health (NIH). (2015). *NINDS cerebral palsy information page.* Retrieved from http://www.ninds.nih.gov /disorders/cerebral_palsy/cerebral_palsy.htm

National Newborn Screening and Global Resource Center. (2014). *General information: History and overview of newborn screening.* Retrieved from http://genes-r-us.uthscsa.edu/resources/newborn/overview.htm

OXO. (n.d.). *Our philosophy.* Retrieved from https://www.oxo.com /our-philosophy

OXO. (n.d.). *Our roots.* Retrieved from https://www.oxo.com/our-roots

Rodriquez, S. (2011, June 14). Equipois' robotic limbs give factory workers and others a hand. *Los Angeles Times.* Retrieved from www .latimes.com/business/la-fi-exoskeleton-20110615,0,6899636

Schachter, S. C., Shafer, P. O, & Sirven, J. I. (2014). *Seizure first aid.* Retrieved from http://www.epilepsy.com/get-help/seizure-first-aid

Shaw, B. (1995, May/June). Ed Roberts: 1939–1995. *Disability Rag, 25.*

U.S. Congress. *Americans with Disabilities Act of 1990,* Pub. L. No. 101-336, 104 STAT.327.

U.S. Congress. *Individuals with Disabilities Education Improvement Act of 2004.* Pub. L. No. 108-446. 118 STAT. 2647.

U.S. Congress. *Rehabilitation Act of 1973.* Section 504, 19 U.S.C. section 794.

U.S. Department of Education. (2002). *Twenty-fourth annual report to Congress on the implementation of the Individuals with Disabilities Education Act.* Washington, DC: U.S. Government Printing Office.

U.S. Department of Education. (2006, August 14). 34 CFR Parts 300 and 301, Assistance to states for the education of children with disabilities and preschool grants for children with disabilities; Final Rule (pp. 1263–1264), *Federal Register,* Washington, DC: Author.

U.S. Department of Education, Office of Special Education Programs, Data Analysis System (DANS). (2012). *Children with disabilities receiving special education under Part B of the Individuals with Disabilities Education Act-2011.* Data updated as of July 15, 2012. Retrieved from www.ideadata.org

U.S. Food and Drug Administration (FDA). (2014, June 26). *FDA news release: FDA allows marketing of first wearable, motorized device that helps people with spinal cord injuries to walk.* Retrieved from http://www .fda.gov/NewsEvents/Newsroom/PressAnnouncements /ucm402970.htm

U.S. Department of Health and Human Services. (n.d.). *Bullying and children and youth with disabilities and special health needs.* Retrieved from http://www.stopbullying.gov/at-risk/groups/special-needs/ bullyingtipsheet.pdf.

U. S. Department of Justice, Civil Rights Division, Disability Rights Section (2011). *Revised ADA requirements: Service animals.* Retrieved from http://www.ada.gov/service_animals_2010.htm

Washington State University (n.d.). *Distance education: Expanding the classroom.*

Retrieved from https://ucomm.wsu.edu/distance-education- expanding-the-classroom/

Wheelchair Pride. (2011, August 1). *Exoskeleton to be controlled by brain waves.* Retrieved from www.wheelchairpride.com/2011/08 /exoskeleton-to-be-controlled-by-brain.html

Wynter, K. (2015, August 27). *Paralyzed teen walks for the first time in nearly a year thanks to robotic exoskeleton.* Retrieved from http://ktla .com/2015/08/27/paralyzed-teen-walks-for-1st-time-in-a-year- thanks-to-robotic-exoskeleton/

Chapter 12

Adams, M. E. (1929). 1865–1935: A few memories of Alexander Graham Bell. *American Annals of the Deaf, 74,* 467–479.

Ahearn, E. M. (2011, September). Children who are deaf/hard of hearing: State of educational practices. *In Forum: Brief Policy Analysis.* Alexandria, VA: National Association of State Directors of Special Education, Project Forum.

Alby, J. F. (1962, Spring). The educational philosophy of Thomas Hopkins Gallaudet. *Buff and Blue,* 17–23.

Alternative Communication Services. (n.d.). *CART.* Retrieved from http://www.acscaptions.com/subpages/CART.asp

Antia, S. D., Jones, P., Luckner, J., Kreimeyer, K. H., & Reed, S. (2011). Social outcomes of students who are deaf and hard of hearing in general education classrooms. *Exceptional Children, 77,* 489–504.

Aud, S., & Hannes, G. (Eds.). (2011). *The condition of education 2011 in brief* (NCES 2011-034). U.S. Department of Education, National Center for Education Statistics. Washington, DC: U.S. Government Printing Office. Retrieved from https://nces.ed.gov/pubs2011/2011034.pdf

Beltone. (2016). *Little ear buds spell big trouble for hearing health.* Retrieved from https://www.beltone.com/hearing-health/ear-buds .aspx

Boys Town National Research Hospital. (n.d.). *Hearing aid choices.* Retrieved from http://www.babyhearing.org/HearingAmplification /AidChoices/styles.asp

Branson, J., & Miller, D. (2002). *Damned for their difference: The cultural construction of deaf people as disabled.* Washington, DC: Gallaudet University Press.

Centers for Disease Control and Prevention (CDC). (2015, October 23). *Hearing loss in children.* Retrieved from http://www.cdc.gov /ncbddd/hearingloss/facts.html

Centers for Disease Control and Prevention (CDC). (2015, October 23). *Summary of 2013 national CDC EHDI data.* Retrieved from http://www.cdc.gov/ncbddd/hearingloss/2013-data/2013_ehdi_ hsfs_summary_e.pdf

Commission on the Education of the Deaf. (1988). *Toward equality: Education of the deaf.* Washington, DC: U.S. Government Printing Office.

Davey, M. (2005, March 21). As town for Deaf takes shape, debate on isolation re-emerges. *New York Times, National Desk.* Retrieved from nytimes.com

Digital Trends. (2011, August 26). *Sony "subtitle glasses" could be a hit with deaf movie goers.* Retrieved from www.digitaltrends.com/cool-tech /sony-subtitle-glasses-could-be-a-hit-with-deaf-moviegoers/

DO-IT. (2015). *What is real-time captioning?* Retrieved from http://www.washington.edu/doit/what-real-time-captioning

Drasgow, E. (1998). American Sign Language as a pathway to linguistic competence. *Exceptional Children, 64,* 329–342.

Echo Initiative. (n.d.). *Overview of otoacoustic emissions (OAE) hearing screening.* Retrieved from http://www.infanthearing.org/earlychild- hood/docs/OAE_overview.pdf

Felzien, M. (2011). Why early audition is important. *Volta Voices, 18,* 22–27.

Flipsen, P., Jr. (2011). Examining speech sound acquisition for children with cochlear implants using the GFTA-2. *The Volta Review, 111,* 25–27.

Gallaudet Research Institute. (2011, April). *Regional and national summary report of data from the 2009–10 Annual Survey of Deaf and Hard of Hearing Children and Youth.* Washington, DC: GRI, Gallaudet University.

Gallo, C. (Ed.). (2011, October). Prepare teams to field mounting requests for real-time captioning. *Special Education Report, 37,* 6.

Gannon, J. R. (1989). *The week the world heard Gallaudet.* Washington, DC: Gallaudet University Press.

Gannon, J. R. (2011). *A narrative history of Deaf America.* Washington, DC: Gallaudet Press.

Gleason, J. B., & Ratner, N. B. (2013). *The development of language* (8th ed.). Boston, MA: Allyn & Bacon.

Gordon-Langbein, A. L., & Metzinger, M. (2000). Technology in the classroom to maximize listening and learning. *Volta Voices, 7,* 10–13.

Greenwald, B. H. (2007). Taking stock: Alexander Graham Bell and eugenics, 1883–1922. In J. V. Van Cleve (Eds.), *The deaf history reader.* Washington, DC: Gallaudet University Press.

Groce, N. E. (1985). *Everyone here spoke sign language: Hereditary deafness on Martha's Vineyard.* Cambridge, MA: Harvard University Press.

Harrington, M. (2003). Hard of hearing students in the public schools: Should we be concerned? *Volta Voices, 11,* 18–22.

Hignett, S. (1983). *Brett from Bloomsbury to New Mexico: A biography.* New York, NY: Franklin Watts.

Houston, K. T., Bradham, R. S., Muñoz, K. F., & Guignard, G. H. (2011). Newborn hearing screening: An analysis of current practices. *The Volta Review, 111,* 109–120.

Institute of Education Sciences, National Center for Educational Statistics. (2011). *Student effort and educational progress: Students with disabilities exiting school with a regular high school diploma.* Retrieved from http://nces.ed.gov/programs/coe/2008/section3/indicator22.asp

James, S. D., & Nathanson, K. (2015, June 8). Generation deaf: Doctors warn of dangers of ear buds. *NBC News.* Retrieved from http://www.nbcnews.com/health/health-news/generation-deaf-doctors-warn-dangers-ear-buds-n360041

Johnson, C. D., & Seaton, J. (2012, revised 2014). IEP/504 Checklist: Accommodations and modifications for students who are deaf and hard of hearing. *Educational Audiology Handbook* (2nd ed.). Clifton Park, NY: Delmar, Cengage Learning.

Kageliery, J. (2002). *The island that spoke by hand.* Martha's Vineyard Chamber of Commerce. Retrieved from www.mvy.com

Kena, G., Hussar W., McFarland J., de Brey C., Musu-Gillette, L., Wang, X., Zhang, J., Rathbun, A., Wilkinson- Flicker, S., Diliberti M., Barmer, A., Bullock Mann, F., & Dunlop Velez, E. (2016). *The Condition of Education 2016* (NCES 2016-144). U.S. Department of Education, National Center for Education Statistics. Washington, DC. Retrieved from http://nces.ed.gov/pubsearch

Laurent Clerc National Deaf Education Center and Boston Children's Hospital. (2015). *Students with cochlear implants: Guidelines for educational program planning.* Retrieved from http://www.gallaudet.edu/Documents/Clerc/Guidelines2015Cochlear.pdf

Liberman, M. C. (2015). Hidden hearing loss. *Scientific American,* 49–53.

Lowenbraun, S. (1995). Hearing impairment. In E. L. Meyen & T. M. Skrtic (Eds.), *Exceptional children and youth: An introduction* (4th ed., pp. 453–486). Denver, CO: Love.

Luckner, J. L., Bruce, S. M., & Ferrell, K. A. (2015). A summary of the communication and literacy evidence-based practices for students who are deaf or hard of hearing, visually impaired, and deafblind. *Communication Disorders Quarterly,* 1–17. doi: 10.1177/1525740115597507

Luckner, J. L., Slike, S. B., & Johnson, H. (2012). Helping students who are deaf or hard of hearing succeed. *TEACHING Exceptional Children,* 44, 58–67.

MacKenzie, D. J. (2007). Audiology and hearing loss. In R. E. Owens, Jr., D. E. Metz, & A. Haas (Eds.), *Introduction to communication disorders: A life span perspective* (3rd ed., pp. 404–463). Boston, MA: Allyn & Bacon.

Marschark, M., Shaver, D. B., Nagle, K. M., & Newman, L. A. (2015). Predicting the academic achievement of deaf and hard-of-hearing students from individual, household, communication, and educational factors. *Exceptional Children,* 81, 350–369.

Martin, F. N., & Clark, J. G. (2012). *Introduction to audiology* (11th ed.). Boston, MA: Pearson.

National Center for Hearing Assessment and Management (NCHAM). (2011). *Newborn hearing screening.* Retrieved from www.infanthearing.org/screening/index.html

National Dissemination Center for Children with Disabilities (NICHCY). (June 2010). *Deafness and hearing loss.* Retrieved from http://nichcy.org/disability/specific/hearingloss

National Institute on Deafness and Other Communication Disorders (NIDCD). (2015, May 15). *Noise-induced hearing loss.* Retrieved from https://www.nidcd.nih.gov/health/noise-induced-hearing-loss

National Institute on Deafness and Other Communication Disorders (NIDCD). (2016, May 3). *Cochlear implants.* Retrieved from https://www.nidcd.nih.gov/health/cochlear-implants

National Institute on Deafness and Other Communication Disorders (NIDCD). (2016, May 11). *Brainstem implant.* Retrieved from https://www.nidcd.nih.gov/glossary/brainstem-implant

National Institute on Deafness and Other Communication Disorders (NIDCD). (2016, May 11). *Hearing aids.* Retrieved from https://www.nidcd.nih.gov/health/hearing-aids

National Institutes of Health. (1993). Early identification of hearing impairment in infants and young children. *NIH Consensus Statement 1993 Mar 1–3,* 11(1): 1–24. Retrieved from http://consensus.nih.gov/1993/1993HearingInfantsChildren092html.htm

National Technical Institute for the Deaf (NTID). (2012). *C-Print: Speech-to-text system.* Retrieved from www.ntid.rit.edu/cprint/what_cprint.php

Nelson, L., Bradham, R. S., & Houston, K. T. (2011). The EHDI and early intervention connection. *The Volta Review,* 111, 133–149.

Nemours Foundation. (n.d.). *Earbuds.* Retrieved from http://kidshealth.org/en/teens/earbuds.html

Nikolaraizi, M., & Makri, M. (2004/2005). Deaf and hearing individuals' beliefs about the capabilities of deaf people. *American Annals of the Deaf,* 149, 404–414.

Northern, J. L., & Downs, M. P. (2002). *Hearing in children* (5th ed.). Philadelphia, PA: Lippincott, Williams & Wilkins.

Owens, R. E., Jr. (2012). *Language development: An introduction* (8th ed.). Boston, MA: Allyn & Bacon.

Ramsey, C. L. (2011). *Cochlear implants: Evolving perspectives.* Washington, DC: Gallaudet Press.

Rosica, M. J., & Dagel, D. D. (2011). The three "dreaded t's:" Managing time, tasks, and temptation. *Volta Voices,* 18, 18–21.

Scheetz, N. A. (2012). *Deaf education in the 21st century: Topics and trends.* Boston, MA: Pearson.

Turnbull, K. L. P., & Justice, L. M. (2012). *Language development from theory to practice* (2nd ed.). Boston, MA: Allyn & Bacon.

U.S. Department of Education. (2006). *Assistance to states for the education of children with disabilities program and the early intervention program for infants and toddlers with disabilities; Final regulations. Federal Register,* 34 CRF Parts 300, 301, and 304.

U.S. Department of Education. (2015). *Number of students ages 6 through 21 served under IDEA, Part B, by disability and state: 2014-15.* [IDEA Section 618 Data Products: Static Tables, 2014-2015 Part B *Child Count and Educational Environments*]. Retrieved from http://www2.ed.gov/programs/osepidea/618-data/static-tables/index.html#part-b

U.S. Department of Education, Office of Special Education Programs (OSEP), Data Accountability Center. (2012). *IDEA data: Analytic tool Part B educational environments.* Retrieved from www.ideadata.org

U.S. Department of Education, Office of Special Education Programs, Data Analysis System (DANS). (2012). *Children with disabilities receiving special education under Part B of the Individuals with Disabilities Education Act-2011.* Data updated as of July 15, 2012. Retrieved from www.ideadata.org

U.S. Government Accountability Office (GAO). (2011, May). *Deaf and hard of hearing children: Federal support for developing language and literacy.* Report #: GAO-11-357.

Van Cleve, J. V. (2007). *The deaf history reader.* Washington, DC: Gallaudet University Press.

Werfel, K. L., & Hendricks, A. E. (2016). Identifying minimal hearing loss and managing its effects on literacy learning. *TEACHING Exceptional Children,* 48, 213–217.

White, K. R., & Blaiser, K. M. (2011). Strategic planning to improve EHDI programs. *The Volta Review,* 111, 83–108.

World Heath Organization. (2015, February 27). *1.1 billion people at risk of hearing loss.* Retrieved from http://www.who.int/mediacentre/news/releases/2015/ear-care/en/

Yoon, J.-O., & Kim, M. (2011). The effects of captions on Deaf students' content comprehension, cognitive load, and motivation in online learning. *American Annals of the Deaf,* 156, 283–289.

Zazove, P., Meador, H. E., Derry, H. A., Gorenflo, D. W., & Saunders, E. W. (2004). Deaf persons and computer use. *American Annals of the Deaf,* 148, 376–384.

Chapter 13

Achilles International. (2016). *Who we are.* Retrieved from http://www.achillesinternational.org/who-we-are/

American Foundation for the Blind. (2008). *Statistics and sources for professionals.* Retrieved from http://www.afb.org/section.aspx?SectionID=15

American Foundation for the Blind. (2015). *Helen Keller Achievement Awards 2015.* Retrieved from http://www.afb.org/info/about-us/events-and-awards/helen-keller-achievement-awards/123

American Foundation for the Blind. (2017). *School experience for children and youth with vision loss.* Retrieved from www.afb.org/section.aspx?FolderID=2&SectionID=15&TopicID=411&DocumentID=4897

American Foundation for the Blind. (n.d.). *Mobility devices for young children*. Retrieved from http://www.afb.org/section.asp?SectionID=40&TopicID=168&DocumentID=804

American Foundation for the Blind. (n.d.). *Types of accommodations*. Retrieved from http://www.afb.org/info/living-with-vision-loss/for-job-seekers/for-employers/accommodations-for-workers-with-vision-loss/types-of-accommodations/12345

American Foundation for the Blind. (n.d.). *What is braille?* Retrieved from http://www.afb.org/info/living-with-vision-loss/braille/what-is-braille/123

Bailey, I. L., Lueck, A. H., Greer, R. B., Tuan, K. M., Bailey, V. M., & Dornbusch, H. G. (2003). Understanding the relationships between print size and reading in low vision. *Journal of Low Vision and Blindness, 97*, 325–333.

Barraga, N. C. (1964). *Increased visual behavior in low vision children*. New York: American Foundation for the Blind.

Barraga, N. C., & Collins, M. E. (1979). Development of efficiency in visual functioning: Rationale for a comprehensive program. *Journal of Visual Impairment & Blindness, 73*, 121–126.

Beech, M. (2010). *Accommodations: Assisting students with disabilities* (3rd ed.). Tallahassee, FL: Florida Department of Education. Retrieved from www.fldoe.org/core/fileparse.php/7690accomm-educator.pdf

Bennett, J., Ashtari, M., Wellman, J., Marshall, K. A., Cyckowski, L. L., Chung, D. C., McCague, S., Pierce, E. A., Chen, Y., Bennicelli, J. L., Zhu, X., Ying, G., Sun, J., Wright, J. F., Auricchio, A., Simonelli, F., Shindler, K. S., Mingozzi, F., High, K. A., & Maguire, A. M. (2012, February 8). AAV2 gene therapy readministration in three adults with congenital blindness. *Science Translational Medicine, 4*(120), 120–135.

Bouchard, D., & Tetreault, S. (2000). The motor development of sighted children and children with moderate low vision aged 8–13. *Journal of Visual Impairment & Blindness, 94*, 564–573.

Braille Authority of North America (2011). *Guidelines and standards for tactile graphics, 2010*. Retrieved from www.brailleauthority.org/tg/index.html

Brown, L., Brown, S., & Glaser, S. (2013). Improved transition outcomes for students with visual impairments through interagency collaboration. *Journal of Visual Impairment & Blindness, 107*, 406–408.

Buhrow, M. M., Hartshorne, T. S., & Bradley-Johnson, S. (1998). Parents' and teachers' ratings of the social skills of elementary-age students who are blind. *Journal of Visual Impairment & Blindness, 92*, 503–511.

Celeste, M. (2008). Social skills intervention for a child who is blind. *Journal of Visual Impairment & Blindness, 101*(9), 521–533.

Centers for Disease Control (CDC). (n.d.). *Vision loss fact sheet*. Retrieved from http://www.cdc.gov/ncbddd/actearly/pdf/parents_pdfs/VisionLossFactSheet.pdf

Cho, H., & Palmer, S.B. (2008). Fostering self-determination in infants and toddlers with visual impairments or blindness. *Young Exceptional Children, 11*, 26–34.

Clarke, K. L., Sainato, D. M., & Ward, M. E. (1994). Travel performance of preschoolers: The effects of mobility training with a long cane versus a precane. *Journal of Visual Impairment & Blindness, 88*, 19–30.

Cmar, J. L. (2015). Orientation and mobility skills and outcome expectations as predictors of employment for young adults with visual impairments. *Journal of Visual Impairment & Blindness, 109*, 95–106.

Corn, A. L. (1989). Instruction in the use of vision for children and adults with low vision: A proposed program model. *RE:view, 21*, 26–38.

Corn, A., & Koenig, A. J. (2002). Literacy for students with low vision: A framework for delivering instruction. *Journal of Visual Impairment & Blindness, 96*, 305–321.

Cox, P., & Dykes, M. (2001). Effective classroom adaptations for students with visual impairments. *TEACHING Exceptional Children, 33*, 68–74.

De Mario, N., & Caruso, M. (2001). The expansion of outreach services for specialized schools for students with visual impairments. *Journal of Visual Impairment & Blindness, 95*, 488–491.

Dixon, J. M. (2011). Braille: The challenge for the future. *Journal of Visual Impairment & Blindness, 105*(11), 742–745.

Eaton, S. B., & Wall, R. S. (1999). A survey of social skills instruction in preservice programs for visual disabilities. *RE:view, 31*(1), 40–45.

Erin, J. N., & Corn, A. L. (1994). A survey of children's first understanding of being visually impaired. *Journal of Visual Impairment & Blindness, 88*, 132–139.

Evans, S., & Douglas, G. (2008). E-learning and blindness: A comparative study of the quality of an e-learning experience. *Journal of Visual Impairment & Blindness, 102*(2), 77–88.

Frank, J. (2000). Requests by persons with visual impairment for large-print accommodation. *Journal of Visual Impairment & Blindness, 94*, 716–719.

Fruchterman, J. R. (2003). In the palm of your hand: A vision of the future of technology for people with visual impairments. *Journal of Visual Impairment & Blindness, 97*, 585–591.

Gompel, M., van Bon, W. J., & Schreuder, R. (2004). Reading by children with low vision. *Journal of Visual Impairment & Blindness, 98*(2) 77–89.

Goodrich, G. L., & Lueck, A. H. (2010). Vision rehabilitation services at a crossroads. *Journal of Visual Impairment & Blindness, 104*(10), 593–597.

Hadrill, M. (2011, June). Congenital cataracts. *All About Vision*. Retrieved from http://www.allaboutvision.com/conditions/congenital-cataracts.htm

Hatton, D. (2001). Model registry of early childhood visual impairment: First-year results. *Journal of Visual Impairment & Blindness, 95*, 418–433.

Hatton, D. D., Bailey, D. B., Burchinal, M. R., & Ferrell, K. A. (1997). Developmental growth curves of preschool children with vision impairments. *Child Development, 68*, 788–806.

Healthday. (2012). *More success with gene therapy for blindness*. Retrieved from http://www.nlm.nih.gov/medlineplus/news/fullstory_121711.html

Healy, M. (2011, October 10). Electrical stimulation creates images that could help blind see. *Los Angeles Times*. Retrieved from http://www.latimes.com/health/boostershots/la-heb-prosthetic-eyes-blind-20111010,0,5647631.story

Herron, M. (2009). Blind visionary. *Engineering &Technology, 4*(8), 84–85.

Holbrook, M. C. (2008). Teaching reading and writing to students with visual impairments: Who is responsible? *Journal of Visual Impairment & Blindness, 102*(4), 203–206.

Holton, B. (2015, June). Apple receives AFB's prestigious Helen Keller Achievement Award. *AFB AccessWorld Magazine, 16*(6). Retrieved from http://www.afb.org/afbpress/pub.asp?DocID=aw160602

Hughes, M., Dote-Kwan, J., & Dolendo, J. (1998). A close look at the cognitive play of preschoolers with visual impairments in the home. *Exceptional Children, 64*, 451–462.

IRIS Center. (2006a). *Accommodations to the physical environment: Setting up a classroom for students with visual disabilities*. Retrieved from http://iris.peabody.vanderbilt.edu/module/v01-clearview/

IRIS Center. (2006b). *Instructional accommodations: Making the learning environment accessible to students with visual disabilities*. Retrieved from http://iris.peabody.vanderbilt.edu/module/v02-successsight/

IRIS Center. (2007). *Serving students with visual impairments: The importance of collaboration*. Retrieved from http://iris.peabody.vanderbilt.edu/module/v03-focusplay/

Jamieson, W. E. (2013, March 2). The crime of his childhood. *The New York Times*. Retrieved from http://www.nytimes.com/2013/03/03/nyregion/40-years-after-an-acid-attack-a-life-well-lived.html?_r=0

Jindal-Snape, D. (2005). Use of feedback from sighted peers in promoting social interaction skills. *Journal of Visual Impairment & Blindness, 99*, 403–412.

Kaine, N., & Kent, R. (2013). Activities to encourage employability skills in middle childhood. *Journal of Visual Impairment & Blindness, 107*, 524–528.

Kelly, S. M. (2013). Labor force participation rates among working-age individuals with visual impairments. *Journal of Visual Impairment & Blindness, 107*, 509–513.

Kendrick, D. (2010, July). Refreshabraille portable braille display and keyboard: A product evaluation. *AccessWorld, 11*(3). Retrieved from http://www.afb.org/afbpress/pub.asp?DocID=aw110303

Koenig, A., & Holbrook, M. (2000). Ensuring high-quality instruction for students in braille literacy programs. *Journal of Visual Impairment & Blindness, 94*, 677–694.

Levin, A. V. (1996). Common visual problems in classrooms. In R. H. A. Haslam & P. J. Valletutti (Eds.), *Medical problems in the classroom: The teacher's role in diagnosis and management* (pp. 161–180). Austin, TX: PRO-ED.

Lighthouse for the Blind and Visually Impaired. (2012, February 3). *Braille and tactile maps*. Retrieved from http://lighthouse-sf.org /braille-and-tactile-maps/

Look into my eyes. (2011, June 2). *The Economist*. Retrieved from http://www.economist.com/node/18750624

Lueck, A. H., Bailey, I. L., Greer, R. B., Tuan, K. M., Bailey, V. M., & Dornbusch, H. G. (2003). Exploring print-size requirements and reading for students with low vision. *Journal of Low Vision and Blindness, 97,* 335–355.

Lynch, K. A. (2013). Survey reveals myths and misconceptions abundant among hiring managers about the capabilities of people who are visually impaired. *Journal of Visual Impairment & Blindness, 107,* 408–410.

MacCuspie, P. A. (1992). The social acceptance and interaction of visually impaired children in integrated settings. In S. Z. Sacks, L. S. Kekelis, and R. J. Gaylord-Ross (Eds.), *The development of social skills by blind and visually impaired students* (pp. 83–102). New York: American Foundation for the Blind.

McGaha, C., & Farran, D. (2001). Interaction in an inclusive classroom: The effects of visual status and setting. *Journal of Visual Impairment & Blindness, 95,* 80–94.

McHugh, E., & Lieberman, L. (2003). The impact of developmental factors on stereotypic rocking of children with visual impairments. *Journal of Visual Impairment & Blindness, 97,* 453–474.

McMahon, E. (2014). The role of specialized schools for students with visual impairments in the continuum of placement options: The right help, at the right time, in the right place. *Journal of Visual Impairment & Blindness, 108,* 449–459.

Miele, J.A. (2012). *Descriptive video exchange: Enhancing the experience by empowering the consumer*. Retrieved from https://nfb.org/images /nfb/publications/fr/fr31/4/fr310412.htm

Miller, J. (2014). Meeting the expectations of the workplace in the schoolplace. *Journal of Visual Impairment & Blindness, 108,* 495–499.

Miller, M. M., & Menacker, S. J. (2007). Vision: Our window to the world. In M. L. Batshaw, L. Pellegrino, and N. J. Roizen (Eds.), *Children with disabilities* (pp. 137–156). Baltimore: Paul H. Brookes Publishing.

Mogk, L., & Goodrich, G. (2004). The history and future of low vision services in the United States. *Journal of Visual Impairment & Blindness, 98,* 585–600.

Monson, M. R., & Bowen, S. K. (2008). The development of phonological awareness by braille users: A review of the research. *Journal of Visual Impairment & Blindness, 102*(4), 210–220.

Mraz, S. (2012, March 1). *Innovations: Artificial retina lets blind see*. Retrieved from http://medicaldesign.com/electrical-components /artificial-retina-0312/

National Center for Educational Statistics (NCES) (2011). *Fast facts: Students with disabilities*. Retrieved from http://nces.ed.gov /fastfacts/display.asp?id=64

National Eye Institute (NEI) (n.d.). *Facts about retinopathy of prematurity (ROP)*. Retrieved from https://nei.nih.gov/health/rop/rop

National Industries for the Blind (2012, November). NIB decision-maker study. Alexandria, VA: Author. Retrieved from http://www .nib.org/sites/default/files/NIB%20Hiring%20Manager%20 Study%20(Releasable).pdf

National Instructional Materials Accessibility Standard (NIMAS). (2006). *State director of special education suggested responsibilities regarding NIMAS and NIMAC*. Retrieved from http://nimas.cast.org /about/resources/sea_sped

Packer, J., Vizenor, K., & Miele, J. (2015). An overview of video description: History, benefits, and guidelines. *Journal of Visual Impairment & Blindness, 109,* 83–93.

Parviz, B. A. (2009, September). Augmented reality in a contact lens. *IEEE Spectrum*. Retrieved from http://spectrum.ieee.org/biomedical /bionics/augmented-reality-in-a-contact-lens/0

Pinquart, M., & Pfeiffer, J. P. (2011). Associations of extroversion and parental overprotection with forming relationships with peers among adolescents with and without visual impairments. *Journal of Visual Impairment & Blindness, 105*(2), 96–107.

Pogrund, R. L., Fazzi, D. L., & Schreier, E. M. (1993). Development of a preschool "Kiddy Cane." *Journal of Visual Impairment & Blindness, 86,* 52–54.

Prevent Blindness America (2010). *Quick facts: Children's eye problems*. Retrieved from http://www.preventblindness.org/sites/default/files /national/documents/fact_sheets/MK03_QuickFactsChildren.pdf

Prevent Blindness America (2013). *Children's vision screening*. Retrieved from http://www.preventblindness.org/childrens-vision-screening

Prevent Blindness America (2013). *Signs of possible eye problems in children*. Retrieved from http://www.preventblindness.org/signs-possible-eye-problems-children

Rettig, M. (1994). The play of young children with visual impairments: Characteristics and interventions. *Journal of Visual Impairment & Blindness, 88,* 410–420.

Roberts, M. (2011, November 21). Bionic contact lens "to project emails before eyes." *BBC News*. Retrieved from http://www.bbc.co.uk /news/health-15817316

Rosenblum, L. P. & Herzbert, T. S. (2015). Braille and tactile graphics: Youths with visual impairments share their experiences. *Journal of Visual Impairment & Blindness, 109,* 173–184.

Sacks, S. Z., & Rosen, S. (1994). Visual impairment. In N. G. Haring, L. McCormick, & T. G. Haring (Eds.), *Exceptional children and youth* (6th ed., pp. 403–446). Columbus, OH: Merrill.

Schiller, P. H., Slocum, W. M., Kwak, M. C., Kendall, G. L., & Tehovnik, E. J. (2011). New methods devised specify the size and color of the spots monkeys see when striate cortex (area V1) is electrically stimulated. *Proceedings of the National Academy of Sciences, 106*(43), 17809–17814.

Shapiro, D. R., Moffett, A., Lieberman, L., & Dummer, G. M. (2008). Domain-specific ratings of importance and global self-worth of children with visual impairments. *Journal of Visual Impairment & Blindness, 102*(4), 232–244.

Sifferlin, A., & Park, A. (2015, September 21). Stepping into the light. *Time, 186,* 54–59.

Smith, D. W., & Amato, S. (2012). Synthesis of available accommodations for students with visual impairment on standardized assessments. *Journal of Visual Impairment & Blindness 106*(5), 299–304.

Social Security Administration. (2015). *If you're blind or have low vision—how we can help*. Retrieved from http://www.ssa.gov/pubs /EN-05-10052.pdf

Space Camp. (n.d.). *Special programs*. Retrieved from http://www .spacecamp.com/specialprograms

Spungin, S. (Ed.). (2002). *When you have a visually impaired student in your classroom: A guide for teachers*. New York: American Foundation for the Blind.

Stangl, A., Kim, J., & Yeh, T. (2014). *3D printed tactile picture books for children with visual impairments: A design probe*. Retrieved from http:// idc2014.org/wp-content/uploads/2014/09/p321-stanglA.pdf

Stuart, M. E., Lieberman, L. J., & Han, K. (2006). Parent-child beliefs about physical activity: An examination of families of children with visual impairments. *Journal of Visual Impairment & Blindness, 100*(4), 223–234.

Tröster, H., & Brambring, M. (1992). Early social-emotional development in blind infants. *Child: Care, Health and Development, 18,* 421–432.

Tröster, H., & Brambring, M. (1994). The play behavior and play materials of blind and sighted infants and preschoolers. *Journal of Visual Impairment & Blindness, 88,* 421–432.

Tuttle, D. W., & Ferrell, K. A. (1995). Visually impaired. In E. L. Meyen and T. M. Skrtic (Eds.), *Exceptional children and youth: An introduction* (4th ed., pp. 487–531). Denver, CO: Love.

Weihenmayer, E. (2001). *Touch the top of the world*. New York, NY: Dutton, the Penguin Group.

Weihenmayer, E., & Stoltz, P. (2010). *The adversity advantage: Turning everyday struggles into everyday greatness*. New York, NY: Fireside, a division of Simon & Schuster.

Wilkinson, M. E., & Trantham, C. S. (2004). Characteristics of children evaluated at a pediatric low vision clinic: 1981–2003. *Journal of Low Vision and Blindness, 98,* 693–702.

Wolffe, K. (2009, April). *Lifelong learning in career education* (Webcast presentation). New York: American Foundation for the Blind.

Retrieved from http://www.afb.org/info/living-with-vision-loss/for-job-seekers/webcast-presentations/lifelong-learning-in-career-education-audio/1235

Wolffe, K., & Kelly, S. M. (2011). Instruction in areas of the expanded core curriculum linked to transition outcomes for students with visual impairments. *Journal of Visual Impairment & Blindness, 105*(6), 340–349.

Wormsley, D. P. (2004). *Braille literacy: A functional approach.* New York: AFB Press.

Chapter 14

29 USC Chapter 21–Helen Keller National Center for Youths and Adults who are Deaf-Blind.

Alsop, L., Berg, C., Hartman, V., Knapp, M., Levasseur, C., Prouty, M., & Prouty, S. (2012). *A family's guide to interveners for children with combined vision and hearing loss.* Logan, UT: Utah State University SKI-HI Institute. Retrieved from http://intervener.org/wp-content/uploads/2012/06/A-Familys-Guide-to-Interveners.pdf

Alwell, M., & Cobb, B. (2006). *Teaching functional skills to youth with disabilities: Executive summary.* National Secondary Transition Technical Assistance Center. Retrieved from https://interwork.sdsu.edu/sp/tscp/files/2015/06/life_skills_executive_summary.pdf

American Foundation for the Blind. (n.d.) *Helen Keller biography.* Retrieved from http://www.afb.org/info/about-us/helen-keller/biography-and-chronology/biography/1235

Bambara, L. M., Koger, F., & Bartholomew, A. (2011). Building skills for home and community. In M. E. Snell and F. Brown (Eds.), *Instruction of students with severe disabilities* (7th ed., pp. 529–568). Upper Saddle River, NJ: Pearson Education, Inc.

Best, S. J. (2011). Understanding individuals with physical, health, and multiple disabilities. In S. J. Best, K. W. Heller, & J. L. Bigge (Eds.), *Teaching individuals with physical or multiple disabilities* (6th ed., pp. 1–31). Upper Saddle River, NJ: Pearson Education, Inc.

Bolay, J. (n.d.). *Including students with multiple/severe disabilities in the general education classroom: Tips and resources for teachers.* Retrieved from http://kc.vanderbilt.edu/kennedy_pdfs/TipSheets/tipsheet_ClassroomInclusion.pdf

Brown, F., & Snell, M. E. (2011). Measuring student behavior and learning. In M. E. Snell & F. Brown (Eds.), *Instruction of students with severe disabilities* (7th ed., pp. 186–223). Upper Saddle River, NJ: Pearson Education, Inc.

Carnes, S., & Barnard, S. (2003). Oregon deaf-blind project intervener training program. *Deaf-Blind Perspectives, 10,* 1–3.

Center for Parent Information and Resources. (n.d.). *Traumatic brain injury.* NICHCY Disability Fact Sheet 18. Retrieved from http://www.parentcenterhub.org/repository/tbi/

Centers for Disease Control and Prevention (CDC). (2010). *A journalist's guide to shaken baby syndrome: A preventable tragedy.* Retrieved from https://stacks.cdc.gov/view/cdc/5865/Email

Centers for Disease Control and Prevention. (2011). *Non-fatal brain injuries related to sports and recreation activities among persons aged ≤ 19 years—United States, 2001–2009.* Retrieved from www.cdc.gov/mmwr/preview/mmwrhtml/mm6039a1.htm?s_cid=mm6039a1_w#tab2

Centers for Disease Control and Prevention. (2016, January 22). *Prevention: What can I do to help prevent traumatic brain injury?* Retrieved from www.cdc.gov/traumaticbraininjury/prevention.html

Centers for Disease Control and Prevention (CDC). (2016, January 22). *TBI: Get the facts.* Retrieved from http://www.cdc.gov/traumaticbraininjury/get_the_facts.html

Centers for Disease Control and Prevention. (2016, April 5). *Preventing abusive head trauma in children.* Retrieved from http://www.cdc.gov/violenceprevention/childmaltreatment/abusive-head-trauma.html

Courtade, G. R., Test, D. W., & Cook, B. G. (2015). Evidence-based practices for learners with severe intellectual disabilities. *Research and Practice for Persons with Severe Disabilities, 39,* 305–318.

D'Luna, D. (2006). The intervener: Big idea, substantial results. *reSources, 12,* 1–5.

Drew, C. J., & Hardman, M. L. (2007). *Intellectual disabilities across the lifespan* (9th ed.). Columbus, OH: Merrill/Pearson.

Federal Communications Commission. (2011, April 6). *FCC acts to ensure that deaf-blind individuals have access to 21st century communications technologies.* Retrieved from http://hraunfoss.fcc.gov/edocs_public/attachmatch/DOC-305587A1.pdf

Giangreco, M. F. (2011). Educating students with severe disabilities: Foundational concepts and practices. In M. E. Snell & F. Brown (Eds.), *Instruction of students with severe disabilities* (7th ed., pp. 1–30). Upper Saddle River, NJ: Pearson Education, Inc.

Grandinette, S., & Best, S. J. (2009). Traumatic brain injury. In K. W. Heller, P. E. Forney, P. A. Alberto, S. J. Best, & M. N. Schwartzman (Eds.), *Understanding physical, health, and multiple disabilities* (2nd ed., pp. 118–138). Columbus, OH: Merrill/Pearson.

Hartshorne, T. S., Hefner, M. A., Davenport, S. L. H., & Thelin, J. W. (2010). *Charge syndrome.* San Diego, CA: Plural Publishing, Inc.

Heller, K. W. (2009). Learning and behavioral characteristics of students with physical, health, or multiple disabilities. In K. W. Heller, P. E. Forney, P. A. Alberto, S. J. Best, & M. N. Schwartzman (Eds.), *Understanding physical, health, and multiple disabilities* (2nd ed., pp. 18–34). Columbus, OH: Merrill/Pearson.

Heller, K. W., & Bigge, J. L. (2011). Augmentative and alternative communication. In S. J. Best, K. W. Heller, & J. L. Bigge (Eds.), *Teaching individuals with physical or multiple disabilities* (6th ed., pp. 221–254). Upper Saddle River, NJ: Pearson Education, Inc.

Holcomb, M., & Wood, S. (1989). *Deaf woman: A parade through the decades.* Berkeley, CA: DawnSignPress.

Jordan, B. (2001). *Considerations when teaching students who are deaf-blind. (PEPNet Tipsheet).* Shawnee Mission, KS: Helen Keller National Center. Retrieved from http://www.pepnet.org/sites/default/files/65PEPNet%20Tipsheet%20-%20Considerations%20when%20teaching%20students%20who%20are%20DeafBlind.pdf

Killoran, J. (2007). *The national deaf-blind child count: 1998–2005 in review.* Monmouth, OR: National Technical Assistance Consortium for Children and Youth who are Deaf-Blind. (NTAC).

Kochar-Bryant, C. A., Shaw, S., & Izzo, M. (2007). *What every teacher should know about transition and IDEA 2004.* Boston, MA: Allyn & Bacon.

Kreutzer, J., & Hsu, N. (2011). *Accommodations guide for students with brain injury.* Retrieved from http://www.brainline.org/content/2011/10/accommodations-guide-for-students-with-brain-injury.html

McWilliams, R. A., Wollery, M., & Odom, S. L. (2001). Instructional perspectives in inclusive preschool classrooms. In M. J. Guralnick (Ed.), *Early childhood inclusion: Focus on change.* Baltimore, MD: Brookes.

Miles, B. (2005, January). *Overview on deaf-blindness.* Retrieved from www.dblink.org/lib/overview.htm

Morgan's Wonderland. (2015). *Just the facts.* Retrieved from http://www.morganswonderland.com/park-info/newsroom/just-the-facts

Naraian, S. (2010). "Why not have fun?" Peers make sense of an inclusive high school. *Intellectual and Developmental Disabilities, 48,* 14–30.

National Center on Deaf-Blindness. (2015, October). *The 2014 national child count of children and youth who are deaf-blind.* Retrieved from https://91372e5fba0d1fb26b72-13cee80c2bfb23b1a8fcedea15638c1f.ssl.cf1.rackcdn.com/cms/2014_National_Deaf-Blind_Child_Count_Report_v112015_641.pdf

National Center on Deaf-Blindness. (2016). *National deaf-blind child count maps, 2014.* Retrieved from https://nationaldb.org/childcount

National Center on Educational Outcomes. (n.d.). *Alternate assessments based on alternate achievement standards (AA-AAS).* Retrieved from https://nceo.info/Assessments/aa-aas

National Dissemination Center for Children with Disabilities (NICHCY). (2013). *Multiple disabilities.* Retrieved from http://www.parentcenterhub.org/repository/multiple/

National Institute on Deafness and Other Communication Disorders (NIDCD). (2014, April 30). *Usher syndrome.* Retrieved from https://www.nidcd.nih.gov/health/usher-syndrome

National Institute of Neurological Disorders and Stroke. (2016, February 11). *NINDS traumatic brain injury information page.* Retrieved from https://www.ninds.nih.gov/Disorders/All-Disorders/Traumatic-Brain-Injury-Information-Page

Project IDEAL. (n.d.). *Multiple disabilities.* Retrieved from http://www .projectidealonline.org/v/multiple-disabilities/

Prouty, S., & Prouty, M. (2009). Interventions: One key to success. *Deaf-Blind Perspectives, 17,* 1–4.

Quenemoen, R. F., & Thurlow, M. L. (2015, June). *AA-AAS: Standards that are the "same but different"* (NCSC Brief #1). Minneapolis, MN: University of Minnesota, National Center and State Collaborative.

Schaefer, J. M., & Andzik, N. R. (2016). Switch on the learning: Teaching students with significant disabilities to use switches. *TEACHING Exceptional Children, 48,* 204–212.

Schein, J. D., & Wolf-Schein, E. G. (n.d.). *A brief history of services for deafblind people in the United States.* Retrieved from www.deafblind .ufl.edu/PDF_attachments/PepNetCh1.pdf

Snell, M. E., & Brown, F. (2011). *Instruction of students with severe disabilities* (7th ed.). Upper Saddle River, NJ: Pearson Education, Inc.

Sprout. (2015). *Our mission.* Retrieved from http://gosprout.org /about-us/

Sprout. (2015). *Travel program.* Retrieved from http://gosprout.org /vacation-programs/

Sproutflix. (n.d.). *About Sproutflix.* Retrieved from http://sproutflix .org/about/

Test, D., & Mazzotti, V. L. (2011). Transitioning from school to employment. In M. E. Snell & F. Brown (Eds.), *Instruction of students with severe disabilities* (7th ed., pp. 569–611). Upper Saddle River, NJ: Pearson Education, Inc.

Towles-Reeves, E., Kleinert, H., & Muhomba, M. (2009). Alternate assessment: Have we learned anything new? *Exceptional Children, 75,* 233–252.

U.S. Department of Education. (2006, August 14). Assistance to states for the education of children with disabilities and preschool grants for children with disabilities; Final Rule (pp. 1263–1264), *Federal Register,* 34 CFR Parts 300 and 301, Washington, DC.

U.S. Department of Education. (2015). Number of students ages 6 through 21 served under IDEA, Part B, by disability and state: 2014-15. [IDEA Section 618 Data Products: Static Tables, 2014-2015 Part B *Child Count and Educational Environments*]. Retrieved from http:// www2.ed.gov/programs/osepidea/618-data/static-tables /index.html#part-b

Westling, D. L., & Fox, E. (2004). *Teaching students with severe disabilities* (3rd ed.). Upper Saddle River, NJ: Merrill/Pearson Education.

Chapter 15

Armstrong, T. (2009). *Multiple intelligences in the classroom* (3rd ed.). Alexandria, VA: Association for Supervision and Curriculum Development.

Assouline, S. G., Colangelo, N., Heo, N., & Dockery, L. (2013). High-ability students' participation in specialized instructional delivery models: Variations by aptitude, grade, gender, and content area. *Gifted Child Quarterly, 57*(2), 135–147.

Assouline, S. G., Colangelo, N., & VanTassel-Baska, J. (2015). *A nation empowered: Evidence trumps the excuses holding back America's brightest students (Vol. 1).* Iowa City, IA: The Belin-Blank Center.

Assouline, S. G., Colangelo, N., & VanTassel-Baska, J. (2015). *A nation empowered: Evidence trumps the excuses holding back America's brightest students (Vol. 2).* Iowa City, IA: The Belin-Blank Center.

Bell, S. M., Taylor, E. P., McCallum, R. S., Coles, J. T., & Hays, E. (2015). Comparing prospective twice-exceptional students with high-performing peers on high-stakes tests of achievement. *Journal for the education of the gifted, 38*(3), 294–317.

Benbow, C. P., & Lubinski, D. (2007). *Future career path of gifted youth can be predicted by age 13.* Nashville, TN: Vanderbilt News.

Benbow, C. P., & Stanley, J. C. (1996). Inequity in equity: How "equity" can lead to inequity for high-potential students. *Psychology, Public Policy, and Law, 2,* 249–292.

Berger, S. (1991). *Differentiating curriculum for gifted students* (Eric Digest No. E510). Retrieved from Eric Database (ED342175).

Berger, S. (n.d.). *How can I help my gifted child plan for college?* Retrieved from http://www.davidsongifted.org/db/Articles_id_10516.aspx

Berger, S. L. (1998). *College planning for gifted students* (2nd ed.). Reston, VA: The Council for Exceptional Children. Retrieved from ERIC database (ED439566).

Berger, S. L. (2014). *College planning for gifted students* (4th ed.). Waco, TX: Prufrock Press, Inc.

Bernal, E. M. (2003). To no longer educate the gifted: Programming for gifted students beyond the era of inclusionism. *Gifted Child Quarterly, 47,* 183–191.

Bianco, M., Harris, B., Garrison-Wade, D., & Leech, N. (2011). Gifted girls: Gender bias in gifted referrals. *Roeper Review, 33,* 170–181.

Binet, A., & Simon, T. (1905). Méthodes nouvelles pour le diagnostic du niveau intellectuel des anormaux. *L'Année psychologique, 11,* 191–336.

Biography.com Editors. (n.d.). *Bill Gates biography.* Retrieved from http://www.biography.com/people/bill-gates-9307520#early-career

Biography.com Editors. (n.d.). *Mark Zuckerberg biography.* Retrieved from http:ww.biography.com/people/mark-zuckerberg-507402

Biography.com Editors. (n.d.). *Steve Jobs biography.* http://www .biography.com/people/steve-jobs-9354805#departure-from-apple

Biography.com Editors. (n.d.). *Taylor Swift biography.* Retrieved from http://www.biography.com/people/taylor-swift-369608# commercial-success

Biography.com Editors. (n.d.). *Whoopi Goldberg biography.* Retrieved from http://www.biography.com/people/whoopi-goldberg-9314384

Biography.com Editors. (n.d.). *Will Smith biography.* Retrieved from http://www.biography.com/people/will-smith-9542165

Bleske-Rechek, A., Lubinski, D., & Benbow, C. P. (2004). Meeting the educational needs of special populations: Advanced Placement's role in developing exceptional human capital. *Psychological Science, 15,* 217–224.

Briggs, C. J., Reis, S. M., & Sullivan, E. E. (2008). A national view of promising programs and practices for culturally, linguistically, and ethnically diverse gifted and talented students. *Gifted Child Quarterly, 52,* 131–145.

Brulles, D., Cohn, S. & Saunders, R. (2010). Improving performance for gifted students in a cluster grouping model. *Journal for the Education of the Gifted, 34*(2), 327–350. Retrieved from http://www .davidsongifted.org/Search-Database/entry/A10691

Callahan, C. M. (2008). Assessing and improving services provided to gifted students: A plan for program evaluation. In F. A. Karnes & K. R. Stephens (Eds.), *Achieving excellence: Educating the gifted and talented* (pp. 230–245). Columbus, OH: Merrill/Pearson Education.

Callahan, C. M., Moon T. R., & Oh, S. (2013). *Status of elementary gifted programs: 2013.* Charlottesville, VA: The National Research Center on the Gifted and Talented. Retrieved from http://www.nagc.org/ sites/default/files/key%20reports/ELEM%20school%20GT% 20Survey%20Report.pdf

Callahan, C. M., Moon T. R., & Oh, S. (2013). *Status of high school gifted programs: 2013.* Charlottesville, VA: The National Research Center on the Gifted and Talented. Retrieved from http://www.nagc.org/sites /default/files/key%20reports/HighSchool%20GT%20Survey%20 Report.pdf

Callahan, C. M., Moon T. R., & Oh, S. (2013). *Status of middle school gifted programs: 2013.* Charlottesville, VA: The National Research Center on the Gifted and Talented. Retrieved from http://www.nagc.org/sites /default/files/key%20reports/MIDDLE%20school%20GT% 20Survey%20Report.pdf

Callahan, C. M., Moon, T. R., & Oh, S. (2014). *National surveys of gifted programs: Executive summary 2014.* Charlottesville, VA: The National Research Center on the Gifted and Talented. Retrieved from http://www.nagc.org/sites/default/files/key%20reports/2014% 20Survey%20of%20GT%20programs%20Exec%20Summ.pdf

Callahan, C. M., Moon, T. R., Oh, S., Azano, A. P., & Hailey, E. P. (2015). What works in gifted education: Documenting the effects of an integrated curricular/instructional model for gifted students. *American Educational Research Journal, 52*(1), 1–31.

Clark, B. (2008). *Growing up gifted: Developing the potential of children at home and school* (7th ed). Upper Saddle River, NJ: Merrill/Pearson Education.

Clemens, T. L. (2008). *Underachieving gifted students: A social cognitive model.* Storrs, CT: National Research Center on the Gifted and Talented, University of Connecticut.

Colangelo, N., Assouline, S., & Gross, M. (2004). *A nation deceived: How schools hold back America's brightest students* (Vol. 1). Iowa City, IA: University of Iowa Press.

Colangelo, N., Assouline, S., & Gross, M. (2004). *A nation deceived: How schools hold back America's brightest students* (Vol. 2). Iowa City, IA: University of Iowa Press.

Coleman, L. J., Micko, K. J., & Cross, T. L. (2015). Twenty-five years of research on the lived experience of being gifted in school: Capturing the students' voices. *Journal for the Education of the Gifted, 38*(4), 358–376.

Contreras, F. (2011). Strengthening the bridge to higher education for academically promising underrepresented students. *Journal of Advanced Academics, 22*(3), 500–526.

Cooper, E. E., Ness, M., & Smith, M. (2004). A case study of a child with dyslexia and spatial-temporal gifts. *Gifted Child Quarterly, 48*, 83–94.

Corwin, M. (2001). *And still we rise: The trials and triumphs of twelve gifted inner-city students.* New York, NY: HarperCollins.

Council for Exceptional Children. (2015, June). *Federal outlook for exceptional children: Fiscal year 2016.* Arlington, VA: Author. Retrieved from https://www.cec.sped.org/~/media/Files/Policy/Current%20Sped%20Issues%20Home/Federal%20Outlook%202016%20FINAL.pdf

Cukierkorn, J. R., Karnes, F. A., Manning, S. J., Houston, H., & Besnoy, K. (2007). Serving the preschool gifted child: Programming and resources. *Roeper Review, 29*, 271–276.

Dare, L., & Nowicki, E. (2015). Conceptualizing concurrent enrollment: Why high-achieving students go for it. *Gifted Child Quarterly, 59*(4), 249–264.

Davidson Institute for Talent Development. (n.d.). *Gifted education policies.* Retrieved from www.davidsongifted.org/db/StatePolicy.aspx

Davidson Institute for Talent Development. (n.d.). *IQ and educational needs.* Retrieved from http://presskit.ditd.org/Davidson_Institute_Press_Kit/ditd_IQ_and_Educational_Needs.html

Davidson Institute for Talent Development. (n.d.). *Talent search opportunities.* Retrieved from http://www.davidsongifted.org/db/Articles_id_10260.aspx

Davidson Institute for Talent Development. (n.d.). *Types of acceleration.* Retrieved from http://www.davidsongifted.org/Search-Database/entry/A10313

Davis, G. A., Rimm, S. B., & Siegle, D. (2011). *Education of the gifted and talented* (6th ed.). Boston, MA: Pearson Education, Inc.

Duke University Talent Identification Program. (2014, September). The social and emotional transition to middle school. *Digest of Gifted Research.* Retrieved from https://tip.duke.edu/node/1640

Esping, A., & Plucker, J. A. (2008). Theories of intelligence. In F. A. Karnes & K. R. Stephens (Eds.), *Achieving excellence: Educating the gifted and talented* (pp. 36–48). Upper Saddle River, NJ: Merrill/Pearson Education.

Farkas, S., & Duffett, A. (2008). Results from a national teacher survey. In Thomas B. Fordham Institute, *High-achieving students in the era of NCLB.* Washington, DC: Thomas B. Fordham Institute.

Finn C. E., Jr., & Petrilli, M. J. (2008). Foreword. In Thomas B. Fordham Institute, *High-achieving students in the era of NCLB.* Washington, DC: Thomas B. Fordham Institute.

Firmender, J. M., Reis, S. M., & Sweeny, S. M. (2013). Reading comprehension and fluency levels ranges across diverse classrooms: The need for differentiated reading instruction and content. *Gifted Child Quarterly, 57*(1), 3–14.

Ford, D. (2015). Culturally responsive gifted classrooms for culturally different students: a focus on invitational learning. *Gifted Child Today, 38*(1), 67–69.

Ford, D. Y. (2011). *Reversing underachievement among gifted Black students* (2nd ed.). Waco, TX: Prufrock Press, Inc.

Ford, D. Y., & Whiting, G. W. (2007). A mind is a terrible thing to erase: Black students' underrepresentation in gifted education. *Multiple Voices, 10*, 28–44.

Francis, R., Hawes, D. J., and Abbott, M. (2016). Intellectual giftedness and psychopathology in children and adolescents: A systematic literature review. *Exceptional Children, 82*(3), 279–302.

Freeman, J. (2003). Gender difference in gifted achievement in Britain and the U.S. *Gifted Child Quarterly, 47*, 202–211.

Friend, M., & Bursuck, W. D. (2006). *Including students with special needs: A practical guide for classroom teachers* (4th ed.). Boston, MA: Allyn & Bacon.

Gagné, F. (2004). An imperative, but, alas, improbable consensus. *Roeper Review, 27*, 12–14.

Gardner, H. (1983). *Frames of mind: Theory of multiple intelligences.* New York, NY: Basic Books.

Gardner, H. (1993). *Multiple intelligences: The theory in practice.* New York, NY: Basic Books.

Gardner, J. W. (1984). *Excellence: Can we be equal and excellent too?* (Rev. ed.). New York, NY: Norton.

Gibbons, M. M., Pelchar, T. K., & Cochran, J. L. (2012). Gifted students from low-education backgrounds. *Roeper Review, 34*, 114–122.

Gifted Development Center. (n.d.). *Highly–profoundly gifted: Educational planning for highly to profoundly gifted children.* Retrieved from http://www.gifteddevelopment.com/about-our-center/our-services/k-12-educational-planning/highly—profoundly-gifted

Gilman, B. J., Lovecky, D. V., Kearney, K., Peters, D. B., Wasserman, J. D., Silverman, L. K., Postma, M. G., Robinson, N. M., Amend, E. R., Ryder-Schoeck, M., Curry, P. H., Lyon, S. K., Rogers, K. B., Collins, L. E., Charlebois, G. M., Harsin, C. M., & Rimm, S. B. (2013). Critical issues in the identification of gifted students with co-existing disabilities: The twice-exceptional. *SAGE Open*, 1–16. doi: 10.1177/2158244013505855

Grantham, T. C. (2002). Underrepresentation in gifted education: How did we get here and what needs to change? *Roeper Review, 24*, 50–51.

Grantham, T. C. (2004). Multicultural mentoring to increase Black male representation in gifted programs. *Gifted Child Quarterly, 48*, 232–245.

Green, N. (2006, Spring). New school for profoundly gifted learners opens this fall in Nevada. *Compass Points, 1*, 7.

Grissom, J. A., & Redding, C. (2016). Discretion and disproportionality: explaining the underrepresentation of high-achieving students of color in gifted programs. *Aera open, 2*(1), 1–25. doi: 10.1177/2332858415622175

Gross, M. (1999). Small poppies: Highly gifted children in the early years. *Roeper Review, 21*(3). Retrieved from http://www.davidsongifted.org/db/Articles_id_10124.aspx

Guenther, A. (1998). *What parents and teachers should know about academic acceleration.* [Practitioners' Guide #A9815]. The National Research Center on the Gifted and Talented: Storrs, CT. Retrieved from http://nrcgt.uconn.edu/wp-content/uploads/sites/953/2015/04/A9815P.pdf

Guibault, K. M. (2012). *Early enrichment for young gifted children.* Retrieved from http://mcgate.org/early-enrichment-for-young-gifted-children/

Halpern, D. H., Aronson, J., Reimer, N., Sipkins, S., Star, J. R., & Wentzel, K. (2007). *Encouraging young girls in math and science [IES Practice Guide].* Washington, DC: U.S. Department of Education, Institute for Educational Sciences, National Center for Educational Research.

Hébert, T. P. (2006). Gifted university males in a Greek fraternity: Creating a culture of achievement. *Gifted Child Quarterly, 50*, 26–41.

Hébert, T. P., & Olenchak, F. R. (2000). Mentors for gifted underachieving males: Developing potential and realizing promises. *Gifted Child Quarterly, 44*, 196–207.

Henderson, L. M., & Ebner, F. F. (1997). The biological basis for early intervention with gifted children. *Peabody Journal of Education, 72*(3/4), 59–80.

Henfield, M. S., Moore, J. L., III, & Wood, C. (2008). Inside and outside gifted education programming: Hidden challenges for African American students. *Exceptional Children, 74*, 433–453.

Hertberg-Davis, H., & Callahan, C. M. (2008). A narrow escape: Gifted students' perceptions of advanced placement and International Baccalaureate programs. *Gifted Child Quarterly, 52*, 199–216.

Hoagies Gifted Education Page. (2016). *Distance learning programs.* Retrieved from http://www.hoagiesgifted.org/distance_learning.htm

Hoh, P. S. (2005). The linguistic advantage of the intellectually gifted child: An empirical study of spontaneous speech. *Roeper Review, 27*, 178–185.

Holdren, J. P. (2011, January 6). *America COMPETES Act keeps America's leadership on target. The White House Blog.* Retrieved from www.whitehouse.gov/blog/2011/01/06/america-competes-act-keeps-americas-leadership-target

Hunsaker, S. L. (1995). The gifted metaphor from the perspective of traditional civilizations. *Journal for the Education of the Gifted, 18*, 255–268.

Inheritance Wiki. (n.d.). *Christopher Paolini*. Retrieved from http://inheritance.wikia.com/wiki/Christopher_Paolini

Jeffrey, T. (2008, Spring). Differentiating content using a conceptual lens. *Compass Points*, THP 8–9.

Johnsen, S. K. (2008). Identifying gifted and talented learners. In F. A. Karnes & K. R. Stephens (Eds.), *Achieving excellence: Educating the gifted and talented* (pp. 135–153). Upper Saddle River, NJ: Merrill/Pearson Education.

Karnes, F. A., & Stephens. K. R. (Eds.). (2008). *Achieving excellence: Educating the gifted and talented*. Upper Saddle River, NJ: Merrill/Pearson Education.

Kim, M. (2016). A meta-analysis of the effect of enrichment programs on gifted students. *Gifted Child Quarterly, 60*(2), 102–116.

Kirschenbaum, R. J. (1998). The creativity classification systems: An assessment theory. *Roeper Review, 21*, 20–26.

Kornhaber, M., Fierros, E., & Veenema, S. (2004). *Multiple intelligences: Best ideas from research to practice*. Boston, MA: Allyn & Bacon.

Kottmeyer, C. (n.d.). *What is highly gifted? Exceptionally gifted? Profoundly gifted? And what does it mean?* Retrieved from http://www.hoagiesgifted.org/highly_profoundly.htm

Kowalske, K. (2015). Portrait of Olivia: A case study of a spiritually gifted student. *Gifted Education International*, 1–13. doi: 10.1177/0261429415602586

Kroesbergen, E. H., van Hooijdonk, M., Viersen, S. V., Middel-Lalleman, M. M. N., and Reijnders, J. J. W. (2016). The psychological well-being of early identified gifted children. *Gifted Child Quarterly, 60*(1), 16–30.

Landis, R. N., & Reschly, A. L. (2013). Reexamining gifted underachievement and dropout through the lens of student engagement. *Journal of the Education of the Gifted 36*(2), 220–249.

Lee, S., Matthews, M. S., & Olszewski-Kubilius, P. (2008). A national picture of talent search and talent search educational programs. *Gifted Child Quarterly, 52*, 55–69.

Lee, S., Olszewski-Kubilius, P., Makel, M. C., & Putallaz, M. (2015). Gifted students' perceptions of an accelerated summer program and social support. *Gifted Child Quarterly, 59*(4), 265–282.

Loveless, R. (2008). An analysis of NAEP data. In Thomas B. Fordham Institute, *High-achieving students in the era of NCLB*. Washington, DC: Thomas B. Fordham Institute.

Lubinski, D., & Benbow, C. P. (1995). Optimal development of talent: Respond educationally to individual differences in personality. *Educational Forum, 59*, 381–392.

Lubinski, D., & Benbow, C. P. (2006). Study of mathematically precocious youth after 35 years: Uncovering antecedents for the development of math-science expertise. *Perspectives on Psychological Science, 1*, 316–345.

Lubinski, D., Benbow, C. P., and Kell, H. J. (2014). Life paths and accomplishments of mathematically precocious males and females four decades later. *Psychological Science, 25*(12), 2217–2232.

Lubinski, D., Benbow, C. P., Webb, R. M., & Bleske-Rechek, A. (2006). Tracking exceptional human capital over two decades. *Psychological Science, 17*, 194–199.

Maker, C. J. (1977). *Providing programs for the gifted handicapped*. Reston, VA: Council for Exceptional Children.

Maker, C. J. (1986). Education of the gifted: Significant trends. In R. J. Morris & B. Blatt (Eds.), *Special education: Research and trends* (pp. 190–221). New York, NY: Pergamon.

Manning, S., & Bosnoy, K. D. (2008). Special populations. In F. A. Karnes & K. R. Stephens (Eds.), *Achieving excellence: Educating the gifted and talented* (pp. 116–134). Upper Saddle River, NJ: Merrill/Pearson Education.

Marland, S. P., Jr. (1972). *Education of the gifted and talented. Vol. 1. Report to Congress of the United States by the U.S. Commissioner of Education*. Washington, DC: U.S. Government Printing Office.

McGee, C. D., & Hughes, C. E. (2011). Identifying and supporting young gifted learners. *Young Children, 66*(4), 100–105.

Mendaglio, S. (2013). Gifted students' transition to university. *Gifted Education International, 29*(1), 3–12.

Moon, S. M. (2009). Myth 15: High-ability students don't face problems and challenges. *Gifted Child Quarterly, 53*(4), 274–276.

Naglieri, J. A., & Ford, D. Y. (2005). Increasing minority children's participation in gifted classes using the NNAT: A response to Lohman. *Gifted Child Quarterly, 49*, 29–36.

National Association for Gifted Children. (1998). *Collaboration between gifted and general education programs [Position Statement]*. Retrieved from www.nagc.org/index.aspx?id=462

National Association for Gifted Children. (2004). *Acceleration [Position Statement]*. Retrieved from www.nagc.org/policy/pp_acceleration.html

National Association for Gifted Children. (2006). *Early childhood [Position Statement]*. Retrieved from https://www.nagc.org/sites/default/files/Position%20Statement/Early%20Childhood%20Position%20Statement.pdf

National Association for Gifted Children. (2008). *The big picture: Gifted education in the U.S.* Retrieved from www.nagc.org/index.aspx?id=532

National Association for Gifted Children. (2014). *Differentiating curriculum and instruction for gifted and talented students* [Position Statement]. Retrieved from https://www.nagc.org/sites/default/files/Position%20Statement/Differentiating%20Curriculum%20and%20Instruction.pdf

National Association for Gifted Children. (n.d.). *Asynchronous development*. Retrieved from http://www.nagc.org/resources-publications/resources/social-emotional-issues/asynchronous-development

National Association for Gifted Children. (n.d.). *Definitions of giftedness*. Retrieved from https://www.nagc.org/resources-publications/resources/definitions-giftedness

National Association for Gifted Children. (n.d.). *Gifted education in the U.S.* Retrieved from https://www.nagc.org/resources-publications/resources/gifted-education-us

National Association for Gifted Children. (n.d.). *Instructional strategies*. Retrieved from https://tip.duke.edu/node/347#Enrichment

National Association for Gifted Children and The Council of State Directors of Programs for the Gifted. (2015). *2014–2015 State of the states in gifted education: Policy and practice data*. Retrieved from http://www.nagc.org/sites/default/files/key%20reports/2014-2015%20State%20of%20the%20States%20%28final%29.pdf

National Center for Education Statistics. (2007). *Digest of education statistics: 2011 tables and figures*. Retrieved from http://nces.ed.gov/programs/digest/d11/tables/dt11_050.asp

National Center for Education Statistics. (2015). *Student readiness and progress through school*. (Data table: Types of state and district requirements for kindergarten entrance and attendance, by state: 2014). Retrieved from https://nces.ed.gov/programs/statereform/tab5_3.asp

National Education Association. (2006). *The twice-exceptional dilemma*. Washington, DC: Author.

National Society for the Gifted and Talented. (n.d.). *Giftedness defined*. Retrieved from http://www.nsgt.org/giftedness-defined/#9

Neag Center for Creativity, Gifted Education, and Talent Development. (n.d.). *Schoolwide Enrichment Model (SEM)*. Retrieved from http://gifted.uconn.edu/schoolwide-enrichment-model/

Nichols, H. J., & Baum, S. (2000, December). High achievers: Keys to helping youngsters with stress reduction. *Parenting for High Potential*, 9–12.

Nielsen, E., & Mortorff-Albert, S. (1990). The effects of special education programming on the self-concept and school attitude of learning disabled/gifted elementary students. *Roeper Review, 12*, 29–36.

Nielsen, M. E. (2002). Gifted students with learning disabilities: Recommendations for identification and programming. *Exceptionality, 10*, 93–111.

Nielsen, M. E., & Higgins, L. D. (2005). The eye of the storm: Services and programs for twice-exceptional learners. *Teaching Exceptional Children, 38*, 8–15.

Noble, K. D., Childers, S. A., & Vaughan, R. C. (2008). A place to be celebrated and understood: The impact of early university entrance programs from parents' points of view. *Gifted Child Quarterly, 52*, 256–268.

Oden, M. H. (1968). The fulfillment of promise: 40-year follow-up of the Terman gifted group. *Genetic Psychology Monographs, 77*, 3–93.

Olszewski-Kubilus, P., & Lee, S. Y. (2008). Specialized programs serving the gifted. In F. A. Karnes & K. R. Stephens (Eds.), *Achieving excellence: Educating the gifted and talented* (pp. 192–209). Columbus, OH: Merrill/Pearson Education.

Paik, S. J., & Walberg, H. J. (Eds.). (2007). *Narrowing the achievement gap: Strategies for educating Latino, Black, and Asian students.* New York, NY: Springer.

Park, G., Lubinski, D., & Benbow, C. P. (2008). Ability differences among people who have commensurate degrees matter for scientific creativity. *Psychological Science, 19,* 957–961.

Park, G., Lubinski, D., & Benbow, C. P. (2012). When less is more: Effects of grade skipping on adult STEM productivity among mathematically precocious adolescents. *Journal of Educational Psychology.* doi: 10.1037/a0029481

Plucker, J., Giancola, J., Healey, G., Arndt, D., & Wang, C. (2015). *Equal talents, unequal opportunities: A report card on state support for academically talented low-income students.* Retrieved from http://classcoalition.org/wp-content/uploads/2015/09/JKCF_ETUO_Report.pdf

Peterson, J. S. (2009). Myth 17: Gifted and talented individuals do not have unique social and emotional needs. *Gifted Child Quarterly, 53*(4), 280–282.

Preckel, F., Goetz, T., Pekrun, R., & Kleine, M. (2008). Gender differences in gifted and average-ability students: Comparing girls' and boys' achievement, self-concept, interest, and motivation in mathematics. *Gifted Child Quarterly, 52,* 146–159.

Reis, S. (2003). Gifted girls, twenty-five years later: Hopes realized and new challenges found. *Roeper Review, 25,* 154–157.

Reis, S., & Housand, A. M. (2008). Characteristics of gifted and talented learners: Similarities and differences across domains. In F. A. Karnes & K. R. Stephens (Eds.), *Achieving excellence: Educating the gifted and talented* (pp. 62–81). Upper Saddle River, NJ: Merrill /Pearson Education.

Reis, S. M. (n.d.). *Major turning points in gifted education in the 20th century.* Retrieved from http://gifted.uconn.edu/schoolwide-enrichment-model/major_turning_points/

Reis, S. M., & McCoach, D. B. (n.d.). *Underachievement in gifted and talented students with special needs.* Retrieved from http://gifted.uconn.edu/schoolwide-enrichment-model/gifted_underachievers/

Renzulli, J. S. (1999, October). A rising tide lifts all ships: Developing the gifts and talents of all students. *Phi Delta Kappan, 80,* 104–111.

Renzulli, J. S. (2000). Gifted dropouts: The who and the why. *Gifted Child Quarterly, 44,* 261–271.

Renzulli, J. S. (2004). The myth: The gifted constitute 3–5% of the population. In J. S. Renzulli (Ed.), *Identification of students for gifted and talented programs.* Thousand Oaks, CA: Corwin Press and the National Association for Gifted Children.

Renzulli, J. S. (2005). *Equity, excellence, and economy in a system for identifying students in gifted education programs: A guidebook.* Storrs, CT: The National Research Center on the Gifted and Talented.

Renzulli, J. S. (2012). Reexamining the role of gifted education and talent development for the 21st century: A four-part theoretical approach. *Gifted Child Quarterly, 56,* 150–159.

Renzulli, J. S. (n.d.). *A practical system for identifying gifted and talented students.* The National Research Center on the Gifted and Talented. Retrieved from http://gifted.uconn.edu/schoolwide-enrichment-model/identifygt/

Renzulli, J. S., & Reis, S. M. (2007). *Enriching curriculum for all students.* Thousand Oaks, CA: Sage.

Renzulli, J. S., & Reis, S. M. (n.d.) *The Schoolwide Enrichment Model executive summary.* Retrieved from http://gifted.uconn.edu /schoolwide-enrichment-model/semexec/

Rimm, S. (2008). Parenting gifted children. In F. A. Karnes & K. R. Stephens (Eds.), *Achieving excellence: Educating the gifted and talented* (pp. 262–277). Upper Saddle River, NJ: Merrill/Pearson Education.

Rinn, A. N., & Bishop, J. (2015). Gifted adults; A systematic review and analysis of the literature. *Gifted Child Quarterly, 59*(4), 213–235.

Roberts, J. L. (2008). Teachers of the gifted and talented. In F. A. Karnes & K. R. Stephens (Eds.), *Achieving excellence: Educating the gifted and talented* (pp. 246–261). Columbus, OH: Merrill/Pearson Education.

Robinson, A. (2006, Spring). Blueprints for biography: Differentiating the curriculum for talented readers. *Compass Points,* 7–8.

Robinson, G. (2016). *What is International Baccalaureate?* Retrieved from http://www.greatschools.org/gk/articles/what-is-ib-international-baccalaureate/

Robinson, N., & Weminer, L. (1991). Selection of candidates for early admission to kindergarten and first grade. In W. T. Southern and E. Jones (Eds.), *The academic acceleration of gifted children* (pp. 29–50). New York, NY: Teachers College Press. Retrieved from http://www.davidsongifted.org/db/Articles_id_10123.aspx

Robinson, S. M. (1999). Meeting the needs of students who are gifted and have learning disabilities. *Intervention in School and Clinic, 34,* 195–204.

Rogers, K. B. (1999). The lifelong productivity of the female researchers in Terman's genetic studies of genius longitudinal study. *Gifted Child Quarterly, 43,* 150–169.

Rogers, K. B. (2002). Grouping the gifted and talented: Questions and answers. *Roeper Review, 16,* 8–12.

Rosalind, L. W., Kemp, C. R., Hodge, K. A., & Bowes, J. M. (2012). Searching for evidence-based practice: A review of the research on educational interventions for intellectually gifted children in the early childhood years. *Journal for the Education of the Gifted, 35*(2), 103–108.

Schader, R. M., & Eckert, R. D. (2006). What do we need to know about children who have already mastered pre-school or kindergarten skills prior to entering the classroom? *Connecting for High Potential* (Issue 3). Retrieved from http://www.nagc.org/sites/default/files /Publication%20CHP/CHP%20Issue%203_0.pdf

Schweinhart, L. J. (2005). *The High/Scope Perry Preschool study through age 40: Summary, conclusions, and frequently asked questions.* Ypsilanti, MI: High/Scope Educational Research Foundation. Retrieved from www.highscope.org

Siegle, D. (2008a, Spring). Message from the NAGC President. *Compass Points, 1,* 6.

Siegle, D. (2008b). The time is now to stand up for gifted education: 2007 NAGC presidential address. *Gifted Child Quarterly, 52,* 111–113.

Siegle, D. (2015). Technology: Learning can be fun and games. *Gifted Child Today, 38*(3), 192–197. doi: 10.1177/1076217515583744

Siegle, D., Gubbins, E. J., O'Rourke, P., Langley, S. D., Mun, R. R., Luria, S. R., Little, C. A., McCoach, D. B., Knupp, T., Callahan, C. M., & Plucker, J. A. (2016). Barriers to underserved students' participation in gifted programs and possible solutions. *Journal for the Education of the Gifted, 39*(2), 103–131.

Silverman, L. (2005). *What we have learned about gifted children.* Denver: Gifted Development Center. Retrieved from www.gifteddevelopment .com

Sisk, D. A. (2015). Spiritual intelligence: Developing higher consciousness revisited. *Gifted Education International,* 1–15. doi: 10.1177 /0261429415602567

Smith, M. K. (2008). Howard Gardner, multiple intelligences and education. *The encyclopaedia of informal education.* Retrieved from www .infed.org

Stambaugh, T. (2010). The education of promising students in rural areas: What do we know and what can we do? In J. VanTassel-Baska (Ed.), *Patterns and profiles from promising learners of poverty* (pp. 59–83). Waco, TX: Prufrock Press, Inc.

Steenbergen-Hu, S., & Moon, S. M. (2011). The effects of acceleration on high-ability learners: A meta-analysis. *Gifted Child Quarterly, 55*(1), 39–53.

Sweeney, N. S. (2007). Gifted children have special needs, too. *Earlychildhood NEWS.* Retrieved from http://www.earlychildhoodnews.com /earlychildhood/article_view.aspx?ArticleID=248

Terman, L. (1925). *Genetic studies of genius* (Vol. 1). Stanford, CA: Stanford University Press.

Terman, L. M., & Oden, M. H. (1959). *The gifted group at midlife.* Stanford, CA: Stanford University Press.

Tornatzky, L. G., Pachon, H. P., & Torres, C. (2003). *Closing achievement gaps: Improving educational outcomes for Hispanic children.* Los Angeles: Center for Latino Educational Excellence, Tomás Rivera Policy Institute, University of Southern California.

Tomlinson, C. A., & Hockett, J. A. (2008). Instructional strategies and programming models for gifted learners. In F. A. Karnes & K. R. Stephens (Eds.), *Achieving excellence: Educating the gifted and talented* (pp. 154–169). Upper Saddle River, NJ: Merrill/Pearson Education.

U.S. Congress. *Every Student Succeeds Act of 2015.* PL 114-95.

U.S. Congress. *Individuals with Disabilities Education Improvement Act of 2004.* PL No. 108–446.

U.S. Congress. *Jacob K. Javits Gifted and Talented Students Education Act of 1988*. PL 100–297.

U.S. Congress. *No Child Left Behind Act of 2001*. PL 107–110.

U.S. Department of Education. (2015). *Thirty-seventh annual report to Congress on the implementation of the Individuals with Disabilities Education Act, 2015*. Retrieved from http://www2.ed.gov/about/reports/annual/osep/2015/parts-b-c/37th-arc-for-idea.pdf

VanTassel-Baska, J., & Stambaugh, T. (2006). *Comprehensive curriculum for gifted learners* (3rd ed.). Boston, MA: Allyn & Bacon.

VanTassel-Baska, J., & Wood, S. (2008). Curriculum development in gifted education: A challenge to provide optimal learning experiences. In F. A. Karnes & K. R. Stephens (Eds.), *Achieving excellence: Educating the gifted and talented* (pp. 209–229). Upper Saddle River, NJ: Merrill/Pearson Education.

Wai, J., Lubinski, D., & Benbow, C. P. (2009). Spatial ability for STEM domains: Aligning over 50 years of cumulative psychological knowledge solidifies its importance. *Journal of Educational Psychology, 4*, 817–835.

Wai, J., Lubinski, D., & Benbow, C. P. (2010). Accomplishment in science, technology, engineering, and mathematics (STEM) and its relation to STEM educational dose: A 25-year longitudinal study. *Journal of Educational Psychology, 102(4)*, 860–871.

Warne, R. T. (2012). History and development of above-level testing of the gifted. *Roeper Review, 34*, 183–193.

Washington Partners. (2008, June). *Funding table for selected FY 2009 education programs*. Washington, DC: Author.

Young Exceptionally Gifted Students. (n.d.). *YEGS Hall of Fame*. Retrieved from http://yegs.org/yegs-hall-of-fame-main-page/

Index

Note: Bold page numbers denote key terms.

A

AA-AAA (alternate assessments based on alternate achievement standards), 422
AAC. *See* Augmentative and alternative communication
AAIDD. *See* American Association of Intellectual and Developmental Disabilities
ABA. *See* Applied behavior analysis
ABC analysis, 216
Above-level testing, **445**
Absenteeism, 7
Abuse
  intellectual disabilities and, 266–267, 271
  of persons with disability, 11, 12
Academic achievement
  alternate standards, **259**
  gender differences, 476
Academic and Behavioral Response to Intervention Project, 297
Academic aptitude, 450
Academic competition, 465
Academic language, 67. *See also* Cognitive academic language proficiency
Academic outcomes, future, 20–21
Acceleration, **456**–460
  resources for, 460
  types of, 458
Accessibility, 23–25
Accessibility Technologies, Apple's, 408
Accident prevention, 337–339
Accommodations, **21**, 23–25, 82–83, **90**
  ADHD, 183–184
  ASD, 217–219
  compared with modifications, 89–91
  for deafness and hearing impairments, 357–359
  EBD, 291–292
  frequently used, 90
  gifted and talented, 457–458
  learning disabilities, 151–153
  low incidence disabilities, 421–423
  mutual, **64**
  physical and health disabilities, 325–327
  speech and language impairments, 118–119
  visual disabilities, 389–392, 405
  websites, 91
Achievement gaps, **9**, 54
Achilles International, 405
Active supervision, **295**
ADA. *See* Americans with Disabilities Act
Adaptive behavior, **244**, 245
  intellectual disabilities, 249–250
  skills, 245, 255
Additive bilingualism, **67**
ADDM. *See* Autism and Developmental Disabilities Monitoring Network
ADHD. *See* Attention deficit hyperactivity disorder
Advanced placement (AP) courses, **53**, 452, **458**, 459, 476
Advance organizers, 152
Adventitious hearing loss, **348**
Adventitiously blind, **379**
Advocacy, intellectual disabilities, 241, 268–269
African Americans, 4, 12, 319, 320, 333, 475
Age of onset, visual disabilities, 379

Aggression, **214**, **281**
AIR (Anonymous. Inspiring. Relatable.), 310
Air conduction audiometry method, **347**
Albinism, **381**
Alcamus, 478
Alexander Graham Bell Association for the Deaf and Hard of Hearing, 367
Allen, Edward, 403
Alliance for Inclusion in the Arts, 12
ALS. *See* Amyotrophic lateral sclerosis
Alternate academic achievement standards, **259**
Alternate achievement standards, **422**–423
Alternate assessments, **259**, **422**–423
Alternate curriculum, **426**
Alvarez, Luis, 468
Amblyopia, **381**
American Academy of Pediatrics, 271
American Association of Deaf-Blind, 433
American Association of Intellectual and Developmental Disabilities (AAIDD), 244
American Federation of Television and Radio Artists, 12
American Institute for Stuttering, 101
Americanization, **50**
American Psychiatric Association (APA), 170, 172, 173
American Sign Language (ASL), 13, 19, 78–79, **352**, 356, 364–365
  foreign language, studied as, 356
  as second language, 356, 360, 365
American Speech-Language-Hearing Association (ASHA), 105, 106, 127
Americans with Disabilities Act (ADA), **23**, 24, 71, 76, 333–334, 411
  passage, 76, 268
Amyotrophic lateral sclerosis (ALS), 313
Anonymous. Inspiring. Relatable. (*AIR*), 310
Anorexia, **281**
Anxiety disorders, **281**
AP. *See* Advanced placement
APA. *See* American Psychiatric Association
Aphasia, **131**
Applied behavior analysis (ABA), **216**–217, 234, 304
Apps and smartphones, 272–273, 408
  ADHD, 200
  for EBD, 308
  for mental health, 310
  speech and language, 133–134
Articulation errors, 106, 121
ASD. *See* Autism spectrum disorder
ASHA. *See* American Speech-Language-Hearing Association
Ashwell, Nicki, 340
ASL. *See* American Sign Language
Asperger, Hans, 229
Asperger's syndrome, **206**, 229
Assessments. *See also* Data-based decision making
  alternate, **259**
  vision, 379–380, 407
Assistive listening devices, 357–358. *See also* Hearing aids
Assistive Technology Act of 2004 (ATA), 76
Assistive technology (AT) and technologists, 95, 96. *See also* Technology
  checklist, 164

deafness and hearing impairments, 355, 356, 357–358, 373. *See also* Cochlear implants; Hearing aids
learning disabilities, 146, 164–165
  video, 165
visual disabilities, 388, 390, 400–402, 405, 408
  website, 165
AssistiveWare, 133–134
Asthma, 320
Asynchrony, **454**, 456, 466
Attention deficit hyperactivity disorder (ADHD), 160–161, 165–201, **169**–170, 320
  504 plans, 82
  accommodations, 91, 183–184
  challenges and solutions, 180–182
  characteristics, 174–175
  defined, 169–171
  diagnostic criteria, 171
  early intervention, 185–187
  future perspectives, 196–200
  gender, 180, 193
  IDEA and, 170, 187
  identification, 185
  intervention, early, 185–187
  medications, 181, 182
  origins, 193–194
  people and situations, 192–196
  personal stories, 194–196
  placement, 175–178
  prevalence, 175–178
  prevention, 197–198
  research, 197–198
  school years, 187–189
  services, 170, 175–177, 185, 187–188, 190, 191
  solutions and challenges, 180–182
  symptoms, 170–171
  technology, 199–200
  transition, 190–192
  treatment types and clinical care, 186
  types of, 171–173
  videos, 175, 187
  websites, 191–192, 200
Attributions, 149, 151
Audiogram, **346**, 349, 350
Audiologists, 96, **347**
Audiometer, **347**
Auditory brainstem implant, **373**
Auditory canal, **344**, 345
Auditory nerve, 345
Auditory neuropathy spectrum disorder, **348**
Auditory processing, **143**
Augmentative and alternative communication (AAC), **118**, **132**, 218, 424, **436**–437
Autism and Developmental Disabilities Monitoring (ADDM) Network, 210, 212
Autism Society of America, 230
Autism Speaks, 230
Autism spectrum disorder (ASD), 7, 146, 202–240, **204**
  ABA and, 216–217
  accommodations, 217–219
  CDC on, 205, 210, 219
  challenges and solutions, 214–217
  characteristics, 207–210
  cues and support, 222–224
  cultural considerations, 227

Autism spectrum disorder (ASD) (*Continued*)
  defined, 204–206
  described, 203–212
  diagnostic criteria, 208, 209
  early intervention, 219–221, 234
  employment and, 225–227
  evidence-based supports, 222–224
  family members and, 232–234
  future perspectives, 235–239
  gender and, 210
  genetic counseling, 235
  IDEA and, 75, 76, 77
  mental health issues, 215
  origins, 229–231
  PECS for, 216, 219–221
  people and situations, 228–234
  personal stories, 231–234
  placement, 210–212
  pregnancy and, 235–236
  prevalence, 210–212
  prevention, 235
  resources, 237–238
  routines and schedules, 218, 222
  school years, 221–224
  social impairments, 205, 208
  solutions, 214–217
  speech and language impairments, 105, 128
  stimuli and, 209, 218
  symptoms, 207
  TEACCH for, 216
  technology, 237–239
  terminology, 19
  transition, post-secondary, 225–227
  types of, 206–207
  vaccination controversy, 228, 230–231, 431
  videos, 219, 223, 224, 232
  websites, 237
  YAP for, 229
Autistic savants, **206**

B

Balbus Balaesus, the Stutterer, 127
Barraga, Natalie, 404
Basic interpersonal conversation skills (BICS), **66**
BCBA. *See* Board Certified Behavior Analyst
Bedlam, 302
Beethoven, Ludwig van, 447
Behavioral expectations, 60, 63
Behavior intervention plans (BIPs), **88, 221,**
  285, 298–289. *See also* Functional behavioral
  assessment
Behavior therapy, **181,** 185–186
Behavior Tracker Pro, 238, 239
Behind-the-ear (BTE) hearing aids, 370–371
Bell, Alexander Graham, 364–365
Bell-shaped curve. *See* Normal curve
Benetech, 161
Best Buddies International, **257,** 268, 272
Bethlem Royal Hospital, 302
Bettelheim, Bruno, 230
BICS. *See* Basic interpersonal conversation skills
Bilingual education, 68
Bilingualism, ASL, 356, 360, 365
Bilingual students, 5
Binet, Alfred, 468
Bionics, 340
BIPs. *See* Behavior intervention plans
Black Enterprise Magazine, 129
Blanton, Smiley, 127
Blatt, Burton, 11, 267, 268
Bleuler, Eugen, 229
Blindness, **378**–379. *See also* Visual disabilities
Blind persons, **378**–379
Board Certified Behavior Analyst (BCBA), **216**

Bode, Patty, 47
Bondy, Andy, 220
Bone conduction audiometry method, **347**
Bookshare, 161, 390, 395
Bower, Eli, 304
Braille, **388, 391, 397,** 403
  IDEA and, 398
  JAWS screen reader, **400**
  mobile keyboard, 408
Braille, Louis, 403
Braille writer, **401**
Brain Injury Association of America, 432
Brain mapping, 163–164
Brainport V100, 408
Brett, Dorothy, 364
Bridgman, Laura Dewey, 378
A Brief History of Time (Hawking), 313, 336
Britain's Missing Top Model, 336
British Sign Language (BSL), 356
Brown v. Board of Education, 12, 53
Bulimia, 276, **281**
Bullying, **29**
  resources, 5, 29
  website, 29
Bush, George W., 129, 131
Butler, Belinda, 202, 227, 232–233, 236

C

California Department of Vocational
  Rehabilitation, 13
CALP. *See* Cognitive academic language
  proficiency
Camp Shriver, 268
Captions, **24,** 358
Career awareness, visual disabilities and, 399
Career-readiness, 21–22, **28**
Carroll, Kelsey, 306
CARS. *See* The Center for Adolescent Research
  in Schools
CART. *See* Communication Access Real-time
  Translation
Carter-Long, Lawrence, 12
Case manager, **330**
CAST, 161
Catheter use, **82**
CBI. *See* Community based instruction
CBM. *See* Curriculum-based measurement
CDC. *See* Centers for Disease Control and
  Prevention
CDD. *See* Childhood disintegrative disorder
CEC. *See* Council for Exceptional Children
Center for Adolescent Research in Schools
  (CARS), 292
Center for Parent Information and Resources,
  305, 306
Center for Positive Behavioral Interventions and
  Supports, 297
Center on Technology and Disability, 437
Centers for Disease Control and Prevention
  (CDC), 175
  on ASD, 205, 210, 219
Cerebral palsy (CP), 133, **319,** 320
Challenges and solutions
  ADHD, 180–182
  ASD, 214–217
  deafness and hearing impairments, 354–356,
  367
  EBD, 288–291
  gifted and talented, 454–457
  intellectual disabilities, 254–258
  learning disabilities, 149–151
  physical and health disabilities, 321, 322–324
  speech and language impairments, 114–118
  visual disabilities, 387–389

Charles, Ray, 404
Check & Connect, **292**
Check-In/Check Out (CICO), **44,** 297–298
Chervin, Claudius, 127
Child abuse. *See* Abuse
Child development milestones, 80
Child Find, 79–81, **80**
  IEP process, 81
  resources, 80, 81
Childhood disintegrative disorder (CDD),
  206, 229
Child of a Deaf Adult (CODAs), **356**
Child Psychiatry (Kanner), 304
Child study team, 81
Christmas in Purgatory (Blatt), 11, 268
Chronic illnesses, **318**
CICO. *See* Check-In/Check-out
Civil Rights Act of 1964, 12
Civil Rights Data Collection Website, 57
Civil rights movement, 12–14. *See also* Section
  504 of the Rehabilitation Act of 1973
CLD. *See* Culturally and linguistically diverse
  learners
Cleft lip, **131**
Cleft palate, **131**
Clerc, Laurnet, 364
Closed captions, **358**
Cluster grouping, **452**
Cluttering, **107**
Cochlea, **344,** 345
Cochlear implants, **355,** 361, 371–372
CODAs. *See* Child of a Deaf Adult
Cognition, **249**
Cognitive academic language proficiency
  (CALP), 66
Collaboration for physical and health
  disabilities, 330–332
Collaborative Strategic Reading (CSR), **124**
College readiness, 21–22, **28**. *See also* Post-
  secondary education; Transitions
Colorblindness, 47
Color scanner, **401**
Communication, 18–19. *See also* Augmentative
  and alternative communication; Deafness
  and hearing impairments
  culture and, 59–60
  PECS, 216, 219–221
  people first language, **19**
  sign language, 133
  styles, 59–60
  total communication approach, hearing
  impairments, **361**
Communication Access Real-time Translation
  (CART), **358**
Communication board, **132,** 436
Communication disorder, **105**
Communicative competence, **109**
Communities. *See also* Deaf community
  of practice, **325**
Community-based instruction (CBI), **261**–262,
  428
Community presence, **12, 23**–25, **250**
Comorbidity, **180**
Comprehensible input, **69**
Compton, Don, 159
Conceptual adaptive behavior skills, 245
Concussions, preventing, 436
Conduct disorder (CD), **180**
Conduct disorders, **280**
Conduction audiometry method, **347**
Conductive hearing loss, **347,** 349
Conflict resolution, IDEA, **77**
Confucius, 468
Congenital cataracts, **382**

Congenital hearing loss, **348**
Congenitally blind, **379**
Consulting teachers, **95**
Contact lenses, 380, 407
Content, **35**, **108**
Content-based acceleration, 458
Cooper, Anderson, 231
Copy This! (Orfalea), 160
Corporal punishment, **303**
Co-teaching, **95**
Council for Exceptional Children (CEC), 129, 135, 341
Counselors, 96
Court cases, 12
  Brown v. Board of Education, 12, 53
  Diana v. State Board of Education, 55
  inequitable education, 55
  Larry P. v. Riles, 55
  Lau v. Nichols, 55
Covarrubias, Justin, 340
CP. *See* Cerebral palsy
Creativity, 8, **443**
Crichton, Alexander, 192, 193
Cross-cultural communication, 59–60
Cross-cultural dissonance, 58–64, **60**
  preventing, 60–61
  providing culturally responsive instruction, 62–64
  teacher self-reflection, 61
  understanding, 58–60
Cruickshank, William, 194
CSR. *See* Collaborative Strategic Reading
Cued speech, **361**
Cultural discontinuity, 60
Cultural diversity. *See* Culturally and linguistically diverse learners
Culturally and linguistically diverse (CLD) learners, 47–70
  attitudes toward school, 62
  disproportionality, understanding, 55–57
  EBD, 279
  intellectual disabilities, 245
  landscape, 49–52
  perceptions, 52–54, 56, 59, 62, 63, 67
  social justice, 52–55
  speech or language disorder, 110
  understanding second-language acquisition, 65–67
Culturally competent teachers, **62**
Culturally diverse students, **58**. *See also* Culturally and linguistically diverse learners
  misinterpretations, culturally based, 59
Culturally responsive instruction, 62–64, **63**
  teacher tips, 63
  videos, 59, 61, 62
Cultural perspective, 17
Cultural pluralism, **50**
Culture. *See also* Cross-cultural dissonance
  communication and, 59–60
  Deaf culture, **346**, **356**, 364–365
  influences, 58, 61–64
  multicultural education, **51**
Curb cuts, **24**
Curricular representation, 60
Curriculum, **33**
  alternate, 426
  expanded core, **388**
  functional, **261–262**
Curriculum-based measurement (CBM), **38**–39, **159**
  data, 159
  probes, **38**–39
Curriculum compacting, **459**–460, 463

D

Daily organizer, 258
Dart, Justin, 13
Data. *See also* Demographics; Prevalence
  Civil Rights Data Collection Website, 57
  IDEA, enrollment data and, 57
Data-based decision making, **37**–40
Davidson, Helen, 158
Davidson Gifted Database, 471
Davidson Institute for Talent Development, 471
Davidson Young Scholars, 471
dB. *See* Decibels
Deaf-blindness, 385, **416**–417
  accommodations, 421–423
  characteristics associated with, 416
  community participation, 431–432
  definitions, 416–417
  differentiated instruction, 426
  early intervention, 423–424
  functional skills instruction, 428
  grade-school interventions, 425–426
  Helen Keller, 430
  incidence following rubella epidemic of (1960s), 430–431
  organizational/agency support, 432–433
  placement, 419–420
  prevalence, 418–419
  severity of vision/hearing loss in, 417
  technology aids, 436–438
  transition activities/services, 427–428
Deaf community, 13, 19, 366–367. *See also* Deaf culture
  Deaf pride, 366
  as minority, 356
Deaf culture, **346**, **356**, 364–365
Deafness and hearing impairments, 342–374, **345**, **350**
  accommodations for, 357–359
  advances, 370–373
  adventitious loss, **348**
  challenges and solutions, 354–356, 367
  characteristics, 348–350
  communication methods, 361
  conductive hearing loss, **347**, 349
  congenital hearing loss, **348**
  definitions and types, 344–348, 350
  Down syndrome and, 351
  early intervention, 346, 359–360, 369
  expectations, 360
  future perspectives, 368–373
  hard of hearing, **345**, **350**
  IDEA definitions, 345
  interpreters, 362
  LRE, 352
  mixed hearing loss, **348**
  NIHL, **349**–**350**, 369
  origins and history, 364–366
  overview, 343–352
  people and situations, 363–368
  placement, 351–352
  post-secondary education, 362–363
  prevalence, 351–352
  prevention, 369–370
  residual hearing, **350**
  school years, 360–362
  sensorineural hearing loss, **348**
  social justice, 364–365
  specialized education, 364
  technology, 370–373. *See also* Hearing aids
  transition, 362–363
  videos, 342, 345, 358, 366, 367, 372
  websites, 348, 352, 357, 363, 365–367
Deaf of Deaf, **356**

Deaf President Now (DPN), 13, 366
Deaf pride, 366
Deaf West Theater, 366
Decibels (dB), **346**, **347**
Deep End Games, 24
Deer, Brian, 230
Deficits. *See also* Attention deficit hyperactivity disorder
  performance, 288
  perspective, 16
  skill, 288
Deinstitutionalization movement for people with intellectual disabilities, 267–268
de León, Pedro Ponce, 364
Delinquency, **281**
Demographics, **3**–5
Deno, Stan, 159
Department of Education. *See* U.S. Department of Education
Depression, **281**
Descriptive Video Exchange, 405
Deshler, Don, 159, 161
Destination ImagiNation, 464
Developmental bilingual education, **68**
Developmental disability, **244**
Developmental milestones, 80
DI. *See* Differentiated instruction
Diabetes, **319**, 320
  sample 504 plan, 83
Diagnostic and Statistical Manual of Mental Disorders (DSM-5), 170, 172, 173, 279
Diagnostic assessments, **37**
Diana v. State Board of Education, 55
Differences, 16
Differentiated instruction (DI), **35**–36, 181, 188
  comparison to UDL, 36
  gifted and talented, 462–464
  low incidence disabilities, 426
  research, 36
Digital pens, 152
Digital textbooks. *See* Electronic textbooks
Disabilities, 5–8. *See also* Impairments; Individuals with Disabilities Education Act; Traumatic brain injury; Visual disabilities; *specific disabilities or impairments*
  academic outcomes, 20–21
  advocacy, 13–15
  better future, 19–25
  changing landscape, 19–25
  community presence, **12**, 23–25
  discrimination and, 10–12, 14, 16–17, 23
  educating students with, 73–83
  gifted and talented and, 9, 447–448
  high incidence, **7**
  language and, 18–19
  legal protections. *See* Americans with Disabilities Act; Individuals with Disabilities Education Act; Section 504 of the Rehabilitation Act of 1973
  low incidence, **7**, 426
  mathematics/learning, 141–142
  as minority group, 12–13
  movies, portrayal in, 11–12
  multiple, 385, 404, 406
  multiple severe, 6
  participation in education, 14–15
  perceptions, 10–13, 16–18
  post-secondary education, 21–22
  prevalence, **6**–8, 284
  primary, 177
  public awareness of, 12
  reading, **141**
  social justice and, 9–15

Disabilities (*Continued*)
   students transitioning, 21–22
   in television and film, 10–12
   underachievement and, 454
   videos, 1, 10, 13, 18
   websites, 1, 3, 7, 11, 13, 17
Disability Rights International, 11
Disability Rights Movement, 13
Disability Social History Project, 267
Di Salvo, Anthony, 431, 432
Discrimination and bias. *See also* Civil rights
      movement; Section 504 of the Rehabilitation
      Act of 1973
   disabilities and, 10–12, 14, 16–17, 23
   intellectual disabilities and, 266–268
Disorders. *See also* Attention deficit hyperactivity
      disorder; Autism spectrum disorder;
      Emotional or behavioral disorders
   ASD, 105, 128
   communication, 105
   conduct, 280
   FASD, **249**, 271
   language, 108–109
   ODD, 282
Disproportionality, understanding, 55–57
Disproportionate representation, **56**
Distance education, **324**, 325
Distance learning, **324**, 478
Diverse learners. *See* Culturally and
      linguistically diverse learners
Dix, Dorothea, 304
Down, John Langdon, 249
Down syndrome, **249**, 250
   actors, 12
   Child Find, **79**
   deafness and hearing impairments, 351
   identification, 261
DPN. *See* Deaf President Now
Dropout
   economic burden, 5
   prevention, 5
   warning signs, 5
   websites, 29
DSM-5. *See Diagnostic and Statistical Manual of
      Mental Disorders*
Dual language learners, **65**. *See also* Bilingual
      education; Bilingualism
Due process under IDEA, **77**
Dugdale, Richard, 267
Duke University Talent Identification Program
      (Duke TIP), 471, 478
Dyscalculia, 142
Dysfluencies, **107**
Dysgraphia, 141, 142
Dyslexia, 136, 141, 142, 160
   video, 161

E

EAHCA. *See* Education for All Handicapped
      Children Act
Ear. *See also* Deafness and hearing impairments
   anatomy of, **344–345**
Eardrum, **344**, 345
Early Childhood Technical Assistance Center, 86
Early Hearing Detection and Intervention
      (EHDI), 328, 369
Early intervening services, **42**
Early intervention, 42, 153–154
   ADHD, 185–187
   ASD, 219–221, 234
   deaf-blindness, 423–424
   deafness and hearing impairments, 346,
      359–360, 369

EBD, 292–294
gifted and talented, 460–462
intellectual disabilities, 259–261
learning disabilities, 153–154
low incidence disabilities, 423–424
multiple disabilities, 423–424
physical and health disabilities, 327–328
services, **42**, **75**, **92**
speech and language impairments, 119–123
TBI, 423–424
visual disabilities, 392–394
EBD. *See* Emotional or behavioral disorders
EBPs. *See* Evidence-based practices
E-Buddies, **272**
Echolalia, **208**
Edison, Thomas, 447
Educating Emotionally Disturbed Children (Haring,
      Phillips), 304
Education. *See also* Department of Education;
      Individualized education program;
      Individualized education programs;
      Individuals with Disabilities Education Act;
      Instruction; School years; Special education;
      Special education teachers
   bilingual, 68
   developmental bilingual, 68
   distance learning, 324, 325, 478
   EBD placements, 284
   EHA, **75**, 76
   equal *vs.* equitable, 55
   exclusion in, 14–15
   FAPE, **78**
   gifted and talented policies, 469–470
   IAES, 285
   inclusive, 261
   Jacob K. Javits Gifted and Talented Students
      Education Act of 1988, 443, 454, 469–470, 474
   multicultural, 51
   NEA, 448
   preschool programs, 260
   special education, 14–15
   special education services, **92**. *See also*
      Individuals with Disabilities Education Act
Education for All Handicapped Children Act
      (EHA), **75**, 76. *See also* Individuals with
      Disabilities Education Act
EHA. *See* Education for All Handicapped
      Children Act
EHDI. *See* Early Hearing Detection and
      Intervention
Einstein, Albert, 471
Electrical stimulation, 407
Electronic textbooks (e-texts), 325, 390, 391
Elementary and Secondary Education Act
      (ESEA), 76, 443, 470
ELLs. *See* English language learners
ELs. *See* English language learners
Email for those with intellectual disabilities, 272
Emotional disturbance, **278**, 279, 280
Emotional or behavioral disorders (EBD), 276–312
   accommodations, 291–292
   challenges and solutions, 288–291
   characteristics, 282–283
   corporal punishment, restraint, seclusion, 303
   cultural considerations, 279
   defined, **278**, 278–279
   descriptions of, 277–286
   early intervention, 292–294
   early warning signs, 294
   evidence-based practices, 298
   future perspectives, 307–311
   IDEA and, 278–279
   learning disabilities, 145

origins and history, 302–305
PBIS and, 295–299
people and situations, 301–307
personal stories, 305–307
prevalence and placement, 283–286
prevention, 308–309
resources, 297
school years, 295–299
special education, 287–301
technology, 308, 310–311
transitions, 299–301
types, 280–281
videos, 294, 297, 307, 310
websites, 301, 306, 307, 310
English as a Second Language (ESL), **68**
English language learners (ELLs), 5, **51**. *See
      also* Culturally and linguistically diverse
      learners; Linguistic diversity
   definition, 65
   effective practices, 67–69
   mathematics and, 67–69
   resources, 63
   videos, 69
   websites, 69
English learners (ELs). *See* English language
      learners
Enlarged print, **390**
Enrichment, **464**
Enrollment, diverse students, 51
Environmental interventions for speech and
      language impairments, 130–132
Environments, continuum of, 97–99
EPGY. *See* Stanford University Educational
      Program for Gifted Youth
Epilepsy, 320, **329**
Equal education, **55**
Equitable education, **55**
ESEA. *See* Elementary and Secondary Education
      Act
ESL. *See* English as a Second Language
e-texts. *See* Electronic textbooks
Eugenics, **267**
Eustachian tube, **344**, 345
Every Student Succeeds Act (ESSA), 32, 76, 470
Evidence-based practices (EBPs), 21, **30–32**
   ASD, 222–224
   EBD, 298
   interventions, 425
   self-determination instruction, 262
Excellence gaps, **9**
Exceptionalities, thinking about, 1–25
Exceptional students, **448**
Exclusion
   in education, 14–15
   in society, 14–15
Executive functions, **174**, 180, 181, 197
Exide battery recycling plant, 270–271
Expanded core curriculum, **388**
Expectations
   gifted and talented, 465
   teachers, 54
   visual disabilities, 375
Explicit instruction, **117**, **150**, 153–156, 159
Expressive language, **66**, **109**–110, 118–119, 126,
      132–133
Externalizing behaviors, **281**, 283
Eye, **378**. *See also* Visual disabilities
Eye to Eye, 160–161

F

False positives, **140**, 328
Families, 424
FAPE. *See* Free appropriate public education

FAS. *See* Fetal alcohol syndrome
FASD. *See* Fetal alcohol spectrum disorder
FBA. *See* Functional behavioral assessment
Federal legislation, 74–76
   basic guarantees, 77–79
Feebleminded, 267
Fetal alcohol spectrum disorder (FASD), **249**, 271
Fetal alcohol syndrome (FAS), **249**, 250, 271
Fidelity (of implementation), 31
Field of vision, **380**
Field trips, 464
Film and television
   culturally responsive education, 61
   portrayal of disabilities in, 10–12, 61, 206,
      265–266, 404
   Steve Jobs, 472
   Straight Outta Compton (movie), 472
Finger spelling, **361**
Firth, Colin, 129
Fisher, Carrie, 305
504 plan. *See* Section 504 of the Rehabilitation
      Act of 1973
The 5000 Initiative: Autism in Tech Workforce, 227
Flexible scheduling, 325
Flink, David, 160
Flint, Michigan, 53, 271
Fluency, **104**
   deficit, 288
   letter, 143
   reading, 154
FM transmission device, **357**
Food insecurity, **52**
Form, **107**
Formative assessments, 37
Fowler, Micah, 336
Foxx, Jamie, 404
Fragile X syndrome, **248**, 250
Free appropriate public education (FAPE), **78**.
      See also Individualized education programs;
      Individualized family service plans
Freeing Voices, Changing Lives Award
      (American Institute for Stuttering), 101
Frequency modulated (FM) devices, **357**
Frequency of sound, **347**
Frostig, Marianne, 160
Fuchs, Doug, 159
Fuchs, Lynn, 159
Full inclusion, **78**
Full potential, 30
Functional behavioral assessment (FBA), **44**, 88,
      216, 298–289
   data collection, 238
Functional curriculum, **261–262**
Functional skills, learning, 428
Future perspectives
   ADHD, 196–200
   ASD, 235–239
   deafness and hearing impairments, 368–373
   EBD, 307–311
   intellectual disabilities, 269–274
   learning disabilities, 161–165
   physical and health disabilities, 337–340
   speech and language disorder, 130–134
   speech and language impairments, 130–134
   visual disabilities, 406–408
Future Problem Solving, 464

G

Gaining Early Awareness and Readiness for
      Undergraduate Programs (GEAR UP), 466
Gallagher, James J., 477
Gallaudet, Edward, 364–365
Gallaudet, Thomas Hopkins, 364

Gallaudet University, 13, 362, 366
Galton, Francis, 468
Games, learning, 477
GarageBand, 478
Gardner, Howard, 447
Gates, Bill, 471
GEAR UP program, 466
Gender differences
   academic achievement, 476
   ADHD and, 180
   ASD and, 210
   gifted and talented, 476
   traumatic brain injury, 435
General education curriculum, **78**
Generalization, **149**
General outcome measures (GOM), **38**
Generational poverty, 52
Genetics and visual disabilities, 407
Geographically correct terminology, 52
Geographic information system (GIS), 405
George VI (King), 129
Gifted and talented, 8–9, 440–479
   acceleration, 456–460
   accommodations made, 457–458
   accomplishments, 471
   African Americans, 472
   assessment and identification, 444–445
   categorizing, 446–448
   challenges faced by, 454–457
   characteristics, 449–450
   curriculum compacting, 459–460, 463
   defined, 442–443
   differentiated instruction, 462–464
   disabilities and, 9, 447–448
   early intervention, 460–462
   education policies, 469–470, 473–474
   enrichment, 464
   fostering, 477–479
   IDEA and, 443
   identifying, 443–445
   impact on daily life, 470
   inconsistent commitment to, 468–470
   IQ categorizations, 446
   Jacob K. Javits Gifted and Talented Students
      Education Act of 1988, 443, 469–470, 476
   multiple intelligences, 447
   organizational support for, 470–471
   potential and loss, 477
   preschoolers, 460–462
   prevalence, 451–452
   by race and ethnicity, 475–476
   resources, 478
   social-emotional development, 450–451
   special considerations for, 475–476
   Talent Pool identification system, 444–445
   technology, 477–478
   tips for teachers, 449
   transition activities/services, 465–466
   twice-exceptional, **9**
   underachievement, 454–455
   videos, 478
   websites, 478
Girma, Haben, 426, 427
   presentation by, 438
   TED talk excerpt, 410–411
   WWDC speech outline, 438
Gizmos, 478
Glaucoma, 407
Glee, 241
Goddard, Henry, 267
Goldberg, Whoopi, 136
Goldstein, Kurt, 194
GOM. *See* General outcome measures

Good Behavior Game, **296**, 297
Government Accountability Office, 303
Governor's School program, **464**
GPS systems, 24, 273
Grade-based acceleration, 458
Grade-skipping, 459–460
Grandin, Temple, 209, 231–232
Graphic organizers
   ADHD, 184, **189**, 200
   intellectual disabilities, 258
   learning disabilities and, 153, 156
   speech and language impairments, 119, 126,
      134
Gross motor development, **393**
Group home, **24**
Grouping practices, **452**
Guide dogs for visual disabilities, 396

H

Hair cells (ear), **344**, 345, 348, 359, 369
Hall, Frank, 403
Hallahan, Dan, 159
Hamilton, Bethany, 336
Hammill, Don, 159
Handicaps caused by society, **12**. *See also*
      Disabilities
Hard of hearing, **345**, 350. *See also* Deafness and
      hearing impairments
Haring, Norris, 304
Harkin, Tom, 23, 71
Haüy, Valentin, 403
Hawking, Stephen, 313, 336, 447
Head Start, 293
Health care, 93, 96
   learning disabilities advances, 162–164
   school nurses, **330**, 330–331
   speech and language impairments, 130–132
Health disabilities. *See* Physical and health
      disabilities
Health progress timeline, 333
Hearing. *See* Deaf community; Deafness;
      Deafness and hearing impairments; Vision
Hearing aids, 350, 364, 370–371
Hearing impairments. *See* Deafness and hearing
      impairments
Hearing loss. *See* Deafness and hearing
      impairments
Hearing trumpet, **364**
Helen Keller National Center, 431
Helmets, TBI prevention, 435
Hertz (Hz), **346**, **347**
Heterogeneity, **144**
Heumann, Judy, 13, 333
Hewett, Frank, 304
Higher education. *See* Post-secondary education
Higher Education Opportunity Act, 32, 76
High-incidence disabilities, **7**, 145
High-quality instruction, 27–40
High-risk behaviors, traumatic brain injury, 435
High-tech devices, **132**
Hippocrates, 332
Hispanics, 475
"Historically underrepresented," 52
History. *See* Origins and history
Hobbs, Nicholas, 304
Hoffmann, Heinrich, 193
Holder, William, 364
Hole in the Wall Gang camps, 335
Hollingworth, Leta, 468
Holocaust, 333
Honors classes, **452**
Hoover canes, 396
Horne, LeDerick, 1, 9, 75

Horner, Rob, 304
Howe, Samuel Gridley, 266, 403, 430
Human Connectome Project, 163
Human ear. *See also* Deafness and hearing
　　impairments
　　anatomy of, **344–345**
Human eye, 378. *See also* Visual disabilities
Human Rights Watch, 11
The Hunchback of Notre Dame, 11
"Hundred Years War," 364–365
Hyperactivity, 171, **172**, 173, **281**. *See also*
　　Attention deficit hyperactivity disorder
Hyperresponsiveness in individuals with ASD,
　　209
Hyporesponsiveness in individuals with ASD,
　　209
Hz. *See* Hertz

I

IAES. *See* Interim alternative educational setting
IDEA. *See* Individuals with Disabilities
　　Education Act
IEP. *See* Individualized education program
IEPs. *See* Individualized education programs
IFSPs. *See* Individualized family service plans
IHP. *See* Individualized Healthcare Plans
Illinois School for the Blind, 403
Illinois Test of Psycholinguistic Abilities (ITPA), 158
Immigrants, 5, 49–51. *See also* Bilingualism;
　　Culturally and linguistically diverse learners
Immunization programs, 271
Impairments. *See also* Deafness and hearing
　　impairments; Speech and language
　　impairments
　　hearing, 328
　　neuromotor, 317, 329
　　OHI, 177, 316
　　orthopedic, **316**, 317
　　social, 205, 208
　　TVIs, **386**, **395**
Implants
　　auditory brainstem implant, **373**
　　cochlear implants, **355**, 361, 371–372
　　corneal, 407
　　retinal microchip, 407
Impulsivity, 171, **172**–173, **281**
Inattention, 171–172, 173. *See also* Predominantly
　　Hyperactive ADHD
Incidence. *See* Prevalence
Inclusion, rates of, **98**
Inclusive education, 261
Independent study, 464
Individualized education, 83–91. *See also*
　　Individualized education programs;
　　Individualized family service plans;
　　Individuals with Disabilities Education Act
Individualized education programs (IEPs),
　　78, 84–89, 99. *See also* Accommodations;
　　Behavior intervention plans; Individualized
　　transition plans; Modifications
　　annual reviews, 82
　　assistive technology, 164
　　basic elements, 86–87
　　Child Find and, 81
　　college and, 156–157
　　comparison with IFSPs, 85, 94, 96
　　costs, 85, 93
　　development, 82
　　elements, 86–87
　　eligibility, 82
　　evaluation, 82
　　implementation, 82
　　for low incidence disabilities, 426, 427

multi-tiered system of support, 81
pre-referral process, 81, 82
process, **81**–83
re-evaluation, 82
referral, 82
resources, 86, 87
services, individualized, 92–94, 96, 99
settings, 99
specialized personnel, 94–96, 99
special setting, 146, 153, 159
steps in the process, 81–83
team, 77–78, 81–82, 88–89, 95
transition components, 87
videos, 85
websites, 86, 87
Individualized family service plans (IFSPs), **77**,
　　83–88
　　basic elements, 86–87
　　comparison with IEPs, 85, 94, 96
　　costs, 85
　　low incidence disabilities, 424
　　services, individualized, 92–94, 96, 99
　　settings, 99
　　specialized personnel, 94–96, 99
　　video, 85
　　websites, 86
Individualized Healthcare Plans (IHP), **324**,
　　329–330
Individualized services, 92–94
　　comparison of IEPs and IFSPs, 94, 96
　　website, 94
Individualized transition plans (ITPs), **88–89**,
　　125–126
Individuals with Disabilities Education Act
　　(IDEA), **15**, 32, 71, **75**. *See also* Individualized
　　education programs; Individualized family
　　service plans
　　ADHD and, 170, 187
　　comparison to Section 504, 77
　　deaf-blindness definitions, 415
　　definitions in, 5–6, 205, 211, 316
　　disciplinary procedures flowchart, 286
　　EBD and, 278, 279
　　enrollment data and, 57
　　funding, 469–470
　　gifted and talented and, 443, 469–470
　　hearing impairments defined, 345
　　learning disabilities, 146
　　mandates, 390, 398, 404
　　multiple disability definitions, 414
　　passage, **75**, 128, 145, 268
　　placement in, 319–320
　　reauthorizations, 15, 75, 76
　　school discipline and, 285
　　video, 75
　　visual disabilities defined, **378**–379
　　websites, 75
Induction hearing loops, **357**–358
Infants
　　identifying multiple disabilities/deaf-
　　　blindness in, 423
　　newborn screenings, **79**, **327**, 328, 369
　　traumatic brain injury in, 423–424
Infectious diseases, **318**
Inner ear, 345
Inspiration, 134, 200
Institute of Stammering, Paris, 127
Instruction. *See also* Culturally responsive
　　instruction
　　community-based, 428
　　differentiated. *See* Differentiated instruction
　　explicit, **150**, 153–156, 159
　　high-quality, 27–40

learning strategy, **188**
primary. *See* Primary instruction
RTI, 81
sheltered, 68
SIOP, 68
Instructional accommodations, **90**
Instructional behaviors, 54
Instructional scaffolding, **44**
Intellectual disabilities, 8, 18, 105, 128, 241–275,
　　244
　　accommodations, 258–259
　　adaptive behavior, 249–250
　　adaptive skills, 255
　　ADHD accommodations, 259
　　advocacy, 241, 268–269
　　causes of, 248–249
　　challenges and solutions, 254–258
　　characteristics, 249–250
　　classification by severity, 247
　　cultural or linguistic diversity, 245
　　defined, 243–246
　　deinstitutionalization movement, 267–268
　　discrimination and bias, 268
　　early intervention, 259–261
　　environmental protections, 270–272
　　future perspectives, 269–274
　　gender and, 248
　　IDEA and, 244
　　inappropriate labeling, 55
　　inclusion rates, 252–253
　　inclusive education, 261
　　individualized programs and special services,
　　　72, 76, 77, 79, 91, 98
　　IQ tests and scores, 245, 246–247, 251
　　normal curve, 247
　　origins and history, 265–267
　　overview, 242–253
　　people and situations, 264–269
　　perceptions, 267–268
　　preschool programs, 260
　　President's Committee on Intellectual
　　　Disabilities, 241, 268
　　prevalence and placement, 248, 250–253
　　prevention, 270–272
　　school years, 261–262
　　self-advocacy, 241
　　settings for education, 251–253
　　severity, 247, 248
　　technology, 258–259, 272–274
　　terminology, 244, 267–268
　　transitions, 263–264
　　types, 246–249
　　videos, 241, 265–266, 268, 271
　　websites, 257, 263, 264, 267, 272
Intellectual functioning, **244**
Intensity, **107**
Intensive services, **93**
Interim alternative educational setting (IAES),
　　76, **285**
Internalizing behaviors, **281**, 283
Internships, 464
Interpreters, 96, 362
Intervener, **426**
Interventions. *See also* Early intervention;
　　Response to intervention
　　BIPs, **88**, 285, 298–299
　　early. *See* Early intervention
　　evaluating, 32
　　evidence-based practices, 425
　　primary intervention, **41**–43, **44**
　　secondary intervention, **41**–43, 44–45
　　tertiary intervention, **41**–43, 44–45
In-the-ear (BTE) hearing aids, 370–371

Iowa Acceleration Scale, 460
iPad, 24, 239
iPhone, 408
IQ tests and scores, 245, 246–247, 251
    discrepancy, IQ/achievement, **139**
    distribution, 446
Irwin, Robert, 403
Itard, Jean-Marc-Gaspard, 14, 265–266
ITPA. *See* Illinois Test of Psycholinguistic
    Abilities
ITPs. *See* Individualized transition plans

J

Jackson, Samuel L., 101, 109
Jacob K. Javits Gifted and Talented Students
    Education Act of 1988, 443, 454, 469–470, 474
JAWS screen reader, **400**
Jefferson, Thomas, 469
JetBlue, 175
Jet Propulsion Laboratory (JPL), 477
Job coach, **264**
Jobs, Steve, 442, 471
Joey Pigza Swallowed the Key (Gantos), 195
Johns Hopkins' Center for Talented Youth, 478
Johnson, Lyndon B., 241, 268
Joint attention, **219**
Jordan, I. King, 13, 366
JPL. *See* Jet Propulsion Laboratory
Jukes family, 267
Junior Great Books, 464
Juvenile diabetes. *See* Type 1 diabetes

K

Kallikak, Deborah, 267
Kanner, Leo, 229, 304
Karsner, Nancy, 454
Keller, Helen, 430, 447
Kennedy, Edward (Ted), 268, 269
Kennedy, Jean, 269
Kennedy, John F., 268, 269
Kennedy, Joseph, 269
Kennedy, Robert, 268
Kennedy, Rose, 269
Kennedy, Rosemary, 268, 269
Kenney, Michael, 471
Kephart, Newell, 194
Khan Academy, 478
Kidspiration, 134, 200
King, Martin Luther, Jr., 447, 471
The King's Speech, 129
Kirk, Sam, 158, 159
Kurzweil Reader, 408

L

Lancet, 230–231
Landmark College, 156
Language, **104**. *See also* American Sign
    Language; English language learners;
    Speech-language pathologists
    ASHA, 105, 126, 127
    CALP, 66
    disabilities, 18–19
    ESL, 68
    expressive, 66, 109–110, 118–119, 126, 132–133
    people first language, 18
    receptive, 109, 118, 119, 133
    receptive language skills, 66
    samples of five-year-old girls, 122
    second-language acquisition. *See* Culturally
        and linguistically diverse learners; English
        language learners; Linguistic diversity
    SLP, 95, 96
    social *vs.* academic language, 67
Language acquisition skills, comparison, 121

Language delays, **120**
Language disorders, **105**, 108–109
Language impairments, **104**. *See also* Speech and
    language impairments
Language minority students, **65**
Language-rich environments, **123**
Language-sensitive environments, **125**
Larry P. v. Riles, 55
Larsen, Steve, 159
Laser canes, 24
Laurent Clerc National Deaf Education Center,
    367
Lau v. Nichols, 55
Lawrence, D. H., 364
Lawrence, Jennifer, 306
Laws. *See* Americans with Disabilities Act;
    Federal legislation; Individuals with
    Disabilities Education Act; Section 504 of the
    Rehabilitation Act of 1973; *specific laws*
LD. *See* Learning disabilities
Lead poisoning, 53, 270–271
Learned helplessness, **149**
Learning. *See also* Universal Design for Learning
    online, 477–478, 479
Learning centers, 35
Learning Disabilities Association of America,
    142, 161
Learning disabilities (LD), 6, 136–166, **138**
    accommodations, 151–153
    advances in health care and technology,
        162–164
    challenges and solutions, 149–151
    characteristics, 143–144
    defined, 138–140
    early intervention, 153–154
    fads and unproven practices, 160
    future perspectives, 161–165
    IDEA, 146
    identification of students with, 147
    individualized programs and special services,
        76, 77, 79, 81, 87, 91
    National Center for Learning Disabilities, 161
    origins and history, 158–160
    overlap, 142
    people and situations, 157–161
    personal stories, 160–161
    prevalence and placement, 144–147
    prevention, 162–164
    process/product debate, **159**
    school years, 154–155
    special education, 148–157
    speech and language impairments, 111–112
    technology for, 162–164
    transitions, 156–157
    types, 139–142
    videos, 153, 161
    websites, 160, 161
Learning experiences, 60
Learning games, 477
Learning menus, **36**
Learning strategies, **123**, **150**–151, 155
Learning strategy instruction, **188**
Least restrictive environment (LRE), 76, **78**, 79,
    82, 97
    deafness and hearing impairments, 352
Legally blind, **378**–379
Legal protections. *See* Americans with
    Disabilities Act; Federal legislation;
    Individuals with Disabilities Education Act;
    Section 504 of the Rehabilitation Act of 1973;
    specific laws
Lego toys, 24
Lehtinen, Laura, 158, 194

L'Enfant Sauvage, 265–266
LEP, **65**
Letter fluency, 143
Levine, Adam, 165
Life skills training, 79
Limited English proficient (LEP), **65**
Linguistically diverse students, **65**
Linguistic diversity, 64–69. *See also* Culturally
    and linguistically diverse learners; English
    language learners
    definitions of linguistically diverse learners, 65
    understanding second-language acquisition,
        65–67
Listening. *See* Deafness and hearing
    impairments
Little people, 10
Livescribe Smartpen, 405
Logue, Lionel, 129
Longmore, Paul, 11
Long-term negative outcomes, 293
Long-term positive outcomes, 293
Louvre, 478
Lovaas, Ivar, 229
Lovato, Demi, 276, 305
Lovitt, Tom, 159
Low incidence disabilities, **7**
    characteristics shared with other disabilities,
        411
    deaf-blindness, **416**–417. *See also*
        Deaf-blindness
    multiple disabilities, 413–414. *See also* Multiple
        disabilities
    traumatic brain injury, 414–415. *See also*
        Traumatic brain injury
Low-income situations
    culturally and linguistically diverse learners,
        52, 53
    gifted and talented, 466, 476
    intellectual disabilities, 267, 270–271
Low-tech devices, **132**
Low vision, **378**–379. *See also* Visual disabilities
LRE. *See* Least restrictive environment
Luke's assistive technology, 133

M

Ma, Yo-Yo, 471
Macular degeneration, 407
Magnification devices, **390**
Make-a-Movie Program, 431
Maker, June, 448
Manifestation determination, **285**
Marcellino, Rosa, 268
Marland, Sidney, 443
Martha's Vineyard, deaf citizens of, 365
Massive Open Online Courses (MOOC), 478
Mastery measurement (MM), **38**
MATHCOUNTS, 464
Mathematics disabilities, **141**–142
McFarland, USA, 61
Measles, mumps, and rubella vaccine (MMR),
    230–231, 271–272
Mechanical restraint, 303
Medical interventions for speech and language
    impairments, 130–132
Medically fragile, **317**
Medical services. *See* Health care
Medications
    ADHD, 181, 182
    stimulant, 181
Melting pot, **50**
Meningitis, deafness and hearing loss
    prevention, 370
Mental health condition, 279

"Mental retardation," 18, **244**, 268. *See also* Intellectual disabilities
Mentorships, 464
Metacognitive strategies, **150**–151
Miele, Joshua, 405, 408
MindSpark, 227
Minority
    deaf community as, 356
    disability as, 12–13
    language minority students, **65**
    terminology, **52**
Misarticulation, **106**
Misinterpretations, culturally based, 59
Mixed hearing loss, **348**
MM. *See* Mastery measurement
MMR. *See* Measles, mumps, and rubella vaccine
Mnemonics, **115**, **154**
Mobility, **317**
Modifications, 89–91
Money scanners, **401**, 408
Mooney, Jonathan, 160–161
Morgan's Wonderland, 432
Morphology, **107**
Mother Teresa, 447
Motor functioning, 319
MTSS. *See* Multi-tiered system of support
Multicultural education, **51**
Multiple disabilities, 385, 404, 406, 413–414
    accommodations, 421–423
    characteristics associated with, 414
    community participation, 431–432
    definitions, 414
    differentiated instruction, 426
    early intervention, 423–424
    functional skills instruction, 428
    grade-school interventions, 425–426
    organizational/agency support, 432–433
    placement, 419–420
    prevalence, 417–418
    technology aids, 436–438
    transition activities/services, 427–428
Multiple intelligences, **447**
Multiple-severe disabilities, 6
Multiple talents, 465
Multi-tiered frameworks, 140, 146
Multi-tiered system of support (MTSS), 40–45, **41**, 81
Muscular/skeletal conditions, **317**
Mutual accommodation, **64**
Myopia, **381**

N

NAGC. *See* National Association for Gifted Children
NAMI. *See* National Alliance on Mental Illness
Naranjo, Michael, 375
National Alliance on Mental Illness (NAMI), 276, 305, 307, 310
National Assessment of Educational Progress (NAEP), 28–29
National Association for Gifted Children (NAGC), 443, 445, 451, 461, 470
National Center for Learning Disabilities, 161
National Center on Deaf-Blindness (NCDB), 419, 420, 433
National Deaf-Blind Census, 419
National Deaf-Blind Equipment Distribution Program, 437
National Disability Rights Network, 303
National Education Association (NEA), 448
National Health and Nutrition Examination Study (NHANES), 310
National Institute of Neurological Disorders and Stroke, 432

National Institute on Deafness and Other Communication Disorders (NIDCD), 367
National Institutes of Health (NIH), 142
National Organization on Disability, 10
National Professional Development Center on Autism Spectrum Disorder, 224
National Research Center on the Gifted and Talented, 469
National Technical Assistance Center on Transition (NTACT), 301
National Technical Institute for the Deaf (NTID), 362
Native Americans, 475
Nativism, **50**
Natural environments and IFSPs, 85
Natural settings, 97, **428**
NCLB. *See* No Child Left Behind
NEA. *See* National Education Association
Need for supports, **244**, 255–258
Neeleman, David, 175
Networks of support, **245**–246, 248, 250, 255–258
Neuromotor impairments, **317**, 329
Newborn screenings, **79**, **327**, 328
    hearing, 369
Newman, Paul, 335
New York Institute for the Blind, 403
NHANES. *See* National Health and Nutrition Examination Study
Nieto, Sonia, 47
NIH. *See* National Institutes of Health
NIHL. *See* Noise-induced hearing loss
Nirje, Bengt, 267
No Barriers, 405
No Child Left Behind (NCLB), 76, 443, 470
Noise-induced hearing loss (NIHL), **349**–350, 369
No Limits, 366–367
Noncompliance, **281**
Normal curve, **17**
    IQ scores, 446
Normalization, **76**, 267
Northwestern Center for Talent Development, 478
Note takers, 152
NTACT. *See* National Technical Assistance Center on Transition
Nursing service staff, 96
N.W.A (hip-hop group), 472

O

OAEs. *See* Otoacoustic emissions
Obama, Barack, 241, 268, 410
Occupational therapy and therapists (OT), 93, 96, **330**–331
O'Connor, Sandra Day, 471
ODD. *See* Oppositional Defiant Disorder
Odyssey of the Mind, 464
Office of Special Education Programs (OSEP), 419
OHI. *See* Other health impairment
Omaze, 305
Online learning, 477–479
Open captioning, 24, **358**
Operation Smile, 131
Opportunities to respond (OTRs), **295**, 296
Opportunity gap, **53**
Oppositional defiant disorder (ODD), **180**, 282
Opticians, 380
Optic nerve, **378**, 381
Optometrists, 380
Oral response, 152
Orfalea, Paul, 160, 195
Orientation and mobility (O&M) instructors, 96, **386**, 397

Orientation skills, 397
Origins and history
    ADHD, 193–194
    ASD, 229–231
    deafness and hearing impairments, 364–366
    EBD, 302–305
    intellectual disabilities, 265–267
    learning disabilities, 158–160
    physical and health disabilities, 332–335
    speech and language impairments, 127–129
    speech language impairments, 127–129
    visual disabilities, 403–404
Orthopedic impairments, **316**, 317
Orton, Samuel, 158
Ossicles, **344**, 345
OT. *See* Occupational therapy and therapists
Other health impairment (OHI), 177, 316, **318**
Otitis media, **132**, 348
Otoacoustic emissions (OAEs), **369**
OTR. *See* Opportunities to respond
Overrepresentation, **56**

P

PACER Center's Children's Mental Health and Emotional and Behavioral Disorders Project, 305, 307
Pandey, Helen, 202, 233
Pandey, Justin, 202, 214, 227, 232–233, 236
Paolini, Christopher, 471
Paraprofessionals, **95**
Parks, 23
Partial sight, **378**–379
PBIS. *See* Positive Behavioral Interventions and Supports
PDD-NOS. *See* Pervasive developmental disorder-not otherwise specified
PECS. *See* Picture Exchange Communication System
Peer buddy systems, **218**
Pennsylvania Institution for the Instruction of the Blind, 403
People and situations
    ADHD, 192–196
    ASD, 228–234
    deafness and hearing impairments, 363–368
    EBD, 301–307
    intellectual disabilities, 264–269
    learning disabilities, 157–161
    physical and health disabilities, 332–336
    speech and language impairments, 127–129
    visual disabilities, 402–406
People first language, 18, **19**
Pepnet 2, 367
Perceptions
    CLD learners, 52–54, 56, 59, 62, 63, 67
    of disabilities, 10–13, 16–18
Perception (video game), 24
Percy Jackson & the Olympians (Riordan), 195–196
Perfectionism, 465
Performance deficits, 288
Peripheral vision, **380**
Perkins School for the Blind, 403, 430
Personal stories
    ADHD, 194–196
    ASD, 231–234
    EBD, 305–307
    learning disabilities, 160–161
    physical and health disabilities, 335–336
    speech and language impairments, 128–129
Person-centered planning, **427**
Personnel, specialized, 94–96
Perspectives
    cultural, 17
    deficit, 16

sociological, 17–18
Pervasive developmental disorder-not otherwise specified (PDD-NOS), 206, 229
Petty, Julie Ann, 241
Phelps, Debbie, 195
Phelps, Michael, 195, 447
Phenylketonuria (PKU), **79**, 328
Phillips, Lakin, 304
Phonation, **107**
Phonemic awareness, **153**
Phonological awareness, **107**, 153
Phonology, **107**
Physical and health disabilities, 313–341, **315**
  accommodations, 325–327
  challenges and solutions, 322–324
  characteristics, 318–319
  collaboration for, 330–331
  conditions, 317–318, 320
  defined, 315–317
  described, 314–321
  early intervention, 327–328
  future perspectives, 337–340
  origins and history, 332–335
  OT collaboration, 331, 332
  people and situations, 332–336
  personal stories, 335–336
  prevalence and placement, 319–321
  prevention, 337–339
  progress across time, 333
  PT collaboration, 331, 332
  related services, 330–331
  school nurse collaboration, 330–331
  school years health emergencies, 328–330
  seizures and, 320, 328–330
  special education, 321–331
  technology, 339–340
  types, 317–318
Physical education teachers, 96
Physical restraint, 303
Physical therapy and therapists (PT), 93, 96, 261, 330–**331**
Pica, **215**
Picture Exchange Communication System (PECS), **216**, 219–221
Pinel, Philippe, 304
Pinna, **344**, 345
Pitch, **107**
PKU. *See* Phenylketonuria
PL. *See* Public Law 94-142
Placement. *See* Prevalence and placement
Polio
  eradication campaign, 333
  survivors, 13, 15
Politically correct terminology, 52
Ponce de León, Pedro, 364
Positive Behavioral Interventions and Supports (PBIS), **43–45**, **290**
  core principles, 44
  EBD and, 295–299
  FBA and, 44
  multi-tiered systems of support, 43–45
  Pyramid Model, 296
Posse Foundation, 466
Postlingual deafness, **348**
Post-secondary education, 21–22, **28**, **84**
  deafness and hearing impairments, 362–363
  Higher Education Opportunity Act, 32, 76
  learning disabilities, students with, 156–157
Potter, Lauren, 241
Poverty, 52, 267, 270–271
Powered exoskeleton, **340**
Practical adaptive behavior skills, 245
Pragmatics, **108**, 109, 119

Predominantly Hyperactive ADHD, 170, 171, 173
Predominantly Inattentive ADHD, 170, 171, 173, 175, 183
Preferential seating, **391**
Prelingual deafness, **348**
Pre-referral process, **81**, 82
Preschoolers and preschool programs, 260, 460–462
President's Committee on Intellectual Disabilities, 241, 268
Prevalence and placement
  ADHD, 175–178
  AP, 53, **452**, 459, 476
  ASD, 210–212
  deaf-blindness, 418–420
  deafness and hearing impairments, 351–352
  disabilities, 6–8, 284, 417–418
  EBD, 283–286
  gifted and talented, 451–452
  IDEA, 319–320
  intellectual disabilities, 248, 250–253
  language impairments, 111–112
  learning disabilities, 144–147
  multiple disabilities, 417–420
  physical and health disabilities, 319–321
  speech and language impairments, 111–112
  TBI, 418–420
  variability, 8
  visual disabilities, 385–386
Prevention
  ADHD, 197–198
  ASD, 235
  bullying, 5
  cross-cultural dissonance, 60–61
  deafness and hearing impairments, 369–370
  diseases, 337–339
  dropout, 5
  EBD, 308–309
  intellectual disabilities, 270–272
  learning disabilities, 162–164
  physical and health disabilities, 337–339
  primary prevention, **41–44**
  secondary prevention, **41–45**
  speech and language impairments, 130–132
  TBI, 435–436
  tertiary prevention, **41–45**
  visual disabilities, 382, 406–407
Primary disability, 177
Primary instruction, **41–43**
Primary intervention, **41–43**, 44
Primary prevention, **41–43**, 44
The Princess Diarist, 305
Probes, **38–39**
Process, **35–36**
  IEP, 81–83
  pre-referral process, 81, 82
Process/product debate, **159**
Product, **35**, 36
Progress monitoring, **38–40**, 140, 143, 154, 159
  steps, 39
Project Re-Ed, 304
Prosthetics, 339–340
Providers, specialized, 94–96
Psychological services, 93
Psychologists, school, 96
PT. *See* Physical therapy and therapists
Public Law 94-142, **75–76**. *See also* Education for All Handicapped Children Act; Individuals with Disabilities Education Act
Pupil, **378**
Pure sounds, **347**
Pyramid Model for Promoting Young Children's Social-Emotional Competence, 294

R
Rain Man, 206
Ramps, 24
Randomized controlled trials, **31**
Rapid letter naming, **143**
Rates of inclusion, 98
Ray, 404
REACH program, University of Iowa, 263
Reading
  difficulties, 258–259
  disabilities, **141**
  fluency, 154
Real-time captioning (RTC), **358**
Receptive language, **109**, 118, 119, 133
Receptive language skills, **66**
Recreation specialists, 96
Refrigerator mothers, 230
Rehabilitation Act of 1973. *See* Section 504 of the Rehabilitation Act of 1973
Rehabilitation counselors, 96
Related service providers, 94–96
Related services, **14**, **93**
Renzulli, Joseph, 444, 449
Research
  ADHD, 197–198
  speech and learning impairments, 124
Residual hearing, **350**
Residual vision, **378–379**
Resistant to instruction, **139**
Resistant to treatment, **139**
Resonance, **107**
Resources
  anti-bullying, 5, 29
  ASD, 237–238
  Center for Parent Information and Resources, 305, 306
  EBD, 297
  ELLs, 63
  gifted and talented, 478
  IEP, 86, 87
Response to intervention (RTI), **41–43**, **140**, 159
  framework, 81
Restraint, **303**
Restricted central vision, 381
Restrictive settings, 98–99
Retina, **378**, 381, 407. *See also* Retinopathy of prematurity
Retinal microchip implants, 407
Retinitis pigmentosa, 407
Retinopathy of prematurity (ROP), **381**, 404, 407
Rett syndrome, **206**, 229
ReWalk, 340
Rh blood incompatibility, 271
Rice, Condoleeza, 471
Rimland, Bernard, 230
Riordan, Rick, 195–196
Roberts, Ed, 10, 13, 333
Robotics, 24, 339–340, **340**
Rochester Institute for Technology, 362
Roosevelt, Franklin Delano, 10, 447
ROP. *See* Retinopathy of prematurity
Rosa's Law, 18, 76, 268
RTC. *See* Real-time captioning
RTI. *See* Response to intervention
Rubella, 271–272
  deafness and hearing loss, 370
  epidemic, 430
  MMR, 230–231
  visual disabilities and, 404, 406
Rush, Benjamin, 304

S
St. Mary of Bethlehem hospital, 302
Sander's Chart, 120

Santa Monica Project, 304
Saturday programs, 464
Scaffolded instruction, **44**
Schizophrenia, **281**
Scholastic Aptitude Test (SAT), 445
School discipline, 285
School nurses, **330**, 330–331
School psychologists, 96
Schoolwide Enrichment Model (SEM), **464**
School-wide PBIS (SWPBS), **43**–45
School years
  ADHD, 187–189
  ASD, 221–224
  deafness and hearing impairments, 360–362
  EBD, 295–299
  intellectual disabilities, 261–262
  learning disabilities, 154–155
  physical and health disabilities, 328–330
  speech and language impairments, 123–125
  visual disabilities, 394–398
Schwab, Charles, 160, 161, 163, 447
Science, Technology, Engineering, and
  Mathematics (STEM), 452, 459, 460, 475
Screen Actors Guild, 12
Screen readers, **400**, 408
Seat belts, TBI prevention, 435
Seclusion, **303**
Secondary intervention, **41**–43, 44–45
Secondary prevention, **41**–43, 44–45
Second-language acquisition. *See* Culturally
  and linguistically diverse learners; English
  language learners; Linguistic diversity
Section 504 of the Rehabilitation Act of 1973,
  74, 187
  504 plan, **82, 187**, 316, 325, 331, 333
  comparison to IDEA, 77
  higher education and, 157
  physical and health disabilities, 316, 325, 331, 333
  websites, 83
Segregated or self-contained settings, 98–99
Segregation, 12, 14–15, 75, 78
Seguin, Edouard, 266
Seizures, 320, 328–330, **329**
Self-advocacy, **126**, 241
Self-determination, **262**
Self-injury, **214**
Self management strategies, **189**
Self-reflection, teachers, 61
Self-regulation strategies, **181, 189**
SEM. *See* Schoolwide Enrichment Model
Semantics, **108**
Sensorineural hearing loss, **348**
Separate settings, 98–99
Service animals, 326
Service coordinator, 86
Services
  ADHD, 170, 175–177, 185, 187–188, 190, 191
  Department of Education, 177, 188
  individualized, 92–94
  related, **93**
  related service providers, 94–96
  special education, **92**
Settings, continuum of, 97–99
  websites, 97
Shaken baby syndrome, **423**–424, 435, 436
Sheltered instruction, **68**
Sheltered Instruction Observation Protocol
  (SIOP), **68**
Shockley, William B., 468
Shriver, Anthony Kennedy, 257, 268
Shriver, Eunice Kennedy, 268, 269
Shriver, Maria, 269
Shriver, Tim, 268

Sickle cell disease, **79, 319**, 320, 324
  tips for teachers, 324
Signed English, **361**
Sign language, 133. *See also* American Sign
  Language
Silver Linings Playbook, 306
Single-case design studies, **31**
SIOP. *See* Sheltered Instruction Observation
  Protocol
Skill deficits, 288
Skill Tracker Pro, 238
Skinner, B. F., 216
SLP. *See* Speech-language pathologist
Smith, Jean Kennedy, 269
Smithsonian, 478
Snellen chart, **379**
Social adaptive behavior skills, 245
Social anxiety disorder, 283
Social-emotional development, 450–451
Social impairments, 205, 208
Social justice, 9–15, **11**
  for diverse learners, 52–55
Social language, 67. *See also* Basic interpersonal
  conversation skills
Social maladjustment, **280**
Social skills deficits, 289
Social *vs.* academic language, 67
Social workers, 96
Society, exclusion in, 14–15
Socioeconomic status (SES), **3**–4, 53, **61**
Sociological perspective, 17–18
Solomon, Sara, 129, 133, 447–448
Soul Surfer, 336
Sound intensity, **347**
Space race, 469
Special education, 5, 14–15
  EBD, 287–301
  learning disabilities, 148–157
  physical and health disabilities, 321–331
  services, **92**. *See also* Individuals with
    Disabilities Education Act
  speech and language disorder, 113–126
Special education teachers
  highly effective, 76
  IEPs, 79, 82, 94, 95
Special health care needs, **318**
Specialized personnel, 94–96
Special Olympics, 257–258, 268, 269
Special settings, 97–99, 146, 153, 159
  segregated or self-contained, 98–99
Specific praise, **295**, 296
Speech, **104**. *See also* Deafness and hearing
  impairments
  body's systems for generating, 104
  cued speech, **361**
Speech and language disorder, **105**
Speech and language impairments, 101–135, **104**
  accommodations, 118–119
  apps for, 133–134
  challenges and solutions, 114–118
  characteristics, 109–110
  cultural and linguistic considerations, 110
  defined, 103–106
  early intervention, 119–123
  future perspectives, 130–134
  medical and environmental interventions,
    130–132
  origins and history, 127–129
  people and situations, 127–129
  personal stories, 128–129
  prevalence and placement, 111–112
  prevention, 130–132
  research-based practices, 124

  school years, 123–125
  special education, 113–126
  technology for, 132–134
  tips for supporting students with, 119
  transitions, 125–126
  types, 106–108
  videos, 101, 107, 121, 122, 133
Speech disorder, **105**
Speech-language pathologist (SLP), **116**, 117,
  127–128
  individualized programs, 95, 96
  intellectual disabilities, 261
Speech-language therapy, **116**
Speechless, 336
Speech sound disorder, **105**
Speech synthesizer, **132**
Speech therapy, 355
Splinter skills in individuals with ASD, **206**
Sprout Film Festival, 431
Sproutflix, **432**
Sprout vacation program, 429, 431
Sputnik, 469
Standard deviations (SDs) in IQ testing, 246–247,
  251
Standardized tests
  bias in, 468
  intellectual ability, 245
Stanford University Educational Program for
  Gifted Youth (EPGY), 478
Stanley, Julian, 445
Star Wars, 305, 335
Statutes. *See* Americans with Disabilities
  Act; Federal legislation; Individuals with
  Disabilities Education Act; Section 504 of the
  Rehabilitation Act of 1973; *specific laws*
Staying Strong 365 Days a Year (Lovato), 276
STEM. *See* Science, technology, engineering, and
  mathematics
Stem-cell treatments for visual disabilities, 407
Stereotypies, **219**
Stereotyping, 61
Steve Jobs (movie), 472
Still, George, 193
Stims, individuals with ASD, **209**
Stimulant medication, 181
"The Story of Fidgety Philip," 193
Strabismus, **381**
Straight Outta Compton (movie), 472
Strategic Instruction Model (SIM), 159
Strauss, Alfred, 158, 194
Struggling learners, 38, 42
Students
  demographics, 3–5
  exceptional, 448
  exceptionalities, thinking about, 1–25
  Jacob K. Javits Gifted and Talented Students
    Education Act of 1988, 443, 454, 469–470, 474
  language minority, **65**
  miscommunications, 116, 125–126
  outcomes, 20–21
  transitioning, 21–22
  twice-exceptional, 447–448
Students of color, 51, **52**, 53, 54
Student support team, 81
Study of Mathematically Precocious Youth
  (SMPY), 459
Study skills
  gifted and talented, 465
  training, **189**, 190–191
Stuttering, 101, **107**, 109, 127, 129
Sugai, George, 304
Suicide, EBD related, 309
Sullivan, Anne, 430

Summative assessments, 37
Summer programs, 464
Support, systems or networks of, **245**–246, 248, 250, 255–258
Supported employment, **264**
Support for all learners, 26–46
Supports Intensity Scale, 248
Supreme Court, U.S., 12. *See also specific cases*
Switched at Birth, 367
Switches, communication, **437**
SWPBS. *See* school-wide PBIS
Symbol communications boards, 118
Syntax, **107**
Systems or networks of support, **245**–246, 248, 250, 255–258

T
Tactile Children's Book Project, 393
Tactile experiences, 391, 393, 405
Talent Pool identification system, 444–445
Talents, 8–9, 444–445. *See also* Gifted and talented
Talent search concept, **445**
TASH, 432
Task commitment, **444**, 449
TBI. *See* Traumatic brain injury
TEACCH, **216**
Teachers. *See also* Orientation and mobility instructors
  consulting, **95**
  co-teaching, **95**
  culturally responsive instruction, 62–64
  expectations, 54
  of gifted and talented, 449
  instructional behaviors, 54
  self-reflection, 61
  TVIs, 6, **386**, **395**
  for visual disabilities, **386**, **395**
Teachers of the visually impaired (TVIs), 6, **386**, **395**
Technology. *See also* Assistive technology and technologists; Augmentative and alternative communication; Implants; Robotics
  ADHD, 199–200
  ASD, 237–239
  Assistive Technology Act of 2004 (ATA), 76
  assistive technology specialists, 95, 96
  CART, **358**
  deaf-blindness, 436–438
  deafness and hearing impairments, 370–373. *See also* Hearing aids
  EBD, 308, 310–311
  gifted and talented, 477–478, 479
  hearing aids, 350, 364, 370–371
  high-tech devices, 132
  intellectual disabilities, 258–259, 272–274
  iPad, 24, 239
  iPhone, 408
  learning disabilities, 162–164
  low-tech devices, 132
  multiple disabilities, 436–438
  physical and health disabilities, 339–340
  for physical and health disabilities, 339–340
  prosthetics, 339–340
  RTC, **358**
  speech and language impairments, 132–134
  for speech and language impairments, 132–134
  STEM, 452, 459, 460, 475
  TBI, 436–438
  visual disabilities, 405, 407–408
  VoiceOver, 408
Television. *See* Film and television
Terman, Lewis, 450, 475, 486
Terminology, 18–19, 244, 268
  intellectual disabilities, 244, 267–268
  student diversity, 52

Tertiary intervention, **41**–43, 44–45
Tertiary prevention, **41**–43, 44–45
Testing accommodations, 90
Tests of intelligence, 246
Therapeutic recreation specialists, 96
Think College, 263
Thinking in Pictures and Other Reports of My Life with Autism (Grandin), 232
Thomson, Polly, 430
Three-dimensional printing (3-D), 393–394
Tiered activities, 36
Tiered content, **35**
Tiered products, 36
Toddlers. *See also* Preschoolers and preschool programs
  identifying multiple disabilities/deaf-blindness in, 423
  traumatic brain injury in, 423–424
Total communication approach, **361**
Toxins and intellectual disabilities, 270–272
Tracking, **452**
Trails of Tears Passage, 115
Transition activities/services, 21–22, 156–157. *See also* Post-secondary education
  ADHD, college transitions, 190–192
  ASD, 225–227
  bilingual education, 68
  deaf-blindness, 427–428
  deafness and hearing impairments, 362–363
  EBD, 299–301
  gifted and talented, 465–466
  IEP components, 87
  individualized transition plans, **88**–89
  intellectual disabilities, 263–264
  ITPs, **88**–89
  learning disabilities, 156–157
  low incidence disabilities, 427–428
  multiple disabilities, 427–428
  speech and language impairments, 125–126
  statements of transitional services, 89
  TBI, 427–428
  visual disabilities, 398–402
  websites, 263, 264
Transitional bilingual education, **68**
Transition services, **92**
Transition specialist, **95**
Traumatic brain injury (TBI), 7, 414–415
  accommodations, 421–423
  causes (birth through age 24), 434–435
  characteristics associated with, 415
  community participation, 431–432
  definitions, 415
  differentiated instruction, 426
  early intervention, 423–424
  functional skills instruction, 428
  gender differences, 435
  grade-school interventions, 425–426
  organizational/agency support, 432–433
  placement, 419–420
  prevalence, 418
  prevention, 435–436
  shaken baby syndrome, 423–424, 435, 436
  sports-related, 435
  technology aids, 436–438
  transition activities/services, 427–428
Trisomy 21, 249
Tunnel vision, **380**
TVIs. *See* Teachers of the visually impaired
Twice-exceptional students, 9, **447**–448, 476
  underachievement and, 454
Two-way immersion, **68**
Tympanic membrane, **344**

Type 1 diabetes, **319**, 320
Type 2 diabetes, **319**

U
UDL. *See* Universal Design for Learning
Underachievement, **454**, 455
Underrepresentation, 56
Unexpected underachievement, **138**
United Children's Fund (UNICEF), 478
Universal design, **334**, 334–335
Universal design architectural concept, 34
Universal Design for Learning (UDL), **31**–34, 181, 188, **334**
  comparison to differentiated instruction, 36
  Haben Girma on, 438
  learning disabilities, 151–152
Universal health care precautions, **338**
Universal screening, 42
University of California (UC) at Berkeley, 13
University of Illinois at Urbana-Champaign, 22
University of Iowa REACH program, 263
University of North Carolina-Chapel Hill, 260
U.S. Department of Education, 303
  Center on Technology and Disability, 437
  Office of Special Education Programs, 419
  services, 177, 188
Use, of language, **108**
Usher syndrome, 423

V
Vaccines, 228, 230–231, 431
  deafness and hearing loss prevention, 370
  intellectual disabilities and, 271–272
Vaughn, Sharon, 159
Verbal repetition for language impairments, 118
Very Special Arts, 269, 375
Video modeling, **219**, 223, 224, 232. *See also* Picture Exchange Communication System
Videos
  ADHD, 175, 187
  assistive technology, 165
  captioned, 358
  Child Find, 80
  cochlear implants, 372
  culturally responsive instruction, 59, 61, 62
  deafness and hearing impairments, 358, 366, 367, 372
  DI, 37
  disabilities, 1, 10, 13, 18
  dyslexia, 161
  EBD, 294, 297, 307, 310
  ELLs, 69
  IDEA, 75
  IEPs, 85
  IFSPs, 85
  intellectual disabilities, 241, 265–266, 268, 271
  lead poisoning, 271
  learning disabilities, 136, 153, 161
  retinopathy of prematurity, 407
  RTI, 43
  specialized personnel and providers, 96
  speech and language impairments, 101, 107, 121, 122, 133
  UDL, 34
  visual disabilities, 391, 396, 400–401, 404, 405, 407, 408
Vision. *See also* Visual disabilities
  assessment, 379–380, 407
  field of vision, 380
  low, **378**–379
  peripheral, 380
  residual vision, 378–379
  restricted central, 381
  tunnel, 380

Visual acuity, **380**
Visual cues, **390**
Visual disabilities, **378–379**
  accessibility, 391
  accommodations, 389–392, 405
  age of onset, **379**
  canes, walking, 396
  causes, 379–382
  challenges, 387–389
  characteristics, 382–385
  conditions of the eye, 380–382
  definitions, 377–379
  early intervention, 392–394
  employment and, 398–399
  expanded core curriculum, 394–398
  future perspectives, 406–408
  guide dogs, 396
  IDEA and, **378–379**, 390, 398, 404
  inclusivity, 403–404
  medical advances, 406–407
  medical technology and therapies, 407
  motor development and, 392–394
  origins and history, 403–404
  overview, 376–386
  people and situations, 402–406
  play skills, 383–384
  prevalence and placement, 385–386
  prevention, 382, 406–407
  reading, 393–394
  school years, 394–398
  signs of vision problems, 382–385
  social skills, 384–385
  technology, 405, 407–408
  tips for teachers, 385
  transitions, 398–402
  types, 379–382
  videos, 391, 396, 400–401, 404, 405, 407, 408
  websites, 391, 394, 402, 405
Visual efficiency, **383**
Visual impairments. *See* Visual disabilities

Visual processing, **143**
Visuals for language impairments, 118
VoiceOver, 408
Voice problems, **107**

W

Wakefield, Andrew, 228, 230–231, 430–431
Wallis, John, 364
Warm Springs, 10
Warning signs
  depression in children, 281
  EBD early, 294
Wayne County Training School in Michigan, 158
Websites
  accommodations, 91
  ADHD, 175, 176, 187, 189, 191–192, 200
  assistive technology, 165
  bullying, 29
  CBM, 39, 40
  Child Find, 80, 81
  culturally responsive instruction, 64
  deafness and hearing impairments, 352, 357, 363, 365, 366, 367
  disabilities, 1, 3, 7, 11, 13, 17
  dropout, 29
  EBD, 301, 306, 307, 310
  ELLs, 69
  gifted and talented, 478
  IDEA, 75
  IEPs, 86, 87
  IFSPs, 86
  individualized services, 94
  intellectual disabilities, 257, 264, 267
  interactive, 200
  language and speech impairments, 109, 131
  learning disabilities, 160, 161
  PBIS, 45
  progress monitoring, 40
  RTI, 43, 140
  Section 504, 83

settings, continuum of, 97
transitioning, 263, 264
visual disabilities, 391, 394, 402, 405
Weihenmahyer, Erik, 404–405
Well-baby visits, **80**
Werner, Heinz, 194
What's Wrong with Timmy (Shriver), 269
White, Jim, 61
Who Cares About Kelsey?, 306
Wild Child of Averyon, 14, 265–266
The Wild Child or *L'Enfant Sauvage*, 265–266
Willowbrook Institution, 268
Wolfensberger, Wolf, 267
Wonder, Stevie, 391
Word processing software, 326
Working memory, **143**
World Health Organization (WHO), deafness and hearing loss, 369
World Institute on Disability, 13
Worldwide Developers Conference (WWDC), 438
Wraparound supports, **290**
Wright, Bob, 230
Wright, Suzanne, 230
Writing disabilities, 141

X

X-linked genetic syndrome, 423

Y

Yale Center for Dyslexia and Creativity, 160
YAP. *See* Young Autism Program
Young, Andre (Dr. Dre), 472
Young Autism Program (YAP), 229
Yousafzai, Malala, 26

Z

Zone of proximal development, **462**
Zuckerberg, Mark, 471